The**Green**Guide
Ireland

Mural of a pub in Glenariff, County Antrim Photo: © Patrick Frilet/hemis.fr

THEGREENGUIDE **IRELAND**

Editorial Director	Cynthia Clayton Ochterbeck
Editor	Sophie Friedman
Contributing Writer	Darragh Geraghty
Production Manager	Natasha George
Cartography	Peter Wrenn
Photo Editor	Yoshimi Kanazawa
Interior Design	Chris Bell
Layout	Natasha George
Cover Design	Chris Bell, Christelle Le Déan

Contact Us

Michelin Travel and Lifestyle North America
One Parkway South
Greenville, SC 29615
USA
travel.lifestyle@us.michelin.com

Michelin Travel Partner
Hannay House
39 Clarendon Road
Watford, Herts WD17 1JA
UK
&01923 205240
travelpubsales@uk.michelin.com
www.ViaMichelin.com

Special Sales

For information regarding bulk sales,
customized editions and premium sales,
please contact us at:
travel.lifestyle@us.michelin.com

HOW TO USE THIS GUIDE

PLANNING YOUR TRIP

The blue-tabbed PLANNING YOUR TRIP section at the front of the guide gives you **ideas for your trip** and **practical information** to help you organise it. You'll find tours, practical information, a host of outdoor activities, a calendar of events, information on shopping, sightseeing, kids' activities and more.

INTRODUCTION

The orange-tabbed INTRODUCTION section explores **The Country Today**, then **History** covers from Celtic Ireland to Partition and Independence. **Architecture**, **Art**, **Literature**, **Music and Dance**, **Religion** and **Myths and Lore** are then explored. **Nature** delves into the geology, landscape and climate of Ireland.

DISCOVERING

The green-tabbed DISCOVERING section features Principal Sights by region, featuring the most interesting local **Sights**, **Walking Tours**, nearby **Excursions**, and detailed **Driving Tours**. Admission prices shown are normally for a single adult.

ADDRESSES

We've selected the best hotels, restaurants, cafés shops, nightlife and entertainment to fit all budgets. See the Legend on the cover flap for an explanation of the price categories. See the back of the guide for an index of hotels and restaurants.

Sidebars

Throughout the guide you will find blue, orange and green-coloured text boxes with lively anecdotes, detailed history and background information.

😊 A Bit of Advice 😊

Green advice boxes found in this guide contain practical tips and handy information relevant to your visit or to a sight in the Discovering section.

STAR RATINGS ★★★

Michelin has given star ratings for more than 100 years. If you're pressed for time, we recommend you visit the ★★★, or ★★ sights first:

★★★	**Highly recommended**
★★	**Recommended**
★	**Interesting**

MAPS

- 😊 Regional Driving Tours map and Principal Sights map.
- 😊 Region maps.
- 😊 Maps for major cities and towns.

All maps in this guide are oriented north, unless otherwise indicated by a directional arrow. The term "Local Map" refers to a map within the chapter or Tourism Region. A complete list of the maps found in the guide appears at the back of this book.

© Gareth McCormack/Getty Images

PLANNING YOUR TRIP

Michelin Driving Tours 10

When and Where to Go 14
Climate 14
Themed Tours........................14
Short Breaks 14
Other Ways of Exploring 18

What to See and Do 20
Historic Properties 20
Nature Reserves and National Parks ...20
Traditional Music 20
Cultural Festivals 21
Irish Banquets 21
Theatres 21
Classical Music 21
Adventure Sports 21
Horse Riding 22
Cycling.............................22
Golf 22
Rambling 22
Hunting & Fishing 22
Horse Racing 22
Greyhound Racing 22
Water Sports 23
Spas 24
Retreats 24
Books..............................24
Films 25
Shopping 26
Activities for Kids...................28

Calendar of Events 29

Useful Words and Phrases 33

Know Before You Go 34
Useful Websites 34
Tourist Offices.......................34

International Visitors 34
Entry Requirements 35
Customs Regulations 35
Domestic Animals 36
Health 36
Accessibility.........................36

Getting There and Getting Around 37
By Plane 37
By Sea 37
By Coach/Bus 37
By Car 37
Driving in Ireland 38
By Train............................40

Where to Stay 40
Accommodation Types 40
Useful Websites 41

Where to Eat 44
Eating out 45
Specialities 45
Tipping 45

Basic Information 46

INTRODUCTION TO IRELAND

The Country Today 52
People..............................52
Gaelige 57
Government 58
Economy............................59
Irish Cuisine 60

History 61
Timeline 61

Architecture 67
Prehistoric Era 67
Irish Monastic Settlements...........68
Middle Ages 70
Plantation Period 74
18C–19C Classical 74
19C–20C 79
Irish Distinction 79

Art 83
Celtic Art 83
Painting 84
Sculpture 85
18C to the Present 86

CONTENTS

Literature	87
Celtic Influence	87
Irish Themes	88
Irish Literary Renaissance	88
Literary Exiles	89
Modern Writing in Ireland	90
Music and Dance	91
Religion	94
Myths and Lore	98
Cinema	100
Nature	102

DISCOVERING IRELAND

© Christopher Hill/Tourism Ireland

Dublin	**110**
Southside	113
Old Dublin	123
Northside	129
Phoenix Park	134
Northside and Southside	134
Excursions	138
The Mid-East	**150**
Boyne Valley	151
Dundalk and the Cooley Peninsula	165
Co Kildare	169
Wicklow Mountains	175
The Midlands	**187**
Co Longford	188
Co Westmeath	190
Co Offaly	193
Co Laois	201
The Southeast	**203**
Co Tipperaray	205
Co Kilkenny	216

Co Wexford	223
Co Waterford	235
The Southwest	**243**
Cork	244
Around Cork	252
South Coast	261
Mizen Head and Bantry Bay	268
Beara Peninsula	272
Ring of Kerry	275
Dingle Peninsula	288
The West	**299**
Limerick	301
Shannon Valley	314
The Burren and West Clare	321
Aran Islands	331
Galway	335
Connemara	344
South Mayo and Westport	355
North Mayo and Achill Island	363
The Northwest	**369**
Co Sligo	371
Donegal and the Donegal Coast	381
Northern Peninsulas	389
Co Monaghan	399
Co Cavan	401
Northern Ireland	**404**
Belfast	408
Around Belfast	421
Lough Neagh	430
Ards Peninsula and Strangford Lough	434
Downpatrick and around	441
Mourne Mountains	448
Newry and Slieve Gullion	454
Armagh and around	456
Co Fermanagh and Lough Erne	464
Sperrin Mountains	472
Londonderry/Derry	479
Causeway Coast	486
Glens of Antrim	494
Index	500
Maps and Plans	514
Map Legend	515

Welcome to Ireland

Stunning seascapes, green pastureland, lively villages filled with music and good food, the dynamic and compact capital cities of Dublin and Belfast, prehistoric sites galore – all in a part of western Europe that for a century or two time almost forgot.

DUBLIN *(pp110-149)*

One of Europe's most accessible capital cities, Dublin is a rewarding mixture of modern fast-paced living and laid-back Irish charm. A modern tramway will trundle you silently around city streets where the best of the old has been preserved in ancient churches, Georgian buildings, medieval street patterns, Viking remains and pretty parks. Top quality hotels are abundant; it would take a month to try the city's many excellent restaurants and a year to check out its famous pubs. And despite all the modernisation, Dubliners' wry charm, wit and curiosity is still intact.

THE MID-EAST *(pp150-186)*

This area was once part of the Pale, the defendable part of the island, held by the English against the hostile Irish forces. The highlight is the soaring Wicklow Mountains – visible from Dublin but unspoiled by its expansion – dotted with tiny villages and filled with good walking routes. Kildare is rich farming country, home of the National Stud with prosperous towns such as Maynooth and Athy, their architecture and tone revealing their Anglo-Irish origins.

THE MIDLANDS *(pp187-202)*

The landlocked central counties of Ireland, Longford, Westmeath, Offaly and Laois have some of the richest farmland in Ireland. They sit in a central plain, their highest points being the Slieve Bloom Mountains, the oldest range in Europe. These are quiet counties, rarely visited and all the more authentic for it. Killarney may be the ad man's idea of Ireland; the Midlands are the authentic hard working, rural Ireland.

THE SOUTHEAST *(pp203-242)*

An area of two contrasting halves: inland Tipperary and Kilkenny, rich farmlands, with some of the country's most interesting sights; and coastal Waterford and Wexford with their ancient Viking origins and long meandering coastlines punctuated by pretty seaside towns, good beaches and historic harbours.

Bank of Ireland, Dublin

© P. Unger/Getty Images

THE SOUTHWEST *(pp243-298)*

The southwest is an essential part of any Ireland visit, with County Cork's pretty coastline and fishing villages, and County Kerry's stunning scenery. From Kinsale southwards, the coast of County Cork is quaint and natural with lots of harbours, wildlife areas and pretty villages to explore. The trip from Cork into Kerry is one of the most spectacular drives in Ireland. As you explore the peninsulas further north, pretty, unspoiled towns give way to

Dog's Bay along The Wild Atlantic Way, the West

© Big Smoke Studio/Tourism Ireland

fuchsia-covered mountains, which in turn lead down to sunny sheltered sandy beaches.

THE WEST (pp299-368)

This long ragged coastline offers endless scenic drives (particularly The Wild Atlantic Way), pit stops at quiet, empty beaches and some of Ireland's most exciting water sports. The Burren often seems like another place altogether with its strange moonscape hills and unusual wildlife. Even more remote are the Aran Islands, beaten by the Atlantic gales, their stones heaved up to divide the barren land into tiny divisions.

THE NORTHWEST (pp369-403)

Sligo is well known for its connection to the Yeats family, however the long coastline of Donegal is the chief attraction, with mountain ranges offering challenging cliff walks and stunning sea views.

NORTHERN IRELAND
(pp404-499)

The six counties which make up the British province of Northern Ireland – Derry, Down, Armagh, Fermanagh, Tyrone and Antrim – were once part of the historic province of Ulster but were separated from Donegal, Monaghan and Cavan by the British in 1921. The three major urban areas

to visit in the province are Belfast, Derry and Armagh, once war torn but now in recovery. Belfast is a major capital city, small enough to get around on foot with a couple of bus rides thrown in. It is a little like one of the United Kingdom's northern cities with bombastic Victorian architecture overlaid with sleek 21C- lines. Its inner city has regenerated into a fascinating cultural centre and its murals, once a cry of pain and anger, have become tourist attractions. The city of Derry has also emerged from the dark years, perhaps not as well as Belfast, but it is a small and fascinating place, its city walls intact and its museum offering an objective version of the Troubles. Armagh is the province's ancient religious capital, its observatory and cathedral well worth a visit. Antrim and Down are the wealthiest of the counties, with small prosperous towns and some beautiful countryside. Fermanagh offers a special lakeland environment and the lively small town of Enniskillen. The highlight of any visit to Northern Ireland is the coastal drive taking in the amazing Giant's Causeway. The North is a very different prospect to the Republic, the long years of warfare are not forgotten but visitors will find a warm welcome and gracious people.

Giant's Causeway, County Antrim, Northern Ireland

© Spila Riccardo/Sime/Photononstop

Healy Pass, Beara Peninsula, Southwest
© Gareth McCormack/Getty Images

PLANNING YOUR TRIP

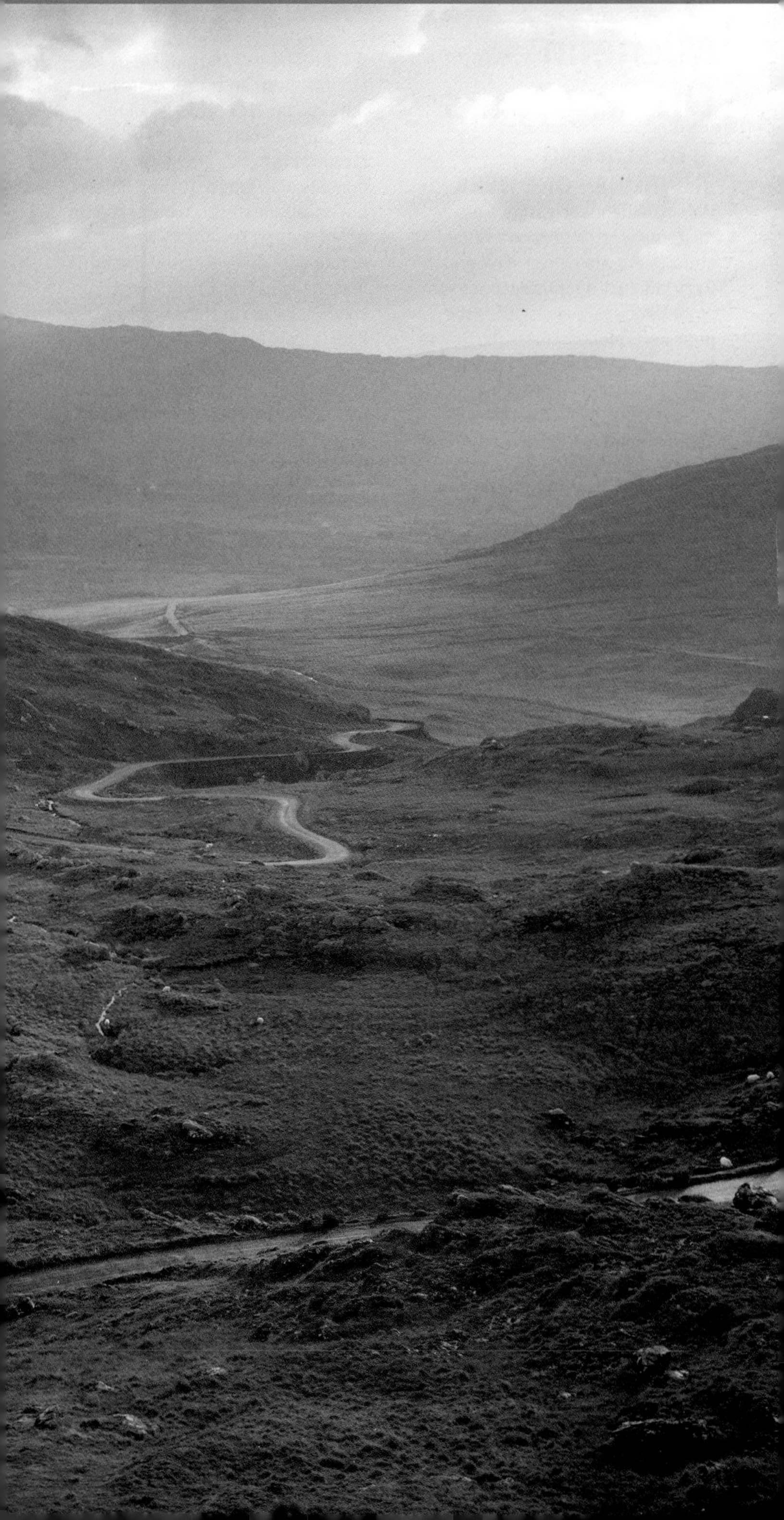

Michelin Driving Tours

1 DUBLIN AND ENVIRONS – ONE WEEK

Dublin demands at least two days for its many attractions and vibrant atmosphere, after which it is good to foray into the countryside to see some of the country's major sights – the prehistoric monuments of the **Boyne Valley**, great houses and gardens, early-Christian Glendalough in its remote valley, busy country towns and charming seaside harbours.

From **Dublin**, head north to picturesque Howth, the aristocratic demesne (former estate lands) of Malahide and bustling Drogheda, the nearby prehistoric grave sites of Newgrange and Knowth, and the tranquil setting for the decisive Battle of the Boyne.

West of the capital, follow the road to the vast Anglo-Norman castle at Trim, the splendid Palladian mansion of Castletown, and Curragh: the heartland of Irish horse-breeding and racing near Kildare. Proceed to the Great House at Russborough. Climb up into the **Wicklow Mountains** but leave some time for the highly evocative monastic remains at Glendalough. After a night in the seaside town of Wicklow, return to Dublin via the magnificent gardens of Powerscourt and the capital's attractive southern suburbs.

2 ASPECTS OF ULSTER – ONE WEEK

Northern Ireland comprises only six of Ulster's nine counties: to get a view of the whole province, consider a longer itinerary (*see Route* 7). Route 2 takes in the major towns, wonderful natural landscapes and an array of man-made attractions, including a number of world-class museums.

Head east out of **Belfast**, pausing at the fascinating Ulster Folk and Transport Museum, to the coastal resort of Bangor. On the way to St Patrick's town of Downpatrick, visit the great houses and gardens of Mountstewart and Castle Ward before driving on to Newcastle. Continue through the spectacular **Mourne Mountains** before arriving at Ireland's holy city of **Armagh**. The less grand but equally interesting country houses of Ardress and The Argory are worth a detour on the way to **Lough Neagh**, Ireland's largest lake. From here, consider calling in at the Peatlands Park to learn about local wildlife and turf-cutting, before going to Ardboe to see the High Cross, and the archetypal plantation towns of Cookstown and Draperstown. Visit the Ulster-American Folk Park on the way to the last walled city to be laid out in Europe, **Derry (Londonderry)**. Follow the **Causeway Coast** road east through Portrush and Portstewart to the spectacular Giant's Causeway and the pretty seaside resort of Ballycastle. Return to Belfast via the imposing landscapes of the **Antrim Glens** and the corniche of the Antrim Coast Road.

3 SIGHTS OF THE SOUTHEAST – ONE WEEK

Follow in the footsteps of the Anglo-Normans as they spread across Ireland, building great castles, churches and abbeys, and relish one of the great sights of ancient Ireland: the holy hill of Cashel. The Republic's second city, **Cork**, has its own distinctive character, while the southeastern coast is renowned for its beauty.

From the ferry port of Rosslare, and the Viking city of **Wexford**, make your way to Johnstown Castle and the Irish Agricultural Museum.

Drive through the National Heritage Park to the old towns of Enniscorthy and New Ross, past the lovely abbey ruins at Jerpoint to medieval **Kilkenny** (two nights), one of Ireland's most compelling cities.

The Rock of Cashel is magical. From here, head south through Caher with its castle, and Fermoy with its splendid river, crossing to the Republic's second city, **Cork** (two nights).

From Cork take the road east along the coast to Cobh, overlooking the broad waters of Cork Harbour, and on via delightful old **Youghal** to the southeast's other Viking city of **Waterford**, renowned for its street arts festival and lively cultural life. A ferry crosses Waterford Harbour to the abbeys, gardens, castles and beaches of the Hook Peninsula. The return is then direct to Rosslare.

④ THE SOUTHWEST: COUNTIES CORK, KERRY AND LIMERICK – 10 DAYS

The Southwest corner – with its rocky peninsulas stretching far into the Atlantic, the country's highest mountains and lush inland landscapes – is perhaps the most alluring region for visitors to Ireland.
From Shannon Airport, follow the road to 15C Bunratty Castle and its Folk Park to the Republic's third largest city, historic **Limerick**. Explore the country towns of Kilmallock and Mallow on the way to bustling **Cork** (two nights). The coastal road west of Cork takes you through attractive fishing villages and little maritime towns like Kinsale. More coastal delights include Skibbereen, Skull and Bantry on its great sea-inlet and **Bantry Bay**, famous for its fish. The splendidly scenic coastal road, the Ring of Beara, runs around the **Beara Peninsula**, to pretty Kenmare.

The panoramic Ring of Kerry offers wonderful views of the glorious **Iveragh Peninsula** to the distant drowned mountain top of Great Skellig Island, once an austere monastic retreat, before reaching the world-famous lake and mountain setting of **Killarney** (two nights). From here, continue to the Gaelic harbour town of Dingle and the tip of the **Dingle Peninsula**, with its beehive huts and panoramic views of the wave-battered Blasket Islands, before turning inland via Tralee, Ardfert Cathedral and Glin Castle. Return to **Limerick** and Shannon.

⑤ GLORIES OF GALWAY, CONNEMARA AND SLIGO – ONE WEEK

Connemara sometimes appears to consist more of sky, sea, bog and lake than terra firma, despite its mountains, including the splendidly rounded Twelve Bens – very different to the bleak arid limestone landscapes of **The Burren** and lively city of **Galway**.
From Knock airport, head north to the cheerful regional capital of **Sligo** with its many associations with W.B. Yeats. From here, head west to **North Mayo** through vast stretches of bog, to Stone Age vestiges at Ceide Fields and the high cliffs of Achill Island.
On the way to the elegant town of Westport, featuring Westport House,

Grey seals, Bantry Bay, County Cork

© imageBROKER/hemis.fr

one of the finest Great Houses in the West, detour to Castlebar and its state-of-the-art National Museum of Country Life at Turlough. From the road southwest, you will see St Patrick's holy mountain, Croagh Patrick. Continue south through the Sheffry Hills, round the end of Killary Harbour (Ireland's only fjord) and past the opulent 19C country house of Kylemore Abbey to charming little Clifden.

Archetypal **Connemara** landscapes can be enjoyed on the way to Inverin. From here there are flights to Inishmore, the largest of the **Aran Islands**, where Gaelic is spoken and life is steeped in traditional ways.

Back on the mainland, it is tempting to linger at the vibrant city of **Galway**. The South of Co Galway includes the strange moonscapes of **The Burren** and the lofty Cliffs of Moher, some of the tallest in Europe.

The tour returns to Knock via Ennis, (the miniature capital of Co Clare), the Heritage Town of Athenry and the little cathedral city of Tuam.

6 THE HEART OF IRELAND, THE UNKNOWN MIDLANDS – ONE WEEK

As well as outstanding monuments like the great monastic complex of Clonmacnoise and the enigmatic earthworks around Tulsk, this itinerary introduces a few hidden treasures: castles and country houses, bustling small towns off the tourist trail, unexpected uplands, the banks of the Shannon, and one of the country's most extensive and well-preserved boglands.

Head northwest out of **Dublin** to Trim, with its great Anglo-Norman castle, to the prehistoric burial mounds of Loughcrew and the ancient seat of the Pakenham family at Tullynally, before arriving at the Midland market town of Mullingar for the night.

Co Longford has some intriguing features, notably the delightful estate village of Ardagh. Co Roscommon boasts Strokestown House, which has its own estate village and an authoritative Famine Museum; the small town of Boyle is graced by handsome abbey ruins. From here, head south to Tulsk, where the Cruachan visitor centre provides an insight into the mysteries of the Celtic past, then continue to Ballinasloe and Athlone at the southern end of Lough Ree on the River Shannon.

The monastic precinct of Clonmacnoise is one of the great ecclesiastical sights of Ireland, as is the extraordinary little Romanesque cathedral of Clonfert. This itinerary now leaves the Shannon for the little Georgian town of Birr, the anteroom to the great house and grounds of the Birr Castle Demesne. To the East of Birr rise the green summits of the relatively little-visited **Slieve Bloom Mountains**, while to the northeast, close to little Tullamore, lies the vast, strange and potentially perilous expanse of Clara Bog. From here, it is a straight run back to **Dublin**.

7 ULSTER ODYSSEY – TWO WEEKS

This near-comprehensive tour of the old province of Ulster, including the six counties of Northern Ireland and three in the Republic, takes in the quiet countryside of **Co Cavan** and **Co Monaghan**, and the wild scenery of **Co Donegal**'s coast and mountains. From **Belfast** take the road to the old coastal resort of Bangor. Visit the great houses and demesnes at Mountstewart and Castle Ward before taking the ferry across the mouth of Strangford Lough to St Patrick's city of Downpatrick, and heading for the seaside town of Newcastle.

Snake your way through the **Mourne Mountains** to **Armagh**, another holy city, the seat of two Archbishops of Ireland (Roman Catholic and Church of Ireland). The following day, head southwest into the Republic through Co Monaghan and Co Cavan, before turning northwest to **Co Fermanagh** and its little capital, Enniskillen. After **Belleek**, with its famous pottery, cross into **Co Donegal**. West of Donegal Town rise the dramatic cliffs of **Slieve League**, where the village of Glencolumbkille is perched, still breathing the spirit of its founder, St Columba. From here, the route heads north via Glenveagh National Park to the quiet little resort of **Dunfanaghy** in the lee of Horn Head.

Take the N 56 back past the ancient fortress of Grianan of Aileach to the renowned walled city of **Londonderry** in Northern Ireland. Divert to the **Sperrin Mountains** for the Ulster-American Folk Park. East of the mountains is the typical plantation settlement of Cookstown, a famous High Cross at Ardboe on the shores of **Lough Neagh**, the country's greatest lake, and the 17C planter's house of Springhill. Drive north to Draperstown, another plantation settlement and continue to the favourite seaside resorts of Portrush and Portstewart. The Giant's Causeway and the **Causeway Coast** demand a day of anyone's time, and a choice of accommodation is available at the seaside resort of Ballycastle.

The return to **Belfast** is along the Antrim Coast Road through the superlative landscapes of the **Glens of Antrim**, with a final stop at the great Anglo-Norman castle at Carrickfergus.

8 IRISH HIGHLIGHTS, GRAND TOUR – TWO WEEKS

This route highlights the very best that Ireland has to offer the first-time visitor. From **Dublin**, drive out to one of the country's finest mansions, Russborough, and on through the **Wicklow Mountains** to the monastic ruins of Glendalough in their deep wooded valley, before arriving at the historic city of Kilkenny (two nights). Spend a day absorbing the atmosphere of Ireland's Acropolis, the Rock of Cashel, before heading for the Republic's second city, **Cork**, and then west on to **Killarney** (two nights) in its incomparable setting of lakes and mountains. The classic drive around the **Iveragh Peninsula**, the Ring of Kerry, is a great experience, as is the **Dingle Peninsula**, with its ancient

Blasket Islands

© G. Karbus Photography / Cultura / Photononstop

stone huts and enclosures, and views of the rocky Blasket Islands.

Limerick is an up-and-coming town, while Co Clare offers its little capital, Ennis, the mighty Cliffs of Moher and the weird limestone landscapes of **The Burren**.

North of The Burren is one of Ireland's most attractive towns, **Galway**.

From here, make your way to Clifden, through what many regard as the most Irish of landscapes: the bogs, shining lakes, and rounded mountains of **Connemara**. Pass close to St Patrick's mountain, Croagh Patrick, to Westport. After Castlebar and the excellent Museum of Country Life at Turlough, follow signs to the busiest town in the northwest, **Sligo**.

Enter Northern Ireland at Enniskillen, in the heart of the glorious **Fermanagh** Lakeland. An essential stop on the way to the walled city of **Londonderry** is the Ulster-American Folk Park. Don't miss the country's greatest natural attraction, the Giant's Causeway, before driving on to the province's capital, **Belfast**. Return to **Dublin** along the **Boyne Valley**, with its battle site and magnificent prehistoric monuments.

When and Where to Go

CLIMATE

Extreme temperatures are rare in Ireland but unfortunately there is the probability of rain throughout the year. The Southeast enjoys the most sun and the East Coast is drier than the West.

The best time to visit the country is the summer, with the sunniest months of the year in May–June and the warmest in July–August. However, whatever time of year you go, rainproof clothing and umbrellas are a must!

Information about the weather in both the Republic and Northern Ireland is available at www.met.ie, or www.metoffice.gov.uk.

THEMED TOURS

HISTORIC ROUTES

Sarsfield's Ride

This historical route (70mi/113km signed) makes a wide loop around Limerick along byroads through small villages and unspoilt countryside, following the route taken by General Patrick Sarsfield when he set out to intercept an English siege train. In August 1690 King William III of England was encamped at Caherconlish (8mi/12.9km east of Limerick) awaiting the arrival of heavy siege guns from Dublin, while his army besieged Limerick. Acting on information from a deserter, Sarsfield slipped out of King John's Castle in Limerick with 600 cavalry and headed northeast along the right bank of the Shannon via Bridgetown, fording the river upstream of Killaloe Bridge, which was held by the Williamites. At about this point he was joined by local guides, who showed him a route by Kiloscully and Ballyhourigan Wood, pausing to rest before climbing over the Silvermine and the Slievefelim Mountains via Toor and Rear Cross. From Doon they continued south on the county boundary to Monard, and turned west. In Cullen they discovered the password for the Williamite camp was Sarsfield; so after midnight they travelled the last two miles to Ballyneety, where they destroyed the siege train.

Siege of Kinsale

The sites of the various camps and engagements of the opposing forces are marked by a dozen signs erected by the roadsides around Kinsale.

SCENIC ROUTES

Several Scenic Routes, designated by the local Tourist Boards, are marked by signs (Slí) – **Inis Eoghain Scenic Drive** in Donegal, **Arigna Scenic Drive** around Lough Key near Boyle, **Slea Head Drive** on the Dingle Peninsula, the **Ring of Kerry** round the Iveragh Peninsula west of Killarney and the **Ring of Beara** round the Beara Peninsula west of Glengarriff.

LITERARY ROUTES

Explore the places where Oliver Goldsmith spent his childhood (see LONGFORD), visit the towns where Anthony Trollope lived (see CO OFFALY) during his residence in Ireland, or follow the trail of sights associated with Patrick Kavanagh. Dublin Literary Pub Crawl (www.dublinpubcrawl.com) is highly recommended.

SHORT BREAKS

Always allow plenty of time when touring Ireland: part of the enjoyment is stopping for an idle chat, a pint of Guinness or a spectacular view.

TWO-DAY BREAKS

Dublin City

Begin with a visit to Trinity College and that masterpiece of Irish art, the Book of Kells, before going up Grafton Street and its side streets, enjoying the buskers and Dublin's elegant shopping area. Wander around the gardens of St Stephen's Green before crossing to the north side to find a place for lunch. In the afternoon, visit the National Museum or the National Gallery, walk through Merrion Square and admire the Georgian houses, notably Number Twenty Nine. Spend the evening exploring Temple Bar. On the second day explore the old town and the art in the Chester Beatty Library, then refresh yourself with a tour around the Guinness Storehouse. Alternatively, enjoy a guided tour of Dublin Castle or look into Christ Church Cathedral or St Patrick's Cathedral. After lunch, take the bus to Kilmainham Gaol for a lesson in recent Irish history and pop in to admire displays in the Irish Museum of Modern Art installed in the Royal Kilmainham Hospital.

Co Kilkenny
Visit Kilkenny Castle and the Kilkenny Design Centre. After lunch, plunge into Dunmore Cave. Head south down the Nore Valley to the magnificent ruins of Jerpoint Abbey, calling in on Inistioge, and on over Brandon Hill to Graiguenamanagh on the River Barrow.

Co Sligo
Visit the Niland Gallery, featuring paintings by Jack B. Yeats, and stroll through the Abbey ruins. After lunch, take a boat trip on Lough Gill, visiting the lake isle of Innisfree and Parke's Castle.
Drive through Yeats' country to the tomb of W.B. Yeats at Drumcliff in the shadow of Benbulben, and Lissadell, home of Countess Markievicz, before turning inland to Glencar Waterfall.

THREE-DAY BREAKS
Cork City
Highlights include the English Market, Grand Parade and St Patrick's Street. Admire the exuberant architecture of William Burges at St Fin Barre's Cathedral. After lunch, cross the river to try your hand at ringing Shandon Bells and to the west of the city, see how criminals were treated in Cork City Gaol.
On the second day take a trip to Blarney Castle to kiss the Blarney Stone and make a round trip to Mallow

National Gallery, Dublin

© L. Maisant/hemis.fr

and Fermoy on the Blackwater River. On the third day drive out to Fota House and the Wildlife Park, make a lunchtime visit to Cobh and end the day sampling whiskey at the Old Midleton Distillery.

Westport and District
Stroll round the charming little town and the Quayside, a good spot for lunch, then visit Westport House. Drive west to explore the Murrisk Peninsula, which presents some of the most beautiful landscapes in the West of Ireland – Croagh Patrick and Killary Harbour.
Take the road north to the Marian Shrine at Knock and stop in at the Museum of Country Life at Turlough near Castlebar.

Enniskillen
Stroll through the town and visit Enniskillen Castle and its museums. In the afternoon tour the stately rooms of Castle Coole.
Drive southwest to Florence Court, a less austere country house, with flamboyant plasterwork, and the Marble Arch Caves, part of which is visited by boat.

Make a tour round the shores of Lower Lough Erne, taking in Devenish Island, Castle Archdale and White Island, the Janus Figure, Belleek Pottery, the Cliffs of Magho viewpoint and Tully Castle.

Londonderry (Derry)

Walk around the walls and visit the Tower Museum, the Cathedral and Long Tower Church.

Make a tour in the Sperrins Mountains – Roe Valley Country Park, Glenshane Pass, Dungiven Priory, Wellbrook Beetling Mill, Beaghmore Stone Circles, Ulster Plantation Centre in Draperstown, Springhill, Ulster History Park, Sperrin Heritage Centre, Ulster American Folk Park and Gray's Printery in Strabane.

Tour north round the Inishowen (Inis Eoghain) Peninsula – visiting the many prehistoric and early Christian relics – Grianán of Aileach, Carrowmore High Crosses, Clonca Church and Cross. Visit Malin Head, famous from the shipping forecasts, and Fort Ree Military Museum.

FOUR-DAY BREAKS
Dublin and District

♿ *For your first two days, explore Dublin City, as described under two-day breaks.*

Drive south into the Wicklow Mountains to Russborough or Powerscourt and further on to the monastic ruins at Glendalough. Take the motorway north via Slane to Newgrange in the Boyne Valley and return via Trim and Tara or Malahide and Newbridge House.

Killarney and District

Wander around the town centre and explore the National Park on foot – Knockreer Demesne and Ross Castle – or by car – Muckross House, Muckross Friary and the Muckross Peninsula, and Torc Waterfall and Ladies View. Take a guided tour through the Gap of Dunloe if it is a fine day, or drive round the Ring of Kerry, enjoying the fine views of the landscape.

Go north to the Dingle Peninsula, part of the Gaeltacht, which has many relics dating from a former way of life.

Limerick and District

Visit the treasures in the Hunt Museum and walk up to the Castle and St Mary's Cathedral.

Drive northwest into Co Clare to visit Bunratty Folk Museum and Castle, Quin Friary, Knappogue Castle and Cragganunowen Centre.

Make a round trip south of Limerick visiting the prehistoric remains at Lough Gur Interpretive Centre, the walled town of Kilmallock and the childhood haunts of Eamon de Valera in Bruree, before returning down the Maigue Valley via Croom, Monasteranenagh Abbey and charming Adare, with its pretty thatched cottages.

Drive north via Ennis and Ennistimon to the barren landscape of the Burren – the Cliffs of Moher, Lisdoonvarna, Corkscrew Hill and Aillwee Cave.

Belfast and District

Visit the city centre and the waterfront. Visit Titanic Belfast and lunch in the Crown Liquor Saloon. In the afternoon visit the Ulster Museum and take a stroll in the Botanic Gardens with its two glasshouses. Alternatively take a tour of the city's famous political Murals.

On day two, drive east to the Ulster Folk and Transport Museum at Cultra; after lunch explore the splendours of Mount Stewart on the east shore of Strangford Lough.

Head south up the Lagan Valley to learn about the traditional Irish linen industry in the Lisburn Museum. Visit charming Hillsborough and see the plants and shrubs at Rowallane. Take a full day out to drive north via Ballymena and Ballymoney to marvel at the volcanic columns of the Giant's Causeway. In the afternoon drive south along the coast and glens of Antrim, not missing the Carrick-a-rede Ropebridge.

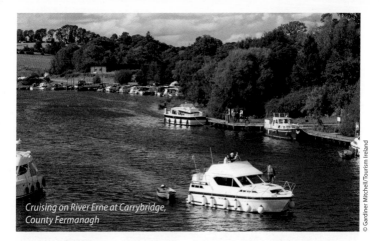

Cruising on River Erne at Carrybridge, County Fermanagh

© Gardiner Mitchell/Tourism Ireland

FIVE-DAY BREAK

Galway and District

Stroll round the medieval city centre and in the afternoon take the road to Aughnanure Castle and the charming fishing village of Oughterard on Lough Corrib.

Take the road up the east shore of Lough Corrib via Annaghdown and Ross Errily Abbey to Cong. Take the road west through Connemara to Clifden, returning by the coast.

In Kiltartan country, south of Galway, visit Athenry heritage town, Thoor Ballylee, once the home of William Butler Yeats, and Coole Park.

Book a day trip to Inis Mor, the largest of the Aran Islands, where tourism has softened the once-harsh island way of life.

ACTIVITY HOLIDAYS

♿See WHAT TO SEE AND DO.
Discover Ireland (the Irish tourist board) provides information on all kinds of holidays and summer schools.

Horse-Drawn Caravan

The caravan provides accommodation as well as a leisurely way of exploring the Irish country roads:

♦ **Irish Horse-drawn Caravans** Mayo, Galway, Wicklow and Laois, www.irishhorsedrawn caravans.com.

Boating and Cruising

Ireland is blessed with many lakes and waterways, and is surrounded by sea. Good waterways for cruising include the River Shannon, Shannon–Erne Waterway and Lough Erne; canal barges are recommended on the River Barrow, the Grand Canal and the River Shannon. Details of local operators are given in the relevant chapters. Visit **www.waterwaysireland.org** for general information. Try to hire from a boat operator who is a member of the Irish Boat Rental Association: **www.boatholidaysireland.com**.

Walking, Cycling and Horse Riding

Holidays – even chauffeur-driven – can be organised around a variety of activities, including tracing ancestors, gardens and golf.

♦ **See Ireland Differently**
☎0844 873 6110
www.seeirelanddifferently.co.uk

Irish Language and Culture

Several courses are on offer in the Irish speaking districts (the Gaeltacht), either specialising in language or combining language with culture. Workshops include tin-whistle playing, Bodhrán playing, set-dancing, sean-nós singing, hill-walking, lectures on Irish folklore, poetry reading, traditional music concerts, cultural activity courses on

Cycling on Inisheer, Aran Islands

© Brian Morrison/Tourism Ireland

archaeology, marine painting, Celtic pottery and much more.

♦ **Oideas Gael**
Gleann Cholm Cille,
Co Donegal. ℘074 973 0248;
www.oideas-gael.com.

Cooking
Various country hotels have set up cookery schools. **Berry Lodge** (Annagh, Miltown Malbray, Co Clare; ℘065 708 7022; www.berrylodge. com) for example, offers individual morning and weekend courses.

OTHER WAYS OF EXPLORING
In addition to the ideas listed below, you may like to check out rail and bus trips from the major towns organised by Irish Rail Service (Iarnród Éireann), Northern Ireland Railways, Bus Eireann and Ulster Bus (♿see GETTING THERE).

BY TOURIST TRAIN
There are a few tourist railways in Ireland that occasionally operate steam trains on the national network. Advance booking is essential.

♦ **Railway Preservation Society of Ireland (RPSI)**
www.steamtrainsireland.com.
♦ **Irish Steam Preservation Society Ltd**
Steam Museum,

Stradbally, Co Laois.
℘086 389 0184;
www.irishsteam.ie.

BY BICYCLE
Ireland is an ideal place to cycle because much of the country is gently undulating. Bicycles can be taken on planes, trains and buses so travelling around is generally straightforward. There are also various tour operators offering well-organised group itineraries and independent holidays (♿see WHAT TO SEE AND DO; Cycling).

♦ **Cycle Holidays Ireland**
Gortanumera, Portumna,
County Galway
℘01 878 321 200;
www.cycleholidaysireland.com.
♦ **Irish Cycling Safaris**
℘01 260 0749;
www.cyclingsafaris.com.

The Táin Trail
This trail (365mi/585km) retraces as closely as possible the route through the Midlands from Rathcroghan to the Cooley Peninsula and back taken by Maeve's armies in pursuit of the Brown Bull of Cooley, a tale told in the *Cattle Raid of Cooley* (*Táin bó Buailgne*), one of the great Irish legends.
The circular route can be joined at any point as it passes through historic

places of interest – on the northern leg, starting from Rathcroghan, the trail goes through Strokestown, Longford, Fore, Kells, Louth, Dundalk and Omeath to Carlingford; on the southern leg, starting in Carlingford, it runs through Monasterboice, Slane, Kells, bypasses Mullingar, and continues through Kilbeggan, Clara, Athlone and Roscommon to Rathcroghan.

ON FOOT

Ireland has over 30 waymarked routes *(yellow arrow and walking figure)* following disused roads, lanes and forest trails across the country. As the weather can quickly change, it is important to let someone know where you are going and when you expect to return and to be properly equipped with suitable clothing, compass, maps and guidebook. In addition to the trails described below, you will find others listed in the appropriate chapter – Beara Way (*see RING OF KERRY*), Burren Way (*see THE BURREN AND WEST CLARE*) and Wicklow Way (*see WICKLOW MOUNTAINS*). Newcastle is a good base for walking in the Mourne Mountains, and the town is the starting point for the Mourne International Walking Festival (*see MOURNE MOUNTAINS*).

The Bangor Trail

This is an old drovers' trail (approx. 20mi/32km) in the West of Ireland from Newport on the shores of Clew Bay northwards through the Nephin Beg Mountains to Bangor Erris. This area of northwest Connacht consists of hills encircled by a vast area of trackless bog, without trees or houses, nothing between the heather and the sky but the occasional shepherd or farmer.

The Cavan Way

In northwest Co Cavan between Blacklion and Dowra (16mi/25km) over the hills to Shannon Pot, the source of the River Shannon, and then mainly by road to Dowra, where it links up with the Leitrim Way (*see below*).

The Dingle Way

A circular walk (104mi/168km), to and from Tralee, which takes in the beautiful scenery of the Dingle Peninsula.

The East Munster Way

This walk (44mi/70km) starts from Carrick-on-Suir, passes through Clonmel and finishes in Clogheen, Co Waterford; it includes forest tracks, open moorland and a river towpath.

The Kerry Way *(Slí íbh Ráthach)*

Ireland's longest waymarked walk (133mi/214km) can be done clockwise or anti-clockwise, starting and finishing in Killarney. It winds through the Macgillycuddy Reeks before reaching the coast at Glenbeigh and running south and east through Caherciveen, Waterville, Derrynane, Sneem and Kenmare.

The Leitrim Way *(Slí Liatroma)*

Consists of old and new tracks (30mi/48km) from Drumshanbo, along the East shore of Lough Allen at the foot of Slieve Anierin, through Dowra, the first town on the River Shannon, up the Owennayle Valley, over a moorland plateau, past Doo Lough (panoramic views), through lowland and forest, over the Tullykeherny Plateau and down a country road into Manorhamilton.

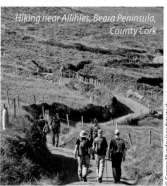

Hiking near Allihies, Beara Peninsula, County Cork

© George Munday/age fotostock

What to See and Do

HISTORIC PROPERTIES

The Irish Heritage Service **Dúchas** is the State body responsible for the protection and conservation of natural and built heritage. The **Heritage Card** provides unlimited admission to nearly all the sites managed by The Office of Public Works, available at most properties or from Dublin Tourism. ☏01 647 6592; www.heritageireland.ie.

◆ **Heritage Towns**
Fifteen towns have been designated Heritage Towns for their architecture, history or character, which is illustrated in the local heritage centre. www.heritagetowns.com.

◆ **Historic Monuments**
In Northern Ireland these are the responsibility of the Department of the Environment. www.doeni.gov.uk.

◆ **National Trust**
The Trust owns over 200 historic houses and gardens and 49 industrial monuments and mills in the UK. Members may use their membership cards to visit NT properties in Northern Ireland. Annual membership offering free admission to all NT sites is available at most sites. Head Office in Northern Ireland. ☏028 9751 0721; www.nationaltrust.org.uk.

◆ **National Heritage Week/ European Heritage Open Days** In August there are walks, lectures, exhibitions, music recitals, pageants and demonstrations at several historic properties. www.heritageweek.ie.

NATURE RESERVES AND NATIONAL PARKS

Ireland has four national parks: Glenveagh, Connemara, Wicklow Mountains and Killarney. Many forest parks and country parks are managed for public use and recreation.

There are numerous nature reserves (wildfowl sanctuaries, peat bogs and sand dunes) both sides of the border:

◆ **National Parks and Wildlife Service** – www.npws.ie.
◆ **Birdwatch Ireland (BWI)** www.birdwatchireland.ie.
◆ **Irish Peatland Conservation Council** – www.ipcc.ie.
◆ **Royal Society for Protection of Birds (RSPB)** www.rspb.org.uk/nireland.

TRADITIONAL MUSIC

Typically Irish, and also generally the most popular form of evening entertainment, is the traditional music and singing performed in bars up and down the country, in cities, towns and rural areas. The instruments played are commonly the violin – called the fiddle by traditional musicians – the flute, the goatskin drum (*bodhrán*) and free-reed instruments such as the accordion, melodeon and concertina; more recently the guitar and banjo have joined in. That other, very genteel and quintessentially Irish instrument, the Irish harp, is now rarely played in public

Irish dance

© Northern Ireland Tourist Board

though there are two harp festivals (⟳ see CALENDAR OF EVENTS).
Ask at the tourist Information centre for bars with traditional music.
A feature of Irish traditional music is dancing, including individual old-style (*sean-nós*) dancing and particularly **set dancing**, an adaptation of military dances to existing tunes such as jigs, reels, hornpipes and polkas.
Set dancing has enjoyed a huge revival in popularity largely thanks to the efforts of the ebullient, American-born Michael Flatley, whose lavish stage production of *Riverdance* (followed by *Lord of the Dance and Feet of Flames*) became an international phenomenon in the mid-1990s.

CULTURAL FESTIVALS

Ireland hosts a number of literature and music festivals in honour of individual artists, or groups of artists. Many are accompanied by bands, parades, horse races and regattas.

IRISH BANQUETS

For a truly Irish evening's entertainment, try a medieval banquet accompanied by music and poetry – they take place at Knappogue Castle; Bunratty Castle; Dunguaire Castle; Killarney Manor and Brú Ború in Cashel.

THEATRES

Ireland has a lively theatrical scene with theatres in many provincial towns, as well as Dublin and Belfast. In Dublin, modern and classic plays are performed at the Abbey Theatre and the Gate Theatre.
The traditional seasonal festivals and rural way of life are evoked in music, song, dance and mime in the performances of the National Folk Theatre of Ireland in Tralee, which draw on the local Gaelic tradition. Productions in the Irish language are put on by the Irish Theatre (*Taibhearc na Gaillimhe*) in Galway, which is a state-sponsored body.

CLASSICAL MUSIC

In Dublin, the **National Concert Hall** (Earlsfort Terrace) has a regular programme of classical and modern orchestral music. The **Waterfront Hall, in Belfast,** offers a varied programme of events.
Concerts of **chamber music** are given by Irish and international musicians in some of the great Irish houses in the summer; details are available from the National Concert Hall in Dublin. Opera is performed in Dublin and Belfast and also at various **opera festivals**, notably in Wexford.

ADVENTURE SPORTS
CLIMBING AND MOUNTAINEERING

The magnificent mountain ranges that fringe the Atlantic coast from north to south provide exhilarating locations for walking, rambling, orienteering and mountaineering.

♦ **Tollymore Mountain Centre**
Northern Ireland's National Centre for mountaineering and canoeing activities. Bryansford, Newcastle. ✆ 028 4372 2158. www.tollymore.com.

MULTI-SPORT CENTRES

♦ **Killary Tours**
Sailing, kayaking, surfing, bungee jumping, high ropes, cycle tours, clay pigeon, etc. Leenane, Connemara, Co Galway. ✆ 095 43411. www.killaryadventure.com.

GLIDING

♦ **Irish Hang-Gliding and Paragliding Association**
www.ihpa.ie or www.uhpc.f9. co.uk (for Northern Ireland).

PARACHUTING

♦ **Irish Parachute Club**
Clonbullogue Airfield Edenderry, Co. Offaly. ✆ 01 850 260 600 www.skydive.ie.

HORSE RIDING

Hunting and horse racing are concentrated in the flatter, agricultural counties of the South and Midlands; pony trekking is available country-wide. Information on all activities is available from tourist boards.

- **Equestrian Holidays Ireland** www.ehi.ie.

CYCLING

Cycling is becoming increasingly popular in Ireland. As a result, bicycle hire is available almost everywhere. For maps and information on routes, visit www.cycle-route.com. Dublinbikes is a public bicycle rental scheme operating in Dublin city since 2009 with over 40 bike stations dotted throughout the city (www.dublinbikes.ie).

TOUR OPERATORS:

- **Irish Cycling Safaris** University College Dublin, Dublin 4. ☎01 260 0749. www.cyclingsafaris.com.
- **Celtic Cycling** Celtic Cycling, 22 Ballybricken, Waterford,. ☎051 850228.
- **Cyclewest Ireland** 12 Dun Na Mara, Renmore, Co Galway. ☎091 877 323. www.cyclewest.com.

GOLF

For golfers there are both inland and links courses.
To view details of over 400 courses and specialist tour operators, visit www.irishgolfcourses.co.uk.

RAMBLING

For **national waymarked trails** in the Republic of Ireland visit www.irishtrails.ie. Detailed information sheets for individual long-distance walks are available from the relevant tourist information offices. Waymarked ways are reserved for walkers and are unsuitable for horses or mountain bikes. For details on all kind of walks, from short city and rural strolls to serious waymarked treks, visit www.discoverireland.com/walking, or www.discovernorthernireland.com/walking.

If you are only visiting the eastern half of the Republic of Ireland, note that East-West Mapping are specialists in recreational and tourism mapping of **Leinster**: http://eastwestmapping.ie.

HUNTING & FISHING

For hunting with hounds, contact the Hunting Association of Ireland – www.hai.ie. The Irish Tourist Board lists details on game **angling**, sea angling and coarse angling, river trout angling, pike angling, River Moy angling, a Lough Derg fishing guide and more. For extensive details on fishing in both the North and South of the country, just search the tourist board websites. A licence is required to fish for salmon or seatrout in both the Republic and Northern Ireland. Fishing licences and permits are available from tackle shops and fishery authorities:

HORSE RACING

There are racecourses dotted across much of Ireland. Those in the Dublin area include The Curragh, Punchestown, Leopardstown and Fairyhouse.The most popular festivals are **Fairyhouse** (Easter), **Killarney** (May), **Curragh** (June), **Killarney** (July), **Galway**, **Tramore** and **Tralee** (August), **Galway** and **Listowel** (September) and **Leopardstown** and **Limerick** (December)
To see what's on when throughout the year, visit the excellent Horseracing Ireland website, www.goracing.ie.

GREYHOUND RACING

There are 18 race tracks for this popular evening entertainment: Ballyskeagh, Cork, Dublin, Dundalk, Dungannon, Enniscorthy, Galway, Kilkenny, Lifford, Limerick, Londonderry, Longford, Mullingar, Newbridge, Thurles, Tralee, Waterford and Youghal.

The Sport of Kings

The Irish are passionate about racing and their horses, which have a worldwide reputation for excellence. Some people believe that the country's legendary emerald pastures are so rich in calcium and other nutrients that they produce horses with strong, light bones. The Ballydoyle Stables in County Tipperary is world-famous, producing some of the finest horses ever raced, including Ninjinsky, Sir Ivor, Alleged and The Minstrel.

Although horseracing in Ireland is popular with every class of folk, it is known as "the sport of kings". This may go back to Celtic times, when Brehon law dictated it should be limited to princes and noblemen.

To see what's on when throughout the year, and to book a night "at the dogs" visit the Irish Greyhound Board website: www.igb.ie.

WATER SPORTS

The long, indented coastline provides facilities for bathing, scuba-diving, wind-surfing, sailing, sea-angling and deep-sea fishing.

CANOEING AND KAYAKING

- **Canoeing Northern Ireland** www.canoeni.com.
- **Waterways Ireland** www.waterwaysireland.org
- **Kayaking tours in Galway** www.kayakmor.ie.

SAILING / CRUISING

The many inland lakes and waterways are good for cruising, canoeing and water-skiing and attractive to anglers. **Ireland Waterways** co-ordinates the management and promotion of inland navigable waterways: www.waterwaysireland.org.

There are sailing marinas all round the coast of Ireland and on the inland lakes. All yacht clubs are linked to the Irish Sailing Association which lists racing, training and cruising activities on its website.

- **Irish Sailing Association** www.sailing.ie.
- **Cruise Ireland** Cruising on the Shannon and Erne waterways. 𝒫01 278 1666. www.cruise-ireland.ie.

SCUBA DIVING

Ireland has a beautiful underwater coastline, particularly on the West Coast, where the Gulf Stream brings an abundant marine life into the clear Atlantic waters.

- **Irish Underwater Council** 𝒫01 284 4601; www.diving.ie.
- **Activity Ireland Dive Centre** Based on the Dingle Peninsula, Waterworld is Ireland's largest diving and leisure centre – 𝒫066 713 9292 www.waterworld.ie.

Kayaking at Portrush, Causeway Coast

© Northern Ireland Tourist Board

SURFING

The best conditions are to be found on the Northwest and the Mid-West coasts; good conditions prevail on the North, Southwest and South Coasts. Surfing on the East Coast is practicable only during a storm or strong southerly winds. Surfboards are available for hire.

- **Irish Surf Association**
  096 49428; www.isasurf.ie.
- **Irish Sailing Association**
  See Sailing.

WATER SKIING AND WAKEBOARDING

Top spots include Macroom, Cork; Craigavon Lakes in County Armagh; Upper and Lower Lough Erne; The Lower Bann; Farran Forest Park, Parknasilla, Ring of Kerry; Blessington Lakes, Co Wicklow; Ballymore Eustace, Co Kildare; and Lough Muckno in Co Monaghan.

- **Irish Water Ski & Wakeboard Federation** – www.irishwwf.ie

WINDSURFING

The elite of the windsurfing community regard Ireland as one of the best locations in the world; top venues include Brandon Bay, Clew Bay and Portstewart. Inland, hundreds of lakes offer excellent opportunities. Some of the most popular places for windsurfing (also known as sailboarding or boardsailing) are in Northwest Ireland on the coast of Co Mayo at **Easky**, where international championships have been held, and on the coast of Co Donegal at **Bundoran**, where the European championships draw large crowds.

- **Oysterhaven Centre** – One of Ireland's leading centres for sailing and windsurfing, 6mi/10km from Kinsale, Co Cork. 021 4770 738; www.oysterhaven.com.

SPAS

Spas in this guide are highlighted with the `Spa` symbol. The only active spa resort in Ireland is **Lisdoonvarna** in The Burren, which has been popular since the 18C. The waters contain magnesia, iodine and iron and are reputed to have restorative and therapeutic powers. The Victorian Spa Complex and Health Centre features sulphur baths, massage, wax treatments and saunas. The Victorian Pump House is open daily.

THALASSOTHERAPY

The abundant supplies of seaweed on the Irish coast are used not only as food but also in hot seaweed baths at Enniscrone, West of Sligo, and for therapeutic purposes at the outdoor baths in Ballybunnion, North of Tralee, and at Waterworld in Bundoran, Co Donegal, where you can enjoy various health treatments using heated sea water, local seaweed and sea water drench showers.

BOOKS

ART

The Painters of Ireland
by Anne Crookshank and the Knight of Glin (1978-9)
A Guide to Irish Country Houses
by Mark Bence-Jones (1988)
Exploring the Book of Kells
by George Otto Simms (1988)

AUTOBIOGRAPHY

Twenty Years A-Growing
by Maurice O'Sullivan (1953, 1992)

Seaweed Baths

Seaweed baths, once again popular in Ireland, date from Edwardian times, when they were much more widespread than now, with baths in most large seaside towns. Seaweed baths are individual baths filled with hot seawater and seaweed – generally wracks such as *Fucus serratus*. The wrack is usually steam-treated prior to use so that it releases minerals, trace elements and polysaccharides such as alginates. Ask at the tourist office for your nearest baths.

Wheels within Wheels
by Dervla Murphy (1981)
The Speckled People by Hugo
Hamilton (2003)

FICTION

The Macdermots of Ballycloran,
The Kellys and the O'Kellys,
Castle Richmond and *The*
Landleaguers by Anthony
Trollope (1847, 1848, 1860, 1883)
The Playboy of the Western World
by J.M. Synge (1907)
A Portrait of the Artist as a Young Man
by James Joyce (1916, 1960)
Ulysses by James Joyce (1922)
The Last September
by Elizabeth Bowen (1929)
At Swim-Two-Birds by Flann O'Brien
(1939)
Troubles by J.G. Farrell (Fontana, 1970)

GEOGRAPHY

The Personality of Ireland – Habitat,
Heritage and History
by E. Estyn Evans (Lilliput, 1992)
Atlas of the Irish Rural Landscape
edited by F.H.A Aalen, Kevin
Whelan and Matthew Stout
(Cork University Press, 1997)
Reading the Irish Landscape
by Frank Mitchell and
Michael Ryan (TownHouse, 2001)

HISTORY

Brendan the Navigator by George Otto
Simms (O'Brien Press, 1998, 2006)
The Celts edited by Joseph Raftery
(The Mercier Press, 1988)
Ireland: A History by Thomas
Bartlett (2010)

FILMS

The Quiet Man (1952)
A slice of stereotypical pre-
industrial Irishness directed
by John Ford (of Irish descent
himself), starring John Wayne in a
memorable role as a homecoming
brawling boxer.
Darby O'Gill and the Little People (1959)
Classic "Oirish" Disney film that
leaves no quaint Irish image or
myth unturned.

Ryan's Daughter (1970)
A young married Irishwoman
falls for an officer of the British
garrison amid the magnificent
wild and very wet landscapes and
seascapes of the West.
The General (1988)
John Boorman directs Brendan
Gleeson in the intriguing story of
a Dublin crime boss.
My Left Foot (1989)
Poignant Oscar-winning
performance from Daniel Day-
Lewis as a cerebral palsy victim.
The Committments (1991)
The "World's Hardest Working
Band", not only brought sweet
soul music to the people of
Dublin, but also a great film and a
spin-off touring band.
The Crying Game (1992)
Neil Jordan's gripping account
of the relationship between an
IRA gunman and a black British
bisexual soldier.
In the Name of the Father (1993)
The failure of justice following the
IRA's bombing of a Guildford pub.
Michael Collins (1996)
Neil Jordan's blockbusting
biopic of the life and times of the
charismatic, doomed Republican
leader.
The Wind that Shakes the Barley (2006)
Ken Loach's bloody epic tells of
the painful struggle for freedom
from occupation as the Irish
Republican Army, having fought
against British rule, cannot agree
on the terms of the settlement.
Hunger (2008)
The disturbing story of Republican
prisoner Bobby Sands, and his
famous 1981 hunger strike in
The Maze.
The Guard (2011)
This black comedy starring
Brendan Gleeson is about an
unorthodox Garda joining forces
with a strait-laced FBI agent to
take on an international drug
smuggling gang in Connemara.

SHOPPING

Irish arts and crafts products provide the best buys when shopping in the Republic as most other goods cost less outside of the country. Irish craftsmen manufacture a number of internationally renowned products, such as Waterford Crystal, Aran sweaters and Donegal tweed. The Kilkenny Design Centre, set up in the early 1960s, infused new life into domestic and industrial design in Ireland and markets a good range of craftwork (*see CO KILKENNY*).

Throughout the country there are many less well-known enterprises and individual craftsmen and women producing quality hand-made articles. Manufacturers of textiles, glass and porcelain usually offer a tour of the factory and have showrooms and shops on the premises; their goods are often available in department stores, specialist shops in the major towns and tourist shops in popular country districts.

Some craft workers are grouped in certain regions, such as weavers in Donegal. Others congregate in special **craft villages**, set up by the Government in Dingle, Donegal town, Blennerville near Tralee or Roundstone in Connemara. Folk museums and folk villages usually organise craft demonstrations.

GLASS

The most famous and oldest glass factory in Ireland is in **Waterford** (*see WATERFORD*), but since its revival in 1951 several smaller enterprises have started to produce hand-blown lead crystal, which is cut, engraved or undecorated – Cavan Crystal, Galway Crystal, Grange Crystal, Sligo Crystal, Tipperary Crystal, Tyrone Crystal. Most have factory shops where first- and second-quality pieces can be bought. Many offer a guided tour of their workshops.

KNITWEAR

The thick cream-coloured (undyed) knitwear associated with the Aran Islands is the best known of Irish knitwear and is on sale throughout the country. Ireland produces a great variety of other knitted garments in a variety of textures and colours, particularly thick sweaters to keep out the wind and rain, using the traditional stitches – basket, blackberry, blanket, cable, diamond, moss, plait, trellis and zigzag.

House of Waterford Crystal, Waterford

© Andrew Bradley/Fáilte Ireland, Tourism Ireland

LACE

In the 19C there were many lace-making centres in Ireland, but few have survived. In most cases the skill was fostered by nuns; the traditional lacemakers of Clones and Carrickmacross have now formed themselves into cooperatives. Kenmare needlepoint lace is the most difficult to make; Clones is a crochet lace, but the other centres produce "mixed lace" on a base of machine-made cotton net.

LINEN

The demand for bed linen, table linen and tea towels keeps some 20 Irish linen houses in business. The popularity of linen as an apparel fabric has revived in recent years, since blending with synthetic or other natural fibres has reduced its tendency to crease. It is now used by top fashion designers all over the world, who appreciate its sheen and interesting texture, its durability and versatility – it is cool in summer and a good insulator in winter; it also dyes well in bright, clear colours.
Some tour guides offer a *Linen Homelands Tour* which visits the **Irish Linen Centre** (*see AROUND BELFAST*), as well as various linen manufacturers in and around Lisburn.

METALWORK

Throughout the country, and especially in the craft villages, artists are employing traditional techniques in gold, silver, bronze, pewter and enamel to produce flatware and jewellery; the traditional Claddagh rings (*see GALWAY*) worked in gold show a heart with two clasped hands.

PORCELAIN AND POTTERY

The largest and most famous porcelain factory in Ireland is at **Belleek** (*see CO FERMANAGH*), which produces fine translucent Parian ware and specialises in woven basket pieces and naturalistic floral decoration. Similar wares are produced by Donegal Irish Parian

Aran Islands' knitwear

© Fáilte Ireland

china. The Irish Dresden factory preserves and develops the tradition of delicate ornamental porcelain figures, which originated in Germany. There are many studio potteries in Ireland producing hand-turned articles, including some in Connemara.

TWEED

Donegal tweed is now mainly produced on power looms by four firms in Ardara, Donegal Town, Downies and Kilcar. Three of these companies also employ outworkers using hand-looms; most have diversified into the production of knitwear and ready-made garments or into weaving with other natural fibres – linen, cotton and silk.
Avoca Weavers was founded in 1723, the Kerry Woollen Mills later in the 18C. Foxford and Blarney were started in the 19C.

WOODWORK

There are a number of craftsmen producing hand-turned articles such as bowls, lamp stands and ornaments; the unique pieces are the graceful and delightful carvings produced by artists from skeletal pieces of bogwood. Some wood-turners produce musical instruments, such as pipes and hand-held drums (*bodhráns*) (*see Roundstone in CONNEMARA*).

ACTIVITIES FOR KIDS

Sights of interest to children are indicated in this guide with a ♙♙ symbol. At first glimpse Ireland may not seem the ideal place for children: the classic Irish holiday itinerary of scenic tours, a game of golf, long walks and enjoying the *craic* in the pub listening to traditional music is hardly likely to appeal to youngsters. Neither are there theme parks, or the kind of major family attractions to be found on the British mainland. However, with a bit of planning and creativity, there is no reason why the whole family can't have a great time.

ANIMAL MAGIC

Dublin Zoo, Fota Wildlife Park and Belfast Zoo present a variety of animals to view. Connemara ponies roam wild in the Connemara National Park and there are herds of deer in several parks – Glenveagh National Park in Co Donegal, Doneraile Wildlife Park, near Mallow and Parkanaur Forest Park, near Dungannon. There are many riding schools offering the chance of a pony or horse ride (⟲ *see WHAT TO SEE AND DO*) or you can take a trip in one of the jaunting cars in Killarney.

Mitchelstown Cave, County Tipperary

© Brian Morrison/Tourism Ireland

RAILWAY CHILDREN

A number of the old railways are being brought back into service. The longest is the Tralee-Blennerville Railway; there are shorter rides on the Fintown Railway in Co Donegal; the Foyle Valley Railway Centre in Londonderry, Downpatrick; and on two former peat bog trains – the Clonmacnoise and West Offaly Railway, near Birr and the narrow gauge railway at Peatlands Park, between Dungannon and Lough Neagh. There are model railways at the West Cork Model Railway Village near Clonakilty and the Fry Model Railway at Malahide.

THE GOOD OLD DAYS

Most children enjoy watching demonstrations of old crafts at the open-air museums – try Muckross Farms, near Killarney, Ulster Folk and Transport Museum, near Bangor and the Ulster-American Folk Park, north of Omagh in the Sperrin Mountains. Children are also likely to enjoy seeing how Irish ancestors lived in earlier centuries at the Craggaunowen Centre near Ennis, where the Brendan is on view, at the Lough Gur Interpretive Centre south of Limerick, at the Irish National Heritage Park near Wexford and the Ulster History Park, north of Omagh in the Sperrin Mountains.
A great selection of vintage vehicles is on view at the Museum of Transport in Clonmel, the National Transport Museum in Howth Castle, north of Dublin, the Museum of Irish Transport in Killarney and the Ulster Folk and Transport Museum near Bangor. Other delights for the mechanically minded are the Great Telescope at Birr Castle, which has been restored to working order.

GOING UNDERGROUND

The action of water on the landmass has produced several caves that can be safely explored – Aillwee Cave in The Burren, Mitchelstown Cave, near Caher, Dunmore Cave, near Kilkenny, Crag Cave, near Tralee and Marble Arch Caves, near Enniskillen.

Writer's Week, Listowel

© Domnick Walsh/Tourism Ireland

Calendar of Events

FEBRUARY
All Ireland Irish Dancing Championships – Different town every year. www.clrg.ie.

MARCH
17 March: St Patrick's Day Parade – Dublin and all major towns. Four-day spectacle of fireworks, carnival, marching bands and theatre. www.stpatricksday.ie.
Feis Ceoil – Dublin. Ten-day classical music festival. http://feisceoil.ie.

APRIL
All Ireland and International Dancing Championships – Different town every year. Competition between over 4,000 dancers from around the world (six days at Easter). www.irishdancingorg.com.
Pan Celtic International Festival – Letterkenny, Donegal. Inter-Celtic poetry, dancing, musical and arts extravaganza. www.panceltic.ie.

MAY–JUNE
Raft Race Weekend – Portrush Bands, street theatre, parachute displays and the Raft Race, raising funds for the RNLI. www.portrushraftrace.co.uk.

Writers' Week – Listowel. Ireland's oldest literary festival with workshops, exhibitions and a book fair. http://writersweek.ie.
Burren in Bloom. – North Clare. A series of illustrated talks and organised walks to give visitors a greater appreciation of the Burren. www.burreninbloom.com

JUNE
Fleadh Amhrán agus Rince – Ballycastle. Traditional festival of song, music and dance.
16 June: Bloomsday – Dublin. Annual celebration of James Joyce's great novel *Ulysses* – readings, re-enactments, music, theatre, street theatre. www.jamesjoyce.ie.
Galway Hookers' Regatta – *(Crinniú na mBád)* – Portaferry. Traditional boat gathering and regatta on Strangford Lough.
Irish Game Fair and Country Lifestyle Festival – Shanes Castle, Co Antrim. Game fair, carriage-driving, clay pigeon shooting, dog shows; Irish Medieval Festival. www.irishgamefair.com.
Loughcrew Garden Opera – Loughcrew. In the round production in Loughcrew Gardens. www.loughcrew.com (search under Calendar).

29

Ould Lammas Fair, Ballycastle

© Northern Ireland Tourist Board

JUNE–JULY

County Wexford Strawberry Festival – Enniscorthy. Strawberries and cream, arts and crafts exhibitions, Irish dancing and mumming, horse and greyhound racing, band recitals… www.strawberrryfest.com.

JULY

Willie Clancy Summer School – Milltown Malbay, Co Clare. Major festival of traditional Irish music (particularly *uilleann* pipes) and dance. www. scoilsamhraidhwillieclancy.com.

James Joyce Summer School – Dublin. Lectures, seminars and social events in Newman House, St Stephen's Green, where Joyce himself studied (two weeks). www.jamesjoyce.ie.

Twelfth of July Parades – Belfast. Bands, banners and brethren of the Orange Order celebrate the anniversary of the Battle of the Boyne (take local advice on safety issues).

International Rose Week – Dixon Park, Belfast. International rose trials.

Galway Arts Festival – Theatre, dance, music and street entertainment; Ireland's premier multi-disciplinary arts festival (13 days). www.giaf.com.

Summer Sensational – Temple Bar, Dublin. Four days of clowning around plus spectacular outdoor performances from Irish and international circus acts, including musical comedy, daring acrobatics and a lot more. www.temple-bar.ie.

West Cork Literary Festival – Bantry. Writers and workshops. www.westcorkliteraryfestival.ie.

JULY–AUGUST

Yeats Festival (Summer School) – Sligo. Literature, music and drama. www.yeatssociety.com.

All-Ireland Road Bowls Finals – Armagh. Ancient game, played only in Co Armagh and Co Cork, in which competitors used to throw cannonballs. www.irishroadbowling.ie.

AUGUST

O'Carolan Harp and Traditional Music Festival – Keadew. Performance of his works, international harp competition, Irish music, ceilidhs, concerts, song and set dancing, many open-air events. August Bank Holiday. www.ocarolanharpfestival.ie.

Steam Engine Rally – Stradbally. Stradbally Steam Museum annual steam and vintage show. August Bank Holiday. www.irishsteam.ie.

Failte Ireland Dublin Horse Show – International team jumping competitions held at the Royal Dublin Society ground in Ballsbridge; a grand equestrian and social event. www.dublinhorseshow.com.

Kilkenny Arts Festival – Ten days of music, visual art, theatre, literature, children's arts and outdoor events. www.kilkennyarts.ie.

10–12 August: Puck Fair – Killorglin. One of the oldest street festivals in Ireland, centred on a billy goat enthroned in a chair, with a traditional horse fair, busking, open-air concerts, parades and fireworks. www.puckfair.ie.

Gathering of the Boats – Kinvara. *(Crinniú na mBád)* Galway hookers' regatta. www.kinvara.com/cnb.html.

Clifden Connemara Pony Show – Grand showing of Ireland's only native pony. www.cpbs.ie.

Fleadh Cheoil na hEireann – The biggest traditional Irish music festival (seven days, different venue each year). Largest showcase of traditional Irish musicians, singers and dancers, with over 10,000 performers taking part. http://2014fleadh.ie.

Rose of Tralee Festival – Bands, parades, a famous beauty parade, dancing, horse racing and many other activities to celebrate Irish culture. http://roseoftralee.ie.

Ould Lammas Fair – Ballycastle. Oldest traditional Irish fair with horse trading, street entertainment, competitions and market stalls.

Masters of Tradition – Bantry. Celebrates traditional music over four days. www.westcorkmusic.ie/mastersoftradition.

AUGUST–SEPTEMBER

Lisdoonvarna Matchmaking Festival – Europe's biggest matchmaking event with music and dance and horse racing *(late August to early October)*. www.matchmakerireland.com.

Appalachian and Bluegrass Music Festival – Ulster American Folk Park, Omagh. Europe's premier bluegrass music festival attracts thousands of visitors to watch International stars and award-winning Irish artists. www.folkpark.com.

All Ireland Hurling Finals – Dublin. Annual national hurling championships at Croke Park. www.gaa.ie.

Clarenbridge Oyster Festival – Mid-Sept. Food and stout, music, dance. www.clarenbridge.com

Laytown Strand Races – Mid-Sept Unique horse race held annually on the beach in East Meath at low tide. www.laytownstrandraces.ie.

All Ireland Football Finals – Dublin. Annual Gaelic football championship finals at Croke Park. www.gaa.ie.

Galway International Oyster Festival – World Oyster-opening Championships, held in the pubs; oyster tasting, music, song and dance. http://galwayoysterfestival.com.

SEPTEMBER–OCTOBER

Dublin Theatre Festival – Best of world theatre and new productions from all the

Fleadh Season

Festivals are an essential part of the Irish experience; there are so many in summer that you would have to go out of your way to avoid them. A term you may well come across is the gaelic *Fleadh* (pronounced *flaa*), which simply means festival and is now synonymous with typical Irish entertainment.

The biggest Fleadh of all is simply titled "Fleadh (plus the year)", each August, over 200,000 people gather from all over the world for a week-long cultural celebration (the venue location changes). The world record for the largest Irish traditional music session was set at Fleadh 2007, when 2,700 musicians performed together in O'Connor Square, Tullamore.

Electric Picnic Festival, Stradbally

© Tourism Ireland

major Irish companies.
www.dublintheatrefestival.com

Electric Picnic Festival – Stradbally, Co.Laois. Ireland's preeminent arts and music festival, hosting dozens of international acts every year

OCTOBER

Cork International Film Festival – Ireland's oldest film event presents the best of international and new Irish cinema. www.corkfilmfest.org.

O'Carolan Harp Cultural and Heritage Festival – Nobber. Harp and instrumental workshops and competitions, traditional Irish music concerts, step and set dancing, traditional festival Mass in Irish, seminars and lectures. www.carolanfestival.com

Kinsale International Gourmet Festival – Kinsale. The best of fine food and wines in a convivial party atmosphere with music, dance and wine tasting. www.kinsalerestaurants.com.

Ballinasloe October Fair – Ballinasloe, Co Galway. One of the three great country fairs of Ireland for buying and selling horses; also features traditional music, tug-of-war competitions, bareback riding, show jumping, a carnival and street traders. www.ballinasloe octoberfair.com.

Cork Guinness Jazz Festival – Great jazz and an imperative rendezvous for the greatest names in this genre. www.guinnessjazzfestival.com.

Baboro – International Arts Festival for Children – Galway. Workshops, storytelling, theatre. (6 days). www.baboro.ie.

OCTOBER–NOVEMBER

Wexford Festival Opera – Production of rare operas and other cultural activities *(10 days)*. http://wexfordopera.com.

Belfast Festival at Queen's – Largest arts festival in Ireland: music from classical to folk and jazz, drama, ballet and cinema. www.belfastfestival.com.

Useful Words and Phrases

	Translation
Alt	Cliff
Ard	High, Height, Hillock
Áth	Ford
Bád	Boat
Baile	Town, townland, homestead
Bawn	Area around house
Beag	Little
Beal	Opening, Entrance, River mouth
Bealtaine	1 May, month of May
Boireann	Large rock, rocky district
Boreen	A small road
Bóthar	Road
Brogue	Boot, Shoe
Buchaill	Boy
Buí	Yellow
Bullan	A hollow in stone
Bun	End, bottom
Cabhán	Hollow
Caiseal	Castle, circular stone fort
Caisleán	Castle
Caladh	Harbour, Landing place
Capall	Horse
Carraig	Rock
Cath	Battle
Cathair	Circular stone fort, City
Cealtrach	Old burial ground
Céide	Hillock
Cill	Church
Cloch	Stone
Cluain	Meadow
Cno	Hill
Colleen	Girl
Crúbeen	Sheep's or Pig's foot
Cruishkeen	A Jug
Dearg	Red
Dia Dhuit	Hello

	Translation
Díseart	Desert, hermitage
Droichead	Bridge
Dubh	Black
Dún	Fort
Eaglais	Church
Eas	Waterfall
Fear	Man
Féile	Festival
Fir	Men
Gall	Foreigner
Go Raibh Maith Agat	Thank you
Gorm	Blue
Gort	Field
Inis	Island
Lár	Centre
Leithinis	Peninsula
Lios	Fairy fort
Mór	Large
Óg	Young
Oileán	Island
Piseog	Superstition
Poitín	Illegal whiskey
Poll	Hole, Cave
Puc	To strike a ball with a hurley
Rath	Fort
Sagart	Priest
Sceách	Thorn bush
Sean	Old
Sláinte	Cheers
Sleán	Turf spade
Slí	Route, way
Sliabh	Mountain
Tay	Tea
Teach	House
Togher	Road through a bog
Trá	Beach, Strand
Túr	Tower
Uachtar	Top, upper part

Know Before You Go

USEFUL WEBSITES

www.ireland.com
The official tourist board website for all of Ireland. A wide range of information for the visitor.

www.discovernorthernireland.com
The official regional tourist board website for Northern Ireland.

www.discovering Ireland.com
The website of My Guide Ireland, customized Irish holiday specialists.

www.irishgenealogy.ie
The Irish Genealogical Project, answering questions about Irish ancestry.

www.wildatlanticway.com)
At over 2,500km this is Ireland's first long-distance touring route, and the longest defined route in the world.

www.irelandsancienteast.com
Covering a vast swathe of territory east of the river Shannon, the Ancient East encourages visitors to explore the history of the area.

TOURIST OFFICES

For information, brochures, maps and assistance in planning a trip, contact:

IRISH TOURIST BOARD (FÁILTE IRELAND)

- **Australia**
  Level 5, 36 Carrington Street, Sydney, NSW 2000.
  ✆029 299 6177.

- **Canada**
  2 Bloor Street West, Suite 3403, Toronto ON M4W.
  ✆1 416 925 6368.

- **United Kingdom**
  London: 103 Wigmore Street, W1U 1QS. ✆020 7518 0800.
  Glasgow: James Millar House,

7th Floor, 98 West George Street.
✆0141 572 4030.

- **United States**
  345 Park Avenue, 17th Floor, New York, NY 10154.
  ✆212 418 0800.

NORTHERN IRELAND TOURIST BOARD (NITB) OFFICES

- **United Kingdom**
  24 Haymarket, London SW1 4DG.
  ✆020 7766 9920.

- **Republic of Ireland**
  Suffolk Street, Dublin 2.
  ✆01 605 7732
  www.discovernorthernireland.com

LOCAL TOURIST OFFICES

In this guide the contact details for Tourist Information Centres are identified by the 🚺 symbol.
Some local tourist offices are only open during the summer months. The centres can supply town plans, timetables and information on sightseeing, local entertainment and sports facilities. Many have bureau de change facilities and a hotel reservation service.

INTERNATIONAL VISITORS
IRISH EMBASSIES

- **Australia**
  20 Arkana Street, Yarralumla, Canberra. ✆06214 0000.
  www.embassyofireland.au.com
  Consulate General –
  Level 26, 1 Market Street.
  Sydney NSW 2000.
  ✆612 9264 9635.

- **Canada**
  Suite 1105, 130 Albert Street, Ottawa, Ontario KIP 5G4.
  ✆613 233 6281.
  www.embassyofireland.ca

- **New Zealand**
  Level 3, National Bank Tower, 205 Queen Street, Auckland.
  Post address:

PO Box 279, Auckland 1140.
📞09 977 2252.

- **South Africa**
2nd Floor, Parkdev Building,
Brooklyn Bridge Office Park,
570 Fehrsen Street. Brooklyn 0181.
PO Box 4174, Pretoria 0001, SA.
📞(27) 12 342 5062.

- **United Kingdom**
17 Grosvenor Place, London
SW1X 7HR.
📞020 7235 2171.
www.embassyofireland.co.uk

- **United States**
2234 Massachusetts Avenue NW,
Washington DC 20008-2849.
📞202 462 3939.
www.embassyofireland.org

FOREIGN EMBASSIES AND CONSULATES IN IRELAND

- **Australia**
Fitzwilton House (7th floor),
Wilton Terrace, Dublin 2.
📞01 664 5300.
www.ireland.embassy.gov.au

- **Canada**
(3rd floor), 7–8 Wilton Terrace,
Dublin 2.
📞01 417 4000.
www.canada.ie

- **South Africa**
Alexandra House, Earlsfort Centre,
Earlsfort Terrace, Dublin 2.
📞01 661 5553

- **United Kingdom**
29 Merrion Road,
Ballsbridge,
Dublin 4.
📞01 205 3700.
www.britishembassy.ie

- **USA**
42 Elgin Road, Ballsbridge,
Dublin 4.
📞01 668 8777.
http://dublin.usembassy.gov

ENTRY REQUIREMENTS

Visitors entering Ireland must be in possession of a **valid national passport** (except British nationals). In case of loss or theft, report to the appropriate embassy and the local police. Visitors who require an **entry visa** for the Republic of Ireland or Northern Ireland should apply at least three weeks in advance to the Irish Embassy or the United Kingdom Embassy.Useful information for US nationals on visa requirements, customs regulations, medical care etc. for international travel can be found by visiting www.travel.state.gov. Visitors from outside the EU should have comprehensive travel insurance. Visitors from EU countries should carry a **European Health Insurance Card (EHIC)** and have adequate travel insurance for the duration of their stay. In case of the loss or theft of any document, report it to the local police.

CUSTOMS REGULATIONS

Tax-free allowances for various commodities are governed by EU legislation. Details of these allowances are available at most ports of entry to the Republic of Ireland/ United Kingdom and from customs authorities. It is against the law to bring into the Republic of Ireland firearms, explosives, illicit drugs, meat and meat products, plant and plant products (including seeds). It is against the law to bring into the United Kingdom drugs, firearms and ammunition, obscene material featuring children, counterfeit merchandise, unlicenced livestock (birds or animals), anything related to endangered species (furs, ivory, horn, leather) and certain plants (potatoes, bulbs, seeds, trees).

- **Customs and Excise** – Passenger Terminal, Dublin Airport, Co Dublin. 📞01 844 5538; www.revenue.ie
- **Customs and Excise** – Custom House, Belfast BT1 3ET. 📞0845 010 9000 www.hmrc.gov.uk

Giant's Causeway Visitor Information Centre

© Hufton and Crow/Northern Ireland Tourist Board

For US nationals returning to the US after travelling abroad there is useful information in the leaflet *Know Before You Go,* available as a downloadable pdf from www.cbp.gov.

DOMESTIC ANIMALS

No animals, pets or otherwise, may be brought into the Republic of Ireland, except from the United Kingdom. Domestic animals (dogs, cats) with vaccination documents are allowed into the UK (Great Britain and Northern Ireland).

♦ **Department of Agriculture, Food and Rural Development** – Agriculture House, Kildare St, Dublin 2. ℘01 607 2000.

HEALTH

For emergencies, dial ℘999.
In Ireland hospital treatment is available in emergencies, but it is not free of charge. Emergency help can be obtained from the Casualty Department of a hospital or from a pharmacy/chemist.
Nationals of non-EU countries should take out comprehensive insurance. Nationals of EU countries should apply to their own National Social Security Offices for a **European Health Insurance Card (EHIC)** (not obligatory for UK nationals; proof of identity only necessary), which entitles them to emergency medical treatment under an EU Reciprocal Medical Treatment arrangement from a hospital or from a doctor in Ireland whose name is on the Health Board Panel of Doctors (list available from the local health board).

ACCESSIBILITY

Where sights described in this guide are accessible, or mostly accessible to disabled visitors, they are indicated by the ♿ symbol. Absence of a symbol does *not* indicate there are no facilities for disabled visitors at the site or attraction in question, just that there are certain difficulties to overcome. As ever, call ahead to plan your visit. The red-cover **Michelin Guide Great Britain and Ireland** indicates hotels with facilities suitable for disabled travellers. The following organisations provide further information:

♦ **Tourism for All**
www.tourismforall.org.uk
℘0845 124 9971
National UK charity dedicated to making tourism welcoming to all.

♦ **Ableize**
www.ableize.com/
Disability-Ireland
Information and advice, including arts, sports, accommodation and many other useful links.

♦ **Discover Ireland**
www.discoverireland.ie
Enter disabled in the search tab for links to a variety of websites in Ireland that cater to the needs and interests of visitors with disabilities.

Getting There and Getting Around

BY PLANE

Many international airlines operate flights to the international airports in Ireland – Dublin, Shannon, Knock and Belfast. All airports are linked by bus to the neighbouring towns.

Regional airports offering scheduled flights to Dublin, the UK and Europe are Kerry Airport (Farrannfore), Galway Airport, Knock International Airport, Sligo, Donegal and Derry (Londonderry) Airports.

Several airlines offer non-stop trans-Atlantic flights to Dublin and Shannon. Others fly to Belfast and to Knock. Information, brochures and timetables are available from the airlines and from travel agents. Fly-Drive schemes are operated by most airlines.

- **Aer Lingus**
  www.aerlingus.com
- **Air France**
  www.airfrance.co.uk
- **British Airways/bmi**
  www.britishairways.com
- **easyJet**
  www.easyjet.com
- **flybe**
  www.flybe.com
- **Jet2.com**
  www.jet2.com
- **Manx2**
  www.manx2.com
- **Ryanair**
  www.ryanair.com

BY SEA

Details of passenger ferry and car ferry services to Ireland from the United Kingdom and France can be obtained from travel agencies or from the main carriers. Information about ferries to the offshore islands is given in the *Discovering* section of the guide.

- **Brittany Ferries**
  www.brittany-ferries.com
  General enquiries:
  ☎0871 244 0744 (UK).
  Roscoff (France)-Cork
- **Irish Ferries**
  www.irishferries.com
  General enquiries: ☎0818 300 400. Holyhead (Wales)–Dublin; Pembroke Wales)–Rosslare. Cherbourg and Roscoff (France)–Rosslare.
- **Stena Line**
  www.stenaline.com
  ☎01 907 5555 (Dublin). Fishguard–Rosslare; Holyhead–Dublin; Belfast-Liverpool. Belfast-Cairnryan (Scotland)
- **P&O Ferries**
  www.poferries.com
  ☎08716 64 64 64 (UK).
  ☎01 407 34 34 (Dublin).
  Larne-Troon or Cairnryan (Scotland); Dublin–Liverpool.
- **Steam Packet Company**
  www.steam-packet.com
  Isle of Man–Belfast and Dublin (also Larne during TT races).
  ☎08722 992 992.

BY COACH/BUS

Regular coach services operate between the major Irish towns and the major cities in Great Britain and the Continent via the car ferry ports at Rosslare, Dublin Ferryport and Larne. As an example of journey times, it takes around 9 hours to get from London to Dublin.

- **National Express**
  www.nationalexpress.com
- **Bus Éireann**
  www.buseireann.ie
- **Dublin Bus (Bus Atha Cliath)**
  ☎01 873 4222
  www.dublinbus.ie
- **Ulsterbus**
  www.translink.co.uk
  (♿*See By Rail*).

BY CAR

Nationals of EU countries wishing to drive in Ireland require a **valid national driving licence**; nationals of non-EU countries require an **International Driving Permit (IDP)**.

This is obtainable in the US from the National Auto Club (see www.thenac.com for details) or from a local branch of the American Automobile Association (www.aaa.com). Nationals of other non-European countries should check before leaving their home country.

If you plan to bring your own car to Ireland you will need the vehicle's **registration papers** ("log-book") and an approved **nationality plate**. **Vehicle insurance cover** is compulsory. Although no longer a legal requirement, the **International Insurance Certificate (Green Card)** is the most effective proof of insurance cover and is internationally recognised by the police and other authorities.

In the case of loss or theft of any document, report it to the local police.

CAR HIRE/RENTAL

There are car rental agencies at airports, railway stations and in all large towns throughout Ireland. European cars usually have manual transmission; automatic cars need to be specified at the time of booking.

Before crossing the border between the Republic and Northern Ireland it is important to check that the insurance cover extends to the other country. It is invariably cheaper to return a hire car to its pick-up point than to leave it elsewhere.

DRIVING IN IRELAND

The road network consists of a limited network of motorways, some high standard major roads and plenty of narrow country roads. In the peatlands, where the road surface may be undulating, it is a good idea to slow down.

HIGHWAY CODE

- Traffic drives on the **left.**
- The **minimum driving age** is 17 throughout Ireland.
- Traffic on main roads and on roundabouts has priority.
- Give way to traffic coming from the right at roundabouts.
- The driver and front-seat passenger must wear **seat belts**. Rear-seat belts must be worn where they are fitted; children under 12 must travel in the rear seats.
- Full or dipped **headlights** should be switched on in poor visibility and at night; use **sidelights** only when the vehicle is stationary in an area without street lighting.
- It is obligatory to carry a red warning triangle or to have hazard warning lights to use in the case of a **breakdown** or **accident**.

PARKING

There are multi-storey car parks in cities; in towns disc systems, parking meters and paying parking zones; in the last two cases, small change is necessary and in the last case tickets must be obtained from the ticket machines and displayed inside the windscreen.

In Northern Ireland the usual regulations are as follows:

- **Double red line** – no stopping at any time (freeway)
- **Double yellow line** – no parking at any time
- **Single yellow line** – no parking for set periods, as indicated on panel
- **Dotted yellow line** – parking limited to certain times only.

PENALTIES

In the Republic

Parking offences may attract an on-the-spot fine. Drivers suspected of **speeding** are liable for an on-the-spot fine. Drivers suspected of **driving while under the influence of alcohol** are liable to be checked with a breathalyser and to prosecution.

In Northern Ireland

Failure to display a parking ticket may result in a fine. Illegal parking will lead to a Penalty Charge Notice and, in some cases, to the vehicle being clamped or towed away.

Driving along the north coast, County Antrim

© Northern Ireland Tourist Board

Drivers suspected of **driving while under the influence of alcohol** are liable to be checked with a breathalyser and to be prosecuted. Drivers suspected of **speeding** are liable to be prosecuted; there are speed camera warning signs beside the road before you enter a speed check area. Speed cameras are yellow.

ROAD SIGNS

The colour code for different types of road signs is as follows:

- **blue** for motorways
- **green** for major roads
- **black on white** for local
- **brown** for tourist signs

ROAD TOLLS

Tolls are levied on the East Link Bridge (Dublin), which spans the Liffey estuary; the West-Link Bridge (Dublin), which runs north–south on

SPEED LIMITS
Republic of Ireland:
30mph/50kph: in built-up areas
50mph/80kph: on regional and local roads
62mph/100kph: on national roads
74mph/120kph: on motorways
Northern Ireland:
30mph/50kph: in built-up areas
60mph/96kph: on country roads
70mph/112kph: on dual carriageways and motorways

the Western edge of the city; on the M1 Drogheda By-pass; and the M4 Kinnegad-Enfield-Kilcock road.

PETROL/GAS

Most service stations have dual-pumps; **unleaded pumps** are identified by a green stripe or green pump handles. Prices tend to vary between the Republic and Northern Ireland but not significantly.

MOTORING ORGANISATIONS

In Ireland and the UK accident insurance and breakdown service schemes are available through motoring organisations. Members of the American Automobile Club should obtain the brochure.

Automobile Association (AA)

- **Ireland:** ✆01 617 9104; www.theaa.ie.
- **UK:** ✆0800 085 2721 (sales); ✆0870 600 0371 (general enquiries); www.theaa.com.

Royal Automobile Club (RAC)

- **Ireland:** ✆0800 015 6000 (sales and customer service). www.rac.co.uk.
- **Northern Ireland:** ✆0844 273 5928 (sales); www.rac.co.uk.

MAPS AND PLANS

For Route Planning use the maps in this guide, **Michelin Map 712 Ireland** and the **Michelin Atlas Great Britain and Ireland**. The atlas and map 712 show the major roads (N or A) and many of the minor roads (R/L or B).

BY TRAIN

Irish Rail Service, Northern Ireland Railways and the various British railway companies operate train services between the major cities in Ireland and the United Kingdom.

- ◆ **Iarnród Éireann / Irish Rail**
  Online timetables and ticket reservation; ✆ 1850 366 222; www.irishrail.ie.
  Iarnród Eireann Travel Centre, 35 Lower Abbey Street, Dublin 1. ✆ 01 703 4070.
- ◆ **Railtours Ireland** –
  (using train and coach).
  Dublin Tourism Centre, Suffolk Street, Dublin 2 or opposite

Connolly Station; ✆ 01 856 0045. www.railtoursireland.com. Toll free from US: ✆ 011 800 5008 0200.

- ◆ **CIE** – national coach/rail/Dublin Bus operator. International and national routes, timetables, fares on www.cie.ie.
- ◆ **Northern Ireland Rail**
  Online timetables and journey planner for public transport by rail and road.
  Central Station, Belfast BT1 3PB. ✆ 028 9066 6630 (enquiries). International services and short breaks. ✆ 028 9024 2420; www.translink.co.uk.

Where to Stay

A variety of different types of accommodation is available in Ireland. Hotels and restaurants are described in the Address Books within the *Discovering* section.

In town centres, **parking** can be a problem but many hotels have a car park on site or a short walk away. In a small town, the only hotel may double as the **local disco** and it may be very noisy until the early hours on a Saturday night, especially if there is a wedding party.

Most establishments offer a light **Continental-style breakfast** of coffee and bread and jam, as well as the traditional **cooked breakfast**. The latter is often a feature of bed and breakfast accommodation and traditionally comes in generous portions.

ACCOMMODATION TYPES
HOTELS
Traditionally hotels tend to be medium to large establishments, where the bedrooms have ensuite facilities and a full range of services.

Throughout Ireland you can now find some of the finest five-star, deluxe, state-of-the-art design and boutique hotels in the British Isles.
Country houses and even castles have seized on the resort trend and many now offer luxurious spas, golf courses and a complete outdoor sports and leisure pursuits package within their estates.

GUESTHOUSES

The term guesthouse describes a smaller operation than a hotel, with fewer facilities, which generally appeals more to visitors on holiday than to those on business.
The properties vary from modern purpose-built premises to Georgian and Victorian houses.

INNS/PUBS WITH ROOMS

In the smaller towns and villages a local pub often has rooms to let.

BED AND BREAKFAST

The distinction between bed-and-breakfast places and guesthouses is often blurred but the traditional bed-and-breakfast is a family-run affair, offering one or two bedrooms at a moderate price.

This simple form of accommodation is found all over Ireland in properties ranging from a simple bungalow to a "Great House" (stately home).

FARM HOLIDAYS

Being a predominantly agricultural country, Ireland has a great range of farms, many of which welcome visitors in the summer season.

SELF CATERING

In many parts of the country, particularly the tourist districts, there are purpose-built holiday villages consisting of a cluster of well-appointed cottages. *See Budget Accommodation.*

UNIVERSITY RESIDENCES

Accommodation in universities (single rooms and self-catering apartments) is available during school vacations, particularly in Dublin, Cork and Galway. *See Budget Accommodation.*

HOSTELS

There are around 50 **hostels** in the Republic and six in Northern Ireland. *See Budget Accommodation.*

CAMP SITES

Ireland has many officially graded caravan and camping parks with modern facilities and a variety of sports facilities. The past couple of years has seen a dramatic rise in the number of upmarket camping sites, or "glamping" sites. Here the focus is on comfort, with guests staying in decked-out yurts or cabins.

USEFUL WEBSITES

http://ireland.com/accommodation
An accommodation booking service developed for the Irish Tourist Board (Bord Fáilte) and the Northern Irish Tourist Board (NITB), and their networks of regional tourist boards. Information on flights, ferries, special interest holidays. ℘01850 668668

in Ireland; ℘+353 66 9791804 (international).
www.discoverireland.com
Has thousands of offers on accommodation, travel, holiday packages, attractions and activities and more.

HOTELS AND GUESTHOUSES

- **The Irish Hotels Federation**
  ℘1 800 989 909 within Ireland; ℘+353 1 2939170 from elsewhere. www.irelandhotels.com.
- **Manor House Hotels and Irish Country Hotels**
  ℘0818 281 281 from within the Republic of Ireland; ℘877 905 6789 US Toll Free; ℘+353 1295 8900 from elsewhere. Includes castles.
  www.manorhousehotels.com.
- **The Hidden Ireland**
  Accommodation in historic Irish houses in town and country. ℘01 662 7166 or 098 66650; www.hiddenireland.com.
- **Ireland's Blue Book**
  Irish country houses, historic hotels and restaurants affiliated to the Historic Hotels of Europe. ℘01 676 9914. www.irelands-blue-book.ie.
- **Irish Farmhouse Holidays**
  B&B and self-catering options on farms across the land. ℘0 71 982 2222; www.irishfarmholidays.com.

BED AND BREAKFAST ACCOMMODATION

- **Town and Country Homes Association**
  Over 1,100 B&Bs in town, city and countryside locations across Ireland. They also publish *Bed and Breakfast Ireland.* ℘071 982 2222; www.townandcountry.ie.
- **Elegant Ireland**
  Exclusive rented castles, country houses and cottages. ℘01 473 2505; www.elegant.ie.
- **Premier Collection of Ireland**
  Twenty-nine guesthouses. ℘01 205 2826; www.premierguesthouses.com

Places to stay

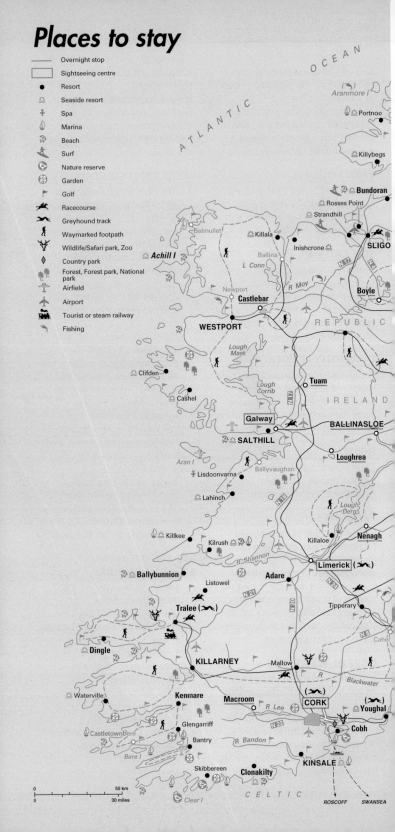

- — Overnight stop
- ▭ Sightseeing centre
- ● Resort
- ⌂ Seaside resort
- ⚇ Spa
- ⚓ Marina
- ﻬ Beach
- ⚐ Surf
- ⊛ Nature reserve
- ⊛ Garden
- ⚑ Golf
- ⚞ Racecourse
- ⚟ Greyhound track
- ⚡ Waymarked footpath
- ⚡ Wildlife/Safari park, Zoo
- ◊ Country park
- ♣ Forest, Forest park, National park
- ✈ Airfield
- ✈ Airport
- ⛟ Tourist or steam railway
- ⚲ Fishing

ATLANTIC OCEAN

Aranmore I
Portnoo
Killybegs
Bundoran
Rosses Point
Strandhill
Belmullet
Killala
Inishcrone
SLIGO
Achill I
Ballina
L Conn
R Moy
Boyle
Newport
Castlebar
REPUBLIC
WESTPORT
Lough Mask
OF
Lough Corrib
Clifden
Cashel
Tuam
IRELAND
Galway
BALLINASLOE
SALTHILL
Loughrea
Aran I
Lisdoonvarna
Ballyvaughan
Lahinch
Lough Derg
Killee
Kilrush
Killaloe
Nenagh
R Shannon
Limerick
Ballybunnion
Adare
Listowel
Tralee
Tipperary
Caher
Dingle
KILLARNEY
Mallow
Waterville
Kenmare
Macroom
R Lee
R Blackwater
CORK
Youghal
Castletownbere
Glengarriff
Bantry
Bere I
R Bandon
Cobh
KINSALE
Skibbereen
Clonakilty
CELTIC
0   50 km
0 30 miles
Clear I
ROSCOFF   SWANSEA

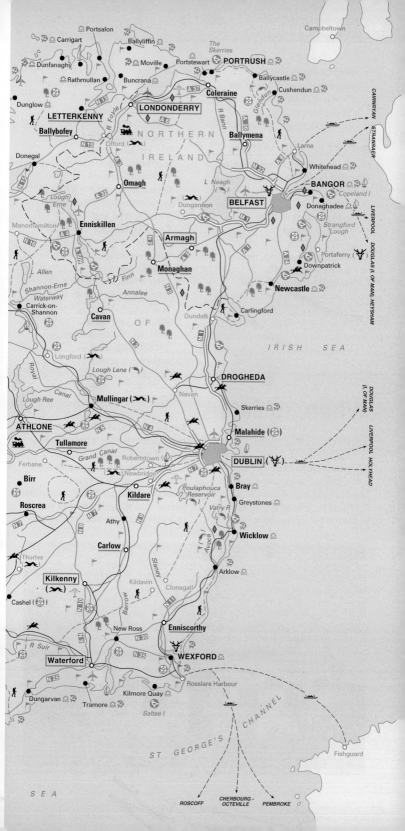

◆ **Irish Cottages and Holiday Homes Association**
Over 5,000 holiday cottages and houses to rent. ✆01 205 2777; www.irishcottageholidays.com

BUDGET ACCOMMODATION

Simple accommodation is available in hostels (single, twin and four–six-bedded rooms) through the following organisations:

◆ **Independent Holiday Hostels Ireland**
✆01 836 4700; www.hostels-ireland.com.

◆ **Northern Ireland Hostelling International**
Modern smart hostels in Armagh, Belfast, Bushmills, Enniskillen, Newcastle and Whitepark Bay.
✆028 9032 4733; www.hini.org.uk

◆ **An Oige**
Youth Hostel Association. Twenty-six youth hostels throughout the country.
✆01 830 4555; http://anoige.ie

◆ **Ireland in Summer**
B&B and self-catering accommodations on seven universities campuses in Dublin, Galway, Cork and Limerick. www.irelandinsummer.com.

◆ **Irish Caravan and Camping Council**
Over 100 camping and caravan parks. www.camping-ireland.ie

◆ **Travelodge**
Value-for-money rooms in 12 Travelodge hotels located in Dublin, Cork, Limerick, Galway, Waterford, Belfast and Derry.
✆01890 709 709 (Ireland); ✆08719 848 484 (UK); www.travelodge.ie

Where to Eat

Ireland offers a huge range of places to eat, from top-class restaurants offering the highest quality produce and the latest in the culinary art; wine bars, bistros and brasseries; and fast food outlets such as pizzerias, cafés and fish & chip shops. Many historical sights, like the National Trust properties in Northern Ireland, also provide lunch and tea.

For a selection of the eating choices available, try the Restaurants Association of Ireland, whose website (www.rai.ie) lets you search for your nearest affiliated restaurant. See also

Café, Inishmore, Arran Islands

© Christophe Boisvieux/hemis.fr

Whiskey or Whisky

The origins of Irish whiskey (usually but not always spelled with an "e") are lost in the mists of time, but it was being distilled and drunk throughout Ireland by the 16C and Elizabeth I seems to have had a taste for it. Illicit whiskey *(poteen)* appeared in the 17C when the government introduced a tax on distilling (1661) and set up a department of Excisemen (Gaugers) to police the distilleries. By the end of the 17C, the substance was being exported all over the British Empire. Exports to the USA dwindled with prohibition in the 1920s and the British Empire market was closed off by the War of Independence. In 1966 the few surviving distilleries joined to form the Irish Distillers Company and founded a new distillery in Midleton; in the early 1970s they took over Bushmills but were taken over by Pernod-Ricard in 1989.

Despite the popularity of blended whisky from Scotland, Irish distillers have preferred to maintain the lightness and fuller flavour of their traditional product, achieved by **Triple Distillation.** The grain, including the husks, is milled to produce "grist" which is mixed with hot water in a large vessel (mash tun) to release the sugars; the liquid is then drawn off. This process is repeated twice and the liquid from the first and second mashing (wort) is pumped into vessels called washbacks; yeast is added, which reacts with the sugars to produce a light brown liquid. When fermentation is complete the liquid is distilled three times. The spirit is matured in old sherry or Bourbon casks and then blended (vatted) for two or three days.

www.travel.viamichelin.com for its choice of restaurants and information on nearby visitor attractions.

EATING OUT

Restaurants are usually open at lunchtime from noon until after 2pm depending on their location; in the evening from around 6.30pm to 10pm. Many close one day a week and they may also close early on Sundays and Mondays (between 7pm and 8pm in Northern Ireland).

It is always advisable to book in the evening, particularly at the weekend. Portions are usually generous.

SPECIALITIES

see also INTODUCTION, Irish Cuisine.

Being an agricultural country, Ireland produces very good home-reared meat, particularly beef and lamb, and excellent dairy products – local cheeses, butter and cream.

Near the coast there should be a good choice of fish; salmon is usually available everywhere. In the less-expensive restaurants the menu may not offer much in the way of fresh fruit and vegetables but the potatoes are usually very good. Look out for soda bread, potato cakes (even at breakfast), oysters and Guinness, black pudding – a speciality in Co Cork – and for *carrageen*, a form of seaweed that is used in savoury and sweet dishes.

TIPPING

Tipping is optional but it is common to leave 10 percent if the service has been good. Often a discretionary service charge (frequently 12.5 percent) is included in the bill, which you may choose not to pay if the service has been poor. Some unscrupulous restaurants may make a service charge *and* leave the total open on a credit card slip, encouraging customers to unwittingly tip twice. To ensure the staff get your tip, always leave cash.

OTHER PUBLICATIONS

Consult the red-cover **Michelin Guide Great Britain and Ireland** or the **Michelin Eating Out in Pubs in Britain and Ireland** for even more places to stay and eat throughout Ireland. The red guide provides comprehensive coverage of hotels, guesthouses and restaurants, while the pub guide covers all the best spots for a good pint and pub lunch. Specialist guides and information about places to eat, drink and stay in Ireland is also available at www.

ireland-guide.com. **Good Food Ireland** and its website, www.goodfoodireland.ie, brings together information on various types of accommodation, places to eat, cookery schools, food producers, farm shops across Ireland and special events related to these areas.

Basic Information

ABBREVIATIONS

Dúchas – Heritage of Ireland, Gaeltacht and the Islands;
HM – Historic Monuments Branch of the Department of the Environment in Northern Ireland;
NT – National Trust.

COMMUNICATIONS
TELEPHONES

The main telephone service in the Republic of Ireland is Eircom (www.eircom.ie).

Pre-paid callcards for national and international calls from public phones are available from post offices and some shops (newsagents, tobacconists). It is usually more expensive (+ 30 percent) to make a long-distance telephone call from a hotel than from a pay phone.

To make an **international call**, dial 00 followed by the country code, followed by the area code (without the initial 0). The codes for direct dialling to other countries are printed at the front of telephone directories. When dialling from the Republic to Northern Ireland, substitute the 028 prefix with 048, followed by the number. You should be able to make and receive calls with your mobile phone while in Ireland.

DISCOUNTS

If you are intending to apply for a reduced price pass, take some passport-size photos with you and all relevant documentation to qualify for your entitlement as a senior citizen or student.

SEASON TICKETS AND PASSES

For a one-off payment **The Dublin Pass** includes transport from the airport to the city, entrance to 34 of Dublin's top attractions and special offers in many of Dublin's top shops, restaurants, tours and entertainment venues: www.dublinpass.ie/dublin pass.**The Belfast Visitor Pass** offers unlimited central bus and rail travel and over 90 offers and discounts on key visitor attractions, tours, cafes, restaurants and shops. You can buy the pass online at www.gotobelfast.com, at the Belfast Welcome Centre (47 Donegall Place), Belfast airport tourist information desks or at any Translink station in Belfast.

The annual **Heritage Card** provides free admission to all Heritage Ireland sites, available from most fee-paying sites, or purchase online from www.heritageireland.ie.

DIALLING CODES	
Australia:	☏ **00 61**
Canada:	☏ **00 1**
Republic of Ireland:	☏ **00 353**
New Zealand:	☏ **00 64**
United Kingdom: (including Northern Ireland)	☏ **00 44**
United States of America:	☏ **00 1**

DISCOUNT RAIL/BUS FARES

Open Road, **Irish Rover**, **Irish Explorer**, **Irish Rambler** and **Emerald Card** tickets are available, which enable passengers to travel throughout all of Ireland, by rail only or by rail and bus. Ask for details at any major station or tourist office, or visit www.buseireann.ie and www.irishrail. ie. The latter also has details of the SailRail scheme.

Non-European residents should visit the **Eurail** site: www.railpass.com.

DISCOUNTS FOR US NATIONALS

Eurorail Pass, **Flexipass** and **Saver Pass** are options available in the US for travel in Europe and must be purchased in the US: ✆212 308 3103; ✆1 800 4 EURAIL, 1 888 BRITRAIL and 1 888 EUROSTAR (automated lines for callers within the US only); www.raileurope.com/us.

DISCOUNTS FOR STUDENTS

Students with an **International Student Card** can apply for **Student Travelsave** to obtain reductions on Irish Rail and Bus Éireann.
USIT – Dublin ✆01 602 1906; www.usit.ie.

ELECTRICITY

The electric current is 230 volts AC (50 hertz); three-pin flat or two-pin round wall sockets are standard.

EMERGENCIES

✆**999** – Ask for Fire, Police, Ambulance, Coastguard and Sea Rescue, Mountain Rescue or Cave Rescue.

MAIL

Irish postage stamps must be used in the Republic, British stamps in Northern Ireland; they are available from post offices and some shops (newsagents and tobacconists).

OPENING HOURS

In the Republic post offices are open Mon–Sat, 8am–5pm or 5.30pm; they are closed on Sun and public holidays and for 1hr 15min at lunchtime; sub-post offices usually close at 1pm one day a week.

In Northern Ireland post offices are open Mon–Fri, 9am–5.30pm, and Sat, 9am–12.30pm; sub-post offices close at 1pm on Wednesdays.

MEDIA

In the **Republic of Ireland** the national newspapers on sale include *The Irish Times*, *The Independent* and *The Irish Examiner*.

In **Northern Ireland** the national newspapers include *The Times*, *The Independent*, *The Daily Telegraph* and *The Guardian*. There are the same terrestrial television channels as on the British mainland, including the BBC channels, ITV, Channel 4 and Channel 5.

MONEY

In the Republic of Ireland the currency is the euro (€1 = 100 cent); in Northern Ireland it is Pounds Sterling (£). There is no limit on the amount of currency visitors can import into the Republic of Ireland.

BANKS

Money can be withdrawn from banks using a credit card and a PIN. There is no commission charge for EU travellers on cash drawn from Cashpoint/ATM machines in the Republic of Ireland.

CREDIT CARDS

Most major credit cards are widely accepted in shops, hotels, restaurants and petrol stations in towns.

There may well be a minimum transaction value however (for example €10). If you are travelling to rural areas, particularly more remote places, cash is usually preferred and in some cases, the only method of payment that is accepted.

1 January	New Year's Day
17 March	St Patrick's Day (Republic only)
Monday nearest 17 March	(Northern Ireland only)
Good Friday	Friday before Easter Day
Easter Monday	Monday after Easter Day
Monday nearest 1 May	May Day Holiday (Northern Ireland only)
Last Monday in May	Spring Bank Holiday (Northern Ireland only)
First Monday in June	June Holiday (Republic only)
12 July	Orangeman's Day (Northern Ireland only)
First Monday in August	August Bank Holiday (Republic only)
Last Monday in August	August Bank Holiday (Northern Ireland only)
Last Monday in October	October Holiday (Republic only)
25 December	Christmas Day
26 December	St Stephen's Day / Boxing Day

◆ **American Express Travel Services**
www.americanexpress.com/uk.

PUBLIC HOLIDAYS

On public holidays, shops, museums and other monuments may be closed or may vary their times of admission. In the Republic of Ireland, national museums and art galleries are usually closed on Mondays.

In addition to the usual school holidays at Christmas and in the spring and summer, there are mid-term breaks at Hallowe'en (31 October) and around St Patrick's Day (17 March).

SIGHTSEEING

ADMISSION TIMES

Ticket offices usually shut 30 minutes before closing time; only exceptions are mentioned. Admission times and charges vary, the information printed in this guide is for guidance only.

Churches

Many Church of Ireland (Anglican) and Presbyterian churches are locked when not in use for services.

CHARGES

Charges in this guide, given in the local currency, are for a single adult. Reductions are nearly always made for families, children, students, senior citizens (old-age pensioners) and the unemployed. Note too that for some of the most popular attractions it is sometimes cheaper to book tickets online and in doing so you can also, usually, avoid having to wait in line. Groups should apply in advance as many places offer special rates for group bookings and some have special days for group visits.

SMOKING

Smoking is prohibited in enclosed public places – including pubs and bars, restaurants and places of entertainment.

TIME

In winter, standard time throughout Ireland is Greenwich Mean Time (GMT). In summer (mid-March to October), clocks are advanced by one hour for British Summer Time (BST), which is the same as Central European Time.

Time may be expressed according to the 24-hour clock or the 12-hour clock.

VAT

The Value-Added Tax (VAT) refund is available to non EU residents. Stores participating in the Tax Back Service must be members of the Retail Export Scheme. Details are available in major department stores.

CONVERSION TABLES

Weights and Measures

1 kilogram (kg)	**2.2 pounds (lb)**	**2.2 pounds**	*To convert*
6.35 kilograms	14 pounds	1 stone (st)	*kilograms*
0.45 kilograms	16 ounces (oz)	16 ounces	*to pounds,*
1 metric ton (tn)	**1.1 tons**	**1.1 tons**	*multiply by 2.2*
1 litre (l)	**2.11 pints (pt)**	**1.76 pints**	*To convert litres*
3.79 litres	1 gallon (gal)	0.83 gallon	*to gallons, multiply*
4.55 litres	1.20 gallon	1 gallon	*by 0.26 (US)*
			or 0.22 (UK)
1 hectare (ha)	**2.47 acres**	**2.47 acres**	*To convert*
1 sq kilometre	**0.38 sq. miles**	**0.38 sq. miles**	*hectares to*
(km²)	**(sq mi)**		*acres, multiply*
			by 2.4
1 centimetre (cm)	**0.39 inches (in)**	**0.39 inches**	*To convert metres*
1 metre (m)	**3.28 feet (ft) or 39.37 inches**		*to feet, multiply*
	or 1.09 yards (yd)		*by 3.28; for*
			kilometres to miles,
1 kilometre (km)	**0.62 miles (mi)**	**0.62 miles**	*multiply by 0.6*

Clothing

Women					Men			
	35	4	2½			40	7½	7
	36	5	3½			41	8½	8
	37	6	4½			42	9½	9
Shoes	38	7	5½		**Shoes**	43	10½	10
	39	8	6½			44	11½	11
	40	9	7½			45	12½	12
	41	10	8½			46	13½	13
	36	6	8			46	36	36
	38	8	10			48	38	38
Dresses	40	10	12		**Suits**	50	40	40
& suits	42	12	14			52	42	42
	44	14	16			54	44	44
	46	16	18			56	46	48
	36	6	30			37	14½	14½
	38	8	32			38	15	15
Blouses &	40	10	34		**Shirts**	39	15½	15½
sweaters	42	12	36			40	15¾	15¾
	44	14	38			41	16	16
	46	16	40			42	16½	16½

Sizes often vary depending on the designer. These equivalents are given for guidance only.

Speed

KPH	10	30	50	70	80	90	100	110	120	130
MPH	6	19	31	43	50	56	62	68	75	81

Temperature

Celsius (°C)	0°	5°	10°	15°	20°	25°	30°	40°	60°	80°	100°
Fahrenheit (°F)	32°	41°	50°	59°	68°	77°	86°	104°	140°	176°	212°

To convert Celsius into Fahrenheit, multiply °C by 9, divide by 5, and add 32.
To convert Fahrenheit into Celsius, subtract 32 from °F, multiply by 5, and divide by 9.
NB: Conversion factors on this page are approximate.

Long Room, Trinity College Old Library, Dublin
© Rob Durston/Fáilte Ireland

The Country Today

Ireland's prosperous economy, initially fuelled by enthusiastic membership of the European Union (EU) and then by government policies favouring property investment, came to a traumatic halt as the first decade of the 21C drew to a close. Until then, the effects of newfound affluence could be seen everywhere. Social change had been profound, but when the country went into economic meltdown, people began to question the materialistic values rewriting their culture. Many of the characteristics of the more traditional Irish way of life, which so endear the country to visitors, have begun to reassert themselves in a newfound spirit of humility. Irish identity, which had seemed in danger of being eroded by the country's wholehearted entry into the mainstream of contemporary international life, is chastened, but alive and well.

PEOPLE
ORIGINS

The Irish are commonly thought of as being a Celtic people, but this is more of a cultural than ethnic definition. Around 8,000 BC, long before the arrival of the Celts, the coastal areas and river valleys were settled by Mesolithic hunter-gatherers who had moved across the land-bridge that still connected Ireland with Scotland. The dominant Celts seem to have come in several waves during the second half of the last millennium BC, pushed to the Western fringe of the continent by the expansion of the Roman Empire and pressure from Germanic tribes in Central Europe. By the time of the coming of Christianity in 5C, the population may have amounted to a quarter of a million. Viking attacks began towards the end of the 8C and although the Norsemen's original objective was pillage, they later settled, founding coastal towns and eventually

becoming absorbed into the local population. Subsequent immigration mostly originated from Britain, the Anglo-Norman invaders and their followers being succeeded in the 16C and 17C by a planned influx of settlers and colonists. By the beginning of the 18C, perhaps a quarter of the population of just over two million was of English, Welsh and Scottish origin. Other groups, though far less numerous, added their distinctive flavour; Huguenots in the late 17C, Jews mostly in the late 19C and early 20C. Before the last decades of the 20C, the backwardness of the economy meant that immigration from non-European countries remained statistically insignificant.

DEMOGRAPHICS

The country has a population of around 5.7 million, of whom 1.7 million or so live in Northern Ireland and 4 million in the Republic. This represents a substantial increase over the low point of the early 20C of about 4.5 million, the result of a falling birthrate and continuing emigration. The size of the current population is largely due to net inward migration, but it is still well short of the total of over 8 million in the period immediately preceding the Famine.

Population density compared with other Western European countries is low – 52 people per sq km – and a large proportion of the population still lives in small towns or the countryside. Villages are relatively few and the isolated family farm is the most typical form of rural settlement; many places that elsewhere in Europe would be classified as villages with a total population of perhaps a few hundred have a full range of urban functions such as a market, shops, pubs and professional offices.

Recent rural building has confirmed the scattered nature of settlement, with new farmhouses and homes standing proudly in the middle of fields and a ribbon development of bungalows along the roads.

The larger towns are all on the coast. Greater Dublin has a disproportionate number of inhabitants, with over a million in total; Greater Belfast has well over a quarter of a million. No other regional centre in the Republic approaches the capital in population size; Cork has around 180,000 inhabitants, while the other leading cities have under 100,000. In the Republic, birth rates have fallen recently, but the population is relatively young, with more than 40 percent under the age of 25, and 24 percent under 15.

SOCIETY
Education
Education is compulsory up to the age of 16 and compared to other countries, a high proportion of pupils are educated in single-sex schools. The Catholic Church has a strong institutional presence in the Republic's education system and in Northern Ireland almost half the total number of pupils attend Catholic-managed schools. Third-level education is non-denominational and there are universities in a number of Irish cities, including Dublin (principally Trinity College and University College), Cork, Galway and Belfast.

Rights
In recent years, legislation has corrected many human rights issues affecting the lives of Irish citizens. Homosexuality was legalised in the Republic in 1993 and two years later the constitutional ban on divorce was abolished in a referendum, though by a very narrow margin. A move to remove the constitutional ban on abortion was rejected in a 2002 referendum and in Northern Ireland a woman's right to abortion remains very restricted.

Media
The main national newspapers in the Republic are *The Irish Times*, *Irish Examiner* and *Irish Independent*. *The Belfast Telegraph* is the leading daily in Northern Ireland. The main Irish-run TV stations are RTE1 and RTE2 but BBC channels and British commercial stations are widely available and popular.

Minorities
Ethnically indistinguishable from their fellow-citizens, travellers are perhaps the most visible minority in southern Ireland. Previously known by the now demeaning name of "tinkers", they move their lorries and caravans from one roadside site to another and earn a living mostly from scrap-metal dealing. There are small numbers of Chinese and other Asians, significantly in Northern Ireland and Dublin. The Republic, especially its remoter western areas, has long attracted individuals from other European countries, particularly Germany, Holland and Britain.

Religion
In recent years, the power and authority of the Roman Catholic Church may have been sapped by recurrent scandals, but the Republic of Ireland is still a demonstratively Catholic country, with 91 percent of the population declaring their adherence to the Roman Catholic Church. Attendance at Mass is high, though no longer universal, and much lower in inner-city districts of Dublin than in rural areas.

The Church's teachings on matters such as abortion continue to command widespread respect; attempts to liberalise restrictions on termination of pregnancy have been defeated when put to referendum. Protestants, who once formed

Ulster-Scots – Scotch-Irish

Speaking of her family, who came from Co Antrim, Theodore Roosevelt's mother described them as:

"A grim, stern people, strong and simple, powerful for good and evil, swayed by gusts of stormy passion, the love of freedom rooted in their very hearts' core… relentless, revengeful, suspicious, knowing neither ruth nor pity; they were also upright, resolute and fearless, loyal to their friends and devoted to their country."

Irish Diaspora

Forty million people of Irish descent live in the USA, 5 million in Canada, 5 million in Australia and innumerable millions in Great Britain. Estimates suggest that over 60 million people in the world are of Irish origin. The influence of Irish people worldwide is immeasurable in comparison to the country's size.

The imposition of the Anglican Reformation in the reign of Elizabeth I caused many to leave Munster for Spain and Portugal. The conquest of 1603 caused more departures to Spain and Brittany. Cromwell transported whole regiments, possibly 34,000 men, to Spain and Portugal, while many civilians were shipped to the West Indies, where they could be sold as slaves. The Treaty of Limerick in 1691 was followed by the flight of the so-called *Wild Geese*, military men who,

Oliver Cromwell

© Steven Wynn Photography/iStockphoto.com

together with their wives and children, emigrated to France, where they served in the French Army until 1697; some of them moved on to Spain, where three Irish regiments were formed. The most famous name among the merchants who settled on the Western coast of Europe is that of Richard Hennessy, from Cork, who started the Cognac company.

The first transatlantic emigrants were mostly Presbyterians, the Ulster-Scots (known in the USA as Scots-Irish or Scotch-Irish), descendants of lowland Scots who had settled in Ulster in the 17C. Whole families emigrated early in the 18C owing to religious strictures and rising rents. The Roman-Catholic Irish tended to emigrate as single young adults, both men and women.

The Scotch-Irish have enjoyed great influence in America despite their limited numbers, particularly in the War of Independence and in education. The heartland of Ulster settlement was in the Appalachian back country; the name "hillbilly" derives from King William III. Many of the settlers were involved in pushing the frontier westwards and building the American railways. Over a quarter of the Presidents of the USA are descended from Scotch-Irish settlers. This Irish-American connection is traced in detail at the Ulster-American Folk Park (⌖*see SPERRIN MOUNTAINS*) and Andrew Jackson Centre (⌖*see AROUND BELFAST)*, as well as several other family homesteads. Allied military leaders in World War II of Ulster stock include Alanbrooke, Alexander, Auchinleck, Dill and Montgomery.

Following the Napoleonic Wars emigration recommenced and during the next 25 years over a million Irish men and women emigrated to Great Britain and the USA. Emigration reached its peak during the Great Famine when Ireland lost 4 million through death and emigration. During the worst years about 1 million fled and another 2.5 million emigrated in the following decade. The great wave of 19C emigrants was largely composed of Roman Catholics from Donegal, Connaught, Munster and Leinster; counties that until then had not seen much emigration. Many landed first in Canada then later crossed the frontier into the USA to escape British rule. Their descendants include John Fitzgerald Kennedy, Ronald Reagan and William Jefferson Clinton.

The numbers who emigrated to Australia and New Zealand were smaller and included some who were transported to the penal colonies.

The flow of immigrants into Great Britain has waxed and waned since the Irish established colonies in Wales and Scotland in the 5C. Many, particularly those who left Ireland during the Famine in the hope of reaching America but were too weak or penniless to continue, settled in Liverpool and Glasgow. London has a flourishing Irish community, particularly north of the river. Margaret Thatcher, former prime minister of the UK (1978–91), is descended from Catherine Sullivan, who emigrated in 1811 from Kenmare and became a washerwoman in England.

Many Irishmen who went to work in Britain on the canals or in agriculture and the building trade in the 18C and 19C returned home for the winter. Those who went to America or Australasia seldom went back to the mother country. Despite their rural origins, most Irish emigrants settled in the big cities rather than on the land of their adopted countries.

Tracing Ancestors

Many visitors, particularly from Australia, New Zealand and the USA, hope to trace ancestors who have left Ireland and settled abroad. This task is more difficult than it might have been due to the destruction during the Civil War of the National Archives, whose records went back to 1174. In the later years of the 20C a great project was set in motion to collect all the information available from parish records, tombstones and other sources throughout Ireland. Access to these computer records and assistance in tracing ancestors can be obtained through the many regional Genealogical Centres that are listed in the Address Books of the appropriate chapters in the *Discovering Ireland* sections. The task is considerably more difficult if you have no idea where in Ireland your ancestors came from; in this case it is best to consult one of the national organisations in Dublin (&see *Planning Your Trip*).

Irish emigrants in the late 20C and early 21C are highly qualified young men and women seeking employment not only in English-speaking countries like the UK and the USA, but also throughout the European Union. In recent years emigration has declined and immigration has increased. In 1997 there was a net inflow of 15,000 people, the highest figure since the 1970s. Many were former emigrants, returning to a higher standard of living and a culturally revitalised society. The present economic woes have since reversed this trend.

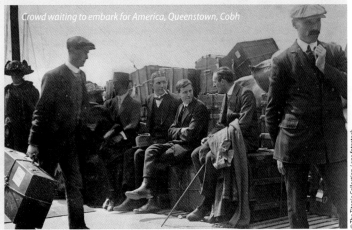

Crowd waiting to embark for America, Queenstown, Cobh

© The Titanic Collection / age fotostock

Gaelic football - Dublin vs Derry at Croke Park, Dublin

© Fáilte Ireland, Tourism Ireland

a quarter of the total population, and almost 50 percent of the inhabitants of Dublin, have declined in number, either through emigration or intermarriage. Today they number around 3 percent of the Republic's population, most of them members of the Church of Ireland. The strength of religious observance is paralleled in Northern Ireland, whose majority Protestant population is split between Presbyterians, Methodists, members of the Church of Ireland and of various minor denominations. Roman Catholics form about one third of the Northern population, a proportion that is steadily increasing.

Sports

Most forms of sport are played enthusiastically in Ireland, none more so than those that are uniquely Irish: **hurling** *(iománaíocht)* and **Gaelic football** *(peil)*, These, together with **handball** *(liathróid láimhe)* and rounders, are administered by the **Gaelic Athletic Association** *(Cumann Lúthchleas Gael)*, a largely rural movement founded in 1884 in Thurles. The national 80,000-spectator GAA stadium – Croke Park, Dublin – is named after the Association's first patron, Archbishop Croke (1824–1902). The high point of the Gaelic sporting year comes in September, when both the hurling and football national finals are held at Croke Park. The history of the Asso-

ciation and the exploits of the hurling and football champions are excellently illustrated in the GAA Museums at Croke Park and in Thurles.

Hurling is a high-scoring and fast-moving game of great antiquity, played by two teams of 15 using long, curved hurley *(camán)* sticks to hit the cork and leather ball into, or over the rugby-style goal. Allowing the ball to be handled under certain circumstances increases the excitement of the game, which can seem violent and chaotic to the non-initiated. *Camogie* is a version of hurling adapted for women participants, with a shorter playing time, teams of 12 and a smaller pitch.

Gaelic football is played with a spherical ball, uses the same pitch as hurling and has similar rules; neither game is played outside Ireland to any extent, but Australian Rules football owes much to its Gaelic ancestor.

Bars and Pubs

More varied and more interesting than its derivatives, which have been such a marketing success worldwide, the Irish pub or bar remains the centre of much social life, particularly in the country-side and in small towns, where some still double as general stores. Big-city pubs in both Belfast and Dublin can be places of almost Baroque splendour, redolent with literary or political associations.

Drinking and conversation remain the patrons' principal preoccupations but more and more pubs serve good food and very few remain an exclusively male preserve. Strangers seeking company are unlikely to remain lonely for long, and the pub is the best place to enjoy fun and good talk, the famous *craic*, as well as a variety of traditional or contemporary music.

Horse Racing

The horse plays a special role in Irish life and the great Horse Fairs still figure in the country's calendar. Breeding and racing horses have deep roots in Irish culture; the earliest horse races were part of pre-Christian festivals. Swimming races, which ceased only recently, also had Celtic origins, in the ritual of immersion. The focal point of Ireland's breeding, racing and training is at the Curragh in Co Kildare.

There are about 28 race courses in Ireland. At Laytown Strand, south of Drogheda, the times of races are dictated by the tide and horses are often exercised on the seashore. The first recorded prize is a plate donated in 1640 by the Trustees of the Duke of Leinster. In 1684 King James II presented the King's Plate at Down Royal "to encourage the sport of horse racing". The first steeplechase, a race over obstacles invented by Lord Doneraile, took place in 1752 from Buttevant Church to St Leger Church near Doneraile (4.5mi/7km). In the past, men challenged one another to pounding matches, in which the participants, accompanied by their grooms, had to follow the leader over any selected obstacle or admit defeat.

GAELIGE

Gaelige, Irish or Gaelic – whichever name is used – is a subtle and extremely expressive language. Although rarely used, it has had a profound influence on the way the Irish use English, which has largely replaced it. Irish is an Indo-European language, one of the Celtic group – Scots Gaelic, the extinct Manx, Welsh, Cornish and Breton – and is closest to Scots Gaelic and Manx. Its stylish

alphabet, abandoned in the 1960s, can still be seen in old road signs and where its decorative qualities are exploited. Once the natural language of the whole island, Irish has been remorselessly displaced by English and is today spoken as a first language by only a small minority, some 60,000 in all. Nevertheless it enjoys its status as the first official language of the Republic, remains an important badge of Irish identity and has been consistently promoted by government and cultural organisations since independence – over 40 percent of adults claim to be able to speak Irish. It has a complex grammar and a pronunciation that most outsiders find difficult to grasp; consonants may remain mute or change their sound according to position. Even monoglot English speakers have become familiar with the use of the Irish language in official expressions; the prime minister is always referred to as the *Taoiseach*, the Parliament as *Dáil Éireann*, the Tourist Board as *Bord Fáilte*, the national railway as *Iarnród Éireann*, and all buses heading for the city centre in Dublin bear the direction *An Lár*.

OGHAM SCRIPT

The earliest known form of writing in the Irish language is in **Ogham script**, which survives in inscriptions on memorials to the dead dating from the 4C to 7C.

The script is based on the Latin alphabet and was probably adapted by poets and wise men before the Latin alphabet became more generally familiar in Christian Ireland. The script consists of 20 characters written as groups of a maximum of five straight lines on either side of, or horizontally or diagonally through a central line which was usually cut into the vertical edge of a standing stone – many of which are to be found in the southern districts of Ireland.

TRANSITION TO ENGLISH

The decline in the use of Irish was caused by the gradual imposition of English law and administration in the 16C and the repressive clauses of the Penal Laws (see HISTORY) in the 17C. Many Irish people turned to English to achieve a position in society. This trend was accelerated by the teaching of English in the National Schools, which were set up in 1831. During and after the famine (1845–49), many Irish speakers died or emigrated. In 1835 half the population was estimated to speak Irish; in 1851 one-quarter was recorded as Irish-speaking; by 1911 the number had fallen to one-eighth.

GAELIC REVIVAL

The 19C saw a revival of interest in Ireland's Gaelic heritage, largely because of its close association with nationalist politics, precipitating various societies set up to promote Irish language and culture.

The **Irish Literary Society** was founded in 1892; early members included William Butler Yeats, Edward Martyn and Lady Gregory; in 1899 the society became the **Irish Literary Theatre** (later the Irish National Theatre at the Abbey Theatre) and George Moore returned to Dublin especially to take part in the new movement.

In 1893 the **Gaelic League** (Conradh na Gaeilge) was founded by Douglas Hyde, who was dedicated to the "de-Anglicisation of Ireland" through the revival of Gaelic as a spoken language and a return to Irish cultural roots. It instituted an annual festival of native culture and campaigned successfully for St Patrick's Day (17 March) to be a national holiday. In 1922 the Constitution stated that Gaelic was an official language and its

study was made compulsory in primary schools. The following year it became an obligatory qualification for entry into the Civil Service of the Irish Free State and the Constitution of 1937 named it the first official language.

In 1925, in order to foster the use of Irish, the new government set up a Commission to investigate conditions in the Gaelic-speaking districts. As a result of its report two organisations – **Gaeltarra Éireann** (1935) and **Údarás na Gaeltachta** (1980) – were established to develop the resources of these areas, collectively known as the **Gaeltacht**. With a total population of over 80,000 (not all of whom are Irish speaking), these are mostly sparsely populated, remote and beautiful western parts of the country – Donegal, Mayo, Galway and Kerry – though there are pockets in the south – near Cork, in Co Waterford and Co Meath. Today, the government's Department of Arts, Heritage, Gaeltacht and the Islands is charged with their social and economic welfare and with promotion of the Irish language. The radio station *Raidío na Gaeltachta* has broadcast in Irish since 1972 and since 1996 there has been a national television service, *Telefís na Gaeilge*. The summer schools started during the 19C Gaelic revival have become a permanent feature of the Gaeltacht, inspiring and entertaining each new generation.

GOVERNMENT

The Republic's government consists of a president and a two-chamber parliament made up of a house of representatives *(Dáil Éireann)* and a Senate *(Seanad Éireann)*.

The President is democratically elected and although the office carries no executive powers it is invested with important formal and ceremonial functions. General elections for *Dáil Éireann* must take place at least once every five years and a system of single transferable voting, a form of proportional representation, is used. In recent elections this tends to result in no single party having an overall majority and a coalition government must be formed. The second chamber,

Seanad Éireann, is elected by various bodies and not by universal suffrage. There are two main political parties: Fianna Fáil and Fine Gael, historically differentiated by the opposing sides they took in the Civil War.

Government in Northern Ireland is run by a democratically elected Assembly, with exective power belonging to a first minister, a deputy first minister and ten departmental ministers. These executive posts are shared by parties representing the Catholic nationalist and Protestant loyalist populations. There is also a North/South Ministerial Council which brings ministers from Northern Ireland and the Republic together for co-operation on policies affecting the island of Ireland as a whole.

ECONOMY

In the 19C, Union with Britain failed for the most part to bring Ireland the benefits or indeed the problems of the Industrial Revolution. The great exception was Belfast, where the linen and food processing industries stimulated the growth of general engineering. The city joined the ranks of British industrial centres, its role confirmed in the first half of the 20C, when Harland and Wolff built liners like the *Titanic*.

In contrast, in the years following independence, the Republic concentrated on being self-sufficient rather than modernising its economy, which remained over-reliant on farming and on the export of agricultural products to Britain. Some stimulation came from government initiatives like the Shannon hydro-electric scheme, but the high level of emigration of people of working age was a fundamental weakness. The world depression of the 1930s and a trade war with Britain further hindered progress. Ireland's neutral stance during 1939–45 may have made political sense but brought none of the benefits of intensified production nor of the American aid that helped restore postwar economies of other European countries.

However, from the 1950s onwards a series of measures were taken to open up the economy and stimulate growth; tax concessions and incentives encouraged export-based, modern industries and attracted foreign investment. A further boost was given when the country joined the European Economic Community (European Union) in 1972. Despite intermittent setbacks, the highly qualified workforce, together with investment in research and development, brought about astonishing economic expansion; by the 1990s the country's growth rate was twice the European Union's average and modern industries like chemicals, pharmaceuticals, electronics, biotechnology and information technology constituted 75 percent of the total industrial output.

The strength of the "Celtic Tiger's" economy meant that Ireland was able to join the single European currency project as one of the few countries complying with the criteria set by the Maastricht Treaty of 1992. Those years of prosperity came to an abrupt end in 2008 with a crisis in banking and a collapse of the property market. The country is currently trying to cope with a massive debt brought about by the Government's need to subsidise most of the major banks. Northern Ireland, once in advance of the South in terms of industry and employment, has suffered similarly to the rest of the UK by the decline in traditional heavy industries. Government sponsored initiatives have not always ended in success and the halting progress of the peace process has inhibited the inflow of investment. A mitigating factor is the exceptionally high level of employment in the public sector.

Tourism has become the Republic's second largest indigenous industry. Six million overseas visitors arrive here every year, drawn by unspoilt landscapes, clean rivers and lakes, peace and quiet, the Celtic heritage and the friendly welcome extended by local people. Fishing and golf remain major attractions.

The previous, somewhat carefree attitude to conservation has given way to the meticulous work of Dúchas, the government body charged with preservation of national heritage.

59

IRISH CUISINE

Traditional meals based around potatoes and beef retain their popularity alongside familiar dishes from contemporary European cuisine. A new Irish cuisine has also developed, using the country's traditional ingredients in innovative and imaginative ways.

BREAKFAST

The traditional and ubiquitious **Irish Fry**, known in the North as an "Ulster Fry", consists of fried egg, sausage, bacon, black pudding, potato farls, mushrooms, tomatoes and sometimes soda bread. Alternatives, such as smoked salmon and scrambled eggs, are available in quality guesthouses.

FISH AND MEAT

The king of the freshwater fish is the **salmon**, wild or farmed; as a main dish it is usually poached or grilled. Irish smoked salmon is traditionally cured with oak wood. The other most frequently served freshwater fish is **trout**, farmed or wild. **Shellfish**, such as crab, lobster, scallops, mussels and Dublin Bay prawns (also known as langoustines or scampi) are usually available near the coast, particularly in the Southwest.

The Irish fishing grounds produce Dover sole (known locally as Black sole), lemon sole, plaice, monkfish, turbot, brill, John Dory, cod, hake, haddock, mackerel and herring.

Prime **beef** is raised on the lush pastures in the East and South of Ireland; lamb comes from the uplands. **Pork** is presented in many ways: as joints and chops; as ham or bacon; as pigs' trotters *(crúibíní)*, known in English as crubeens; in white puddings; in black puddings *(drisheen)* flavoured with tansy and eaten for breakfast. Though game is not common, hare and pheasant are sometimes served.

TRADITIONAL DISHES

There is no official recipe for **Irish stew**, which consists of neck of mutton layered in a pot with potatoes, onions and herbs. **Colcannon** is a Harvest or Hallowe'en dish of mashed potatoes, onions, parsnips and white cabbage, mixed with butter and cream. **Champ** is a simpler dish of potatoes mashed with butter, to which are added chopped chives or other green vegetables such as parsley, spring onions (scallions), chopped shallots, nettles, peas, cabbage or even carrots (cooked in milk that is added to the purée). Nettles are also made into soup. To make **coddle**, a forehock of bacon, pork sausages, potatoes and onions are stewed in layers. **Collar and cabbage** is composed of a collar of bacon, which has been boiled, coated in breadcrumbs and brown sugar, baked and then served with cabbage cooked in the bacon stock. Various sorts of **seaweed**, a highly nutritious source of vitamins and minerals, were traditionally used to thicken soups and stews. **Carrageen** seaweed is used to make a dessert with a delicate flavour and **Dulse** is also made into a sweet.

Irish cookery makes liberal use of butter and cream. Ice-cream is particularly popular as a dessert. In recent years many hand-made **cheeses** have appeared on the market, such as **Cashel Blue** (a soft, creamy, blue-veined cheese made from cow's milk in Tipperary; milder than Stilton), **Cooleeny** (a Camembert-type cheese from Thurles in Co Tipperary), **Milleens** (a distinctive spicy cheese from West Cork) and **Gubbeen** (a soft, surface-ripening cheese from Skull in Co Cork).

A wide variety of breads and cakes is baked for breakfast and tea. The best-known is **soda bread**, made of white or brown flour and buttermilk. **Barm Brack** is a rich fruit cake made with yeast *(bái-rín breac* – speckled cake).

BEVERAGES

Stout made by **Guinness** or **Murphys** is the traditional thirst-quencher in Ireland, but the drinking of ales (bitter) and lagers is equally popular. Black Velvet is a mixture of stout and champagne. Most pubs serve coffee, though it may be of the instant-mix kind. Cappuccino, espresso, latte and the like are commonly available throughout the country in cafés.

History

Ireland may carry the scars of its troubled history more than most European countries but no longer in so noticeable ways. The Republic of Ireland enjoyed a booming prosperity after joining the European Union and one which lasted until 2008. Since the political breakthroughs of recent years, Northern Ireland, and Belfast in particular, has also begun to harvest the fruits of peace.

TIMELINE
CELTIC IRELAND

6000-1750 BC Stone Age; c. 3000 BC hunter-gatherer people begin farming. Construction of passage graves.

1750–500 BC Bronze Age.

500 BC–AD 450 Iron Age; Celtic invasion from Europe; inter-tribal strife for supremacy and the title of High King (*Ard Rí*).

55 BC – early 5C AD Roman occupation of Britain (not Ireland): trade links proven by coins and jewellery found.

4C–5C Irish Celts (known as Scots) colonise the West of England and Scotland.

432–61 **St Patrick's mission** to convert Ireland to Christianity.

6C–11C **Monastic age**; Irish missionaries travel to the Continent.

795 **Viking Invasions** – Vikings from Norway and Denmark raid the monasteries near the coasts and waterways; from around 840 they begin to settle.

1014 **Battle of Clontarf** – **Brian Ború**, King of Munster, defeats the Danish Vikings and the King of Leinster's allied forces.

1156 Death of Turlough O'Connor, last powerful native ruler.

1159 Henry II (1154–89), receives the title "Lord of Ireland" from Pope Adrian IV and is permitted to invade Ireland.

ANGLO-NORMAN IRELAND

1169 Invited by Dermot, King of Leinster, to oust his opponents, Strongbow (Richard de Clare) lands with his Anglo-Norman army and in 1171, Strongbow declares himself King of Leinster to the discomfiture of Henry II. England's involvement in Irish affairs is now constant, though the interests of the two frequently diverge.

1177 **Anglo-Norman** invasion of Ulster by John de Courcy.

1185 **Prince John**, "Lord of Ireland", visited the country, to which he returned in 1210.

1297 First **Irish Parliament** convened.

1315–18 **Bruce Invasion** – Edward Bruce, brother to King Robert of Scotland, lands at Carrickfergus with 6,000 Scottish mercenaries (gallowglasses); he is crowned king in 1316, but dies at the Battle of Faughart, near Dundalk, in 1318.

1348–50 **The Black Death** kills one-third of the population.

1366 **The Statutes of Kilkenny** promulgated to maintain the distinction between Anglo-Normans and native Irish. Prohibition of fosterage, bareback riding, hurling, the Irish language, and Irish dress and patronage of Irish storytellers and poets largely fail in their purpose.

1394 & 1399 **Richard II** landed in Ireland with an army to re-establish control.

1446 First mention of **The Pale** to describe the area of English

The Wrecks of the Spanish Armada

In 1588 some 30 ships of the Spanish Armada were wrecked off the Irish coast between Antrim and Kerry, with an estimated loss of 8,000 sailors and gunners, 2,100 rowers, 19,000 soldiers and 2,431 pieces of ordnance.

The *Gerona*, a galleass (oar-propelled galley), went down at Port na Spaniagh on the Giant's Causeway; all perished. Treasures recovered by divers in 1968 are displayed in the Ulster Museum. The *Juliana, La Levia* and *La Santa Maria de Vision* all foundered at Streedagh Point, north of Sligo; over 1,300 are thought to have died. *La Duquesa St Anna and La Trinidad Valencia* was wrecked on the Inishowen Peninsula at Kinnagoe Bay. A map on the clifftop *(at the road junction)* plots the sites of the many ships that were lost during those fateful storms.

One survivor who came ashore at Streedagh, Captain Francisco de Cuellar, wrote an account of his escape from Sligo through Leitrim, Donegal and Derry to Antrim, from where he sailed to Scotland, then on to Antwerp and Spain.

influence; by the 15C it was only a narrow coastal strip from Dundalk to the south of Dublin.

1471 The Earl of Kildare appointed **Lord Deputy**, marking the rise to power of the Geraldines.

1487 **The pretender** Lambert Simnel crowned Edward V of England in Dublin by the Earl of Kildare.

1491 Perkin Warbeck, pretender to the English throne, landed in Cork without the opposition of the Earl of Kildare.

1494 Sir Edward Poynings appointed Lord Deputy: under **Poynings' Law** the Irish Parliament could not meet or propose legislation without Royal consent.

1534–40 Failure of the **Kildare (Geraldine) Revolt** and the end of Kildare ascendancy.

REFORMATION AND PLANTATION

1539 **Reformation** and **Dissolution of the Monasteries**.

1541 Henry VIII declared **King of Ireland** by the Irish Parliament.

1556 Colonisation of Co Laois (Queen's County) and

Offaly (King's County) by English settlers.

1579 **Desmond (Munster) Rebellion** severely crushed by Elizabeth I; confiscation and colonisation.

1585 Ireland mapped and divided into counties; 27 sent members to Parliament.

1588 **Spanish Armada** – After its defeat in the English Channel, the Spanish Armada, driven by the wind, sailed up the East Coast of Great Britain and round the North Coast of Scotland. Stormy weather off the Irish coast further depleted its ranks.

1598 **Hugh O'Neill**, **Earl of Tyrone**, leads rebellion and defeats the English Army at the **Battle of the Yellow Ford** (⟨ see *Bloody Battlefields*; ARMAGH AND AROUND).

1601 **Siege of Kinsale** – 4,000 Spanish troops land in Kinsale to assist Hugh O'Neill but withdraw when besieged.

1603 Submission of Hugh O'Neill (Earl of Tyrone) and Rory O'Donnell (Earl of Tyrconnell) at Mellifont to **Lord Mountjoy**, Queen Elizabeth's Deputy. In 1607 they sail from Rathmullan

(♦see DONEGAL) into exile on the continent. This **Flight of the Earls** marks the end of Gaelic Ireland's political power.

1607–41 **Plantation of Ulster** under James I: Protestants from the Scottish lowlands settle in the northern part of Ireland.

1641 **Confederate Rebellion** provoked by policies of the King's Deputy and the desire of the dispossessed to recover their land: widespread slaughter of Protestant settlers.

1642 **Confederation of Kilkenny** is an alliance between the Irish and Old English Catholics to defend their religion, land and political rights.

1649 **Oliver Cromwell** "pacifies" Ireland with great brutality, storming Drogheda and Wexford, and sending thousands of Irish to the West Indies.

1653 Under the **Cromwellian Settlement** most Roman-Catholic landowners judged unsympathetic to the Commonwealth were dispossessed and ordered to retreat west of the Shannon.

1660 **Restoration** of Charles II and restitution of some land to Roman-Catholic owners.

1678 **The Oates Conspiracy** was a pretext for the arrest, imprisonment and even death of various Roman Catholics, among them Oliver Plunkett, Archbishop of Armagh (♦see BOYNE VALLEY).

1685 Revocation of the Edict of Nantes in France forces many **Huguenots** (Protestants) to flee to England and Ireland.

1688 **Glorious Revolution:** James II is deposed; William of Orange accedes to the English throne. Thirteen Londonderry Apprentice Boys shut the city gates in the face of King James' troops; the following year the city endures a three-month siege by a Jacobite army.

1690 **Battle of the Boyne** – King William III of England and his allies representing the Protestant interest defeat King James II, who flees to France.

1691 **Siege of Limerick** – Following the battles of Athlone and Aughrim, the Irish army retreats to Limerick. After a siege it surrenders "with honour" as per the military terms of the **Treaty of Limerick**; known as the **Wild Geese**, these soldiers are granted leave to

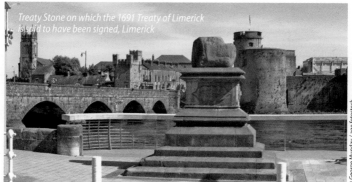

Treaty Stone on which the 1691 Treaty of Limerick is said to have been signed, Limerick

© George Munday / age fotostock

sail to France; many join the French Army.

ANGLO-IRISH ASCENDANCY

1695 The provisions of the Treaty of Limerick guaranteeing Roman-Catholic rights are soon ignored; **Penal Laws** (⟲see *Religion*) impose severe restrictions on their rights to property, freedom of worship and education.

1711 **Linen Board** established to control quality of linen for export; other improvements to canals, roads and urban planning contribute to growing prosperity.

1778 **Volunteers** rally to defend Ireland against the French; support a call for an independent Irish parliament.

1782 **Repeal of Poynings' Law** and the establishment of an independent Irish Parliament, known as Grattan's Parliament after Henry Grattan, a leading campaigner for independence.

1791 Formation in Belfast of the mostly Presbyterian **United Irishmen** to promote the idea of a republican country with no religious distinctions.

1791–93 **Catholic Relief Acts**.

1795 Rural violence between Protestant Peep O'Day Boys and Catholic Defenders and the foundation of the **Orange Order** (⟲see ARMAGH).

1796 Abortive French invasion in Bantry Bay (⟲see BANTRY).

1798 **Rebellion of the United Irishmen** launched by Wolfe Tone; main engagements in Antrim, Wexford and Mayo; the rising was brutally suppressed and 30,000 rebels killed. Tone is captured and commits suicide in prison.

IRELAND IN THE UNITED KINGDOM

1800 **Act of Union** and suppression of the Irish Parliament: members take up 100 seats in the House of Commons and 32 in the Upper-House in London.

1803 The abortive **Emmet Rebellion** led by Robert Emmet (1778–1803) ends with his hanging but provides inspiration for future nationalists.

1823 **Daniel O'Connell** (1775–1847), a Roman Catholic lawyer, is elected MP for Co Clare after campaigning for the rights of Catholics

The Great Famine (1845–49)

When potato blight (*phytophthora infestans*) destroyed the potato crop on which much of the population depended, around 800 000 people died of hunger, typhus and cholera. Thousands of starving people overwhelmed the workhouses and the depot towns distributing the Indian corn imported by the government; the workhouse capacity was 100 000 but five times that number qualified for relief. The Quakers did most to provide relief: soup kitchens were set up by compassionate landlords and by Protestant groups seeking converts; public works were instituted to provide employment relief. Other landlords evicted penniless tenants (in 1847 16 landlords were murdered) or arranged for their emigration, though so many people died en-route or in quarantine that the vessels became known as coffin ships. Over one million emigrated to England, Scotland, Canada and the USA.

and the repeal of the Act of Union. The **Roman Catholic Emancipation Act**, passed in 1829, enables Roman Catholics to enter Parliament.

1845–49 A blight destroys potato crops, leading to the **Irish Potato Famine** and the deaths of an estimated 800,000 people. Even more emigrate to Great Britain and the USA.

1848 Abortive **Young Ireland Uprising** led by William Smith O'Brien (1803–64).

1858 Founding of the rebel **Irish Republican Brotherhood (IRB)** known as Fenians.

1867 **Manchester Martyrs**: three Fenians are executed for the death of a policeman during an attack to release two Fenian prisoners. The conviction on doubtful evidence undermines Irish confidence in British justice.

1869 Disestablishment of **Anglican Church of Ireland**.

1870–1933 Seventeen **Land Acts** transfer ownership of large estates from landlords to tenants.

1874–59 **Home Rulers** elected to Parliament. In 1875 Protestant landowner **Charles Stewart Parnell** (1846–91) takes his seat, lobbying for home rule and landowner rights.

1879–82 **Land League** formed by Michael Davitt to campaign for the reform of the tenancy laws and land purchase.

1886 The **First Home Rule Bill** granting Ireland autonomy to decide certain domestic matters is rejected by Parliament.

1891–1923 **Congested Districts' Board** uses funds from the disestablished Church of Ireland to build harbours, promote fishing, fish curing and modern farming methods in poor areas.

1893 **Second Home Rule Bill** rejected by Parliament.

1905–08 **Sinn Féin** (Ourselves) founded to promote the idea of a dual monarchy.

1912 **Third Home Rule Bill** introduced by Asquith: fierce opposition in Ulster, where 75 percent of the adult population represented by **Sir Edward Carson** sign a convenant to veto it. Rival militias are armed with smuggled weaponry to form the Ulster Volunteer Force *(north)* and Nationalist Irish Volunteers *(south)*.

1914 **World War I** Postponement of Home Rule and civil strife. Irishmen volunteer for the British Army.

1917 **Sinn Féin** reorganised under Eamon de Valera to campaign for an independent Ireland.

1918 **General Election:** Redmond's Home Rulers defeated; Sinn Féin win 73 seats.

1919 **Declaration of Independence** in the Irish Assembly *(Dáil Éireann)*.

1919–20 **War of Independence –** Irish Republican Army **(IRA)** aims to block the British administration; martial law proclaimed; the Royal Irish Constabulary reinforced by British ex-servicemen (Black and Tans), notorious for their brutal tactics.

1920 **Government of Ireland Act** provides for partition: six Ulster counties remain part of the UK as per the will of the majority, to be ruled by a separate parliament; dominion status granted to the remaining 26 counties, which form the Free State.

The Easter Rising, 1916

While **John Redmond**, leader of the moderate Nationalists, hoped that Irish contribution to the British war effort would be rewarded by Home Rule, the Military Council of the Irish Republican Brotherhood secretly organised a national uprising. Despite the capture of Sir Roger Casement and a cargo of arms from Germany, the plan went ahead. On Easter Monday, columns of volunteers marched into Dublin and seized various key sites. Outside the General Post Office, Patrick Pearse announced the establishment of a republic, but the insurgents were hopelessly outnumbered and outgunned; on Saturday they surrendered. Initially the insurrection was not especially popular, but attitudes changed when the ringleaders were court marshalled and executed.

PARTITION AND INDEPENDENCE

1921	**Anglo-Irish Treaty**
1922–23	**Civil War:** Michael Collins and the Free State Army clash with the Republicans against the terms of the treaty. Casualty numbers surpass those of the War of Independence. Collins is assassinated; the Republicans are defeated.
1922	**Irish Free State**; the two-tier legislature comprises the Senate and *Dáil Éireann*.
1937	Change of name to **Éire**.
1938	Three British naval bases granted under the Anglo-Irish Treaty are returned to Ireland.
1939–45	**World War I**): Éire is neutral but gives covert aid to the Allies.
1949	Éire renamed the **Republic of Ireland**; withdrawal from the Commonwealth.
1952	Ireland joins the United Nations.
1965	Anglo-Irish Free Trade Area Agreement.
1973	The Republic of Ireland and the UK join the EU. EU funds stimulate development in the Republic.
1998	The Northern Ireland Assembly is established as a result of the Belfast Agreement of April 10, 1998.
2002	**Euro currency** goes into circulation in the Republic.
2004	Sinn Fein fail to provide Unionists (DUM and UUP) evidence that the IRA has been decommissioned. Hope of achieving a devolved Parliament is suspended.
2005	The Provisional IRA orders its units to disarm and cease all activity unrelated to peaceful political programmes.
2006	The Republic population rises to its highest level since 1861 (4,234,925).
2007	Following an historic meeting between Ian Paisley (leader of the DUP) and Gerry Adams (Sinn Fein leader) at Stormont, both parties agree to an **Executive Committee** in a Northern Ireland Assembly. Devolved powers restored on May 8, 2007.
2008–9	**Irish Referendum** on a new EU constitution rejected. An economic crisis engulfs the Republic; a second referendum approves the new constitution.
2010	The final obstacle to political power-sharing in Northern Ireland, regarding policing, is finally overcome.
2012	Loyalist riots return to Belfast over the union flag flying at Belfast's city hall.
2015	Ireland becomes first country to legalise by popular vote same-sex marriage.

Architecture

Architecture in Ireland has been strongly influenced by stylistic developments originating in Britain or continental Europe, but Irish building has many distinctive features. For example, the medieval round towers with their conical caps have become an emblem of Irishness. The array of prehistoric monuments and medieval fortified structures is extraordinary, while the town and country buildings of the Georgian era are particularly fine.

PREHISTORIC ERA

Although the first traces of human habitation in Ireland date from c. 7,000 BC, the first people to leave structural evidence of their presence were Neolithic farmers who lived in Ireland from their arrival, c. 4,000 BC, until 2,000 BC. Traces of their huts have been found at Lough Gur (&see Limerick).

MEGALITHIC TOMBS

The most visible and enduring monuments to these people are their elaborate **burial mounds**.

The most impressive are the **passage tombs** at Newgrange, Knowth and Dowth in the Boyne Valley, on Bricklieve Mountain, at Loughcrew, at Fourknocks and Knockmany. Each grave consists of a passage leading to a chamber roofed with a flat stone or a corbelled structure, sometimes with smaller chambers off the other three sides and sometimes containing stone basins. They are covered by a circular mound of earth or stones, retained by a ring of upright stones. Passage graves date from 3000–2500 BC.

The earliest Megalithic structures, **court tombs**, consist of a long chamber divided into compartments and covered by a long mound of stones retained by a kerb of upright stones. Before the entrance a semicircular open court is flanked by standing stones, as at Ossian's Grave (&see ANTRIM GLENS). A third style of Megalithic tomb is known as the **portal tomb**; like Proleek (&see DUNDALK), they mostly found near the East Coast of Ireland. The tomb consisted of two standing stones in front, with others behind supporting a massive capstone, hauled into place up an earth ramp long since removed. They date from c. 2,000 BC.

BRONZE-AGE STRUCTURES

Stone circles, which date from the Bronze Age (1750–500 BC), are mostly, but not only, found in the southwest of the country (&see DONEGAL, KENMARE, DOWNPATRICK, SPERRIN MOUNTAINS). The circle at Drombeg (&see SOUTH COAST) seems to have been used to determine and/or celebrate the shortest day of the year.

Knowth burial mounds

© macmillan media/Tourism Ireland

Single standing stones probably marked boundaries or grave sites. Some were made into Christian monuments with a cross or an Ogham inscription (*see Gaelige*). Of similar antiquity is the cooking pit *(fulacht fiadh),* which was filled with water; hot stones were placed inside to boil the water.

IRON-AGE DWELLINGS

By the Iron Age men were living in **homesteads**, approached by a causeway. A ringfort *(ráth or dún)* was enclosed by an earth bank or by a stone wall *(caiseal)* and was surrounded by a ditch. An artificial island *(crannóg)* was formed by heaping up stones in a marsh or lake. Many such dwellings were in use from the Iron Age until the 17C. There is a replica at Craggaunowen (*see ENNIS*). Stone forts *(cashels)* like Dún Aonghasa (*see ARAN ISLANDS*) and Grianán of Aileach (*see NORTHERN PENINSULAS*), although restored at various periods, illustrate the type, built on a hill with massive walls and mural chambers.

Within the homestead individual huts were built of wattle and daub, or of stone with a thatched roof. In the West, beehive huts *(clocháin)* were built entirely of stone using the same technique of **corbelling** inwards to form a roof that was used in the passage graves. Similar stone huts are also found in the monastery on Great Skellig and at Clochan na Carraige on the Aran Islands. They demonstrate the use of drystone construction in a treeless land.

At the centre of the homestead was often an underground stone passage, called a *souterrain*, used for storage or refuge.

IRISH MONASTIC SETTLEMENTS

Little remains of most early Christian settlements as the buildings were made of perishable material – wood or wattle and daub. The records describe beautiful wooden churches made of smooth planks constructed with great craft and skill. Unfortunately none has survived. Early monasteries consisted of an area enclosed by a circular wall or bank and divided into concentric rings or into sectors assigned to different uses. The most important sector was the graveyard, since it was seen as the gateway to heaven.

ROUND TOWERS

The sites of early monasteries are marked by slender tapering round towers, just as much a symbol of Ireland as the high crosses. Almost unique to Ireland, they were built between about AD 950 and 12C as bell-towers, where hand bells, the only kind available, were rung from the top floor to announce the services. The towers were also used to store treasures and possibly as places of refuge; in almost every case the entrance was several feet (10ft/3m) above ground level. Intact towers vary in height (from 50ft/17m to over 100ft/30m).

All were surmounted by a conical cap, sometimes replaced by later battlements. About 65 survive in varying condition, with 12 intact. Most were constructed without foundations and all are tapered.

TOMB SHRINES

Some saints' graves are marked by a stone **mortuary house**, which resembles a miniature church. These structures, such as St Ciaran's at Clonmacnoise, are among the earliest identifiable stone buildings in Ireland.

CHURCHES

Most **early stone churches** consisted of a single chamber with a west door and an east window; churches with a nave and chancel date from the 12C. None of the surviving churches are very large, but there are often several churches on one site. The very large stones employed accentuate the smallness of the churches. Roofs would have been made of thatch or shingles.

The rare **stone-roofed churches**, an Irish peculiarity, employ the corbelling technique. The simplest is Gallarus Oratory; St Doulagh's near Malahide is a 13C church still roofed with stone slabs; St Columba's House, St Mochta's House, St Flannan's Oratory and Cormac's

Ecclesiastical Buildings

Romanesque (Norman)

CLONFERT CATHEDRAL, Co Galway – West door – 12C

The inner arch immediately surrounding the door is 300 years later than rest of the doorway, which consists of five rows of columns and five rows of round-headed arches framing the door, surmounted by a hood moulding containing a triangular pediment, the whole capped by a finial.

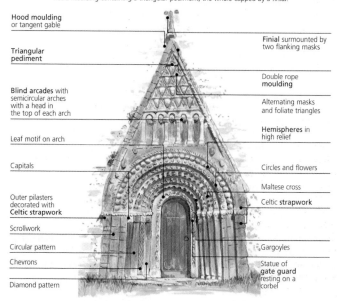

Hood moulding or tangent gable

Triangular pediment

Blind arcades with semicircular arches with a head in the top of each arch

Leaf motif on arch

Capitals

Outer pilasters decorated with **Celtic strapwork**

Scrollwork

Circular pattern

Chevrons

Diamond pattern

Finial surmounted by two flanking masks

Double rope **moulding**

Alternating masks and foliate triangles

Hemispheres in high relief

Circles and flowers

Maltese cross

Celtic **strapwork**

Gargoyles

Statue of **gate guard** resting on a corbel

Medieval

JERPOINT ABBEY, Co Kilkenny – 12C with 15C tower

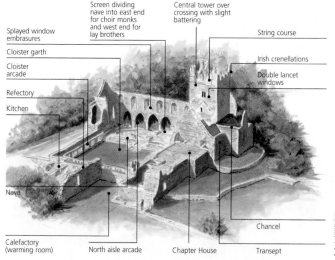

Splayed window embrasures

Cloister garth

Cloister arcade

Refectory

Kitchen

Nave

Calefactory (warming room)

North aisle arcade

Screen dividing nave into east end for choir monks and west end for lay brothers

Central tower over crossing with slight battering

String course

Irish crenellations

Double lancet windows

Chapter House

Transept

Chancel

R. Corbel/MICHELIN

Chapel have a small room between the vaulted ceiling and the roof. The earliest examples are devoid of ornament; an exception to this rule is found on White Island in Co Fermanagh, where seven figurative slabs are attached to the walls – these may be later insertions.

MIDDLE AGES
NORMAN/ROMANESQUE

The first church in the Romanesque style introduced from the Continent in the 12C, was Cormac's Chapel of 1139 at Cashel. In Ireland, Romanesque churches are always small; their typical features, to which carved decoration is limited, are round-headed doorways, windows and arches.

Ornament includes fantastic animals, human masks and geometric designs such as bosses, zigzags and "teeth". Cormac's Chapel has fine carvings, several series of blind arcading, painted rib vaults and the earliest extant frescoes. Profusely ornamented west doorways are perhaps unique to Ireland, exemplified by Clonfert (after 1167), Ardfert and St Cronan's in Roscrea.

GOTHIC CHURCHES

Gothic architecture, introduced to Ireland in the late 12C, is on a much smaller scale than elsewhere and few examples have survived. Most cathedrals show English and Welsh influences, whereas monasteries, founded by Continental monastic orders, are built according to their usual plan of a quadrangle enclosed by cloisters bordered by the church on the north side, the sacristy and chapter-house on the east, the refectory and kitchens on the south and the store on the west, with dormitories above the east and south ranges.

Early in the 13C many cathedrals were remodelled; the two Anglican cathedrals in Dublin underwent building works in this period, although they have been much altered since. St Patrick's Cathedral in Dublin, completed in 1254, to which a tower was added in 1372, is very English in its form and decoration. A second period of building occurred in the 15C and coincided with the construction of many Franciscan houses in the west. Most existing churches were altered to conform to the new fashion. Broad traceried windows were inserted,

Gothic

ST PATRICK'S CATHEDRAL, Dublin – 13C
Construction begun in the Early English style but extensively restored in the 19C.

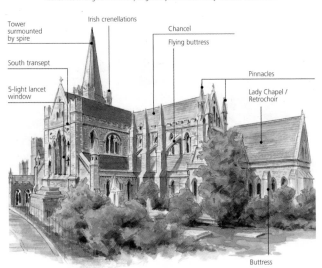

Tower surmounted by spire

Irish crenellations

Chancel

Flying buttress

South transept

Pinnacles

5-light lancet window

Lady Chapel / Retrochoir

Buttress

R. Corbel/MICHELIN

Neo-Classical

CHRIST CHURCH CATHEDRAL, Waterford – 18C

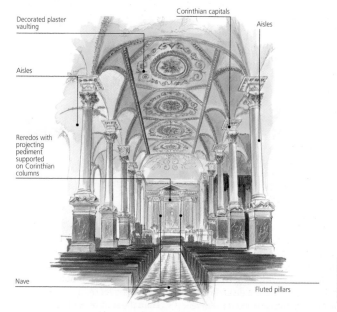

Decorated plaster vaulting

Corinthian capitals

Aisles

Aisles

Reredos with projecting pediment supported on Corinthian columns

Nave

Fluted pillars

R. Corbel/MICHELIN

Neo-Gothic

CHURCH OF THE MOST HOLY TRINITY (formerly Chapel Royal), Dublin Castle – 19C

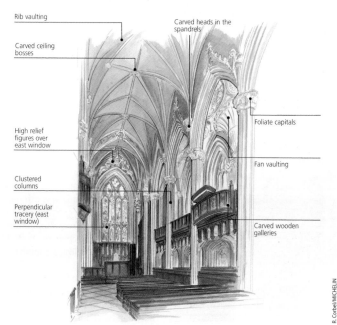

Rib vaulting

Carved heads in the spandrels

Carved ceiling bosses

High relief figures over east window

Foliate capitals

Fan vaulting

Clustered columns

Perpendicular tracery (east window)

Carved wooden galleries

R. Corbel/MICHELIN

Norman

Motte and bailey

In the immediate post-invasion years, the Normans built timber castles, surmounting a natural or artificial earthern mound (motte). A outer stockaded enclosure (bailey) contained stables, storehouses etc. Later castles were built of stone.

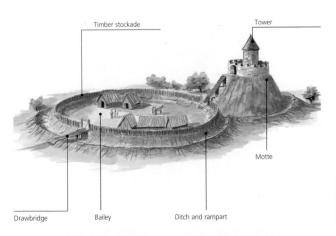

Timber stockade

Tower

Motte

Drawbridge   Bailey   Ditch and rampart

R. Corbel/MICHELIN

which let in more light and provided the stonemasons with opportunities for decoration. There is a distinctive Irish character to the capitals and high relief carving in the cloisters at Jerpoint (15C).

NORMAN CASTLES

The first castles built by Normans were of the **motte and bailey** type. The motte was a natural or artificial mound of earth surrounded by a ditch and usually surmounted by a wooden tower as at Clough in Co Down; the bailey was an area attached to the motte and enclosed by a paling fence.

From the start of the 13C, the Normans built more solid stone donjons (keeps), which were square with corner buttresses, as at Trim, Carrickfergus and Greencastle; polygonal as at Dundrum and Athlone, or round, as at Nenagh. During the 13C entrance towers became more important and barbicans were added for additional defence. In the latter half of the 13C a new symmetrical design was developed, consisting of an inner ward with four round corner towers and a combined gatehouse/donjon in the middle of one wall, as at Roscommon.

TOWER HOUSES

After the Black Death (1348–50), building resumed on a more modest scale. In 1429 a £10 subsidy was offered by Edward VI for the construction of a castle or tower. Over 70 percent of tower houses, which were erected by native and settler alike, are south of the Dublin–Galway axis.

The most distinctive feature is their verticality, one room on each of four to five storeys, sometimes with a hidden room between two floors.

Jerpoint Abbey Cloisters

© O. Forir / Michelin

15C-17C

DUNGUAIRE CASTLE, Co Galway – 1520 restored in the 19C

Fortified dwelling, consisting of a **tower house** surrounded by a courtyard, known as a **bawn**, enclosed by defensive wall; the main living accommodation with windows was on the upper floors.

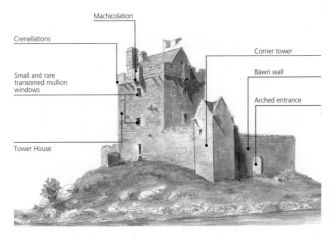

Machicolation

Crenellations

Small and rare transomed mullion windows

Tower House

Corner tower

Bawn wall

Arched entrance

R. Corbel/MICHELIN

17C

CHARLES FORT, Co Cork – c 1670

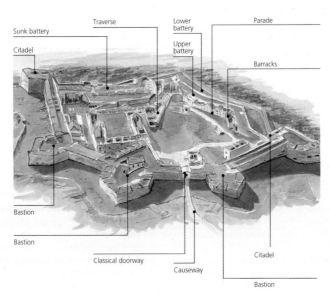

Sunk battery

Traverse

Lower battery

Upper battery

Parade

Citadel

Barracks

Bastion

Bastion

Classical doorway

Causeway

Citadel

Bastion

R. Corbel/MICHELIN

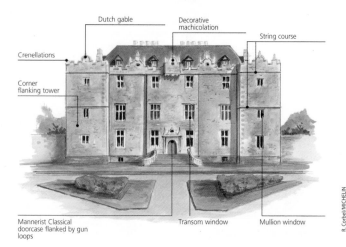

16C

PORTUMNA CASTLE, Co Galway – 1518
Semi-fortified house, with symmetrical fenestration, approached through formal walled gardens.

Dutch gable

Decorative machicolation

String course

Crenellations

Corner flanking tower

Mannerist Classical doorcase flanked by gun loops

Transom window

Mullion window

R. Corbel/MICHELIN

Defences consisted of corner loop holes, battering at the base, double-stepped merlons, known as **Irish crenellations**, and external machicolations over the corners and the entrance. Most such towers, which were built between 1450 and 1650, were surrounded by a **bawn**, an area enclosed by a defensive wall. Only in the later and larger castles is decoration evident.

PLANTATION PERIOD
PLANTATION CASTLES

As the country came more firmly under English control in the late 16C, more luxurious rectangular houses were built with square corner towers, as at Kanturk (c. 1603), Portumna (c. 1618), Glinsk (c. 1620) and Ballygally (1625). Often an existing tower house was extended by the addition of a more modern house, as at Leamaneh, Donegal and Carrick-on-Suir. These buildings show a Renaissance influence in plain and regular fenestration with large mullioned windows.

PLANTER'S GOTHIC

This style was introduced in the early 17C by settlers from England and Scotland, who built many parish churches throughout Ireland, a few of which survive unaltered. One of the best examples

is St Columb's Cathedral in Derry (&see *LONDONDERRY/DERRY*).

COASTAL FORTIFICATIONS

In the Restoration period several important towns were provided with star forts; the most complete surviving fortification is Charles Fort in Kinsale (from 1671). Signal towers were built on the coast after the French invasion of Bantry Bay in 1796 and Killala in 1798. The building of Martello towers began in 1804; about 50 of these squat structures with very thick walls punctuate the coast from Drogheda to Cork and along the Shannon estuary. The so-called Joyce Tower in Sandycove, built of ashlar granite, is typical.

18C–19C CLASSICAL
COUNTRY HOUSES

Between the Battle of the Boyne (1690) and the Rebellion (1798), there was a period of relative peace and prosperity, during which most of the important country houses were built. While Dutch gables and red brick are attributed to the influence of William of Orange, in general English and French inspiration predominated in the late 17C. In the 18C the influence was mainly Italian sources, often distilled through England and

17C

SPRINGHILL, Co Tyrone – c 1680 with 18C additions
Unfortified house with symmetrical facade and large and regular fenestration.

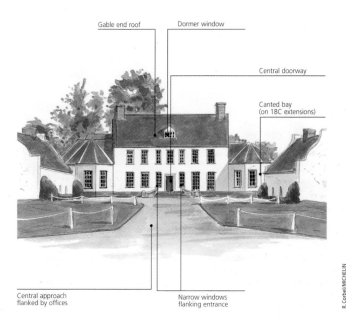

Gable end roof

Dormer window

Central doorway

Canted bay
(on 18C extensions)

Central approach
flanked by offices

Narrow windows
flanking entrance

R. Corbel/MICHELIN

latterly Greek-inspired architects, while in the 19C the English Gothic and Tudor revivalists were influential. Most country houses were built of local stone.

The most popular style in the 18C was the **Palladian villa**, which consisted of a central residence – two or three storeys high – flanked by curved or straight colonnades ending in pavilions (usually one storey lower), which housed the kitchens or stables and farm buildings.

The major architect of the first half of the 18C was **Richard Castle** (originally Cassels) (1690–1751), of Huguenot origin. Castle's many houses – Powerscourt, Westport, Russborough, Newbridge – tend to be very solid. He took over the practice of **Sir Edward Lovett Pearce**, who had the major role in designing Castletown (*see CO KILDAARE*) and who built the Houses of Parliament (from 1729), now the Bank of Ireland in Dublin.

The influence of **Robert Adam** (1728–92) arrived in Ireland in 1770, the date of the mausoleum he designed at Templepatrick. Sir William Chambers' work in Ireland is exemplified by The Marino Casino (1769–80), an expensive neo-Classical gentleman's retreat-cum-folly. James Gandon (1742–1823) was brought to Ireland in 1781 to design Emo Court. His Classical style is well illustrated by the Customs House and the Four Courts in Dublin.

The chief work of **James Wyatt** (1746–1813) was at Castle Coole, but he also contributed to Slane Castle.

One of the best-known Irish architects was **Francis Johnston** (1761–1829), an exponent of both the Classical and the Gothic styles, the former exemplified by Dublin's General Post Office, the latter by Dublin Castle's Chapel Royal.

18C

RUSSBOROUGH, Co Wicklow – 1743-56
House in the **Palladian style** consisting of a main **residential block** linked by curved or straight colonnades to two **flanking service blocks** containing the kitchens and stables.

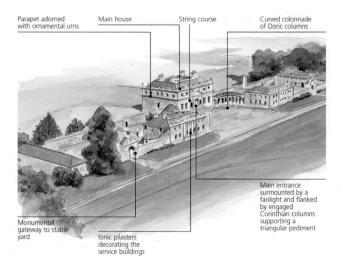

Parapet adorned with ornamental urns

Main house

String course

Curved colonnade of Doric columns

Main entrance surmounted by a fanlight and flanked by engaged Corinthian columns supporting a triangular pediment

Monumental gateway to stable yard

Ionic pilasters decorating the service buildings

18C plasterwork

FLORENCE COURT, Co Fermanagh – 1740s

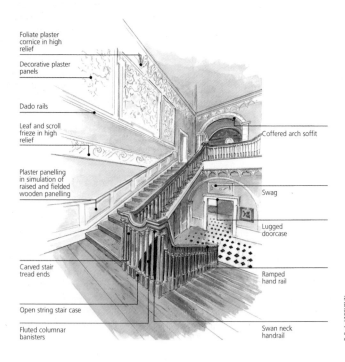

Foliate plaster cornice in high relief

Decorative plaster panels

Dado rails

Leaf and scroll frieze in high relief

Plaster panelling in simulation of raised and fielded wooden panelling

Carved stair tread ends

Open string stair case

Fluted columnar banisters

Coffered arch soffit

Swag

Lugged doorcase

Ramped hand rail

Swan neck handrail

R. Corbel/MICHELIN

Belfast Castle

© Northern Ireland Tourist Board

Interior Decoration

Many interiors were decorated with exuberant stuccowork executed by the Swiss-Italian **Lafranchini** brothers, one of whom executed the stairwell plasterwork at Castletown. Contemporary work of a similar quality was carried out by Robert West and at Powerscourt House in Dublin by **Michael Stapleton**, principal exponent of Adam décor.

Churches

Classical details began to be used in the 17C. St Michan's in Dublin (c. 1685) and Lismore (1680) by William Robinson retain some details of 17C work. The early Georgian St Anne's in Shandon, Cork, has an imposing west tower with an eastern flavour.

The neo-Classical rectangular building with a pillared portico, inspired by the Greek temple, was popular with all the major denominations: St Werburgh's (1754–59), St George's (1812), St Stephen's (1825) and the Pro-Cathedral (finished after 1840) in Dublin, St John the Evangelist (1781–85) at Coolbanagher by Gandon and St George's (1816) in Belfast.

REVIVAL STYLES

The Gothic Revival style first appeared in Ireland in the 1760s at Castle Ward and at Malahide Castle, where two tall Gothic towers were added to the medieval core. At first Gothic features and intricate stuccowork vaulted ceilings were added to buildings that were basically Classical and symmetrical, such as Castle Ward. In addition to crenellations, machicolations and pointed arches, one of the key features of the Gothic style was asymmetry. Existing medieval castles or tower houses, or Classical mansions, such as Kilkenny Castle (c. 1826) by William Robertson, and Dromoland Castle (1826) by George and James Pain, were enlarged and reworked in Gothic or Tudor style. Johnstown Castle and Ashford Castle are later examples of such Gothicising, which was romantic in flavour though distinctly Victorian in convenience.

Some new houses were built entirely in an antiquated style; Gosford Castle is neo-Norman; Glenveagh was designed in the Irish Baronial style; for Belfast Castle, Lanyon and Lynn chose the Scottish Baronial style, which was also used for Blarney Castle House.

Gothic Revival Churches

Many early 19C Gothic churches, such as the Church of the Most Holy Trinity (formerly the Chapel Royal) in Dublin Castle, are filled with ornament, with decorative galleries, plaster vaulting and rich oak carvings. Later, the influence of Augustus Welby Pugin, who practised widely in Ireland, and J.J. McCarthy, promoted antiquarian correctness, as at St Fin Barre's in Cork (1862) by William Burges. McCarthy's greatest achievement was probably the completion

MONAGHAN MARKET HOUSE, Co Monaghan – 1791

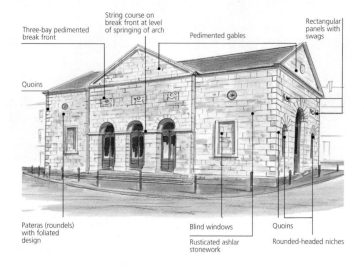

Three-bay pedimented break front

String course on break front at level of springing of arch

Pedimented gables

Rectangular panels with swags

Quoins

Pateras (roundels) with foliated design

Blind windows

Rusticated ashlar stonework

Quoins

Rounded-headed niches

Revival styles

Medieval styles such as Gothic and Norman were revived featuring asymmetric façades and fenestration and varied rooflines.

LISMORE CASTLE, Co Waterford – 19C Neo-Gothic

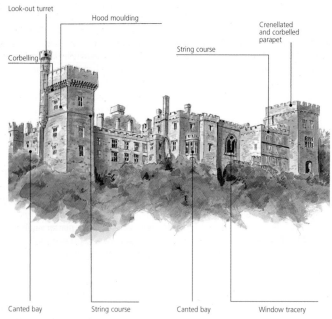

Look-out turret

Hood moulding

Crenellated and corbelled parapet

Corbelling

String course

Canted bay

String course

Canted bay

Window tracery

R. Corbel/MICHELIN

in Decorated Gothic style of the great new cathedral at Armagh (after 1853). This was only one example, albeit an outstanding one, in the spate of building that followed the Emancipation Act when many Roman Catholic cathedrals and parish churches were constructed in eclectic Gothic variations.

19C–20C

The Gothic style was often used in the second half of the 19C for civic buildings, as well as detached houses and mansions; Trinity College Museum (completed in 1857) by Deane and Woodward is a classic of the Venetian Gothic revival. The Arts and Crafts movement did not find much architectural expression in Ireland; Cavan Town Hall (1908) by William Scott is a notable exception with expressive use of planes and textures. University College Dublin in Earlsfort Terrace (1912) by R.M. Butler and the College of Sciences in Upper Merrion Street (1904–13) by Sir Aston Webb exemplify the Classical revival. Perhaps the most grandiose structure of this period is the huge City Hall (1906) in Belfast, a "great wedding cake of a building" (J. Sheehy), with a dome and corner towers. The young Free State restored with admirable promptness the bombed General Post Office, the Four Courts and the Custom House, but the record of new design is relatively poor.

MODERNISM

Architectural Modernism was slow to come to Ireland but an early and very striking example was the Church of Christ the King (1927) at Turner's Cross in Cork by Barry Byrne of Chicago. The changes in practice introduced by Vatican II favouring worship in the round have inspired many exciting church designs, some of which reflect local physical features – St Conal's Church, Glenties, Co Donegal; St Michael's Church, Creeslough, Co Donegal; Dominican Church, Athy; Prince of Peace Church, Fossa, near Killarney; Holy Trinity, Bunclody. Modern civic architecture arrived in Ireland with the construction of the Ardnacrusha hydroelectric plant

St Patrick's RC Cathedral, Armagh

© Northern Ireland Tourist Board

in 1929 and the Dublin Airport terminal building of 1940.

IRISH DISTINCTION
TOWNS AND CITIES

Early Irish villages *(clachans)* were formed of clusters of wattle-and-daub cottages arranged in a haphazard manner. The first towns were founded by the Vikings, invariably on estuaries; among them were Drogheda, Dublin, Waterford and Wexford. Most such places had a Tholsel (toll stall), often an arch or gateway several storeys high, where payment for rights of privilege or passage was made. Norman settlements were mostly confined to the South and East of the country. Towns were often enclosed within town walls, parts of which have survived at Athenry, Kilmallock, Youghal, Fethard and Londonderry.

The first widespread foundation of towns occurred in the late 16C and 17C during the plantations of Ulster, Munster and some parts of Leinster; they consisted of timber-framed houses, which have not survived, set out round a green or lining a street. The green was often known as "The Diamond", many of which survive in Ulster. In many Irish towns one of the most elegant buildings is the market and the courthouse, sometimes combined in one structure.

TOWN PLANNING

In the 18C and 19C many country landlords indulged in town planning, setting out wide streets as in Strokestown and

18C

GEORGIAN URBAN HOUSING

Urban terrace houses built of red brick, with 4 storeys over basement, three bays wide, with regular fenestration, composed of sash windows with wooden glazing bars. The tall windows emphasized the importance of the first floor reception rooms.

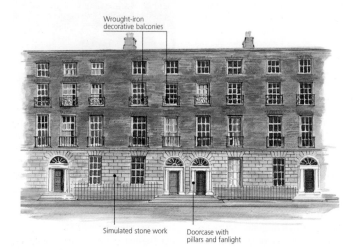

Wrought-iron decorative balconies

Simulated stone work

Doorcase with pillars and fanlight

Doorcases and fanlights (1740s)

Door case capped by a lantern fan light and flanked by pillars with Ionic capitals

Door case capped by a decorated fan light and flanked by pillars with Ionic capitals

Door case capped by a decorative fan light and flanked by pillars with Ionic capitals and by side lights and door scrapers

Door case capped by a decorated fan light and flanked by pillars with Ionic capitals

R. Corbel/MICHELIN

Moy, tree-lined malls as in Westport, Birr and Castlebar, unusual formal street plans, such as the X-shape in Kenmare, rows of cottages built of local stone, as at Glassan, northeast of Athlone, and Shillelagh in Co Wicklow or the picturesque thatched houses of Adare.

In the major towns elegant terraces of houses of Classically inspired design were built of local stone or red brick, some of which was imported from Somerset via Bristol. In 19C Dublin the materials used were grey brick from local clays, local limestone and grey Wicklow granite.

Although most terraces were erected piecemeal and lack a unified aesthetic, the influence of the **Wide Streets Commissioners** (in Dublin from 1758) led to distinctly Irish Georgian doorways – usually flanked by columns – and ordered fenestration. The tallest windows are on the principal floor, decreasing in size towards the roofline parapet. Some later terraces by the Wide Streets Commissioners and others were more standardised – Fitzwilliam Street and Square (south side) in Dublin, and Pery Square in Limerick. Internal decoration was often of a very high standard, with Classical motifs common in chimneypieces, plasterwork and timberwork.

Twentieth century town planning in Ireland has had few notable successes. Grandiose plans for the reconstruction of Dublin following the devastation of 1916 were drawn up but never implemented. Many of the close-packed terraced streets of late 19C Belfast have been replaced by planned housing schemes of various kinds, the least successful of which consisted of Brutalist blocks of flats.

The attempt to create the "New Town" of Craigavon on the British model, based on the existing urban areas of Lurgan and Portadown, has only been partially realised. In the South, rural prosperity and lax planning controls have led to the abandonment of the picturesque but sub-standard cabin with a scatter of comfortable but visually inappropriate houses and bungalows.

VERNACULAR HOUSES

The Irish countryside is full of buildings and other structures of traditional vernacular architecture – not only dwellings and outhouses but also structures such as sweathouses and forges.

The small stone sweathouse was used to treat pleurisy and other ailments and also as a type of sauna. A fire was lit inside and, when the interior was hot, the ashes were raked out and a layer of

Reconstruction of a vernacular house, Bunratty Folk Park

© Chris Hill Photographic/Tourism Ireland

81

rushes placed on the floor to protect one's feet from the heat.

The 1841 Census identified four grades of housing, of which the most modest was a windowless one-room mud cabin with a thatched roof *(bothán)*, a type of dwelling that predominated west of a line from Londonderry to Cork. Such houses contained little or no furniture; more windows or rooms meant higher rents. The half door, which is to be found all over Ireland, allowed in light while keeping out animals.

The middle grades of house, single- and two-storey farmhouses, have survived in greater numbers, with glazed windows, hearths and a hierarchy of rooms for distinct social uses.

The Irish **long house**, in which all the rooms were interconnecting with the stairs at one end, was a style that lasted from the Middle Ages to the 18C; the one at Cratloe *(see LIMERICK)* is a rare example.

The box-style Georgian house with symmetrical elevation, some Classical detailing, such as Venetian or Wyatt windows and a fanlit and columnated doorcase, was very popular with people of more substantial means.

Simple dwellings were often destroyed during evictions or fell into decay. Some have been discovered under layers of modernisation; others, threatened with demolition, have been reconstructed or recreated in Bunratty Folk Park, Glencolmcille Folk Village, the Ulster-American Folk Park and the Ulster Folk Park, near Bangor.

STAINED GLASS

No medieval stained glass has survived in-situ in Ireland but there was a revival of interest in this craft in the 1770s with the enamelling work of Thomas Jervais and Richard Hand, much of which was secular. The fashion for the neo-Gothic style of architecture in the 19C for both churches and houses created a great demand for stained glass; good examples from this period are St Patrick's Roman Catholic Church in Dundalk, which has glass by Early of Dublin, Hardman of Birmingham and Meyer of Munich, the east window of St Patrick's Anglican Church in Monaghan by the German F.S. Barff, and the altar window of the Cathedral of the Assumption in Tuam by Michael O'Connor (1801–67).

The outstanding contribution made by 20C Irish artists in this field was nurtured by the foundation of **An Túr Gloine** (the Tower of Glass) (1903–63) at the instigation of Edward Martyn and Sarah Purser. The portrait painter Sarah Purser did designs for several windows including Cormac of Cashel in St Patrick's Cathedral, and another founder member was Michael Healy (d. 1941) whose work can be seen in Loughrea Cathedral.

Wilhelmina Margaret Geddes worked for An Túr Gloine from 1912 to 1925 and works by her can be seen in the Municipal Gallery of Modern Art in Dublin and in the Ulster Museum.

Evie Hone joined An Túr Gloine in 1934. Her work, which was often inspired by Irish medieval sculpture, includes *The Ascension* (1948) for the Roman Catholic church in Kingscourt, Co Cavan, and *The Beatitudes* (1946) for a chapel in the Jesuit Retreat House at Tullabeg, near Tullamore.

Harry Clarke (1889–1931) developed a distinctive personal style as early as 1915, drawing from iconography and legends in a symbolist manner. His first public commission, 12 windows for the Honan Chapel in University College Cork, is one of his greatest works. His "Geneva Window" (1928) is in the Municipal Gallery of Modern Art in Dublin. Just before his death he executed his most important ecclesiastical commission, *The Last Judgement with the Blessed Virgin Mary and St Paul,* for St Patrick's Church in Newport.

A current revival is headed by James Scanlon and Maud Cotter, both based in Cork.

Art

Constantly receptive to influences from Britain and the rest of Europe and often giving them a specifically local flavour, Irish art was unsurpassed in its originality and creativity in the Early Christian era, when sculptors, jewellers, illuminators and other artists found inspiration in the country's glorious heritage of Celtic arts and crafts. Outstanding examples from this period, such as the Ardagh Chalice, are on show in the National Musuem in Dublin. A fainter echo of Celtic achievement came in the paintings and graphic arts associated with the Gaelic revival of the late 19C and early 20C, but before this, Ireland, quite as much as England, had become a stronghold of the arts and crafts of the Georgian era. The brilliant and sometimes eccentric life of the Anglo-Irish Ascendancy is reflected in the painting of the time as much as in architecture and the decorative arts.

CELTIC ART

Circles are an integral part of Celtic art; the outline of the design was marked out on the piece to be decorated with an iron compass. Other decorative motifs were S-and C-shaped curves, spirals and swirls and zig-zags, with intricate, interlaced patterns in the interstices. Similar designs, identified by archaeologists as **La Tène** (after the continental Celtic centre found at La Tène which flourished during the last five centuries BC), are found on two granite monuments – Castlestrange (🔊see SHANNON VALLEY) and Turoe – which date from the 3C BC. The only two such monuments to have survived in Ireland, they were probably used in religious ceremonies. They resemble the Greek *omphalos* at Delphi, a site raided by the Celts in 290 BC.

The finest Celtic pieces are designed in gold. In making a torc (a neckband), the goldsmith stretched the metal into long narrow strips and then twisted them around each other to make a golden rope, which was then shaped to fit around the warrior's neck. The Celts made personal ornaments – brooches, horse harnesses and sword sheaths – which they often decorated with enamel, favouring the colour red but also using blue, yellow and green. A regular motif in Celtic design is the triskele, a figure with three arms or legs, symbolising earth, fire and water.

Some early sculptures display a nude (and invariably very lewd) female figure with open legs, known as *Sheila-na-gig*, which owes much to pagan traditions but is usually found in or about churches. Many interpretations have been given to these often grotesque carvings, which were probably linked to a fertility cult.

A GOLDEN AGE

The first important example of an illuminated manuscript is a copy of the Psalms dating from around AD 600 and traditionally attributed to St Columba. Compared with later achievements, it is relatively simple, its principal feature being a large decorated initial at the beginning of paragraphs. Its ornamentation of Celtic spirals and stylised animals is further developed in the course of the 7C in the **Book of Durrow**, where a variety of coloured inks is used, as well as the black of Columba's manuscript. Whole "carpet pages" are given over to decoration rather than text, and the characteristic motif of interlaced bands makes its appearance.

Over the next century and a half the scribes' increasing skill resulted in ever-greater intricacy and exuberance, culminating in the sublime achievement of the **Book of Kells** dating from around 800. Of equal virtuosity are a number of products of the metalworker's and jeweller's art. The almost monumental **Ardagh Chalice** (c. 700) is a masterpiece of colourful decoration; its extraordinarily elaborate base, with three friezes in gold around a central rock crystal, would have been visible only briefly when raised during Mass. In a similar way, the splendid ornamentation of the underside of the renowned

Monogram page from Book of Kells

© Print Collector/Hulton Archive/Getty Images

Tara Brooch (also c. 700) would have only been seen by its owner.

PAINTING

When Gaelic culture waned in the 17C the chief influences on art in Ireland were English and European. A guild of painters was founded in Dublin in 1670, but there was little development until the Dublin Society's Schools were set up in 1746 to promote design in art and manufacture.

The first master, Robert West (d. 1770), and his assistant, James Mannin (d. 1779), trained in France. The School's most outstanding pupil was probably **Hugh Douglas Hamilton** (1739–1808), who excelled at pastel portraits; in 1778 he visited Italy and while in Rome developed as a painter in oils.

Susanna Drury (1733–70), whose paintings of the Giant's Causeway are in the Ulster Museum, was a member of the Irish school of landscape painting, which emerged in the 18C.

George Barret (c. 1732–84), who moved to England in 1763, introduced the Romantic element into his landscapes. Several Irish artists travelled to Italy. Thomas Roberts (1748–78), a pupil of

Clonmacnoise

© Liam Murphy/Fáilte Ireland

the Dublin Society's Schools and a brilliant landscape artist, was familiar with Dutch and French painting and exhibited several works in the style of Claude Vernet. The dominant figure of the 18C is **James Barry** (1741–1806), who produced large-scale works in the neo-Classical tradition. He travelled widely, including in Italy, studying painting and sculpture. Joseph Peacock (c. 1783–1837) from Dublin was famous for his outdoor fair scenes.

Among the visitors to 18C Dublin were Vincent Valdré (1742–1814), who painted three ceiling panels for Dublin Castle, and Angelica Kauffmann (1741–1807), the guest of the Viceroy, Lord Townshend, for several months in 1771.

In 1823 the **Royal Hibernian Academy** was incorporated by charter to encourage Irish artists by offering them an annual opportunity to show work. After the Act of Union in 1800 many Irish artists moved to London, including Martin Archer Shee (1769–1850), who became President of the Royal Academy in 1830, and Daniel Mac Lise (1806–70), a popular historical painter. Nathaniel Hone (1831–1917) spent 17 years in France, painting outside like the painters of the Barbizon school.

Roderic O'Conor (1860–1940) studied in Antwerp and in France where he met Gauguin, whose influence, together with that of Van Gogh, is obvious in his work.

Sir John Lavery (1856–1948), who also studied in Paris, is known for his portraits although he also painted scenes from the French countryside. Another artist who studied abroad is **Sarah Purser** (1848–1943), a prolific portrait painter and a founder of *An Túr Gloine*. The 20C produced several artists of note. **Jack B. Yeats** (1871–1957), brother of the poet, painted his views of Irish life with bold brushstrokes in brilliant colours. **Paul Henry** (1876–1958) is known for his ability to represent the luminous quality of the light in the West of Ireland. **William Orpen** (1878–1931), who trained at the Metropolitan School of Art in Dublin and the Slade in London, became a fashionable portrait painter and an official war artist; among his Irish pupils were **Seán Keating** (1889–1977) and **Patrick Tuohy** (1894–1930). Cubism was introduced to Ireland by **Mainie Jellett** (1897–1944) and **Evie Hone** (1894–1955), who is better known for her work in stained glass.

In 1991 the National Gallery and the Hugh Lane Gallery were joined by the Irish Museum of Modern Art at Kilmainham, all in Dublin.

SCULPTURE
CROSS-SLABS AND PILLAR-STONES

Among the earliest stone monuments are the slabs laid flat over an individual grave between the 8C and the 12C. The largest collection is at the monastic site at Clonmacnoise. Of somewhat earlier date are cross-decorate pillar-stones, some set up as grave markers.

A number of them may be recycled pre-historic standing stones.

HIGH CROSSES

One of the great symbols of Ireland, the free standing highly-decorated crosses, are most numerous in the East of Ireland but they are also found in western and northern Britain. The best groups are at Monasterboice, Clonmacnoise, Kells and Ahenny. It is thought that high crosses are the successors to small painted or bronze-covered wooden crosses used as a focus for kneeling congregations. Most stand on a pyramidal base; the head of the cross, usually ringed and surmounted by a finial, often in the shape of a small shrine.

The early carving on late 8C crosses is mostly decorative consisting of spirals and interlacing. In the 9C and 10C, panels of figures appear illustrating stories at first from the New Testament and then from the Old. Interestingly, such biblical figures or scenes are rare in early Christian art. Animal scenes are often executed on the base.

The 12C crosses are not a direct continuation and often lack a ring. By this date the figure of a bishop or abbot in the Continental style predominates.

Ardboe Cross, County Tyrone

© Lough Neagh Partnership/Northern Ireland Tourist Board

MIDDLE AGES TO THE RENAISSANCE

A distinctive feature of the medieval period is the box tomb found in the chancel of many churches. These often have lids bearing a carved effigy of the deceased and sometimes that of his wife, while the sides are decorated with figures of the Apostles and saints. In the 15C and 16C, figures and scenes from the Crucifixion were carved in high relief (⟲ *see KILDARE and KILKENNY Cathedrals*). Although predominantly religious, 17C sculpture, such as the Jacobean Segrave or Cosgrave stucco tableaux in St Audeon's Church in Dublin, widened in scope to include stone and timber carved chimneypieces; there are two fine examples of the former in the castles in Donegal and Carrick-on-Suir. Renaissance-inspired 17C tombs are to be found in St Mary's Cathedral in Limerick, St Nicholas' Church in Carrickfergus and in Youghal Parish Church. Carvings from the Restoration period survive, some at Kilmainham Hospital.

18C TO THE PRESENT

A spate of building in the 18C provided much work for sculptors. The figures of **Justice** and **Mars** above the gates of Dublin Castle are the work of **Van Nost**, as is a statue of George III, now in the Mansion House. **Edward Smyth** (1749–1812) created the riverine heads on the keystones of the arches, the arms of Ireland on the Custom House and also worked on the Four Courts under James Gandon and on the Bank of Ireland; he had been apprenticed to Simon Vierpyl (c. 1725–1810), who worked on the Marino Casino. Vierpyl's work at the Casino includes the urns flanking the external steps; the lions adjacent are the work of the English sculptor Joseph Wilton.

The 19C saw the dominance of a taste in Greek Revival detailing; in St Patrick's Church in Monaghan there is a good collection of monuments, notably the one to Lady Rossmore (c. 1807) by Thomas Kirk (1781–1845). John Hogan (1800–58) is acknowledged as a most distinguished sculptor – see his fine plaster, *The Drunken Faun*, in the Crawford Art Galley in Cork. Among his contemporaries, two stand out: Patrick MacDowell (1799–1870), who carved the group of Europe on the base of the Albert Memorial in London, and John Henry Foley (1818–74) who sculpted the bronze figure of Prince Albert. Foley's best work in Dublin is the O'Connell Monument and the statues of Burke, Goldsmith and Grattan on College Green. The best work of Thomas Farrell (1827–1900) is the Cullen Memorial (1881) in the Pro-Cathedral in Dublin. The Wellington Testimonial (c. 1817), in Dublin's Phoenix Park, by English architect Sir Robert Smirke, has bronze reliefs on the base by the sculptors Joseph Robinson Kirk, Farrell and Hogan. The work of Oliver Sheppard (1864–1941) is strongly influenced by the Art Nouveau style. The Parnell Monument in O'Connell Street, Dublin, was designed by Augustus St Gaudens in 1911. The portrait sculptor **Albert Power** (1883–1945), a resident of Dublin, was elected Associate of RHA in 1911; there are examples of his work in Cavan Cathedral, Mullingar Cathedral and in Eyre

Statue of Justice, Dublin Castle

© Marek Slusarczyk/Bigstockphoto.com

Square in Galway. The Belfast sculptor F.E. McWilliam (1909–92) is represented by a series of bronze figurative sculptures in the Ulster Museum.

More recent work of note includes the *Children of Lir* by Oisin Kelly (1916–81) in the Garden of Remembrance, Dublin. A pleasing aspect of contemporary urban renewal is the placing of sculpture in places where it is readily encountered by the public, who have often responded with affection and amusement.

Literature

Irish Men and Women of Letters have made a significant contribution to English literature through poetry, novels and drama. Poetry was an art form practised by the Celtic bard and medieval monk, but theatrical performances were unknown to Gaelic society. The Irish brought a talent for fantasy, wit, satire and Gaelic speech patterns to the English language. Four Irish writers have been awarded the Nobel Prize for Literature: William Butler Yeats (1923), George Bernard Shaw (1925), Samuel Beckett (1969) and Seamus Heaney (1995).

CELTIC INFLUENCE

The Celts may not have left a written record but their oral tradition has bequeathed a rich legacy of myth and history to inspire later generations.

The work of the monks in the scriptorium of a Celtic Church was to copy biblical and other religious texts and to write their own commentaries. They decorated their work, particularly the first capital letter of a chapter, with highly ornate Celtic patterns. Several of these **illuminated manuscripts**, of which the most famous is the Book of Kells, are displayed in the Old Library of Trinity College in Dublin. One account from this early period is *Navigatio*, written in medieval Latin, an account of the voyage from Ireland to America made by St Brendan in the 6C (*see ENNIS*).

ANGLO-IRISH LITERATURE

The first flowering of Anglo-Irish literature came in the late 17C and 18C, when George Farquhar (1678–1707) wrote his

William Butler Yeats

stage works, Oliver Goldsmith (1728–74) composed poetry, novels and plays and Richard Brinsley Sheridan (1751–1816) published his satirical comedies – *School for Scandal*.

The major figure of this period was **Jonathan Swift** (1667–1745) who was born in Ireland, studied at Trinity College, Dublin, then spent many years in England before being appointed Dean of St Patrick's Cathedral in Dublin where he stayed until his death. *Gulliver's Travels* is the most famous of his satirical writings on 18C Irish society. His friend and fellow student, **William Congreve** (1670–1729), meanwhile, wrote witty costume dramas such as *The Way of the World*, which inspired Wilde and Shaw. After spending his early childhood among his mother's relatives in Ireland, **Laurence Sterne** (1713–68), made his name in England as an innovator among novelists with *Tristram Shandy* and *A Sentimental Journey*; he is also seen as a forerunner of the stream of consciousness technique practised by James Joyce.

Many Irish writers who achieved success and fame moved to London, where they made a significant contribution to English literature and theatre. The name of the novel *Dracula* is better known than its author **Bram Stoker** (1847–1912), who worked for several years as an Irish civil servant, writing drama reviews,

before moving to London as Henry Irving's manager.

Only his first novel, *A Snake's Pass*, is set in Ireland. George Moore (1852–1933) described high society in Dublin *(Drama in Muslin)* and introduced the realism of Zola into the novel *(Esther Waters)*. **Oscar Wilde** (1854–1900) achieved huge success in the London theatre with his poetry, comic plays *(Lady Windermere's Fan, The Importance of Being Earnest)* and in society with his distinctive dress and style, his disgrace and prison term in Reading Gaol. **George Bernard Shaw** (1856–1950) commented on the Anglo-Irish dilemma in his journalism and his play, *John Bull's Other Island,* and explored the contradictions of English society *(Pygmalion)*.

IRISH THEMES

Several successful authors chose Irish themes for their work. Maria Edgeworth (1767–1849) achieved international fame and the admiration of Sir Walter Scott with her novels *Castle Rackrent* and *The Absentee*; William Carleton (1794–1869) wrote about rural life in County Tyrone. The theme of the novel *The Collegians* by Gerald Griffin (1803–40) was reworked by Dion Boucicault for the stage as *The Colleen Bawn* and by Benedict as an opera, *The Lily of Killarney*. **Anthony Trollope** (1815–82), who began his literary career while working for the Post Office in Ireland, wrote several novels on Irish themes. Canon Sheehan (1852–1913) was admired in Russia by Tolstoy and in the USA for his novels about rural life. Somerville and Ross, a literary partnership composed of **Edith Somerville** (1858–1949) and her cousin, Violet Florence Martin (1862–1915), whose pen-name was **Martin Ross**, produced novels about Anglo-Irish society, *The Real Charlotte* and the highly humorous *Experiences of an Irish RM*, adapted for TV in the 1980s.

IRISH LITERARY RENAISSANCE

At this time, as part of the **Gaelic Revival** (*see* THE COUNTRY TODAY, *Gaelige*), a literary renaissance deeply rooted in folklore was taking place in Ireland. One of its early influential figures was George Russell (1867–1935), known as AE, mystic, poet and painter, economist and journalist. The leader of this literary movement and the dominant writer of traditional Irish myths and legends was **William Butler Yeats** (1856–1939), who established his name as a poet and playwright and was a founder member of the Abbey Theatre. He lived for a number of years in County Sligo and came to recognise the power of the native imagination in Irish oral tradition, especially in the heroic tales and in mythological material, which greatly influenced his writing. His own understanding of the occult influenced his involvement in, and interpretations of, Irish lore. His *Fairy and Folk Tales of the Irish Peasantry*, first published in 1888, was followed by *Irish Fairy Tales* in 1892. Here he made the distinction among folktale, legend and myth; he was among the first writers to interpret Irish folklore. He admired Douglas Hyde because of Hyde's honest commitment to the Irish language and to native Irish lore. Yeats was part of a group of people who associated Anglo-Irish writing as part of a revival of a culture in danger of disappearing, to a large extent owing to social development. Another leading light in this movement was **Isabella Augusta, Lady Gregory** (1852–1932), who lived in County Galway and became friendly with Yeats. They were much influenced by one another and collected folklore together. Among her best-known works is *Visions and Beliefs in the West of Ireland* (1920), which is based on 20 years of work in this area with Yeats.

The *Kiltartan History Book* (1909) contained, for the first time, accounts and descriptions of many aspects of historical lore, unchanged from the oral narration of local people. She was one of the first to publish unedited folklore material, faithfully reproducing what she had collected. In common with Yeats, she recognised the richness of folklore among the "farmers and potato-diggers and old men" in her own district, the unbroken chain of tradition and the wealth of ballads, tales and lore that played such an important part in the everyday life of the ordinary people around her in County Galway.

Some of the greatest successes written for the **Abbey Theatre** were the plays of **John Millington Synge** (1871–1909). These included *Riders to the Sea* and *Playboy of the Western World*, inspired by the Aran Islands, and *The Shadow of the Glen*, inspired by the Wicklow Mountains, where language dominates in the bleak landscape; and the pacifist plays of **Sean O'Casey** (1880–1964), *The Shadow of a Gunman, Juno and the Paycock* and *The Plough and the Stars*, written in the aftermath of World War I.

LITERARY EXILES

The narrow-mindedness of Irish society is expressed in the drama and fiction of George Moore (1852–1933), who spent part of his early life in Paris, and even more so in the work of **James Joyce** (1882–1941), often considered to be the greatest and certainly the most innovative of 20C writers in English.

The appearance of his short story collection, *Dubliners*, was long delayed because of the publisher's attempts to impose cuts. Joyce's alienation from Irish society led him to leave Dublin in 1904 for exile, first in Trieste, then in Zürich and Paris. His most influential

Statue of James Joyce by Marjorie Fitzgibbon on North Earl Street, Dublin

© Eurasia Press/Photononstop/Getty Images

work, the vast novel *Ulysses*, recounts a day in the life of Jewish Dubliner Leopold Bloom as he moves around the city in a strange reprise of the wanderings of Homer's hero. The novel revels in the English language and pushes it to its limits, exploiting the devices of interior monologue and stream of consciousness to extraordinary effect. Dwelling on the most intimate details of everyday life, it was banned not just in Ireland but in Britain and America as well. The even more monumental *Finnegan's Wake* takes these developments even further, exploiting not just the potential of English but of scores of other languages and delighting in word-play and paradox of the utmost complexity.

Much influenced by Joyce, and an associate of his during the older writer's sojourn in Paris, **Samuel Beckett** (1906–89) is remembered mainly as one of founders of the Theatre of the Absurd. Like Joyce, Beckett found life in Ireland unbearably constricting and spent most of his life in France, being decorated for his work in the Resistance in World War II. Unlike Joyce, Beckett honed his language to the bare minimum required to convey his grim vision of human life as an "intolerable existence not worthwhile terminating". His best-known work is the play *En Attendant Godot/Waiting for Godot*, written in French and then translated by the author himself.

First produced in 1953 and provoking acclaim and bafflement in equal measure, it is the austere and apparently inconsequential tale of two tramps waiting in vain for a mysterious being who never makes an appearance.

MODERN WRITING IN IRELAND

The early 20C produced the bleak realistic poetry of **Patrick Kavanagh** from Monaghan (1904–67; *Ploughman and Other Poems*) – whose influence can be seen in the work of John Montague (b. 1929; *Poisoned Lands* and *Rough Field*) and Northern poet **Seamus Heaney** (1939–2013; *The Death of a Naturalist*) – and of Louis MacNeice (1907–63), who was a member of Auden's circle and an early influence on the poet/playwright Derek Mahon (b. 1941; *The Hudson Letter*). Novelists included Flann O'Brien (1911–66, real name Brian O'Nolan), who wrote a famous newspaper column as Myles na Gopaleen.

The theme of the Big House survives in the work of Elizabeth Bowen (1899–1973; *The Last September*), **Molly Keane** (1897-1974) writing as M.J. Farrell (1905–97; *The Last Puppetstown*), Aidan Higgins (b. 1927; *Langrishe, Go Down*), Jennifer Johnston (b. 1930; *The Illusionist*) and *Woodbrook* (1974) by David Thompson. Influential writers include **John B. Keane** (1928–2002), whose work is firmly set in Co Kerry – his first play *Sive* won the all-Ireland drama festival; *The Field* was made into a film in 1990 and his best novel is *The Bodhran Makers*; also **Edna O'Brien** (b. 1932; *The Country Girls*), whose frank accounts of female sexuality in the 1950s were banned in Ireland on first publication and publicly burned in her home village in Co Clare, and the highly acclaimed short-story writer **John MacGahern** (1934–2006 *Amongst Women*) who grew up in Co Leitrim. *Troubles* by **JG Farrell** (1935–79) brings rare humour to the grim reality of the War of Independence. **Maeve Binchy** (b. 1940) writes in lighter vein about episodes in Irish family life. **Brendan Behan** (1923–64), who was involved in IRA activity at an early age and imprisoned in both Britain and Ireland, made use of these experiences in the vivid and humorous writing of the plays *The Quare Fellow* and *The Hostage* (the latter originally written in Irish) and in his autobiography, Borstal Boy.

Northern Irish writers Brian Moore (b. 1921; *The Lonely Passion of Judith Hearne*), Patrick McCabe (b. 1955 *Butcher Boy*) and Eoin MacNamee (b. 1960 *Resurrection Man*) have all seen their work quickly turned into films, as have many writers from the south, including **Roddy Doyle** (b. 1958; *The Commitments* and *Paddy Clarke Ha Ha Ha*, which won the Booker Prize) and Colin

Bateman (b. 1962; *Cycle of Violence, Belfast Confidential*), or from outside Ireland such as **Frank McCourt**, who won the Pulitzer Prize in 1997 with *Angela's Ashes*, about his childhood in Limerick.Among the established pillars of Irish drama are **Brian Friel** (b. 1929; *Dancing at Lughnasa*, adapted as a film in 1998), Thomas Kilroy (b. 1934; *The Secret Fall of Constance Wilde*), Thomas Murphy (b. 1935; *A Whistle in the Dark, Bailegangaire*) and Frank McGuinness (b. 1956; *Observe the Sons of Ulster Marching towards the Somme*). Alongside them a new wave of young Irish writers is making an international impact. Encouraged by the Abbey and the Gate Theatres in Dublin, the Royal Court in London and independent theatre companies, such as Rough Magic in Dublin, the Druid Theatre Company in Galway and Red Kettle in Waterford, this new wave includes Martin McDonagh (*The Leenane Trilogy*), Conor McPherson (b 1971 *The Weir*), Marina Carr (b. 1964; *The Mai*) and Enda Walsh (*Disco Pigs*).

The Gaelic Revival at the end of the 19C was responsible for the rescue of writing in Irish, which, at the start of that century had fallen to a very low point indeed. An important figure was Fr. Peter O'Leary (An tAthair Peadar) (1839–1920); his folktale Séadna of 1910 eschewed archaic literary convention in favour of the vigour of the contemporary spoken language, as did the short stories of Pádraig O'Conaire (1882–1928). Among the best-known authors is the Connemara-born Máirtín Ó Cadhain (1906–70), former professor of Irish at Trinity College, whose novel *Cré na Cille (The Clay of the Graveyard* – 1949*)* is the best-known prose writing in recent times. Those who lived and worked on the Great Blasket Island, off the coast of Co Kerry, have produced several works describing island life before the people left in the early 1950s.

Modern Irish poetry, composed by Seán O Ríordéin, Máirtín O Direáin and Nuala ní Dhomhnaill among others, has appeared in a number of languages.

Music and Dance

Ireland is unusual in having a musical instrument – the harp – as its national emblem. Music plays a very important role in Irish life. Traditional music, song and dance are among the most vibrant aspects of Irish culture. Performances take place frequently and spontaneously in all parts of the country and it is this very unpredictability which is responsible for much of its attraction.

The harp dominated the musical scene from the Middle Ages until it was proscribed by the English because of its nationalist allure. It was used to accompany the singing or recitation of poetry. Irish harpists, who trained for many years, were admired for their rapid fingerwork

and their quick and lively technique; they enjoyed high social status. Turlough O'Carolan (Carolan) (1670–1738) started too late in life to reach the highest standard of skill but he was an outstanding composer, much in demand. He left over 200 tunes, which show remarkable melodic invention and are still played today. The first documented mention of mouth-blown pipes in Ireland occurs in an 11C text and the earliest depiction dates from the 15C; these pipes appear to have been primarily for entertainment purposes. The particularly Irish form of pipes, the *uilleann* (elbow) pipes, which have regulators and drones operated by the fingers, emerged in the 18C. They are renowned for the unique sound produced by highly skilled musicians and are closely identified with Irish traditional music, which in recent years has become an important industry.

TRADITIONAL MUSIC TODAY

During the 20C traditional Irish music, which formerly had been played as the accompaniment to dancing, came to be valued in its own right and is no longer confined to isolated regions. Nowadays, traditional musicians come together in pubs throughout the country for sessions that may be formal, commercial and structured, while others are informal and free of charge. Apart from the pipes, the most popular instruments tend to be the fiddle, flute, tin whistle, accordion, concertina, melodeon, banjo, guitar, *bodhrán*, keyboard and the spoons.

Schools and festivals are held throughout the year with people coming from far and wide to learn an instrument or study some other aspect of Irish music. Several schools celebrate the name of a local musician, the best known being the **Willie Clancy Summer School**, which runs in early July in Milltown Malbay, County Clare. Specialist classes in regional styles of instrumental playing are also held at many schools, such as the fiddle classes in Glenties, Co Donegal, each October.

TRADITIONAL TO POP

Traditional music was popularised through the recordings made by the Irish in America and the formation of *Ceoltóirí Chualann* by Seán O'Riada in the early 1960s. This group of the highest calibre of traditional musicians created a more formalised style and generated an appreciation of Irish music. Out of it the **Chieftains** were formed and brought Irish traditional music to a worldwide audience. In the same decade in the United States the Clancy Brothers and Tommy Makem achieved the popularisation of the Irish ballad tradition. In subsequent years many traditional music groups emerged, including the **Dubliners**, the **Bothy Band**, **De Dannan**, **Planxty** and **Altan**.

Members of the Brennan family of the Irish-speaking region of Donegal penetrated the realm of popular music singing in both Irish and English as the group **Clannad**, while another member of the family, **Enya**, forged a highly successful international career as a solo artist.

During the 1950s and 1960s showbands entertained in ballrooms throughout Ireland. Musicians such as **Rory Gallagher** and **Van Morrison** began in showbands before pursuing solo careers.

Country/Irish music has a large fan base in Ireland. Traditional Irish music has influenced the bands of recent decades, so

Traditional music session in a pub, Donegal

© Fáilte Ireland

Irish dancing in Analong

© Northern Ireland Tourist Board

much so that Irish rock has often been described as "Celtic Rock". **Thin Lizzy** and **Rory Gallagher** were among the first to gain international celebrity. **Van Morrison** and **U2** continue to maintain their positions on the international stage, entertaining new generations with their brand of Irish music.

More recent international celebrities **The Pogues**, **The Cranberries**, **Sinéad O'Connor** and **The Corrs** have created a worldwide interest in "Celtic" music. Rather bland by comparison, **Boyzone**, **B*witched** and **Westlife** have had huge commercial success. Boyzone members have embarked on solo careers; Ronan Keating has the largest following to date.

Bands who came to the fore in the 1990s, making the charts in both Ireland and the UK, are Northern Ireland's Divine Comedy and Ash. At the forefront of the Club Scene is David Holmes, a DJ turned popstar, who has gained a considerable reputation for his remixing and soundtrack work.

Many bands that have not yet entered the charts, nor ever will, still have many loyal fans who flock to their gigs – this underground music scene was brilliantly captured in Roddy Doyle's book and subsequent film *The Commitments*.

SONG AND DANCE

Singing forms part of many of the music festivals held in Ireland and at least one festival is devoted solely to this art and is held each June in Ennistymon, Co Clare. Traditional singing is usually called old style *(sean-nós)* singing, and is especially closely identified with singing in Irish; songs are also sung in English in this style. Traditional songs in Irish date for the most part from the last two or three hundred years, although some are older and the style is a good deal older still. Songs in English include recently composed songs and also many songs from the medieval ballad traditions. The style is individual, unaccompanied, free and ornate, with many regional variations. The Irish-speaking area of Rath Cairn, Co Meath, hosts the Irish-language singing festival, *Eigse Dharach Uí Chatháin,* in October each year. **Set dancing** originated in Ireland in the 18C; it consists of figure dances, developed by travelling dancing masters, who adapted the original French dance movements to suit Irish music. Set-dancing is very popular and can be seen at many public venues. Classes are held on a regular basis at hundreds of venues. Although it could not strictly be described as "traditional", the phenomenon of **Riverdance**, created in 1994 and seen on five continents, has done for Irish dance what the Chieftains did for Irish music.

Religion

Christianity was probably introduced to Ireland from Roman Britain or Gaul in the 4C. Palladius, the first bishop, was appointed in 431 by Pope Celestine I but his mission met with little success and it is Patrick, the country's much-revered patron saint, who is held responsible for the country's definitive conversion.

The majority (75 percent) of the population of Ireland is Roman Catholic but most of the country's Catholic churches are of recent date; the traditional religious sites are usually occupied by Anglican churches, a reminder that for many years the Protestant Church of Ireland was the country's established church. Many Catholic churches stand in new centres of population though others were built close to a ruined monastery, where the faithful heard Mass in the Penal Days, and where they continue to be buried.

NATIONAL SAINTS
ST PATRICK
The patron saint of Ireland was born on the West Coast of Roman Britain, where he was captured as a young man by Irish raiders. After six years of slavery near Sliabh Mis (Slemish in Co Down), he escaped to France and then returned to his birthplace. Inspired by a vision that the people of Ireland were calling him, he went to France to study, possibly at the monasteries of Lérins, Tours and Auxerre. In 432, in middle age, he returned to Ireland to convert the people to Christianity. He is thought to have founded his first church at Saul and then travelled to Slane, where he challenged the power of the High King and his druids.

In 444, after a visit to Rome, he founded the cathedral church of Armagh, still the ecclesiastical capital of Ireland, as well as many other churches. When he died, probably at Saul in 461, the country was organised into dioceses based on the petty Irish kingdoms.

Patrick is the subject of numerous tales and legends, according to which he banished monsters and drove the snakes out of Ireland.

On St Patrick's day (17 March) people wear a sprig of **shamrock** *(seamróg)*, a comparatively recent custom, being first documented in the later part of the 17C. It is claimed that the saint used this trefoil plant to illustrate the doctrine of the Holy Trinity.

ST BRIDGET
Brigit was a Celtic goddess, whose name means "the exalted person"; it is significant that the same name is given to the most popular female saint in Irish

Saint Patrick's Day celebrations, Belfast

© Northern Ireland Tourist Board

Irish Missionary Monks

Monks from Ireland played a leading role in re-Christianising Europe, particularly in the conversion of the powerful Frankish kingdom. In the late 6C, **Columbanus** founded monasteries in Luxeuil, Annegray and Fontaines in France and Bobbio in Italy. His disciple **Gall** gave his name to Switzerland's most renowned monastery, which has preserved a fine collection of Irish manuscripts. **Columba (Colmcille** in Irish) left his native country to found the monastery on Iona; monks from there moved on to Lindisfarne in the North of England and to the court of Charlemagne. **Fursey** founded a monastery at Lagny, near Paris, while **Johannes Eriugena** achieved renown as a philosopher at Laon. Several Irish monks went to Germany and beyond; **Kilian** to Würzburg, **Virgil** in the 8C to Salzburg, **Marianus Scottus** in the 11C to Cologne, Fulda and Mainz, and a namesake, a member of an important Donegal family, to Regensburg. The most-travelled monk, however, was probably **Brendan** (*see ENNIS*), who may have reached America.

tradition and second only to St Patrick among all the saints. This Leinster saint ("Bríd"), who died c. AD 524, established a convent in Kildare (*Cill Dara* meaning "the church of the oak tree") and this may have been a sacred spot in pre-Christian times. Bridget is perceived to be the protectress of animals and crops, with which she is closely associated.

The most popular legend of St Bridget is associated with Kildare, where she wished to build a convent. The local king refused to grant her more land than could be covered by her cloak, but when she spread the garment it expanded to cover a vast area.

On St Bridget's day (1 February) it is customary to honour the saint by making straw or rush crosses *(Cros Bhríde)*, which have numerous regional variations in design and form.

CELTIC CHURCH

As continental Europe was overrun by barbarians, the church in Ireland developed a distinctive form of organisation based on monasticism. In the mid-6C and 7C, a great many monasteries were founded and by the 8C the administration of the Church had been taken over by the abbots.

Although bishops continued to perform the sacramental duties and new bishops were consecrated, they were not appointed to particular sees.

Some **monasteries** grew up round a hermit's retreat but many were founded by the head of a clan; members of the family entered the religious life and filled the various offices, as abbot, bishop, priest, teacher or ascetic. The manual work was done either by the monks or by the original tenants of the land: married men with families, whose elder sons usually received a clerical education in the monastery school.

Most monasteries were self-sufficient communities, providing their own food, clothing, books, tools and horses. Some monasteries seem to have been founded on sites with pagan religious associations; others were set up by the main highways, often on the boundaries of a kingdom.

The monastic **libraries** contained copies of the Scriptures, the early Fathers, some classical authors and some history; much early Christian scholarship was preserved in Ireland after the fall of the Roman Empire. In the scriptorium the monks made copies of existing texts or wrote their own learned works, using meticulous techniques which are well described and illustrated at the Colmcille Heritage Centre (*see NORTHERN PENINSULAS*).

Irish monks developed a strong tradition of **asceticism** with a threefold classification of martyrdom. Ascetics seeking to contemplate the presence of God would form small monastic communities in remote places, particularly on islands like the harsh and remote rock of Great Skellig.

ROMANISATION

Following four synods held in the first half of the 12C, the Irish Church lost its distinctive character and was gradually reorganised on the Roman pattern. Four provinces and 33 new dioceses were created, each with a bishop. Some monastic churches became cathedrals, others were used as parish churches.

Monastic orders from the Continent were introduced. The Augustinians took over earlier monastic centres to be near the people. The Cistercians chose new and remote sites in accordance with their ascetic rule, which attracted many Irish monks; by 1272 there were 38 Cistercian houses in Ireland. The Franciscans settled in the towns in the 13C; in the 15C the Observants spread to the West and North.

The Irish Church was further diminished by the Normans with the encouragement of King Henry II and Popes Adrian IV and Alexander III so as "to extend the bounds of the Roman Church". Under the Statute of Kilkenny (1366), Irishmen were forbidden to enter English-run monasteries, and English-speaking clergy were to be appointed to English-speaking parishes.

REFORMATION

In the 16C the churches in England and Ireland were declared independent of Rome; the monasteries were suppressed. Trinity College in Dublin was founded in 1591 to provide Irish priests for the established church; although Roman Catholics were admitted to degrees in 1793, membership was confined to Anglicans until 1873. The 16C reforms were only intermittently enforced in Ireland; the majority of the people remained faithful to the Roman church and many monasteries continued until suppressed by Cromwell. Early in the 17C the Plantation of Ulster with lowland Scots introduced fervent Presbyterianism.

PENAL LAWS

Under the repressive measures introduced after the Battle of the Boyne (1690), Roman Catholics were barred from the Armed Forces, law, commerce, from civic office or office under the crown, from land purchase; Roman Catholic estates could pass *in toto* to an eldest son if he converted to the established church but otherwise had to be divided among all the sons. No Roman Catholic could attend school, keep a school or go abroad to school. Education was conducted in **hedge schools**, which taught Latin, Greek, arithmetic, Irish, English, history and geography. The masters, who were paid in money or kind, were respected members of the Irish community; several were poets. All Roman-Catholic bishops and regular clergy were banished from Ireland, and Roman-Catholic worship was forbidden. Roman Catholic priests travelled the country in disguise and said mass outdoors in remote places or in ruined monastery churches; they used sacramental vessels, which could be dismantled to avoid detection.

DISSENTERS

Roman Catholics were not alone in suffering repression. The Scottish Presbyterians who had migrated to Ulster were frequently regarded with disfavour, though the Protestant Ascendancy could not afford to alienate them completely. The Toleration Act of 1719 granted them freedom of worship, but they continued to endure various disabilities and particularly resented the obligation to pay tithes to the established Church of Ireland. In the 18C, many of them emigrated to America, though the majority remained. Their dissatisfaction with the existing order found expression in widespread support for the rebellion of 1798, when a large proportion of the membership of the United Irishmen was composed of Presbyterians. The English Quakers, who came to Ireland during the Civil War period, also faced discrimination of various kinds, though by the beginning of the 18C this had diminished. Like their

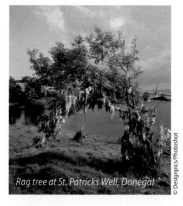
Rag tree at St. Patricks Well, Donegal

counterparts elsewhere, and despite their generally humble beginnings, many Quakers later achieved prominence in commerce and industry.

DENOMINATIONAL FREEDOM

The Catholic Relief Acts of 1791 and 1793 finally allowed freedom of worship and education. In 1795, **Maynooth Seminary** was established for training Roman Catholic clergy. In 1820, Edmund Rice (1762–1844), a former pupil of a hedge school, obtained papal recognition of the **Christian Brothers** (♿ *see CO KILK-ENNY*), an order that established many boys' schools in Ireland. In 1831, the 18C

hedge schools were replaced by the National Schools. In 1869, the Church of Ireland, a member of the Anglican Communion, was disestablished. Apart from Trinity College and two short-lived 16C colleges at Maynooth and Galway, Ireland had no medieval universities. In 1845, charters were issued to incorporate three colleges in Belfast, Cork and Galway, but owing to Roman-Catholic opposition, only Queen's College in Belfast thrived. The Catholic University, founded in Dublin in 1854, with Cardinal Newman as rector, was incorporated as University College when the National University of Ireland was founded in 1908. Two years later, Maynooth was also recognised as a college of the National University.

PILGRIMAGES AND PATTERNS

Since the 8C, by which time Ireland was an almost entirely Christian country, the lives of the **saints** have played a major role in popular devotion and also stimulated an entire body of related legends and lore. Saints were seen to be powerful in many spheres of life on earth and in the afterlife; in many instances, they were seen as popular heroes and heroines. Some were said to have had

Pilgrims climbing Croagh Patrick, County Mayo

a miraculous birth; others wielded supernatural powers and could triumph against the enemy. Saints had healing powers and even their possessions or relics could effect a cure.

Oral tradition has been profoundly influenced by biographies of saints; the lore of saints is widespread throughout Ireland. Thousands of **holy wells**, many associated with local saints, are scattered throughout the countryside. They are said to have curative powers – of a general type or more specific – and are visited frequently, particularly on saints' days.

People still observe the feast days of local saints and the **pattern** (modern Irish *pátrún*; the word is a corruption of patron) when they make a communal visit to a holy well or other religious site under the protection of the local patron saint. In many places holy wells are associated with **rag trees**, named after the hundreds of coloured pieces of cloth attached to their branches, and used to invoke divine assistance, often of a curative kind.

Many traditional religious sites are still visited by pilgrims: Glencolumbkille on St Columba's Day (9 June); Clonmacnoise on St Kieran's Day (9 September); Croagh Patrick in July, when people climb barefoot to the summit. The most rigorous pilgrimage takes place at St Patrick's Purgatory, an island in Lough Derg (southeast of Donegal), where St Patrick spent 40 days in prayer and fasting; during the season (1 June to 15 August) pilgrims spend three days barefoot, take part in an all-night vigil and exist on one meal a day of bread and hot black tea or coffee.

Myths and Lore

Some of the best sources for understanding the Celtic mind and imagination are the Irish myths and tales populated with colourful descriptions of gods and goddesses, and the fabulous exploits of mortal heroes and heroines. Although most of the earlier stories originated in Ireland, they were written down by Christian monks.

RELIGION

The Celts seem to have acknowledged many divinities – gods of war and hunting, goddesses of fertility, harvest and healing. Among those worshipped in Ireland were Brigit, Daghdha and Cernunnos – god of animals, plants and forests, whose emblem was a set of antlers. Different tribes venerated their own tribal god or goddess, who might reside in a special sacred well and hold the power to cure and protect people who regarded not only wells, but trees and certain springs and rivers – particularly the River Boyne – as sacred. Indeed, they carved images of their gods on tree-trunks. Assemblies, at which games and races took place, were held at ancient royal or assembly sites, such as Tara and Tullaghoge. The Celts buried their dead, sometimes cremated, with offerings of food and ornaments; they believed that after death they went on to join their ancestors, the gods of the Otherworld, who were thought to live in sacred mounds, now known to be prehistoric burial mounds such as at Newgrange, Tara and Rathcrogan.

FAIRYLORE

The belief in the **Otherworld** is still an important factor in Irish tradition. This "Otherworld" may exist in a fort or in a mountain, under a lake or beneath the sea. Hundreds of tales and legends associated with the fairies and their world survive, as the landscape and its placenames bear witness. In Irish the fairies are called *sí* or *na daoine maithe* – the good people, or *na daoine beaga* – the little people. They are said variously to be fallen angels, the ancient gods – the *Tuatha Dé Danann* or sometimes the Community of the Dead. These supernatural beings are invisible to mortals, inhabiting the earth, the air and water. The earthen tumuli – known as *rath* and *lios* – are often said to be fairy forts and sometimes fairy music can be heard to emanate from them. Many legends are told describing how the fairies "borrowed" or "stole" a mortal to assist them in some task of their own, such as nursing a fairy child or playing music at a fairy wedding. On occasions, fairies have been said to remove a mortal child, leaving one of their own in its place; when the unsuspecting parents returned from their chores, they would be shocked to discover a sick or dying child in the cradle, referred to as a "**changeling**".

BANSHEE

The Banshee *(Bean Sí)* is a solitary female spirit, whose eerie cry is said to portend death. Superstition associated with the banshee is still very strong and an excuse for the retelling of many legends, often depicting her combing her long hair. One story describes how a man found her comb and brought it home; the following night he heard wailing and knocking at his window and so, catching the comb in a pair of tongs, he passed it out of the window. The comb was removed by the banshee and the tongs broken as a warning that had the man put out his hand, it would have met with the same fate.

The banshee is associated with lamenting, keening and death. The keen *(caoineadh)* was performed by women at funerals and at wakes as part of the Lament for the Dead. Certain – usually older – women in the community came to the house where the corpse was laid out and took it in turns to perform the keen, which was usually composed *ex tempore* and sung to music with a regular refrain during the days of the wake and later at the graveyard. During the wake people also told stories, smoked clay pipes, drank whiskey and played games. The clergy disapproved of many of the wake customs and of the keen.

THE MYTHOLOGICAL AND HISTORICAL CYCLES

The stories from the four great ancient Irish cycles are arguably among the finest expressions of Irish imagination and still a source of artistic inspiration.

The **Mythological Cycle** tells of the heroes or gods who inhabited Ireland before the arrival of the Celts and contains the story of the Battle of Moytura, the Children of Lir and the Wooing of Etain.

The **Ulster Cycle** *(Rúraíocht)* recounts the deeds of the Red Branch Knights of Navan Fort; it includes the **Cattle Raid of Cooley** *(Táin Bó Cuailgne)*, an epic poem that describes how Queen Maeve of Connaught set out to capture the famous brown bull of Cooley and how Ferdia, the Connaught champion, was defeated by the Ulster champion, Cúchulain, which translates as the hound of Culann.

The **Ossianic Cycle**, also known as the **Fenian Cycle** *(Fiannaíocht)*, is set in the time of Cormac mac Airt, who is said to have reigned at Tara in the 3C, and tells about Fionn mac Cumhaill and the Fianna, whose capital was on the Hill of Allen. The Fenian tales and lore tell of the great deeds of the Fianna or Fenian warriors.

Hundreds of neolithic tombs are called Diarmuid and Gráinne's bed *(Leaba Dhiarmuid agus Ghráinne)* in the belief that these lovers from the Fenian tales slept here during their travels in Ireland.

The **Historical Cycle**, which is also known as the **Cycle of the Kings**, is probably a mixture of history and fiction. Many place-names and sites identify with characters and episodes from mythological tales.

A vast number of tales and episodes from these cycles were central to the living storytelling tradition in Ireland until very recently. In addition to their preservation in written literature, the stories were kept alive in oral form, both in Irish and in English, and formed an important part of the repertoire of the storyteller *(seanchaí)*, a person of great social importance.

Cinema

Cinema first appeared in Ireland on 20 April 1896 with a projection of a film by the Lumière brothers in Dublin and by 1909 the Volta in Dublin had been opened by James Joyce himself. Very soon the movies were playing a major role in Irish life. They continue to do so, and in recent years, government support has encouraged cinematic activity; many foreign films have been shot in Ireland and the local industry has produced some memorable works.

In 1904 J.T. Jameson, a newsreel cameraman, founded the Irish Animated Company (IAC); together with the American cinema, which was anxious to please the many Irish immigrants in the States, it made cinema acceptable in Ireland and launched the local industry. In 1916 and 1917 two more companies were set up – Film Company of Ireland (FCOI) and General Film Supply (GFS). It was not, however, until the founding of the Free State in 1922 that Irish cinema truly flourished in Ireland. Political events supplied the first themes such as the Easter Rising of 1916 in *Irish Destiny* (1926) by Isaac Eppel; incidents in the War of Independence feature in *Guest of the Nation* (1935) by Denis Johnston and Tom Cooper's *The Dawn* (1936).

Perhaps the internationally best-known film made in Ireland in the 1930s was the documentary *Man of Aran*. The work of an American of Irish descent, Robert O'Flaherty, it presents a compelling and beautiful picture of the harsh traditional life of the people of the Aran Islands, but is more a romantic evocation of humanity's epic struggle against the elements than an accurate record of a particular place, period or people.

One of the earliest non-Irish films to make extensive use of Ireland as a location was Laurence Olivier's *Henry V*. Shot in 1944 as a deliberate wartime morale booster, it used the Powerscourt estate in neutral Ireland as a setting for the large-scale recreation of the Battle of Agincourt. Hundreds of local farmers hired as extras proved themselves more than adequate as stalwart cavalrymen. Plenty of other films have exploited Ireland as a background to films set elsewhere, among them Mel Gibson's *Braveheart* (1996), in which the town of Trim, its great castle and its surroundings stand in for the Scotland of rebel William Wallace. In 1956, the little port of Youghal was transformed into New Bedford, Massachusetts, becoming the harbour town from which Captain Ahab sets out in search of the great whale in *Moby Dick*. More often, however, the cinematic role of Ireland has been as itself, or at least as a version of itself. In what is probably the most celebrated of all films with an Irish setting, *The Quiet Man* (1952), the country appears as a kind of mysterious, pre-industrial rural paradise, inhabited by quaint, stereotypical Irishmen and Irishwomen.

The film revolves around the return to his native land of a boxer, played by John Wayne, and features one of cinema's longest fight scenes, in which Wayne and his rival brawl their way through the village from farmyard to pub.

Conflict of another kind was portrayed by David Lean in *Ryan's Daughter* (1970), in which a young married Irishwoman falls for an officer of the British garrison. Its evocation of the wild landscapes and seascapes of the west has never been excelled.

In more recent years, film-makers from home and abroad have moved beyond this backward-looking vision of the country, taking their themes from contemporary politics and social questions as well as from history and from literature. Neil Jordan's blockbusting biopic *Michael Collins* (1996), an account of the life and times of the charismatic but doomed Republican leader, was second only to *Titanic* in its success with Irish audiences. Liam Neeson was only one of several Irish stars like Gabriel Byrne, Stephen Rea and Pierce Brosnan, to emerge in this period with international reputations. Jordan's earlier *The Crying Game* (1992) dealt with the relationship of an

Forest Whitaker and Stephen Rea in The Crying Game (1992) by Neil Jordan

© ZUMA Press/age fotostock

IRA gunman and a black British soldier, while his *The Butcher Boy* (1997), in which a young boy from a dysfunctional family descends into madness and murder, has been seen as a metaphor for a country still coming to terms with its troubled history. Jim Sheridan's *The Field* (1991) was equally sombre in its treatment of a farmer's refusal to let his land pass into alien hands. Previously, in 1989, Sheridan had filmed the poignant story of the cerebral palsy victim Christy Brown in *My Left Foot*, for which Daniel Day-Lewis won an Oscar. Day-Lewis also appeared in *In the Name of the Father* (1993), Sheridan's account of the failure of justice following the IRA's bombing of a Guildford pub.

Numerous works of literature have been translated onto the screen with varying degrees of success. Among them are James Joyce's *Dubliners* (1987) and *Ulysses* (1967). *Angela's Ashes* (1999) was a not an altogether convincing adaptation by Alan Parker of Frank McCourt's best-selling autobiographical memoir of his rain-soaked and wretched Limerick childhood. A similarly grim social story is retold in *The Magdalene Sisters* (2003), set in a women's asylum run by Roman-Catholic nuns.

Roddy Doyle's sensitive and sometimes hilarious novels of contemporary Dublin's low life have inspired *The Commitments* (1991) by Alan Parker and *The Van* (1996) by Stephen Frears.

Mention should also be made of the work of the socialist director **Ken Loach** – *Hidden Agenda* (1990), *Land and Freedom* (1995), *Carla's Song* (1997) and *Sweet Sixteen* (2002). In 2006, his film, *The Wind that Shakes the Barley* was awarded the prestigious Palme d'Or at Cannes for his portrayal of the struggle for freedom from occupation: in this instance the Irish Republican Army fights against the yoke of British rule, whose escalating loss of control was epitomised in the 1920s by the Black and Tans, with intense scenes of violence on both sides.

Three Irish TV series have earned great popularity in the UK – *Father Ted, The Ambassador* starring Pauline Collins and partly filmed in Ely Place in Dublin, and *Ballykissangel,* filmed in Avoca in the Wicklow Mountains.

More recently there have been a string of hit films, both indie and mainstream. With the coming-of-age tale *Sing Street*, John Carney follows the massive success of *Once* with another musical, this time set in 1980's Dublin. The sweeping scope of *Brooklyn* brings to vivid life the experience of many emigrants leaving Ireland in the 1950's.

Nature

Visitors come to Ireland for many reasons: to meet the friendly and convivial people and explore their Celtic heritage; for the folk music and the Guinness or to visit the western-most edge of the European continent, but the country's greatest draw is the wonderful scenery. The "Emerald Isle" is wondrously green, variegated by its bare mountains and strange rock formations, stark cliffs and sandy strands, flower-rich boglands and tree-canopied desmesnes.

LAY OF THE LAND

Unlike the archetypal island, which is supposed to rise from coastal lowlands to a mountain core, Ireland's heartland is mostly low-lying country, enclosed by highland ramparts.

Only from Dublin northwards is there an extensive opening of the land to the sea, a 50-mile doorway of fertile land, through which successive waves of invaders have entered the country. Overlooking Dublin from the South, the Wicklow Mountains rise to a peak of 3 035ft/925m at Lugnaquilla, but the country's highest point and the most dramatic mountain scenery are to be found in the far Southwest, where Carantuohill (3414ft/1038m) and Macgillycuddy's Reeks preside over the glories of the Killarney lakelands and the Iveragh Peninsula. This peninsula is one of several and forms part of a much wider set of parallel mountain folds running roughly east to west, which were violently folded in Hercynian times, and which include the granites of Brittany and the Harz massif in Germany. In Ireland they also include a whole series of ranges dividing the Midlands from the island's southern coastline. Their equivalents in the North are the Northeast to Southwest pointing ranges, folded in the Caledonian period and crossing the Atlantic edge in Donegal and Connaught, and the narrow strait separating Ulster from Scotland. Bounded by these ancient mountain systems, the central regions of the country are largely underlaid by a much-eroded foundation of carboniferous limestone: the basis of the rich pasturelands for which Ireland is famous, it is far from monotonous, producing such dramatic features as the great escarpment of Benbulben, glowering over Sligo, and the eerie moonscapes of The Burren in Co Clare.

Much of the Midlands' landscape is profoundly marked by the impact of the Ice Ages. The retreating glaciers left unconsolidated deposits of clay, sand and gravel, great tracts of which remain badly drained today, though the worm-like, winding ridges of sandy gravel called *eskers* – deposited by streams running beneath the glaciers – have always provided dry areas in an otherwise almost impenetrable land. The ice sheets also moulded great swarms of **drumlins**, low egg-shaped mounds, most clearly visible when partially submerged as in Clew Bay and Strangford Lough. In the North, a broad band of drumlins extends right across the island, the waterlogged land around them forming a barrier to communication, which may well have helped establish Ulster's distinctive identity in ancient times.

PEAT BOGS

One of the most intriguing features of the Irish landscape is its peat bogs, the most extensive in Europe, occupying something like a sixth of the land surface and playing an important role in the country's history, economy and collective memory.

There are two types of bog in Ireland although the peat in both is formed in water-logged conditions by the accumulation of dead and incompletely decomposed plant material. **Blanket bog** occurs in areas of high rainfall and humidity, mostly in the mountains of the western seaboard, and comprises dead grass and sedge. It is usually shallower (6ft/2m to 20ft/6m) than **raised bog**, which is more of a lowland phenomenon, occurring where there is less rainfall, growing above the ground-water level, and formed by dome-shaped bog moss (sphagnum). This type of peat-bog,

Galway - Connemara landscape with peat bog

© Derek Cullen/Fáilte Ireland

up to 19ft/12m deep, is scattered over much of the Midlands, where it forms a distinctive, open and natural-seeming landscape in contrast to the farmland beyond. Raised bogs have developed over time without appreciable human interference, whereas the blanket bog has been fashioned by burning and the clearance of scrub and woodland for grazing.

The history of the land is preserved by the peat layers, revealing the nature of forests and of Neolithic fields beneath the blanket bogs of the West.

In more recent times the Irish bogs have provided places of refuge for rebels and outlaws, while their inaccessibility and unfamiliarity have made it difficult for invaders to extend their control over the whole country.

The early disappearance of tree cover and scarcity of coal deposits meant that peat – known locally as turf – became the most important source of fuel. Turfs are traditionally cut with a *slane*, a narrow spade with a side blade set at a right angle, and laid out to dry. When thoroughly dry, they are stacked into clamps near the house. In a fine summer, a family can harvest enough fuel for several years. The cuts sliced deep into the bog and the stacks of drying peat make distinctive patterns in the landscape that appear quite alien to visitors from abroad, while the sight, sound and smell of the turf fire glowing in the corner of a living room or pub evokes strong emotions in every Irish heart.

Since the mid-20C peat has been harvested on an industrial scale to provide the country with electric power as well as yielding moss peat for horticultural purposes. The mechanical harvesters of the *Bord na Móna* (Peat Development Authority) are an impressive sight as they scrape huge quantities of sun-dried milled peat from a bog (drained for five to seven years). The harvested peat is made into briquettes for domestic use or burned in one of five electricity generating stations.

CLIMATE

Confronting the Atlantic as it does, Ireland has an oceanic climate, tempered by the influence of the warm waters of the Gulf Stream flowing northwards along its western shores. Successive weather systems blow in from the Southwest, bringing abundant precipitation and ever-changing cloudscapes.

The temperature range is limited; it is rarely very hot nor very cold. In the coolest months of January and February temperatures vary between 4° and 7° Celsius, in the warmest months of July and August between 14° and 16°.

Snowfalls are uncommon except on the highest mountains, where the total annual precipitation can exceed 2.4m. The Southwest is the wettest part of the country and the East the driest, but it is not so much the amount of rainfall, rather its persistence that is characteristic. However, although there may not be many days without rain or a touch of drizzle, it should always be remembered that its occurrence is in no small part responsible for the freshness of the atmosphere and the luminous look of the landscape.

COAST

The country's rock foundation is most dramatically exposed at the interface of land and ocean, particularly in the West, where mountainous peninsulas frequently end in bold headlands, while sea inlets and fjords penetrate far inland. The northern shore of Co Antrim boasts what is surely Ireland's most famous natural wonder, the countless clustered columns of the Giant's Causeway, formed 60 million years ago by violent volcanic disturbances. Few natural ramparts are as spectacular as the bands of shale and sandstone making up the 5mi/8km stretch of the Cliffs of Moher, rising 200m over the Atlantic breakers on the edge of The Burren in Co Clare. The limestones of The Burren leap seaward to form the Aran Islands, where the abrupt cliffs of Inishmore, though less high, are equally awe-inspiring. The discontinuous archipelago along the Western coast offers other equally extraordinary sights, none more so than the rocky mountaintop of Skellig Michael. The tallest cliffs are those of the Slieve League peninsula, where a great bastion of quartzite stands some 1,972ft/601m above the waves.

In the East of the country coasts are characterised by splendid natural harbours formed by drowned valleys, low limestone cliffs and glorious beach.

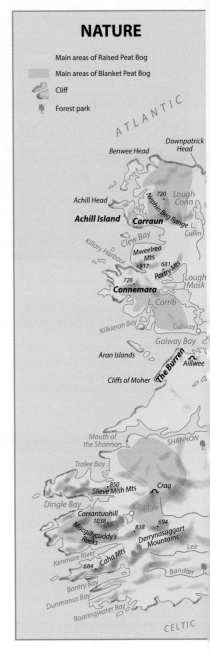

NATURE

Main areas of Raised Peat Bog

Main areas of Blanket Peat Bog

Cliff

Forest park

FIELDS AND FARMS

Despite recent economic trends, Ireland is still very much an **agricultural country**, with more than 80 percent of the land used for farming. Most of this is

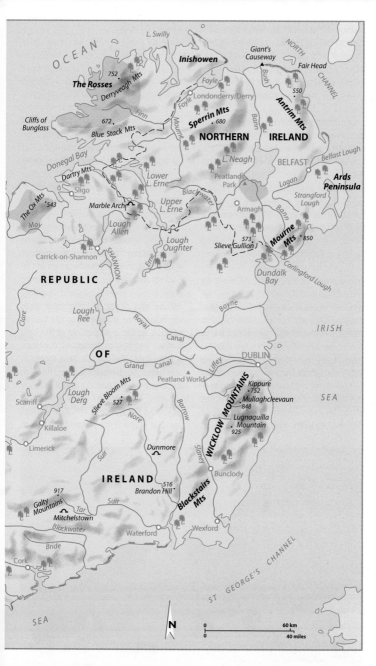

pasture; it is estimated that Ireland has around 95 percent of the best grassland in the whole European Union, but **arable farming** prospers in the drier East, notably in the Ards Peninsular in Ulster and in Co Wexford, where barley is grown on a large scale.

As elsewhere in Atlantic Europe, farmland is **enclosed** rather than open, with a variety of field patterns reflecting a complex historical development. The typical field boundary is a hedgebank topped with native shrubs and trees, often allowed to grow spontaneously rather than laid to make them stock-proof. It is these leafy banks that make up for the country's lack of woodland, transforming the rolling landscape into picturesque scenery. In the rocky penin-sulas of the West and elsewhere, stone is used to form boundary walls: most notably in the Aran Islands, where tiny enclosures are bounded by drystone walls built to be permeable to strong local winds. In areas of poor soil and high rainfall, "**lazy beds**" were made. These were cultivation ridges, created by laying a strip of manure and inverting sods over it from both sides. The raised bed drained easily into the trenches on either side and its soil was warmed by the sun from the side as well as the top, highly advantageous characteristics in a cool, wet country. Lazy beds came into their own with the widespread cultiva-tion of the potato in the pre-Famine years and whole landscapes are marked by the wrinkled pattern of the subse-quently abandoned ridges, sometimes at an elevation where cultivation of any crop would seem doomed to failure.

VEGETATION

Most of the country was originally covered in trees, particularly forests of sessile oak. Clearance for agriculture began in Neolithic times and continued until virtually no natural or even semi-natural woodlands were left. One of the last assaults on the native forest was made by the British in the 17C and 18C, on the one hand for building materials and for smelting, on the other to deny refuge to the rebellious Irish. Remnants of natu-ral forest can be found in the southern Wicklow Mountains and around Killarney, where there are also marvellous speci-mens of the arbutus or strawberry tree. In the 18C considerable replanting efforts were made by many owners of demesnes eager to landscape their estates in the English manner. Exotic trees like Scots pine, beech, sweet chestnut, monkey puzzle and cedar of Lebandon were introduced to supplement the native species. As some six percent of the land surface was held in demesnes, the land-scape impact was considerable, though it was subsequently much reduced through the break-up and parcelling-out of many estates. The fate of the Anglo-Irish so-called Big House is well known; less familiar is the felling of its heritage of

Glen Keen Farm, County Mayo

© Kelvin Gillmor/Fáilte Ireland, Tourism Ireland

© Suzanne Clark/County Carlow/Fáilte Ireland, Tourism Ireland

River Barrow at Fenniscourt, County Carlow

trees and ornamental woodland and their conversion into ordinary farmland or conifer plantations. Nevertheless a number of demesnes have survived, some in the form of **Forest Parks** in public ownership, others in the hands of the National Trust in Northern Ireland. Generations of gardeners have exploited the country's favourable, frost-free environment to create gardens famous for their broad spectrum of plants, notably in areas sheltered from the wind. Several sub-tropical paradise gardens such as Garinish Island in Glengarriff Harbour, manage to have flowers in bloom all year round. Conditions favoured by rhododendrons and fuchsias account for why these shrubs grow in woodlands and hedgerows. Botanically speaking, Ireland's most fascinating landscape is perhaps The Burren, where a profusion of acid- and lime-loving plants grow in harmonious co-existence.

RIVERS AND LAKES

Not surprisingly, water is ever-present in the Irish landscape. The country's rivers have a total length of 16,530mi/ 26,000km and lakes/loughs cover an area of 560sq mi/1,450sq km. Ireland's low population density and the relative lack of polluting industries means that most of this water is unpolluted and well-stocked with fish and other wildlife. The watercourses rising on the seaward side of mountains tend to be short and steep, draining straight into the sea. Those that rise inland form slow-moving lowland streams, lined by water-meadows and often widening out into lakes. The Shannon, the country's longest river (230mi/370km) behaves in this way, winding sluggishly through the Midlands countryside and forming the great expanses of Lough Ree and Lough Derg, before discharging into its immensely long estuary below Limerick. In Ulster, Lough Neagh is far more impressive than the River Bann, which flows through it – though shallow, it is Ireland's largest body of water, covering an area of 153sq m/400sq km, and teeming with eels.

The country's loveliest lakeland is that which has developed along the course of the Erne, comprising countless lesser lakes as well as island-studded Upper and Lower Lough Erne themselves.

In the South, rivers rising far inland have cut their way through upland chains to reach the sea; the valleys thus formed by the Blackwater, Nore, Suir, Barrow and Slaney are often of great beauty.

Cliffs of Moher, County Clare
© Christopher Hill/Tourism Ireland

Ireland's famous capital – the fair city – bestrides the River Liffey and looks seawards to its port and the broad waters of Dublin Bay. The distinctive outline of the Wicklow Mountains forms a magnificent backdrop to the South, while suburbs stretch far inland as well as north to the Ben of Howth and south to Dalkey Headland. Something like a third of the country's population lives in the greater Dublin area and the majority of the country's business is carried out here. Georgian architectural elegance and the increasingly cosmopolitan café, restaurant and bar scene make the city an irresistible destination, not only for a weekend but for longer periods of exploration.

Highlights

1 The fascinating Book of Kells exhibition at **Trinity College** (p113)

2 Ireland's hoards of gold, Viking artefacts and sheelagh-na-gigs at the **National Museum** (p121)

3 The medieval **Christ Church Cathedral** disguised by a Victorian upgrade (p127)

4 The extensive collection at the **Hugh Lane Gallery of Modern Art** (p132)

5 Touring the castle at the seaside resort of **Malahide** (p140)

▶ **Population:** 506,211 (Dublin City).

ℹ **Info:** Dublin Tourism Centres: 25 Suffolk St.; 14 Upper O'Connell St.; Arrivals Hall, Airport (terminals 1 and 2). ☎01850 230 330; ☎0800 0397 000 (from UK); ☎+353 669 792 083 (international) www.visitdublin.com.

▶ **Location:** Dublin is set on the East Coast, on the estuary of the River Liffey and the shores of Dublin Bay. It has direct connections with all the major provincial towns. It is served by an international airport (north of the city centre) and by shipping lines from Britain.

🅿 **Parking:** There are car parks throughout the city (though public transport is recommended).

👥 **Kids:** Dublinia, Dublin Zoo.

☺ **Don't Miss:** Trinity College, Dublin Castle and Kilmainham Gaol are special.

🕐 **Timing:** Allow at least three days for the highlights.

The City Today

Low-rise but high-tech, elegant and yet raucous, Dublin retains the feel of a small city while flaunting its modernity. Shivering a little in the icy winds of recession, the city has seen the end of its boom years but fortunately much of its cultural heritage has survived the developers. A robust realism replaces the hubristic confidence of the years of the "Celtic Tiger" and Dubliners, fierce survivors, remain proud of their history and identity.

A Bit Of History
Viking Settlement

The name Dublin (*Baile Átha Cliath*) is derived from *Dubh Linn*, the Dark Pool at the confluence of the Poddle and the Liffey; the Irish name, *Baile Átha Cliath*, means the city by the hurdle ford.

The first permanent settlement beside the Liffey was established at Wood Quay in the 9C by the Vikings, who then spread north of the river, where their settlement was known as Oxmantown; at the Battle of Clontarf on the north shore of Dublin Bay in 1014 their power was curbed by Brian Ború.

Irish Bronze Age goldwork, National Museum

© Tony Pleavin/Tourism Ireland

Anglo-Norman Stronghold

After the Anglo-Norman invasion late in the 12C Dublin was granted to the port of Bristol as a trading post by Henry II in 1172. Under constant harassment by the Irish tribes and an unsuccessful attack in 1316 by Edward Bruce of Scotland, the extent of the Anglo-Normans' influence waxed and waned but they never lost control of Dublin, which gradually became the seat of Parliament and the centre of government.

Early Lord Deputies operated from their own power bases in the Pale – Trim, Maynooth and Kilkenny – but in the 16C Sir Henry Sidney, who was four times Lord Deputy, took up residence in the castle and put it in good repair. Gradually the medieval fortress evolved into an administrative centre and viceregal court.

Kildare Revolt

The most serious incident occurred in 1534, when Thomas Fitzgerald, known as "Silken Thomas" because of the silk embroidery on his men's apparel, renounced his allegiance to Henry VIII and launched a rebellion, which became known as the Kildare or Geraldine Revolt. He laid siege to the castle but the citizenry turned against him; the besieged proclaimed the arrival of the King's army and made a sortie, whereupon the besiegers took fright and scattered.

Fitzgerald himself escaped but was forced to surrender some months later and was executed in London, together with his five uncles.

Georgian Dublin

In the relative peace of the 18C, restrictions eased and trade flourished. Buildings were constructed to house public bodies; terraces of fine houses were erected first north and then south of the river; men of property, drawn to the capital on parliamentary and other business, commissioned fine mansions. Under the activities of the Wide Streets Commissioners, established in 1758, Dublin developed into an elegant city, embraced by the Royal and Grand Canals and bisected by the Liffey, now embanked between quays and spanned by several bridges. With the Act of Union (1800), political affairs removed to London and although known as the "second city of the Empire", Dublin stagnated. Despite many grievous losses, Dublin can still claim to be the finest Georgian city in the British Isles.

Capital of the Republic

There was much destruction during the Easter Rising and the Civil War but key buildings like the Four Courts, the GPO and the Custom House were eventually restored to something like their former glory. More recent renovation work has transformed Temple Bar from a dilapidated district into a network of pedestrian streets, vibrant with pubs, cafés, restaurants, nightspots, crafts and clothes shops.

GETTING THERE

BY AIR - Dublin International Airport – ✆01 814 1111; www.dublinairport.com. **Airlink 747** is a bus service operated by Dublin Bus (**⬇see below**) between Dublin Airport and central Dublin; pick-up points include O'Connell Street, Central bus and railway stations, International Financial Centre and Convention Centre. A similar service is provided by Aircoach. www.aircoach.ie.

GETTING AROUND

Dublin city is served by a bus network and a railway line along the coast. The **DART** (Dublin Area Rapid Transport) is a **rail service** along the coast (25mi/40km) from Howth in the North to Greystones in the South, administered by the national rail operator, Iarnród Éireann (Irish Rail) so Trekker and Explorer tickets are valid. It serves three stations in central Dublin – Connolly, Tara Street and Pearse. The service operates daily between around 6.30am (9am Sunday) and 11.45pm with trains running every 5–10min during peak times and every 15min off-peak; ✆01 703 3504 (Passenger information); www.dublin.ie/transport/dart.htm.

The **Dublin LUAS System** is a **light rail transit system** with routes from the city centre – Abbey Street southwest via Drimnagh to Tallaght; St Stephen's Green south via Ranelagh and Dundrum to Sandyford. For visitors the most useful line is the red line, which travels west to Heuston Station and east past Bus Aras to The Point (3 Arena). Trams run Mon–Sat 5.30am (6.30am Sat)–12.30am; Sun 7am–11.30pm, every 5 to 10min (every 15min, 10.30pm onwards). Ticket prices from €2 (single), €3.30 (return). ✆1850 300 604; www.luas.ie.

Dublin Bus (CIE) operates the **bus network**, which covers the whole city from the Central Bus Station (Busáras) in Store Street (behind the Custom House). Note that exact change in coins is required. No change is given, though you will be given a receipt that can be refunded at the Dublin Bus office, (59 Upper O'Connell Street office) so if you intend making several journeys it is worth considering a prepaid card. Tours are available north along the coast to Howth and Malahide; south along the coast to Bray and Greystones, returning inland via Enniskerry. Further details: ✆01 873 4222; www.dublinbus.ie.

Nitelink buses run from the city centre to the suburbs, every Fri–Sat on the hour, 12.00am–4am; fare is €6.50. In the city centre there are **paying car parks**, **parking meters**, **pay and display machines** and **disc parking areas**.

There is no parking on **double yellow lines** at any time; no parking on **single yellow lines** during the hours indicated on the time plate; no parking in **clearways and bus lanes** during the hours indicated on the time plate. **Parking bays** for **disabled drivers** require a disabled parking permit on display. Cars parked illegally may be **clamped**; declamping costs at least €80. A system of numbered car parks linked to numbered road junctions on the outskirts of Dublin makes it much easier to find the right route into the city centre.

The major **toll roads** are the Dublin East-Link, which spans the Liffey estuary, and the Dublin West-Link, which runs North–South on the Western edge of the city. The M1 Drogheda bypass and M4 motorway also collect a toll, at Enfield). There is a toll on the M50 radial route around the city and on the Port Tunnel. Tolls vary; expect €3.30; at peak times the Port Tunnel toll is over €10). See www.eflow.ie/tolls for all charges.

WALKING TOURS

These three walks through the city centre start and finish at O'Connell Bridge or Ha'penny Bridge.

1 SOUTHSIDE

Thie southside of the Liffey is the city's youngest quarter, vulnerable as it was to Irish raiding parties swooping down from the Wicklow Mountains. Until the construction of the Old Parliament in 1728, there was little building east of the old town except for Trinity College. The district began to develop into a fashionable suburb in the 1750s when the Duke of Leinster erected the first nobleman's house south of the river; his prediction that fashionable society would follow soon proved true. Some of the most elegant Georgian terraces are to be found east and south of his mansion. In 1815 the Leinster property was bought by the Royal Dublin Society, and the National Museum, the National Library and the National Gallery were built in the grounds. After 1922 the mansion was converted to serve as the Parliament of the newly established Free State.

From O'Connell Bridge walk south along Westmoreland Street passing (right) the Bank of Ireland.

Bank of Ireland★★

Foster Place. ♿ ◐*Open Tue–Fri 10am–4pm (5pm Thu).* ◐ *guided tour, Tue 10.30am, 11.30am, 1.45pm.* ◐*Closed Bank Hols.* ✆*01 661 5933.*
Ireland was governed from this elegant building in Foster Place from when it was completed (1728) until 1800, when the Act of Union abolished the country's jurisdiction and transferred it to Westminster. Several eminent architects contributed to its appearance – Sir Edward Lovett Pearce, James Gandon and Francis Johnston, who converted it for use by the Bank of Ireland in 1803. The old House of Commons is now the banking hall. The **House of Lords** is still largely intact, with a magnificent coffered ceiling, a great chandelier

of Irish glass, an oak mantelpiece to a design by Inigo Jones and splendid 17C Flemish tapestries depicting the Battle of the Boyne and the siege of Londonderry.

In the **Story of Banking** a short video and display of currency, bank notes and an old money cart form part of an excellent interpretation of the role of the Bank of Ireland in the commercial development of the country since its establishment in 1783.

College Green

This triangular open space, formerly known as Hoggen Green, was an old Viking burial ground *(haugen)* and meeting place *(thengmote)*. At the centre stands a statue of **Henry Grattan** by John Foley (1879) and a modern iron sculpture designed by Edward Delaney in memory of **Thomas Davis** (1814–45), poet, leader of the Young Ireland movement and founder of *The Nation.*

Trinity College★★

Trinity College, Dublin, sometimes known as TCD, was founded in 1592 by Elizabeth I on the site of All Hallows, an Augustinian monastery suppressed at the Dissolution.

It developed according to the tradition of the Oxford and Cambridge colleges and long remained an Anglican preserve. Roman Catholics were excluded until 1873, while the Roman-Catholic Church for its part strongly disapproved of the faithful studying here well into the 1960s. Women were first admitted in 1903. The College stands in its own grounds, **College Park**: an open space set aside for sport – cricket, rugby, running and hurling – although this has been encroached upon by the science and medical faculties. The film *Educating Rita*, starring Michael Caine and Julie Walters, was filmed here.

Beside the entrance gates stands an elegant Georgian house built for the Provost in 1758. Statues by Foley of Oliver Goldsmith and Edmund Burke flank the main gate.

The buildings in **Front Court** date from the mid 18C; the wings termi-

DUBLIN
Map I

0 ——— 1 km
0 ——— 1/2 mile

WHERE TO EAT

Bistro One..①
Nancy Hands Pub & Restaurant......②
Roly's Bistro..③
Seagrass..④

STREET INDEX

Denmark St.. 2
Mount St Upper................................... 4
Thomas St West.................................... 7
Western Way.. 9

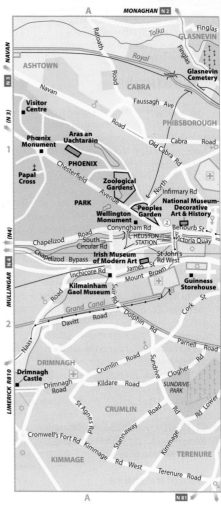

nate in the **Theatre** *(south)* and the **Chapel** *(north)*, both designed by Sir William Chambers, with stuccowork by Michael Stapleton. The chapel is mainly lit by high semi-circular windows. The theatre (1777–91) is used for degree ceremonies, Senate meetings, musical and theatrical events; it is hung with portraits of Elizabeth I, Edmund Burke, George Berkeley and Jonathan Swift.

Library Court is dominated by the **Campanile** (1853), designed by Charles Lanyon. Among the trees in the centre is *Reclining Connected Forms* (1969), a sculpture by Henry Moore. The area behind the north range is called **Botany Bay**, after the Australian penal colony (possibly because of unruly student antics). The red-brick range on the East side, known as Rubrics, is the oldest building in the college: the South side is closed by the Old Library and Treasury.

The **Museum** (1850) *(south side of New Square)* was designed by Sir Thomas Deane and Benjamin Woodward in the Venetian style promoted by Ruskin; the delightful stone carving of flowers, leaves and animals is by the O'Shea brothers from Cork.

R 105 HOWTH

NORTH BULL ISLAND

DOUGLAS, HOLYHEAD

LIVERPOOL, MOSTYN

Rd Old — Griffith — Collins — Road — KILLESTER — Road — ST ANNE'S PARK

National Botanic Gardens

Casino Marino ■ L 87

Avenue — Port — Tunnel — Malahide — Howth — Road — L 80

DRUMCONDRA — St-Alphonsus Rd — Iona Rd — Tolka — MARINO — Howth — CLONTARF

Canal — Circular — Clonliffe Road — Fairview — FAIRVIEW PARK — Alfie Byrne Rd — Clontarf — Road

Phibsborough — Berkeley Rd — Dorset St — GAA Museum — L 47

Mountjoy Square — see map II — East Wall Rd — TOLL — 1

NORTHSIDE — POINT VILLAGE — Sheriff — St — Tolka Quay — Road

SAMUEL BECKETT BRIDGE — Liffey — East Wall — TOLL

Castle — TRINITY COLLEGE — SOUTHSIDE — GRAND CANAL DOCK — Ringsend Rd — WATERWAYS IRELAND VISITOR CENTRE — RINGSEND

Mount St — Bath Ave — Beach — DUBLIN

Shaw Birthplace — NATIONAL CONCERT HALL — St Stephen's Church — SANDYMOUNT — Strand — BAY — 2

Jewish Museum — Adelaide Rd — Grand Canal — Haddington — Shelbourne Rd — Merrion — R 131

HAROLD'S CROSS — Grove Rd — Grand Parade — Ranelagh — Leeson St Upper — Clyde Lane — HERBERT PARK — Anglesea — Shrewsbury Rd — Ailesbury Rd — Rock Rd

Canal Rd — Morehampton Rd — Donnybrook Rd — Dodder

RATHMINES — DONNYBROOK — Sandford Rd — Eglinton Rd — Clonskeagh — Stillorgan — BOOTERSTOWN

Palmerston Park — Dodder — UNIVERSITY COLLEGE

Terenure Rd East

N

Trinity College

© CEZARY ZAREBSKI PHOTOGRAPHY/Moment/Getty Images

On the north side of College Park, on Pearse Street is TCD's latest initiative, the excellent **Science Gallery** (☞*see p136*).

▷ Turn left into Nassau St.

Trinity College Old Library★★★

Entrances in College Green and Nassau St. ♿ ⊙*Open Mon–Sat, 8.30am–5pm (Sun, Oct–Apr 9.30am-5pm).* ⊙*Closed 22 Dec–2 Jan.* ⊛⊛€9 🔊College tour *(30min, including the Colonnades and Book of Kells): mid-May–Sept, 10.15am–12.45pm every 25–35 mins, then 2.15pm, 3pm and 3.40pm (no tours Sun 3.40pm) from the Front Arch.* ⊛⊛€10-13. *⌕01 896 1661. www.tcd.ie/visitors.*

This austere building (1712–32) was designed by Thomas Burgh, chief engineer and surveyor-general of Her Majesty's Fortifications in Ireland. The library acquired its books by purchase or donation until 1801, when it became a copyright library, receiving copies of every book published in the Commonwealth. Since then the increased pace of acquisition has required new buildings: the Reading Room built in 1937 and the Berkeley Library designed by Paul Koralek in 1967. Until 1892 the ground floor was an open colonnade designed to protect the books from damp; in 1992 part of it was converted to provide two galleries: The Colonnades for annual themed exhibitions, and the Treasury.

Treasury★★★ – This gallery displays the great treasures of Trinity College Library. The *Book of Kells★★★*, the most famous of them, is an illuminated manuscript of the four Gospels in Latin on vellum, produced c 800 and kept at Kells until the 17C. The *Book of Durrow★* (c. 700) is another illustrated manuscript of the Gospels in a simpler style. The *Book of Armagh★★* (c. 807) contains the complete text of the New

Grand Canal

© Rob Durston/Fáilte Ireland

Dublin Waterways

The urban landscape of Dublin is greatly enhanced by the five waterways which traverse the city – **River Liffey**, personified as Anna Livia Pluribella, which flows through the city centre before entering the sea in Dublin Bay; two tributaries, the **River Dodder** on the Southside and the **River Tolka** on the Northside; and two canals, the **Grand Canal** (1757–1803), which passes through the southern suburbs to join the Shannon at Shannon Harbour, north of Birr, and the **Royal Canal** (1790–1817), which passes through the Northside to join the Shannon west of Longford. ☞*Visit remote sections of the canals in the daytime only.*

Georgian house, Merrion Square

© SGM/age fotostock

Testament in Latin, as used by the Celtic Church, as well as the lives of St Patrick and St Martin, and the Confession of St Patrick. The *Book of Dimma*★★ contains both the Gospels and some liturgical text; its silver shrine dates from c. 1150.

Long Room★★ – Above the entrance door at the top of the stairs are the arms of Elizabeth I, a relic of the original college. The Long Room (209ft/64m x 40ft/12m) is lined with bookcases. The original flat ceiling was replaced in the mid-19C by the present higher barrel vault. The 29-string Irish harp (c. 15C, restored), made of willow, is the oldest in Ireland, found in Limerick in the 18C.

◗ On the corner with Kildare Street stands the former home of the *Kildare Street Club*, the oldest and most staunchly Unionist of Dublin's gentleman's clubs. Continue along Nassau St and Clare St to Merrion Sq.

Merrion Square★

The jewel of Georgian Dublin was laid out in 1762 by John Ensor for the 6th Viscount Fitzwilliam under the policy of the Wide Streets Commissioners. Delicate fanlights surmount the elegant doorways of the perfectly proportioned red-brick houses; commemorative plaques mark the homes of famous people – Oscar Wilde's father, Sir William Wilde, at no. 1, William Butler Yeats at no. 82. The West side is graced by the gardens of Leinster House, flanked by the Natural History Museum and the National Gallery. The Southeast vista is closed by **St Stephen's Church**, designed in 1821 by John Bowden and completed by Joseph Welland: its domed tower, known as the "Pepper Canister", was inspired by three Athenian buildings – the Erechtheum, the Tower of the Winds and the Monument of Lysicrates. ✆*01 2880663 (vicarage)*

◗ Rejoin Merrion Square East.

Among the many handsome Georgian houses are the town house of the Wellesley family, where the Duke of Wellington spent some of his childhood, and the Merrion Street Hotel, with its splendidly restored interior.

Number Twenty Nine★

🕔*Note: Number Twenty Nine is closed through 2020.* ⌚€6. ✗ ✆*01 702 6163. www.numbertwentynine.ie.*
This 18C terrace house evocatively re-creates domestic life in Dublin in the Georgian era. It is decorated throughout with appropriate furniture, carpets, curtains and paintings, and is crammed

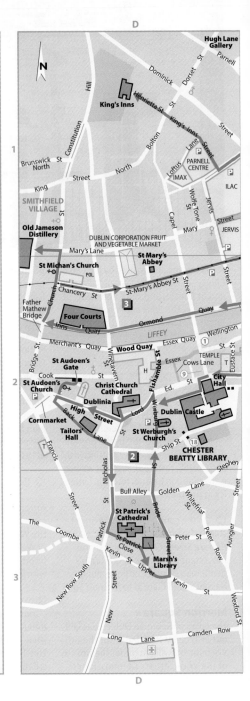

DUBLIN
Map II

0   200 m
0   200 yards

WHERE TO STAY

Clarence (The)........................ ①
Harrington Hall...................... ②
Mercer (The)........................... ③
Merrion (The)......................... ④
Pembroke Townhouse............ ⑤
Trinity Lodge......................... ⑥

WHERE TO EAT

Bad Ass Café (The)................. ①
Balzac.................................... ②
Bang Café............................... ③
Bentley's Oyster Bar and Grill...... ④
Bleu.. ⑤
Cellar Bar (The)...................... ⑥
Chapter One........................... ⑦
Cliff Townhouse (The)............ ⑧
Ely CHQ Brasserie.................. ⑨
Fallon & Byrne....................... ⑩
Gueuleton (L')........................ ⑫
Old Spot (The)........................ ⑬
Patrick Guilbaud..................... ⑭
Pichet..................................... ⑮
Pig's Ear (The)........................ ⑯
Rustic Stone........................... ⑰
Silk Road Cafe........................ ⑱
Super Miss Sue....................... ⑲

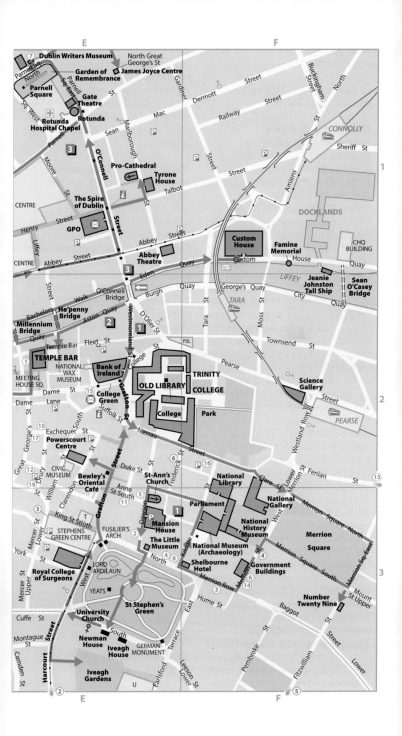

with the paraphernalia of everyday living. Among the wealth of objects are a wine cistern designed by Francis Johnston and a curved belly-warmer.

▷ Return up Merrion Street via Merrion Square South.

National Gallery★★

Entrance on Clare St. (Dúchas). ♿
🕐*Open daily 9.15am (11am Sun)–5.30pm (8.30pm Thu).* 🕐*Closed Good Fri, 24–26 Dec.* 🗣*Guided tour: Sat 12.30pm, Sun 11.30am, 12.30pm, 1.30pm.* ✕ ☎*01 661 5133.*
www.nationalgallery.ie.

Ireland's National Gallery, inaugurated in 1864, has one of the finest collections of art in Europe. By the Merrion Street entrance stands the statue of William Dargan (1799–1867), a railway magnate and the promoter of the Irish Industrial Exhibition of 1853 which included a Fine Art Hall, and it is these works that formed the founding collection. Other benefactors have included Sir Hugh Lane, Sir Henry Vaughan and G.B. Shaw, whose donation included royalties from *My Fair Lady*. The Milltown Rooms were built to house the Milltown Collection. The latest addition is the controversial Millennium Wing, a striking stone-clad edifice providing a spacious new entrance area and space for loaned exhibitions from abroad.

Understandably, the gallery's collection of Irish art is outstanding, with examples by the country's major painters and sculptors from the 17C to the 20C, displayed alongside select items of furniture. There are fascinating topographical pictures, portraits and a whole room devoted to the work of Jack B. Yeats (1871–1957), who ably captured the colour and spirit of contemporary life in Ireland and its landscapes, as did, of course, his brother, W.B. Yeats.

The gallery's British paintings include works by Hogarth, Wilson, Gainsborough, Reynolds and Romney; lovely watercolours by Bonington and Crome. There is an important Italian collection ranging from early altarpieces to paintings by Fra Angelico, Mantegna and Titian, and a superbly dramatic Caravaggio, *The Taking of Christ*. French art is represented by Claude and Poussin, by several artists of the Rococo and a number of Impressionists. Outstanding Dutch paintings include works from Vermeer, Ruisdael and Hobbema.The Spanish collection is substantial, with El Greco, Velázquez, Murillo, Zurbaran and Goya.

Natural History Museum★

Merrion Street Upper. 🕐*Open Tue–Sat 10am–5pm and Sun 2pm–5pm.* ☎*01 677 7444. www.museum.ie/naturalhistory.*

Reopened in 2010 after a major restoration project, this museum isstill based on the original Victorian layout, the building's pillared hall and galleries are as fascinating as their contents, which include three skeletons of the Great Irish Deer, now extinct. The specimens, still exhibited in the original display cabinets, cover the complete range of creatures ever to have lived in Ireland, which explains its rather grim nickname - The Dead Zoo.

Government Buildings

Upper Merrion St. 🗣*Visit by guided tour only (30–40mins), Sat 10.30am, 11.30am, 12.30pm. Tickets required (no charge), available from National Gallery, Merion Square.* ☎*01 619 4116. www.taoiseach.gov.ie.*

This imposing structure in Edwardian Baroque, opened in 1911 by George V, was the last major public building project completed in Dublin under British rule. Until 1989, parts of the building were occupied by Trinity College. Modern furniture and a fascinating range of contemporary art provide a fitting workplace for government committees and the Prime Minister *(Taoiseach)*.

▷ Turn right onto the north side of St Stephen's Green.

The **Shelbourne Hotel** (1867), still a centre of Dublin's social life, was built by Martin Burke on the site of Kerry

House, residence of the Earl of Shelburne, in 1824.

▷ Turn right into Kildare St.

National Museum (Archaeology)★★

Kildare St. ♿ 🕐*Open Tue–Sun 10am (2pm Sun)–5pm.* 🕐*Closed Good Fri, 25 Dec.* 🐾*Guided tour (45min) see website Calendar of Events.* 👓€2. ✕ 📞*01 677 74444. www.museum.ie.*
The Kildare Street branch of the National Museum was purpose-built in 1890 to display treasures from the national archaeological collections.
A short video contextualises the masterpieces of Irish art now on show in **The Treasury★★★**. Precious objects range in date from the Bronze Age to the 15C and include: a model boat in gold from the Broighter Hoard (1C); the Loughnashade Trumpet (1C BC); the Ardagh Chalice (8C); the Tara Brooch (8C); the Shrine of St Patrick's Bell in bronze, gold and silver (c. 1100); the "Cathach", a book shrine made to contain the Psalter of St Columba (Colmcille) (12C–15C); the Kavanagh Charter Horn of ivory and brass, the only surviving object associated with Irish kingship (12C–15C).
The section on **Prehistoric Ireland** has a reconstruction of a passage tomb as well as the huge Lurgan Longboat from around 2500 BC. **Ireland's Gold★★★** displays a gleaming array of artefacts, some from hoards preserved for millennia in the Irish boglands.
Among the objects shown in **Viking Ireland** are items from the Viking settlement at Wood Quay in Old Dublin: iron, bone, wood utensils, clothing and ornaments. St Manchan's Shrine, a spectacular reliquary, is one of several ecclesiastical treasures on display in the section entitled **The Church**.
The small but exquisite objects from **Ancient Egypt** are dramatically lit. There is also a small but fascinating collection of ancient Cypriot artefacts, including glassware.

Houses of the Oireachtas/ (National Parliament)

🐾*Visit by guided tour only (30min). Meet at Kildare Street Gate 15 min before tour time. Walk-up tours: when parliament is sitting: Mon & Fri 10.30am & 2.30pm; during recess, Mon–Fri 10.30am & 2.30pm. Tours by arrangement through your embassy: during recess Mon–Fri 10.30am, 11.30am, 2.30pm, 3.30pm (in session, also Tue, Wed 7pm, 8pm).* 📞*01 618 3271/3781. www.oireachtas.ie.*
The two houses (**Dáil Éireann and Seanad Éireann**) meet in **Leinster House**, which was designed in 1745 by Richard Castle for the Duke of Leinster and converted to house the Republican parliament in 1922. Visitors are admitted to the public gallery when the house is in session *(Tue–Thu)*.

National Library★

Kildare St. ♿ 🕐*Open Reading Room Mon–Wed 9.30am–7.45pm, Thu–Fri 9.30am–4.45pm, Sat 9.30am–12.45pm. Exhibitions Mon–Wed 9.30am–7.45pm, Thu–Fri 9.30am–4.45pm, Sat 9.30am –4.30pm, Sun 1–4.45pm.* ✕ 📞*01 603 0213. www.nli.ie.*
Opened in 1890, this classical-style building mirrors the National Museum opposite. Its attraction for visitors lies in its free first-class **exhibitions** – two of which are staged at a time, in the modern part of the main building and in the adjacent 2–3 Kildare Street address, in the classic domed reading Room of the Library (portrayed in *Ulysees*). There is also a **Genealogy Room** where visitors in search of their roots can seek advice (a lot of these services are now available for free on their website).

▷ Turn into Molesworth St then left into Dawson St.

St Ann's Church

🕐*Open 10am–4pm.* 📞*01 676 7727. http://stann.dublin.anglican.org/*
St Ann's was one of the earliest Georgian churches in Dublin, an elegant and fashionable place of worship designed by Isaac Wills and not really improved

by the addition of a Victorian neo-Romanesque west front and stained glass. The bread shelf in the chancel was established in 1723 by a charitable bequest to provide 120 loaves of bread each week for the poor. The church is highly regarded for the quality of its regular concerts.

Mansion House

Mansion House was built in 1705 by Joshua Dawson and bought by the City of Dublin in 1715 as the residence of the Lord Mayor. The spacious Round Room was added for the visit of George IV in 1821; it was here that the first Irish parliament met in 1919 to adopt the Declaration of Independence.

▷ At the top of Dawson St turn left onto St Stephen's Green North.

The Little Museum★

15 St Stephen's Green North.
🕐*Open daily 9.30am–5pm (8pm Thu).*
🕐*Closed Christmas and New Year holidays.* ✆€8. ℘01 661 1000. *www. littlemuseum.ie.*

Opened in 2011 and already a favourite, this imaginative charming small collection is set on the upper floors of a Georgian House. It tells the story of the modern city through the voices and artefacts of the people of Dublin. These include art, photography, advertising, letters, postcards, objects and ephemera relating to cultural, social and political life in Dublin between the years 1900 and 2000. Most of the items have been donated by members of the public, including a very rare first-edition English language copy of James Joyce's *Ulysses* and a death mask of the writer. An eclectic exhibition programme, with subjects ranging from Bram Stoker to U2 is also staged.

▷ Cross the road into the gardens of St Stephen's Green.

St Stephen's Green ★

(Dúchas) 🕐*Open daily 7.30am (9.30am Sun and Bank Hols)–dusk.* ℘01 475 7816. www.heritageireland.ie/en.*

St Stephen's Green

© IIC / age fotostock

Formerly common land first enclosed in 1663, the beautifully landscaped and well-maintained gardens (22 acres/9ha) are a wonderful asset in this densely built-up part of the city. They were laid out in 1880 by Lord Ardilaun, a member of the Guinness family, who is honoured with a statue on the west side. The bronze sculpture by Henry Moore was erected in memory of William Butler Yeats in 1967. The Fusiliers' Arch *(northwest entrance)* commemorates those who died in the Boer War and the German Monument *(southeast entrance)* expresses the gratitude of the people of the Federal Republic of Germany for help they received after World War II.
The **Royal College of Surgeons** *(west side),* designed by Edward Parke in 1806, was captured during the Easter Rising in 1916 by a party of insurgents led by Constance Markievicz.
On the south side are **Newman House, Iveagh House** (designed by Richard Castle and now the Department of Foreign Affairs) and the **University Church** (1854), designed at the behest of Cardinal Newman by John Pollen in the highly ornate Byzantine and Italian early-Christian style advocated by John Ruskin.

Newman House★★

St Stephen's Green South. Visit by guided tour only (40min), Jun–Aug, Tue–Fri, 2pm–4pm on the hour; otherwise by appointment. ⊜€7. ✆01 716 7422 or 475 7255.

The two 18C town houses named after Cardinal Newman honour the memory of the first Rector of University College, which started here in 1854. Still almost completely intact, they provide an insight into the 18C city. The smaller house was designed by Richard Castle in 1738 and retains many original features like the glazing bars he devised. The larger house dates from 1765; the Bishops' Room has a portrait of Cardinal Newman and his Rector's Chair, while the staircase is decorated with lovely Rococo plasterwork by Richard West. An antiques and collectibles fair is held here every other Sunday.

▷ From the SE corner of the square turn left into Harcourt St then Clonmel.

Iveagh Gardens

Entrance Hatch St. (wheelchair access also Clonmel St.). (Dúchas) ◷*Open 8am (10am Sun and Bank Hols)–dusk (5pm Feb and Nov; 6pm Mar–Oct; 4pm Dec–Jan). www.heritageireland.ie/en.* Lawns and tree-lined walks, enhanced by statuesque fountains, a rosarium and a maze, provide respite from the city bustle.

▷ Return to St Stephen's Green; walk south and into Grafton St.

Grafton Street★

Dublin's finest shopping street is now a bustling pedestrian precinct and a favourite haunt of street musicians; in the 19C it was paved with pine blocks to deaden the sound of carriage wheels. **Bewley's Oriental Café**, with its distinctive mosaic façade and stained-glass windows by Harry Clarke, started in the 1840s but was reopened in 1927. The previous building there was Whytes School, attended by

Robert Emmet, Thomas Moore, Richard Sheridan and the Duke of Wellington.

▷ Turn left into Johnson Ct.

Powerscourt Centre★

◷*Open Mon–Fri 10am–6pm (8pm Thu), Sat 9am–6pm, Sun noon–6pm.* ✆01 6794 144. www.powerscourtcentre.ie. This 18C townhouse with fine stucco ceilings was designed in 1771 by Robert Mack for Viscount Powerscourt; it now houses a shopping centre.

A few doors down at number 58 is the old Dublin Civic Museum, now sadly closed to the public. It was originally built in the 18C for the Society of Artists as an exhibition hall, but in 1791 became the City Assembly Hall. During the War of Independence (1919–1921) the outlawed Irish Supreme Court sat here. In 2011 the Irish Georgian Society acquired the property and are renovating and refurbishing the building

▷ Return to Grafton St and continue north to College Green and O'Connell Bridge.

② OLD DUBLIN ★

The heart of old Dublin occupies the ridge between the Liffey and its southern tributary, the Poddle River, which now flows underground. Excavations (1974–81) at **Wood Quay**, where the modern Civic Offices of Dublin Corporation now stand, revealed the remains of 150 Viking buildings at 13 different levels (AD 920–1100).

The town expanded eastwards along Dame Street to meet the development taking place around Leinster House, and also westwards along the **High Street** into the **Cornmarket**, where vast quantities of grain were sold for export in the Middle Ages. Little remains of the old buildings in **Fishamble Street**, where Molly Malone was born and Handel conducted the first performance of the *Messiah* to raise funds for the Rotunda Hospital.

Liffey Footbridges

© IIC / Design Pics RM / age fotostock

The **Liberties** was the name given to the area farther south and west, which lay outside the jurisdiction of the medieval city; here the buildings vary from 17C high-gable houses built by French Huguenot refugees to 19C mansion flats and 20C housing estates.

▷ From the south side of O'Connell Bridge walk upstream on Aston Quay.

Liffey Footbridges
The popular name for the delicate cast-iron footbridge, opened in 1816 as the Wellington Bridge, is the iconic **Ha'penny Bridge★**, so-called because of the ½d toll levied until 1919. It now

has two companions, the **Millennium Bridge** and the **Sean O'Casey Bridge**.

▷ Opposite the Ha'penny Bridge turn from the river through the arch.

Merchants' Hall *(Wellington Quay)* was designed by Frederick Darley for the Merchants' Guild, also known as the Fraternity of the Holy Trinity, the first of Dublin's 25 guilds; the arched passage through the building leads into Temple Bar.

Temple Bar★
The area between the river and Dame Street, now known as Temple Bar (28 acres/11ha) takes its name from Sir William Temple, Provost of Trinity (1628–99), who owned land which included a sand bar on the South Bank of the river. A stroll through its medieval network of narrow streets and courts reveals a variety of old buildings – Georgian houses, warehouses and chapels – restored and converted to new uses, interspersed with new purpose-built property. Derelict sites have been converted into open spaces – Temple Bar Square, Meeting House Square and Central Bank Plaza among the banks and insurance offices of Dame Street. This astonishingly successful case of urban renewal has produced a **cultural district** brimming over with venues for entertainment,

Temple Bar

© F. Fell / Tips / Photononstop

alongside many "alternative" shops, markets, restaurants, hotels and residential areas. It has been one of the city's most popular areas after dark for well over a decade though on weekend nights excessive alcoholic consumption means it can be very boisterous.

The Temple Bar Cultural Trust website (*www.templebar.ie*) provides details of what's on and when. The **Irish Film Institute** (*6 Eustace Square, www.ifi.ie*) shows independent, Irish and international cinema, while the **Temple Bar Gallery and Studios** (TBG+S) (5 - 9 Temple Bar, www.templebargallery. com is a contemporary gallery and artists' studios complex.

▶ Head west up Dame Street. Turn left onto Dame Lane.

City Hall★

Dame St. ◯Open Mon-Sat 10am–5.15pm (Story of the Capital closes 4pm). ◯Closed Good Fri, 25–26 Dec. ✆01 222 2222. www.dublincity.ie.
This magnificent edifice, one of the finest public buildings in Dublin, built in 1769–79 by Thomas Cooley as the Royal Exchange, marked the arrival in Ireland of the neo-Classical style. When economic activity declined after the 1800 Act of Union, the building lost much of its purpose, and in 1852 it was bought by the City Corporation. During the **Easter Rising** of 1916 it was occupied by the insurgents; from the roof they commanded the approaches and main gate of Dublin Castle but after about three hours the regular soldiers regained command of the Upper Yard. The splendid domed **rotunda** has early 20C frescoes illustrating aspects of city history.

The Story of the Capital, a lively introduction to Dublin's past, is housed in the vaulted basement: this excellent multi-media exhibition complements Dublinia, exploring the post-medieval history with plans, photographs, old film, artworks and precious objects like the Civic Sword presented by Henry IV around 1409.

Dublin Castle★★

Entrances in Dame La. and Ship St. (Dúchas) ⚭ ◯Open by guided tour only, (45min) including State Apartments, Chapel Royal and Undercroft), 10am (noon Sun, Bank Hols)–4.45pm. ◯Closed 1 Jan, Good Fri, 25–26 Dec. ⚭€4.50. ✕ ✆01 645 8813. www.dublincastle.ie.
Between 1204 and 1922 Dublin Castle represented British rule in Ireland. People under suspicion languished in its prisons; traitors' heads were exhibited on spikes over the gate. Embedded within the tight-knit urban fabric of the city, the Castle changed over the centuries from a formidable fortress to an administrative complex of almost domestic character. The Castle is now one of the symbols of Irish statehood, its sumptuous State Apartments used to receive foreign dignitaries and other important ceremonial occasions.

Its construction began 30 years after the Anglo-Norman landing in Ireland, when King John ordered a castle to be built on the high ground southeast of the existing town. The original structure expanded into a rough quadrangle with a round tower at each corner on the site of the present Upper Yard. In 1684 much of the medieval castle was destroyed by fire. The Castle's two courtyards now have an essentially Georgian appearance, with the Powder Tower as the most visible reminder of its medieval origin, even though it was much altered in the early 19C.

State Apartments★★ – *Upper Yard.* The upper floor on the south side was built between 1750 and 1780 but the interiors have been subsequently much modified. The Grand Staircase and the Battleaxe Landing lead to a suite of sumptuously furnished and decorated interiors overlooking Castle Green. In 1916, one room served as a prison for James Connolly, one of the leaders of the Uprising. There is Sheraton, Regency and Louis XIX furniture and modern, colourful carpets from Killybegs. The Throne Room features deities probably painted by the Venetian Giambattista Bellucci in the early

18C; in the Picture Gallery are superb Venetian chandeliers and the Wedgwood Room has paintings attributed to Angelica Kauffmann (1741–1807) and black Wedgwood plaques.

Many glittering balls were held in Ascendancy times in St Patrick's Hall, built in the mid-18C. Crests, helmets and banners hang above the stallplates recording the names of the members of the Order of St Pattrick, while the ceiling is a glorification of the relationship between Britain and Ireland.

Castle Hall – The dignified two-storey building *(closed)* on the north side of the upper yard was designed c. 1750 by Thomas Ivory for the Master of Ceremonies. Four days before the state visit of Edward VII and Queen Alexandra in 1907 the Crown Jewels were stolen from the Office of Arms in the Bedford Tower; they have never been recovered. Flanking Castle Hall are two gates surmounted by statues by Van Nost: *Fortitude* on the west gate and *Justice* on the east gate. A figure of Justice stands atop the Tower; Dublin wags liked to point out that her back is turned to the city and her scales dipped unevenly in wet weather; holes were eventually bored in the outer pan to allow the rainwater to drain away.

Powder Tower Undercroft★ – *Lower Yard*. Excavations beneath the Powder Tower have revealed parts of the Viking and Norman defences – a 13C arch and relieving arch in the Old City Wall which enabled boatmen to enter the moat to deliver goods to the postern gate.

Church of the Most Holy Trinity – This fine example of a Regency Gothic building was designed by Francis Johnston and consecrated in 1814. Before reconsecration as a Roman Catholic sanctuary (1943), the building served as the Chapel Royal, on the site of an earlier, smaller church. The exterior is decorated with over 100 heads carved in Tullamore limestone by Edward Smyth and his son John; The Passion of Christ panels in the east window are composed of old Continental stained glass. The arms of all the Viceroys from 1172 to 1922 are represented in the galleries, gallery windows and on the chancel walls.

Chester Beatty Library★★★

Dublin Castle Precinct, Dubh Linn Garden; entrance in Dame Lane or Ship St. &⌚*Open Mon-Fri 10am-5pm (Nov-Feb closed Mon), Sat 11am-5pm, Sun 1pm-5pm).* ⌚*Closed 1 Jan, Bank Hol Mon, Good Fri, 24–26 Dec.* ✕ *✆01 4070750. www.cbl.ie.*

This fabulous collection of Islamic and Far Eastern manuscripts and artworks was bequeathed to the nation by Sir Alfred Chester Beatty (1875–1968), an American businessman who was made the country's first honorary citizen. Among the **Arabic**, **Persian and Turkish manuscripts** are over 270 copies of **the Koran**, some with illuminations by great master calligraphers. The **Biblical material** consists of Syriac, Armenian, Ethiopian and Coptic texts, also early Western Bibles and Books of Hours. Of international importance are the biblical papyri dating from the early 2C to 4C. The Japanese and Chinese collection includes paintings and prints of the highest quality, including Japanese woodblock prints which influenced 19C European art. In addition, there is a large collection of snuff bottles, netsuke, jade books and rhinoceros-horn cups. The Western European collection contains many important printed books as well as prints by Dürer, Holbein, Piranesi, Bartolozzi and many others. The attached Silk Road Cafe serves excellent food.

Christ Church Cathedral★★

&⌚*Open Mon-Sat 9.30am-7pm (6pm Mar & Oct, 5pm Nov-Feb), Sun 12.30pm-2.30pm, 4.30pm-6pm (7pm Apr-Sept, closed 2.30pm Nov-Feb). Last admission 45 mins before closing.* ⌚*Closed 26 Dec.* ✎€6.50. ☞*Cathedral tours (free) several days per week, less frequently during low season - for details phone the office. Belfry tours* ✎€4. *Combination ticket with Dublinia* €14.50. *✆01 677 8099. www.christchurchcathedral.ie.*

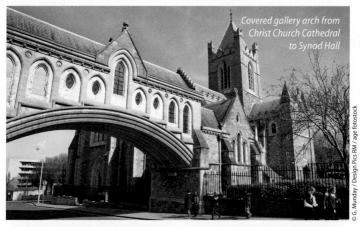

Covered gallery arch from Christ Church Cathedral to Synod Hall

© G. Munday / Design Pics RM / age fotostock

Like the Castle, Christ Church Cathedral became a symbol of the Ascendancy, and the Romanesque/Early English building is still the seat of the Anglican Bishop of Dublin and Glendalough. Largely rebuilt in the 19C by George Scott, it is nevertheless an important link to the city's very earliest days, being the successor to the wooden church built in 1038 by Dunan, the first Bishop of Dublin. Soon after 1170 this building was replaced by a stone church built on the orders of Strongbow, Richard de Clare, Earl of Pembroke.

A number of medieval features survived the 19C rebuilding: the elegant **Romanesque south door** overlooking the ruins of the Chapter House, the **brass eagle lectern** and some of the original encaustic tiles in the Chapel of St Laud. Hanging on the chapel wall *(right)* is a casket containing the heart of St Laurence O'Toole, second Archbishop of Dublin.

In the south aisle is the **"Strongbow" monument**; though the effigy in chainmail is certainly not the great Anglo-Norman commander, the half figure beside it may well belong to the original tomb.

Of all the Cathedral interiors, the 12C Norman **crypt** *(access in the south aisle)* is perhaps the most evocative. Measuring over 200 ft (63m) long it is the largest in Britain and Ireland and an audio visual presentation relates its colorful history; it has been used for services, let to shopkeepers and was used for burials until the mid-19C.

▶ A covered gallery arch spans Wine Tavern Street, to the cathedral's Synod Hall.

♟♙ Dublinia

High St. ♿⏰*Open Mar–Sept, 10am–6.30pm; Oct–Feb 10am–5.30pm. Last admission 1hr before closing.* ⏰*Closed 24–26 Dec.* ᨀ€*8.50, child* €*5.50. Combination ticket with Christ Church Cathedral* €*14.50.* ✆*01 679 4611. www.dublinia.ie.*

This entertaining interactive exhibition, featuring costumed guides, provides a multi-sensory experience of Viking Dublin and the medieval city. There are tableaux, clothes to try on, a superb model of Dublin from around 1500, a mock-up of part of an important archeological excavation along the Liffey and key finds, plus a reconstruction of the face of a medieval Dubliner, whose skeleton was found nearby. The 17C tower of St Michael's (96 steps) offers a panoramic view of the Dublin Hills.

▶ Walk west along High Street.

St Audoen's Church

(Dúchas). ♿⏰*Open late Apr–late Oct, 9.30am–5.30pm (4.45pm last admission).* ✆*01 6770 088. www.heritageireland.ie/en.*

Jonathan Swift (1667–1745)

Swift was born in Dublin in 1667 and educated at Kilkenny and Trinity College, Dublin. In 1689 he became Secretary to Sir William Temple of Moor Park in England but failed to secure advancement. Back in Ireland he was ordained (1694) and appointed prebendary of Kilroot, near Carrickfergus, where he wrote his first book, *A Tale of a Tub*, a satire on "corruptions in religion and learning", published in 1704 together with *The Battle of the Books*. He went back to England but, on Temple's death in 1699, returned to Ireland. He became Vicar of Laracor, south of Trim (1701) and was appointed dean of St Patrick's Cathedral in 1713.

Today, Jonathan Swift is best remembered for *Gulliver's Travels*, despite all that he wrote on church matters, politics and Ireland – including the wickedly satirical *A Modest Proposal* (1729) – in which he suggested (tongue in cheek) how to dispose of unwanted babies. His *Journal to Stella*, a collection of intimate letters, was addressed to Esther Johnson; according to some she and Swift were married in the Deanery garden but they never lived together.

Swift spent one-third of his income on the poor and saved another third, which he bequeathed for the founding of a hospital for the insane. At the end of his life he suffered from Ménière's disease and lost the use of many of his faculties.

The old church (now Anglican) was founded by the Anglo-Normans and dedicated to St Audoen of Rouen in France. The west doorway is 12C, the nave is 13C. **St Audoen's Gate** (1275), leading to the river, is one of 32 gates in the Norman city walls.

▶ Go left on Back Lane.

Tailors' Hall

The Tailors' Hall (1703–07) is the only surviving guildhall in Dublin. The Great Hall has a stage, a handsome marble fireplace and a minute gallery with a wrought-iron railing: the building (*closed to the public*) is now used by *An Taisce*, the Irish National Trust.

St Patrick's Cathedral★★

&🕓*Open year-round Mon–Fri. 9.30am–5pm, Sat 9am–6pm (Nov–Feb 5pm). Sun 9–10.30am, 12.30–2.30pm, 4.30–6.30pm (Nov–Feb closes 2.30pm)* 🕓*Closed 1 Jan and 25–26 Dec.* €6.50. *Guided Tours (30 mins, free) Mon–Sat 2.30pm.* 📌 ✆*01 453 9472. www.stpatrickscathedral.ie.*
John Comyn, appointed Archbishop of Dublin in 1181, objected to being subject to the laws and regulations of the city. He therefore moved his seat out of the city jurisdiction, to the site of a holy well, used, according to tradition, by St Patrick to baptise converts. His church was promoted to a cathedral and rebuilt in the Early English style in the mid-13C.

The cathedral is strongly associated with **Jonathan Swift** (🕓*see "Jonathan Swift" box, above*), its Dean from 1713 to 1745. His tomb is marked by a bronze plaque in the floor near the main door, beside it that of his friend "Stella". Swiftian memorabilia includes his death-mask and a replica of his skull (in the bookcase).

Swift wrote his own epitaph; he also composed an epitaph for the black marble tomb of the **Duke of Schomberg** *(north choir aisle)* and put up a plaque *(south transept)* to his faithful servant, Alexander McGee.

The vaulted **baptistery** in the south-west corner of the nave was probably the entrance to the original church. The 13C floor tiles have been copied throughout the cathedral. The huge and splendid **Boyle Monument** (1632), erected by the great Earl of Cork in memory of his second wife Catherine, is adorned with no fewer than 16 polychrome figures.

In the north aisle stands a fine statue by Edward Smyth of the Marquess of Buckingham, Viceroy and first Grand

Master of the **Order of St Patrick;** until 1871 the cathedral was the chapel of the Order, hence the banners and escutcheons.

In the north transept stands the old door of the Chapter House; the hole was cut in 1492 so that the Earl of Kildare could, quite literally, "chance his arm" in a conciliatory gesture to Black James Ormond, who had taken refuge in the Chapter House; they had quarrelled because Ormond had been appointed Lord Deputy in place of Kildare.

Marsh's Library★★

St Patrick's Close. ⏱*Open Mon, Wed–Fri, 9.30am–5pm, Sat 10am–5pm.* ⏱*Closed 24 Dec–1 Jan.* ⊛€3. ✆01 454 3511. www.marshlibrary.ie.

Marsh's Library was designed in 1701 by Sir William Robinson to house the first public library in Ireland. A portrait of the founder, Archbishop Narcissus Marsh, hangs above the stairs. The dark oak bookcases, surmounted by a mitre, divide the long room into seven bays. Beyond the office are three "cages", where precious books can be consulted. The total of 25,000 books is composed of four individual collections.

▶ Take a left on Bridge Street

St Werburgh's Church

⏱*Open by appointment.* ✆01 4783710. The 1715 church replaced an early 12C one; it was remodelled in 1759 after a fire and has one of the city's most elegant Georgian interiors.

③ NORTHSIDE

In the Middle Ages, the Viking settlement by the Liffey, known as Oxmantown, was dominated by **St Mary's Abbey**. In the 17C it was built up on a grid plan around Oxmantown Green, now Smithfield. By the 18C, the Northside, centred on O'Connell Street (then known as Gardiner's Mall) had become the most fashionable residential district of Dublin. No one today would describe O'Connell Street as fashionable but it retains its generous dimensions and remains a vital part of the city centre. Farther north, Parnell Square was developed to raise money for a maternity hospital, which occupied the south side. Many of the once-elegant Georgian terraces in the neighbourhood, particularly **Mountjoy Square**, have passed through neglect to demolition, some to restoration and conversion.

Two of Dublin's major theatres are located on the northside. The **Gate Theatre** was founded in 1928 by Hilton Edwards and Micheál MacLiammóir. The earlier **Abbey Theatre**, now a national institution, was founded in 1904 by Lady Gregory and W.B. Yeats as part of the Irish literary revival. In 1924 it became the first state-subsidised theatre in the English-speaking world, and for a while its productions continued to cause controversy, even riots, notably with the plays of Sean O'Casey. The original theatre was destroyed by fire in 1951.

▶ Starting from the north side of O'Connell bridge, walk east along Eden Quay.

Custom House★★

Custom House Quay; entrance in south front. ⏱*Visitor Centre open Thur-Fri 2pm-4pm, Sat-Sun & public holidays 11.30am-4.30pm.* ✆01 888 2538.

The Custom House, with its long façade and central dome, is one of the great landmarks of Dublin. It was designed by James Gandon, completed in 1791, and restored after being set on fire by anti-Treaty forces at the beginning of the Civil War in 1921. The **Visitor Centre**, in the ceremonial vestibules behind the south portico, offers a detailed and fascinating history of the building.

Outside on the quay beside the River Liffey stands the **Famine Memorial**: six bronze figures by Rowan Gillespie personify the emotions of the many victims of the **Great Famine** or **Irish Potato Famine** that Ireland suffered between 1845 and 1852.

Jeanie Johnston Tall Ship

© R. Drinkwater / Loop Images /age fotostock

Jeanie Johnston Tall Ship & Famine Museum★★

Custom House Quay. 🚶‍♂️*Open by guided tour only, daily on the hour Apr–Oct 10am–4pm except 1pm; Mar & Oct–Nov 11am, noon, 2pm, 3pm; Feb noon, 1pm, 2pm; Jan (Fri– Sun only) noon, 1pm, 2pm.* ⊕€10. ☏01 473 0111. www.jeaniejohnston.ie.

This wooden sailing ship is an accurate replica of the original *Jeanie Johnston* emigrant ship which sailed between Tralee in Co. Kerry and North America between 1847 and 1855. In all it made 16 voyages and succeeded in carrying over 2,500 emigrants to a new life. Remarkably, while its contemporaries were known as "coffin ships" due to the high number of fatalities—mortality rates of 30 per cent were common on the 3,000 mile voyage—the *Jeanie Johnston* did not lose a single passenger or crew member.

The ship's enthusiastic guides put a human perspective on this dreadful period of starvation, disease and emigration, telling the sometime tragic, sometime stirring stories of the lives of crew members and passengers (traced from original passenger lists) in great detail.

▷ Walk along the docks back to O'Connell Bridge, then continue to Inns Quay.

Four Courts★

🕐*Open Mon–Fri 9am–5pm, subject to official business. No admission to courts.* ☏01 888 6000. www.courts.ie.

The building (1785) accommodating four major courts – Chancery, King's Bench, Exchequer and Common Pleas – was begun by Thomas Cooley and completed by James Gandon. It was seized by the rebels in 1916 and again by anti-Treaty forces.

On the first occasion it escaped serious damage but in 1921, it was shelled by the Free State army from across the river and mined by the insurgents; the building and the irreplacable national archives from 1174 that it contained, were virtually destroyed.

▷ Follow Arran Quay and turn right onto Church Street.

St Michan's Church★

Church St. ♿🕐*Open mid-Mar–Oct, Mon–Fri 10am–12.45pm, 2pm–4.45pm. Nov–mid-Mar Mon–Fri 12.30pm– 3.30pm. Sat all year 10am–12.45pm.* 🕐*Closed Christmas and Bank Hols.* ⊕€5. ☏01 872 4154. www.stmichans.com.

The first church on the site was probably built by the Danes as St Michan is thought to be a Danish saint. The present church dates from 1095 but gained its present appearance in 1686. The **interior** boasts an early 18C organ played by Handel and **vaults** containing **mummified corpses**, preserved for over 300 years by the dry air and constant temperature.

▷ Continue on Church Street and turn left into Smithfield Village.

Old Jameson Distillery

Bow St., Smithfield Village. ♿🚶‍♂️*Visit by guided tour only (1 hr) every 20 mins, daily 9am–6pm (10am Sun). Last tour 5.15pm.* 🕐*Closed Good Fri, Christmas hols.* ⊕ €15 (save 10 *percent booking online).* ✕ ☎*01 807 2348. www.jamesonwhiskey.com.*

Part of the original 1780 distillery has been converted and re-created to show current and earlier methods of production of Jameson's famous Irish whiskey (☞*see p45*). A video and tour explains the processes and mysteries of malting, milling, mashing, fermention, maturation and distillation, warts and all. The tour ends in the bar, where visitors are invited to take part in a whiskey tasting.

▶ Return to Church Street; Chancery Street opposite continues to Abbey Street and O'Connell Street.

O'Connell Street★

This broad, elegant thoroughfare was laid out by Luke Gardiner in the 18C as a tree-lined mall and later converted into a narrow residential square. Renamed Sackville Street, it developed into the most important street in 18C Dublin; later it was extended south to Carlisle Bridge (1794) and renamed after O'Connell in 1922.

Down the centre of the street stands a row of **monuments** by John Foley of *(south to north)* Daniel O'Connell; William Smith O'Brien (1803–64), the leader of the Young Ireland Movement sentenced to death for treason in 1848;

Spire of Dublin by Ian Ritchie Architects

© Dragos Cosmin photos/Moment/Getty Images

Sir John Gray, who organised Dublin's water supply; James Larkin (1876–1947), founder of the Irish Transport and General Workers' Union (1909) and Father Theobald Mathew of the 19C temperance movement.

The **GPO building**★ with its Ionic portico was designed by Francis Johnston in 1814. It was the headquarters of the rebels in the Easter Rising in 1916 and still bears scars of the fighting.

Erected in 2003, the **Spire of Dublin** (officially titled The Monument of Light) was the brainchild of Ian Ritchie Architects. This impressive stainless steel needle-like sculpture, topped by a beacon, measures 120m high, seven times the height of the GPO building. On the east side of the street is Clery's, the world's first purpose-built department store. The present building was erected in 1922 to replace the original, destroyed during the Easter Rising.

▶ Turn right into Talbot Street.

Pro-Cathedral★

🕐*Open Mon–Sat, 7.30am–6.45pm (Sat 7.15pm), Sun 9am–1.45pm, 5.30pm–7.45pm. Bank hols 10am–1.30pm.* ☎*01 874 5441. www.procathedral.ie.*

Dublin's most important Roman-Catholic church was built in 1821 in the style of a Greek Doric temple. Its rather cramped setting is a result of Protestant interests that kept it away from its intended site on O'Connell Street.

Opposite stands **Tyrone House**, an elegant mansion designed by Richard Castle in 1741.

▶ Return to O'Connell St and head north.

Parnell Square★

Rutland Square was renamed in honour of **Charles Stewart Parnell**, whose statue stands at the road intersection. The south side of the square is taken up by the elegant lying-in hospital designed by Richard Castle in 1752. The **Rotunda Hospital Chapel** (🕐 *open Wed 10am–noon, on appli-*

cation in writing; *℘01 873 0700*) is an exuberant Rococo creation, decorated with superb stuccowork and carved mahogany woodwork.

Funds for the hospital were raised from entertainments given in the **Rotunda** (1764) – now a cinema, or in the **Assembly Rooms** (1786), designed by Richard Johnston – now the Gate Theatre. Yet more fundraising was done in the walled **pleasure gardens** (*Dúchas;* ♿ ⏲*open May–Sept 9.30am–8pm, Oct–Apr 11am–7pm (4pm, Nov–Feb); ℘office: 01 647 2498, garden: 01 874 3074*) in the centre of the square, laid out with a wilderness, temples of refreshment and a terrace where music was played – known as the Orchestra. The surrounding houses were completed in the 1770s and inhabited by peers, bishops and members of Parliament.

The north end of the square has been converted into a **Garden of Remembrance** designed by Daithí P Hanly; the gates incorporate Celtic motifs, the central sculpture by Oisín Kelly echoes Yeats' poem *Easter 1916* and the mythological transformation of the Children of Lir into swans. The broken spears in the mosaic reflect the Celtic custom of throwing weapons into water after a battle.

Garden of Remembrance

© T. Bognar/Photononstop

The site is significant because it was here that plans for the Easter Rising (1916) were hatched *(plaque on the north side)* and the rebels were held overnight.

▷ On the north side of the square are the Dublin Writers' Museum and the Hugh Lane Gallery.

Dublin Writers' Museum★

Parnell Sq. North. ⏲*Open daily 10am (11am Sun, Bank Hols)–4.45pm.* ⏲*Closed 24–27 Dec.* ▭*€7.50.* ✗ *℘01 872 2077. www.writersmuseum.com.*

The Irish writers associated with the city of Dublin – Jonathan Swift, Oscar Wilde, Bernard Shaw, James Joyce, Samuel Beckett, W.B. Yeats, Synge, O'Casey, Flann O'Brien, Brendan Behan and Patrick Kavanagh to name just the best known – are remembered with personal items, photos, portraits, busts, manuscripts and copies of their major works. The museum also traces the written tradition in Ireland from the illuminated manuscripts of the Celtic Christian church, such as the Book of Kells, to the present day.

Temporary exhibitions are held in the elegant reception rooms, readings and workshops in the children's section. The museum occupies two Georgian terrace houses with **elegant stucco ceilings★**; the one in the library is by Michael Stapleton. Alterations made in 1891–95 by Alfred Darbyshire for George Jameson include the addition of stained-glass windows bearing the Jameson monogram, four female figures representing Music, Literature, Art and Science, and, in the first-floor saloon, a series of painted door panels by Gibson and an ornamental colonnade and gilded frieze.

Hugh Lane Gallery of Modern Art★

Parnell Sq., North. ♿ ⏲*Open Tue–Fri 9.45am–6pm (5pm Fri), Sat–Sun 10am–5pm (11am Sun).* ⏲*Closed Good Fri, 25 Dec.* ✗ *℘01 222 5564. www.hughlane.ie.*

The extensive collection of late-19C and 20C works by Irish and Continental art-

Literary Dublin

Several Nobel Prize winners figure among the Dublin-born writers who achieved international fame – Swift, Mangan, Wilde, Shaw, Yeats, Synge, O'Casey, Joyce, Behan and Beckett. Their former homes are marked with plaques and/or converted into museums. The major figures are celebrated in a literary parade in St Patrick's Park, while their literary works are marked in the Dublin Writers' Museum.

Jonathan Swift (1667–1745), the satirist and author of *Gulliver's Travels*, was born near Dublin Castle and is buried in St Patrick's Cathedral.

Oscar Wilde's most vivid memorial is the statue in Merrion Square opposite his family home. A statue by Henry Moore is dedicated to Yeats and stands in St Stephen's Green. Sean O'Casey (1880–1964) grew up in Dublin and became involved with Yeats and the Abbey in the early years of the 20C. The Sean O'Casey Bridge is named for him.

Dublin's most famous son, James Joyce (1882–1941), is remembered at the James Joyce Centre (see p134), the new James Joyce bridge and at the Joyce Museum at Sandycove (see p139), where he lived for a brief period. His family home in Bray, 1 Martello Terrace, is the site where a famous Christmas dinner scene from *A Portrait of the Artist as a Young Man* actually took place.

Samuel Becket (1906–1989) was born in Foxrock and attended Trinity College, where a theatre is named after him. He too has a bridge named after him.

Brendan Behan (1923–1964) has no bridge but lots of pubs remember him. There is a statue erected to him on the banks of the Royal Canal (near to Mountjoy Prison) where he lived for four years.

Statue of Oscar Wilde by Danny Osborne, Merrion Square

© Fáilte Ireland

ists supplements the works acquired by **Sir Hugh Lane** (1875–1915), who drowned on the *Lusitania*. The building, a three-storey mansion of Portland stone and granite, flanked by curved screen walls, was designed in 1762 by Sir William Chambers for an earlier connoisseur, **James Caulfield**, 1st Earl of Charlemont, who also built the Marino Casino.

There are works by several Impressionists, Corot and Courbet, and contemporary pieces by the likes of Christo, who swathed the pathways of St Stephen's Green. *Lakeside Cottage* (c. 1929) is a landscape by Paul Henry; *The Rescue of the Prison Van at Manchester* by Maurice MacGonical dramatically portrays a famous Fenian incident from 1867. One room is devoted to Roderic O'Conor (1860–1940), a friend of Gauguin.

However, the gallery's most fascinating room is the (in)famously chaotic **Francis Bacon Studio★★**, relocated here in its entirety (even including its dust) and comprising over 5,500 objects.

▶ Take Denmark Street and turn right onto North Great George's Street.

James Joyce Centre

35 North Great George's St. ⏰*Open Tue–Sun 10am (noon Sun)–5pm.* ⏰*Closed Bank Hols and Christmas & New Year hol period.* 🎟 €5. 🎧*Guided tours available, Apr–Sept Tue, Thu, Sat at 11am, 2pm, Oct–Mar Sat only. Note: Tue & Thu 11am tours require min 4 people to proceed.* 🎟€5. ✕ ✆*01 878 8547. www.jamesjoyce.ie.*
The centre promotes the life and work of James Joyce by hosting talks, tours of the house and walks through the north inner city. As a boy, Joyce lived nearby in Fitzgibbon Street and attended Belvedere College *(Denmark St)*.

The restored terrace house, built in 1784 by Francis Ryan, once served as the town house of Valentine Brown, Earl of Kenmare; the very fine **plasterwork** is mostly by Michael Stapleton. Joyce family portraits line the staircase.

PHOENIX PARK★

The largest enclosed urban park in Europe (1,752 acres/709ha) derives its name from the Gaelic for clear water *(Fionn Uisce)*. The land, confiscated from Kilmainham Priory in 1543 by the Crown, was enclosed in 1662 by the Duke of Ormond, who introduced a herd of fallow deer which still roam the Fifteen Acres (actually approximately 300 acres/121ha). The southeast gate is flanked by the **Wellington Monument**, designed by Sir William Smirke in 1817, and the **Peoples' Garden** sloping to a small lake. From here Chesterfield Avenue, lit by gas lamps, leads to the **Phoenix Monument**, erected by Lord Chesterfield in 1745. To the south stands the residence of the Ambassador of the USA and the **Papal Cross** marking the visit of Pope John Paul II in 1979.

In 1882, at the height of agitation over the Land Act, the newly appointed Chief Secretary, Lord Frederick Cavendish, and the Under-Secretary, Thomas H. Burke, the intended victim, were stabbed to death while walking in the park near the Vice-Regal Lodge by the "Invincibles", members of an extremist Fenian sect. All this and more is told in the **Phoenix Park Visitor Centre**. *(Dúchas)* ♿⏰*Open Apr–Dec daily 10am–6pm; Jan–Mar, Wed–Sun 10.30am–5pm;* ✕; ✆*01 677 0095; www. phoenixpark.ie/visitorcentre.*
If you would like a free tour of **Aras an Uachtaráin,** the **official residence of the President of Ireland**, (🎧*open by guided tour only, 30min, Sat 10.15am–4.30pm (3.30pm in winter);* ⏰*closed 24–26 Dec. & New Year weekend;* ✆*01 677 0095; www.president.ie)* you can book here in the visitor centre. The house was formerly Vice-Regal Lodge, built (1751–54) as a private house by Nathaniel Clements.

Set in some 30 acres (12ha) of Phoenix Park, is the ever-popular 👥**Dublin Zoo** (⏰*open 9.30am–6pm/dusk Oct–Feb, last admission 3pm Dec;* 🎟 €16, child, €12;* ✕; ✆*01 474 8900. www. dublinzoo.ie.* Founded in 1830, besides being a wildlife showcase, the zoo is actively involved in constantly evolving breeding programmes with other zoos. Around 400 animals from almost 100 species can be seen in indoor and outdoor habitats throughout the zoo, including the African Savannah, the Gorilla Rainforest, Asian Rainforest, the South America House, House of Reptiles and (nearer home) the Family Farm.

ADDITIONAL NORTHSIDE SIGHTS

There are two superb national museums of art, while a little further afield Croke Park stadium has a museum dedicated to the history of Gaelic games. Marino Casino, the Botanic Gardens and/or Glasnevin Cemetery all make an excellent summer afternoon's outing.

National Museum★★ (Decorative Arts & History)

Collins Barracks, Benburb Street. ◷*Open Tue–Sat, 10am (2pm Sun) –5pm.* ◷*Closed Good Fri, 25 Dec.* ✖ ℗ ℰ*01 677 7444. www.museum.ie.*
The great barracks which once housed 3,000 men and 1,000 horses, was commissioned in 1700 by King William III and in its day, was the largest institution of its kind in the British Isles, a progressive alternative to the contentious practice of billeting soldiers on the population.

The **West Block** shows an enthralling array of special treasures – 25 highly varied pieces grouped together under the heading of **Curators' Choice**; these might be a rare astrolabe from Prague, an elongated late-13C or early-14C wood statue of St Molaise and Bow figurines made by Thomas Frye, or modelled by his fellow London Irishmen.

The **South Block** displays Irish country furniture and woodcraft *(third floor)* from the Baroque to the Modern era, including fascinating examples of late-19C Neo-Celtic pieces inspired by objects like the Tara Brooch discovered in 1850; scientific instruments *(second floor)*; Irish silver from the early 17C to the present day *(first floor)*.

Casino Marino★★

Off Malahide Rd., Marino. (Dúchas) ▰*Visit by guided tour only, Mar- Oct, 10am–5pm (6pm Jun-Sept) Last entry 45min before closing.* ◷*Closed 1 Jan, 25–26 Dec.* ☜€7. ℗ ℰ*01 833 1618. www.heritageireland.ie/en.*
This centrally-planned French neo-Classical casino (meaning summer house) is built of Portland stone; 12 Doric columns support a frieze and cornice topped by pediments, statues and urn-shaped chimneys. The sculpture is by Simon Vierpyl and Joseph Wilton. The interior contains four elaborate state rooms.

National Botanic Gardens★

Botanic Rd, Glasnevin. (Dúchas). ♿◷*Gardens: Open Mon–Fri 9am–5pm, Sat–Sun & hols 10am–6pm*

National Botanic Gardens

(4.30pm, late Oct–early Feb). Glasshouses close 4.15pm winter. ▰*Guided tours available (☜no charge) Sun, noon, 2.30pm.* ℗✖ ℰ*01 804 0300 or 857 0909. www.botanicgardens.ie.*
The gardens were started in 1795 on a 48acre/19ha site beside the Tolka River. The splendid Victorian glasshouses include the **Curvilinear Range** (1843–69), designed by Richard Turner, and the **Great Palm House** (1884).

There is a delightful **walk** along the river from the **rose garden**, through the **peat garden** and the **bog garden** beside the ornamental pond to the **arboretum**. Further specimens in the rock garden, cactus house and fern house account for the 20,000 species grown here.

Glasnevin Cemetery★

Finglas Rd., Glasnevin. ◷*Open Mon–Sun 10am–6pm (incl Bank hols),* ▰*Tours every hour from 10.30am-3.30pm.* ✖ ℰ*01 830 1133. www.glasnevintrust.ie*
Europe's largest cemetery (120acres/49ha) is the resting place of over a million people: anonymous paupers, cholera victims, and historical figures including Eamon De Valera, Daniel O'Connell and Michael Collins. An excellent new **museum** puts flesh on the bones of the cemetery's many inmates and **tours**, which include a trip

to the crypt of Daniel O'Connell, and are particularly thorough and entertaining.

GAA Museum

Croke Park, St Joseph's Ave, off Clonliffe Rd. ○*Open Mon–Sat, 9.30am (10.30am Sun)–5pm (6pm Jul–Aug); match days, open to Cusack stand ticket holders only.* ○*Closed 1 Jan, 24–28, 31 Dec.* ◌€7. ☞*Museum and stadium guided tour daily on the hour.* ◌€14. ✕ 🕿01 819 2323. www.crokepark.ie/gaa-museum.

Croke Park is the home of the national games of Ireland – hurling and Gaelic football. Recently updated (and in the throes of more developments), the museum traces the development of the **Gaelic Athletic Association** and its influence on the sporting, cultural and social traditions of Ireland. Computers provide highlights of past games, while in the interactive games area, visitors can test their speed of reaction or try hitting the *sliothar* with a *camán* in the practice nets. The **Etihad Skyline Tour** (*book online, 2hr,* ◌€20) takes visitors 144 ft (44m) above pitch level for panoramic views.

ADDITIONAL SOUTHSIDE SIGHTS

The stark, unwelcoming conditions obvious at Kilmainham Gaol contrast sharply with the elegant Museum of Modern Art, while further east the Guinness Storehouse is a modern-day temple to good cheer and a highlight of any trip to Dublin. A trip farther south brings you to Dimnagh Castle, a 13C moated castle.

The Science Gallery

The Naughton Institute, Pearse Street, Trinity College. ○*Open Tue–Fri noon–8pm, Sat–Sun noon–6pm.* ✕ 🕿01 896 4091. http://sciencegallery.com.
While much of TCD (◌*see p113*) harks to the past, its latest intiative is a lively and imaginative cutting edge (part hands-on) gallery, exploring 21C issues of everyday science-related issues via a rotating exhbition programme.

Kilmainham Gaol Museum★★

Inchicore Rd., Kilmainham. (Dúchas) ♿☞*Visit by guided tours only (1hr). 9.30am-5.30pm (Jun-Aug 9am-6.45am).* ☞*book in advance to avoid disappointment.* ○*Closed 24–26 Dec.* ◌€9 (discount online). ✕ 🅿 🕿01 453 5984.
www.heritageireland.com/en.
(Certain areas of the Gaol will be inaccessible to the public from time to time due to major building works until the end of December 2015 and admission prices will be reduced accordingly).
The struggle for political independence is movingly presented in the actual prison where so many Irishmen were incarcerated for offences against the Crown. Collections of souvenirs, photographs, letters and press cuttings illustrate the many incidents and rebellions from 1796 to 1924 and their socio-political contexts.

The **tour** includes the Central Hall (1862) containing 100 cells, the chapel, individual cells in the 1798 corridor and the exercise yards, which were also used for executions. The New Gaol, erected in 1792, consisted of a central range flanked by an east and a west courtyard divided into exercise yards.

Irish Museum of Modern Art★

Military Rd., Kilmainham. ♿○*Open Tue–Fri, 11.30am (10am Sat, noon Sun, Bank Hols)–5.30pm.* ○*Closed Good*

Kilmainham Gaol Museum
© Hoberman / Universal Images Group / age fotostock

Fri, 24–26 Dec. ✗ 🍴 *Guided heritage tours, summer afternoons. Call for tour times and charges.* 🅿 ℘*01 612 9900. www.imma.ie.*

The museum presents 20C Irish and international visual art. Its exciting and wide-ranging programme includes exhibitions of major 20C art and promising contemporary talent. The setting is **Royal Kilmainham Hospital★★**, the earliest-surviving Classical building in Ireland, designed by William Robinson, (1680–84) to provide accommodation for 300 old soldiers, the last of whom left in 1929. The **Great Hall** hosts concerts and government receptions; the ceiling of the **Chapel**, is made of papier maché.

Guinness Storehouse★★

Crane Market St., off Thomas St. ♿ 🕐 *Open 9.30am–5pm (7pm Jul–Aug).* 🕐*Closed Good Fri, 24–26 Dec.* 💶€18 *(€16.20 online).* 🅿 ✗ ℘*01 408 4800. www.guinness-storehouse.com.*

The most popular tour in town provides a complete survey of the Guinness production process and associated activities (including cooperage and worldwide transportation), covering the history of the now globally reknowned family firm. It's a fascinating 250-year old story told over 7 floors of the spectacular and atmospheric renovated 18C storehouse building. En toute there's a whole host of clever multi-media techniques, large scale exhibits, and hands-on installations, such as mastering the art of pouring the perfect pint of the black stuff. The famous Guiness advertising campaigns naturally, get a good airing. The end of the tour is the 7th-floor Gravity Bar, where you receive a complimentary pint of Guinness and enjoy fabulous uninterrupted 360-degree panoramic views across Dublin. Guiness lovers may also wish to extend their drinking knowledge at the Connoisseur Bar, sampling Foreign Extra Stout and Guinness Black Lager. There is also a very good restaurant featuring many dishes made with Guinness.

Rathfarnham Castle★

3mi/5km south of Dublin by N 81 and R 115. (Dúchas). 🕐*Open mid/late May–early Nov Tue–Sun 10am–5.15pm. Nov–mid/late May Wed–Sun & bank hols 10.30am–5pm.* 🕐*Closed 24–26 Dec* ℘*01 493 9462. www.heritageireland. ie/en. (The building will be closed for refurbishment works until June 2015. However, the surrounding parkland will remain open).*

More country house than traditional castle, the forbidding exterior gives no hint of the elegant 18C interior designed by Sir William Chambers and James "Athenian" Stuart. The rectangular central keep with four flanker towers was built c. 1593 by Adam Loftus, a Yorkshireman who became Archbishop of Dublin. The castle's splendid interiors, re-modelled in the 1770s are now home to the **Berkeley Costume and Toy Collection**, an exquisite collection of 18C and 19C toys, dolls and costumes.

Drimnagh Castle

Long Mile Rd. ♿🍴*Tours Mon-Fri 9am-4pm (1pm Fri). Last tour 4pm.* 💶€4. ℘*01 450 2530. www.drimnaghcastle.org*

Drimnagh is a 13C moated castle with a medieval Great Hall and vaulted undercroft, flanked by a battlemented tower. It boasts a formal 17C garden with box hedges, lavender bushes and herbs.

Irish Jewish Museum

Walworth Rd. 🕐*Open May–Oct Sun-Thu 11am–3.30pm; Nov–Apr Sun 11am–3pm.* ℘*01 453 1797. www.jewishmuseum.ie.*

Set in a former synagogue, this museum was opened by Chaim Herzog, President of Israel and son of the first Chief Rabbi of Ireland. It displays material on the history of Irish Jews from the 11C.

The **synagogue** upstairs retains the ritual fittings.

Guns for Independence

In July 1914, 900 German rifles and 25,000 rounds of ammunition for the Irish Volunteers were landed at Howth from the *Asgard*, the yacht belonging to Erskine Childers, a committed Republican, influenced by the time he had spent at Glendalough, his mother's childhood home, which he loved passionately. Strongly opposed to the Anglo-Irish Treaty which partioned the country, he was arrested in 1922 by the Free State government for possessing a revolver and then executed. His novel, *The Riddle of the Sands*, has been made into a film.

EXCURSIONS

THE BEN OF HOWTH★

North side of Dublin Bay by the DART (Raheny Station for North Bull Island) or by the coast road and R 105.
Ben of Howth, on the north side of Dublin Bay, shelters North Bull Island, originally a mere sandbank covered at high tide, which has grown to its present size (3mi/4.5km long) and continues to increase in width seawards, since the

Bull Wall was built in the late 18C to protect Dublin harbour from silting up.

North Bull Island

♿🕐*Open 10am–4.30pm.* 🕐*Closed Easter, Christmas.* ✆*01 833 8341.*
At the heart of the island is the **nature reserve** where wildfowl and waders spend the winter, and where some 30,000 shore birds take daily refuge from the high tide covering their feeding grounds in Dublin Bay.
There is an interpretive centre, the island also has two golf courses and several lovely beaches.

Howth★

This picturesque village (pronounced to rhyme with both) clings to the steep north face of the headland. The harbour (1807–09), which now shelters sailing and fishing boats, was the packet boat station from 1813 until Dún Laoghaire took over in 1833. Offshore lies **Ireland's Eye** (*boats depart from East Pier; open Apr–Sept, 10.30am–6pm on demand;* ⊕€15; ✆*086 845 9154; www.island-ferries.net*), a bird sanctuary, where 6C Christians built a church.
West of the village is **Howth Castle Demesne**, a medieval keep with a 15C gatehouse. The castle is closed to the public but in its grounds are the ruins of **Howth Abbey** (St Mary's), which hold

Howth harbour

the splendid tomb of a late-15C knight and his lady (*instructions on the gate for key and opening times*).

A short walk away the **National Transport Museum of Ireland** (&⊙*open Sat, Sun, bank hols 2pm–5pm; ⊛€4;* ▣; *☎01 832 0427; www.nationaltransportmuseum.org*), is a comprehensively labelled collection of horse-drawn, or motorised, commercial and military vehicles.

DÚN LAOGHAIRE★
South side of Dublin Bay by the DART or by N 31.

Dún Laoghaire (pronounced Leary), the main port of entry to Ireland from Great Britain, has become an attractive residential area, with the amenities of a seaside and boating resort. It grew from a small fishing village into a busy port through the growth of trade with Britain in the 18C; Laoghaire was a High King of Ireland in the 5C, who built a fort here.

For 100 years the port was known as **Kingstown** in honour of **George IV**, who landed here in September 1821; an **Obelisk**, erected in memory of the King's visit to Ireland, stands on the waterfront south of the harbour.

National Maritime Museum of Ireland★
Haigh Terrace. &⊙*Open daily 11am–5pm. ⊛€5. ☎01 280 0969. www.mariner.ie*

Housed in the Mariners' Church (1835–60) on the south side of Moran Park, this small collection belies its name and consists largely of model ships.

James Joyce Museum★
0.5mi/0.8km east by the coast road to Sandycove. ⊙*Open daily 10am-4pm. ☎01 280 9265. www. jamesjoycetower.com*

The Martello Tower (1804) on the point at Sandycove now houses a **Joyce Museum:** first editions, letters, photos, his death-mask, piano, guitar, cabin trunk, walking stick, wallet and cigar case. Joyce stayed there for six days in 1904 as the guest of the writer Oliver

Gogarty, who had rented the tower from the government. The upper room, the location of the breakfast scene in *Ulysses*, is furnished appropriately, while the **view** from the roof embraces Dún Laoghaire Harbour *(northwest)*, the coast to Dalkey Island *(southeast)* and the Wicklow Mountains *(southwest)*.

Dalkey Village
1mi/1.6km S of Dún Laoghaire.

Dalkey (pronounced Dawkey), now designated a Heritage Town, was once a walled town with seven fortified buildings. **Bulloch Castle** by the shore was built in the 12C by the monks of St Mary's Abbey in Dublin to protect the harbour. Two late-medieval tower houses survive in the heart of the village. One is **Archbold's Castle**, the other is **Dalkey Castle and Heritage Centre** (&⊙*open Mon–Fri 10am–5.30pm, Sat, Sun & bank hols 11am–5.30pm, closed Tue; ⊛€9; ☎01 285 8366. www.dalkeycastle.com*) set in a 15C fortified town house with splendid views from the battlements. From here costumed tour guides will show you Dalkey Town Hall (1893) and St Begnet Church and graveyard (10C). There is also a live theatre performance every half hour, an exhibition area with excellent displays on local history, and an art & crafts gallery.

Many writers, including James Joyce, have associations with Dalkey; as a child George Bernard Shaw (1856–1950) lived in Torca Cottage on Dalkey Hill and learnt to swim at Killiney beach. Recent local luminaries include Maeve Binchey and film director Neil Jordan. Offshore lies **Dalkey Island**, which is now a bird sanctuary.

From the coast road south of Sorrento Point there is a magnificent **view** of Killiney Bay extending south to Bray Head. The park covering the south end of Dalkey Hill was opened to the public and includes a **nature trail** which winds through trees and over the heath to an **obelisk**, built by John Mapas in 1742 to provide work for his tenants. From here there are **panoramic views★★★**.

Patrick Pearse (1879–1914) – Teacher, Barrister, Poet, Activist

James Pearse, a stone carver from England, kindled his son's love of English literature while his great-aunt, Margaret, stimulated an interest in the Irish language. Patrick joined the **Gaelic League**, campaigned for the use of Gaelic in schools and set up his own boy's school. Prominent names – W.B. Yeats, Patrick MacDonagh and Padraic Colum – attended pupils' theatrical productions. Over the years his pride in all things Irish evolved into more active political engagement. In November 1913 he joined the Irish Volunteers and then, in February 1914, the IRB. He took a prominent part in the Easter Rising and was executed at Kilmainham Gaol on May 2nd, 1916. His brother William was executed the following day.

SOUTH OF DUBLIN

Pearse Museum

*4.5mi/7.2km S of Dublin by N 81.
In Terenure fork left. In Rathfarnham bear left to Bray; turn first right onto Grange Rd; after 0.5 mile/0.8km turn right onto Sarah Curran Ave. 10min there and back on foot from the car park by the footpath parallel with the road. (Dúchas) ○Open Mar–Oct Wed–Mon 9.30am (10am Sun)–5.30pm (4pm Nov–Jan, 5pm Feb). ℘01 493 4208.
www.heritageireland.ie/en.*

The house (1797) was acquired by the Pearse brothers (℮see "Patrick Pearse" box) in 1910 for their boys' school, to encourage Irish culture and develop talents free from the pressure of exams.

FINGAL★

🛈*Fingal Tourism, Mainscourt,
Main St., Swords. ℘01 890 5144.
www.fingaldublin.ie.*

The area north of Dublin consists of rich farmland fringed by a long coastline. Fingal is the northern sub-division of County Dublin, which includes the city of Dublin and the adjacent suburbs from Balbriggan in the North to Lucan and Brittas in the West and Killiney in the South. The seaside resort of **Skerries** has several beaches, a colony of grey seals and a fishing harbour, where the famous Dublin Bay prawns are landed. **Portmarnock**, another popular resort, is known for its long, sandy Velvet Strand and its championship golf course.

In the Middle Ages Fingal formed part of **The Pale** (℮see TRIM) and contains several historic sites, elegant parks surrounding old stately homes and the charming dormitory town and seaside resort of **Malahide**.

Malahide Castle★★

*8.5mi/13km north of Dublin by R 107 or by M 1 and R 106. ○Open daily 9.30am –5.30pm. ∞€12.50. ✕ ℘01 816 9538.
www.malahidecastleandgardens.ie*

Malahide Castle was the home of the Talbot family for nearly 800 years; the great demesne (estate) was the prize awarded to Richard Talbot, who came to Ireland with Henry II in 1177. Built around the original 14C tower, the castle has been picturesquely extended and recently given a new lease of life.

Visitors can learn about the influential Talbots and see an exhibition on the castle before taking a tour of its four main rooms. Still highly atmospheric, these are hung with portraits from the National Portrait Collection and include wonderful Rococo plasterwork from the 18C. The Great Hall dates from the 15C, with a minstrel's gallery of 1825, and a frieze made up of fragments of 16C and 17C carvings.

The *Battle of the Boyne* by Jan Wyck, recalls the tragic story that 14 Talbot cousins, all Jacobites, breakfasted at Malahide on the morning of the battle and were killed in the fighting.

The **Talbot Botanic Gardens** (19 acres/ 7.5ha with 4 acres/1.5ha of walled garden) were largely created by Milo, the

© Ch. Schmidt/E+/Getty Images

Malahide Castle

last Lord Talbot, between 1948 and 1973, who indulged his passion for plants from the southern hemisphere. The result is a superb collection of trees and shrubs arranged around luscious lawns and a "Secret Walled Garden" with a Victorian glasshouse. There is also a lively interactive garden exhibition to visit.

The castle courtyard is home to a visitor cente and an Avoca foodhall, cafe and shop.

Newbridge House★

10mi/16km N of Dublin by M 1 and then E to Donabate. 🐾🐾*Tour (45min) Apr–Sept, Tue–Sat 10am–1pm, 2pm–5pm, Sun, Bank Hols noon–6pm. Oct–Mar, Sat–Sun and Bank Hols, noon–5pm.* 👓€7 (house), €5 (farm). ✕ 🖋*01 843 6534/6530.*
www.newbridgehouseandfarm.com
George Semple's early-18C Georgian country house, on the edge of Donabate, is set in extensive grounds and is one of the finest remaining examples of a landscaped park in Ireland. It has been the home of the Cobbe family since c. 1740 when it was built for Charles Cobbe, who came to Ireland in 1717 as chaplain to the Lord Lieutenant, and rose to become Archbishop of Dublin (portrait in the hall). Much of the interior has remained unchanged for centuries: some original furniture was made by Dublin craftsmen; the **stucco** and **plasterwork** (18C–early 19C) is superb. The **Red Drawing Room**, added c. 1760, preserves the wallpaper, curtains and carpet fitted in 1820. The family **museum** (1790), decorated in Chinese style is intriguing, crammed with souvenirs, trophies and exotica brought back from foreign travels.

Traditional Farm – A museum of traditional rural life is presented in the outbuildings – dairy (19C), dwelling, carpenter's shop, forge, stables and coach house. Domestic animals live in the paddocks; the large walled garden was converted to an orchard during World War II.

The Down Survey

The confiscation and redistribution of almost half the land in Ireland during the Cromwellian Settlement involved the preparation of accurate maps: these were provided by **Sir William Petty** and his team of surveyors over 13 months (1655–1656). This exercise, known as the Down Survey, has no connection with Co Down, but was so-called because the results were set down on maps rather than in the more usual tabulated form. Several sets of maps were individually drawn and coloured. While at sea between Dublin and London in 1707 the Petty set was captured by the French.

Newbridge House

© Dublin Regional Tourism Authority/Fáilte Ireland, Tourism Ireland

Ardgillan Castle

22mi/35km north of Dublin by M 1 and a minor road east to Balbriggan. ⊙*Open Apr–Sept, Tue–Sun and Bank Hols, 11am–6pm; third week Dec–Jan, Sun 2pm–4.15pm. Rest of year, Wed–Sun and Bank Hols, 11am–4.15pm.* ⊙*Closed 23 Dec –1 Jan.* ↞*Guided tour available.* ⌾€6. ℰ*01 890 5334; www.ardgillancastle.ie.*

On the coast north of Skerries stands the Georgian country house acquired in 1737 by the Taylor family, descendants of Thomas Taylor, a professional surveyor, who had come to Ireland from Sussex in 1650 to work on the **Down Survey**. The elegant interiors contain mementoes and furniture of the Taylor family. Kitchens, larder and scullery occupy the extensive basement, and on the upper floor there is a excellent exhibition on the Down Survey. Beyond the rose gardens are the walled gardens, laid out with lawns, flowers and vegetables in geometric plots. The west front is screened by Irish yew trees.

Skerries Mills

20mi/32km north of Dublin by M 1 and R 127. ↞*Visit by guided tour only, 10am–5.30pm (4.30pm Oct–Mar* ⊙*Closed Good Fri, 20 Dec–1 Jan.* ⌾€8. ✕ ℰ*01 849 5208; www.skerriesmills.ie.*

This rare survival of 17C–19C industrial technology comprises a watermill, two windmills (one with five sails and one with four), mill races, a mill pond and wetlands. The mills have been restored to working order. There is a small industrial heritage museum, cafe and gift shop.

Swords (Sord)

8mi/14km north of Dublin by M 1.

The bustling county town has a history going back to the 6C when St Columba founded a monastery on a low hilltop now marked by the Anglican church, a 9C **round tower** and a 12C **Norman tower**. At the northern end of the town stand the substantial remains of **Swords Castle** (&⊙*open Mon–Fri 10am–noon, 1pm–4pm (Fri 3pm);* ℰ*01 890 5600; www.fingaldublin.ie),* the summer palace of the Archbishops of Dublin.

ADDRESSES

☞ STAY

⊖ **Travelodge Dublin Stephens Green Hotel**– *Lower Mercer St.* ℰ*01 47 20 800; www.travelodge.ie/stephens-green-hotel. 41 rooms. Restaurant*⊖⊜. Keen shoppers and city centre revellers alike will appreciate the price and location of this dependable, if rather anonymous chain hotel, next to Grafton Street in the middle of town.

🛏🛏 **Harrington Hall** – *70 Harcourt St.* *📞01 2958900. https://manorhousehotels. com/hotels/harrington-hall/. 28 rooms.* Standing in an elegant terrace of classic Georgian properties, Harrington Hall offers sophisticated levels of comfort and service. All the bedrooms are of a generous size, especially the three junior suites, which have ornate ceilings and huge windows.

🛏🛏 **Pembroke Townhouse** – *90 Pembroke Rd. 📞01 660 0277. www.pembroketownhouse.ie. Closed 21 Dec–2 Jan. 48 rooms.* A quiet location in a smart suburba 15-min stroll from the bustle of the city centre. Thoughtfully furnished and faithful to its Georgian origins yet with all mod cons.

🛏🛏🛏 **Trinity Lodge** – *12 South Frederick St. 📞01 617 0900. www. trinitylodge.com. 26 rooms.* This modernised Georgian town house with clean, comfortable and well-furnished bedrooms is in one of the quieter streets in the city centre.

🛏🛏🛏🛏 **The Cliff Townhouse** – *22 St Stephen's Green. 📞01 638 3939. www.theclifftownhouse.com. 9 rooms.* Described as a restaurant-with-rooms, it would be hard to beat the location of this beautifully restored Georgian house that overlooks St Stephen's Green in the heart of the city. The original staircase and many period touches add to a relaxing elegant atmosphere.

🛏🛏🛏🛏 **The Clarence** – *6–8 Wellington Quay – 📞01 407 0800. www.theclarence.ie. 43 rooms, five suites. Restaurant🍽🍽🍽.* Its stylish interior, merging the contemporary with the traditional, has made The Clarence (part owned by Bono and The Edge of U2), highly popular with the cognoscenti. Staff are alert to guests' every need.

🛏🛏🛏🛏 **The Merrion** – *Upper Merrion St. 📞01 603 0600; www.merrionhotel.com. 123 rooms. 19 suites. Restaurant Patrick Guilbaud. 🍽🍽🍽🍽.* Sumptuous surroundings and pampered service is the order of the day at this elegant hotel, set in a row of carefully restored, ornately decorated Georgian town houses arranged around a private garden.

🍴 EAT

🍽 **The Bad Ass Café** – *Crown Alley, Temple Bar. 📞01 675 3005. www.badass dublin.com.* It's loud and it's brash but it ain't half bad, and it offers an undemanding menu of assorted grilled dishes and pizza to its many regulars.

🍽– 🍽🍽 **Nancy Hands Pub & Restaurant** – *30–32 Parkgate Street. 📞01 677 0149. www.nancyhands.ie.* Famed for its vast collection of Irish whiskeys and mildly schizophrenic décor that lends a certain Victorian charm; including a collection of Guinness antiques and advertising. Superior pub fare and generously portioned

🍽– 🍽🍽 **Silk Road Cafe** – *Jo St. 📞01 407 0770. www.silkroadcafe.ie.* Set in the Chester Beatty Library building with a view over Dublin Castle garden, the Silk Road bases its cuisine on some of the countries represented in the museum. Middle Eastern, North African, Mediterranean and vegetarian dishes are created by a team of Arabic chefs.

🍽🍽 **Bastible** – *111 South Circular Road 📞01 473 7409. www.bastible.com. Closed Mon & Tues.* One of the finest restaurants to open in recent times, Bastible is a contemporary neighbourhood bistro in the heart of Portobello. The dishes are seasonal and ever-changing, with a set menu from Wednesday to Saturday. Larger cuts of meat are selected for family-style lunches on Sunday.

🍽🍽 **Super Miss Sue** – *2–3 Drury Street. 📞01 679 9009. www.supermisssue.com.* The perfect pit-stop on a busy day of sightseeing, this trendy and welcoming restaurant serves up some fantastic dishes. Ostensibly a fish restaurant, it has enough on the menu to cater to all tastes. Next door they serve fish & chips to go.

🍽🍽 **Fallon & Byrne** – *11–17 Exchequer St. 📞01 472 1010. www.fallonandbyrne.com.* Situated above an artisan food hall and cafe of the same name this restaurant's elegant and simple approach to food is belied by its impressive, red-brick Victorian exterior.Fallon & Byrne prides itself on providing slow-cooked and seasonal Irish recipes alongside more adventurous offerings such as Carlingford Lough Oysters. Extensive selection of wines.

⊖⊜ – ⊖⊜⊟ **Bistro One** – *3 Brighton Rd., Foxrock.* ☏*01 289 7711. www.bistro-one.ie. Closed Mon. Booking advisable.* Gingham tablecloths and a blackboard menu contribute to the relaxed, informal feel. Somewhat hidden in a residential area to the South of the city, it showcases modern cooking with a blend Irish and Italian influences.

⊖⊜⊟ **Featherblade** – *51 Dawson St.* ☏*01 679 8814. www.featherblade.ie.* A no-fuss steak restaurant, this stylish new eatery offers 100% grass-fed Irish beef. The only permanent item on the menu is the sublime featherblade steak, everthing else is seasonal. Walk-ins welcome.

⊖⊜⊟ **Bang Restaurant** – *11 Merrion Row.* ☏*01 400 4229. www.bangrestaurant. com. Closed Christmas Day, and Bank Holiday Mon – Booking essential.* Captures the zeitgeist, with a suitably unstuffy atmosphere that matches the bustle of the surrounding streets. Service is chatty and the open-plan kitchen produces a mix of the classical and the more creative.

⊖⊜⊟ **The Cellar Restaurant** – *Upper Merrion St. (at The Merrion Hotel)* – ☏*01 603 0600. www.merrionhotel.com.* It's best to book at this restored Georgian cellar with its vaulted ceiling and exposed brick walls. The menu features modern Irish dishes by Executive Chef Ed Cooney. The lunchtime fixed price menu (⊖⊜) is excellent value. There is also a popular bar attached.

⊖⊜⊟ **The Old Spot** – *14 Bath Avenue, Sandymount.* ☏*01 660 5599. www. theoldspot.ie. Booking advised.* Perfectly located a stone's throw from the Aviva Stadium, this neighbourhood gastropub has fast established itself as one of the finest in the city. A pub serving food this good is something of a rarity - their Sunday roasts are a particular treat.

⊖⊜ **Ely Bar & Brasserie** – *IFSC, Custom House Quay.* ☏*01 672 0100. www.ely winebar.ie.* On the waterside in Custom House Dock in the newly renovated Docklands area, this restaurant has a stunning interior set in a vaulted converted wine warehouse and a charming outdoor seating area, complete with heaters. Great value Early Bird menu.

⊖⊜ **Rustic Stone** – *17 South George's St.* ☏*01 707 9596. www.rusticstone.ie.* A restaurant established in 2010 by Irish celebrity chef Dylan McGrath, which lives up to its name in more ways than one.

Natural elements in the decor is unusual for a city centre restaurant and hints at the modern twists given to traditional recipes. The most notable dishes are served on a hot volcanic stone which the diner cooks themselves.

⊖⊜ **L'Gueuleton** – *1 Fade St.* ☏*01 675 3708. www.lgueuleton.com.* Rustic restaurant with beamed ceilings, Gallic furnishings and rear terrace. Interesting French menus use local, seasonal produce. Flavoursome country cooking; friendly, efficient service.

⊖⊜ **La Cave** – *28 South Anne St.* ☏*01 679 4409; www.lacavewinebar.com.* Just off Grafton Street is Dublin's oldest French wine bar, serving light French food or full classic Gallic-Irish meals. Excellent value (⊖) Pre-Theatre menu.

⊖⊜⊟ **Pichet** – *14-15 Trinity St.* ☏*01 677 1060. www.pichet.ie. Closed 1-10 Jan.* Popular brasserie with buzzy atmosphere; its long, narrow room is dominated by an open-plan kitchen. Front café/bar, complete with cake and pastry counter for light snacks. Neat, flavoursome modern European cooking. Good value (⊖⊜)early evening menu; order by 6.30pm.

⊖⊜⊟ **Roly's Bistro** – *7 Ballsbridge Terr.* ☏*01 668 2611. www.rolysbistro.ie. Closed 25–27 Dec. Booking advisable.* A veritable institution and one of the city's most celebrated restaurants. The tables are set close together so you virtually rub shoulders with your neighbour but that's all part of the charm. Modern menu; particularly good value lunch. Its evening Cafe Menu (⊖) is superb value.

⊖⊜ – ⊖⊜⊟ **Chapter One** – *18–19 Parnell Sq.* ☏*01 873 2266. www.chapter onerestaurant.com. Closed Sun, Mon, Sat lunch; first fortnight Aug, fortnight from 24 Dec.* Lovely room beneath the Dublin Writers' Museum. Contemporary art hangs on the thick granite walls. The cooking (awarded a Michelin star) is innovative and the service careful. Splendid wines.

⊖⊜ – ⊖⊜⊟ **The Pig's Ear** – *4–5 Nassau St.* ☏*01 670 3865. www.thepigsear.com. Closed Sun & Bank Holidays.* Modern place designed on austere grey lines, serving contemporary Irish cuisine; overlooking Trinity College playing fields. Traditional dishes given a modern innovative twist by head chef Stephen McAllister.

⊖⊜⊜⊜ **Patrick Guilbaud** – *21 Upper Merrion St. ☏01 676 4192. www.restaurantpatrickguilbaud.ie. Closed Good Fri, first week Jan, 25 Dec, Sun and Mon.* The city's most renowned restaurant occupies a Georgian town house adjacent to the Merrion Hotel. The superlative cooking – modern Irish cooking using fresh Irish produce in season – combined with cosmopolitan surroundings and courteous service all help to make this one of the ultimate dining experiences.

TAKING A BREAK

Most pubs open Mon–Sat from 10.30am, Sun from noon and close between 11pm and midnight (perhaps later at weekends).

Abbey Tavern – *Howth. ☏01 839 0307. www.abbeytavern.ie.* This charming 1879 pub, north of the city, exudes a genuine sense of authenticity and a very convivial atmosphere. Known for its long-established "Traditional Irish Night" concerts in the adjacent barn.

Brazen Head – *20 Lower Bridge Street. ☏01 679 5186. www.brazenhead.com.* The oldest pub in the city, on the site of a 12C-tavern. Although popular with tourists, this doesn't seem to detract from the atmosphere. Worth getting there early to get a seat for the nightly music. Has a pleasant terrace.

Butlers Chocolate Café – *24 Wicklow St. ☏01 671 0591. www.butlerschocolates.com. Open daily 7.45am (8.30am Sat, 10.30am Sun)–7pm (9pm Thu).* One of a chain of several Butlers Chocolate Cafés throughout the city, this is not only the best place for sipping a cup of hot chocolate (they also serve a wide range of teas and coffees). For the taste of Ireland, try the Jameson Truffle, filled with Irish Whiskey. This is also a very good place to buy chocolates for presents/souvenirs.

Bewley's Cafe – *78–9 Grafton St. ☏01 672 7720. http://bewleys.com/bewleys-grafton-street-cafe. Mon–Sat 8am–10pm (11pm Sat). Sun 9am–10pm.* An Irish institution, which every Dublin visitor should sample at least once, Bewley's *is* the essence of Irish café society. Come here for a coffee and cake or their famous full breakfast, or pizzas, pastas and salads in the Cafe Bar Deli section. Particularly worth seeing is the Harry Clarke room, renowned for its stained glass windows, and do try to get

tickets for the Café Theatre. Lunchtime drama in the summer months (*www.bewleyscafetheatre.com, doors open daily 12.50pm*). and year-round evening cabaret, jazz and comedy.

Davy Byrne's – *21 Duke St. ☏01 677 5217. www.davybyrnes.com.* This is the most famous of Dublin's many literary pubs and is closely associated with James Joyce. Despite the changes made over the years, Davy Byrne's is still a very pleasant bar with a few remaining Art Deco touches and 1940s murals. It is also renowned for its seafood, particularly the fresh salmon, smoked salmon, crab and oysters.

Doheny & Nesbitt – *4–5 Lower Baggot St. ☏01 676 2945. http://dohenyandnesbitts.com.* A classic pub, recently renovated but still full of character and popular with government workers from the neighbourhood, especially civil servants from the Department of Finance. Hence the reason why Dubliners like to refer to the pub as the Doheny & Nesbitt School of Economics.

Johnnie Fox's – *Glencullen. ☏01 295 5647. www.jfp.ie.* It may look as if it were built for a film set but Johnnie Fox's has been in business since 1798. Situated in Glencullen on top of the Dublin mountains, this is not only one of Ireland's oldest and most famous pubs, it is also the highest pub in the country. Traditional music here every evening; worth the half-hour drive from the city centre.

The Ha'penny Bridge Inn – *42 Wellington Quay, Temple Bar. ☏01 677 2515. www.hapennybridgeinn.com.* Located on the quays by the most famous bridge in the city, the Ha'penny Inn is a pub with real character. Family-run, with regular music and comedy nights, it's the perfect spot to soak up some atmosphere.

J.W. Sweetman – *1–2 Burgh Quay. ☏01 670 5777. www.jwsweetman.ie.* This 19C-building facing the Liffey is a good example of the fusion of the old and the new worlds, combined as all things to all drinkers. It has cosy little nooks and crannies, a library bar, micro-brewery, cafe and brasserie/restaurant serving a fusion of Irish, continental and world cuisine.

Mulligan's – *8 Poolbeg St. ☏01 677 5582. www.mulligans.ie.* This celebrated old pub is the genuine article. James Joyce

Live music at The Temple Bar

© Holger Leue/Getty Images

and John F. Kennedy are just two of the famous luminaries who have enjoyed a pint here. The Victorian interior, with its mahogany and screens, is ideal for those looking for more intimacy and is regularly frequented by journalists and others who take their drinking seriously.

Oliver St John Gogarty – *58–9 Temple Bar. ☎01 671 1822. www.gogartys.ie.* Located in the heart of Temple Bar, this is always a very popular bar with visitors to the city. There's a first-floor restaurant, live music every night until around 2am and it also acts as the starting point for the famed "Musical Pub Crawl".

O'Donoghue's – *14 Merrion Row. ☎01 660 7194. www.odonoghues.ie.* Although a bit touristy, this pub has excellent traditional Irish music nightly and all day Sunday. The famous group, the Dubliners, came roaring onto the music scene here in 1962. Often very crowded, especially at weekends.

Temple Bar – *48 Temple Bar. ☎01 672 5286. www.thetemplebarpub.com.* The most-photographed pub in Dublin (if not Ireland!), this is nonetheless a very agreeable and popular choice for a good night out. The musical programme is varied, the acoustics good and on a summer's day or night it all moves into the garden. There's a shop attached, selling all manner of Temple Bar merchandise.

The Auld Dubliner – *Fleet St. ☎01 677 0527. www.aulddubliner.ie.* Despite the name, this is a relatively recent arrival on the Temple Bar pub scene, which has gained a good reputation for its daily traditional music sessions.

The Church – *MaySt/Jervis St. ☎01 828 0102. www.thechurch.ie.* Magnificently restored church now turned into club, bar, café and restaurant with an open-air barbecue area. Gets a little crowded in mid-summer but if you can find a quiet spot in all the hubbub, then you can sit and admire a beautiful old building.

The Long Hall – *51 South Great George Street. ☎01 475 1590. Open Sun–Wed 4pm–11.30pm, Thu–Sat 1pm–12.30am.* This wonderful Victorian bar has remained largely unchanged since 1880 and is noted for the extraordinarily long counter. It's a welcoming and sociable place, attracting visitors from all parts of the globe.

The Porter House Temple Bar – *16 Parliament St. ☎01 679 8847. www. porterhousebrewco.com.* The city's first micro-brewery has rapidly become a fashionable hangout. It offers a large range of modern beers and thus makes an ideal stop for those wanting a break from the "black stuff". Traditional music at weekends, modern during the week.

ENTERTAINMENT

Abbey Theatre – *26 Lower Abbey St. ☎01 878 7222. www.abbeytheatre.ie.* The Abbey is a proud symbol of Irish culture. Works by Ireland's best-known authors are regularly performed here (Shaw, Synge, Yeats, O'Casey), as are pieces by less-famous dramatists. The Peacock Theatre, in the same building, specialises in contemporary and experimental work.

Gaiety Theatre – *South King St. ☎0818 719388 www.gaietytheatre.ie. Mon–Sat 10am–8pm.* Opened in 1871, and affectionately known as The Grand Old Lady of South King Street, this theatre focuses on big-budget entertainment including Opera and musicals.

Bord Gáis Energy Theatre – *Grand Canal Sq., Docklands. 01 677 7999. www. bordgaisenergytheatre.ie.* Dublin's newest theatre, built in the up-and-coming Docklands area. Look out for big travelling productions of West End and Broadway shows, opera, ballet and concerts.

Gate Theatre – *1 Cavendish Row. 01 874 4045. www.gate-theatre.ie.* A proud Dublin institution, founded in the 1920s, this theatre includes Irish and non-Irish works in its repertoire.

Irish Film Institute – *6 Eustace St., Temple Bar. 01 679 3477. www.ifi.ie.* Film buffs are catered for all year round here. The programme ensures that Irish films as well as foreign-language and classics are always being shown.

The Laughter Lounge – *4–8 Eden Quay. 01 878 3003. www.laughterlounge.com Thu–Sat. Doors open 7.30pm.* Purpose-built comedy theatre with some big names in comedy as well as the often more rewarding local artists performing. Cameras carry the performance into the bars.

National Concert Hall – *Earlsfort Terr. 01 417 0000. www.nch.ie.* Dublin's premier performing arts venue hosts everything from the Irish Youth Orchestra to Japanese drummers and informal ceilidhs.

Olympia Theatre – *72 Dame St. 01 679 3323. www.olympia.ie. Mon–Sat from 10.30am.* Primarily a music venue, it also hosts comedy, theatre and other events. One of the best places to see a gig in Dublin - the setting is a beautifully ornate old-world theatre, and there's always a fantastic atmosphere.

NIGHTLIFE

Rí-Rá – *11 Dame Court. 01 671 1220. www.riraclub.ie. Open Mon–Sat 11pm–2.30am.* Spread over two floors, this night-club is loud, funky, free and despite (probably) having had its best days, stilll popular with a lively crowd. The Globe bar, upstairs is a good place to meet up.

SHOPPING

The **central shopping** area extends from Grafton Street *(southside)* to O'Connell Street *(northside)*. Nassau Street *(parallel with the southside of Trinity College)* contains several good shops selling a range of **Irish goods** from high fashion to modest souvenirs – clothing, craftwork, pottery, Irish music and instruments, family crests. The **Temple Bar** area offers an eclectic mix of individual little shops and outdoor stalls.

For **antiques**, go to Francis Street.

Street market-goers should visit: **Moore Street market** *(Mon–Sat)*, where barrow boys sell fresh fruit and vegetables; **Dublin Corporation Fruit and Vegetable Market** under a cast-iron roof *(Mary's Lane; Sat morning)*: **Temple Bar Market** *(Meeting House Square; Sat morning)* selling local foods and produce (cheeses, sauces, bread, chocolates, vegetable drinks, pizzas, pies and sausages).

Avoca Mills, *Suffolk St – 01 677 4215. www.avoca.ie.* A seven-level mini-department store filled with quirky gifts and fashionable design items. There's a small cafe downstairs selling great food - ideal for a quick mid-shop pit-stop.

Brown Thomas – *88–95 Grafton St. 01 605 6666; www.brownthomas.com.* Dublin's smartest department store deals in designer brands, from fashions and accessories to cosmetics and homewares.

Ulysses Rare Books – *10 Duke Street. 01 671 8676. www.rarebooks.ie.* Located just off Grafton Street, this tiny bookshop is chock-full of first editions and rarities. Specialising in 20th Century Irish literature, the shelves are stacked with one-of-a-kind volumes of Joyce, Yeats, Beckett, Heaney, et al.

Claddagh Records – *2 Cecilia St., Temple Bar. 01 677 0262. www.claddagh records.com.* Specialist in folk, traditional and ethnic music.

House of Ireland – *37 Nassau Street. 01 671 1111. www.houseofireland.com.* If it's made in Ireland then it is probably available in this well-known shop. Although perhaps a little expensive, the range is vast; from woollens to crystal, porcelain to jewellery.

Kevin & Howlin – *31 Nassau St. 01 633 4576. www.kevinandhowlin.com.* The definitive temple of Donegal tweed. The range available at this family firm includes jackets, suits, waistcoats and ties. Alternatively, fabric can be bought by the metre.

Kilkenny Shop – *6 Nassau St.* ☏ *01 677 7066. www.kilkennyshop.com.* Tweeds, Aran sweaters, lace and Celtic jewellery are just some of the goods on sale at what is claimed to be the largest emporium of traditional Irish products. Wilting shoppers can refuel in the café or award-winning restaurant.

Mitchell & Son – *The CHQ Building, IFSC Docklands.* ☏ *01 612 5540. www.mitchellandson.com.* This wine merchants was founded in 1805 and the sixth generation of the family is now at the helm. Celebrated for its famous "Green Spot" whiskey, aged in sherry casks, they also offer a vast range of wines, rare malts, spirits and cigars.

Market Arcades – *South Great George St.* This covered passage is home to over 20 shops, some offering second-hand clothing. There are real bargains to be found, especially in tweed jackets.

National Museum Shop – *Kildare St. and Benburb St.* Top-quality reproductions of items based on exhibits in the country's national museums.

The Powerscourt Centre – *South William St.* ☏ *01 679 4144. www.powersourtcentre.ie.* An 18C town house, now converted into an attractive shopping centre, with 43 individual shops.

Rory's (Fishing Tackle) – *17A Fleet St., Temple Bar.* ☏ *01 677 2351. www.rorys.ie.* A Dublin institution and a must for fishermen. All the equipment you could ever need is here, including a huge range of flies made at the shop. They are more than willing to advise on what to buy and where to fish.

SPORTS AND LEISURE

Croke Park – *Drumcondra.* ☏ *01 819 2300; www.crokepark.ie.* The stadium where the national finals of the Gaelic games – hurling and football – are held. Stadium tours and home to the GAA Museum.

Aviva Stadium – *62 Lansdowne Rd.* ☏ *01 238 2300; www.avivastadium.ie.* Newly-reconstructed stadium where international rugby and football matches, as well as concerts, take place.

Horse Racing is held at **Leopardstown** (south) and **Fairy House** (north). **Punchestown**, the home of Irish National Hunt racing, is 26 mi/42km away.

Greyhound Racing takes place at Shelbourne Park and Harold's Cross.

EVENTS AND FESTIVALS

Temple Bar Trad Festival of Irish Music & Culture (late Jan) *www.templebartrad. com* – Dublin's premier celebration of traditional Irish music and culture.

RBS Six Nations Rugby Internationals (Feb–Mar) *www.rbs6nations.com*– Any rugby international featuring Ireland playing at home in Dublin turns the city into a raucous but good-natured place to be.

St Patrick's Festival (mid-Mar) – *www.stpatricksfestival.ie.* This five-day extravaganza of music, street theatre, carnival, dance, pageantry, comedy and more, is one of the world's biggest street parties, culminating on St Patrick's Day ("Paddy's Day"), 17 March.

Bloomsday (16 June) – Annual celebration) of James Joyce's great novel *Ulysses* – including readings, music, theatre and street theatre.

Rugby match, Aviva Stadium

© P. Walsh / Action Plus Sports - Compete / age fotostock

SIGHTSEEING

The **Dublin Pass** can be purchased online (at a discount) or at any Dublin tourist information office. It entitles the bearer to free airport–city centre transfer, free admission to 34 visitor attractions, and various special offers/discounts at many of Dublin's top shops, restaurants, tours and entertainment venues. Adult passes start at €35 and may be purchased for one, two, three, or six days. *www.dublinpass.ie.*

BUS TOURS

City Sightseeing Dublin (*www.love ireland.com*) offer **hop-on-hop-off circular bus tours** of the city centre aboard a red open-top bus (2hr 45min) A live commentary is given by an approved guide. Tickets (buy online for a discount) are good for 2 days and include a night tour. A very similar, service is offered by **Dublin Bus Tours** (*www. dublinbus.ie*). Their route is not quite so comprehensive, with 20 instead of 25 stops, but their prices (both operators discount their tickets frequently) are often lower. Dublin Bus Tours also run evening **Ghostbus** tours (*www.dublin sightseeing.ie/GhostBus*), a theatrical experience with professional actors and not suitable for children under 14 yrs.

Viking Splash Tours – An Informative and highly entertaining sightseeing tour of Dublin by land and water in a bright yellow amphibious World War II DUKW vehicle. Tours start from St Stephen's Green and eventually enter the water at the Grand Canal Basin in the new Docklands. En route guests don plastic Viking helmets, roar at passing "Celts" and generally enjoy the craic! *Operate early Feb–early Nov daily, 10am–5pm every 30 mins.* €20. *01 707 6000; www.vikingsplash.com.*

Full-day and half-day tours to attractions in the Dublin area are organised by various bus companies, including **Gray Line Tours Ireland** – *Excursions to the Wicklow Mountains, valleys and lakes (including Glendalough); Dublin Bay and Malahide Castle.* €24–38. *01 458 0054; www.grayline.com.* For more tours see *www.loveireland.com.*

For **steam train excursions** visit *www.steamtrainsireland.com.*

Dublin Ghost Bus Tour

© Dublin Bus/Fáilte Ireland

WALKING TOURS

There are many specialist walking tours of the city. Visit www.visitdublin.com and Search Guide Walking Tours for the full list. The following are recommended:

Historical Walking Tours of Dublin – Dublin's development, from the influence of the American and French Revolutions, the Potato Famine, the 1916 Rising, the War of Independence,and Partition to the Peace Process.*Operates May–Sept, daily 11am, 3pm; Aprand Oct, daily 11am; Nov–Mar, Fri–Sun11am.* €12. *087 688 9412; www.historicaltours.ie.*

1916 Rebellion Walking Tour – The stirring story of the people who took part, the key events as they unfolded and the central Dublin locations—some still pockmarked by bullet holes even today—where the Rising took place. No need to book, just turn up at the International Bar, 23 Wicklow Street. *Operates Mar–Oct, Mon–Sat 11.30pm; Sun, 1pm.* €12. *086 858 3847; www.1916rising.com.*

Dublin Literary Pub Crawl – This highly amusing tour is conducted by two actors who introduce the city's most famous writers and re-enact scenes from their works in appropriate locations. *Operates Apr–Nov daily, Dec–Mar Thu–Sun 7.30pm and Sun noon.* €13. *01 670 5602; www.dublinpubcrawl.com.*

Traditional Irish Musical Pub Crawl
Pub tour led by two professional musicians who perform tunes and songs while telling the story of Irish music. Great fun. €12. *Operates nightly 7.30pm (Nov–Mar (Thu–Sat only).* *01 475 3313; www.discoverdublin.ie.*

The regions in this area – County Kildare, County Wicklow, County Meath and Co.Louth– were once part of the area called the Pale, a fortified region around Dublin which the Anglo-Norman invaders of Ireland were able to police and defend. Kildare, formed as a county by the Anglo-Norman Fitzgeralds, was especially important as a buffer zone that secured the Pale against incursions by the Irish to the South. Hugh De Lacy, one of the original Anglo-Norman invaders who arrived in 1169, chose to establish his headquarters at Trim and in this way the town developed as a military base guarding the western side of the Pale. By the Middle Ages, indeed, Trim was secure enough to act as a meeting place for the Irish Parliament.

Highlights

1   The Megalithic Tomb at **Newgrange** (p153)

2   The medieval **Trim Castle** and the ruins of the **Cathedral** (p159/p160)

3   Stunning **Castletown House** and its Gardens (p172)

4   The beautiful setting of the **Glendalough Monastic Site** (p175)

5   **Powerscourt House** and its landscaped gardens (p179)

Meath, Kildare and Louth

Today, Meath and Kildare retain an attachment to the city as an extended hinterland where Dubliners can enjoy the countryside, have fun and in many cases live and commute into the city.

The green rural landscape of County Meath is home to Newgrange, the most important ancient site in Ireland and perhaps the one place that ought to be on every traveller's itinerary. There is also Bective Abbey, a medieval Cistercian complex and once a seat of great political power in the region, and the charming town of Trim, with its Norman fortress and ruined cathedral.

The undulating landscape of Kildare is well known for the National Stud and the Curragh, while the county's highlight is the Georgian Castletown House, built by the then richest man in Ireland and later lovingly restored by the State. The verdant pastures of Kildare are marked by the darker hues of the Bog of Allen,

while high crosses are a reminder of the period in the county's history when a different power dominated the countryside. The solid, Georgian county town of Kildare was once an important monastic site and the 12C round tower and 13C church are well worth a visit.

The small county of Louth boasts the highly interesting Cooley Peninsula, which provides magnificent sea views and sandy beaches.

Wicklow

County Wicklow, to the South of Dublin and on the East Coast, is able to compete with the West of Ireland in terms of stunning mountain scenery. Indeed, the peat-covered mountains of Wicklow constitute the largest area of continuous high ground anywhere in the country. The rugged landscape can be appreciated at Powerscourt and Glendalough, two places with intrinsic attractions that make a visit even more compelling. Glendalough is the site of an early Celtic monastery while Powerscourt is an imposing Palladian mansion with magnificent formal gardens. In addition, the county boasts some excellent long-distance walks that take in pretty sleeper towns and tiny villages. Wicklow's coastline, still relatively undeveloped, contains abundant wildlife, some challenging walks and quiet places to stay.

The bustling county town has a long and proud history and much to attract visitors. This area, like Kildare and Meath, was settled by Anglo-Irish families and throughout the county there are reminders of their history in grand houses and formal gardens.

Boyne Valley ★

Upstream from Drogheda, the River Boyne winds through a fertile and well-wooded landscape with an extraordinary concentration of ancient and prehistoric sites. Huge grave mounds, laboriously constructed and enigmatically decorated, testify to the skill and sophistication of the people who thrived here long before work started on the pyramids of Egypt. Much later, in the pre-Christian era, the High Kings of Ireland held court at the Hill of Tara. Christianity was brought to the region by St Patrick himself; the early monastic site at Monasterboice evokes the Irish church before its 12C Romanisation, in contrast to the later, European style of monastery at Mellifont. The clash of arms on the banks of the river in 1690 was an event of European as well as local importance, and the outcome of the Battle of the Boyne is still a factor in contemporary Irish politics.

Info: The Tholsel, West Street, Drogheda. ☎041 987 2843. www.heritage ireland.ie.

Location: The Boyne Valley runs inland from Drogheda; the sights can be reached from N 51 on the north bank of the River Boyne, from M 1 which passes just west of Drogheda or from N 2, which passes through Slane.

Don't Miss: Newgrange – a UNESCO World Heritage Site, and Monasterboice.

Walking Paths: River Boyne towpath, Oldbridge Estate, Townley Hall grounds (nature trail).

Timing: Allow at least a day for the prehistoric sites.

DROGHEDA★

27mi/43km north of Dublin.
The Tholsel, West Street; ☎041 987 2843. www.drogheda.ie. www.louthholidays.com.
Straddling the River Boyne close to its mouth, Drogheda *(Droichead Átha)* was one of the most important towns of medieval Ireland, with a long and eventful history. It is still a place of some consequence, located on the main Dublin-Belfast road and railway, with varied industries and a harbour. Much of the town centre is set on the steep north bank of the river, with narrow lanes and flights of steps linking the different levels.

A Bit of History

The town was founded in 911 by Norsemen. In the late 12C, Hugh de Lacy, Lord of Meath, made it an important Norman stronghold with two separate parishes, Armagh and Meath. Little remains of the many monasteries which flourished in Drogheda in the Middle Ages and only the **Butter Gate** on Millmount and St Laurence Gate remain of the town walls built in 1234.

Parliament often met in Drogheda and in 1494 it was here declared that the Irish Parliament was to be placed under the authority of the English Parliament.

During the Confederate Rebellion Drogheda was twice besieged, most infamously in 1649 when it was attacked by **Oliver Cromwell**. During the siege, many people took refuge in St Peter's Church and perished when the wooden steeple was set alight by Cromwell's troops.

Eventually the city wall was breached on the southeast side of Millmount near St Mary's Church and, according to Cromwell's own estimate, 2,000 died by the sword; most of the survivors were transported to Barbados.

The Tholsel

At the crossroads in the town centre stands The Tholsel; a clock tower and a lantern surmount the limestone building (1770), where Corporation meetings and law courts were held until 1889.

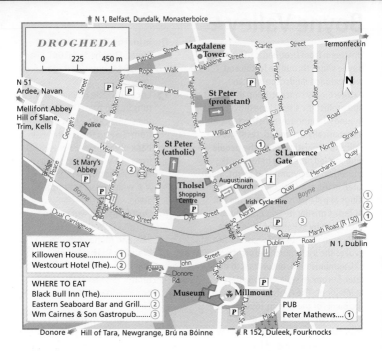

WHERE TO STAY
Killowen House..............①
Westcourt Hotel (The)...②

WHERE TO EAT
Black Bull Inn (The)........................①
Eastern Seaboard Bar and Grill.....②
Wm Cairnes & Son Gastropub.......③

PUB
Peter Mathews....①

St Peter's Roman Catholic Cathedral

&. ⏱*Open year-round 8.30am–6pm.*
☎*041 984 5355 (Sacristan).*

A neo-Gothic building (1881) on West Street which contains the shrine of **Oliver Plunkett** (1625–81), the Roman Catholic Archbishop of Armagh.

The roofless nave and crossing tower of **St Mary's Abbey** stand on the oldest monastic site in Drogheda, where, according to tradition, a monastery was founded after St Patrick's visit in 452. In 1206 a Norman settler, Ursus de Swemele and his wife, founded a hospital which was later administered by the Augustinian Friars until the Dissolution of 1543. The **Courthouse**, with its distinctive weather vane on the corner of Fair Street and Bolton Street, was completed in 1790.

St Peter's Anglican Church

⏱*Open for services and concerts.* ☎*041 982 7345. www.stpetersdrogheda.ie.*

A new church was built in 1753 to replace the medieval church burnt by Cromwell. It suffered a serious arson attack in 1999 and has subsequently been much rebuilt with the provision of a new space for concerts and other performances.

The three rows of Georgian houses (c. 1730) beyond the graveyard, with its **cadaver tombstone**, *(at the east gate)* were built for clergy widows.

Magdalene Tower *(14C)* marks the site of a Dominican monastery founded in 1224 by Lucas de Netterville, Archbishop of Armagh, where in 1395 four Irish princes submitted to Richard II.

St Laurence Gate★ This well-preserved three-storey barbican, an integral part of the 13C gate, is unique in Ireland. It was built by the Normans using stone from the walls erected by the Vikings. A section of the town wall still stands on the south side.

Millmount

South Bank.

Generations of rulers left their mark on the hill dominating the south bank of the Boyne; it was possibly the site of a passage grave and subsequently crowned by an Anglo-Norman motte, then by 18C fortifications. From the **Martello Tower** of **Millmount Fort** there is a fine **view** of the town centre and **railway viaduct** built in 1855 across the Boyne estuary.

Drogheda Millmount Museum★

🕐*Open Mon–Sat 10am–5.30pm, Sun 2pm–5pm.* 👣*Last tour 1 hr before closing.* 🎟€5.50. 🅿 ✆*041 983 3097. www.millmount.net.*

Located in the old Officers' quarters (1820), this museum is dedicated to its military use, local industries, a folk kitchen, geology and archaeology. The Martello Tower (fort) offers fine views over Drogheda.

PREHISTORIC SITES★★★

The prehistoric burial sites at Knowth, Dowth and Newgrange are the oldest in the British Isles. They were built by a farming and stock-raising community in the Neolithic era (3,500–2,700 BC), overlooking the Boyne, then a main through route.

Present knowledge suggests Dowth (*closed to visitors*) was built first to align with the setting sun. It was followed by Newgrange, where the rising sun penetrates the inner chamber at the winter solstice. Knowth was built later, facing east to west to align with the rising sun in March and the setting sun in September.

Altogether, there are some 40 graves, consisting of three major graves and many satellites: only the major graves have been systematically excavated.

Brú na Bóinne Visitor Centre★★★

(Dúchas) ♿👣*Visit by guided tour only (75min) May–Sept, daily, 9am–6.30pm (7pm Jun–mid-Sept). Feb–Apr and Oct, daily, 9.30am–5.30pm. Nov–Jan 9am–5pm.* 🕐*Closed 24–27 Dec.* ℹ*Arrive early in high season as visitor numbers are strictly limited (Newgrange 24 people, Knowth 48 people) so tours sell out quickly.* 🎟*Visitor Centre only, €3; Centre and Newgrange (2hr) €6; Centre and Knowth (Easter to late Oct), 2hr, €5. Centre, Newgrange and Knowth (inc. shuttle bus) €11.* ✖🅿 ✆*041 988 0300. www.heritageireland.ie.*

Informative displays with replicas of the monuments provide an excellent introduction to the archaeological sites: details of the people, their clothing, food and Neolithic dwellings are integrated into descriptions of their expertise and ability to move stones on rollers: 500 years before the pyramids of Egypt.

Newgrange★★★

Newgrange is one of the best examples of a passage grave in western Europe, its dimensions imposing, the enigmatic stone carving a marvel of imagination. The **mound** (1.25 acres/0.5ha, between 260ft/79m and 280ft/85m in diameter, and 37ft/11m high) consists of a cairn of medium-sized stones enclosed within a circle of 97 kerbstones, some of which are decorated, set on their long edges, ends touching, surmounted by a facing of round granite boulders.

Excavations in 1963 made it possible to reconstruct the original south front **revetment** of white quartz stones, except where the entrance has been enlarged to accommodate visitors. Above the entrance, originally closed by an upright slab *(right)*, is the **roof box**, a unique structure with a finely decorated lintel, through which the rays of the rising sun penetrate to the inner

Burial Chamber, Newgrange

© Brian Lynch/Fáilte Ireland

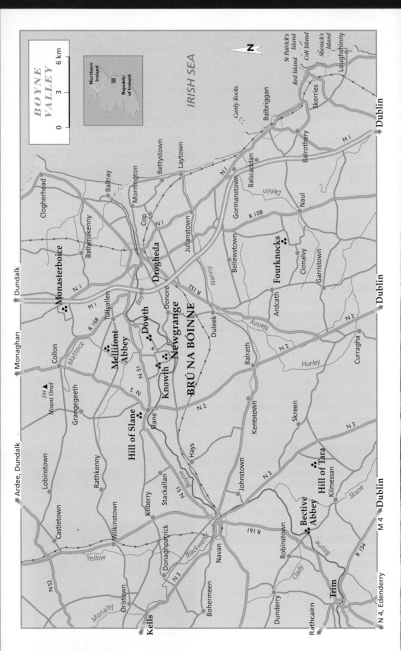

chamber for 17 minutes at the winter solstice (21 December).

The passage, which is lined with large standing stones, some decorated and all dressed, leads into a **corbelled chamber** a third of the way into the mound. The three decorated recesses contain **stone basins**, which held the bones of the dead together with funeral offerings of stone and bone beads and pendants, bone pins and small stone balls resembling marbles. The corbelled

Battle of the Boyne

The battle fought on July 12, 1690 was the decisive engagement in the War of the Two Kings *(Cogadh an Dá Rí)* and ended the Stuart cause. The army of **King James II** of England, supported by Louis XIV of France, numbered some 25,000. King William III of England (**William of Orange**) and his allies (British, Danish, Dutch, Finnish, French, German, Irish, Polish, Prussian and Swiss) counted 36,000. While the French Jacobites were under orders to delay William, the latter was keen for a speedy victory. As he surveyed his troops on the morning of the battle, a bullet tore his coat and grazed his shoulder. The King despatched troops upstream to the French left flank, they forded the Boyne at Oldbridge and attacked the Jacobite army on the south bank; five crossings were made between 10am–2pm.

William lost 500 men; James double that. On hearing William had crossed the river, James left for Dublin, rode on to Duncannon and sailed to Kinsale and France. In the hope of reversing the Cromwellian land settlement, the Irish fought on until the following year when they suffered defeats at Athlone, Aughrim and Limerick.

vaulted roof, completed by a central capstone (4 tonnes), is quite water-proof as the outer faces of the stones are grooved to drain off water.

The mound was surrounded at a distance (39x49ft/12x15m) by a **great circle** of standing stones. The four opposite the entrance are among the largest. South of the mound are traces of a late-Neolithic to early-Bronze Age **pit circle**.

Knowth★

The mound (40ft/12m high, 220ft/67m in diameter) probably dates from 2500 to 2000 BC. It contains two decorated passage graves discovered in 1967 and 1968; one is simply an enlargement of the passageway but the other is circular and corbelled with side chambers. It is aligned east–west and is surrounded by smaller tombs facing the large central mound. In the early centuries AD the central mound was surrounded by deep defensive ditches. In about 8C AD the settlement expanded and several souterrains and rectangular houses were built. From the 12C to 14C the site was occupied by the Normans, who constructed a rectangular stone structure on the top of the mound.

Excavations conducted since 1962 have made it possible to reconstruct the smaller tombs which had collapsed owing to the passage of time and conversion of the material to other uses.

Dowth

The mound (⚰ *closed for excavation*), which was raised by man in 3000 BC (1 acre/0.4ha, 280ft/85m in diameter, 50ft/15.24m high), contains two tombs and a souterrain connecting with the north tomb.

The base of the mound was enclosed by about 100 kerb stones, many ornamented, although most are covered by landslip.

OTHER SITES
Hill of Tara★

5mi/8km S of Navan by N 3. (Dúchas)
♿ 🕐 *Site: Open all year. Visitor Centre and guided tour: mid/late-May–mid-Sept, 10am–6pm (5pm last tour).* ◈€3.
✕ 🅿 ✆ *046 902 5903.*
www.heritageireland.ie.

The name Tara conjures up the spirit of Irish Celtic greatness; the Hill of Tara, also known as Tara of the Kings, played a significant part in Irish legends. Its origin as a religious site is lost in prehistory; it achieved greatest prestige under the pagan High Kings of Ireland and even after the introduction of Christianity it retained significance as the nominal seat of the High King until it was abandoned in 1022.

During the 1798 rebellion a skirmish took place on the hill. In the 19C Daniel O'Connell chose it as the site of one of his huge rallies ("monster meetings") in

Hill of Tara

© Stefano Torrione/hemis.fr

the cause of Roman-Catholic emancipation; 250,000 people came to hear him speak.

The **bare hill** pockmarked with earthworks does not readily suggest a royal palace. An effort of the imagination is required to envisage the many small buildings, of wood or wattle and daub, where the King held his court.

The history of Tara is recounted in an audio-visual presentation in the early-19C **St Patrick's Church**, which incorporates a medieval window.

In the churchyard stands a red sandstone pillar stone, known as **St Adamnán's Cross**, which bears a carved figure which may be the ancient Celtic god **Cernunnos**.

West of the graveyard is the **Rath of the Synods**, a ringfort with three banks. Farther south is an Iron-Age ringfort, enclosed by a bank and a ditch, known as the **Royal Enclosure**. Within is the **Mound of the Hostages**, a small passage grave which dates from about 1800 BC. In the centre of the enclosure are two ringforts, known as the **Royal Seat** and **Cormac's House;** beside the statue of St Patrick is a standing stone known as the **Lia Fáil**, which was moved from its original position near the Mound of the Hostages to be a memorial to those who died in 1798.

South of the Royal Enclosure is part of another earthwork known as **King Laoghaire's Rath**. To the north of the churchyard is a hollow flanked by two long parallel banks, which may have been the grand entrance but which is known as the Banqueting Hall. On the west side are three circular earthworks; the first is known as Gráinne's Fort, the other two as the Sloping Trenches.

South of the hill *(0.5mi/0.8km – visible from the road)* is part of another ringfort, known as **Rath Maeve**, surrounded by a bank and ditch.

Fourknocks

11mi/18km S of Drogheda by R 108; after 10mi/16km turn right.
www.knowth.com/fourknocks.

This **passage grave** (*key available from Mr White;* ℰ*041 980 9950, make arrangement in advance*), dates from c. 1500 BC, and is unusually large compared with the size of the mound. The interior contains stones decorated with zigzags and other prehistoric designs and a human face. It contained over 60 burials.

BATTLE SITE
Battle of the Boyne Visitor Centre

&⃝*Open Mar–Apr daily, 9.30am–5.30pm. May–Sept, daily 10am–6pm. Oct–Feb, daily 9am–5pm.*
Last admission 1hr before closing.
Site may close in poor weather.
⊛€4. ✕ℰ*041 980 9950.*
www.battleoftheboyne.ie.

The battlefield site, now part of the Oldbridge estate, granted to the Williamite commander Coddington, contains a museum and interpretive centre including an audio-visual presentation. There are Living History weekends *(May–Sept)* and riverside walks on the estate and beside the river from the Obelisk Bridge.

MONASTIC SITES
Monasterboice★★

8mi/13km N of Drogheda by N 1.
Overlooked by a half-ruined **round tower**, three **high crosses★** of outstanding beauty and interest mark the site of the famous 6C monastery founded by **St Buithe** (**Boethius**), an

important centre of learning closely connected with Armagh.

The **South Cross** was erected by Muiredach in the 9C. The west face shows the Crucifixion, Christ with Peter and Paul, the raised Christ flanked by Apostles and the Mocking of Jesus; on the east face are the Last Judgement, the Adoration of the Magi, Moses striking the Rock, David and Goliath, the Fall of Man and Cain slaying Abel.

The **West Cross** *(between the two ruined churches)* is unusually tall (23ft/7m) and the subjects of the carvings are unusual: the Crucifixion, the Arrest of Christ, Christ surrounded by Apostles, the Resurrection of the Dead, the Soldiers at the Tomb; Christ Militans, Christ walking on the water, Simon Magus and the Fiery Furnace, Goliath, Samuel anointing David, the Golden Calf, the Sacrifice of Isaac and David killing a lion.

The **North Cross** *(NE corner of the graveyard)* also shows the Crucifixion. The original shaft is contained in the same enclosure as well as a monastic sundial indicating the hours of the Divine Office. Behind the north church lies an early **grave slab** bearing the name Ruarcan. The **tower** and its treasures were burned in 1097.

Old Mellifont Abbey★

6mi/10km W of Drogheda by N 51, R 168 and a minor road west of Tullyallen. (Dúchas) ♿⏱*Visitor Centre: Open late Apr/May–late Sept, 10am–6pm (5.15pm last admission).* ₱€4. 🅿 ✆*041 982 6459. www.heritageireland.ie.*

The first Cistercian house in Ireland was founded here, on the banks of the **River Mattock** by St Malachy in 1142 with four Irish and nine French monks. No doubt it owed its name ("Honey fountain" in Latin) to the beauty of the surroundings.

Still standing are the ruined **gatehouse**, the vaulted **Chapter House** (14C) and four faces of the two-storey **octagonal lavabo** (12C). The 12C church, consecrated in 1157, was designed by one of the Frenchmen; it had a crypt at the west end and three transept chapels. In 1225 the chancel and transepts were extended. In 1556 the abbey became a private house, which was abandoned in 1727.

Hill of Slane

This hilltop with its wide-ranging views is one of the key sites in the story of Irish Christianity. In 433 St Patrick travelled from Saul (in Co Down) by sea and on foot to Slane, where he lit a fire on the hilltop on Easter Eve to challenge the druids, who were holding a festival at Tara. As anyone who kindled a fire within sight of Tara did so on pain of death, Patrick was brought before Laoghaire, the High King, to whom he preached the Gospel. Although the King remained a pagan, he allowed his subjects free-

Old Mellifont Abbey

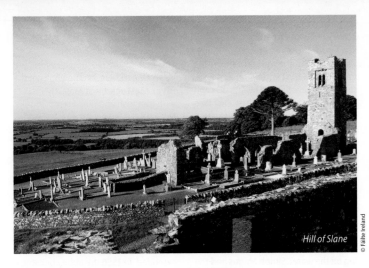

Hill of Slane

© Fáilte Ireland

dom of conscience. One of them, Erc, converted and founded a monastery at Slane; he is said to be buried in the ruined mortuary house in the graveyard. The church, which was in use until 1723, was part of **Slane Friary**, a Franciscan house founded in 1512 by Sir Christopher Flemyng, whose arms are on the west wall of the courtyard. The friary, which housed four priests, four lay-brothers and four choristers, was suppressed in 1540, occupied by Capuchins in 1631 and abandoned under Cromwell. On the west face of the hill is a motte raised by Richard le Flemyng of Flanders, who arrived in Ireland in 1175.

Termonfeckin★

6mi/10km N of Drogheda by R 167 E or R 166 and a minor road E. (Dúchas) Key available from the cottage opposite.

In the graveyard of St Fechin's Church stands a 10C **high cross** depicting the Crucifixion and Christ in Glory; it marks the site of a monastery founded by St Fechin of Fore. Close to the shore stands a 15C or 16C three-storey **tower house** which has an unusual corbelled roof *(45 steps)*: **view** of the coast from Drogheda *(S)* to Clogher Head *(N)*.

SLANE

The "square" at the centre of the village was laid out by Viscount Conyngham in the late 18C; it is lit by oil lamps and bordered by four nearly-identical Georgian houses, each flanked by two smaller ones. The Gothic Gate *(South of the crossroads)* was designed by **Francis Johnston** (c. 1795) as an entrance to Slane Castle. From the bridge over the Boyne there is a **view** of Slane Castle, Slane Mill (1766), the weir and the canal; the towpath goes upstream to Navan and downstream to Drogheda.

Slane Castle

0.25mi/0.5km W of Slane by N 51.
Guided tour Jun–Aug, Sun–Thu noon–5pm. €7. Whisky tours and tasting also available, from €17; booking min two weeks ahead required. ☎041 982 4080. www.slanecastle.ie.

The impressive raised **site** overlooking the **River Boyne** is surmounted by an elegant assembly of turrets, crenellations and machicolations. The present house was built between 1785 and 1821 on the site of a confiscated **Fleming** fortress purchased by the Conynghams in 1641. Only the best architects were employed, among them James Gandon, James Wyatt, Francis Johnston and Thomas Hopper, while Capability Brown designed the stables and landscaped the grounds.

Ledwidge Cottage Museum

0.5mi/0.8km E of Slane by N 51.
♿ ⊙*Open early Feb–mid-Dec daily,*
10am–3.30pm. ⊚*€3.* ☏*041 982 4544.*
www.francisledwidge.com.

The four-room semi-detached cottage
built under the Labourers' Dwellings Act
(1886), was the childhood home of the
First World War poet **Francis Ledwidge**
(1887–1917), who wrote about his love of
the Meath countryside. Today, it displays
some of his manuscripts.

TRIM★

Population: 1,740. Trim is situated
28mi/45km northwest of Dublin on the
R 154. 🛈 *Town Hall, Castle St.* ☏*046 943*
7227. www.meath.ie/Tourism

Straddling the Boyne by an ancient
ford, little Trim *(Baile Átha Troim)*, a designated Heritage Town, is dominated
by the ruins of its castle, the largest
in Ireland, a medieval monument to
match the great prehistoric structures
farther down the valley. Other imposing
remains recall Trim's important role as a
stronghold and ecclesiastical centre on
the outer edge of the Pale established
by the Anglo-Normans.

Trim Visitor Centre

Town Hall, Castle St. ⊙*Open year-*
round Mon–Sat 9.30am–5.30pm, Sun,
Bank Hols 1–5pm; Oct–Apr Mon–Sat
10am–5pm. Last showing of "Power &
Glory" audiovisual 1hr before closing.
⊚*Multimedia exhibition €3.20.* ✕
☏*046 943 7227. www.meath.ie/*
Tourism.

The Power & Glory multimedia exhibition paints a vivid picture of the historical background of the impressive
medieval ruins of Trim.

Trim Castle★

South bank; access through the
Town Gate or along the river bank
from the bridge. (Dúchas). ⊙*Open*
mid-Mar–Sept daily 10am–6pm; Oct
9.30am–5.30pm.Nov–Jan Sat–Sun
9am–5pm; Feb–mid-Mar 9.30am–
5.30pm. 📷*Castle keep visit by guided*
tour (45min) only (winter tour at 11am).
⊚*€4. Site is extremely busy in summer,*
so come early. ☏*046 943 8619.*
www.heritageireland.ie.

This magnificent medieval castle overlooks the meadows beside the Boyne,
whose waters fed the now-dry moat. An
outer curtain wall with gatehouses and
several towers encloses a broad grassy
space dominated by the formidable
keep (1225) with its two great halls and
sleeping accommodation above.

Trim Castle

© S. Vidler / Prisma / age fotostock

The Pale

In medieval times the Irish living outside Anglo-Norman jurisdiction were "beyond the Pale", from the Latin *palus* for a stake, as applied to a fence (made from palings). The settlement, under Henry II (1154–89), comprised Louth, Meath, Trim, Dublin, Kilkenny, Tipperary, Waterford and Wexford; by the late 15C, as English control weakened, the Pale included Louth, Meath, Dublin and Kildare.

The first stronghold here was built in 1172, in the early days of the Anglo-Norman conquest by Hugh de Lacy, but was soon attacked and destroyed by the native Irish. Rebuilt, it served as King John's headquarters on his sojourn in Ireland and is often called King John's Castle. Protected by two drawbridges and a barbican, the Dublin Gate served as a prison, where the young prince who was to become Henry IV was held prisoner by Richard II. The castle was attacked by Cromwell's troops, who left a breach in the river wall; an adjacent stretch of wall collapsed in 1839, in the course of a storm known as the "Big Wind". Across the river stands a stone arch, the medieval **Sheep Gate**, a fragment of the town's medieval walls; tolls were levied here on flocks bought and sold at the great sheep fairs.

Yellow Steeple

North bank; access from the High Street.
The ruined late-14C tower, which gleams in the sun, marks the site of **St Mary's Abbey**, an Augustinian community, founded by St Malachy of Armagh in the 12C near the point where St Patrick landed in the 5C and converted Foitchern, son of the local chieftain and later first Bishop of Trim. Many pilgrims were attracted to the abbey by Our Lady of Trim, a wooden statue with a reputation for effecting miracles, which disappeared in the Cromwellian period.

In 1425 the west cloisters of the abbey were converted by Lord Lieutenant Talbot into a fortified house, **Talbot's Castle**, which bears the Talbot coat of arms on the north wall. After the Reformation the house became a Latin School, later attended by the young Duke of Wellington, sometime MP for Trim, whose family home was at Dangan *(southeast)*. Unlike many other members of the Ascendancy, the Iron Duke was not particularly proud of his origins, famously denigrating his Irishness by declaring "because a man is born in a stable, it does not make him a horse."

Cathedral

1mi/1.6km east at Newtown Trim.
Among the graves of Newtown Cemetery is a **tomb** bearing the recumbent figures of Sir Luke Dillon, in his Renaissance armour, and his wife, Lady Jane Bathe, in an Elizabethan gown. Separated by a sword, they are referred to as "the jealous man and woman", Lady Jane supposedly having deceived her husband with his brother. People leave pins on the tomb in the belief that their warts will disappear.

Farther west are the lovely ruins of a **cathedral** built early in the 13C to replace the church at Clonard *(southwest)*, which was burned by the Irish at the end of the 12C. To the Southwest, further remains are those of a priory, two walls of its refectory still standing next to the 14C kitchen.

Crutched Friary

1mi/1.6km E at Newtown Trim.
On the south bank of the Boyne are the ruins of a 13C hospital built by the Crutched Friars, an order of mendicant friars who wore a cross on their habits. The buildings consist of a keep with several fireplaces, a ruined chapel with a triple-light window, and the hospital and stores beside the river.

BECTIVE ABBEY★

5mi/8km NE by R161 (T26). After 4mi/6.4km turn right. Park beyond the abbey near the bridge.
The impressive and extensive ruins stand in a field on the west bank of the Knightsbrook River. The abbey, one of

the earliest Cistercian houses in Ireland, was founded in 1150 by the King of Meath, Murcha Ó Maolsheachlainn, and dedicated to the Blessed Virgin; its abbot was a member of the Parliament of the Pale and Hugh de Lacy was buried here in 1195. Little remains of the 12C buildings. The **cloisters**, the tower and the great hall in the South Wing date from the 15C when the buildings were altered and fortified.

The film *Braveheart* (1996) was partly shot among these ruins and at Dunsoghly Castle.

KELLS★

12mi/20km west of Slane on R163.
🅸*Headfort Place.* ✆*046 9248 856.*
www.meath.ie/Tourism.

This little market town, a designated Heritage Town in the valley of the River Blackwater, owes its fame to the wonderful illuminated manuscript now in the library of Trinity College, Dublin. A perfect (modern) copy of it is on display in the tourist office.

The town also retains some fascinating relics of the monastery from which the Book of Kells was taken, and a courthouse and a church designed by the Georgian architect Francis Johnston.

A Bit of History

The Book of Kells – The monastery at Kells (Ceanannas Mór) was founded by St Columba in the 6C. In the 9C his relics were brought here by monks fleeing the Viking raids on Iona. Even here they were not secure and Kells itself was attacked by the Vikings, by the native Irish in the 12C and by the Scotsman, Edward Bruce, in the 14C. The great illuminated manuscript may have been produced at Kells or brought here from Iona. In 1007 it was stolen from the sacristy but found two months later minus its gold ornament. During Cromwell's campaigns, it was taken to Dublin for safe keeping and presented to Trinity College in 1661, where it has stayed ever since.

Round Tower and one of the high crosses

© Fáilte Ireland

Round Tower and High Crosses★★

St Columba's Church, Market St.
♿🕐*Church open daily outside service times.* 🗣*information for a self-guided tour of the site is avaliable from the tourist office.*

Parts of the monastery survive in the grounds of **St Columba's Anglican Church**. The **round tower**, built before 1076, has lost its conical cap, but still rises to an impressive height (100ft/30m). A number of well-weathered heads adorn the doorway.

Next to the tower stands the **South Cross**, considered to be from the 9C. The lively biblical scenes, among the interlacing, foliage, birds and animals include Daniel in the Lions' Den, the Three Children in the Fiery Furnace, Cain and Abel and Adam and Eve; the Sacrifice of Isaac, St Paul and St Antony in the desert, David with his harp, the miracle of the loaves and fishes, the Crucifixion and Christ in Judgement. South of the church stands an unfinished cross with raised panels ready to be carved and the Crucifixion.

Detailed information about the monastery, the crosses, the Kells Crozier (in the British Museum) and the Book of Kells is displayed in the gallery of the church.

Dark Ages Missionary

St Kilian was born in the 7C in Mullagh, Co Cavan and was educated at the monastic school in Rosscarbery, Co Cork. As a pilgrim for Christ, he went to Würzburg in Franconia to make Christian converts. Legend has it that he disapproved of the local ruler, Gozbert (one of his converts) marrying his brother's wife. As a result he had St Kilian beheaded. In 782 his remains were moved to Marienberg.

St Columcille's House★

Key available: enquire at the tourist office.

Higher up the lane stands a beautifully preserved ancient stone oratory with a steep corbelled stone roof, probably from the 11C/12C. The original entrance is visible in the west wall; the intervening floor is missing; between the ceiling vault and the steep roof is a tiny chamber *(access by ladder)*.

St Kilian's Heritage Centre, Mullagh

8mi/13km north of Kells by R 164.
Open Easter–Oct Tue–Fri 10am–6pm, Sat–Sun, Bank Hol Mon 2pm–6pm.
€3. 046 924 2433.

This centre celebrates the life of St Kilian (640–689), born in Mullagh, the "Apostle of the Franks" and patron saint of Würzburg. Maps, photographs, statuettes, manuscript facsimiles and art reproductions bring to life a glorious era in Irish Church history and the work of Irish missionaries in Europe in the 6th and 7th centuries. The exhibition also traces the development of Gaelic script for the Ogham writing of the 4th to the 7th centuries and the Wurzburg Glosses (the earliest example of written Irish c 750) to the illuminated script of the book of Kells.

North of Mullagh stands a ruined church known as Kilian's Church *(Teampall Ceallaigh)*. People still pray at his holy well, although formal observances ended early in the 19C.

Castlekeeran High Crosses

5mi/8km west of Kells by R 163.
After 3mi/5km turn right at the crossroads. Through the farmyard and across the field and stile.

The graveyard has three undecorated early crosses which pre-date the scriptural crosses at Kells; beside the yew tree stands an Ogham Stone. They mark the site of an early monastery which grew up around the hermitage of Kieran, a monk from Kells.

Loughcrew Gardens

15mi/24km from Kells by R 163 and R 154 and a minor road west to Millbrook.
Open Mar–Oct 12pm–6pm. €6. 049 854 1060. www.loughcrew.com.

Loughcrew Gardens are an extraordinary historically layered arrangemet of ruins, earthworks, and ancient avenues, once owned by the Plunkett family – including St Oliver Plunkett. Around the church (roofless) extends the skeleton of an early 17C formal garden with an avenue of venerable yew trees leading to a medieval motte.

Close by are the foundations of the original Loughcrew House, replaced in the early 19C by an imposing neo-Classical mansion devised by Charles Cockerell, which has also disappeared, although its portico survives as a folly beyond the gardens.

Loughcrew Cairns★

15mi/24km west of Kells by R 163.
Beyond Ballinlough bear right onto R 154. After 3mi/4.6km turn left; after 0.5mi/0.8km turn left again onto a narrow rough road. (Dúchas). Open early-Jun Thu–Mon only, then daily mid-Jun–Aug 10am–6pm. 049 854 1240. www.heritageireland.ie.
Steep climb to Cairn.

Far less famous than the Neolithic tombs of the Boyne valley, but almost as impressive, these passage tombs are prominently sited on the Loughcrew Mountains and are also known as

Loughcrew Cairns

© Tony Pleavin/Tourism Ireland

"The Hills/Mountain of the Witch". The cemetery covers the adjoining peaks, Cairnbane East and Cairnbane West, and Slieve na Calliagh (908ft/277m).

There are at least 30 graves, some of which have been excavated, most dating from 2500–2000 BC. In 1943, however, excavations in Cairn H on Cairnbane West uncovered objects bearing Iron Age La Tène style decoration.

Inside **Cairn T** (120ft/37m in diameter), the largest grave, lies a cruciform chamber, a corbelled roof and concentric circles, zigzag lines and floral motifs; some of the most beautiful examples of Neolithic art in Ireland.

During the Vernal and Autumn Equinox crowds gather in Cairn T at dawn to watch sunlight enter the chamber and illuminate the inside of the tomb.

The owner of the land on Carnbane West where Cairn L is located does not permit public access to the site.

Visit www.mythicalireland.com for more information and images on the cairns at Loughcrew.

The Last Catholic Martyr to Die in England

Oliver Plunkett (1629–81) was a member of a notable Anglo-Irish family from Loughcrew in Co Meath. Educated in Rome, Plunkett was appointed Archbishop of Armagh and Primate of Ireland in 1670. Using family connections with the establishment, he used his authority to reverse years of neglect following the Cromwellian era and the Penal Laws, travelling extensively in the North of Ireland. In his wake, a school for pupils of all ages was set up, priests were ordained and bishops annointed.

Repression following the marriage of Charles II's brother, James Duke of York, to the Roman-Catholic Mary of Modena, prompted Plunkett to go into hiding. Anti-monarchists in London accused him of complicity in the "Popish Plot" fabricated by Titus Oates and implicated in the organisation of an invasion of 40,000 men in Carlingford. He was arrested in 1679 and brought to trial in Dundalk but no one would give evidence against him. Convicted of treason in London, he was condemned to be hanged, drawn and quartered at Tyburn. He was canonised in 1975.

ADDRESSES

DROGHEDA

STAY

⊖ **Killowen House** – *Woodgrange, Dublin Rd.* ℘*041 983 3547. www.killowen house.com.* This modern two-storey house just south of town, occupies a three quarters acre site and offers comfortable, spacious, airy well-appointed bedrooms.

⊖–⊖⊖ **The Westcourt Hotel** – *West St.* ℘*041 983 0965. www.westcourt.ie. 27rm.* A major refurbishment in 2011 has transformed, the Westcourt Hotel into a smart designer hotel and guests have free access to the vibrant Earth nightclub. Beware possibility of noise.

Ⓨ/EAT

⊖ **The Black Bull Inn** – *Dublin Rd.* ℘*041 983 7139. www.blackbullinn.ie.* Local pub serving traditional Irish and Modern Irish cooking.

⊖ **Wm Cairnes & Son Gastropub** – *The D Hotel, Scotch Hall, Marsh Rd.* ℘*041 980 6464. www.wmcairnes.com.* Traditional favourites, gourmet burgers and contemporary European dishes are served in this lively space (set in the old Cairnes Brewery) in the city's top hotel.

⊖⊖ **Eastern Seaboard Bar & Grill** – *Bryanstown Centre, Dublin Rd. Booking advisable.* ℘*041 980 2570. www.glasgow-diaz.com.* Quirky, highly likeable (and popular) contemporary American themed restaurant, serving excellent well-priced modern dishes on a very informal choose-what-you-like menu, from crab cakes to pig cheeks.

⊖⊖⊜ **Brabazon** – *Tankardstown House, Slane, 9 mi (14km) west of Drogheda. Booking advisable. Dinner & Sun lunch.* ℘*041 982 4621. www.tankardstown.ie.* Rustic restaurant set in the former piggery of the manor house, with modern interior, painted wooden tables and beautiful terrace overlooking the landscaped courtyard. Superb contemporary cooking.

PUBS

Peter Matthews (McPhails)– *9 Laurence St.* ℘*041 983 7371.* A very lively pub with original features dating back over 100 years. Live music and a beer garden attract locals in large numbers.

SHOPPING

Millmount Craft Centre *by Martello Tower. Open Tue–Sat, 10am–1.30pm, 2.30 –5pm.* ℘*041 984 1960.* Designers and craftsmen working from their studios: jewellery, hand-painted silks, ceramics and knitwear.

SPORTS & LESIURE

Extensive beaches at Bettystown (south).

KELLS

STAY

⊖–⊖⊖ **Headfort Arms Hotel** – *Headfort Pl.* ℘*046 924 0063. www. headfortarms.ie.* A smart blend of old and new with comfortable, often large bedrooms, spa facilities and the excellent Vanilla Pod restaurant (◑*see below*).

Ⓨ/EAT

⊖⊖ **Vanilla Pod Restaurant** – *Headfort Arms Hotel, Headfort Pl.* ℘*046 924 0063. www.headfortarms.ie.* The "Pod" has been serving International and Irish cuisine in a contemporary bistro setting for over a decade . The menu is seasonal and includes some terrific specialities - the locally reared lamb is a stand-out.

TRIM

STAY

⊖⊖ **Knightsbrook Hotel**– *Trim.* ℘*046 948 2100. www.knightsbrook.com. 27rm.* Set in sweeping parklands, just outside Trim, on the Dublin Road, this highly popular luxury golf and spa resort hotel offers all mod cons and facilities.

Ⓨ/EAT

⊖⊖ **Franzini O'Briens** – *next to Trim Castle.* ℘*046 943 1002. www.franzinis.com.* Varied International food in this eaterie, popular with locals and visitors.

EVENTS AND FESTIVALS

Opera in Loughcrew Gardens – Two performances under canvas in late July. ℘*49 85 41356. www.loughcrew.com.*

Dundalk★ and the Cooley Peninsula★

At the head of Dundalk Bay, midway between Dublin and Belfast, Dundalk *(Dún Dealgan)* is one of the country's largest urban centres, with a harbour and a range of industries. It makes a good centre for exploring the many attractions of the nearby coast and countryside. Apart from the town itself, the chief attraction of this area is the Cooley Peninsula.

DUNDALK★

In medieval times it was fortified by the Anglo-Normans, who used it as a base for incursions into the Gaelic strongholds of Ulster; subsequent repeated attacks and sieges have left little early heritage intact.

> ▶ **Population:** 37,816.
> 🔢 **Info:** Market Sq. ☏042 935 2111. www.discoverireland.ie/eastcoast.
> ◐ **Location:** Dundalk is served by the main road *(N 1)* north up the coast to the border with Northern Ireland.
> 👓 **Don't Miss:** Carlingford and the Cooley Peninsula

Dundalk was comprehensively re-planned in Georgian times by the then owner, James, 1st Earl of Clanbrassil. To the south of the bridge over the Castletown River *(Church Street)* stands one of the few reminders of the place's medieval past, the 14C tower of **St Nicholas' Church** (Anglican); the church was rebuilt in 1707 and later given a spire by Francis Johnston.

The **Courthouse** *(south)* is a formidably austere neo-Classical structure with a Doric portico, designed by Park and Bowden in 1813.

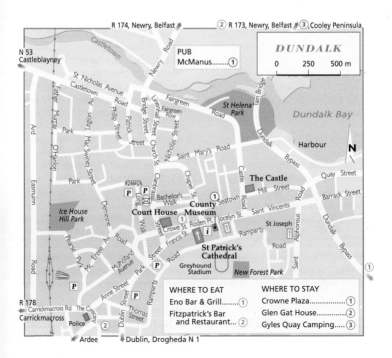

An elaborate porch-screen (*Roden Place – east*) leads to **St Patrick's RC Cathedral**, modelled on King's College Chapel in Cambridge; the sanctuary and the side chapels are richly decorated with mosaics.

County Museum Dundalk

Jocelyn St. ○*Open Tue–Sat 10am–5pm.* ℘*042 932 7056. www.dundalkmuseum.ie*
A restored 18C warehouse houses a clear and comprehensive review of local history (archaeological finds, farming and industry, the port and railway) through audio-visual presentations, touch-screens, films and graphics.

🚗 DRIVING TOURS

COOLEY PENINSULA★
Approx 34mi/55km round tour.

The Cooley Peninsula is a mountainous granite promontory, providing magnificent landscapes and seascapes – *(south)* over Dundalk Bay and – *(north)* over Carlingford Lough to the glorious outline of the Mourne Mountains in Northern Ireland. This is excellent walking country and features in many a legend; in particular it is associated with Cuchulain, hero of the epic tale, *The Cattle Raid of Cooley (Táin bo Cuainlge).*
Fine sandy beaches stud the edge of Carlingford Lough.

▶ Take the N 1 N and R 173 E.

Proleek Dolmen★
Ballymascanlon Hotel. 20min return on foot through the yard and along the tarmac path between the fields.
A massive capstone (35 tonnes) resting on two tall supporting stones (portals) and a third smaller one at the back dates from 3000 BC; according to legend the wish will be granted of anyone who can make three pebbles land on the top. Nearby is a wedge-shaped gallery grave.

▶ Continue E and turn left into the mountain road north to Omeath.

Windy Gap★★
The road climbs towards Carlingford Mountain (1,932ft/587m). Beyond the site of the Long Woman's Grave *(plaque)* the road enters the aptly named **Windy Gap**, a narrow pass between rocky crags; fine view south over Dundalk Bay. Farther north is a **viewpoint** overlooking the mouth of Newry River at Warrenpoint and the Mourne Mountains rising from the eastern shore.

Omeath
Once a Gaelic-speaking fishing village, Omeath is now a little resort with a rocky shoreline, where one can savour freshly caught seafood. In summer, jaunting cars carry fares to the outdoor Stations of the Cross at the monastery of the Rosminian Fathers and the Carlingford Lough Ferry plies across the border to Warrenpoint.

▶ From Omeath take the coast road R 173 S.

Carlingford★
Viking and Norman monuments add to the charm of this attractive resort at the foot of the Cooley Mountains, facing the Mourne Mountains across Carlingford Lough (marina and boat trips). Carlingford oysters are a local delicacy with an international reputation.
Local history is traced on great triptychs in the **Carlingford Heritage Centre** (○*open Mon–Fri 9.30am–1pm, 1.30–4.30pm/summer 2–5pm;* ○*closed Bank Hols;* ℘*042 937 3888; www.carlingfordheritagecentre.com*), housed in the deconsecrated Anglican church; the starting point for a guided tour of the town centre. Spanning the main street is the **Tholsel**, a gateway once three storeys high, where Parliament is said to have promulgated laws for the Pale. South of the town square stands a 15C fortified house *(right)* decorated with Celtic mouldings; although it is known as the **Mint**, there is no proof that the local mint, founded in 1467, ever operated there. Overlooking the harbour is **Taaffe's Castle**, a late-15C square tower fortified with machicolations,

Carlingford

© Fáilte Ireland

crenellations, arrow slits and murder holes; the vaulted basement may have been a boat-house since the tide used to reach the foundations. It was built by the Taaffe family, created Earls of Carlingford in 1661. The ruins of **King John's Castle** stand on a bluff north of the harbour commanding the entrance to Carlingford Lough.

▶ Return to Dundalk on the R 173.

BETWEEN THE FANE AND THE DEE
Approx 31mi/50km round tour

▶ From Dundalk take the R 171 SW to Louth.

St Mochta's House★
It is hard to believe that little Louth was once the centre of the 11C/12C Kingdom of Oriel. In a field behind the ruins of a Franciscan friary (14C–15C) stands a stone oratory with a **corbelled roof**, which has been much restored; it is said to have been built in a night as a resting place for St Mochta, who died in 534.

▶ From Louth take the minor road N via Chanonrock to Inniskeen.

Inniskeen
The village is the birthplace of **Patrick Kavanagh** (1904–67), poet, author and journalist, who is buried in the old churchyard; his life and work are presented in the **Patrick Kavanagh Centre** (◷*open early Mar–20 Dec, Tue–Fri 11am–4.30pm (Jun–Sept also Sun 3–5.30pm);* ◷*closed mid-Dec–early Mar;* ◷€5; ℘042 937 8560; www.patrickkavanaghcountry.com), alongside information about the local history. The remains of a round tower mark the site of a 6C monastery founded by St Daig beside the Fane River.

▶ From Inniskeen take the road W to Carrickmacross.

Carrickmacross
Known today as a good angling centre, the town grew up round a castle built by the Earl of Essex, to whom the land was granted by Elizabeth I.
For two centuries it has enjoyed a reputation for hand-made lace: the **Carrickmacross Lace Gallery** (*Market Square at the north end of the main street;* ◷*open Tues–Fri 10am–5.30pm (4pm Sat, Mon);* ◷*closed Bank Hols, 25 Dec–1 Jan;* ℘042 966 4176; www.carrickmacrosslace.ie) displays examples of the local "mixed lace", composed of cambric patterns applied to machine net and embellished with point stitches and loops.
The Roman-Catholic church (1866) was designed by J.J. McCarthy, with stained glass (1925) by Harry Clarke.

▶ Take R 179 SW to Kingscourt.

Dún A' Rí Forest Park★

The forest park, until 1959 part of the Cabra estate, is set in a valley beside the Cabra River.

A **nature trail** and four signposted **walks** provide access to the red deer enclosure, a waterfall downstream from Cromwell's Bridge, a wishing well, Cabra Cottage – the Pratt family mansion until Cabra Castle *(east)* was built in 1814 – a ruined flax mill, an ice house and the ruins of Fleming's Castle (1607) – named after an Anglo-Norman family, who lost their land for supporting James II.

▶ Take R 165 SE via Drumcondra; at the crossroads turn left into N 52.

Ardee (Baile Átha Fhirdhia)

The name means the Ford of Ferdia. On the east side of the main street stand two fortified buildings: **Hatch's Castle**, a late-medieval fortified house, and **Ardee Castle**, built in 1207 by Roger de Peppard, though much of the present building dates from the 15C.

ADDRESSES

DUNDALK

🏠 STAY

🛏 **Glengat Guesthouse** – *18/19 The Crescent. ☎042 933 7938. www.glengat house.com.* Very popular characterful period house with a tranquil atmosphere and friendly helpful family hosts.

🛏 **Crowne Plaza** – *Inner Relief Rd., Green Pk. ☎042 93 94 900, www.cpireland. crowneplaza.com. 129 rm.* A favourite among business travellers during the week this modern 14-storey high chain hotel boasts good facilities and a restaurant on the top floor with stirring views over the Cooley Mountains and sea beyond. Good value.

🛏 **Innisfree Guest House** – *Carrick Rd. ☎042 933 4912. www.innisfreehouse.ie. 5rm.* A town house built around a century ago and offering a comfortable night's stay. Strictly non-smoking premises.

CAMPING

Gyles Quay Camping – *Riverstown. 12mi/16km north on the R173. Follow the signs for Carlingford for 7mi/11km, turn right for Gyles Quay. Mar–Sept. ☎042 937 6262. €22 per tent.* A large area (3.24ha/8acre), mostly devoted to mobile homes but also with space for camping.

🍴 EAT

🍽 **Fitzpatrick's Bar & Restaurant** – *Rockmarshall, Jenkinstown. 5mi/8km north of Dundalk, reached by taking the road to Carlingford. ☎042 937 6193.* A pretty pub and restaurant with lots of character, flower-filled beer garden and a choice of settings for a meal or drink. Expect the usual International-Irish pub-style menu. Great for outdoor drinks in the summer.

🍽 **Eno Bar & Grill** – *5 Roden Pl., ☎042 935 5467. www.eno.ie. Closed Mon.* A stylish and comfortable family bistro serving Mediterranean food. The impressive wood-fired oven takes centre stage so the emphasis is on pizza, but there's plenty more besides. Cocktails upstairs.

PUBS

McManus' – *Seatown. ☎041 42 933 1632.* A lively traditional pub with lots of live music (the Corrs started here).

SIGHTSEEING

Historical walking tour – Dundalk has a marked heritage trail for visitors to follow – details from the tourist office.

SPORTS AND LEISURE

Táin Trail – Long-distance footpath *(19mi/30km)* encircling the **Cooley Peninsula** starting and finishing in Carlingford.

Sailing – Dundalk and Carlingford Sailing Club ☎042 937 3238; carlingford-sailingclub.net

Riding – Ravensdale Lodge offers tuition, trails and hacking ☎042 937 1034; www.ravensdalelodge.com

Beaches – South at **Blackrock**, north at **Clogherhead** (Long Strand) and northeast on the Cooley Peninsula at **Giles Quay**, facing south, and at **Omeath**, on the shore of **Carlingford Lough**. The salt-marshes and mud-flats *(east)* are a vast **bird sanctuary**.

EVENTS AND FESTIVALS

Annual Patrick Kavanagh Weekend
(last weekend Sept) – Celebration of the
poet Patrick Kavanagh, held at the Patrick
Kavanagh Centre in Inniskeen. *042
937 8560.*

INNISKEEN

STAY

◶ **Gleneven Guest House** – *Inniskeen.*
042 937 8294. www.gleneven.com. 5rm.
A traditional-looking, Georgian-style
house with spacious rooms and a
rural setting.

CARLINGFORD

STAY AND EAT

◶ **Ghan House** – *Carlingford. 042 937
3682. www.ghanhouse.com. 12rm.* An
18C-house on the edge of the village,
with hard-to-beat views of the Mourne
Mountains. The bedrooms are full
of character, four of which are in the
main house. The superb meals at the
restaurant (◶◶) are very much part
of the Ghan House experience and it
is open to non-residents (booking is
advisable in the summer months). To
underline the importance of food here,
there is also a cookery school attached
to the hotel.

Co Kildare★

Kildare is rich in farmland and home
to the Curragh and National Stud.
Its great age as a settled area is
attested by the Celtic crosses which
are scattered around the county
and its importance as an Anglo-Irish
settlement is written in the many
Georgian buildings.

KILDARE★

*Kildare town is situated on the main
road (N 7) leading southwest from
Dublin to Limerick.*
Kildare *(Cill Dara)* is intimately associated
with the nearby Curragh; the extensive plain
covered in short springy turf and famous
for horse racing and breeding. This neat
little county, cathedral and Heritage Town,
traces its origins to the 5C religious community founded by St Brigid and St Conleth;
one of the few convents for women in the
Celtic period.

St Brigid's Cathedral &
Round Tower★

*Market Sq. Open May–Sept Mon–Sat
10am–1pm, 2pm–5pm. Sun 2pm–5pm
Round Tower €7. 045 441 654.*
Kildare Cathedral is a late-19C building
incorporating 13C sections, a medieval
stone font, stained-glass windows, and a
number of tombs with effigies, including
the superb figure of Bishop Wellesly, dating

▶ **Population:** 222,130.
Info: Heritage Centre.
Market Sq., **Kildare** 045
530 672. Athy 059 863
3075. www.discoverireland.
ie/visit-kildare-wicklow.
http://kildare.ie.
◔ **Location:** Bordering
Co Dublin, served by M4,
M7 and M9 roads.
◉ **Don't Miss:** A visit to the
Irish National Stud or
looking over the
magnificent interior of
Castletown House.

from around 1539. Beside the cathedral
stands a **round tower** (108ft/30m high
– the tallest climbable tower in Ireland)
which has been substantially restored in
recent years. Opposite, a small road leads
to **St Brigid's shrine** and **well**.

Kildare Heritage Centre

*Market Sq. Open Mon–Sat 9.30am–
1pm, 2–5.00pm; 045 530 672.
www.kildareheritage.com.*
The history and heritage of Kildare are
clearly described through video and sto-
ryboards in the beautifully restored 18C
Market House, which is also home to the
Kildare tourist office.

169

Irish National Stud

© Brian Morrison/Tourism Ireland

EXCURSIONS

Irish National Stud and Japanese Gardens★★

1mi/1.5km SE of Kildare (sign) at Tully. ₺ Open mid-Feb–Nov 9.00am–6pm. Last admission 5pm. Guided tours of Stud available daily 10.30am, noon, 2.00pm, 4pm (35min). €12.50. 045 522 963.
www.irishnationalstud.ie.

Lord Wavertree, a wealthy Scotsman from a brewing family, began breeding horses at Tully in 1900; in 1915 he gave his stud to the British Crown and it continued as the British National Stud until it was handed over to the Irish Government in 1943.

The **Irish Horse Museum** traces the story of horse racing in Ireland and contains the skeleton of Arkle, an outstandingly successful racehorse during the 1960s. A video "Birth of a Foal", made on the Stud, is available to view and a stroll down the **Tully Walk** to see any mares and foals that might be out and about is a good idea.

The grounds contain a large lake, created by Eida (see below), and the ruins of the **Black Abbey**, founded as a preceptory of the Knights Hospitaller of St John after the Anglo-Norman invasion of Ireland in 1169. According to tradition it is connected by a tunnel (1mi/1.5km) to Kildare Cathedral. When the abbey was suppressed in the mid-16C, it passed into the possession of the Sarsfield family, of which **Patrick Sarsfield** was leader

of the Irish at the Siege of Limerick. Among the most ambitious of their kind outside Japan, the **Japanese Gardens** were created for Lord Wavertree between 1906 and 1910 by the Japanese gardener **Eida** and his son Minoru. The main garden depicts the story of the life of man, beginning with the **Gate of Oblivion** and the **Cave of Birth**, continuing across the bridges of engagement and marriage to the **Hill of Ambition** and the **Well of Wisdom**. Formerly the concluding feature, the **Gateway to Eternity** now leads into the **Garden of Eternity** (1974) and onto the **Zen meditation garden** (1976), where visitors might pause for contemplation. **St. Fiachra's Garden**, which celebrates the patron saint of gardeners, recreates the type of natural environment which inspired the spirituality of the monastic movement in Ireland during the 6C and 7C. Seeking to capture the power of the Irish landscape in its rawest state, this rock and water garden is within a natural setting of woodlands, wetlands, lakes and islands.

Bog of Allen Nature Centre★

12mi/19km N by R 401 and R 414 at Lullymore. ₺ Open Mon (exc bank hols)–Fri 9am–5pm (last entry 4pm), also special weekends (see website). Closed Christmas. €5 donation requested. 045 860133. www.ipcc.ie/visitor-attraction.

Bog Allen is the largest complex of raised bog in Ireland. As the visitor centre will tell you, 90 percent of this fragile eco-system has been lost through drainage and mining over the past four centuries.

Hill of Allen
6mi/10km N by R 415.
The summit of a 19C tower (676ft/206m) provides **views** of the vast Bog of Allen stretching west to the Shannon.

Robertstown *(Inis Robertaig)*
10mi/16km N by R 415.
This tranquil village is strategically located where the Grand Canal divides bound for Waterford and the Shannon. The water-front is dominated by the stately red-brick **Canal Hotel**, built in 1803 to serve the passengers on the flyboats.

Punchestown Standing Stone
15mi/24km E by N 7 to Naas and R 411.
North of the famous racecourse stands a granite long stone (20ft/6m high), which is thought to date from the early Bronze Age.

MAYNOOTH
Maynooth is 18 mi/30km west of Dublin on the Grand Canal, and main roads out of the capital; bypassed by the M 4.
Maynooth is synonymous with the great seminary which for more than 200 years, has prepared priests for the Roman Catholic Church. Today it is a growing commuter and university town, with transport con-nections to Dublin.

Maynooth Castle
Open May-Sep, Wed-Sun (including Bank Holidays) 10am–6pm. Access to the keep by guided tour only, last tour 4.30pm before closing. 01 628 6744. www.heritageireland.ie.
The ruins of the 12C Fitzgerald castle predate the period when the Earls of Kildare reached pre-eminence serving as Lord Deputy from 1471 to 1534. Dur-ing this time Maynooth was effectively the political capital of Ireland. In 1535, following the Silken Thomas rebellion of 1534, it was successfully besieged by the royal forces and Thomas was executed. In 1656, the castle was aban-doned in favour of a new residence at Carton House. There is an exhibition in the Keep on the history of the castle and the family.

St Patrick's College, Maynooth
Open: Visitor Centre May–Sept Mon–Fri, 11am–5pm; Sat–Sun 2–6pm. 01 708 4700. www.maynoothcollege.ie
St Patrick's College is Ireland's National Seminary and Pontifical University. The history of the college, town and district is presented in the **Visitor Centre**, which organises guided tours of the Chapel, Stoyte House, the Pugin build-ing and the gardens. The latter includes the Silken Thomas Yew – Ireland's oldest native tree, magnificent magnolias and Dawn Redwoods, billed as "Maynooth's living fossils".
St Patrick's College was founded in 1795 by refugee French priests on the aca-demic staff. Since then, it has educated churchmen who have served congre-gations throughout the British Empire, most notably across India, China and Africa. In 1966, the first lay students were admitted.
The college is laid out around two spa-cious courtyards: the first dates from the early 19C, the second is one of Pugin's finest Gothic Revival projects, completed in mid-century despite the Great Famine and inadequate fund-ing. The Chapel, with its tall spire and splendid oak choir stalls, are by Pugin's pupil, J.J. McCarthy. The grounds also include the **National Science Museum** (open May–Sept Tue, Thu 2pm–4pm, Sun 2pm–6pm; Oct–Apr by appoint-ment; €4; 01 708 3576; www.nuim. ie/museum) displaying scientific and ecclesiastical artefacts.

EXCURSIONS
Castletown House★★
Celbridge; 4mi/6.4km SE of Maynooth by a minor road. (Dúchas) Open Mar-Nov, 10am-5pm, last admission 4pm. €8. 01 628 8252. www.castletown.ie.
At the time of its completion in 1722, this great Palladian mansion was the largest private house in Ireland, setting a precedent for scores of other palatial residences. The final result, facing south

Castletown House

© Mark Wesley/Tourism Ireland

over the Liffey valley to the Wicklow Mountains, consists of a 13-bay central block by the Italian architect Alessandrio Galilei, linked by curving colonnades to two pavilions designed by Sir Edward Lovett Pearce: all built for William "Speaker" Connolly (*see 'Speaker Conolly' box*), reputedly the richest commoner in Ireland.

Work on Castletown's sumptuous interiors spanned two generations. The original decorative scheme, using only local wood and stone, is preserved in the Brown Study (tall and narrow oak doors and pine panelling).

The Lafranchini brothers transformed the stairwell with exuberant stuccowork, Sir William Chambers gave the ground-floor rooms a neo-Classical decor, the print room was hung with Old Master prints, and the magnificent Long Gallery was modelled on Pompeii and provided with hand-blown chandeliers from Venice.

Castletown Follies

The extraordinary **Castletown Obelisk**, also known as the **Conolly Folly** *(visible from the windows of the Long Gallery and from the Maynooth–Castletown road)*, north of the house, comprises two tiers of arches designed by Richard Castle. It was erected in memory of Speaker Conolly by his wife, in part to provide employment during the severe winter of 1739.

The **Wonderful Barn** *(private)* which closes the northeast vista *(3mi/5km east via the R 403 and R 404)* was built in 1743. The conical structure, with an external spiral staircase and four diminishing brick domes, was used for drying and storing grain.

The Steam Museum & Lodge Park Walled Garden

5mi/8km south of Maynooth on the R 406. ○*Open May & Sep, Sat-Sun and Bank Hols 2pm-6pm, Jun–Aug, Fri–Sun and Bank Hols 2pm–6pm. Engines steamed up on Sun.* €7.50. ✕ ☏*01 628 8412. www.steam-museum.com.*

The restored 18C garden attached to the Palladian house *(private)* built in 1773

"Speaker" Conolly

William Conolly (1662–1729) was a lawyer of humble origins from Ballyshannon, who made a fortune from shrewd dealing in forfeited estates after the Battle of the Boyne. Member of Parliament for Donegal in 1692, Commissioner of the Revenue in 1709, he was elected Speaker of the Irish House of Commons in 1715, becoming one of the country's most powerful politicians.

provides quite a contrast to the Gothic-Revival church used by the engineers of the old Great Southern & Western Railway. Transferred from Inchicore, near Dublin, it now holds the Model Hall in which a fascinating collection of over 20 18C–20C locomotives are displayed. In the Power Hall is an array of engines that once powered mills, distilleries and breweries, and a steamship.

Coolcarrigan Gardens

10mi/16km SW of Maynooth.
&@*Limited opening Mar–Oct, phone or see website for dates and admission prices.* &*045 863 527. www.coolcarrigan.ie.*
The parkland laid out in the 19C has been enriched by subsequent planting. Roses and herbaceous borders add colour to the formal gardens near the handsome Victorian house. The **glasshouse** hosts a vine, a passion flower, peaches and nectarines. At the end of the **woodland walk** *(30min)* there is a fine view across the Bog of Allen. The **church** (1881) is in the Hiberno-Romanesque revival style and decorated with stained glass.

ATHY

Athy stands on the N 78, and the county boundary between Kildare and Carlow.
Athy is a bustling centre for an extensive rural area and attracts streams of visitors looking to cruise, sail and fish the River Barrow, the Barrow Line and the Grand Canal.

Town Centre

Facing onto the main square housed in the mid-18C Courthouse and Town Hall is the **Athy Heritage Centre-Museum**(@*Open Mon–Fri 10am–5pm, Sat&Sun 12pm-4pm;* @€5; *Book in advance for guided tours* &*059 863 3075, www.athyheritagecentre-museum.ie*), which houses an information centre, a genealogy and heritage centre. It also celebrates the arctic explorer Sir Ernest Shackelton, born locally.

🚗 DRIVING TOUR

EAST OF BARROW VALLEY
20mi/32km.

▶ From Athy take the N 67 E and a minor road (right) via Burtown.

Ballitore

The great Irish statesman and political theorist Edmund Burke (1729–97) was at school here.
The **House of Mary Leadbetter** now accommodates the Ballitore Library and a **Quaker Museum** (@*open Tue–Sat, noon–5pm;* ✗; &*059 862 3344, http://kildare.ie*) devoted to the life and times of Mary Leadbeater and other Quaker families associated with Ballitore from the 18C onwards.

▶ Take the N 9 S

Moone High Cross★

The scant ruins of a 6C monastery founded by **St Columba** enclose an unusual, early 9C high cross (17.5ft/5.3m high) with carved panels of biblical scenes: one shows the Feeding of the Five Thousand with five loaves, two highly stylised eels and a pair of smiling fish.

▶ Continue S by N 9 to Castledermot; continue 9.5mi/16km SE by R 418.

Castledermot High Crosses★

The site of a monastery founded by **St Dermot** is marked by two granite **high crosses** carved with biblical scenes and a 10C **round tower** topped by medieval battlements.

▶ From Castledermot take minor road E; in Graney turn left to Baltinglass.

Baltinglass

The main square of the tiny town is dominated by a memorial to Michael Dwyer, who escaped British soldiers in 1798, when his comrade Sam MacAllister selflessly drew their fire onto himself.

Beside the 19C Anglican church are the ruins of **Baltinglass Abbey**, founded in 1148 and suppressed in 1536: six Gothic nave arches, the 19C tower and parts of the original cloisters (restored) still stand.

ADDRESSES

KILDARE TOWN

STAY

⊜ **Lord Edward** – *Dublin St, Market Square.* ℘*045 522 232. www.lordedward kildare.com.* In the heart of Kildare town as part of the Silken Thomas complex of restaurants and bars, this cosy hotel sits in the shadow of an impressive Norman Castle that was once among the most important in Leinster. Good value bed and breakfast offers available.

⊜⊜ **Kildare House Hotel** – *Dublin Rd.* ℘*045 520 002. www.kildarehousehotel.com.* This recently renovated hotel boasts a stylish and modern new look while maintaining many hints at its more traditional and unpolished past.

⚏/EAT

⊜⊜ **Hartes of Kildare** – *Market Square.* ℘*045 533 557. www.harteskildare.ie.* A stylish and cosy gastropub which caters for both traditional and more contemporary tastes. The menu offers classic dishes with a modern twist a very reasonable price.

MAYNOOTH

STAY

⊜ **Ashford House** – *Enfield Rd., Kilcock.* ℘*01 628 7585. www.ashfordhousebnb.com.* Just north of Maynooth this peaceful and welcoming guesthouse maintains the feel of a typical Irish countryside homestead.

⊜⊜⊜ **Carton House Hotel** – *Dublin Rd.* ℘*01 505 2000. www.cartonhouse.com.* One of the premier hotels on the island where no expense is spared in providing beautifully restored decor and excellent service. The hotel often acts as a temporary home to the country's international soccer and rugby squads.

⚏/EAT

⊜⊜ **Bistro 53** – *Main St.* ℘*01 628 9001.* A new addition to the Kildare dining scene and already receiving national acclaim, this restaurant is relaxed and puts together some very impressive dishes. Excellent value early bird menu.

⊜⊜ **Avenue Café** – *Main St.* ℘*01 628 5003. www.avenuecafe.ie.* This restaurant-bar offers very contemporary cuisne alongside more traditional dishes in a relaxed, family-friendly setting. Regularly features live music.

NAAS

STAY

⊜ **Moate House** – *Rathmore, 5mi east of Naas.* ℘*045 862 154. www.moatehouse.ie.* This is a beautifully furnished country village guesthouse with a tennis court and indoor swimming pool available to guests.

⊜⊜ **Lawlors Hotel** – *Poplar Sq.* ℘*045 906 444. www.lawlors.ie.* This pretty boutique hotel in the heart of Naas acts as a perfect base camp for those visitors wishing to enjoy Dublin city as well as access the west of the country.

⊜⊜⊜ **The Kildare Hotel (The K Club)** – *Straffan, 8mi north of Naas.* ℘*01 6017 200. www.kclub.ie.* As part of the golfing resort which hosted the 2006 Ryder Cup on its Arnold Palmer designed course, this hotel is one of the most luxurious that Ireland has to offer. Also home to The River Room Restaurant (⊜⊜⊜), voted the best hotel restaurant in Ireland in 2013.

⚏/EAT

⊜⊜ **Vie de Châteaux** – *The Harbour.* ℘*045 888 478. www.viedechateaux.ie.* The home of fine dining in Kildare which aims to blend French culinary expertise and high quality Irish produce. Excellent value for this level of dining.

SHOPPING

Kildare Village Shopping Outlet. *Open Sat–Wed, 10am–7pm (8pm Thu, Fri).* ℘*045 520 501. www.kildarevillage.com.*

Wicklow Mountains★★★

The Wicklow Mountains, south of Dublin, provide high peaks and spectacular views, lakes, reservoirs and waterfalls, open moorland and verdant valleys, some landscaped into elegant gardens. The rolling heights are covered in peat bog, where the rivers form broad shallow treeless corridors; on the harder schist they create deep and narrow wooded gorges, like Dargle Glen, Glen of the Downs and Devil's Glen. In the past the mountains were even wilder and far less accessible than today and served as a refuge for outlaws and rebels; some of the 1798 insurgents found sanctuary here for several years, prompting the construction by the British of the Military Road. The mountains fall eastwards to the shingle ridge and sand dunes of the coast, with its string of resorts: Bray, Greystones, Wicklow and Arklow.

What helps to make the landscape of the Wicklow Mountains so attractive, in addition to the mountains, valleys and gorges, are the peat-covered areas, where purple-covered species of heather mix with the bright yellow of gorse. The close proximity to Dublin ensures a steady stream of walkers and motorists in the spring and summer months.

GLENDALOUGH★★★

Population: 257. Glendalough stands 30mi S of Dublin in the Wicklow Mountains and can be reached by the coast route (M 11 and N 11 S to Ashford and R 763 to Annamoe, R 755 S to Laragh and R 756 W or by the inland route (N 7, N 81 and R 756); slower but more scenic routes take the road through the Sally Gap (R 115) or via Enniskerry, Roundwood and Annamore (R 117, R 760, R 755 and R 756).

From Dublin take St Kevin's Bus Service, which departs from Dawson St. on the north side of St Stephen's Green, daily 11.30am and 6pm; from Bray at 12.10pm and 6.40pm. ℘01 281 8119.

Info: Fitzwilliam Sq., **Wicklow**; ℘0404 69117. **Arklow**; ℘0402 32484. www.wicklowmountains nationalpark.ie

Location: Extending south from Dublin for about 30m/48km as far as Arklow. Between the coast road (N 11) and the inland road (N 81) there is a network of steep and narrow country roads providing magnificent views of the lakes and moorland.

Kids: Powerscourt Waterfall, National Sea Life Centre, Bray, Clara Lara Fun Park and Wicklow Historic Gaol.

Don't Miss: Glendalough's monastic site. Bring a picnic; food is not available to buy on site. Powerscourt, Russborough.

www.glendaloughbus.com. Day tours are also operated by Bus Éireann.

This once-remote valley among the Wicklow Mountains, where St Kevin sought solitude and later founded a great monastery, has long been a place of pilgrimage. It continues to be one of Ireland's most popular sites and today attracts over one million visitors each year. Despite this, the "Glen of the Two Lakes" *(Gleann Dá Locha)* is one of the most evocative of all Irish monastic sites, both for the beauty of its setting and for the array of buildings left over from the early days of Christianity in Ireland. The monastery founded by St Kevin flourished long after his death (c. 617), drawing pilgrims deterred from journeying to Rome by war and conflict: seven pilgrimages to Glendalough were said to be the equivalent of one to Rome. Despite repeated raids and destruction by the Vikings and Irish, the monastery enjoyed a golden age in the 10C and

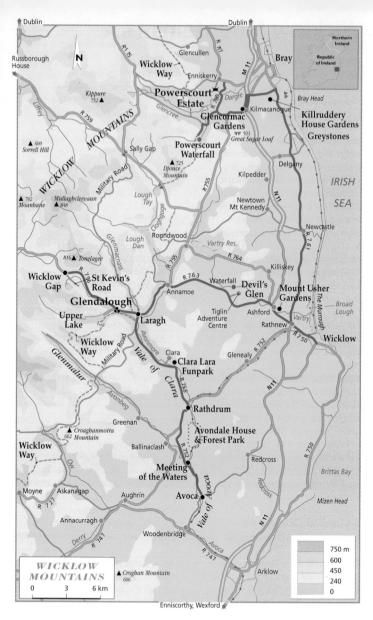

Enniscorthy, Wexford

11C, a period of Celtic revival. Glendalough also prospered under St Laurence O'Toole (1128–80), who became abbot in 1153 and Archbishop of Dublin in 1163. Decline began in the 13C and an English attack in 1398 caused much destruction. Dissolution followed during the reign of Henry VIII but the pilgrimages continued until disorderly behaviour caused their suppression in the 1860s. The two lakes at Glendalough, once one stretch of water, are set in a beautiful valley shaped by an Ice Age glacier descending from the Wicklow Mountains. The splendidly-wooded southern shore of the Upper Lake, associated with St Kevin, is particularly striking, with cliffs (100ft/30m) dropping precipi-

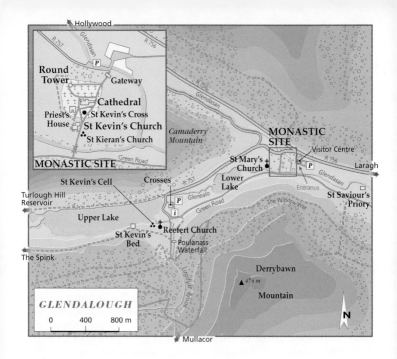

GLENDALOUGH

0   400   800 m

tously into the dark waters of the lake. For many years the area was mined, so the woods were cut to smelt the lead, zinc, iron, copper and silver ores. The Miners' Road, which runs along the northern shore of the lake to a deserted mining village at the top of the valley, provides the best view of St Kevin's Bed and the ruins of Temple-na-Skellig.

Visitor Centre

The spacious modern **visitor centre** (*Dúchas* &⏰ *open daily 9.30am–6pm (5pm mid-Oct–mid-Mar). Last admission 45min before closing.* ⏰*Closed 24–27 Dec.* ⊜€3. *www.heritageireland.ie*) presents various displays, including a fine model, based on Glendalough, of a typical medieval monastery complex. Old photographs show the site before and after restoration; a video narrates the history of monastic Ireland.

Monastic Site★★★

The ruins of the later monastic settlement, east of the Lower Lake, form the most important part of the Glendalough site, approached through the gateway,

a unique example to a monastic enclosure. Set in the wall just beyond the first of two arches is a great slab of mica schist with an incised cross, probably marking the point at which sanctuary would be granted to those seeking it.

The **Round Tower★★** (100ft/30m high) is an iconic landmark probably constructed in the early 10C. It would have served as a six-storeyed storehouse, bell-tower, look-out and refuge.

The roofless **Cathedral★★**, once the focal point of the community, continues to be a substantial presence on the site, its nave one of the widest of early Irish churches. Built in stages, perhaps from the late 10C, it consists of a nave and chancel with a small sacristy.

St Kevin's Cross, the early, undecorated Celtic high cross (12ft/3.5m high) is the best preserved.

St Kevin's Church★★ is an early 11C Irish oratory with a high-pitched roof of overlapping stones. Its alternative popular name – St Kevin's Kitchen – was perhaps prompted by its unusual circular chimney-like tower or the scullery-like sacristy.

Round Tower and St Kevin's Church, Glendalough

© Bertrand Rieger/hemis.fr

St Saviour's Priory★

The Priory (*east of the Lower Lake by the Green Road*) is said to have been founded by St Laurence O'Toole, Abbot of Glendalough, but may be earlier in origin. The buildings (reconstructed in 1875), now enclosed in a forestry area, include a church nave and chancel with fine carving typical of the Irish Romanesque style.

Upper Lake★★

1.5mi/2.5km on foot west of the Visitor Centre by the Green Road, or 0.5mi/0.8km on foot from the Upper Lake car park. The way up to St Kevin's Cell is very steep in places. The **crosses**, which originally marked the boundary of the monastic site on the east shore, were later used by pilgrims as Stations of the Cross.

Reefert Church★, set above the lake among oaks and hazels, is deemed to be the traditional burial place of kings, and maybe of St Kevin. The roofless late-10C church has a plain but beautiful chancel arch, nave windows and an imposing granite doorway with sloping jambs. Nothing remains of **St Kevin's Cell** save a ring of foundation stones, colonised by three oak trees.

St Kevin's Bed and Temple-na-Skellig

(⊶*No access*)
The tiny cave known as **St Kevin's Bed** (30ft/9m above the lake) was probably a Bronze Age tomb. For as long as it was

The Recluse and the Blackbird

St Kevin – Probably born some time in the mid-6C, the young Kevin soon attracted attention for his ability to work miracles, but entrusted to the care of clerics, he instead sought solace from Nature, living in the hollow of a tree above the Upper Lake at Glendalough. Although he returned to his studies, he remained bewitched by Glendalough. The monastery in the lower part of the valley flourished under his leadership, until he retreated once more to the wilderness, living in complete solitude, probably somewhere above the Upper Lake (Temple-na-Skellig). One story tells how a blackbird laid her egg in his hand as he stood in ascetic contemplation, his arms outstretched in the shape of the Cross, forcing him to remain there standing still *"in the sun and rain for weeks, until the young are hatched and fledged and flown."* (Seamus Heaney, *St Kevin and the Blackbird*).

believed to be where St Kevin would come to pray and fast, it attracted pilgrims to Glendalough; after landing at Temple-na-Skellig by boat, they would walk along the lake shore and up the steps hewn into the cliff, to be helped, one by one, into the "bone-rock bed of the austere saint" (Richard Hills).

The first church at **Temple-na-Skellig** (about 20ft/6m above the lake) may date from the time of St Kevin, though the present ruins are probably 12C.

National Park Information Centre

Call in here to obtain information on the various waymarked walking routes in the valley (⏰*Open 10am–6pm or dusk* ✆*0404 45425*). Close by a path follows the Lugduff Brook steeply upstream to the lovely **Poulanass Waterfall**.

INLAND WICKLOW

There are a number of noteworthy places to visit away from the coast in Wicklow, best visited as part of a driving tour through the area.

Powerscourt★★

&⏰*House and gardens: open year-round daily 9.30am–5.30pm (garden close at dusk in winter). Ballroom & Garden Rooms Sun 9.30am–1.30pm; May–Sept Mon 9.30am–1.30pm.* ⏰*House and Gardens closed 25–26 Dec.* ⌾*Gardens €10, waterfall €6, house and exhibition free.* ✗ ✆*01 204 6000. www.powerscourt.ie.*

Restored after a terrible fire in 1974, the Palladian mansion designed by Richard Castle in 1730 looks out over a magnificent landscaped park with grassy terraces, stone stairways, antique statuary, fountains, woodland and specimen trees, set against the backdrop of mountains beyond, including the near-perfect cone of Great Sugar Loaf (1,654ft/503m). The house is now home to several high quality Irish gifts, clothes, and furniture shops, plus an exhibition on the rich history of the estate. A recent arrival is **Tara's Palace, Museum of Childhood,** where the prize exhibit is one of the finest **doll's houses** in the world,

meticulously constructed by some of Ireland's top craftsmen over two decades to encapsulates the grandeur and elegance of Ireland's three great 18C mansions; Castletown House, Leinster House and Carlton House.

The museum also displays a collection of historic doll's houses, toys and childhood memorabilia.

The estate is named after Eustace le Poer, a Norman knight. In 1609 the land was granted to Sir Richard Wingfield by James I, who made him Viscount Powerscourt. In 1961, the estate was sold to Mr. and Mrs. Slazenger.

The **gardens★** may have first been laid out by Richard Castle. They were then added to by successive viscounts, mostly in the course of the 19C. In 1843, the 6th Viscount employed the architect Daniel Robertson to design the terraces. The 7th Viscount added the superb wrought-iron gates and much of the statuary, some of it brought from Europe, some of it specially commissioned, like the Triton Fountain in the lake, which spews a jet of water 100ft/30m into the air. Many of the ornamental trees were planted at this time, among them numerous superb conifers. New features continued to be added in the early 20C, among them the Pepper Pot Tower and the jungle-like **Japanese gardens★**, created in 1908 on reclaimed bogland.

▷ Take the R 760 south; after 2mi/3.2km turn right (signposted); at the crossroads drive straight on for 2mi/3.2km to Valclusa.

♟♟ Powerscourt Waterfall★

&⏰*Open May–Aug 9.30am–7pm (10.30am–dusk rest of year).* ⏰*Closed two weeks up to 25 Dec, reopens 26 Dec.* ⌾*€6, child €3.50.* ✗ *(daily summer, weekends winter).* ✆*01 204 6000. www.powerscourt.ie. 5min on foot from car park to waterfall;* ⚠*Climbing the rock face is dangerous.*

Part of the Powerscourt estate, the highest waterfall in Ireland is formed by the Dargle River, which plunges (400ft/122m) in a spray of thick white

Powerscourt Waterfall

© Tourism Ireland

spume down a jagged grey rockface in a horseshoe of hills. This is a popular picnic spot with pleasant walks and nature trails by the river, and a good play area for children.

Killruddery★

Gardens: open May–Sept daily 9.30pm–6pm, Apr & Oct Sat–Sun 9.30pm–6pm. House by guided tour only, Jul–Sept daily 1–5pm. €14; gardens only, €7.50. 01 286 3405. www.killruddery.com.

The **formal gardens** at Killruddery were designed by a Frenchman in 1682 for the Earl of Meath (whose descendants still inhabit the house). They are a fascinating rarity, being a particularly complete example of the kind of formality which went out of fashion in the following century, when most desmesnes were landscaped (or re-landscaped) in an informal, naturalistic manner.

The major features are a pair of parallel canals (550ft/168m long), the **Long Ponds**, prolonged by the **Lime Avenue** leading uphill to the 18C park. The **Angles** consists of a number of intersecting walks lined with high hedges; the wilderness of trees bisected by broad walks; a bay hedge encloses the **Sylvan Theatre**, while the **beech hedge pond** consists of two concentric circular beech hedges, surrounding a round pond (60ft/18m in diameter) and a fountain.

The **house**, which dates from the 1650s, was considerably remodelled in the 1820s in neo-Tudor style by Richard and William Morrison. The west front is enhanced by a lovely conservatory with a domed roof and an ornamental octagonal dairy. Above the stableyard entrance is a clock and striking mechanism, both operated by water power and built by members of the family in 1906–09.

Military Road★★

After the 1798 Rebellion the British Government built a military road running south from Dublin through some of the most rugged and isolated parts of the Wicklow Mountains.

The original barracks in Glencree now house **The Glencree Centre for Peace and Reconciliation**, an organisation seeking to promote reconciliation between people of different religious traditions on both sides of the border.

Russborough's Stolen Treasures

Russborough's magnificent painting collection has proved too great a temptation to thieves on several occasions. In 1974 a gang, including the British heiress Rose Dugdale, took 19 pictures worth £8m, using them in a vain attempt to get IRA prisoners in England transferred to Belfast. All the paintings were swiftly found by the police. In 1986 another raid netted £30m worth of pictures. Their fame made them almost impossible to sell and most have been subsequently recovered. In 2001 and in 2002 there were thefts involving fewer and less valuable paintings. All of these paintings have now been recovered.

Kilmacanogue

The headquarters of the acclaimed **Avoca Weavers** (⏰*open year-round daily 9am–6pm; ☎01 274 6939; Fern House Café, reservations advisable; ☎01 274 6990; www.avoca.ie*) stands on the site of **Glencormac House**, built in 1864 by James Jameson of the famous whiskey family. The grounds contain various rare species of tree – a weeping cypress, Blue Atlantic cedars, several Wellingtonias, various types of eucalyptus and pine, and 13 yew trees said to be 700 to 800 years old that originally formed part of an avenue leading to Holybrook Abbey.

Such is the popularity of Avoca that there are two cafés to accommodate the many shoppers who come for the high-quality Irish designed Avoca range of goods, plus a gourmet foodhall and a garden nursery.

Russborough★★

📷*House open by guided tour (50min) each hour 10am–5pm, May–Sept daily. Apr & Oct Sun and Bank Hol Mon only. ☜€10, 3D Exhibition €6 (combined house and 3D €12), maze €3. ✕☎045 865239. www.russborough.ie.*

This is one of the grandest country houses in Ireland, a Palladian palace in Wicklow granite facing a lake which mirrors the mountains rising to the east. Commissioned in 1742 by JoSepth Leeson, heir to a brewing fortune, it is the masterpiece of the architect Richard Castle, its central block reaching far out into the landscape via curving colonnades, side pavilions, walls, archways and minor buildings.

Leeson – later Earl of Milltown – is depicted in stucco over the door linking the staircase and entrance halls; he was a great traveller and collector and, when

Russborough

Sally Gap

© Tourism Ireland

his line died out at the end of the 19C, his paintings passed into the ownership of the National Gallery in Dublin.

The outstanding features are the almost incredibly rich **stucco ceilings** by the Lafranchini brothers and their pupils. The thick and heavy stuccowork on the staircase is by a less accomplished hand. Gorgeous stucco panels frame exquisite seascapes by Vernet, now back in place after being sold in 1926.

Before visiting the house see the fascinating **3D Exhibition** which draws on cinema footage left by the last private owner of the house Sir Alfred Beit.

Sally Gap★★

The crossroads on the Military Road offers splendid views of the surrounding blanket bog on the Wicklow Mountains.

Loughs Tay and Dan★

Scree slopes plunge directly into the dark waters of Lough Tay, which is linked to Lough Dan by the Cloghgoge River.

Glenmacnass Waterfall★

The mountain river streams dramatically down an inclined rockface.

Wicklow Gap★★

The road west from Glendalough to Hollywood follows the course of the medieval pilgrims' path, **St Kevin's Road**, through the Vale of Glendasan. Where the modern road loops northeast, hikers may follow the old direct route (2mi/3km) closer to Lough Nahanagan. The motor road rejoins the old route to pass through the Wicklow Gap between Tonelagee (2,686ft/816m north) and Table Mountain (2,302ft/700m west).

Devil's Glen

The Vartry River makes a spectacular **waterfall** (100ft/30m) by cascading into the Devil's Punchbowl, a deep basin in the rock. There are **walks** in the immediate vicinity and good views of the coastline.

Mount Usher Gardens★★

&〇Open year-round10.30am–5.20pm (last admission), includes café and shopping courtyard. ⚏€7.50. ✕ ℘0404 40116.
www.mountushergardens.ie.

Set on the outskirts of Ashford village, these romantic natural-style gardens (20 acres/8ha), planted with over 5,000 species, many sub-tropical, are renowned for the collections of eucryphia and eucalyptus. They were laid out in 1868 by Edward Walpole, a member of a Dublin linen-manufacturing family, and restored in 1986.

Two suspension bridges lead to the woodland walks on the east bank of the River Vartry, which has been attractively developed with the addition of weirs.

The Uncrowned King of Ireland

Charles Stewart Parnell (1846–91) entered Parliament in 1875. He became vice-president of the Home Rule Confederation of Great Britain and president of the Land League, campaigning for tenants' rights to their homesteads. Parnell travelled regularly to America and Canada to raise funds and was so well received there that he was dubbed the "uncrowned King of Ireland". In 1882, he founded the National League to campaign for Home Rule.

The life and career of one of the greatest political leaders in Irish history ended in tragedy, however, when in 1886 he became the third party in a bitter high-profile divorce case, involving a Mrs Kitty O'Shea. Parnell refused to resign; his party split and he died in October 1891, four months after marrying Kitty.

Vale of Clara

The road, which follows the lushly-wooded course of the Avonmore River, links Laragh, a natural junction of roads and glens, to the attractive village of Rathdrum.

Glenmalur★

The road beside the upper reaches of the Avonbeg River ends in a remote and desolate spot at the northeast foot of Lugnaquilla, Ireland's second-highest mountain (3,039ft/926m high).

Avondale★★

⏱Park: Open to dusk. House open Easter–Oct daily 11am–6pm. Last admission at 5pm. ⏱Closed Mon (open Bank Hol Mon) Apr–May and Sept–Oct; Good Fri. ⊜Car park: €5; House: €7. ✕ ☎0404 46111. www.heritageisland.com.

The Avondale estate was the home of the Parnells, a prosperous Protestant landlord family, and it was here that **Charles Stewart Parnell** (&see "The Uncrowned King of Ireland" box), was born. The two-storey **neo-Classical house** has been restored to its appearance during Parnell's lifetime when it was much used for social occasions.

It was designed in 1759 by Samuel Hayes; there is Coade stone ornamentation by the **Lafranchini brothers** in the dining room. The life of Charles Parnell, the history of his family in Ireland, his role in 19C Irish politics, are all traced by a video. Among the furniture and memorabilia are Parnell's stick and chair (he was 6ft 3in/1.9m tall), photos of Parnell and Kitty O'Shea, her wedding ring of Avonmore gold mined by the Parnell family and a set of folding library steps made of Irish bog oak.

Avondale

© Photoshot

The **forest park★** (512 acres/207ha)
covers a steep slope facing east across
the Avondale River. The oldest surviving trees – two gigantic silver firs by
the river as well as oaks, beeches and
larches – were planted by Samuel Hayes
in the 18C. The stump of a beech tree,
planted nearly 250 years ago, has its
rings delineated in relation to subsequent historical events.

There are several trails and woodland
walks along the banks of the Avonmore
River and along the Great Ride.

Meeting of the Waters★

The confluence of the rivers Avonbeg
and Avonmore is set amid the forests
of south Co Wicklow; it was here that
Thomas Moore (1779–1852) is said to
have celebrated the "valley so sweet"
in his poem *The Meeting of the Waters*
of 1807.

Motte Stone

The name of the large glacial boulder is
derived from the French word for half
(*moitié*), as it used to mark the halfway
point between Dublin and Wexford
before the advent of mileposts.

Vale of Avoca

The village of Avoca has attracted visitors in great numbers ever since it was
chosen as the setting for the hugely
popular television series, *Ballykissangel*.
There are forest walks in the wooded
river valley. **The Mill at Avoca Village** (⏰*open daily, summer 9am–6pm,
winter 9.30am–5.30pm;* ✕; ✆*0402 35105;
www.avoca.ie*) was founded in 1723 and

is therefore the oldest surviving business
in Ireland. Visitors flock in large numbers to watch the traditional production
methods used to make the famous Avoca
textiles (ও*see Addresses, Shopping*).

COASTAL WICKLOW★★★

An alternative to the main N 11 road
from Bray to Wicklow town and Arklow
is the R 761 as far as Wicklow and then
the R 750 to Arklow.

Bray

Bray is an old-established resort with a
sand and shingle beach at the south end
of Killiney Bay.

The public park on Bray Head provides a
fine **view** of the coastline. Local history
is traced through photographs, maps
and artefacts in the **Heritage Centre**
(ও⏰*open Jan–Nov Mon–Fri 9.30am–
1pm;* ▨*€3;* ✆*01 27 867 128)*; also home
to a tourist information office.

On the seafront, the **National Sea-Life
Centre** (▨▴ও⏰*open Mar–Oct daily
10am–6pm; Nov–Feb Mon–Fri 11am–
5pm, Sat–Sun 10am–6pm;* ▨*€10 (online),
child €7.50;* ⌂*buy tickets online for a 20
percent discount;* ✆*01 286 6939, www.
visitsealife.com/Bray*) presents more than
30 displays populated by over 90 species
of marine and freshwater creatures, and
Ireland's largest collection of sharks.

Greystones★

As the southern terminus of Dublin's
DART suburban railway line, Greystones
has become a fashionable commuter
haven from the capital. Developed from
a small fishing village, it is now home to
a vibrant collection of cafés, restaurants
and boutique shops. There is a newly
built marina flanked by shingle beaches.

The Murrough

0.5mi/0.8km north of Wicklow.
A long shingle beach (3mi/5km) backed
by a broad grass bank is flanked by the
sea and the **Broad Lough**, a lagoon
noted for wildfowl and golden plover.

Black Castle, Wicklow

© Tourism Ireland

Wicklow

At the eastern foot of the mountains, the harbour town of Wicklow is the main commercial centre for the area as well as the county town and a Heritage Town. The statue of a pikeman in the Market Square represents all those who fought in nationalist uprisings.

The **Halpin Memorial** commemorates Captain Robert C. Halpin (1836–94), a native of the town, who commanded the *Great Eastern*, the ship built by Brunel which laid the first transatlantic telegraph cable.

Black Castle, which stands on a rocky promontory immediately south of the harbour, was built in 1176. The ruins form a fine vantage point for **views** of the town and coast.

The 18C **Anglican Church** has an onion-shaped copper cupola, donated in 1777, and incorporates a 12C Irish-Romanesque doorway. The interior contains a fine king-post roof and a 12C font. In the grounds of the parish priest's house are extensive ruins of a **Franciscan friary**, founded by the Fitzgeralds in the 13C.

♣♣ Wicklow's Historic Gaol★

Open daily 10.30am–4.30pm. €7.90, child €5. Night tours available, see website, ✗ *℘0404 61599. www.wicklowshistoricgaol.com.*

This stone-built prison dates from 1702 and was in use until 1924. It now houses elaborate exhibits and actors which bring to life its history of rough justice. A warder inducts visitors into the ghastly conditions; local gentleman-rebel Billy Byrne awaits his execution; the life of convicts in the 19C, both here and in Australia, is evoked, and so on. Paranormal tours are also conducted.

Brittas Bay

This long, sandy beach (3mi/5km), backed by dunes, is one of the most popular resorts on the east coast.

Arklow

Founded by the Vikings, on the Avoca estuary, Arklow is a seaside resort, an important east-coast fishing harbour and a base for Ireland's main fleet of coastal trading ships. There are pleasant walks by the harbour and along the south bank of the river.

The **Maritime Museum** (♿🕐*open year-round Mon–Sun 10am–5pm.* €5. *℘0402 32868. www.arklowmaritimemuseum.com)* displays exhibits connected with Ireland's maritime history and traces the development of local commercial shipping since the 1850s. **Arklow Rock** *(2mi/3.2km south)* provides a fine **view** of the coastline.

ADDRESSES

🛏 STAY

⊝ Keppel's Farmhouse – *Ballanagh. 2mi south of Avoca. 5rm.* ☎*0402 35168.* Farmhouse on a dairy estate dating back to 1880 with far-reaching views of countryside. The atmosphere is relaxed and tranquil, the hosts are charming and breakfast is a hearty affair.

⊝⊝ Glendalough Hotel – *Glendalough. 44 rm.* ☎*0404 45135. www.glendaloughhotel.com.* There's no monastic privations here with luxurious modern rooms offering panoramic views of the Wicklow countryside.

⊝⊝ Ballyknocken House and Cookery School – *Glenealy, 3mi south of Ashford. 7rm.* ☎*0404 44627. www.ballyknocken.ie.* This Victorian guesthouse, elegantly furnished with antiques, has charming romantic bedrooms, some with Victorian baths and brass beds. Food is emphasised here, the proprietor is a TV chef and a School of Cookery has been established; note that the restaurant, serving a 4 course set (no choice) dinner (⊝⊝– ⊝⊝⊝) is only open on Fri and Sat nights.

🍴 EAT

⊝⊝–⊝⊝⊝ Ballymore Inn – *Ballymore Eustace.* ☎*045 864 585. www.ballymoreinn.com.* A characterful pub in the middle of town. Choose from the Back Bar or (slightly more formal) restaurant. The food in both is imaginative, with an eclectic range of international and Irish dishes using local ingredients.

⊝⊝ Fern House Cafe (Avoca Weavers) – ☎*01 274 6990. www.avoca.ie. Lunch daily, dinner Thu–Sat (last sitting 9.30pm).* In the charming setting of Glencormac House gardens (*⊙ see Inland Wicklow Driving Tour, Kilmacanogue*), high-quality Italian-influenced cuisine is served. For a cheaper but still very rewarding taste of Avoca's finest, try their self service Sugar Tree Cafe (⊝) for salads, quiches, local wild salmon, etc.

SHOPPING

Avoca Weavers – *www.avoca.ie.* Very popular, ever-fashionable woollen goods and clothes, household accessories, glassware, ceramics, jewellery, foodstuffs and more available at the mill in Avoca or at the shop in Kilmacanogue.

Glendalough Woollen Mills – *Laragh.* ☎*040 445 156. www.glendalough woollenmills.com.* Factory outlet shop with tea rooms.

Kildare Outlet Village – *Kildare.* ☎*045 520 501. www.kildarevillage.com.* Over 60 discounted international designer brands plus a chic Italian restaurant.

SPORTS AND LEISURE

The **Curragh Racecourse** hosts all five Irish Classic **horse races**, including The Irish Derby and 16 other racedays. ☎*045 441205. www.curragh.ie.*

Clara Lara Fun Park 🧍🧍, *Vale of Clara – Open May (Sat–Sun only), daily Jun–Aug 10.30am–6pm.* ☎*€10 (some extra charges).* ☎*0404 46161. www.claralara.com.* Some 50 acres of outdoor activities for young children (up to 12) – assault course, adventure playgrounds, go-karts, radio-controlled boats, bathing, boating and fishing.

WALKING

Wicklow Way – *www.wicklowway.com.* This long-distance footpath (82mi/132km), starts in Marlay Park in Rathfarnham, in the southern suburbs of Dublin, passes near Powerscourt, Lough Tay and Lough Dan, Glenmacnass, Glendalough, Glenmalur and Aghavannagh, and finishes in Clonegal in Co Carlow (access at Moyne, Bridgeland and Kilquiggin). The trail, consisting of forest tracks, bog roads and mountain paths, crosses mountains, switches back and forth through river valleys and presents glorious views.

Wicklow Mountains National Park Information Point by the Upper Lake *(open May–Aug daily 10am–6pm, Apr and Sept Sat–Sun only 10am–5pm). www.wicklowmountainsnationalpark.ie.*

The counties of Longford, Westmeath, Offaly and Laois, forming part of the low-lying central plain of the island, share a landscape dominated by rich fertile grassland supporting large dairy and grain-producing farms, interspersed with small towns and villages, the largest being the county towns of Tullamore, Mullingar, Longford and Portlaoise.

Bogland

The area contains large expanses of bogland, one of Ireland's most characteristic features, which for generations has provided a second industry.

Two fascinating insights into the nature of the bogland can be explored here; at **Corlea Trackway** an Iron-Age roadway has been uncovered and at **Clara Bog**, now protected as a nature reserve, the complex and delicate ecosystem of a raised bog may be visited.

The once-impassable areas of bogland are interspersed with eskers – long raised ridges formed during the last ice age, which in many cases have provided excellent bases for roads.

Highlights

1 Visiting the "Seven Wonders" of **Fore Abbey** (p190)

2 Strolling the lakeside grounds of **Birr Castle Demsne** (p193)

3 Exploring the Monastic Site of **Clonmacnoise** (p193)

4 Taking a gentle walk in the rolling hills of the **Slieve Bloom Mountains** (p198)

5 Admiring restored steam machines at the **Stradbally Steam Museum** (p201)

Rivers and Lakes

The wide, meandering River Shannon, for centuries a major artery in Irish commerce, runs along the western boundary of the area, providing fishing and boating opportunities while the many lakes and smaller rivers offer scenic walking routes, coarse, trout and salmon fishing, and sailing.

Rural Life

Modern life has only lightly touched this rural landscape. Planter towns from the 17C still show their planned layouts beneath the contemporary shops and houses, the 19C love of Gothic overlays the 17C fortress at Tullynally, while the 15C ruins of Fore Abbey overlay an even earlier building.

What these counties lack in seascape and tourist-oriented facilities they make up for in quiet pastoral scenes, bountiful rivers and lakes, unexploited bogland habitats and an archaeology covering centuries of Irish life and industry.

Fore Abbey

© Brian Morrison/Tourism Ireland

Co Longford

A mixture of undulating rich grasslands and bogland, the county's highest point near Lough Gowna is only 276m/905ft. The River Shannon and Lough Ree border the county on the West side and to the South the Royal Canal flows across the land to join the River Shannon. Longford was planted with English settlers in the 1620s and the Anglo-Irish heritage is reflected in its literary associations.

▶ **Population:** 40,810
🐾 **Don't Miss:** A visit to the Corlea Trackway and a walk around the village of Ardagh.
ℹ **Info:** Dublin Street, Longford town. ✆043 334 2577. www.longfordtourism.ie.

LONGFORD

On the N 4 roughly halfway between Dublin, 73mi/118km southeast, and Sligo, 51mi/82km northwest.

The market centre for the surrounding agricultural area, Longford *(An Longfort)* lies on the Camlin River amid pleasant, if undistinguished scenery, a few miles from where the Shannon broadens out into Lough Ree.

Co Longford has important literary associations with Oliver Goldsmith (Lough Ree) and Maria Edgeworth (at Mostrim), and it was at Ballinamuck (10mi/16km north) that the last engagement of the 1798 rebellion was fought, when General Humbert's French troops and Irish volunteers were defeated by the English under General Lake.

St Mel's Cathedral

♿🕐✆ *043 334 6465.*
www.longfordparish.com.
Longford's principle landmark is the monumental neo-Classical Roman-Catholic cathedral with its vast Ionic portico supporting a richly sculpted pediment and tall, octagonal bell-tower capped with a dome – designed by John Keane in 1840. Sadly, on Christmas Day 2009, a fire swept through the cathedral causing massive damage.

The greatest treasure of the **Diocesan Museum** *(right transept)* was **St Mel's Crozier** (10C), a stick of yew encased in bronze, inset with studs and decorated with animal motifs, foliage and interlacing, found at old St Mel's Church in Ardagh in 1860. A portion of the crozier has been recovered, along with over 200 other museum artefacts.

Following the 2009 fire, the community undertook a near impossible restoration project. The Cathedral reopened, on schedule, for Christmas Eve mass in 2014. Setting aside the loss of invaluable artefacts, in many ways the cathedral has been renewed to its former glory and beyond. On your visit, keep an eye out for the Harry Clarke stained glass windows and the unique art glass windows created by Kim en Joong.

ARDAGH

7mi/11km SE of Longford on the N 4 and R 393.

The charming little estate village was largely rebuilt in the 1860s by Lady Fetherstone, who lived at Ardagh House. The ruins of a simple stone church, St Mel's, are said to stand on the site where the saint was buried.

The **Ardagh Heritage Centre** *(🕐open Mon–Sat 9.30am–5.30pm; 🕐closed Bank Hols; ✆043 334 2577)* traces the history of the locality from the pre-Christian era, through the internal rivalries of the local O'Farrell tribe and the 1619 Plantation to the present.

CORLEA TRACKWAY

10mi/16km S of Longford by the N 63 and R 397; in Kenagh, turn right (sign). (Dúchas). ♿🕐*Open Apr–Oct Daily 10am–6pm. Last admission at 5.15pm.* ✕ *✆043 332 2386. www.heritageireland.ie.*

The centre interprets an Iron-Age track built in the year 148 BC across

Ardagh

© Fáilte Ireland, Tourism Ireland

the boglands of Longford, close to the River Shannon. The ancient trackway *(togher)* consisted of a series of oak planks secured by pegs, wide enough to carry wheeled vehicles across the bog, sinking under the weight over time. A 59ft/18m long section of the preserved timber trackway – the largest of its kind to have been uncovered in Europe – discovered in the 1980s, is displayed under cover. The story of its discovery and subsequent preservation are the subject of a video; the accompanying exhibition sets it in its Iron-Age context.

ADDRESSES

LOCAL ART

Michael and Kevin Casey of Newtowncashel are artists in bogwood, ancient tree roots uncovered during peat-harvesting. Keep an eye open for some of their work, which stands round the village green on the east bank of Lough Ree. Their workshop and studio is by the river at Barley Harbour, Newtowncashel and is open 9am–6pm Mon–Sat and at other times by appointment. ✆043 332 5297, www.bogwood.net

Travels in Goldsmith Country

The country around Lough Ree is where the poet, playwright, historian and naturalist **Oliver Goldsmith** (c. 1731–74) spent the first 20 or so years of his life, visiting relatives and attending school in Elphin, Mostrim, Athlone and Lissoy.

Lissoy Parsonage, now in ruins, was the house where the Goldsmith family lived from 1731 to 1747; Lissoy village is recalled as "sweet Auburn" in his poem, *The Deserted Village*.

In Ardagh he experienced the plot of his play, *She Stoops to Conquer*, in mistaking the big house for the village inn. Until 1731 his father was rector of Forgney church, which contains a stained-glass window depicting "sweet Auburn".

Co Westmeath

A county of prosperous farms benefiting from good grassland, Westmeath is also home to patches of raised bogland and some large lakes. The county was initially taken in by the 12C Anglo-Norman conquest, only to remain beyond the Pale when the Gaelic O'Melaghlins and MacGeoghegans once again made it their own.

MULLINGAR

Mullingar is 50mi/80km NW of Dublin via the M 4.

Mullingar *(An Muileann Gcearr)*, the county town of Westmeath, is an important agricultural market in the middle of prime cattle country.

In the 2C AD a royal residence topped **Uisneach Hill** *(6mi/9.6km W by R 390)*, an ancient druidic sanctuary where the Celts held their rituals. The **Catstone** marks the meeting point of the five provinces of ancient Ireland. When the Normans arrived in the 12C, they constructed stone castles and several mottes and baileys across the region. In the 16C, under Henry VIII, Meath was divided in two: Mullingar became the county town of Westmeath, its prosperity assured by good communications with Dublin – the Royal Canal (1790s), the Midland & Great Western Railway (1848) and the main Dublin–Sligo road (which ran through town until the bypass was built). In 1825, a prison and handsome courthouse were erected in Mount Street, the space between used for public hangings.

A Literary Family

The talented **Pakenham family** includes Lord Longford (d. 2001), his wife Elizabeth (d. 2002), who wrote biographies, their son Thomas Pakenham, an author, and daughters Antonia Fraser, biographer, and novelist Rachel Billington.

▸ **Population:** 79,346
Don't Miss: Belvedere House and its grand gardens and Fore Abbey.
Info: Market House, Mullingar. ✆044 934 8650; westmeathtourism.com.

During his student days **James Joyce** came to Mullingar, where his father was reorganising the electoral rolls: hence the reason it features in *Ulysses* and *Stephen Hero*.

Cathedral of Christ the King

The main landmark is the Roman-Catholic cathedral set in parkland that stretches down to the Royal Canal, with its tall, twin towers (140ft/43m), designed by Ralph Byrne in a "last flamboyant fling of Classicism" (J. Sheehy), dedicated in 1939. The portico tympanum **sculptures** of Portland stone are by Albert Power, a pupil of Rodin. The chapel **mosaics** are by the Russian artist Boris Anrep.

The **museum** *(upstairs – ask the Verger)* displays a letter written by Oliver Plunkett, his vestments and other church-related artefacts.

NORTH OF MULLINGAR
Multyfarnham Franciscan Friary★

8mi/13km N via the N 4; in Ballynafid turn right. ✆044 937 1114.

Founded in 1268, the friary was raided six times and twice burnt by the English between 1590 and 1617. It has 14 life-size Stations of the Cross figures among the trees. Still in use, the church is open most mornings from around 7.30am for mass and closes around 8.30pm.

Taghmon Church

7mi/11.5km N via the N 4 and R 394; in Crookedwood, turn right.

On the site of a monastery founded by St Fintan Munna by the stream, stands a fortified church; the four-storey tower contains living accommodation. Note the two sculpted heads facing out from the North and West walls.

Tullynally Castle Gardens★

12.8mi/20.6km N via the R 394 or 0.9mi/1.5km from Castlepollard (sign). ♿🕐*Gardens: open Apr-Sept Thu–Sun and Bank Hols (daily Heritage Week) 11am–5pm. Castle open to pre-booked groups (min 20) only.* ⚊€6, *children* €3. ✗ ☎044 966 1159. *www.tullynallycastle.com.*

Tullynally, the seat of the Pakenham family since 1655, bristles with turrets and crenellations above the treetops of the extensive grounds. The original fortress with massive walls (10ft/3m thick) was converted early in the 18C into a country house, Gothicised by Francis Johnston and extended by Sir Richard Morrison. The interiors reflect the 19C love of all things medieval: it has a **Great Hall** and an octagonal dining room covered in wallpaper designed by Pugin for the House of Lords. The family coach is parked in the courtyard.

By 1760 the early-18C formal layout of canals and cascades was replaced by naturally **landscaped gardens**; the terraces date from Victorian times when tennis and croquet were popular. Two Coad stone sphinxes (1780) guard the huge walled **kitchen garden**, with its Regency glasshouses and avenue of Irish yews.

A **forest walk** leads past a waterfall to the lower lake and **views** of the castle.

Fore Abbey★

15mi/24km N on the R 394 to Castlepollard, the R 195 E, then turn right.

This ancient monastic site is one of the loveliest in the country. The extensive ruins – church, cloisters, chapter house, refectory, kitchen and columbarium – belong mostly to the Benedictine abbey founded in 1200, but **St Fechin's Church** is named after the founder (d. 665) of the earlier 11C–12C complex. In 1436 the buildings were fortified to protect them from attack by the native Irish.

The Abbey's various features have traditionally been known as the **"Seven**

The Children of Lir

Tullynally is an old Irish place name meaning the "Hill of Swans", and Tullynally Castle is set on high ground, sloping south to Lough Darravaragh. According to Irish legend, the Children of Lir spent 300 years there after they were changed into swans by their jealous stepmother.

Wonders of Fore", described in miraculous terms. The "monastery in a bog" (the **abbey** itself), raised on firm ground in the middle of marshland; "water that will not boil" from **St Fechin's Well;** a "tree that will not burn", the three branches of which represented the Trinity; the "stream that flows uphill" to drive the "mill without a race" appeared when the saint beat his crozier on the ground; the "hermit in the stone" was Patrick Beglen, last anchorite in Ireland, who in the 17C languished in a medieval watchtower, later incorporated into a **chapel mausoleum** for the Nugent family. Finally, the "stone raised by St Fechin's prayers" is the huge lintel over the West doorway of the church, which proved too heavy for the masons to lift into place and had to be wafted aloft by the power of prayer!

SOUTH OF MULLINGAR
Belvedere House and Gardens★

3.5mi/5.6km S of Mullinger on the N 52. ♿🕐*Open daily: House year-round 9.30am–5pm (4pm Nov–Feb). Gardens year-round, open: 9.30am; close May–Aug 8pm, Mar–Apr & Sept–Oct 7pm, Nov–Feb 4.30pm.* ⚊€8. ✗ ☎044 934 9060. *www.belvedere-house.ie.*

The beautiful landscape park above Lough Ennell is graced by an elegant villa (1740), probably designed by Richard Castle as a fishing lodge for Robert Rochfort, first Earl of Belvedere.

The house has been restored to its original appearance, complete with finely-carved woodwork and Rococo plasterwork ceilings; the furnishings are in

Kilbeggan Distillery Experience

© Simon Crowe/Fáilte Ireland

Nov–Mar 10am–4pm. ✕ *℘057 933 2134. www.kilbeggandistillery.com.*
On the west bank of the River Brosna stands this distillery (1757–1953) established by John Locke, possibly the oldest licensed pot distillery in Ireland. The process of distilling whiskey is explained and much of the original equipment is still in place: millstones, mash tuns; the huge wooden vats for fermentation; the hogsheads for maturing the whiskey; coopers' tools; the under-shot waterwheel, and the steam engine.
Today Kilbeggan's new malt spirit is flowing from these ancient pot stills and the visit finishes (naturally) with a tasting session.

period. The **visitor centre** gives a history of the estate and owners, including the mountaineer Colonel Charles Howard-Bury (🕯️*see "Tales of the Yeti" box*).
The **gardens** include three terraces overlooking the lake. A **woodland walk** *(2mi/3km)* is dotted with various **follies** including an octagonal gazebo, a Gothic arch, an ice house and two stone bridges over the stream. Built c. 1760, the **Jealous Wall** (148ft/45m high) is described as "Ireland's biggest folly" – erected to blot out the view of the larger Tudenham House (now in ruins) where the Earl's estranged brother lived.

Kilbeggan Distillery Experience
S of Mullingar at Kilbeggan on the N6 Dublin–Galway road. ♿🚶*Visit by guided tour (40min). Apr–Oct 9am–6pm,*

ADDRESSES

MULLINGAR

🛏️ STAY
🛏️ **Annebrook House** – *Pearse St. 111rm. ℘044 935 3300 www.annebrook.ie.* A lovely town-centre hotel with the River Brosna flowing through its grounds. Built around 1810, it has character in its public rooms and luxurious bedrooms.

🍴 EAT
🍽️🍽️ **The Terrace Restaurant** – *Dublin Road, Mullingar. ℘044 93 37 500. www.mullingarparkhotel.com.* Stylish modern European cuisine using the finest of Irish produce is served at this modern hotel dining room.

SHOPPING
Mullingar Pewter Ltd – *5mi/8km east of Mullingar on the N 4; after 4mi/6km, bear left towards Killucan, to The Downs. Open Mon–Thurs 9.30am–4pm, Fri 9.30am–3pm. Gift shop open Mon–Sat. ℘044 934 8791. www.mullingarpewter.com.* Here, you can watch the moulding, soldering, turning, polishing and blackening.Purchase works in theshowroom.

SPORTS AND LEISURE
Fishing and sailing on Lough Ennell, Greyhound Racing in Mullingar.

Tales of the Yeti
In 1921 Col. Charles Howard-Bury led an expedition to Everest. Dressed in Donegal tweed, his party came within 2 000ft/609m of the summit, took the first photos of the mountain and brought back stories told by local porters of "abominable snowmen".

Co Offaly

To the south of Westmeath, County Offaly is separated from County Laois by the Slieve Bloom Mountains. Although small in size, there is a lot to see and appreciate in the county.

BIRR★

Birr is situated on N 52 between Tullamore and Nenagh on the county boundary SW of Tullamore in the O'Carroll country.

With elegant 18C houses lining its shady streets, Birr *(Biorra)* is a fine example of a planned Georgian town laid out at the gates of a great house, and now a Heritage Town.

The principal axis is **Oxentown Mall**, which runs between the castle gates and the Anglican church between rows of elegant houses and mature trees. The town centre is formed by **Emmet Square**; among the best Georgian houses is Dooley's Hotel (1740). **John's Mall** is graced by a statue of the 3rd Earl of Rosse, and beside the delightful little Greek temple (1833) is the **Birr Stone**, a large limestone rock, which may once have marked the supposed meeting place of the mythical Fianna warriors, near Seffin. In 1828 it was removed to a mansion in Co Clare for secret celebrations of the Mass; it was returned in 1974.

The local landowners, the Parsons family, later ennobled as the Earls of Rosse, were also responsible for creating one of the richest collections of exotic trees

> ▶ **Population:** 78,003
> ⊛ **Don't Miss:**
> Clonmacnoise and its high crosses.
> The grounds of Birr Castle.
> ℹ **Info:** Wilmer Road, **Birr**; ℘057 912 0110. Athlone Castle, **Athlone**; ℘090 649 4630. Dew Heritage Centre, **Tullamore**; ℘057 935 2617. www.midirelandtourism.ie.

and shrubs to be found anywhere: one of many bequests left by a line of eminent men, innovators and inventors – another being what for many years was the world's most powerful telescope.

A Bit of History

Birr figures in early records as the site of an important monastery, which produced the Macregol's Gospels and where the Law of Adamnan was accepted by abbots and chieftains at the Synod of Birr in 697. Owing to its central position in Ireland, Birr was referred to in the Down Survey as *Umbilicus Hiberniae*. Until the establishment of the Free State, Birr was known as Parsonstown in King's County (the old name of Co Offaly). In 1620, the village was granted to **Sir Lawrence Parsons**. He started weekly markets, set up a glass factory and built most of the castle. In 1642,

Great Telescope, Birr

© Tourism Ireland

Birr Castle Demesne

© Brian Morrison/Tourism Ireland

much of Birr was destroyed by fire during a siege by local clans; in 1690, it was garrisoned by the Williamites and besieged by the Duke of Berwick. During the more peaceful 18C and 19C, the town, castle and demesne were much extended.

Sir William Parsons, a patron of Handel, enabled the composer to stage the first performance of the *Messiah* in Dublin. His grandson – another Sir William, the 4th baronet – devoted much time to the late-18C Volunteers. **Sir Lawrence**, the 5th baronet, was more nationalist in political sentiment and a friend of **Wolfe Tone** but he retired from politics after the Act of Union in 1800. In the 19C the family genius was invested in **scientific discoveries** and in the 20C was directed towards the collection and propagation of **rare botanical species** for the magnificent gardens.

🚗 DRIVING TOUR

SLIEVE BLOOM MOUNTAINS★

▶ Depart from Birr and take R 440.

🗘*See SHANNON VALLEY for local map.*

A good way to enjoy the scenery of the mountains is to walk sections of the 44mi/70km **Slieve Bloom Way** *(see feature box p199).* Otherwise take this drive east from Birr to the village of Kinnitty. To the east of Birr, the massive green hills of the Slieve Bloom Mountains rise to just over 500m/1,640ft. For details on walking trails contact the **Slieve Bloom Centre** (🕐*open Apr–Sept, Mon–Fri mornings;* ☎*086 2789147; www. slievebloom.ie).* 🗘*See also p199.*

Birr Castle Demesne★★

🗘🕐*Open daily mid-Mar–Oct 9am–6pm, Nov–mid-Mar 10am–4pm.* ⊕€9. ✗ 🅿 ☎*057 912 0336. www.birrcastle.com.*

Each of the many walks through these pleasure grounds *(100 acres/40ha),* either by the water or among thousands of species of trees and shrubs, is a delight. Highlights include tall box hedges and the flora from China and the Himalayas. Extensive herbaceous displays adorn the terraces below the crenellated 17C-castle *(private).*

Great Telescope★★ – In the 1840s, the 3rd Earl of Rosse built a telescope named the Leviathan of Parsonstown, providing a more extensive view of space than was hitherto possible. Its mirror *(72in/183cm)* was cast in a furnace built at the bottom of the castle moat and fired with turf from nearby bogs. Astronomers came from far and wide

Anthony Trollope in Ireland

Having been in the employ of the Post Office since 1834, Anthony Trollope was appointed surveyor's clerk in 1841 and went to Ireland. His first appointment, to which he travelled from Dublin by canal boat, was in **Banagher**, where he took up hunting and visited Sir William Gregory of Coole Park, a contemporary at Harrow School. In 1843, during a visit to Drumsna, he was inspired to begin his first novel, *The Macdermots of Ballycloran*, published in 1847.

© World Illustrated/Photoshot

On June 11, 1844 he married Rose Heseltine. Later that year they moved to **Clonmel**, renting rooms on the first floor of a house in O'Connell Street (then High Street), where their two sons were born – Henry Merivale (March 1846) and Frederic James (September 1847). In 1845 Trollope began his second novel, *The Kellys and the O'Kellys*, published in 1848. The family then moved to **Mallow** (1848–51), where he was able to indulge his passion for hunting with various great hunts including the Duhallow, the oldest in Ireland. While on secondment to the Channel Islands in 1853, Trollope implemented the idea of the first **post boxes**, which were painted sage green. In 1854, after a year in Belfast as acting surveyor, he was appointed surveyor of the northern district of Ireland but obtained permission to reside in Dublin, where he lived at 5 Seaview Terrace, Donnybrook. As his work involved a good deal of travelling, he created a portable desk so that he could write on the train.

In 1859, the year in which he transferred permanently to England, he began his third Irish novel, *Castle Richmond*, which takes place during the Great Famine. Towards the end of his life, Trollope began a fourth Irish novel, *The Landleaguers*, about agrarian reform, but he died in December 1882 before it was finished.

to use the telescope, considered to be the most powerful in the world for 60 years, until 1908.

Ireland's Historic Science Centre – Part of the stableyard is given over to an account of the brilliant family achievements. The building of the first-known example of a wrought-iron suspension bridge by the 2nd Earl; the construction of the great telescope and the discovery of distant galaxies by the 3rd Earl; the invention of the steam turbine engine by Charles Parsons in the 1890s; pioneering work in photography by Mary, Countess of Rosse in the 1850s and the world-wide plant-collecting expeditions conducted by the 5th and 6th Earls.

Kinnitty

The village has considerable charm. The **Kinnitty Pyramid** in the churchyard south of the village (on the Roscrea road) is an extraordinary mausoleum modelled on the pyramid of Cheops in Egypt, honouring the Bernards of Kinnitty Castle.

CLONMACNOISE★★★

Clonmacnoise is situated on the east bank of the River Shannon 13mi/21km south of Athlone on the N 6 and N 62 or 13mi/20km from Ballinasloe along the R357. Allow one–two hours for your visit but be aware that this is a very busy site and delays may be experienced during the summer months.

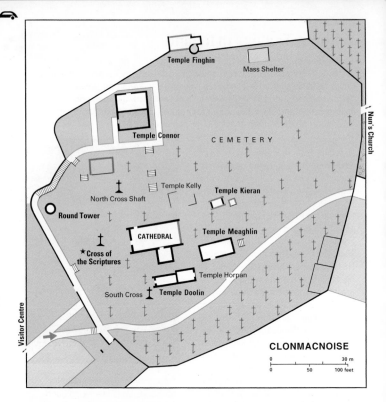

Temple Finghin

Mass Shelter

Nun's Church

Temple Connor

C E M E T E R Y

Temple Kelly

Temple Kieran

North Cross Shaft

Round Tower

CATHEDRAL

Temple Meaghlin

★ **Cross of the Scriptures**

Temple Horpan

South Cross **Temple Doolin**

Visitor Centre

CLONMACNOISE

0 — 30 m
0 — 50 — 100 feet

Founded in 545 by St Kieran *(Ciarán)*, Clonmacnoise *(Cluain Mhic Nóis)* was once a pre-eminent monastic site, second only to Armagh, where the Kings of Connaught and Tara are interred. With its churches, cathedral, high crosses, ancient grave slabs and round towers, it draws thousands of visitors, tourists and pilgrims, most notably on 9 September (St Kieran's Day).

A Bit of History

The monastery's position beside the Shannon now seems remote but in earlier centuries transport was easier by water than over land. The old Pilgrims' Road, approached from the north along the esker (or ridge). As its reputation grew, the settlement expanded from an original wooden oratory to a cluster of stone churches, numerous monks' dwellings and a round tower within an earth or stone enclosure. None of the surviving ruins predate the 9C, having been successively plundered by the Irish, Vikings and Anglo-Normans until finally reduced to ruin in 1552 by the English garrison from Athlone.

Visitor Centre

(Dúchas). ♿ 🕐*Open daily Jun–Aug 9am–6.30pm; rest of year 10am–6pm (5.30pm Nov–mid-Mar); last admission 45min before closing.* 🕐*Closed 25–26 Dec.* ⊚€8. ✕ ✆*090 967 4195. www.heritageireland.ie.*

The **Visitor Centre** displays the original **high crosses** and a collection of **grave slabs★** (those on site are replicas), confirming Clonmacnoise's status as an important stone-carving centre from the 8C to 12C. There is also an audiovisual presentation on the site's history.

Monuments

The most important monuments include the early 9C **South Cross** (12ft/3.6m), with a carving of the Crucifixion, decorative spirals and interlacing, which recall designs on crosses at Kells, on Iona and

Aerial view, Clonmacnoise

© Designpics/Photoshot

Kildalton in Scotland. **Temple Doolin** is the pre-12C church named after Edward Dowling when he restored it (1689) as a mausoleum. **Temple Meaghlin or Temple Rí** has special windows that echo those at Clonfert and O'Heyne's Church at Kilmacduagh. **Temple Kieran** is the tiny church said to contain the grave of St Kieran. The **North Cross Shaft** (c. 800) is decorated with lions biting their tails, and a cross-legged figure thought by some to be the Celtic god Cernunnos. The sandstone **Cross of the Scriptures★**, related to the crosses at Monasterboice, was erected in the 10C, possibly by King Flann (d. 916). Unusually, its arms protrude upwards from the circle – note scenes of the Crucifixion, the Last Judgement, the Passion (soldiers resting on their spears), and one showing Abbot Colman and King Flann founding the monastery.

Cathedral

The simple rectangular building has been modified many times. The oldest parts may date from the 10C when the original wooden church was replaced with a stone structure. The Romanesque west doorway dates from the 12C; the sacristy may be 13C. An elaborate north doorway, with three plaques depicting St Dominic, St Patrick and St Francis, was added by Dean Odo in the 15C at the same time as the chancel was divided into three vaulted chapels.

St Kieran

Born in Roscommon, St Kieran was trained by St Finnian at Clonard before going to Inishmore, among the Aran Islands. His vision of a great tree growing in the heart of Ireland was interpreted by his tutor St Enda as a church growing on the banks of the Shannon. After a stay on Hare Island in Lough Ree, St Kieran and seven companions settled at Clonmacnoise, the field of the sons of Nos. He died months later of the plague, aged 33.

Round Tower

Despite having lost its conical cap, this is a typical round tower, possibly built in the 10C by Fergal O'Rourke and repaired in 1120 by Abbot O'Malone. The arched doorway is most likely 12C.

Temple Connor

The Anglican church may date from 1010 when it was endowed by Cathal O'Connor.

Temple Finghin and Nun's Church

The 12C church was modified in the 17C. Unusual features include the South door and mini round tower incorporated into the chancel.

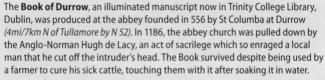

Durrow High Cross

The **Book of Durrow**, an illuminated manuscript now in Trinity College Library, Dublin, was produced at the abbey founded in 556 by St Columba at Durrow *(4mi/7km N of Tullamore by N 52)*. In 1186, the abbey church was pulled down by the Anglo-Norman Hugh de Lacy, an act of sacrilege which so enraged a local man that he cut off the intruder's head. The Book survived despite being used by a farmer to cure his sick cattle, touching them with it after soaking it in water.

The site of the abbey *(private property)* is a gloomily romantic place, with a ruined 18C church, a holy well, a cemetery with 9C to 11C grave slabs, and above all, a fine 10C **high cross**. Its east face shows the Sacrifice of Isaac together with Christ in Glory flanked by David with his harp *(left)* and David killing the Lion *(right)*; the west face depicts the Crucifixion and associated events.

▶ From the centre of the enclosure follow the old path E across the extended graveyard and along the road.

The ruined Nun's Church with nave and chancel was completed according to the Annals of the Four Masters in 1167 by Dervorgilla. The West doorway and chancel arch have striking Irish Romanesque style decoration.

TULLAMORE

Tullamore is 62mi/100km due west of Dublin, on the Grand Canal, south of the Dublin–Athlone road (N 6).

Bustling Tullamore *(Tulach Mhór)* has been the county town of Offaly since 1833. Otherwise undistinguished, the place still has something of its late 18C/early 19C character, when much rebuilding took place and the construction of the Grand Canal brought the town a measure of prosperity.

Tullamore D.E.W. Visitor Centre

&. ◷ *Open year-round daily Mon–Sat 9.30am–6pm, Sun 11.30am–5pm.* ◷ *Closed 24 Dec–1 Jan.* ⊛ €14. ✗ P ℘ *057 932 5015.*

www.tullamoredew.com.

A golden drop of Tullamore Dew whiskey or Irish Mist awaits in the bar but first, it is worth discovering the history of the distillery, via a guided tour and audiovisual presentation. The distillery was founded in 1829 by Michael Molloy. In 1887, Daniel E. Williams, who had been steeped in whiskey production since joining the staff at the age of 15, became general manager and gradually acquired overall control of the business. He used his own initials to provide a brand name, Tullamore Dew, for the distillery's pot still whiskey.

In the 1950s, when sales were low, the distillery began to produce Irish Mist, a whiskey-based liqueur inspired by a traditional Irish recipe for heather wine made with pot still whiskey, herbs and heather honey.

Clara Bog

7mi/10km NW of Tullamore by N 80; in Clara, take a minor road south; car park at the end of a short causeway.

☝ *Visitors should not stray from the causeway unless accompanied by a knowledgeable guide.*

This raised bog (1,640 acres/665ha; 23ft/7m maximum depth) is one of the finest and largest of its kind remaining in Ireland and is of international interest. When efforts were made to preserve the bog, the land was purchased by the Dutch government and donated to the Irish state. In 1987, it was designated a National Nature Reserve.

It has a diverse flora, including at least 10 different bog mosses; in wet areas carnivorous plants, such as sundews and bladderworts, entrap unwary insects.

Slieve Bloom Mountains walking festival

© Fáilte Ireland

Slieve Bloom Mountains★

The Slieve Bloom Mountains (☾ *see p194 for a driving tour that takes in the mountains*) cross the county boundary between Laois and Offaly. As mountains go, they are not very high (rising from the central plains of the country to 1735ft/526m at their highest, at Arderin in the southwest of the range) but they make themselves felt on the landscape of North Laois. When walking there, you definitely feel as if urban civilization has been well and truly left behind.

The rocks of the Slieve Bloom tend to be grit and sandstones from the Old Red Sandstone period. Colours of the rock vary from yellow and white to light browns and reddish-purple. When the light is good, a combination of these colours characterise the mountain scenery.

The mountains take their name from Bladhma *(Anglicized as Bloom)*, a Celtic warrior who fled to their high ground to escape capture.

Given the gentle nature of the Slieve Bloom Mountains, they provide an ideal environment for easy-going walks away from the hustle and bustle of everyday life. Every year, on the May Bank Holiday weekend, organised walks take place in the mountains and in the autumn a two-day walking festival is also organised *(see www.slievebloom.ie)*. The **Slieve Bloom Way** is a waymarked walking route extending for 30mi/48km which offers a surprising variety of terrains, from deciduous woodland to desolate open moorland, passing small farms and plantations of pine trees. There are four main rivers that flow through the mountains: the Barrow, the Silver, the Delour and the Owenass. Once you are on high ground the views are terrific and on a fine day they extend across miles of Irish countryside at its finest. Back at ground level in the foothills of the mountains there are quaint little villages and friendly pubs where visitors are welcome because they are a rare sight.

The Slieve Bloom Mountains, like the counties of Laois and Offaly, are a forgotten part of Ireland in terms of travellers from abroad and this alone is a good reason for spending some time there.

ADDRESSES

BIRR

🛏 STAY

Ring Farmhouse – *Ballinree. 2km from Birr, off N62. 4rm.* ℘057 912 0976. *www.irishfarmhouseholiday.com.* Friendly farmhouse B&B built on the site of a medieval Loretto Castle. Good location for walking in the Slieve Bloom Mountains.

Ardmore House B&B – *The Walk Kinnitty. 5rm.* ℘057 913 7009. *www.kinnitty.com.* This charming Victorian period house makes an ideal base for walks in the Slieve Bloom Mountains.

Maltings Guesthouse – *Castle St. 13rm.* ℘057 91 21345. *www.themaltings birr.com.* Built in 1810 as a maltstore for Guinness, this establishment also houses a craft centre. It offers spacious accommodation and a simple restaurant overlooking the river.

🍴 EAT

Brambles Café & Deli– *Mill St.* ℘087 745 3359. *www.bramblesbirr.ie. Mon–Sat 8.30am–6pm, Sun 11am-2.30pm.* Home-made soda bread, cakes and scones. Produce from the proprietor's farm is also on sale, as well as local cheese and various jams and chutneys.

Stables Emporium & Tea Rooms – *6 Oxmantown Mall. Closed Sun–Mon.* ℘057 912 0263. *www.thestablesbirr.com.* Ideal for a light lunch and home-made desserts before, or after, browsing the Emporium for giftware, glass and jewellery. Rooms (🛏) also available.

The Thatch – *Crinkill. 1.5mi S off N 52.* ℘050 920 682. *www.thethatch crinkill.com.* Thatched pub kept by fifth generation of landlords. Casual bar dining and early bird menus (🍴), more formal dinner in the restaurant.

SPORTS AND LEISURE

Walking: Birr Castle Demesne, along the River Camcor, beside the Grand Canal, and in the Slieve Bloom Mountains.
Boating: On the Shannon, Grand Canal.
Fishing: Shannon and Brosna Rivers for salmon, pike, trout and most coarse species; River Suck and Grand Canal for pike, bream and perch.

EVENTS AND FESTIVALS

Birr Vintage Week *(late Aug) www. birrvintageweek.com.* Events include a Sunday parade, a Georgian Cricket Match played in period costume (according to the 1744 rules) and the Irish Independent Carriage Driving Championships, held in the Castle Demesne, including music, theatre and fireworks.

SIGHTSEEING

Silverline Cruisers – *Banagher Marina.* ℘057 915 1112. *www.silverlinecruisers.com.* Cruisers for hire on the Shannon.

TULLAMORE

🛏 STAY

Tullamore Court Hotel – *O'Moore St.* ℘057 934 6666. *www.tullamorecourt hotel.ie.* A large modern hotel, with a leisure centre that includes a swimming pool. Popular with locals and business travellers.

Annaharvey Guesthouse & Equestrian Centre – *Tullamore. On the main Tullamore to Portarlington road (R420), 3mi from the village of Geashill. 5rm.* ℘057 934 3544. *www. annaharveyfarm.ie.* Most people staying in this lovely farmhouse are attracted by the equestrian activities, suitable for beginners and the experienced, but the locality is also good for walking and cycling and most of Offaly's sites are within a reasonable distance. There is also a cookery school.

🍴 EAT

Jamie's Restaurant – *Harbour St.* ℘057 935 1529. A congenial place for an evening meal, with an early-bird menu from 5pm to 7pm. A small but adequate wine list.

TRACING ANCESTORS

Irish Midlands Ancestry *Bury Quay, Tullamore, Offaly. Enquire online initially. www.offalyhistory.com.*

Co Laois

The inland identity of Co Laois (pronounced "leash") is in harmony with the rich agricultural landscape that greets the visitor whatever part of Laois is being viewed. Although often travelled through on the way to somewhere else, the county has some picturesque towns to offer.

▶ **Population:** 84,732.

ℹ **Info:** Dunamaise Arts Centre, Portlaoise. ✆ 057 866 4132. www.laoistourism.ie.

◉ **Don't Miss:** A trip into the Slive Bloom Mountains on the border with Offaly.

ABBEYLEIX

Abbeyleix lies on N8, 61mi/98km SW of Dublin towards Cork.

At the height of the Anglo-Irish Ascendancy in the mid-18C, Viscount de Vesci followed the contemporary trend for demolishing tenant cottages, re-housing the residents in a carefully planned new settlement at the gates of his great mansion. Scarcely changed since those days, Abbeyleix *(Mainistir Laoise)* is one of the best examples of this type of aristocratic estate development, preserved by its designation as a Heritage Town. However, the origins are much older, since it occupies the site of a late- 12C Cistercian abbey built on an earlier monastery.

Abbeyleix Heritage House

♿ ◷ *Open Tue–Sat, 9am–5pm, (weekends by arrangement).* ◉ €3. 🅿 ✆ 057 873 1653. *www.abbeyleixheritage.com.*

The exhibition in the old school traces the history of Abbeyleix, its industries and role in the evolution of the region.

In the walled garden of the former convent, the **Abbey Sense Garden** has been designed and planted to appeal to all the senses. Other exhibitions include Rural Life, The Carpet Factory, and an impressive model railway.

Excursions

Emo Court★

(Dúchas) 15mi/24km NNE of Abbeyleix by N 8, M 7 and R 422. (Dúchas) Gardens: ◷ *Open: Gardens daylight hours.* 👣 *House, by guided tours only, Easter–29 Sept, 10am–6pm; last tour 5pm.* ◷ *Closed 25–26 Dec. House* ◉ €5. ✕. *(Easter–Sept).* 🅿. ✆ *057 862 6573. www.heritageireland.ie.*

This splendid domed Classical mansion, surrounded by extensive gardens, was designed by **James Gandon** in 1792. After many years of use as a Jesuit seminary, the rotunda and superb stucco work has been restored and re-furnished, including a collection of Wedgwood pottery.

A magnificent avenue of Wellingtonias, the first in Ireland, links the house to

Emo Court

© Tourism Ireland

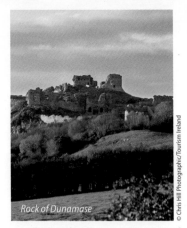

Rock of Dunamase

© Chris Hill Photographic/Tourism Ireland

the Dublin Road; azaleas, rhododendrons and Japanese maples feature in the Clucker Garden; statues of the Seasons and a ring garden adorn the lawns.

Rock of Dunamase★

15mi/24km NE of Abbeyleix by R 245, R 247 and N 80 NW.

The rock rising straight from the plain is crowned by the extensive ruins of the O'More clan fortress, destroyed by Cromwell's army in the mid-17C. It offers excellent **views★** from the summit (200ft/60m high).

STRADBALLY

13mi/21km NE of Abbeyleix by R 245, R 247 and N 80 SE.

In the Stradbally Market Place stands an unusual pagoda-like structure with a red roof. It commemorates Dr William Perceval, a local man who died in 1899 after 54 years of local practice.

The **Steam Museum★** (&see website for opening hours, €7.50; 057 864 1878/086 389 0184; www.irishsteam.ie) displays 1930s-steam-powered farm machinery and a 1895 steam-driven locomotive that transported casks of Guinness around the Guinness brewery in Dublin. A narrow-gauge steam railway *(1mi/1.6km)* runs through the woods.

In the late summer Stradbally plays host to the annual arts and music festival, the Electric Picnic.

TIMAHOE

9mi/15km NE of Abbeyleix by R 430 east and a minor road N.

The fine **Round Tower★** *(96ft/29m high)* leaning 2ft/0.6m from the vertical, was probably built in the 12C; it has a lovely Romanesque double doorway. **Richard Nixon**, President of the USA (1969–74), whose ancestors came from the village, visited Timahoe in 1970.

BALLINAKILL
Heywood Gardens

(Dúchas) 3.5mi/6km SE of Abbeyleix by R 432. Open 8.30am–dusk. 057 873 3563. www.heritageireland.ie.

The gardens were completed in 1912 by **Edwin Lutyens** (1869–1944) and **Gertrude Jekyll** (1843–1932), with terraces, clipped yew hedges, an Italianate sunken garden, ponds and walks with fine prospects of distant towers.

The gardens were cared for by the Salesian Fathers from 1941 until taken over by the Irish state in 1993.

ADDRESSES

NEAR ABBEYLEIX

STAY

Sandymount House – *Oldtown, 2m on R433 road from Abbeyleix.* 057 873 1063. www.sandymounthouse.com. Beautifully restored 1836 Georgian residence, set in mature, tranquil gardens with four period-style guest bedrooms.

BARS

Morrissey's Bar– Many travellers make a point of stopping off at Morrissey's Bar in Main Street, Abbeyleix; a wonderful combination of grocer's shop and pub, which, like the town itself, seems little altered since it was built.

SIGHTSEEING

Grantstown Lake – *8mi/13km W by R 433* – Woodland walks beside a lake with fishing.

The Southeast of Ireland has much to offer the visitor, although compared to the searing wildernesses and tumbled ruins of Co Donegal or the graceful mountains ranges and lakes of Co Kerry, it may seem more domesticated. The legacies of Viking and Norman settlements are still written in the structures of its modern-looking towns while its mountain ranges are accessible by way of long-distance walking routes offering sudden idyllic views and unspoilt areas of natural beauty.

Coastline and Countryside

The long, meandering coastline of the Southeast is dotted with tiny villages, each with their own cultural attractions, with sheltered, sandy beaches where rare and endangered bird life often finds a home. There is a fine network of roads connecting the coast with inland places of interest.

Inland, Co Tipperary and Co Kilkenny offer scenic rural countryside, pretty natural woodland and medieval ruins.

Agriculture and Industry

The least rainy and most sunny region of the country, the Southeast is one of its most fertile and agriculturally productive regions, its limestone plains providing rich grassland and well-drained areas for the cultivation of crops.

Traditional Irish culture flourishes in the urban areas and tourism contributes to the economy. Waterford, famous for its crystal-glass factory (which has survived the threat of closure), is the fifth-largest city in Ireland, and Kilkenny and Wexford are major urban centres.

Highlights

1 The dramatic silhouette of the medieval **Rock of Cashel** (p210)

2 Touring the imposing **Kilkenny Castle** (p216)

3 Learning about Irish emigrants and their descendants at the **Dunbrody Famine Ship** (p229)

4 The remote beaches of the **Hook Head Peninsula** (p231)

5 A factory tour of the **House of Waterford Crystal** (p236)

Hook Head Lighthouse

© Luke Myers/Fáilte Ireland, Tourism Ireland

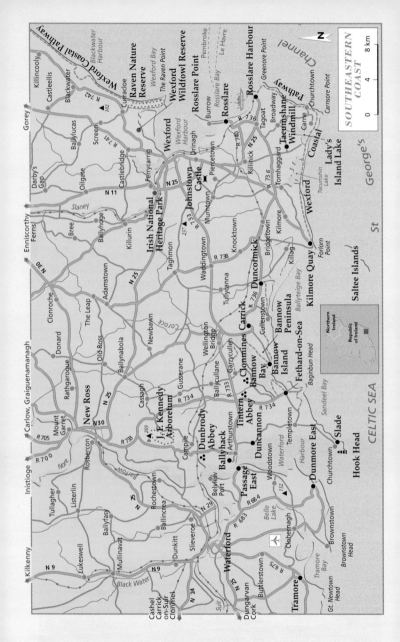

Rivers

Three great rivers flow through the region: the Slaney, rising high up in Lugnaquilla in the Wicklow Mountains and flowing into Wexford Harbour, and the Rivers Barrow and Nore, rising from the Slieve Bloom Mountains in the county of Laois and joining the Suir to form the **Three Sisters** on their route to Waterford Harbour.

Salmon breed in the rivers and some stretches are navigable and connected to the system of inland canals and waterways.

Co Tipperary

Ireland's biggest inland county, Tipperary is an area of rich, dairy farmland, its flat, fertile limestone plain sheltered to the South and West by a semicircle of mountain ranges: the Galtee Mountains, the Knockmealdown Mountains and the Comeragh Mountains, all offering the visitor scenic views and the option of unspoilt hill walks. The River Suir flows through its western side and the stunning limestone outcrop of the Rock of Cashel sits at the heart of the county.

CLONMEL★

30 mi/50km west of Waterford on the N 24 on the boundary between Co. Tipperary and Co. Waterford.

The principal town of Co Tipperary *(Cluain Meala)* stands in a lovely fertile valley. To the south rise the Comeragh Mountains in Co Waterford: a fine backdrop to the many historic buildings of the town, which recall its great period of prosperity in the 18C and 19C.

A Bit of History

The town is said to pre-date the Vikings and its name comes from the Irish words for "a meadow of honey" – an Early Christian reference to the great fertility of the Suir Valley. Viking longships sailed up the River Suir from Waterford and, according to tradition, fought at Clonmel in 916 or 917 against the local O'Neill clan.

Edward I granted the town a charter and the **walls** were built in the early 14C. Later, it became an important stronghold of the Butler family, the Earls of Ormond. In the 17C, the garrison is said to have put up more resistance to Cromwell than any other Irish town.

Four English novelists had close links with Clonmel: **Anthony Trollope** wrote his first two novels here (1844–48); **George Borrow**, who attended a local school, refers to Clonmel in *Lavengro*; **Marguerite Power**, the Countess of Blessington, a noted early-19C literary figure, was born at Suir Island in 1789;

▶ **Population:** 160,441

ℹ **Info:** Main Guard Building, **Clonmel**, ✆052 742 2960; Mitchell St., **Tipperary**, ✆062 80520. www.tipperary.com; Heritage Centre, Main St., **Cashel**, ✆062 62511, www.cashel.ie; Castle St., **Cahir**, ✆052 744 1453, www.visitcahir.ie.

▶ **Location:** Inland, with Co Waterford south and Co Kilkenny east.

✎ **Don't Miss:** The scenic beauty of a drive through Nier Valley.

Laurence Sterne (1713–68), author of *Tristram Shandy*, was born in Mary Street and his family lived at Suir Island.

Landmarks

The Anglican **Old St Mary's Church★**, with its unusual octagonal tower, was built in the 19C incorporating parts of earlier 14C buildings: it now accommodates an information centre.

The town's mock-Tudor gateway (1831) was built on the site of the medieval **Westgate** separating the Anglo-Norman borough from its suburb, Irishtown. Cromwell's troops destroyed Clonmel's original courthouse during the 1650 siege. Its 1674, three-storeyed replacement, **Main Guard**, adorned with the town's coat of arms, is one of Ireland's earliest public classical buildings, inspired by the architecture of Sir Christopher Wren.

Riverside

The 17C **Old Bridge** links Little Island, Suir Island and Stretches Island (named after 16C Italian immigrants called Stroccio). The north bank between the Old Bridge and the 18C **Gashouse Bridge** forms the town **quay**, where ships used to unload their cargo. Note the memorial to the Manchester Martyrs and the elegant **Georgian** terraces of houses and tall warehouses.

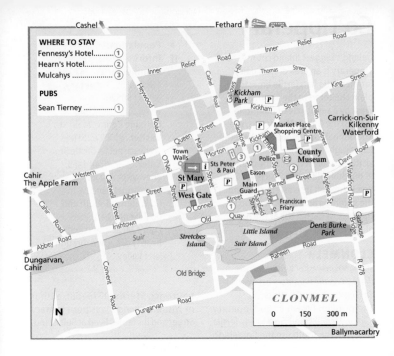

Museums

The **Tipperary County Museum★** (🕐open Tue–Sat 10am–4.45pm; 𝓟052 613 4550; www.tipperarycoco.ie) displays a wealth of artefacts from the Stone Age to the 20C and a good selection of paintings by Irish artists.

🚗 DRIVING TOUR

NIER VALLEY SCENIC ROUTE★★

Round tour of 40mi/64km, crosses the boundary into Co Waterford.

The road goes through the dark green forests, moorland and imposing escarpments of the **Comeragh Mountains★** which culminate in Knockanaffrin at 2,478ft/753m. This route offers beautiful views across the valley.

▶ From Clonmel take the R 678 south. After 5mi/8km turn right; after 4mi/6km make a detour left to a viewpoint. Return to the R 678.

Ballymacarbry★ is a hamlet nestled on the banks of River Nire. It is a good starting point for hiking in the Nier Valley.

▶ From Ballymacarbry turn right onto the R 671 to return to Clonmel.

CLONMEL AREA
Carrick-on-Suir

13mi/21km E on the N 24.

This bustling little town enjoys a prime location on the tidal Suir between Slievenamon and the Comeragh foothills). The 15C Old Bridge is the lowest river crossing before the estuary, built when the wool trade was at its height. You can trace this history at the **Heritage Centre** (♿🕐open Tues-Fri 10am-4pm (closed for lunch); 𝓟051 640 200, www.carrickonsuirheritagecentre.com), located in a 13C church off Main Street, which also serves as a tourist information office.

Ormond Castle★ (Dúchas) (🔊 admission by guided tour only (45min), daily 10am–6pm; ⊜€5; 𝓟051 640 787; www.heritageireland.ie) is the best

Moving the Masses

Charles Bianconi (1786–1875) was the son of an Italian immigrant from Lombardy. He arrived in Dublin as a teenager in 1802 with no English language skills and sold pictures on the street. Eventually making his way to Clonmel he set up business in 1809 (at No. 1 Gladstone Street), as a maker of frames. The quality of his work established his reputation as a "carver and gilder of the first class" and he found himself having to regularly travel, on foot and carrying picture frames on his back, to Waterford in connection with his work. His breakthrough was to come in the area of cheap public transport. Noting from his own hard experience, selling "on the road", how little transport there was in early 19C Ireland, he cleverly bought up cheap ex-army horses, surplus after the defeat of Napoleon, and developed carriages, which became known as "Bians" (after Bianconi). His first service ran from Clonmel to Cahir in 1815 and proved a great success. He extended the business and developed routes to Wexford, Waterford, Cork and Kilkenny through agents in the towns' hotels that serviced the passengers. As demand grew elsewhere, a network of communications, with Clonmel at the hub, spread over the whole of Ireland. At its peak the service employed 1,400 horses and 100 vehicles painted crimson and yellow, creating a nationwide revolution in the carrying of mail, freight and passengers that was only superseded by the advent of railways in the late 19C. Bianconi was voted mayor of Clonmel twice in recognition of his work.

One of the old mail cars ran between Clonmel and Dungarvan well into the 1920s, long after Bianconi retired in 1865. A mail coach horn and the clock (now handless), by which the departures were timed, are preserved in the foyer of Hearn's Hotel.

example of an Elizabethan manor house in Ireland. It was built around 1568 by the **10th Earl of Ormond** to receive his cousin, Queen Elizabeth, who disappointingly never visited Ireland at all. Highlights include fine **ornamental plasterwork**, a long gallery hung with Elizabethan portraits and a fascinating collection of charters tracing the rise in status of the Ormond family.

Kilkeeran High Crosses
17mi/27km E via the N 24 and R 697.
Three crosses, probably from the 9C, mark the site of an early monastery. The **West Cross** has eight horsemen and an unusual cap, like the plainer, possibly unfinished, East Cross. The Long Shaft Cross is the only one of its type in Ireland.

Ahenny High Crosses★
19mi/31km E via the N 24 and R 697.
The decorative interlacing and spirals so characteristic of the Book of Kells are repeated here in stone, which may mean that the two crosses (note their unusual caps) may date from as early as the 8C. The figures on the base represent seven clergymen carrying croziers, led by a cross-bearer.

Fethard★
8mi/13km N by R 689.
Fethard, an Anglo-Norman town of some importance, has retained its late-14C **town walls** and a 15C **castle** in one of three keeps. Its **church** features a late-15C crenellated tower and boasts a huge roof-span; the east window is copied from Kilcooley Abbey.

Among the ruins of a 12C Augustinian **priory** lie tombs dating from the 16C and 17C.

The **Fethard Folk Farm and Transport Museum** (👥♿🕐*open Sun and Bank Hol Mon 11.30am–5pm;* ⊛€5; ✕; ☎*052 613 1516; www.fethard.com/attra/Museum.html*) is dedicated to the rural and domestic life of earlier centuries, including bicycles, washing machines and hearses. One of Ireland's biggest car boot sales takes place here every Sunday afternoon with dealers coming from all over Ireland.

TIPPERARY

24.8mi/40km SE of Limerick by N 24.

This pleasant small county town, with enough old buildings and 19C shop-fronts to merit Heritage Town status, was a centre of Land League agitation and later the headquarters of the 3rd Tipperary Brigade of the IRA, which fought many battles in the War of Independence. It owes much of its fame, however, to the World War I marching song:

> *It's a long way to Tipperary,*
> *it's a long way to go*
> *It's a long way to Tipperary,*
> *to the sweetest girl I know.*
> *Goodbye Piccadilly,*
> *Goodbye Leicester Square,*
> *It's a long, long way to Tipperary*
> *but my heart lies there.*

Glen of Aherlow★

2m/3.2km S of Tipperary by R 664.

This lovely vale runs for 16m/26km between the forests of the Slievenamuck Ridge and the Galty Mountains, Ireland's highest inland range. The glen, once woodland, is now lush farmland. Head for the panoramic **viewpoint★★** above Newtown. A gleaming white statue of Christ the King looks to the Galtees, their splendid swooping ridgeline reaching its highest point (3,018ft/919m) at the summit of Galtymore.

ROSCREA★

Roscrea is 76mi/123km SW of Dublin via the M 7 and 46mi/74km NE of Limerick on the E 20.

Laid out on the steep banks of the Bunnow River, the prosperous agricultural town of Roscrea (*Ros Cré*) nestles between the Slieve Bloom Mountains to the North and Devils Bit Mountain to the South. It has also been nominated a Heritage Town. Ancient roadways converge on the 7C site of a monastery started by St Cronan, and where, in the early 13C, the Anglo-Irish had a strategic castle built.

Roscrea Heritage Centre - Castle and Damer House

(Dúchas). &.③*Apr–Sept 10am–6pm. Last admission 45mins before closing. Restored period gardens open at all times.* ∞€5. ☏*050 521 850. www.heritageireland.ie.*

Dominating the centre of the town is the 13C **Roscrea Castle**, an irregular polygonal enclosure contained by curtain walls and two D-shaped towers. The

Roscrea Castle

medieval gatetower was embellished with gables and chimneys in the 17C.

Damer House★ is an elegant three-storey furnished house started in 1715 by Joseph Damer, a member of a Plantation family who came to Ireland in 1661; when he died in 1720, he was deemed to be the richest man in Ireland. On completion, the house was used by the Anglican Bishop of Killaloe. Today, the rooms display exhibitions relating to local history.

Blackmill, built in 1722, is dedicated to providing information about **St Cronan's Church and Round Tower**, the remains of the monastery sacked no fewer than four times in the course of the 12C, and plundered for building stone in the 19C and then further destroyed when the main Dublin-Limerick road was completed. Little survives other than the west façade of the 12C church, a 12C **high cross** and the 8C round tower *(60ft/18m high)*, which lost its conical cap in 1135 and suffered further damage during fighting in 1798.

ROSCREA AREA
Monaincha Abbey
1mi/1.6km W of Roscrea via the N 7 and a minor road from the roundabout.
An exquisite 12C ruin, with its finely carved doorway and chancel arch, stands on a raised isolated site, which was an island until the bog was drained in the late-18C. In Early Christian times this was a famous retreat associated with various saints, notably St Cronan, which grew to become a major pilgrimage centre in the Middle Ages.

Devil's Bit Mountain
15mi/24km S of Roscrea via the N 62.
Legend has it that the gap at Devil's Bit Mountain was scooped out by the Devil to form the Rock of Cashel; in reality, it was caused by glaciers. An easy climb to the summit (1,577ft/479m) is rewarded by extensive views over the Golden Vale.

CASHEL★★★
Cashel stands on the N 8 between Cork and Portlaoise. Public car park

beside the Rock, come early morning before the coach parties descend on the town.

Rising like a mirage over the vastness of the Tipperary plain, the Rock of Cashel *(Caiseal)* is Ireland's Acropolis; its ruined buildings wonderfully evocative of the spirit of Celtic Christianity and Irish kingship. From the limestone outcrop *(200ft/60m)* rises a cluster of structures – castle and fortress, chapel, cathedral and round tower – forming the country's greatest landmark. At close quarters, the Rock reveals a wealth of pattern and texture, the primordial geometry of triangular gable, high-pitched roof, cubes, cones and cylindrical tower offset by battlements, blind arcades, slender window openings and ornate carving.

A Bit of History
Between c. AD370–1101, the rock was the seat of the kings of Munster and therefore the provincial capital, comparable in regal stature to Tara, home of the High Kings of Ireland. St Patrick visited Cashel in 450 when he baptised King Aengus; there is a legend that during the ceremony, he accidentally pierced the King's foot with the point of his staff but the King, believing it to be part of the ritual, remained composed. Cashel was a place of great importance during the 10C, when it was the stronghold of holy Cormac MacCullinan, king and bishop.

The first cathedral was founded in 1169 and in 1172 the country's clergy assembled to honour the claim of Henry II to rule all Ireland. In 1494 it was burned down by Gerald Mor, the Great Earl of Kildare. In 1647, Lord Inchiquin, seeking the presidency of Munster under the Cromwellian regime, attacked the town of Cashel; hundreds fled to the rock, so Lord Inchiquin ordered turf to be piled up against the walls of the cathedral; in the subsequent fire, many were burnt to death. By the end of that terrible day, most of the population of 3,000 had perished.

In 1749 the Anglican Archbishop of Cashel, tiring of the climb from his palace to the cathedral, decided to move

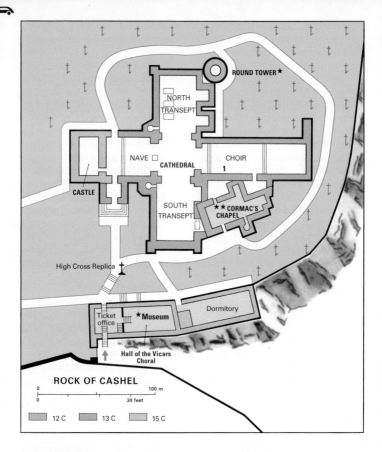

ROUND TOWER ★

NORTH TRANSEPT

NAVE
CATHEDRAL

CHOIR
1

CASTLE

SOUTH TRANSEPT

★★ CORMAC'S CHAPEL

High Cross Replica †

Ticket office   ★ Museum

Dormitory

Hall of the Vicars Choral

ROCK OF CASHEL

0 — 100 m
0 — 30 feet

12 C   13 C   15 C

the cathedral into town. The great storm of 1847 did much damage to the abandoned building.

Rock of Cashel★★★

(Dúchas) ♿ ⏰*Open daily, 9am/9.30am–5.30pm (mid Jun–mid-Sept 7pm; mid-Oct–mid-Mar 4.30pm). Last admission 45min before closing.* 🅰*Due to restoration work, access to Cormac's Chapel will be by guided tour only from May–Sept each year, until the works are complete.* ⏰*Closed 25–26 Dec.* ⌨€8. 📞*062 61437.* www.heritageireland.ie.

Cormac's Chapel★★ – Cashel's greatest treasure is the chapel started by Cormac MacCarthy in 1127. It is a highly ornate Romanesque building with twin towers, decorated with some of the earliest frescoes in Ireland and an array of carv-

ings, the most elaborate of their time. The human heads and animals are Celtic in style, while the interlace carving on a sarcophagus is of Viking inspiration.
Round Tower★ – In perfect condition, the tower, standing 92ft/28m high, is built from irregularly coursed sandstone.
Cathedral – Most of the ruin dates from the 13C, the central tower from the 14C. In the south wall of the choir is the tomb (1) of Archbishop Miler MacGrath, the Scoundrel of Cashel, who changed his religious beliefs several times and served as both Anglican and Roman Catholic bishop of Cashel during the reign of Elizabeth I; he died in 1621 at the age of 100. The west tower *(91ft/28m)*, also called the **castle**, was built as a fortified residence by Archbishop O'Hedigan in 1450.

Rock of Cashel

© Brian Morrison/Tourism Ireland

Museum★ – The museum, in the under-croft of the 15C Hall of the Vicars Choral, displays articles associated with the Rock: the stone cross of St Patrick (12C); an evil eye stone and replicas of the 9C Cashel bell and brooch.

Hall of the Vicars Choral – Extensively renovated in 1970, this was the clergy residence. The main hall *(upstairs)* contains a huge 17C stone fireplace and fine items of medieval-style furniture made by modern craftsmen. The kitchen has been restored to its original state. A video presentation in the Dormitory sets Cashel in the context of Irish history.

Brú Ború

&🕐*Open year-round Mon–Fri 9am– 5pm (mid-Jun–late Aug Tue–Sat until 11pm). Multimedia show Mon–Fri 9am– 5pm. ⊜multimedia show €5, concerts/theatre shows €20. ✕ ℘062 61122, www.bruboru.ie.*
Set at the foot of the Rock on the village green this cultural centre presents performances of native Irish music, song and dance, story-telling and folk theatre. The principal attraction by day is the Sounds of History multimedia show. There is also a genealogy service.

🐾 WALKING TOUR

▷ From the Rock, take Bishop's Walk down through Cashel Palace Hotel★ Gardens into Main St.

Cashel Heritage Centre

Main St. 🕐*Open year-round daily 9.30am–5.30pm (closed weekends Nov–Feb). ℘062 62511. www.cashel.ie.*
Displays trace the history of Cashel, its royal heirlooms and charters, and relics of the house of McCarthy Mor.

▷ From Main St walk up John St.

Cathedral and Library

The austere Anglican cathedral dedicated jointly to St John and to St Patrick of the Rock (1749–84) has a fine panelled ceiling and stalls for Dean and Chapter. In the graveyard a number of 13C carved stone coffin lids have been placed against the walls, which are part of 14C town defences.

▷ Walk through to Friar St.

Parish Church

The Roman-Catholic church of St John the Baptist, the oldest RC church in use in Ireland, was opened in 1795, screened by a row of cottages. The mosaics on the façade were added to commemorate the

Holy Cross Abbey

© Liam Murphy/Fáilte Ireland

Eucharistic Congress in Ireland (1932). The interior is unusual in that two galleries run the full length of the building and the ceiling resembles the upturned hull of a ship.

▶ Walk down to the end of Friar St; turn left into Main St and right into Dominic St.

Folk Village

&. ○ *Open year-round daily 9.30am–4.30/5.30pm (mid-Jun–mid-Sept 9am–7.30pm).* €6. 𝖯 ℘062 63601.
A reconstruction of 18C Irish rural life, including various traditional thatched village shops, a forge, other businesses and a penal Chapel. It also houses a permanent exhibition on the 1916 Easter Rising.

CASHEL AREA
Holy Cross Abbey★★
9mi/16km N of Cashel by R 660. ○ *Open 10am–6pm.* ☞ *Guided tour Feb–Oct every Wed & Sun, 2pm. Any other time by prior arrangement ℘0504 443 124.*
www.holycrossabbey.ie.
Holy Cross is one of the finest examples of 15C church architecture in the country and today serves as a flourishing parish church. It was originally founded for the Benedictines by Donal O'Brien, King of Munster (1168), and became a major

place of pilgrimage, as it was reputed to contain a relic of the True Cross. After the Dissolution it passed to the Earls of Ormond, though the monks (by now Cistercians) continued in residence into the 17C. The popularity of the abbey as a centre of pilgrimage made it wealthy, allowing the 15C rebuilding to be completed to the highest standard.
There are windows with stained glass, fine original stonework and a rare **wall-painting**, showing hunters about to kill a stag beneath an oak tree. The **grounds** contain a replica of the Vatican gardens, including the Stations of the Cross.
The eight-arch **bridge** spanning the River Suir, a copy of the original, was constructed in 1626.

Lár na Páirce
14mi/23km N of Cashel by R 660 to Thurles; Slievenamon Rd. ○ *Open Mon–Sat, 10am–5.30pm.* €5. ℘0504 22702.
This elegant 19C building houses a display on the history of the Gaelic Games.

Hore Abbey
0.5mi/0.8km W of Cashel by N 74.
The last Cistercian house to be founded in medieval Ireland, established by monks from Mellifont in 1272. Most of the present extensive ruins date from the late 13C.

Athassel Priory★

5mi/8km W of Cashel by N 74 and minor road S from Golden; across two fields.

This was once one of the most extensive and prosperous establishments of its kind in Ireland, surrounded by a town. The priory was destroyed in 1447 but parts of the main church survive.

CAHIR

In a fine location on the River Suir at the foot of the Galty Mountains, Cahir (*An Cathair*) – also known as Caher and pronounced *care* – is a busy little cross-roads town. This designated Heritage Town now benefits from a bypass carrying the main Dublin–Cork highway. Its formidable castle, built on a rocky islet in the river, was the residence of Brian Ború, the High King of Ireland, in the 10/11C. The present stronghold was begun in the 13C, then greatly modified and extended by the powerful Anglo-Irish Butler dynasty, which retained possession until it passed to the State in 1961.

Cahir Castle★★

(Dúchas). ⏰*Open daily year-round 9.30am–5.30pm (4.30pm mid-Oct–Feb). Mid-Jun–Aug 9am–6.30pm. Last admission 45mins before closing.*

⏰*Closed Dec 24–30.* ∞€5. ✆*052 744 1011. www.heritageireland.ie.*

Though much restored, Cahir Castle is one of the largest and finest examples of a late-medieval stronghold in Ireland, with a high outer wall, outer, middle and inner wards, a barbican, sturdy towers and a splendid keep. It expresses the power and pride of the Anglo-Norman Butlers, Earls of Ormond, who held sway over much of southeastern Ireland, even though its defences failed to save it from falling to an assault by troops led by Queen Elizabeth I's favourite, the Earl of Essex. A 15-min audio-visual covers its history and guided tours (*30–40min*) explores its passageways, spiral staircases, sentry walks and great hall.

▷ Walk along Castle Street to the Square.

The **Cahir House Hotel**, the former family seat of the Butlers after the castle had fallen into disrepair, and the Market House (now the library) are part of the 18C transformation of the town centre by the Butlers; the mills also date from this period.

▷ Walk along Old Church Street (N 24 to Clonmel).

Cahir Castle

© Liam Murphy/Fáilte Ireland

Swiss Cottage

© Patrick Browne/Fáilte Ireland

The ruined church, last used in the 1820s, had a curtain wall, which allowed Roman Catholics and Protestants to worship simultaneously; in the 19C, when Cahir was an important garrison town, part of the adjoining cemetery was reserved for military burials. Many Cahir men fell in World War I and are commemorated by the Great War Memorial, a rarity in an Irish town.

◗ Return to the Square and turn right into Church Street (N 8 north towards Cashel).

The Anglican **St Paul's Church** was designed in 1820 by John Nash, the famous Regency architect.

CAHIR AREA
Swiss Cottage★
1mi/2km S of Cahir by R 670 or on foot along the riverbank. (Dúchas).
Visit by guided tour (40min) only, 17th-19th Mar, Apr-Nov, 10am–6pm.
This is a very busy site, arrive early to avoid delays during Summer. €5. 052 744 1144.
www.heritageireland.ie.
John Nash designed this elaborate thatched cottage, built in 1812–14, as a fishing and hunting lodge for Lord Cahir. In one of the two ground-floor rooms, the hand-painted French wallpaper shows views of the Bosporus.

Mitchelstown Cave
9mi/14.5km W by N 8; in Boolakennedy, turn left. Open by guided tour only, daily Feb-May, Nov 10am–4pm (4.45pm Jun–Aug). Sep-Oct 10am-4.30pm, Dec-Jan 10am–4pm (weekends only). €9. 052 746 7246.
www.mitchelstowncave.com.
A flight of 88 steep steps leads into three massive caverns (1mi/2km) containing dripstone formations – stalactites and stalagmites, curtains and pipes: the most impressive being the Tower of Babel, a huge calcite column, measuring 250ft/76m long.

ADDRESSES

CASHEL

🏨 STAY

🛏–🛏🛏 **Ladyswell House** – *Ladyswell St. 5rm. ☎062 62985. www.ladyswellhouse.com.* Situated under the Rock of Cashel, this luxury B&B is famed for its breakfasts.

🍴 EAT

🍽🍽🍽 **Chez Hans** – *Moore Lane. ☎062 61177, www.chezhans.net. Dinner only.* A converted church is the setting for this popular restaurant famous for its atmosphere and its steaks, beef and lamb dishes. Next door Cafe Hans (🍽🍽) is also excellent; closes 6pm.

ENTERTAINMENT/NIGHTLIFE

Brú Ború Theatre
For a **traditional Irish evening** (🔆*see Rock of Cashel*).

SHOPPING

Farney Castle Visitor Centre, *Holycross, Co Tipperary. cyrilcullen. wordpress.com/farney-castle. Open Mon–Sat, 10am–5.30pm. Castle 🎫€6; shop free.* ✘ *☎0504 43281.* Farney Castle, built in 1495 and augmented in 1800, is the only round tower in Ireland occupied as a family home. In fact it is the home, design studio and retail outlet of Irish international designer, Cyril Cullen, famed for his rare Jacob sheep wool sweaters and Fine Parian porcelain figurines (on sale here).

TRACING ANCESTORS

Brú Ború – (🔆*see Rock of Cashel*).

Tipperary Family History Research – *Tipperary Exel. Open Mon–Fri, 10am –4.30pm. ☎062 80555. www.tfhr.org.*

CLONMEL

🏨 STAY

🛏 **Fennessy's Hotel** – *Gladstone St. ☎052 612 3680. www.fennessyshotel.com.* Early-19C building and now a family-run hotel. Attractive décor and comfortable rooms.

🛏 **Mulcahys** – *Gladstone St. ☎052 612 5054. www.mulcahys.ie.* From the outside it's just a pub but it also has nice bedrooms, a restaurant and a nightclub.

🛏🛏 **Hearn's Hotel** – *Parnell St. 26rm. ☎052 612 1611.* This 18C family-run hotel is a popular meeting place in town. Its pub with 5 bars, 4 rooms, 3 DJ's, 2 dance floors and a huge beer garden is very lively indeed.

🍴 EAT

🍽🍽 **Befani's Mediterranean & Tapas Restaurant** – *6 Sarsfield St. ☎052 617 7893, www.befani.com.* Not a large menu but a discerning one that offers meat, fish and vegetarian options in a congenial setting.

PUB

Sean Tierney – *13 O'Connell St. ☎052 612 4467, www.seantierneys.com.* Voted best pub in Tipperary 14 times, with a restaurant upstairs, serving typical pub grub.

Co Kilkenny★★

The idyllic countryside of the county of Kilkenny offers more than just pastoral scenes of pretty water meadows filled with well-fed, grazing animals. Its winding country roads and footpaths, meandering rivers and verdant fields are a repository for ancient ruins that tell the story of Ireland in their stones. At its heart the city itself displays its medieval heritage with pride and it serves as the natural base for exploring the county's footpaths and its generous share of tiny, relatively traffic-free roads.

▶ **Population:** 95,419

▤ **Info:** Shee Alms House, Rose Inn Street, Kilkenny City. ☏056 775 1500. www.kilkennytourism.ie.

◖ **Location:** Inland, with Co Wexford SE and Co Waterford SW.

⊛ **Don't Miss:** Kilkenny Castle, St Canice's Cathedral, Jerpoint Abbey.

◷ **Timing:** Kilkenny City is a good base to explore southeast Ireland.

KILKENNY★★

32mi/51.5km N of Waterford.
Kilkenny *(Cill Chainnigh)* is Ireland's outstanding medieval city, set on the banks of the River Nore and dominated by the castle and cathedral. Narrow alleys, known locally as slips, recall the medieval street pattern. The city's historical legacy, splendidly expressed in any number of well-restored ancient buildings, is matched by a strong cultural and artistic tradition.

A Bit of History

Capital of the Kingdom of Ossory – The city is named after St Canice, the 6C founder of a church here, in what was, from the 2C to the 12C, the capital of the Gaelic Kingdom of Ossory, mainly ruled by the MacGiolla Phadruig family, who

Kilkenny
© Aurelie Amiot/Tourism Ireland

constantly struggled for the kingship of Leinster.

Statutes of Kilkenny – Following the Anglo-Norman invasion (12C), Kilkenny quickly assumed strategic and political importance as a major venue for Anglo-Irish parliaments. Under Anglo-Norman rule, the native clans and the invaders lived alongside each other in relative harmony despite frequent incomprehension. Over the centuries, the Anglo-Norman families, led by the dominant Butler clan, integrated into the native Gaelic culture, adopting their dress and language, and intermarrying. Not unnaturally, this process displeased the authorities in Dublin and England: so in 1366, the **Statutes of Kilkenny** were passed by Parliament to prohibit the Anglo-Normans from intermingling with the Irish; but it was too late and the new laws were ignored.

Confederation of Kilkenny – The height of Kilkenny's authority (1642–48) came when the Confederation of Kilkenny functioned as an independent Irish parliament, representing both the old Irish and the Anglo-Irish Roman Catholics. When this body split, the Anglo-Irish sided with the English Viceroy and the Old Irish looked to Pope Innocent X for support. The Old Irish, led by Owen Roe O'Neill, were eventually defeated; following Cromwell's siege of Kilkenny in 1650, the Irish army

© macmillan media/Tourism Ireland

Kilkenny Castle

was permitted to march out of the city. **Nationalist Tradition** – Kilkenny has always had a strongly nationalistic tradition and played a key role in the movement for independence early in the 20C. **William T. Cosgrave**, the first president of the Executive Council, was a steadfast leader in the young Free State, acting as Sinn Féin member for Kilkenny at Westminster and then in the Irish Parliament *(Dáil)*.

Kilkenny Castle and Park★★

(Dúchas)&♿☞*Visit by guided tours only, Jun–Aug 9am–5.30pm; Apr–May 9.30am–5.30pm; Oct–Feb 9.30am–4.30pm; Mar 9.30am–5pm. Last admission, 1hr before closing.* ⏱*Closed Good Fri and Christmas hols.* ♿€8 ✗ ✆*056 770 4100. www.heritageireland.ie.*

The castle, built by William the Earl Marshal (1192–1207), overlooks the River Nore. Uniquely among Irish castles, it was a nobleman's residence: the seat of the Butler family, Earls and Dukes of Ormond, who dominated the Southeast of Ireland. Much of the medieval fabric remains, including three of the four corner towers, though it was acquired by the state in 1967 to save it from dereliction. Today, after much restoration, the great stronghold provides a window on the lifestyle of the Anglo-Irish aristocracy.

The most imposing interior is the 19C **Long Gallery★★** hung with Gobelin tapestries and family portraits, with a hammerbeam roof decorated with pre-Raphaelite neo-Celtic motifs.

In the basement is the **Butler Gallery** *(*&♿*open daily May–Sept 10am–5.30pm; Mar–Apr 10am–1pm, 2pm–4.30pm (5pm Mar); Oct–Feb 10am–1pm, 2pm–4.30pm;* ✆*056 776 1106; www.butlergallery.com)*, which displays 19C–20C Irish art and visiting contemporary art exhibitions. Housed in the monumental 18C stable buildings of the castle, the **Kilkenny Design Centre** *(*&♿*open as castle;* ✆*056 772 2118; www.kilkennydesign. com)*, is a major retail outlet for high-quality souvenirs and provides accommodation for a variety of craftspeople. It was set up in the 1960s as a focal point for improvement in the design of ceramics, textiles, furniture and jewellery. It also incorporates a very good food hall and self-service café-restaurant.

Also in the old stables is **The National Craft Gallery** *(*&♿*Open Tue–Sat & bank hol Mons 10am–5.30pm, Sun 11am–5.30pm;* ✆*056 779 6147; www.national-craftgallery.ie)*, which stages exhibitions of some of the finest contemporary craft and design from Ireland and abroad.

The extensive **park** (50 acres/20ha) has formal gardens and woodland.

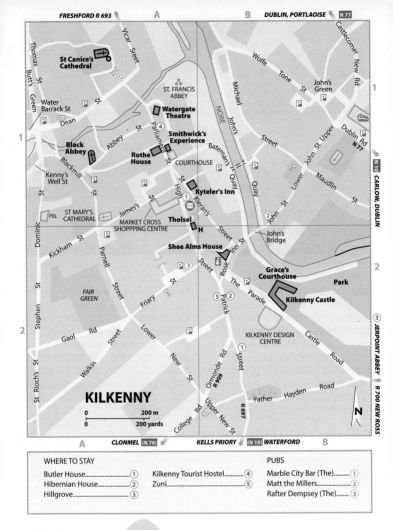

FRESHFORD R 693 A | B **DUBLIN, PORTLAOISE** N 77

KILKENNY

```
0        200 m
0        200 yards
```

CLONMEL N 76 | **KELLS PRIORY** N 10 **WATERFORD** B

WHERE TO STAY

Butler House	①	Kilkenny Tourist Hostel	④
Hibernian House	②	Zuni	⑤
Hillgrove	③		

PUBS

Marble City Bar (The)	①
Matt the Millers	②
Rafter Dempsey (The)	③

WALKING TOUR

Among the vestiges of the old town, is the 16C **Shee Alms House**, Rose Inn Street, once used as a hospice and now the tourist office (*open Mon–Fri 9.30am–6pm, Sat 10am–6pm; 056 775 1500*) and the 18C **Tholsel**, a former toll house, customs house, courthouse and guild hall, now the town hall.
Grace's Courthouse (also known as **Grace's Castle**) stands above the remains of a castle (1210), which served as a prison in the 16C and then a court-house in the 19C.

▶ Walk up Rose Inn Street and turn right into High Street.

Rothe House & Garden★

Open Mon–Sat 10.30am–5pm, Sun 12pm–5pm. Closed 24 Dec–first week Jan. €5.50. Genealogy service. 056 772 2893. www.rothehouse.com.
With its splendid Tudor façade, this is the only remaining town house of the Renaissance period in Ireland. Built in 1594 by a local merchant, John Rothe, it was used in the 17C as a meeting place by religious and political leaders during

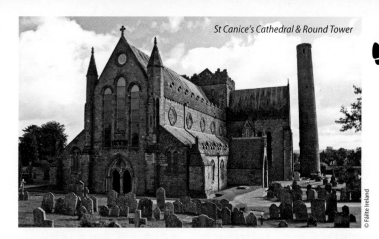
St Canice's Cathedral & Round Tower

© Fáilte Ireland

the Kilkenny Confederation, then in the 19C by the nationalist Gaelic League. It now houses the local museum, featuring an entertaining and rotating programme of local exhibits. Its walled garden, of vegetables, herbs, and fruit trees re-creates its 17C original.

◯ Continue N along Parliament Street over the bridge; cross Dean Street and take the steps up to the Cathedral.

St Canice's Cathedral & Round Tower★★

Open Cathedral: Jun–Aug, 9am (1pm Sun)–6pm. Rest of year Mon–Sat 10am–1pm, 2pm–5pm, Sun 2pm–5pm (closes 4pm Oct–Mar). Open Tower: Mon–Sat noon & 3pm, Sun 3pm (min age 12 yrs). Tower usually closed Oct. €4 Cathedral; €3 Round Tower. Combined ticket: Cathedral/Round Tower €6. 056 776 4971. www.stcanicescathedral.ie.

This 13C Early-Gothic cathedral is thought to stand on the raised site of St Canice's 6C church. It is best approached by St Canice's Steps (SE) laid out in the early 17C when damage inflicted by Cromwell (who stabled horses in the nave) necessitated repairs. There are many fine tombs: most notably that in black Kilkenny marble of Piers Butler, Earl of Ormond, and Ossory (d. 1539) and his wife Margaret Fitzgerald; her effigy has a finely jewelled and embroidered girdle. The oldest tomb (13C) bears part of the original dog-tooth ornament.

The oldest gravestone is the **Kyteler slab**, inscribed in Norman French in memory of Jose Kyteler, probably the father of Dame Alice Kyteler, who was tried for witchcraft in 1323.

In the graveyard stands the **round tower** (100ft/30m high), built between 700 and 1000, offering views of Kilkenny and surrounding countryside .

◯ From Parliament St turn left into Abbey St, through the medieval Black Freren Gate.

Black Abbey★

The **medieval church**, founded c. 1225 for the Dominicans and repressed in 1543, served as the city's courthouse from the 17C. It was re-consecrated in the 19C. The interior is lit by fine early-14C traceried windows and a lovely alabaster carving of the **Most Holy Trinity★** beside the altar from c. 1400 despite the inscription. In the graveyard are 10 stone coffins dating from the 13C and 14C.

THOMASTOWN

11mi/18km S of Kilkenny by R 700.
Little twisting streets converge on the main street close to the old bridge over the Nore, half-obliterated by its modern concrete deck. **The (Ladywell) Water Garden** (open Mar–Nov 9.30am–

5pm; ◷closed Public Hols; ⬮donation requested; ✕; ℘056 772 4690) is an intricate mixture of trees, shrubs and aquatic plants.

KILFANE GLEN AND WATERFALL★

14mi/23km S of Kilkenny by R 700 and N 9 N from Thomastown. ◷*Open Jul–Aug 11am–6pm.* ⬮€7. ℘056 7727105. *www.kilfane.com.*

This wonderful, unusual Romantic creation from the late-18C nestles in a wooded ravine, with more formal contemporary gardens and modern sculpture added later – including an installation by the American artist, James Turrell, inviting visitors to contemplate the sky. Precipitous walks, steps and bridges, a waterfall and a delightful thatched cottage orné set in a grassy glen testify to the Power family's interest and love of the landscape since the 1790s.

The ruined church in the village contains a famous effigy, the **Cantwell Knight★**, a fine carving of a Norman nobleman, Thomas de Cantwell, who died around 1320. The effigy is quite a sight and gives a remarkable impression of just how daunting an armed Norman could have appeared to the native Irish.

JERPOINT ABBEY★★

12mi/19km S of Kilkenny by R 700 and N 9 S from Thomastown. (Dúchas) ♿ ◷*Open early Mar–Sept 9am–5.30pm, Oct 9am–5pm, Nov–early Dec 9.30am–4pm.* ⬮€5. ℘056 772 4623. *www.heritageireland.ie.*

A sturdy tower, with its stepped Irish battlements rising over the Little Arrigle River, is a landmark for the ruins of what was once one of the country's foremost Cistercian monasteries.

Cistercian monks from Baltinglass in Co Wicklow (♿*see ATHY*) arrived here in 1180, and constructed their own complex on an earlier Benedictine house. In the mid-13C there were 36 monks and 50 lay-brothers; after the Dissolution (1540), the monastery, its farm buildings, fisheries and considerable estates passed to the Earl of Ormond. The **visitor centre** has a small exhibition devoted to medieval stone carving. The abbey **church** has the classic Cistercian cruciform plan. The transepts, which belong to the original late-12C construction, have two chapels each. In the **chancel** are splendid effigies of two bishops, one believed to be Felix O'Dulany, first abbot of Jerpoint and bishop of Ossory (1178–1202). The church is also home to a fine sculptured tomb of a harper and his wife,

Jerpoint Abbey

© Chris Hill Photographic/Tourism Ireland

a rare example of a 16C civilian effigy anywhere in Ireland. On the north wall are remains of a 15C–16C wall painting showing the heraldic shields of Jerpoint's main benefactors.

The columns of the 14C or 15C **cloisters★** (restored) bear remarkable carvings of animals, saints, knights and ladies in contemporary attire and armour.

KELLS PRIORY★★

8mi/13km S of Kilkenny by R 697.

The tranquil remains of this priory by the Kings River are some of the largest and most spectacular ruins in Ireland. Founded in 1193 by Geoffrey de Marisco, with four Augustinian canons from Bodmin in Cornwall, the priory suffered repeated attacks; the extensive *(5 acres/2ha)* site is enclosed by a curtain wall with towers and a gateway. Most of what you see dates from the 14C and 15C, and the site as a whole gives a good impression of what a medieval settlement in Ireland would have looked like.

EDMUND RICE HERITAGE CENTRE

Callan; 10mi/16km SW of Kilkenny via the N76. &. ⏱*Open year-round daily 10am–1pm 2pm–6pm (Oct–Mar 5pm).* ⏱*Closed Good Fri, 25 Dec.* ✆*056 772 5993. www.edmundrice.net*

This complex with its visitor centre and chapel, is built around his cottage **birthplace**. The kitchen has a stone-flagged floor, open hearth and spinning wheel, as in Rice's day: other rooms are similarly preserved with furniture of the period. In the town of Callan there are substantial remains of a 15C-Augustinian priory.

BRÓD TULLAROAN

10mi/16km W of Kilkenny by a minor road. ⏱*Open Mar–Nov Mon–Fri 10am–5.30pm, Sun 2pm–5pm; Storytelling/ music nights (min party size, 20 people).* ⊜€4. ✗ ✆*087 668 8881.*

The "Pride of Tullaroan" heritage centre, set in deep countryside, is devoted to the memory of **Lory Meagher**, the "prince of hurlers" who dominated the sport in Co Kilkenny in the 1920s and 1930s. The thatched farmhouse where he was born and lived has been restored and furnished to evoke the period around 1884, the year in which the Gaelic Athletic Association was founded by Lory's father among others. The **Museum of Hurling** presents the fascinating local history of the sport.

KILCOOLY ABBEY

21mi/32km NW of Kilkenny by R 693; from Urlingford, take R 689 S for 3.5mi/ 5.5km; 500yd/0.5km on foot from the parish church car park.

The substantial ruins of this Cistercian abbey, founded c 1200, include a massive tower and a cloister; in the field stands a large dovecot.

DUNMORE CAVE★

7mi/11km N of Kilkenny by N 77 and N 78. (Dúchas). ⮕ *Visit by guided tour only (1hr), Open all year, 9.30am–5pm (6.30pm Jun–Sep), Nov–Mar Wed-Sun only. (last admission 1hr to 90mins before closing).* ⊜€5. ✗ ✆*056 776 7726. www.heritageireland.ie.*

Beneath the isolated Castlecomer limestone outcrop is this large cave encrusted with stalagmites and stalactites. The visitor centre explains the site's geology and history. The 10C tale of a horrible massacre by Vikings seemed partially confirmed when 40 or so human skeletons were found in 1973, adding to the Viking remains, coins, brass buckles and delicate silverwork of North African origin recovered in the 1880s.

CASTLECOMER

11.5mi/19km N of Kilkenny by N 77 and N 78.

The village was laid out in Italian style by Sir Christopher Wandesforde in 1635; his family mined coal in the region for three centuries. There is no more coalmining, but plenty of mementoes are preserved at the Coal Mine Lounge pub. The town's name comes from an Anglo-Norman castle that once stood here, but now there is only a mound marking its former location.

ADDRESSES

KILKENNY

🛏️ STAY

Hillgrove–*Warrington, Bennettsbridge Rd.* ✆*056 772 2890. http://homepage. eircom.net/~hillgrove.* If you don't mind being on the outskirts of town then the friendly helpful hosts, boasting a National Breakfast Award, make this comfortable retreat very popular.

Kilkenny Tourist Hostel – *35 Parliament St.* ✆*056 776 3541. www.kilkennyhostel.ie. 60 beds.* Centrally located, this hostel's rooms offer from four to eight beds but private rooms are also available. Fully equipped kitchen and free wi-fi.

Zuni – *26 Patrick St.* ✆*056 772 3999. www.zuni.ie. 13 rms.* The building's origins as Kilkenny's first cinema are reflected in the original façade and contrast with the stylish and modern interior, following its conversion into a boutique hotel and restaurant. Excellent value.

Hibernian House – *St Patrick St. 10rm.*✆*056 776 4848. www.hibernian-housekilkenny.com.* Smart B&B accommodation very close to Kilkenny Castle.

Butler House – *16 St Patrick St.* ✆*056 772 2828. www.butler.ie.* Built as part of Kilkenny Castle Estate and restored in the 1970s, Butler House offers superbly classy accommodation, in a beautiful location in manicured gardens. Breakfast is served across the way in the Kilkenny Design Centre.

🍴 EAT

Zuni – *26 Patrick St.* ✆*056 772 3999. www.zuni.ie.* The city's trendiest restaurant, voted Best in Ireland 2012 by one reputable Irish food guide, mixes modern Irish cuisine with Mediterranean, Middle Eastern and Asian influences. For informal eating there is also the Cafe & Tapas Bar.

PUBS

The Marble City Bar& Tearooms – *66 High St.* ✆*056 776 1143. www.langtons.ie/ bars.* One of the oldest public houses in the county, the Marble City has retained many of its original features and exudes a warm & friendly atmosphere. The Marble City Bar offers an informal menu boasting fresh local dishes in The 67 room (with live music nightly), and an extensive range of teas, plus coffee, wine and beer in The Tea & Wine Rooms.

Rafter Dempsey's–*Friary St.* ✆*056 772 2970. www.rafterdempseys.ie.* A pub, restaurant and guesthouse with decent pub grub and live music.

Matt The Millers–*John St.* ✆*056 776 1696. www.mattthemillers.com.* A large place, with different bars on four floors, (some catering to an up-for-it young crowd) with trad weekday sessions at 6.30pm and also live music at weekends.

SHOPPING

In addition to the craft outlets in the Castle stables, a number of craft studios including **Nicholas Mosse** *(www.nicholasmosse.com)*, are grouped in the **Irish Country Shop & Cafe** in Bennettsbridge *(7mi/11km south)*, housed in an old flour mill.

For hand-blown glass, where the craftsmen can be seen at work, visit **Jerpoint Glass Studio** *(south of Stoneyford on the Thomastown road; www.jerpointglass.com)*.

SPORTS AND LEISURE

The magnificent estate of **Mount Juliet** (1,400 acres/567ha) offers many sporting facilities, the star attraction being a golf course designed by Jack Nicklaus. Other activities include horseriding, archery, clay target shooting, angling and a spa. *www. mountjuliet.ie.*

EVENTS AND FESTIVALS

Kilkenny Arts Festival – Ireland's top arts festival, featuring classical music, visual art, theatre, literature, children's arts and outdoor events *(mid-Aug. www.kilkennyarts.ie)*.

The Cat Laughs Comedy Festival – Rated the best comedy festival in the world by some, and featuring comedians from Ireland and abroad at venues across town *(4 days over late May bank hol weekend, www.thecatlaughs.com)*.

Co Wexford★

Bounded on the Southwest by the River Barrow, the Northwest by the Blackstairs Mountains and on the East by a long, sandy and constantly eroding coastline, County Wexford is an excellent area for bird watching and has many beaches to explore. The county town has a long history and a vibrant cultural life while quaint fishing villages such as Kilmore Quay still show off their 19C architecture.

▶ **Population:** 145,273
ℹ **Info:** Crescent Quay, **Wexford**, ℘053 912311, www.visitwexford.ie; 1798 Visitor Centre, Mill Park Road, **Enniscorthy**, ℘053 923 7596; The Quay, **New Ross**, ℘051 361 016, www. experiencenewross.com.
☺ **Don't Miss:** The Irish National Heritage Park for a compact history of the country.

WEXFORD★

Wexford lies in the southeast corner of the county, 37mi/60km east of Waterford. The ferry terminal at Rosslare Harbour (5mi/8km southeast) provides passenger and car ferry services from Ireland to South Wales and the ports of northern France.

The county town and the commercial centre of the southeast region, Wexford *(Loch Garman)*, set on the south bank of the River Slaney, where it enters Wexford Harbour, is a place of great antiquity, first granted a charter in 1317. It is a designated Heritage Town with a strong cultural tradition and is famous for its annual international opera festival.

A Bit of History

The site of Wexford was noted by Ptolemy in his 2C AD map, but the town's history really began when the Vikings arrived in 950, naming their settlement Waesfjord (the harbour of the mud-flats). Following the Anglo-Norman invasion (1169), Wexford was captured and the first Anglo-Irish treaty signed at Selskar Abbey. In the 13C the earthen ramparts of the Norse town were replaced by stone walls.

In 1649 Cromwell entered Wexford; Selskar Abbey was destroyed and hundreds, possibly thousands, of citizens were massacred in the market place.

During the rebellion of the United Irishmen in 1798 Wexford was held for a month by the insurgents, some of whom treated their opponents with extreme cruelty.

It was then recaptured, with even more bloodshed by Crown forces.

In the 19C, led by local shipping companies, Wexford built up a strong maritime trade. Silting of the harbour and competition from Waterford led to its decline in the early 20C but the town's proximity to the harbour at Rosslare and its vibrant cultural life have more than compensated for this in recent years.

Crescent Quay

Wexford's long quayside and promenade, facing the broad and tidal River Slaney, is relieved by the curve of Crescent Quay; a statue honours John Barry, a native of Co Wexford, who became senior commodore of the US Navy in 1794. The tourist office is on the quay and **walking tours** (🚶 *daily 11am–Mar–Oct; 1hr 30min, €5; www. wexfordwalkingtours.net*) of the city depart from here.

Main Street★

The commercial centre of Wexford is a long and narrow winding pedestrianised street, fronted by grey slate building typical of the area, and shops that retain their traditional 19C design and style of country town establishments.

St Iberius' Church★

🕐*Open year-round, daily 10am–4pm (occasionally 3pm in winter).*
The Anglican church stands on an ancient Christian site, formerly at the water's edge. The present Georgian

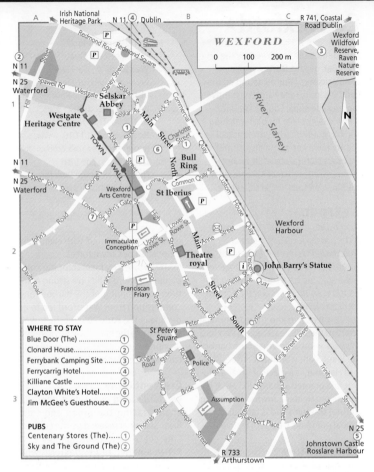

church dates from 1760. The Venetian façade is mid-19C.

Bull Ring

The scene of Cromwell's devastating massacre in 1649 is marked by the **Bull Ring**, once used for bull baiting, a pastime popular in 12C/13C Wexford.

The **1798 Memorial** shows the bronze figure of a pikeman, a dramatic work by Oliver Sheppard (1864–1941), designer of many patriotic monuments.

Selskar Abbey

Only the outer walls and square tower remain of the abbey, founded c. 1190 by the Anglo-Norman nobleman Sir Alexander de la Roche on his return from the Crusades. In 1170–71 Henry II, King of England, spent time in Ireland, partly to assert his authority over the ambitious Strongbow, perhaps partly to escape the opprobrium following the murder of Thomas à Becket, and it was at Selskar that he passed the whole of Lent in 1171 doing penance for the assassination of his archbishop.

West Gate Heritage Centre

Spawell Road. ⊙*Open Feb–Dec, Mon–Sat 10am–5.30pm.* ⊞*Audio-visual €3.* ℗ ℘*053 914 6506.*

This is the only one of the five original fortified gates still standing; it was built by Sir Stephen Devereux c. 1200 and closed to traffic in the late 16C.

There is an audio-visual presentation of the town's history, and Norman rooms in the tower give access to a battlement walk to Selskar Abbey.

Twin Churches★

The **Church of the Immaculate Conception** *(Rowe Street)* and the **Church of the Assumption** *(Bride Street – south)* were both designed by Augustus Pugin in an almost identical Gothic style; their towers are the same height (230ft/70m) and their foundation stones were laid on the same day in 1851.

Franciscan Friary★

🕐 *Open 9.30am–5.30pm (1.30pm Sun).*
📞 *053 912 2758.*

The church founded by the Franciscans in 1230 was confiscated in 1540 at the Dissolution of the Monasteries, but returned in 1622. The present church *(restored)* has an attractive stucco ceiling and works by contemporary Irish artists, including *The Burning Bush Tabernacle* sculpted by Brother Benedict Tutty of Glenstal Abbey.

In 2007, after 750 years in residence at Wexford, a lack of vocations meant that the Franciscans could no longer sustain themselves here. The Friary has been taken over by the Grey Friars brotherhood.

WEXFORD AREA

Rosslare (Ros Láir)

10mi/16km S of Wexford via the N 25.
The popular seaside resort and ferry port has a fine beach *(6mi/10km)* with ample sporting facilities.

Lady's Island

11mi/18km south of Wexford via the N 25 and a minor road from Killinick.
This former centre of pilgrimage developed around an Augustinian friary and Norman castle. **Tacumshane Windmill** *(🔑Key available from Meyler's Millhouse Bar & Restaurant next door; leave a donation if possible)* built in 1846, was restored complete with sails, in the 1950s. **Tacumshin Lake** attracts flocks of wintering wildfowl.

Kilmore Quay★

15mi/24km SW Wexford, N 25 and R 739.
This fishing village retains some of its 19C character, notably where the houses are thatched. The *Wooden House* pub has a fine collection of historic photographs.

Saltee Islands★

www.salteeislands.info. Boat trips from Kilmore Quay; 3mi/4.8km.
The Great and Little Saltee Islands (each about 0.5mi/0.8km long) form Ireland's largest bird sanctuary (gannets, guillemots, puffins).

Irish Agricultural Museum, Johnstown Castle★★

5mi/8km SW of Wexford via the N 25.
♿🕐*Open Mar–Oct daily 9am–5pm (11am–4pm Sat–Sun and Bank Hols). Nov–Feb Mon–Fri 9am–4pm, Sat–Sun and Bank Hols 11am–4pm.* 🎫€6

Johnstown Castle

© Peter Zoeller/Design Pics/Getty Images

museum, €3 gardens, €8 both; gardens free winter. Ⓐ Payment by cash only. ✗ 𝄢 053 918 4671. www.irishagrimuseum.ie. The Johnstown estate was donated to the Irish State in 1945 and **Johnstown Castle** (closed to the public), designed by Daniel Robertson, houses an agricultural research centre.

The park (50 acres/20ha) contains **ornamental grounds** with over 200 species of trees and shrubs, three ornamental lakes, walled gardens and hothouses.

The well-presented **Agricultural Museum** documents Irish agricultural life from the turn of the 18C until the middle of the 20C. The transport section includes tub traps, a late-19C jaunting car, carts, traps and harness; corn winnowing machines and old tractors. There are reconstructions of a cooperage, a harness-maker's workshop, a blacksmith's forge and a carpenter's shop; a re-creation of 19C Irish rural living; a display of fine Irish country furniture and much more. The **Famine Exhibition** is a thorough interpretation of the causes, effects and aftermath of the Great Famine (1845–49), with recreations of a rural home and a soup kitchen.

Irish National Heritage Park★

Ferrycarrig. 2.5mi/4km NW of Wexford via the N 11. ♿Ⓞ*Open year-round daily 9.30am–6.30pm (Sept–Apr 5.30pm, last admission 3pm–3.30pm).* ⬤€9.50. ✗ 𝄢053 912 0733. www.inhp.com.

Some 9,000 years of Irish history, from the first man up to the Normans, are brought to life by 16 separate archaeological and historical reconstructions, all located in their natural settings, linked by a trail.

The **Stone Age**, 7000–2000 BC, is represented by a Mesolithic camp site, an early Irish farmstead and a portal dolmen. The **Bronze Age** is illustrated by a cist burial chamber and a stone circle. The Celtic and early-Christian ages are represented by an early-Christian monastery, an **Ogham stone** showing the earliest form of writing in Ireland, and a **crannóg**, an artificial island protected by a palisade. The horizontal watermill is a reconstruction of a Co Cork mill dating from 833. The round tower is a replica, built in 1857 to commemorate Wexford men killed in the Crimean War.

The only authentic historic relics are the Norman earthworks and fortifications, built by Robert FitzStephen in 1169. Other exhibitions cover the Great Potato Famine and Harry Ferguson and his tractors.

Wexford Wildfowl Reserve

3mi/5km N of Wexford via the R 741. (Dúchas). Ⓞ*Visitor Centre open daily year-round, 9am–5pm.* Ⓞ*Closed 25 Dec.* 𝄢*053 912 3406. www.heritageireland.ie. www.wexfordwildfowlreserve.ie.*

For eight months of the year most of the world's population of Greenland

Irish National Heritage Park

© Chris Hill Photographic/Tourism Ireland

white-fronted geese winters on the north shore of Wexford Harbour. Exhibitions and an audio-visual introduce the reserve to visitors.

Curracloe★

6mi/9km N of Wexford, R 741 and R 742.
Thatched cottages, glorious sand dunes and seemingly endless sandy beaches (7mi/11km) overlook Wexford Bay.

ENNISCORTHY

Enniscorthy sits on the junction of the N 11, running between Dublin and Wexford.

The market town of Enniscorthy *(Inis Córthaidh)* occupies an attractive site on the steep slopes of the River Slaney at its tidal limit. Historically, the town played a key role in the 1798 rebellion. Castle and cathedral dominate a townscape that has scarcely changed since the 19C. Local events are commemorated in the 1798 memorial *(Market Square)* showing Fr Murphy leading the uprising, while the 1916 Easter Rising is marked by Seamus Rafter, a local commander *(Abbey Square)*.

The surrounding country is well suited to the growing of soft fruit, celebrated at the Strawberry Fair in early July.

A Bit of History

Monastic Foundation – The origins of Enniscorthy go back to the 6C, when St Senan arrived from Scattery Island to found a monastic settlement at Templeshannon, on the east bank of the River Slaney. From the 12C, the monastery's fortunes were controlled by the Normans, who ruled from their castle until the 15C, when the MacMurrough Kavanaghs clan gained control. In the late 16C, Queen Elizabeth I appointed Sir Henry Wallop and Philip Stamp to put an end to local rule.

Commercial Development – Commercial exploitation in Elizabethan times: trees were felled and the timber was exported to France and Spain through Wexford; Philip Stamp set up an ironworks, which survived until the 1940s, and brought many English families to settle in Enniscorthy, which expanded across the River Slaney. At the close of the 18C, several distillery and brewery businesses were launched; by 1796, Enniscorthy had 23 malthouses.

Today, the main concerns revolve around bacon curing, fruit growing, cutlery and potteries.

National 1798 Visitor Centre

The Quay, south of town centre.
&🕐Open Mon–Fri 9.30am–5pm, Sat–Sun & Bank holidays noon–5pm. ✆€7.
✕ ☏053 923 7596. www.1798centre.ie.
This visitor centre was opened to mark the bicentenary of the 1798 uprising and to study the birth of popular democracy in Ireland. The rebellion, particularly the three weeks of disruption in Co Wexford, is presented in vivid detail; parallels are made with contemporary events in France and America and the emergence of modern political parties are reviewed. The highlight is the stirring virtual recreation of the Battle of Vinegar Hill (⌚see "Vinegar Hill" box). Enquire about guided tours of the battlefield at the visitor centre, and look out too, if you are

---

Vinegar Hill

21 June 1798 is the most infamous date in the history of Enniscorthy. Following the rebellion that year, centred mostly in Counties Wexford and Wicklow, the insurgents, known as "the pikemen" after their weapons, made their last stand on Vinegar Hill, which they held for nearly a month. The 20,000 insurgents, including many women and children, were faced by an equivalent number of government troops led by General Lake. Following the governement victory hundreds of defenceless civilians were killed by the army. Vinegar Hill marked the end of the 1798 rebellion.

around, for a costumed re-enactment of the battle on the August Bank Holiday weekend.

Enniscorthy Castle★

&○*Open Mon-Fri 9.30am–5pm, Weekends & Bank Holidays noon–5pm. Last admission 4.30pm.* ⊚*€5.* ✗ *℘053 923 4699. www.enniscorthycastle.ie*

With its four corner towers, the castle owes its present formidable appearance to a 1586 rebuilding of the original stronghold, probably erected by Raymond le Gros, who led the first Anglo-Norman soldiers into the town in 1169. After many years in the hands of the MacMurrough clan, the castle became Crown property; Elizabeth I granted it to her favourite poet, Edmund Spenser, who spent a mere three days here before escaping its chilly walls.

The castle has recently been superbly restored to include a spectacular roof top viewing platform (**visit by guided tour only**) and the **Wexford County Museum★**, which displays items relating to the 1798 rebellion, the 1916 Easter Rising and aspects of local history.

St Aidan's Cathedral

This fine Gothic-Revival Roman-Catholic church is one of several built by Pugin (1843–46); much of the stone came from the ruined Franciscan friary in Abbey Square.

ENNISCORTHY AREA
Ferns Castle★

8mi/13km NE of Enniscorthy by N 11. (Dúchas) &○*Grounds: open throughout the year. Castle: open May–Sept 10am–5pm (last admission 45mins before closing).* ✗ *℘053 936 6411. www.heritageireland.ie.*

This modest village was once capital of the province of Leinster and the royal seat of the MacMurroughs: as the significant **ruins** will testify.

The tower and part of the north wall are vestiges of the abbey founded in the 12C by the King of Leinster, Dermot MacMurrough Kavanagh. The 13C **castle**, one of the best of its kind in Ireland, has a rectangular keep and circular towers;

the first-floor **chapel** has a fine vaulted ceiling.

Bunclody

12mi/19km N of Enniscorthy by N 11 and N 80.

The town is attractively sited on the River Clody, a tributary of the Slaney, at the north end of the Blackstairs Mountains. The broad central mall is bisected by a stream that falls in steps. The Church of the Most Holy Trinity, consecrated in 1970, was designed by E. N. Smith.

Bunclody was the last bastion in Co Wexford of the Irish language, commonly used until a century ago.

Mount Leinster★

17mi/28km N of Enniscorthy by N 11 and N 80. In Bunclody take the minor road W; after 4mi/6.4km turn left onto the summit road; it is 0.25 mi/0.4km to the peak.

From the summit (2,602ft/793m) on a clear day, there are great views over southeast Ireland: Wexford and Wicklow; the Welsh mountains across St George's Channel.

Altamont Garden

25mi/40km N by N 11 and N 81; turn right (sign) into minor road. &○*Open Apr–Sep 9am–6.30pm, Dec–Jan 9am–4pm, Nov & Feb 9am–4.30am, Oct & Mar 9am–5pm. ℘059 915 9444. www.heritageireland.ie.*

The formal and informal gardens have many specimen trees, an arboretum and a small garden with species of flowers normally found growing in Ireland's marshy bogs. The lake was dug out by hand to provide employment during the Famine.

On the horizon rise Mount Leinster *(south)* in the Blackstairs Mountains, and the Wicklow Mountains *(northeast)* across the River Slaney.

NEW ROSS

New Ross is 14mi/23km NE of Waterford. Waterford Harbour Ferry Operates between Passage East and Ballyhack daily, 7am (9.30am Sun and Bank Hols)

to 10pm (8pm Oct–Mar) ☜€8.
Single journey per car, return €12 ;
€2 pedestrian. ✆051 382 480.
www.passageferry.ie

Far inland on the tidal River Barrow, this thriving place was once the country's principal port; ocean-going ships still dock at the broad quayside opposite the substantial warehouses and tall houses reminiscent of the 19C. Its history, however, can be traced back to the 6C. Narrow streets, many linked by footpaths and flights of steps, rise steeply from the riverside to Irishtown, site of the ancient monastic settlement on the heights above. Very much a working town, New Ross *(Ros Mhic Treoin)* is an ideal place from which to explore the attractive scenery of the Barrow Valley upstream to Nore, and downstream to the Hook Head Peninsula.

A Bit of History

New Ross was founded below the site of St Abban's late 6C–early 7C monastery, in about 1200 by William le Marshall, Earl Marshal of Ireland, and his wife, Countess Isabelle de Clare, daughter of Strongbow. The first bridge across the River Barrow was built in 1211 and in 1265 the first town walls were constructed. New Ross prospered but by the end of the 17C, Ireland's premier harbour was Waterford.

In 1649, mindful of the massacre suffered by Wexford, the Catholic garrison prudently surrendered the town to Cromwell. In the 1798 rebellion the town was successfully defended against the insurgents, who suffered thousands of casualties. In 1832, a cholera epidemic swept through the region claiming 3,000 lives.

Dunbrody Famine Ship

© Luke Myers/Fáilte Ireland

By the mid-19C New Ross had re-established substantial trading links, with ships sailing to the Baltic and across the Atlantic, some carrying emigrants fleeing the Famine.

👣 WALKING TOUR

Dunbrody Famine Ship★

The Quay . 👣*Open daily by guided tour (50 mins) only, year-round 9am–6pm (Oct–Mar 5pm). Last tour 1hr before closing.* ☜€10. ✆051 425 239. www.dunbrody.com.

The *Dunbrody* is a splendid replica of a 458-tonne three-masted barque (176ft/54m long). The original freighter, built in Quebec by an Irish shipwright for a New Ross merchant, ferried emigrants mainly between 1845 and 1851.

After a 9min audio-visual introduction you will be greeted by your "emigrants" (costumed actors), tour hosts who re-enact the terrible conditions endured on

American Emigrants

The Dunbrody Famine Ship offers access to a fascinating database compiled from the original passenger lists of ships, which sailed from Ireland and the UK in the 19C. Insert any name you like into the database and in a matter of seconds you can see how many people of this name sailed to the USA, how old they were, what ship they travelled on and which port they arrived at.

a trip to New York in 1849. A fascinating exhibition evokes the achievements of members of the Irish diaspora including Patrick Kennedy, who departed the port of New Ross on a wet day in 1848 to set sail for the United States; his descendants were to become one of the world's most famous families (&see *Downstream from New Ross*).

Ros Tapestry

The Quay. ◐*Mon–Sat 10am–5pm, Sun 11am-3pm* ☜€8. ℘*051 445396. www.rostapestry.ie.*
This huge community project , organised by over 150 dedicated volunteers, has produced 15 striking embroidered panels, each measuring 6ft (1.83m) x 4ft (1.22m). The Ros Tapestries depict events around the Anglo-Norman arrival in the South East of Ireland, specifically the founding of the town of New Ross by William Marshal and Isabel de Clare.

◖ Walk up Mary Street.

Tholsel

Corner of South Street and Quay Street. ◐*Open by appointment Mon– Fri 9am–5pm.* ℘*051 421 284.*
The neo-Classical building was erected in 1749 and rebuilt in 1806 after the ground subsided. The front façade is by William Kent. It now houses the local council, together with its volumes of corporation minutes collected since the 17C, the mace of Charles II (1699) and the charter of James II (1688).

◖ Continue up Mary Street.

St Mary's Church★

This early-19C Anglican church was built on the site of what was probably the largest parish church in medieval Ireland, part of the abbey founded by William le Marshall and his wife (1207– 20). Besides the ruined chancel, there are a number of striking late-13C and early-14C effigies.

◖ Walk back down Mary Street, turn left into Bewley Street and right into Michael Street.

Roman-Catholic Parish Church

The building with its high ceiling and Corinthian columns echoes St Mary's Church *(adjacent)*; its completion was delayed by the cholera epidemic in 1832.

◖ Leave by the rear entrance. Walk up Cross Lane; turn right into Neville Street.

Town Walls and Gates

At the junction stands the Three Bullet Gate *(left)*, through which Cromwell entered the town in 1649, and the Mural Tower erected in the 14C. The substantial remains of the Maiden Gate are 15C.

◖ Walk down William Street. Turn right into Priory Street and left into Marsh Lane to return to the Quay.

UPSTREAM FROM NEW ROSS
Graiguenamanagh★

11mi/18km N of New Ross via the N 30, R 700 and R 705.
The commercial quays of Graiguenamanagh (pronounced *Gray-g-na-manor* and meaning "granary of the monks") occupy a particularly attractive stretch of the River Barrow, overlooked by the heather-covered summit of Brandon Hill (1,694ft/516m). The township is dominated by the restored ruins of Duiske (pronounced *Dooishka*) Abbey, established here in the early 13C by William le Marshall for the Cistercians.

Duiske Abbey★★

Despite having been suppressed in 1536, the abbey continued to function for years after. The tower collapsed in 1774 and most of the precincts were subsequently built over. The most outstanding feature of the restoration is the high-pitched church roof, constructed from unseasoned timbers of oak and elm secured with pegged wooden joints. Note the superb effigy of the Knight of Duiske (c. 1300), cross-legged, sword-seizing; his identity remains a mystery. The **Abbey Centre** (◐*open Mon–Fri 10am–5pm;* ℘*059 972 4238*) houses a

Graiguenamanagh

© Jason Baxter/Fáilte Ireland

museum for examples of the Abbey plate and other items; a gallery shows works by contemporary artists.

Inistioge★

10mi/16km N of New Ross via the N 30 and R 700.

Inistioge (pronounced *Inisteeg*), a famously picturesque village, is set on the west bank of the Nore, spanned by a splendid 18C 10-arch bridge. The ruins of the **13C castle** flank the tree-lined **square**. On the west side next to the ruined Tholsel is a curiosity, a large model of an **Armillary Sphere**. The

Roman-Catholic church contains early stone carvings, apparently illustrating the legend of the mermaid being taken from the River Nore in 1118. Up the lane is **St Colmcille's Well**. Adjoining the Anglican Church are the tower, nave and Lady Chapel of the **Augustinian priory**, founded in 1210.

DOWNSTREAM FROM NEW ROSS
The Kennedy Homestead

Dunganstown, 4mi/6.4km S of New Ross via the R 733 and the minor road west. ♿○*9.30am-5.30pm, last admission 5pm. Closed Dec 22-29* ✆€*7.50* ☎*051 388 264; www.kennedyhomestead.ie.*
This is where the great-grandfather of John F. Kennedy, President of the USA (1961–63), was born in 1820. The land is still in family hands, and Kennedy decendants proudly display photographs and souvenirs of the President's visit in 1963 plus much more. A new visitor centre opened here in summer 2013.

The John F Kennedy Arboretum

7.5mi/12km S of New Ross off the R 733. (Dúchas) ♿○*Open daily from 10am: May–Aug until 8pm; Apr and Sept until 6.30pm; Oct–Mar until 5pm.* ○*Closed 25 Dec, Good Fri.* ✆€*5.* ✗ ☎*051 386 171. www.heritageireland.com.*

Inistioge

© Tourism Ireland

Opened in 1968, the arboretum is divided into plant collection, forest plots and mountain heathland. Various lovely walks meander through the estate (667 acres/252ha) and a scenic road winds to the summit of Slieve Coillte, from where expansive views extend.

Kilmokea Country Manor Gardens★

10mi/15km south of New Ross via the R 733 and a minor road west. ⓒOpen Mar–Nov daily 10am–6pm. ⬤€7. ✕ ☏051 388 109. www.kilmokea.com.

Within the earthen ramparts of what was probably an Early Christian monastic foundation stands a handsome Georgian glebe house (now a luxury guesthouse); its assorted gardens, among the most exquisite in Ireland, were developed over half a century.

Dunbrody Abbey★

10mi/16km south of New Ross via the R 733, nr Clonmines. ⓒOpen May–end-Sept 11am–5.30pm (Jul-Aug 6pm). ⬤€4; €7 maze, pitch and putt. ✕ ☏051 388 603. www.dunbrodyabbey.com.

This roofless, but well-preserved cruciform abbey church, was built in 1182 by Cistercian monks from Dublin. It is pleasantly set above an inlet of the river Barrow. After the Dissolution, the abbey passed to the Etchingham family, who erected a fortified dwelling, Dunbrody Castle. Long demolished, on its site is now a visitor centre and the Castle garden houses an intricate **yew hedge maze**. Made with 1,500 yew trees and gravel paths, it is one of only two full-size mazes in the Republic of Ireland.

HOOK HEAD PENINSULA★★

The remote beaches and distinctive landscapes have long drawn holiday-makers to this spot.

Tintern Abbey★

(Dúchas) ♿ⓒOpen Apr-Oct 10am–5pm. ⬤€5. ☏051 562 650. www.heritageireland.com.

A small exhibition tells the story of this ruined Cistercian abbey, a daughter house of Tintern Abbey in Monmouthshire, was founded in 1200 by William le Marshall in thanks for his safe crossing from England in a storm.

Fethard-On-Sea★

The pleasant little resort of Fethard was originally founded by the Anglo-Normans, whose first expedition to Ireland landed in 1169 at Bannow Island.

Slade★

A tiny fishing village, with a double harbour, popular for scuba-diving.
On the pier are the remains of 18C salthouses, where sea water was evaporated to make salt. Beside them stood **Slade Castle**, a tower house (15C–16C).

Hook Head Lighthouse★

⬤Lighthouse open by guided tour only: Jan-Aug daily 9.30am–6pm, Sep-Dec 9.30am-5.30pm. ⬤€9. ✕ ☏051 397 055/4. http://hookheritage.ie.

This lighthouse has served shipping since the beginning of the 13C and is thought to be one of the oldest in operation in the world.
The first cylindrical keep (82ft/25m) was built by the Normans to aid navigation of Waterford Harbour to their port at New Ross. It was automated in 1996.

Duncannon Fort★

Built in 1588 as part of the precautions against the Spanish Armada, the fortress was strengthened and assumed its present star-shaped form with a dry moat (3 acres/1.2ha). In 1690, both James II and William III sailed from Duncannon following the Battle of the Boyne.
Today it houses a **maritime museum** (♿ⓒopen Jun–Sept daily 10am–5.30pm, rest of year Mon–Fri 10am–4.30pm; ⬤guided tours available 10.30am, 12.30pm, 2pm, 3pm, 4.30pm; ⬤€5; ✕; ☏051 389 454; www.discoverireland.ie) charting the history of the Wexford coast, one of the most dangerous coastlines in Ireland.

ADDRESSES

WEXFORD

🏨 STAY

Jim McGee's Guesthouse – *18 Lower John St, Townparks. ℘053 912 2638. 6rm.* Established in the 1840s, with clean and quiet bedrooms, this is a centrally located guest house with lots of character. The attached bar hosts regular live music nights.

The Blue Door – *18 George St. Lower. ℘053 912 1047. www.bluedoor.ie.* Centrally located, well-appointed rooms and a morning menu that includes an alternative to the traditional, cholesterol-rich Irish breakfast.

Clonard House – *Clonard Great. ℘053 914 3141. 9rm.* An 18C-farmhouse suitably furnished with antiques and four-poster beds.

Killiane Castle– *Drinagh (1.5mi/3km from Wexford on the road to Rosslare). ℘053 915 8885. www.killianecastle.com. 8rm.* Quality accommodation in a 17C-house, adjoining an impressive 15C-castle, tucked away in the Wexford countryside. One- and two-bedroomed apartments also available for renting on a weekly basis.

Ferrycarrig Hotel – *Ferrycarrig, 4.5mi northwest. ℘053 912 0999. www.ferrycarrighotel.ie. 102rm. Restaurant 🍴.* This imposing hotel is idyllically set on the River Slaney and its estuary, with each of its stylish, contemporary rooms enjoying the view. A health club, a Kids Club and either fine dining or summer barbecues are good reasons why this hotel has won family-friendly awards.

Clayton Whites Hotel – *Abbey St. ℘053 912 2311. www.claytonwhiteshotel. com. 157rm.* This famous luxury hotel, dating back to 1795, has been enlarged and thoroughly modernised. Facilities include a pool, a spa and a cryotherapy clinic. A good choice of places to eat within the hotel.

CAMPING

Ferrybank Camping Site – *Ferrybank. Just east of Wexford town (over the bridge) on the R 741. ℘053 918 5256.* Overlooking the harbour and open all year this is a well-run campsite with good facilities. From €16.50 to €23 to pitch a tent for up to two adults and two children.

🍴 EAT

Westgate Design – *22 North Main St. ℘053 912 3787. www.westgatedesign.ie. (daytime only).* Westgate Design retails fashion, giftware and jewellery but the big draw for many is the high quality self-service restaurant. There is also a deli offering a take-away service.

Fusion – *Ferryport Hotel, Rosslare Harbour. ℘053 913 3933. www.ferryporthouse.com.* As the name indicates, the menu is a mixture of Asian and European (though it's mostly Chinese). A useful place to eat or stay (🏨) if travelling by ferry.

SHOPPING

The majority of shops are in Main Street – North and South.

PUBS

The Centenary Stores–*Charlotte St. ℘053 912 4424. www.thestores.ie* A lively pub in the centre of town. Good reputation for its sessions of traditional music on Sunday mornings.

The Sky and The Ground–*112 Main St. ℘053 912 1273. www.visitwexford.ie.* Traditional Irish music can be enjoyed here most nights, but there are three levels to the pub and a quiet spot can also be found.

ENTERTAINMENT

Wexford Arts Centre – *Open Mon–Sat 10am–6pm, Sun noon–4pm. ℘053 912 3764. www.wexfordartscentre.ie.* Concerts, plays and art exhibitions are held throughout the year. Good cafe (*www.dlushcafe.ie*).

SPORTS AND LEISURE

Beaches at **Rosslare** (south) and **Curracloe** (north).

Reef and wreck fishing. *Operates Apr–Oct (12 person, maximum). Call for rates. ℘053 912 9704, mobile 087 254 9111.*

Wexford Festival Opera

© CLIVE BARDA/ArenaPAL/Fáilte Ireland

EVENTS AND FESTIVALS

Wexford Festival Opera– *High St.* *℘053 912 2400. www.wexfordopera.com. Open mid-Oct–early Nov; performances from 11am.* This annual event, lasting 18 days from late October onwards, features three productions of "forgotten opera masterpieces" and inlcudes over 50 other events, including lunchtime concerts, afternoon ShortWorks and recitals, late night revues. A vibrant Fringe Festival offers everything from art exhibitions through to singing and swinging pubs. Its home since 2006 has been the landmark **Wexford Opera House** featuring a stunning interior. Book as far ahead as you can.

ENNISCORTHY

¶/EAT

◒◒ **Via Veneto** – *58 Weafer St., Enniscorthy. ℘055 923 6929. www. viaveneto.ie. Dinner only.* Authentic Italian restaurant with a large menu, a homely atmosphere, friendly service and an all-Italian wine list. The owner is also a cineaste who displays his collection of Italian movie history throughout the restaurant.

POTTERIES

Carley's Bridge Potteries – Ireland's oldest pottery. *N30, Enniscorthy to New Ross. ℘ 053 923 3512* for visiting details.

Hillview Pottery – *Carley's Bridge. Open Mon–Sat 9am–5pm, Sun 2pm–5pm. ℘053 923 5443.* All the pottery items are hand thrown on the potters wheel, and finished off in beautiful glazed colours.

Badger Hill Pottery – produces Jack O'Patsy hand-thrown stoneware, ovenware, tablewear and ornamental pots. *Ballinavary. Open Wed–Sun, Bank Hols 10am–1pm, 2pm–5pm. ℘053 35060.*

Kiltrea Bridge Pottery – *3.5mi/5.5km, off the Kiltealy Rd. (R702). ℘053 923 5107. Open Wed–Sat 11am–1pm 1.30–5pm. Closed 23 Dec–early Feb. www.kiltrea pottery.com.* Beautiful hand-thrown pottery and terracotta for house, kitchen and garden.

SPORTS AND LEISURE

Greyhound racing – Show Grounds, Enniscorthy. *Most Mon & Thu, €10. ℘053 92 33172. www.igb.ie/enniscorthy.*

NEW ROSS

ENTERTAINMENT

The Galley Cruising Restaurant – Various trips on the local rivers, most including meals/light refreshments – *Cruises Apr–Sept from New Ross (North Quay to Inistioge, towards St. Mullins or downriver depending on tide). ℘051 421 723. www.rivercruises.ie.*

HOOK HEAD PENINSULA

SPORTS AND LEISURE

Beaches at Duncannon; scuba-diving at Slade; bird-watching In spring and autumn on the Peninsula, where over 200 species have been recorded.

Co Waterford★★

Settled by Celts, then Vikings, then Normans, County Waterford is sheltered by the Knockmealdown and Comeragh mountain ranges to the North, and lower-lying hills to the South. The long, scenic coastline has provided an income for fishing families over the centuries and most of its towns grew up from fishing villages. Inland, rich dairy farms pattern the landscape while the major town of Waterford provides a good base for exploring the countryside.

WATERFORD★

Waterford is situated on the county boundary with Co Wexford on the major coast road between Wexford, 37mi/60km E and Cork 75mi/120km W. The harbour city of Waterford *(Port Láirge)* continues to benefit from its superb location on the tidal River Suir inland from its confluence with the River Barrow and the vast stretch of sheltered water known as Waterford Harbour. Waterford glassware has become a global brand and the city enjoys a prosperity rooted in a mercantile and manufacturing tradition going back to its foundation by Vikings in the 9C. Many memories of this long history are preserved in the mile-long quayside, the close-packed streets and the surviving sections of the once extensive City Walls★ that enclosed the town.

GETTING AROUND

BY SEA – Passage East Car Ferry: Ferry across Waterford Harbour from Passage East (southeast of Waterford via the R 683) to Ballyhack. ℘051 382 480. www.passageferry.ie.

The watchtower (35ft/10m high) surveys a well-preserved section on the south side, near John's River. As well as the Norman extensions, which are mostly 13C, there are traces of the 9C and 10C Danish walls, including the sallyports in Reginald's Bar near Reginald's Tower.

A Bit of History

The Danish Vikings sailed up the Suir in 853, establishing a settlement which they called *Vadrefjord* (meaning weather haven). Despite constant warfare with the local Irish, the Danes retained control of Vadrefjord until 1169, when the Anglo-

Bishop's Palace, Waterford

© Leo Byrne / Fáilte Ireland

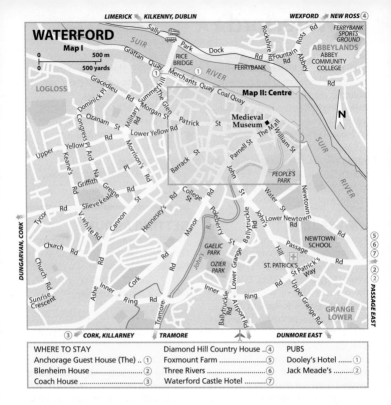

WATERFORD

Map I

0 — 500 m
0 — 500 yards

Map II: Centre

WHERE TO STAY		
Anchorage Guest House (The) .. ①	Diamond Hill Country House ..④	PUBS
Blenheim House ....②	Foxmount Farm ....⑤	Dooley's Hotel ....①
Coach House ....③	Three Rivers ....⑥	Jack Meade's ....②
	Waterford Castle Hotel ....⑦	

Norman Earl of Pembroke (Strongbow) fought his way into the town, subsequently marrying the King of Leinster's daughter in Reginald's Tower.

Reginald's Tower

© Liam Murphy/Fáilte Ireland

Under Anglo-Norman rule Waterford became the second most important town in Ireland after Dublin, with a reputation of fierce loyalty to the English king. In 1649, Waterford was unsuccessfully besieged by Cromwell but it fell to his general, Ireton, the following year.

Reginald's Tower★

(Dúchas) ⌖ ◷*Open 9.30am–5pm (Mar-mid-Dec 5.30pm);* ◷*Closed Christmas period.* ⊛€5. ℘051 304 220. *www.heritageireland.ie.* *www.waterfordtreasures.com.*
This iconic landmark stone fortress, in a commanding location overlooking the River Suir was built by the Vikings in 1013 as part of the town's defences, then strengthened by the Anglo-Normans. It is said to be the oldest complete building in Ireland. Its four floors, linked by a spiral staircase, contain a newly renovated superb collection of historic and archaeological artefacts that tell the story of Waterford's Viking heritage.

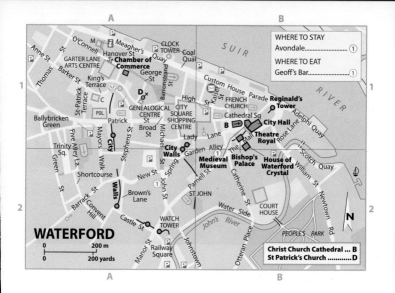

City Hall and Theatre Royal

The **City Hall** is a stately edifice designed by John Roberts in 1788. The building incorporates the newly restored 1876 **Theatre Royal** (℘051 874 402, www. theatreroyal.ie); its Victorian decor is rare in a theatre in Ireland. The three-tier horseshoe design (seating capacity 650) rises to an impressive dome; the specially designed Waterford Crystal chandelier was presented in 1958.

A large selection of often impressive artworks from the Waterford Municipal Art Collection is now on permanent display in the public areas of the theatre.

Christ Church Cathedral★

♿🕐Open Easter-end-Oct mon-Sat 10am-5pm, Oct-Easter noon-3pm. 🕐Closed Bank Holidays. ℘051 858 958. www.christchurchwaterford.com.
The present building was designed by John Roberts (1714–96) in the 18C English Classical style. In 1891 the galleries and square pews were removed. Within is a model of the original Viking church (1050–1773).

Medieval Waterford

When the City Square Shopping Centre was built, 12 layers of housing were found resting on Viking foundations. Stones mark the site of St Peter's church

(12C), the earliest example of an apsed church in Ireland. The mural depicts the area c. 1100.

St Patrick's Church

As it was built during the Penal Period, the church was deliberately constructed to resemble a house from the outside.

Chamber of Commerce

The fine Georgian building (1795) was designed by John Roberts, a noted 18C-Waterford architect.

House of Waterford Crystal★★

The Mall. 🐾*Tours daily in summer 9am–4.15pm (Sun 10.30am). Contact for winter opening times.* ♿€13. ℘051 317 000. www.waterfordvisitorcentre.com. Waterford Glass was first produced in 1783 and the factory has grown to be the largest glassworks in the world; guided tours of the state-of-the-art facility are offered and a visitor centre and retail store are also on site.

Medieval Museum★

The Mall. ♿🕐*Open Mon-Fri 9.15am–6pm (Sep-May 5pm), Sat 9.30am-6pm (Sep-May 10am-5pm), Sun & Bank Holidays 11am-6pm (Sep-May 5pm).* ♿€7. ℘051 849 501. www.waterfordtreasures.com.

Dunmore East

© Chris Hill/Tourism Ireland

Situated between Cathedral Square and the Bishop's Palace, Waterford's latest museum is striking above and below ground carefully preserving several medieval structures within its walls. It houses a fascinating display of Viking and medieval finds plus interactive displays and video.

Bishop's Palace★

The Mall. &. ⓢOpen Mon-Fri 9.15am–6pm (Sep-May 5pm), Sat 9.30am-6pm (Sep-May 10am-5pm), Sun & Bank Holidays 11am-6pm (Sep-May 5pm). ⊛€7. ✕ ℘051 849 650. www.waterfordtreasures.com.

Set In the newly renovated Bishop's Palace this superb interactive exhibition relates the history of Waterford from 1700–1970. Most glittering is its elegant silverware and fine glassmaking, including the oldest piece of Waterford Crystal in the world, a decanter made in the 1780s.

🚗 DRIVING TOUR

WATERFORD COAST

▶ From Waterford take the R 683.

Built originally around a fort, the fishing village of **Passage East** sits beneath a high escarpment with small squares, narrow streets and brightly painted houses; there are no fewer than three quays.

▶ Continue south on the R 685; turn left into a minor road.

Dunmore East★

This Breton-style fishing village comprises several thatched cottages clustered around attractive little coves. There are forest walks beside the Ballymacaw Road *(0.25mi/0.4km west)*.

▶ Take the R 684 and R 685 west via Clohernagh.

Tramore *(Trá Mhór)*

9mi/14.5km S of Waterford by R 675.
Tramore is one of Ireland's main holiday resorts, equipped with a large amusement park (50 acres/20ha), a water park and a long sandy beach (3mi/5km) overlooking Tramore Bay.

There are fine walks along the Doneraile cliffs *(south)*. Great Newtown Head *(west)* across the bay, is marked by three early-19C navigational pillars; the **Tramore Metal Man** is an extraordinary cast-iron figure (14ft/4m high), with a pale blue jacket and white trousers, erected in 1823 as a warning to shipping.

▶ Take the R 675 north to return to Waterford.

DUNGARVAN★

Dungarvan, southwest of Waterford, is on the main N25 route to Cork.

This thriving seaside resort occupies an attractive site astride the Colligan estuary overlooking the broad bay known as Dungarvan Harbour. It is flanked by the Drum Hills (south) and the Monavullagh and Comeragh Mountains (north).

King John's Castle, built by the king in 1185, not long after the Anglo-Norman invasion, consists of a large circular keep surrounded by fortified walls, much modified in subsequent centuries.

The **Waterford County Museum** (◷*open Mon–Fri 10am–5pm;* ℘*058 45960; www.dungarvanmuseum.org*), housed in the old Town Hall, has a nautical theme and local shipwrecks are well documented. On the east bank of the river are the ruins of a 13C Augustinian priory. The walk on the seaward side of the graveyard provides fine views across Dungarvan Harbour south to **Helvick Head★★**.

LISMORE★

Lismore (Lios Mór) is situated on the south bank of the River Blackwater, roughly halfway between Waterford (41mi/66km NE) and Cork.

No bigger than a village, but a designated Heritage Town, this idyllic little place on the banks of the salmon-rich River Blackwater was once a great centre of medieval learning. It still has a cathedral, but the dominant landmark is the castle overlooking the lovely wooded valley.

A Bit of History

The monastery, founded by **St Carthach** in the 7C, was one of Europe's most distinguished universities until 978, when the Danish Vikings raided the town and burned the monasteries. A prosperous town developed around the castle, built in 1185 by King John. In 1589, it came into the possession of Sir Walter Raleigh. The present castle *(private)* is one of the most spectacular in Ireland, rebuilt by Sir Joseph Paxton (of Crystal Palace fame). It is a theatrical neo-Tudor fantasy, looking out over the valley of the River Blackwater.

Lismore Castle Gardens★

♿◷*Open 17 Mar–Oct 10.30am–5.30pm (last entry 4.30pm)* ⊗€8. ℘*058 54424. www.lismorecastle.com*

The gardens are set in seven acres within the 17C outer defensive walls and have spectacular views of the Castle and surrounding countryside. They are divided into two sections, comprising the 17C walled garden and the lower garden. The lower garden, known as the Pleasure Grounds, was laid out c. 1850, although the Yew Walk where, tradition-

Lismore Castle Gardens

Famous Sons of Waterford

Thomas Francis Meagher (1822–67) was a wealthy Catholic lawyer and nationalist who joined the Young Ireland uprising of 1848. For his part in the rising at Ballingarry in Co Tipperary he received a death sentence, which was commuted to transportation to Tasmania. From there, he escaped to the USA, where he studied law and became a journalist. Later, he founded the Irish Brigade and fought in the American Civil War. After the war he became governor of Montana and here, with an irony he was presumably unaware of, organised a series of attacks on the native Sioux, who objected to the breaking of treaties by white settlers. He died in suspicious circumstances while traveling in a steamboat on the Missouri River.

William Hobson (1783–1842), who was born in Lombard Street near The Mall, became the first Governor of New Zealand after many years as a sailor, first as a humble seaman and later as a captain in the West Indies, fighting pirates and twice being captured by them. He fought in the Napoleonic Wars and visited Napoleon's island of exile, Elba, where he was detailed to sink a well for Napoleon's drinking water. Later, after being sent to Australia in 1841, he created the British Crown Colony of New Zealand, negotiating treaties with native groups and organising the first settlers.

Raymond Chandler (1888–1959), not a son but a grandson of the city, graced Waterford with his presence during his childhood summers. Born in Chicago, the son of two lapsed Quakers from Waterford, he visited the old family with his mother every summer. In later years, living in London, he spoke of his great attachment to the city.

ally, Edmund Spenser composed part of *The Faerie Queene*, is much older. Yew, beech and box hedges screen flower and vegetable beds, Paxton's greenhouses date from 1858.

The Broghill Tower *(SW corner)* provides a fine view. Contemporary sculpture by the likes of Anthony Gormley, Emily Young, David Nash and, Marzia Colonna) add a modern twist to this immaculate landscape.

There is a contemporary art gallery in the West Wing of Lismore Castle *(same ticket as gardens)*.

St Carthage's Cathedral (Anglican)★

Surrounded by a picturesque graveyard shaded by yews and lime trees, the parish church is redolent of Lismore's long history. The existing building, the fourth on the site, is largely the result of a rebuild ordered by Sir Richard Boyle in 1633; the **ribbed ceilings** were added by Sir Richard Morrison (c. 1820), and the fine **tower** and **ribbed spire** (1826) by the Payne brothers of Cork. Note the fine stained-glass window donated by Sir

Edward Burne-Jones, the pebbles from the Isle of Iona (Scotland) in the floor of St Columba's Chapel and the elaborate **table-tomb** of 1548.

St Carthach's Church (Roman-Catholic)

Designed by W.G. Doolin in 1881, this is one of the most outstanding Lombardo-Romanesque churches in Ireland, richly detailed and built of red sandstone, with white limestone dressings and a detached bell-tower.

Facing the west entrance to the church is a fine row of 19C artisans' cottages.

Lismore Heritage Centre

🕐 Open year-round Mon–Fri 9am –5.30pm. Mar–Nov also Sat–Sun 10am (noon Sun)–5pm. ✆€5. 📞058 54975. www.discoverlismore.com.

The Old Courthouse provides an audio-visual history of Lismore, an exhibition gallery on the town and the life and works of **Robert Boyle**, the father of modern chemistry, who was born in Lismore Castle.

LISMORE AREA
The Gap★
10mi/16km north via the R 688.
Beyond the Blackwater Valley, rise the Old Red Sandstone Knockmealdown Mountains (2608ft/795m).
The Lismore-Caher road follows the lush valley before climbing to the scenic V Gap with its magnificent **views★**.

ADDRESSES

🛏 STAY

🛏 **The Anchorage** – *9 The Quay. ℘051 854 302. www.anchorage.ie 14rm.* Simple, clean and straightforward accommodation on the edge of the city and fairly priced. The rooms at the front have views of the quay and the river, while those at the back tend to be quieter.

🛏 **Avondale** – *2 Parnell St., Dunmore East. ℘051 852 267.* Personally run, clean and friendly terraced town house, two minutes' walk from the town centre opposite the Waterford Crystal Visitors Centre. Bedrooms are tidy, come in a variety of shapes and sizes and are sensibly priced, but do note that breakfast is not supplied.

🛏 **Diamond Hill Country House** – *Slieveroe. ℘051 832 855. www.diamond hill.ie. 18rm.* Set 2km from town, Diamond Hill lies in 2 acres of delightful mature gardens, for which the owners have won awards. The house itself is modern and rather bland.

🛏🛏 **Coach House** – *Butlerstown Castle, Cork Rd. ℘051 384 656. www. butlerstowncastle.com. 7rm.* Large stone-built house of Victorian origins that lies in the lovely grounds of the ruins of Butlerstown Castle. This characterful accommodation is decorated with grand period furniture sitting alongside modern facilities including a sauna.

🛏🛏 **Foxmount Country Farm** – *Passage East Rd., 4.5mi southeast. ℘051 874 308. www.foxmountcountry house.com. 5rm.* Ideal for escaping the pressures of modern metropolitan life, this charming and luxurious 17C country house is surrounded by a working dairy farm. Elegantly fitted bedrooms look out over the mature gardens; award-winning breakfasts. Very good value.

🛏🛏 **Three Rivers** – *Cheekpoint. 7mi east. ℘051 382 520. 4rm.* This refurbished purpose-built guesthouse enjoys a peaceful setting and excellent views, with the garden and lounge overlooking the estuary, and river views from several rooms.

🛏🛏–🛏🛏🛏 **Waterford Castle Hotel** – *The Island, Ballinakill. 2.5mi east. ℘051 878 203. www.waterfordcastleresort.com. Restaurant (🛏🛏–🛏🛏🛏).* A private ferry serves this luxury resort set around an imposing 15C castle on its own 300 acre/121ha island on the River Suir. Granite arches, gargoyles, oak panelling, log fires and tapestries all add to the authentic baronial experience. Amenities include a spa, championship golf course, horse riding and other country pursuits. Book in advance for some excellent deals.

🍴 EAT

🍴 **McAlpin's Suir Inn** – *Cheekpoint. ℘051 382 220. www.mcalpins.com.* This pretty and immaculately-kept inn on the harbour front in a charming village has served the local fishermen for almost 300 years. Handwritten daily-changing menu of tried-and-trusted favourites; seafood is the speciality.

🍴🍴 **Azzurro at The Ship** – *Dock Rd., Dunmore East. ℘051 383 141. www. azzurro.ie.* One of Waterford's most successful restaurateurs has given an Italian/Mediterranean makeover to this ivy-clad pub in a picturesque fishing village.

🍴🍴 **McLeary's** – *High St. ℘051 853 444. www.mclearys.ie.* Set in a converted 15C wine warehouse, this popular steak and seafood restaurant offers the usual surf'n'turf favourites as well as a few local dishes.

ENTERTAINMENT

Garter Lane Arts Centre – *O'Connell St. ℘051 855 038. www.garterlane.ie.* Regular art exhibitions, recitals, world music, comedy, dance and theatrical productions.

Theatre Royal – *The Mall. ℘051 874 402. www.theatreroyal.ie.* Waterford's leading mainstream drama theatre (see p237).

Spraoi

© Fáilte Ireland

PUBS

Jack Meade's – *9mi/6.5km E, under the viaduct on the road of Cheekpoint.* ✆*051 850 950. www.jackmeades.com.* Winner of Irish Life Magazine, Best Gastro Pub in Co. Waterford 2012, this characterful old pub also serves up musical entertainment in the summer months. There is a wonderful garden with a large children's play area.

Geoff's Bar – *9 John St.* ✆*051 874 787.* A local favourite, Geoff's is a warren of little nooks and crannies serving surprisingly excellent food. Great atmosphere, especially on live music nights.

Dooley's Hotel – *The Quay.* ✆*051 873 531. www.dooleys-hotel.ie.* The bar of this well-known hotel on the waterfront has some excellent musical night with Country & Western and traditional Irish music.

SHOPPING

The main shopping streets are Barronstrand Street, which runs inland from the clock tower in the Quay, and the neighbouring streets (*☙see Sights*).

SPORTS AND LEISURE

Beaches and bathing at Tramore and at Woodstown, south of Passage East and south of Duncannon Fort on the east shore of Waterford Harbour.

Splashworld – Ireland's premier water leisure centre. ✆*051 390 176. www.splashworld.ie.*

Greyhound Racing – Kilcohan Park. ✆*061 448 080. www.igb.ie/waterford.*

EVENTS AND FESTIVALS

Spraoi – pronounced *Spree* (fun/celebration in Gaelic) this festival is the best of national and international street art and music, staged over three days around August Bank Holiday, culminating in a fantastic parade. *www.spraoi.com.*

Waterford Arts Festival (Imagine) – Music (folk, trad, reggae, rock…), literature, film, theatre, comedy children's events and special workshops. Spans 10 days in late Oct. *www.imagineartsfestival.com.*

Waterford Harvest Festival – cookery demonstrations, food tours, foodie films, tastings and workshops. Second week Sept. *www.waterfordharvestfestival.ie.*

SIGHTSEEING

Walking Tours – ✆*051 873 711. www.jackswalkingtours.com.* A daily walking tour of Waterford city, lasting approximately 1 hour, takes place between mid-March and mid-October.

TRACING ANCESTORS

Waterford Heritage Genealogical Service – *Jenkin's Lane. Open Mon–Fri 9am–5pm (2pm Fri).* ✆*051 876 123. www.iol.ie/~mnoc.*

The southwest counties of Ireland, Cork and Kerry, have long been two of Ireland's most popular holidaying areas and it is not difficult to see why. There is only one city, Cork, and the towns are invariably small and usually rural in character. The countryside is characterised by small farms, their fields home to modest herds of cattle or flocks of mountain sheep, and the visitor is rarely far from the sea and stirring views of the Atlantic.

Exploring the Southwest

The major urban area is in and around Cork city, but even here life seems to proceed at a leisurely pace and a walk through the streets early in the morning or after the shops have closed makes it difficult to believe that you are in the Republic's second-largest city.

From Cork city it is a short hop to the fashionable town of Kinsale, famous for its food scene and well-known to gourmets. The coastal route from Kinsale down to Skibbereen is a myriad of tiny fishing villages, seaside resorts and narrow coastal roads, making a slow driving tour of the area a series of delights and the perfect introduction to West Cork. The two most-visited small towns are Killarney and Dingle, and in the summer months they attract large numbers of visitors. While this has its downside, it also means a plentiful supply of good accommodation and activities for visitors with, or without children. These two towns also serve as ideal bases to explore some of the most unspoiled parts of the island of Ireland.

Peninsulas

The highlight of any visit to this corner of Ireland, though, has to be the set of wild, thinly-inhabited, mountainous peninsulas that jut out into the Atlantic Ocean, creating deep, fjord-like bays and long, rugged coastlines with innumerable beaches and places to explore. At the sheltered heart of each of the bays are pockets of near Mediterranean-like microclimates with lush vegetation, rare plants and imaginatively created gardens. Many of the gardens were originally created by the long-gone Anglo-Irish landed gentry and some are now owned by the state.

Highlights

1 Kissing the famous **Blarney Stone** (p252)

2 Relaxing in the picturesque harbour town of **Kinsale** (p261)

3 The remote and rocky **Mizen Head** (p268)

4 World Heritage monastic site on the scenic island of **Skellig Michael** (p283)

5 Stunning coastal scenery from **Dingle** to **Brandon Creek** (p294)

Traditional Ireland

Exploring this corner of Ireland opens up vistas of tiny farms clinging to the mountainsides, evoking a rural past that is fast disappearing from western Europe. Old traditions such as the "Fair Day", when farmers used to bring animals into town to sell, have left their legacy. In Bantry, for example, the first Friday of each month was the traditional Fair Day and it is still the best time to visit the town. Stalls are set up in the main square and locals still bring along hens, ducks and the occasional donkey or horse for sale. Outside of the main towns, large parts of the Cork and Kerry area remain largely undamaged by progress. Visitors will still see horses and donkeys, once an essential part of every farm, browsing in small fields. There are ancient ruins dotted around by the side of roads, islands abandoned by their inhabitants but with boat services (and in the case of Dursey Island at the end of the Beara Peninsula a cable-car) that enable exploratory visits to be made to them. There are also long stretches of sandy beaches with barely another soul to spoil the views.

Cork★★

The Republic of Ireland's second-largest city, **Cork** *(Corcaigh)*, is a major port and commercial centre, with a university established since the mid-19C and a distinct historical and cultural identity. Cork city is far less tourist-oriented than Dublin and, Corkonians would readily testify, all the better for it. It has a vibrant and welcoming atmosphere and a fine cultural life of its own. The Cork Jazz Festival is very well-established and each year attracts some big names in jazz. The city's charming, compact, low-lying centre, with its narrow café-lined passageways, is built on reclaimed marshland between two arms of the River Lee, whose estuary, Cork Harbour, forms the largest natural harbour in Europe. Until the 19C many of the streets were open waterways, where ships moored – likened in 1780, by Arthur Young, to the towns of the Netherlands. Many of the original mooring posts are still in place. To the North of the river the land rises steeply, this is now covered by **Montenotte**, the city's most exclusive residential district, filled with grand mansions set in their own grounds and built by Cork's wealthy 19C traders, their homes now converted to institutions or apartments and rarely visited by tourists. The city of Cork is an excellent place to visit, accessible on foot, with many small cafés and lots of bars for rest stops, small shaded parks and river walks filling in the gaps between the cathedral, the not-to-be-missed English Market, heritage centres and art galleries.

A BIT OF HISTORY

Cork derives its name from the Irish for a "marshy place", where St Finbar founded a church in 650 on the banks of the River Lee, near the present site of University College. Its early development was disrupted in 860 by Viking raids and in 1172 by the invasion of the Anglo-Normans, who eventually

▶ **Population:** 125,622 (Cork city).

Info: Grand Parade. *℘*021 425 5100; www.discoverireland.ie.

Location: 75mi/120km south west of Waterford on the N 25, 65mi/104km south of Limerick on the N 20, and 55mi/88km south east of Killarney on the N 22.

P **Parking:** Disc parking in the street; parking discs available at the Tourist Office and other outlets in Cork.

Don't Miss: The Anglican Cathedral or the Shandon Bells carillon.

Kids: Cork City Gaol.

Timing: Allow at least a day in Cork.

GETTING THERE

BY AIR – **Cork International Airport:** 5mi/8km south of Cork city. *℘*021 431 3131; www.corkairport.com.
BY SEA – **Ferry Terminal, Ringaskiddy:** 10mi/16km south-east of Cork city. *℘*021 437 0779.

broke the Danish hold on the city. Cork's political independence is rooted in its long standing commercial success. In 1492, **Perkin Warbeck**, the pretender to the English throne, arrived and soon won the support of the mayor and other leading citizens, who accompanied him to England, where he proclaimed himself Richard IV, King of England and Lord of Ireland. They were all later hanged at Tyburn.

In the 1640s Cork supported the royal cause; when Cromwell entered the city in 1649, he inflicted great damage on it. Then, in 1690, the city endured a five-day siege until the army of William III breached the walls and destroyed the fortifications. In the early 18C, Cork accom-

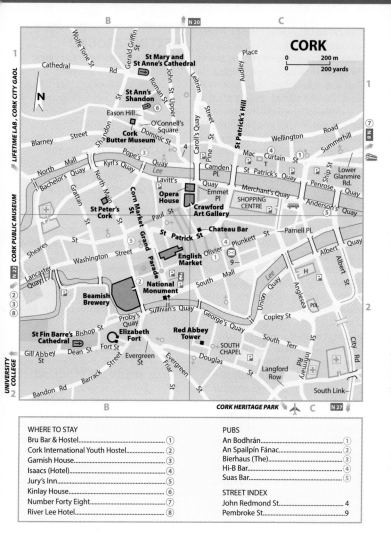

CORK

0   200 m
0   200 yards

WHERE TO STAY	
Bru Bar & Hostel	①
Cork International Youth Hostel	②
Garnish House	③
Isaacs (Hotel)	④
Jury's Inn	⑤
Kinlay House	⑥
Number Forty Eight	⑦
River Lee Hotel	⑧

PUBS	
An Bodhrán	①
An Spailpín Fánac	②
Bierhaus (The)	③
Hi-B Bar	④
Suas Bar	⑤

STREET INDEX

John Redmond St	4
Pembroke St	9

modated many Huguenots fleeing from religious persecution in France – hence the name of French Church Street.

Cork became economically important to the British for its harbour and the export of the county's agricultural products. In the 19C, the city lived up to its rebellious reputation, becoming a stronghold of Fenian (&see HISTORY) agitation. The War of Independence and the subsequent Civil War were bitterly fought in and around Cork. In 1920 the Black and Tans (&see HISTORY) set fire to a substantial portion of the city centre. The political unrest was aggravated by the

deaths of two lord mayors of Cork: Terence McSwiney died on hunger strike in Brixton Prison; while Tomás McCurtain was shot in his bed by Crown Forces in the presence of his wife and children.

Commercial and Industrial Centre – Cork began trading in the 12C, exporting hides and cloth, and importing wine from Bordeaux. By the 18C the city had become a major producer of butter, shipping it to Britain, Europe and America.

In 1852 Cork staged Ireland's first national Industrial Exhibition, modelled on the Great Exhibition in London.

Henry Ford, founder of the great American car firm, was born at Ballinascarty, 28mi/44km southwest of Cork, and in 1917, the Ford car company set up its first overseas factory at the Marina in Cork. Dunlop started its Cork plant in the 1930s. Both Ford and Dunlop ceased operations in 1980 and shipbuilding died shortly afterwards. The principal commercial activity is now related to computer manufacturing.

 WALKING TOURS

The City Centre★
Allow 2hrs.

Cork's centre is small enough to visit on foot: there are two car parks on Grand Parade, close to the Tourist Information Centre, which is an excellent starting point for a visit.

Encircled by the two branches (Channels) of the River Lee, the city centre is crossed by a wide crescent-shaped avenue, St Patrick's Street, the continuation of **Grand Parade**. The latter begins at the South Channel of the river, where you will find the amazing steeple-shaped **National Monument**, erected in memory of the Irish patriots who died in the struggle for independence. Following the avenue, with your back to the river, notice the multicoloured façades of the large 18C houses. On your right you will pass Oliver Plunkett Street, formerly known for its furriers and jewellers.

Further along Grand Parade, you will come to one of the four entrances to the covered **English Market★** (⊙*open year-round Mon–Sat 8am–6pm; www. englishmarket.ie*), established in 1610. At that time, the main aisle was a waterway; it was not filled in until the early 19C. Boats would have docked at the entrance to the market to unload their merchandise. Standing in front of the stalls piled with ready-butchered meat, you'll be struck by the rather strong smells of the vividly coloured produce. Discover local specialities with Irish names, such as *drisheen* (black pudding) *and crúibini* (pig's trotters). The aisles open onto an

GETTING AROUND
BY SEA – Cork Harbour Car Ferry: Across the River Lee between Carrigaloe *(east bank)* and Glenbrook *(west bank)*, operates daily, 7am–10pm. Car €8 (return), €6 single; pedestrian €1.50. ✆*021 481 1485. www.crossriverferries.ie*
BY RAIL – Rail Service: Operates between Cobh and Cork via Fota Island, daily. ✆*021 481 1655 (Cobh Railway Station); www.irishrail.ie*

atrium, which is overlooked by the Farm Gate Café (*www.farmgate.ie*), a popular lunchtime destination.

At the corner where Grand Parade becomes St Patrick's Street, a small road joins up with **Cornmarket Street**. On Saturday mornings, this popular area, with its multicoloured shop-fronts and bold advertising, is home to a street market, **Coal Quay Market** (⊙*open year-round Sat 9am–4.30pm*), which buzzes with the cries of fruit and veg sellers and news vendors.

On North Main Street, which runs parallel to Cornmarket Street, **St Peter's Church** (⊙*open year-round Tue–Sun 10am–6pm (Tue&Wed 5pm, Sun 11am–3pm);* ⊗*no charge;* ✆*021 427 8187, www. stpeterscork.ie*) now houses an engaging exhibition and heritage space. This cultural centre presents the history of Cork (video, exhibition, model of the city) and hosts temporary photographic and art exhibitions. Continue along **St Patrick's Street**, the city's main thoroughfare, which is lined with tall pastel-hued houses and department stores. Don't miss **Le Chateau Bar**, a fine example of an 18C period house. This pub, which dates from 1793, is distinguished by its steps leading to a raised entrance, which at the time it was built would have been on the quayside. The doorway under the stairs would have been used when unloading the casks.

But the real action is to be found in the adjacent alleys. Follow French Church Street, for example, which leads off St Patrick Street to join up with **Paul**

English Market

© Tourism Ireland

Street. Today, this is the trendy part of town, where most of the city's designer and interior decoration boutiques are to found, alongside the most fashionable bars and restaurants.

▷ Turn east along Paul Street to join Emmet Place.

Cork's main gallery is the excellent **Crawford Art Gallery★** (◷ open year-round Mon–Sat 10am–5pm/8pm Thu); ℘021 480 5042; www.crawfordartgallery. ie), featuring a small but impressive permanent collection (art and sculpture and glasswork) alongside temporary exhibitions here. One of the highlights of the gallery's holdings is its collection of 19C and 20C paintings by Irish artists, which includes canvases by Jack Yeats, brother of W. B. Yeats, who received the Nobel Prize for Literature in 1923.
Not far from the gallery, on the water-front of the North Channel, **Cork Opera House**, an imposing and rather ugly grey structure, hosts a variety of cultural events, including a well-known jazz festival at the end of October (♺ see Festivals, p250).

▷ Next, follow the river eastwards and cross over Patrick's Bridge to explore the north hill.

North of the River
Allow 1hr for the hill, 3hrs if you plan to walk to Cork City Gaol. ♺ Resist the temptation to drive: the steeply sloping

and winding lanes form a complex one-way system.
After having crossed the bridge, cut across McCurtain Street, which is strewn with bars and clubs of every kind, and continue to the bottom of **St Patrick's Hill★**. Climb the stepped pavement of the steep hill, lined with multicoloured houses, to enjoy a charming view of the port and city. Walk back down to the junction with McCurtain Street and turn right onto Coburg Street, then continue into Devonshire Street. Take the right-hand fork onto John Redmond Street and you will arrive at the church **St Anne's (Shandon)★** (◷ open Jun–Sept Mon–Sat 10am–5pm, Sun 11.30am–4.30pm; Mar–May and Oct Mon–Sat 10am–4pm, Sun 11.30am–

Shandon Bells

© Brian Morrison/Tourism Ireland

Artistic Cork

Among those sons of Cork who made their mark in the world are **John Hogan** (1800–58), a sculptor whose work is found not only in Cork but elsewhere in Ireland, **Frank O'Connor**, who penned short stories, and **Frank Browne**, a Jesuit and photographer extraordinaire of life in Ireland at the beginning of the 20C, but especially of the first stages of the fatal maiden voyage of the *Titanic*.

museum), retraces the history of the butter industry in Cork.

Not to be missed, in the little road facing the entrance to the centre is a small shop that forms part of the daily life of the neighbourhood; the **Exchange Toffee Works** is the last manufacturer of homemade sweets in the whole of Munster. For four generations, this family-run business has made marshmallows and other sweets that children buy on their way to school. Make time to go in and smell the aromas of hot sugar and fruit syrups.

▷ Turn back in front of St Anne's and turn into Chapel Street.

4.30pm; Nov–Feb daily 11am–3pm; €5; ℰ 021 450 5906, www.shandonbells.ie).
One of the city's symbolic monuments, easily distinguishable by its profile and clocktower, which is topped by a weathervane in the shape of a salmon more than 10ft/3m long.

Built in 1722, the curiously designed church has two façades of red sandstone and two of grey limestone. Inside, it houses a beautiful collection of antiquarian books from the 17C. If the climb to the top of belltower doesn't frighten you then (for a small charge) you can try your hand at bellringing: each of the bells numbered from one to eight has a different sound. You will even be given sheet music to play a tune.

A stone's throw from St. Anne's, the **Butter Exchange**, created in 1770, once centralised the flourishing market in salted butter, which was produced in the surrounding countryside then exported to Europe and as far as India. This trade created wealth for the city throughout the 19C. Now renovated, the building is home to the **Shandon Craft Centre** (*Mon–Fri 8am–4.30pm; Sat 8am–2.30pm*), where you can watch a variety of articles being made: pottery, weaving, sewing, crystal and sculpture. Next door, an interesting little museum, the **Cork Butter Museum** (*open Mar–Oct 10am–5pm/6pm Jul–Aug, Nov–Feb Sat–Sun only 11am–3pm; €4; ℰ 021 4300 600, www.corkbutter.*

St Mary's Cathedral, the other church in the area, this one Catholic, is distinguishable by its entrance of pediment and columns. Its 19C architecture is of little interest, but the building contains registers dating back to 1748, which is very helpful for Irish men and women wanting to trace their roots.

Next, join the quayside via Shandon Street and follow the river to Cork Gaol (*allow 15–20 mins to walk there from St Patrick's Bridge*).

Cork City Gaol (*by guided tour only, Oct–Mar 10am–4pm; Apr–Sep 9.30am–5pm; additional night tours Mon–Fri 5.45pm; last entry 1hr before closing; €8; night tour €10 must book in advance; ℰ 021 430 5022, www.corkcitygaol.com*), the city's old prison, has been completely restored. The reconstructed cells contain lifesize models of prisoners and furniture of the time. The treatment they suffered and the conditions of prison life are realistically evoked. The building also houses a museum devoted to radio, the national radio station having broadcast its programmes from the upper floor of the prison from 1927 until the 1950s. There is a small café where you can relax before you walk back to the city centre.

South of the River

Allow 1hr. From the Tourist Information Office, take the footbridge at the end of Grand Parade to cross the South Channel of the river.

The waterfront on the south side of the river is particularly picturesque and is punctuated with an impressive succession of pubs. On the left after the footbridge, between Sullivan's Quay and George's Quay, Mary Street leads to **Red Abbey Tower**. This square tower, the last vestige of the Medieval town, was part of an old Augustinian monastery built in the 13C. English leaders used it to bombard the city during the siege of 1690.

Next, follow the river westward, in the direction of the cathedral. When you spot the sign for **Elizabeth Fort**, turn into Keyser's Hill, a steep alleyway between two bright-yellow walls. Steps lead up to the old star-shaped fort (1603).

Badly damaged during the siege of 1690, it became a prison and later housed a military corps. The *Garda* (police) has now taken up residence here, but you can still get into the fortification to admire the beautiful view of the city: below, stand the big steel drums of the **Beamish brewery** and, further away, the clock towers of St Anne's Shandon and St Mary's.

▶ Walk back down to the waterfront and continue west along Proby's Quay then Bishop Street.

The Protestant **St Fin Barre's Cathedral**★ (◷ *open year-round Mon–Sat 9.30am–5.30pm; Apr–Nov only, Sunday 12.30–5pm; €5; ℘ 021 4963387, www.corkcathedral.webs.com*) occupies the site of the monastery that was at the heart of the city. The current building was constructed only in 1978, in a highly ornate neo-Gothic style. Inspired by the great cathedrals of France, it is made of white limestone and crowned with a 240ft/73m spire. Note the highly decorative carving on the three great doors of the west façade and inside, the stained-

glass windows and the decorative panelled ceiling, which depict events in the life of Christ.

West of the City

Return to your car and leave the city via Western Rd, heading towards Killarney and Tralee. Parking is free all along this road, bordering the university park, or in the road that runs alongside the Lee.

This residential area is home to **University College Cork**★, founded by Queen Victoria in 1849 *(on Western Rd, on the left when leaving the city, behind large gates opening onto a park)*. Its buildings are an interesting mix of English styles forming a very traditional campus. Stroll among the park's hundred-year-old trees to **Honan Chapel**★, with its collection of colourful stained-glass windows dating from the early 20C.

Leaving the park, cross over Western Road and walk beside the river along Mardyke Walk. You will come to Fitzgerald Park, a large green garden that borders the river. At the heart of this park is the **Cork Public Museum**★ (◷ *Mon–Fri 11am–1pm, 2.15–5pm; Sat 11am–1pm, 2.15–4pm; Sun, Apr–Sept, 3pm–5pm; ℘ 021 427 0679, www.cork city.ie*), which retraces local history since prehistoric times, using models, old documents, engravings and collections of objects. The commercial, artistic, political and social evolution of the city is brought to life through an unsung cultural heritage, which includes superb antique lace, a finely-cut gold bird, exceptional silverwork and paintings.

ADDRESSES

🛏 STAY

🛏 **Bru Bar & Hostel** – *57 MacCurtain St. 20rms. ℘ 021 455 9667. www.bruhostel.com.* Popular with backpackers, this is a lively spot with comfortable beds and a great bar attached. Live music nightly.

🛏 **Cork International Youth Hostel** – *12 Redclyffe, Western Rd. 96 beds. ℘ 021 454 3289. http://anoige.ie.* A good variety of rooms in this large red-brick Victorian hostel, including two- and four-beds. Breakfasts are available, as well as the use of a large kitchen. Nice lounge and breakfast room.

⊜ **Garnish House** – *Western Rd. 14rms.* *℘021 427 5111. www.garnish.ie.* This luxury Georgian Guest House stands right opposite the beautiful University grounds. Its award winning gourmet breakfast menu has over 30 options.

⊜ **Kinlay House** – *Bob & Joan's Walk, Shandon. 31 rms. ℘021 450 8966. www. kinlayhousecork.ie.* A modern hostel close to Shandon's famous church, with a range of private rooms as well as dorm beds; meals available.

⊜ **Number Forty Eight**– *48 Lower Glanmire Rd. 6 rms. ℘021 450 5790. www. bbcorknumberfortyeight.com/en-gb.* Pleasant B&B by the station. The helpful and charming host provides internet access for guests.

⊜⊜ **Hotel Isaacs** – *MacCurtain St. 47 rms. ℘021 450 0011. www. hotelisaacscork.ie.* Intimate, comfortable and friendly boutique hotel, with a delightful waterfall outside, in a secluded spot on a busy road. Excellent value and a good restaurant *(Greenes, Ⓒsee EAT).*

⊜⊜ **Jurys Inn** – *Anderson's Quay. 133rms. ℘021 494 3000. www.jurysinns.com.* Smart, modern hotel in the city centre beside the River Lee.

⊜⊜⊜ **River Lee Hotel** – *Western Rd. 182rms. ℘021 425 2700. www.doyle collection.com.* Set on the banks of the River Lee, this recently refurbished very stylish 4-star boutique hotel boasts a Fitness Centre, state-of-the-art spa, a bistro and bar.

⌘/ EAT

⊜⊜ **Greenes** – *MacCurtain St. ℘021 455 2279. www.greenesrestaurant.com.* Modern Irish cuisine at its best and a superb al fresco setting, next to a charming waterfall, as well as indoor tables. The early-bird menu, from 6–7pm, is good value.

⊜⊜ **Jacobs on the Mall** – *30A South Mall. Closed Sun. ℘021 425 1530. www.jacobsonthemall.com.* Former 19C Turkish baths converted into one of the city's most stylish restaurants,

showcasing modern Irish art. Attentive service and modern cooking using the best local ingredients.

⊜⊜ **Jacques** – *Phoenix St. Lunch Mon–Fri; dinner Mon–Sat. Booking advisable. ℘021 427 7387. www.jacquesrestaurant.ie.* Well-established restaurant located in a colourful little side street in the city centre. Always busy with locals, yet retaining an intimate atmosphere. Modern menu with the emphasis on locally sourced produce.

⊜⊜ **No 5 Fenn's Quay** – *Sheares Street. Closed Sun. ℘021 427 9527. www.fenns quay.net.* Converted mews house, bright and informally run. Open all day for snacks and light lunches; more substantial dinners all freshly prepared.

⊜⊜ **Les Gourmandises** – *17 Cook St. Closed two weeks Mar, two weeks Aug. ℘021 425 1959. www.lesgourmandises.ie.* It's Sunday lunch or dinner only at this relaxed restaurant in the centre of the city. The wine list is impressive and locals have a high regard for the quality of the food and its presentation.

⊜⊜ **Blair's Inn** – *Cloghroe, five mins from Blarney on the R 579. ℘021 438 1470. www.blairsinn.ie.* Friendly attractive traditional pub in a charming and secluded wooded setting by the Owennageara River. Traditional bar menu, Irish craft beers, more elaborate modern restaurant menu. Lovely garden with al fresco dining.

PUBS

Cork has a lively pub scene and its own stouts: Beamish (now part of the Heineken empire and no longer brewed on its own premises) and Murphy's (www.murphys.com). The pubs along Washington Street are popular with the city's student population.

Hi-B Bar (The Hibernian) – *108 Oliver Plunkett St.* A famous Cork pub with a character all of its own. Live music some evenings; good conversation every night of the week.

An Bodhrán– *42 Oliver Plunkett St.* A small pub, good for live trad music. A sociable atmosphere that draws in a loyal crowd of regulars and makes finding a seat next to impossible.

An Spailpin Fánac– *28 Main St.* The Tudor-style building opposite this pub was where Cork's Beamish stout used to be brewed but you can still be sure of finding it on tap in An Spailpin Fánac, a pub with a history dating back to the late-18C. Live music Sunday to Thursday; an open fire in winter months.

Suas– 4–5 South Main St. www.suas bar.com. Roof-top bar with a classy setting; come here to pose with multi-coloured cocktails as a change from quaffing the black stuff.

The Bierhaus– Popes Quay. www.thebierhauscork.com. The pub with the largest selection of world beers in the city, with over 70 to choose from, Including Galway hooker, O'Hara's stout and brews from the Czech Republic and Lithuania.

ENTERTAINMENT

Cyprus Avenue– Caroline St. www.cyprusavenue.ie. Live gigs, mainly featuring rock and guitar bands.

Everyman Palace Theatre – 15 MacCurtain St. ℘021 450 1673. www.everymanpalace.com. Cork's principal theatre, producing a wide range of entertainment.

Cork Cine Club – St. John's Central College (lecture theatre), Sawmill Street. http://corkcineclub.com. Thu (see website for dates) 8pm. Tickets, €8.50/€7, are sold at the door. The best of independent world cinema.

Opera House – Emmet Place. ℘021 427 0022. www.corkoperahouse.ie. Opera, dance, drama, musicals, concerts and family entertainment.

UCC Granary Theatre – Mardyke. ℘021 490 4275. www.granary.ie. New, experimental and sometimes controversial work by various artists.

Triskel Christchurch –Tobin St. ℘021 427 2022. www.triskelartscentre.ie. A hugely popular arts centre where top international and Irish perfomers (2012 concerts included Paul Brady, Christy Moore and Sinéad O'Connor) play in an intimate church setting. It is also a stage for the visual arts, literature, and cinema. Excellent bar-restaurant next door (www.soho.ie).

SHOPPING

The main shopping street is **Patrick Street**. **North Main Street** is one of the oldest shopping areas. Don't miss the **English Market** (♿see p246).

The area around **Paul Street** is dotted with cafés, boutiques and antique shops; the **Shandon Crafts Centre** is fun for crystal, jewellery and textiles (♿see p248).

Merchant's Quay Shopping Centre – 1 Patrick St. Open Mon–Sat 9am–6pm (Fri 9pm), Sun 2pm–6pm. www.merchants quaycork.com is the city's best shopping mall.

EVENTS AND FESTIVALS

Cork International Folk Dance Festival (Damhsafest) (late July) – www.damhsafest.ie.

Guinness Cork Jazz Festival (October) – www.guinnessjazzfestival.com. Spread over four days and packing in over 1,000 performances from 150 or more acts.

Corona Cork Film Festival (mid-November) – www.corkfilmfest.org

SIGHTSEEING

Day Coach Tours to Kinsale, Killarney, Kerry, Kenmare. ℘021 454 5328. www.easytourscork.com

Cork City Tours – operate Mar–Oct. Hop-on hop-off tours of the city centre. ℘021 21 430 9090. www.corkcitytour.com.

TRACING ANCESTORS

Cork City and County Archives – Great William O'Brien St., Blackpool. Open by appointment Tue–Fri, 10am–1pm and 2.30pm–5pm. ℘021 450 5886. www.corkarchives.ie.

Around Cork★

There are a number of attractions on the edge or just outside of Cork city, which require a journey by car or bus, the most famous of these being Blarney Castle or, to be more precise, the single stone in a wall of the castle that promises a special gift, if kissed.

BLARNEY CASTLE★★

5mi/8km northwest via the N 20.
&Castle open year-round Mon–Sat 9am–6.30pm (7pm Jun–Aug; 5pm Nov–Feb, 6pm Ma-Apr & Oct). Sun 9am–6pm (Nov-Feb 5pm). Blarney House (open by guided tour only) Apr–May Mon–Sat 10am–2pm. Closed 24–25 Dec. €15. 021 4385 252. www.blarneycastle.ie.

The central feature of the castle is the massive keep, a fine example of a tower house. In addition there are halls and dungeons, but the main reason why the castle attracts so many visitors is the **Blarney Stone**, said to bestow the gift of eloquent speech on all those who kiss it. Kissing the stone is harder than it sounds since the famous piece of rock is set inside the parapet at the top of the castle and can only be reached by lying upside-down with a guide holding one's legs.

There are a number of legends on the stone's origins: some say it is the pillow

Blarney Castle
© Chris Hill/Tourism Ireland

of Jacob or St Columba, or the Stone of Ezel brought back to Ireland during the Crusades, or the "Stone of Destiny" (a magical part of the king's throne), or even the rock struck by Moses to call the waters of the Nile to crush the pursuing Egyptian army.

In the 16C Queen Elizabeth I commanded the Earl of Leicester to take the castle from the head of the McCarthy clan. The Earl was frustrated in his mission, but he sent back numerous progress reports which so irritated the Queen that she referred to them as "all Blarney".

Blarney House★ built in 1874 in the Scottish baronial style with fine corner turrets and conical-roofed bartizans, has recently been opened to the public for the first time (Open Jun-Aug Mon-Sat 10am-2pm). It is one of the most elegant and gracious of Ireland's stately homes and beautifully situated, overlooking Blarney Lake. Inside is a fine collection of early furniture, family portraits, tapestries and works of art.

On a druidic site beside the Blarney River is the romantically landscaped dell known as **Rock Close★**. Laid out in the 19C, the gardens contain wishing steps – ideally negotiated up and down with eyes closed. Two dolmens are sited in the close, which has a Fairy Glade with a sacrificial rock, also said to have druidic connotations.

Blarney Woollen Mills

Centre of Blarney town. &Open year-round daily, 9.30am–6pm (10am Sun). Closed 25–26 Dec, 1 Jan. 021 451 6111. www.blarney.com.

> **Info:** www.discoverireland.ie.
>
> **Location:** All the excursions here are within an hour's drive from Cork.
>
> **Don't Miss:** An excursion to Blarney Castle.
>
> **Kids:** Fota Wildlife Park.
>
> **Timing:** Allow a day or two for excursions from Cork city.

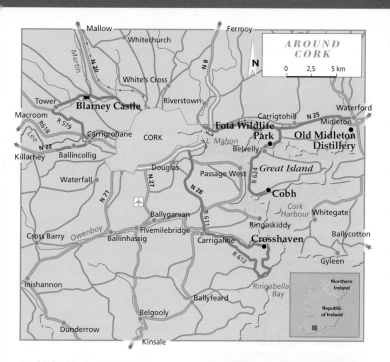

AROUND CORK

0   2,5   5 km

N

Established in the 19C, this is the enormous flagship store of the famous Irish chain and the successor to the 13 mills developed around the castle as an industrial enterprise in the 18C. It is housed in one of Ireland's oldest and most authentic Irish woollen mills and is almost as popular as the Blarney Stone.

COBH★

Cobh lies on the south side of Great Island, linked by road and rail to Fota Island and the mainland, 12mi/19km southeast of Cork. ▯Old Yacht Club, Cobh, ℘021 481 3301, www.visitcobh.com.

Facing the sheltered water of Cork Harbour, Cobh *(An Cóbh)* – pronounced cove – has been an important naval base for generations.

Cobh developed in the late 18C when Royal Navy ships assembled here for operations in the American War of Independence and later against France. The Royal Navy continued to operate from here well after Independence until Cobh was handed back to the Free State with the other "Treaty Ports" (1938). Until the 1960s, large transatlantic cruise liners like the Queen Mary and

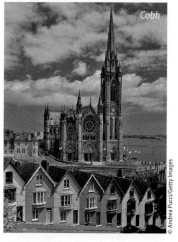

Cobh

© Andrea Pucci/Getty Images

the Queen Elizabeth would stop here: an era recorded in period photographs and paintings hanging in the bar of the Commodore Hotel. On a much sadder note, Cobh also witnessed the departure of around 2.5 million of the 6 million Irish people who emigrated to North America between 1848 and 1950. They are commemorated in the statue of Annie Moore, the very first emigrant to pass

Water Club

The world's first yachting fraternity, the Water Club, was founded in Cobh in 1720. Its successor, the **Royal Cork Yacht Club**, is now based at Crosshaven, but its old headquarters still stands, an elegant waterfront pavilion designed in 1854 by the architect Anthony Salvin.

through the Ellis Island immigration reception centre in New York.

A period as a health resort in the 19C left a fine legacy of Italianate buildings and neo-Gothic villas, which merit the classification of Heritage Town. Cobh was also once known as Queenstown, after Queen Victoria disembarked here in 1849 on her first visit to Ireland.

St Colman's Cathedral★

The neo-Gothic Catholic cathedral designed by Pugin and Ashlin (1868–1915) was clearly modelled on the French medieval cathedrals of Amiens, Chartre and Laon; the sculpture echoes Rheims. The tall **spire** houses a carillon of 47 bells. The interior is typically Victorian.

Lusitania Memorial★

The 1,500 lives lost when the *Lusitania* was torpedoed in 1915 are commemorated by an elaborate sculpture in Casement Square, designed by Jerome Connor (1876–1943), who was born in Cork; it was completed posthumously by Seamus Murphy.

Nearby, in Pierce Square, a more modest memorial recalls the demise of the *Titanic*, which docked at Cobh on April 11, 1912 before sailing out on her fateful maiden voyage.

Museums

At the **Cobh Heritage Centre★** (&Oopen year-round daily 9.30am–6pm; Jan–Apr and Nov–Dec 5pm; Last admissions 1hr before closing; Oclosed 23 Dec–2 Jan; ✕; €9.50; ✆021 481 3591; www.cobhheritage.com),

The Queenstown Story (Cobh's name between 1850 and 1920, commemorating a visit by Queen Victoria) explains how convicts were expelled to Australia and how thousands more emigrated to America from here. A separate display is dedicated to the *Titanic*.

Opposite the Heritage Centre, a house in the former Scots Presbyterian Church, on the High Road, is now the **Cobh Museum** (Oopen Mar–Oct Mon–Sat 11am–1pm and 2pm–5.30pm; Sun 2.30pm–5pm; Nov–Mar Mon–Sat 10am–1pm and 2pm–4pm €4; ✆021 481 4240; www.cobhmuseum.com) displays historical material relating to Cobh and the Great Island.

FOTA ISLAND★

10mi/16km E of Cork by N 8 and N 25; 4mi/6km N of Cobh by R 624.

Until 1975, this 780 acre/316ha island in Cork Harbour belonged to the descendants of its 12C Anglo-Norman Lord Philip de Barri. In the early 19C, the family's hunting lodge was converted by John Smith Barry into a fine neo-Classical gentleman's residence to plans by the leading architects, Richard and William Vitruvius Morrison; other additions included sea defences, walls, lodges, workers' cottages and outbuildings, a landscaped parkland and a famous arboretum. Much of the island is now given over to one of the country's finest wildlife parks, and the house has been saved from near-dereliction.

Fota House Arboretum & Gardens★

&OOpen: House Apr-Sept Mon–Sat 10am–5pm and 11am–5pm, Sun and Bank Hols. OClosed Christmas. House €8; arboretum & gardens free. ✕✆021 481 5543. www.fotahouse.com. This Regency mansion is notable for its series of exquisite interiors set off by fine furniture. The Morrisons' masterly manipulation of space is particularly evident in the entrance hall, while below stairs, the servery, kitchen and scullery are models of their kind.

A short distance from the house is a delightful little **orangery** and a walled

Walled garden, Fota House Arboretum & Gardens

© George Munday/Tourism Ireland

garden. The great **arboretum**★ was laid out by John Barry Smith, a prominent plant collector, and sustained by his successors into the 20C. Its warm brown earth soils and mild climate favour species from North America, Chile, Australasia, Japan and China, and this is one of the finest collections of rare and tender trees and shrubs grown outdoors in Ireland and Britain.

🏛 Fota Wildlife Park★

♿⏱*Open year-round daily 10am (10.30am Sun), last admission 4.30pm.* ⏱*Closed 25–26 Dec*⚲€16, child €10.50. ✕ 🅿€3. ✆021 481 2678. www.fotawildlife.ie.

This spacious park, comprising 70acres/28ha, was established by the Zoological Society of Ireland in 1983 to breed endangered species like cheetah, oryx and macaque. Zebra, antelope and kangaroo roam freely while giraffe, monkeys, flamingoes, pelicans, penguins and other waterfowl thrive in designated areas. A special attraction is the Cheetah Run feeding time, every day at 3pm. Their food is suspended on a wire that travels 10ft/3m off the ground, at approximately 40mph/65kph, which encourages them to act naturally by sprinting after it.

A land train ferries visitors around the grounds.

MIDLETON

On the N 25, between Cork and Youghal. 🛈*Jameson Heritage Centre (seasonal).* ✆*021 461 3702.*

Midleton *(Mainistir An Corann)* is a pleasant old market town, set in the rich fertile plain of East Cork. Its greatest draw is the Jameson Irish Whiskey distillery.

Old Midleton Distillery (Jameson Experience)

♿☛*Visit by guided tours only, Mar–Oct 10am–6pm (tours on demand); Nov–Feb: at 11.30am, 1.15pm 2.30pm, 4pm.* ⏱*Closed Good Fri and Christmas hols.* ⚲€15, €13.50 online. ✕✆*021 461 3594. www.jamesonwhiskey.com.*

The Jameson Irish Whiskey distillery was built in 1975 alongside the old buildings that once accommodated a woollen mill and barracks. The tour begins with a video presentation on the history of

---

Steeplechasing

The **steeplechase** had its origin in Ireland, when huntsmen set wagers with each other on who would be the first to reach a prominent landmark. The first such contest took place from Buttevant in 1752, with the steeple of the Anglican Church as the starting point of a race to St Leger Church near Doneraile (4.5mi/7km).

Old Midleton Distillery (Jameson Experience)

© Chris Hill/Tourism Ireland

the distillery. Then follows a visit to the old buildings, including the Distiller's cottage, the drying kiln, the great storehouse and the giant waterwheel of 1852, which at one stage powered five pairs of millstones and all of the distillery machinery. Today it still turns the cogs and wheels in the Mill Building. Most impressive of all is the **largest copper pot still** (1825) in the world (capacity 33,000 gallons/1,485hl). Finally, there are the oak casks in which the spirit was matured and the tour concludes, naturally, with a whiskey tasting.

MIDLETON AREA
Cloyne
5mi/8km S of Midleton via the R 630 and R 629.

Three people are particularly associated with the cathedral village of Cloyne: Christy Ring, the greatest-ever hurler; **George Berkeley** (1684–1753), the bishop of what was once a vast diocese, and St Colman (522–604), who founded a local monastery, of which only a tiny oratory and 10C **round tower** (100ft/30m high) remain next to the restored 14C **Cathedral★**. Bishop Berkeley was a highly regarded and original philosopher, who also devoted himself to practical matters such as good farming practice; though his attempt to found a college in America came to nothing, he is honoured by Berkeley in California.

YOUGHAL★
30mi/48km E of Cork; roughly half-way between Cork and Waterford.
🛈 *Heritage Centre, Market Place.*
📞 *024 92 447. www.youghal.ie.*
http://youghal4all.com.

An attractive seaside resort, with miles of fine beaches along the lovely estuary of the River Blackwater, the ancient harbour town of Youghal (pronounced *Yawl*) looks back on a long and colourful history, attested to by a fine array of old buildings and the country's most extensive system of defensive walls, enough to merit Youghal the title Heritage Town.

👣 WALKING TOUR

Youghal Heritage Centre
♿🕘 *Open year-round 9am-5pm.*
📞 *024 20170. www.youghal.ie.*
The old Market House now houses the Tourist Information Office and an exhibition on the history of Youghal.
In the Market Square stands a memorial commemorating the *Nellie Fleming*, the last of the old Youghal sailing vessels. The pub on the corner, **Moby Dick's**, displays many photographs taken during the filming of *Moby Dick* on location in Youghal during the summer of 1954.

▷ Walk inland along a side street; turn right into South Main Street.

Clock Gate★

The unusual four-storey building straddling the Main Street was constructed by the corporation in 1777 to replace the Iron Gate, also known as Trinity Castle, part of the walls. The new tower was used as the town gaol until 1837; such was the state of insurrection in the late 18C that it soon became overcrowded; rebels were hanged from the windows as an example to the rest of the populace.

▷ Walk though the Clock Gate and continue north along South Main Street.

Benedictine Abbey

Left side of the street.
All that remains of the abbey is the East gable wall pierced by a moulded Gothic doorway with ornamental spandrels; in the passageway are the arched piscina and square aumbry from the original church. The abbey was founded in 1350 and used by Cromwell as his winter headquarters in 1649–50.

The Red House

Left side of the street.
This fine example of early-18C Dutch domestic architecture creates a marked contrast with its neighbours. The red brick façade with white stone quoins is surmounted by a triangular gable and a steep mansard roof. It was designed in 1710 for the Uniacke family by a Dutch architect-builder Claud Leuvethen.

Tynte's Castle

Right side of the street.
This 15C battlemented building has a device over the front door for pouring boiling oil on rebels and other unwelcome visitors. Once on the waterfront, it is now 200yd/182m from the river.

Almshouses

Left side of the street.
The Elizabethan almshouses, still used for residential purposes, were erected in 1610 by the Earl of Cork, who provided "five pounds apiece for each of ye six old decayed soldiers or Alms Men for ever".

▷ Turn left into Church Street.

Also used for residential purposes is the neighbouring former **Protestant asylum**, dated 1838, now called Shalom House.

St Mary's Collegiate Church★★

The present early-13C edifice is one of Ireland's most impressive ancient churches. It replaced an 11C Danish-built church destroyed in a great storm soon after its construction. During the late-15C wars, the forces of the Earl of Desmond occupied the building and removed the roof of the chancel. Large-scale restoration, including the re-modelling of the chancel, took place between 1851 and 1858.

The church contains a large collection of **grave slabs** and **effigies**, including some from the 13C and 14C with Norman-French inscriptions. None remotely match the monument in the South transept erected by the 1st Earl of Cork to himself. This superbly pompous house-size structure shows him reclining nonchalantly beneath his family tree, surrounded by his wives, children and mother-in-law.

Town Walls★

Partially accessible from the churchyard.
Youghal has the best-preserved town walls in Ireland, their extent even greater than the city walls of Derry. They were built in the 13C and extended in the 17C; large sections are still in excellent condition, although only three of the 13 medieval towers remain. The portion restored in the 19C with a turret and a cannon is accessible from the churchyard; the sentry walk provides a fine **view** of the town and the harbour. The full length of the walls is best seen from the outside *(Raheen Road)*.

MALLOW★

Mallow is 21mi/33km north of Cork via the N 20. ▉*Bridge St.* ✆*022 42222. www.mallow.ie.*
The busy market town of Mallow *(Mala)* in Co Cork is built at a major crossroads, attractively sited above the River Black-

St Mary's Collegiate Church

© Chris Hill/Tourism Ireland

water, sometimes described as the "Irish Rhine". A faint air of nostalgia pervades, the place recalling the glory days when it was the foremost spa in Ireland, frequented by the notorious "Rakes of Mallow", (⊙see "The Rake's Last Resort" box), who today would no doubt be keen patrons of the local racecourse.

Mallow had a late-12C Anglo-Norman castle, built perhaps by King John, that was replaced by a 16C mansion (in ruins just inside the gates of Mallow Castle) as a seat for Sir John Norreys, Lord President of Munster. In 1688, the town was granted a charter by King James II. A spa developed in the 18C after the discovery of a natural hot spring.

As the spa declined in the early 19C, the town became a centre of great political activity, in part because two eminent Nationalists were born here: **Thomas Davis** (1814–45), the Protestant patriot and unchallenged leader of the Young Ireland movement; the noted MP **William O'Brien** (1852–1928). Mallow also has literary connections: **Anthony Trollope** was a resident for some years (Davis St.); **Canon Patrick Sheehan**, the former parish priest at Doneralle (1895–1913) and a popular author (born at 29 O'Brien St.); Elizabeth Bowen, author of The Last September (1929) and other acclaimed novels.

The Rake's Last Resort

The curative properties of Mallow water, said to be good for purifying the blood, were discovered in 1724. The town was not long in becoming a popular spa with a fast reputation; its male patrons infamous as the **Rakes of Mallow**.

Living short but merry lives,
Going where the devil drives,
Having sweethearts, but no wives…

From April to October, visitors would take the waters; in the evening, there was dancing and cards; balls, meetings and gatherings were held in the Long Room as was the fashion in Bath, Tunbridge Wells and Scarborough.

St James's Church★

Mallow's Anglican church is a fine example of Gothic Revival architecture, built in 1824. Substantial ruins remain of the former medieval church of St Anne's, badly damaged in the Williamite wars, in which Thomas Davis was baptised in 1814.

Spa House

The Tudor-style complex housing the pump-room, reading room and baths, was built in 1828 by Charles Jephson. Unfortunately, all traces of the spa have now vanished and the building is now an office of the Energy Agency.

Buttevant Franciscan Friary

© IIC / age fotostock

Clock House

This four-storey timber-framed build-ing flanked by a clock tower, was erected c. 1855 by an amateur archi-tect, supposedly enthused by an Alpine holiday!

Church of the Resurrection

J R Boyd Barratt's Catholic church (1966–69) is shaped like an open fan; the stations of the Cross are of Tyrolean oak; the stained glass is by the Murphy Davitt Studios of Dublin.

MALLOW AREA

Buttevant Friary★

7mi/11km N of Mallow by N 20.
The ruins of the Franciscan friary (1251), stand beside the River Awbeg next to St Mary's Church. The building, used until recently as a place of burial, has two crypts, one above the other; the chancel walls are still largely intact.

Doneraile Wildlife Park★

6mi/10km NE of Mallow by N 20 and R 581. ♿ ⏰ *Open Mon-Fri 8am-8pm (5pm in winter), Sat-Sun & Bank Hols 9am-8pm (5pm in winter).* ✕ ☎*087 251 5965. www.heritageireland.ie.*
The walled Doneraile demesne (395 acres/160ha) is noted for its herds of red, fallow and sika deer. Wooded areas and ornamental lakes punctuate the gently rolling landscaped parkland around **Doneraile Court**, built c. 1700 and remodelled in the early 19C. A stone vault and spiral staircase are all that remains of **Kilcolman Castle**, once the residence of the poet **Edmund Spenser**.

Kanturk (Ceann Toirc)★

13mi/21km west of Mallow on the N 72 and R 576.
This small market town has three great mid-18C **bridges** spanning the River Dalua and River Allua. There is a striking French-Gothic church at the western end of the town.
South of Kanturk is a ruined **castle★** *(take the R 579)* dating from 1609. It was intended by the local chieftain, Mac-Donagh MacCarthy, to be the largest mansion ever to belong to an Irish chief, but was stopped by the Privy Council on the grounds that "it was much too large for a subject (of the English Crown)".

CROSSHAVEN

14mi/23km SE of Cork via the N 28 and R 611 to Carrigaline, then the R 612. Close to Crosshaven, the road follows the River Owenboy estuary. ✆*86 235 2208 www.crosshaven.net.* ⚠*Beware of busy weekend traffic.* It was natural that this cosy fishing village became the marina for the rich citizens of Cork and the prestigious Royal Cork Yacht Club *(⚓ see sidebar p254),* formerly at Cobh, is now based here.

As well as being a favourite with sailors, the village offers spectacular walks with sea, river and land views.

ADDRESSES

COBH

STAY

⊖⊜ **Knockeven House** – *Rushbrooke. 0.1mi NE on the R 624. ℘021 481 1778. www.knockevenhouse.com.* On the outskirts of Cobh in the Cork city direction, this spacious mid-19C house offers comfortable bedrooms and a friendly welcome.

YOUGHAL

⊠STAY AND ℗/EAT

⊖⊜⊜ **Aherne's Townhouse & Seafood Bar** – *163 North Main St. ℘024 92424. www.ahernes.net.* The luxurious country-house style rooms (⊖⊜) were added in the wake of the restaurant's success but for most people, the food is still the star attraction. Oysters, smoked salmon or chowder for starters and a choice of well-cooked main dishes like cod wrapped in bacon. Good French wines and two bars.

MALLOW

⊠STAY AND ℗/EAT

⊖⊜⊜ **Longueville House Hotel** – *Mallow. ℘022 47156. www.longueville house.ie. Both hotel and restaurant close Mon, Tue Apr–Oct and Mon–Thu Nov–Mar.* One of the grandest old country houses in Ireland, a Georgian mansion with elegantly furnished rooms and antiques galore. The restaurant is outstanding, both in its setting, the quality of the food and its presentation. Ingredients are locally sourced whenever possible and the restaurant boasts an excellent list of French wines.

SPORTS AND LEISURE

Safe beaches and coves dot the coast south of Midleton from Roche's Point eastwards to Knockadoon Head.

Trabolgan Holiday Village: *Roche's Point, 12.5mi/20km S of Midleton. ℘21 466 1551. www.trabolgan.com.* This holiday complex has a tropical themed indoor swimming pool, plunge pool, sauna, solarium, fitness centre, tennis, par-3 golf, 10-pin bowling and many adventure sports, all open to day visitors.

There is sailing in Ballycotton Bay *(12mi/19km SE of Midleton)*, at Roche's Point *12.5mi/20km S of Midleton)* and in Cork Harbour, angling from the shore or on the lake.

The area also boasts golf courses, pleasant walks, notably in **Rostellan Wood** on the shore of Cork Harbour. *(6mi/9.7km southeast via the R 630)* or along the **cliff-top** from Roche's Point to Ballycotton overlooking Ballycotton Bay and the lighthouse on Ballycotton Island *(11mi/18km SE of Midleton via the R 630 and R 629).*

South Coast★

West of Kinsale, with its fishing boats and yachts, the coastline is etched with innumerable little coves and river estuaries. The road rarely leaves the coastline and the journey time is filled with stunning ocean views while behind you lies the hilly countryside, with its tiny farms. If time is limited and the West Coast is your destination, skip the coastal route and take the inland route to Bantry. From here, the road heads on to Glengarriff and into Kerry, with smaller roads leading off west to the peninsulas that define this corner of Ireland.

Info: Pier Road, **Kinsale**, ℘021 477 2234, www.kinsale.ie; Ashe Street, **Clonakilty**, ℘023 33226, http://clonakilty.ie; North Street, **Skibbereen**, ℘028 21766, www.skibbereen.ie.

Location: Kinsale, situated south of Cork city and Cork Airport, is easily reached by N 27 and R 600. The coastal route running from Kinsale is stunning.

Kids: The West Cork Model Railway Village, Clonakilty.

KINSALE★★

Pretty little Kinsale *(Cionn Tsáile)*, a designated Heritage Town on the broad estuary of the River Bandon, has had a long history as a harbour town, then as a favoured resort, with charming, narrow lanes and neat Georgian houses stepping up the hillside overlooking the water. Kinsale has become particularly fashionable, with a gastronomic reputation that is celebrated annually with a food festival.

Kinsale Regional Museum★

◷*Open Wed–Sat 10am–5pm; Sun 2pm–5pm.* ℘*021 477 7930. http://homepage.eircom.net/~kinsalemuseum.*
The museum in the late-17C town hall with distinctive Dutch gables has many relics of old Kinsale, including several royal charters. The Great Hall is associated with the famous inquest on the victims of the *Lusitania* (☉*see "The Lusitania" box*). The exhibition room displays a variety of items: Kinsale-made lace which, like the Kinsale cloak, was popular for over a century; footwear and cutlery belonging to "The Kinsale Giant", **Patrick Cotter O'Brien** (1706–1806), who made a lucrative career on the English stage and who lived in Giant's Cottage *(private)* in Chairman's Lane.

St Multose Church (Anglican)★

The original church was built about 1190 and dedicated to St Multose or Eltin, the patron saint of Kinsale, who lived in the 6C. The massive square tower has a 12C Romanesque doorway with zig-zag decoration; a statue of St Multose stands in a niche over the west door. Inside are various interesting 16C tombstones.

Kinsale Early Days

Kinsale was founded in the late 12C by the Anglo-Normans, but only really enters the history books in 1601 when a Spanish force occupied the town, a long way from their ally Hugh O'Neill, fighting the English in far-off Ulster. Kinsale was besieged by an English army, who were besieged in turn by O'Neill after an exhausting march from the North. The combined Irish/Spanish forces should have easily defeated their enemy but the Spaniards watched from the walls as O'Neill was routed. This defeat marked the beginning of the end of the old Gaelic order and clan system; until the end of the 18C, no native Irish were to settle within its 13C walls. In 1641, the town sided with Cromwell and so was spared much damage.

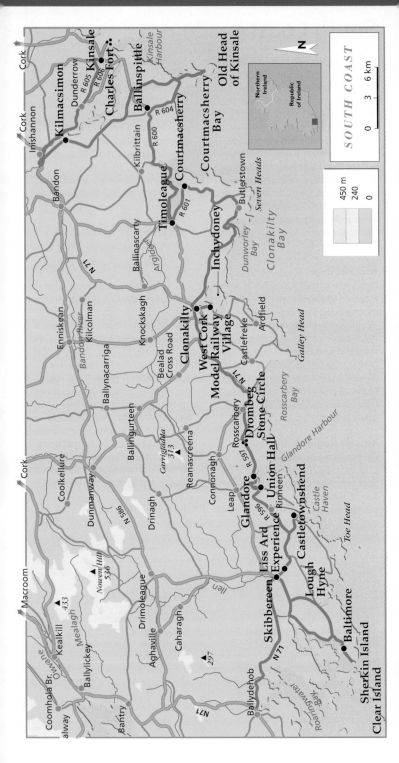

Desmond Castle

(Dúchas). ◷Open Apr–Oct 10am–6pm.
Last admission 5pm. ⌖€5. ✆021 477
4855. www.heritageireland.ie.
The three-storey tower house was built
in the late 15C or early 16C by the Earls of
Desmond as a custom-house. During the
siege of Kinsale it served as a magazine;
in 1641, it served as a gaol for French
and other foreign prisoners. Today It
houses an **International Museum of
Wine** exhibition, reflecting the days
when Kinsale was a port, and highlights
several Irish families connected with
winemaking in France, Spain, Australia
and the USA.

Kinsale Harbour★

There is a pleasant walk (1.5mi/2.4km)
along the east bank of the Bandon
estuary to **Summercove**, where English ships landed guns and supplies for
their army during the siege of Kinsale
(1601–02).
From the graveyard of St Catherine's
Anglican Church there are extensive
views★ across the harbour.
Charles Fort★★ (Dúchas; up the hill; ♿
⛴visit daily by guided tour (1hr) only,
Nov-mid-Mar 10am-5pm, mid-Mar-Oct
10am-6pm; ⌖€5; ✕; ✆021 477 2263,
www.heritageireland.ie), was begun
about 1670 and remained in use until
1922. The vast star-shaped stronghold
is a typical example of Baroque forti-

The Lusitania

On the seabed (12mi/19km S) lies
the wreck of the great transatlantic
liner *Lusitania*, torpedoed by a
German submarine on 7 May 1915
on her way from New York to
Liverpool; her sinking changed the
climate of opinion in the United
States and prepared the way for
the American Declaration of War on
Germany, two years later. Among
the 1,500 who lost their lives was
Sir Hugh Lane, the wealthy art
collector who established the
Hugh Lane Gallery of Modern Art
in Dublin.

fication and is the largest structure of
its date in Ireland. Many of the buildings surrounding the quadrangle of
greensward are derelict, but the old
ordnance-store houses a good interpretive exhibition.
From the fort there are extensive
views★ of Kinsale harbour, guarded
on the west side by **James Fort**, built
1604 (cross the bridge over the Bandon
River and turn left; 0.5mi/0.8km on foot
from the car park). Only the central tower,
blockhouse and portions of the defensive walls are still partially intact.
The harbour entrance is protected by the
headland, **Old Head of Kinsale★** (from

Kinsale at night

© M. Siepmann / imagebroker / age fotostock

the river bridge take R 600 W and R 604 S), with the ruins of a 15C fort. The road stops just short of the modern lighthouse.

🚗 DRIVING TOURS

COURTMACSHERRY BAY★
Approx 40km. Allow 2 hrs.

Ballinspittle
Leaving Kinsale, the R 600 snakes through a landscape of green hills, eventually arriving at Ballinspittle, famous for a while after 1985 when thousands of visitors came after stories spread that a statue of the Virgin Mary could be seen moving. The road then skirts the bay of Courtmacsherry to Timoleague.

Timoleague★
The village on the Argideen estuary is dominated by a ruined **Franciscan friary★**, founded in 1320 and plundered by Oliver Cromwell in 1642. The extensive ruins include the cloisters and the outer yard, and the ruins of a 12C leper hospital.

Courtmacsherry★
3mi/5km detour E by R 601.
This attractive village is a fine base for walking and deep-sea fishing; footpaths lead through the trees to Wood Point, or to a pebble beach at Broadstrand Bay.

▷ Drive 9.3mi/15km W of Courtmacsherry by the R 601 and the R 600.

Clonakilty (Cloich na Coillte)
The town centre is distinguished by **Emmet Square**, with its central garden and tall Georgian houses.
The **West Cork Regional Museum★** (🕐*open May–Oct;* 👤*Enquire at house next door if the museum is closed;* 👜*Donation requested;* 🅿; 𝒫*023 33115),* in the converted schoolhouse traces local history, with special emphasis on the War of Independence and on Michael Collins, who was born at Sam's Cross *(3mi/5km west)* and which is now

the **Michael Collins Centre★** (🕐*open mid-Jun–mid-Sept Mon–Fri 10.30–5pm Sat 11am–2pm;* 𝒫*023 884 6107, www. michaelcollinscentre.com).*
The **West Cork Model Railway Village** (👤👶🕐*open year-round, may close for maintenance Jan, see website; 11am–5pm (Jul–Aug 10am-6pm); Christmas Hols, phone to confirm;* 👜*Village: €8 (child €4.50); Village and land train ride: €11 (child €6.50);* ✕; 𝒫*023 33224; www.mod-elvillage.ie) portrays life (in miniature) as it was in the 1940s and is a delight for young and not-so-young visitors.
The peninsula known as **Inchydoney Island ★***(3mi/5km S by the causeway road),* has a series of lovely, sandy beaches; the large, grass-covered spit of land jutting south into the sea is known as the "Virgin's Bank".

THE ESTUARIES ROAD★★
Approx 15.5mi/25km.

Don't be tempted to take the fast road directly towards Skibbereen as you will miss many charming places on this route. From Clonakilty, follow the N 71 for nearly 8mi/13km until Rosscarbery, then take the picturesque and undulating R 597 route towards Glandore.

▷ From Clonakilty take the N 71 W.

Rosscarbery
This small village at the head of a narrow inlet has an enormous quadrangular square and a much-restored 12C Romanesque building, **St Fachtna's Cathedral** (Anglican), with an elaborately-carved west doorway. That great evangeliser of the Germans, St Kilian, was educated here at the monastic school, founded in AD 590 by St Fachtna, bishop and abbot, before setting out on his mission to Würzburg. Two centuries later, that city repaid the compliment by sending one of its monks, St James, to found a Benedictine community in Rosscarbery.

▷ From Rosscarbery take the R 597 W towards Glandore; after 4mi/6.4km turn left to the Drombeg Circle (sign).

Drombeg Stone Circle★

This is probably the most impressive of the 60 stone circles built in prehistoric times in West Cork. It has 14 evenly-spaced stones which form an enclosed circle *(30ft/9m in diameter)*; usually the number of stones was uneven. Of similar antiquity is the nearby cooking pit.

▷ Continue W on R 597 to Glandore.

Glandore

The original Irish name for this small village, Cuan Dor meaning the "harbour of the oaks", alludes to the days when extensive woodland covered much of West Cork. The semicircular harbour faces two minute islands in the estuary called Adam and Eve; sailors try to "avoid Adam and hug Eve".

▷ Cross the river to Union Hall.

Union Hall

This small port, straight out of a picture book, with its solid stone church, colourful pubs and pretty harbour, safe haven for the fishing fleet and for visiting pleasure boats, owes its name to the Act of Union of 1800, which politically "united" Ireland with England. The buildings sit around a natural-looking lagoon, created by the causeway to the village. Traditional music can be enjoyed in the pubs on summer nights

▷ Take the road via Rineen to Castletownshend.

Castletownshend

The steep Main Street of this tiny village descends to the water's edge, where a small pier offers fine views across the

Drombeg Stone Circle
© Chris Hill/Tourism Ireland

lovely Castle Haven estuary. **St Barrahane's Church** (Anglican) is attractively set at the top of four flights of steps *(50)* at the foot of the Main Street; the colourful Nativity Window was designed by Harry Clarke.

SKIBBEREEN AREA

Skibbereen

This attractive and prosperous little market town owes its existence to Algerian pirates, who raided the neighbouring settlement of Baltimore in 1631, capturing some of the English settlers.

As a result the others fled inland and set up two settlements, of which Skibbereen *(Sciobairín)* was one. The town suffered severely during the 19C Famine but today it is a lively spot, boasting many good restaurants, from which to explore the beautiful coastal scenery and Lough Hyne.

Skibbereen Heritage Centre

Open early-May–late Sept daily 10am–6pm; mid/late-Mar–early-Apr and early Oct–early Nov Tue–Sat 10am–

Somerville and Ross

Castletownshend in West Cork was once a stronghold of the Anglo-Irish Ascendancy: a perfect subject for the novelists Edith Somerville and Violet Martin, second cousins, known as **Somerville and Ross**. The success of *Some Experiences of an Irish RM* (1899) prompted *Further Experiences of an Irish RM* (1908) and *In Mr Knox's Country* (1915). More serious issues appear in *The Real Charlotte* (1894); but *The Big House at Inver* (1925), written by Edith after Violet's death, is perhaps the best. Both lie buried in St Barrahane's Church graveyard.

"Keeping an eye on the Czar of Russia"

In the 1890s a leader in the *Skibbereen Eagle* remarked that the paper was "keeping an eye on the Czar of Russia." The comment, outrageously bombastic for a small provincial newspaper, was picked up by the international wire services and went around the world. Still quoted today, it turned out to be the most famous line ever written in an Irish newspaper. The files of the old *Eagle* may be inspected by appointment at the offices of the *Southern Star* newspaper in Ilen Street.

6pm. €6. 028 40900. www.skibbheritage.com.
Located in the old gas works, **The Great Famine Commemoration Exhibition** is a sombre reminder that the Skibbereen area was one of the worst affected by the Irish Potato Famine. Newspapers of the day depicted Skibbereen as being symbolic of the destitution and hardship caused by the failure of the crop and between 8,000 and 10,000 unidentified souls are buried in a single Famine Graveyard at Abbeystrewery, near Skibbereen. More cheerfully, the Heritage Centre also interprets beautiful **Lough Hyne** (including a trail leaflet) and a genealogy resource.

Take the R 596 2mi/3km S of Skibbereen.

Liss Ard

Open Apr–Nov daily 10am–5pm. Gardens free, crater €5 as part of a guided tour, booking advisable. 028 40 000. www.lissardestate.com.
This exclusive 200-acre estate of country manors, gardens, trails, ponds and lakes is managed to encourage the natural flora and fauna to flourish. A series of isolated contemplative areas allows day visitors to enjoy the peace and tranquility of the place, most notably the extraordinary **James Turrell Irish Sky Garden Crater**, designed by American installation artist, James Turrell (b. 1943), to be appreciated by spectators lying on the stone structures at the bottom of it. The dome-effect that is created in the elliptical frame is a remarkable experience.

2.5mi/4km further along the road towards Baltimore, watch out for the sign on the left.

Lough Hyne Nature Reserve★★

Beware of sea urchin spines, if moving about barefoot.
Set among low hills, this unpolluted saltwater lagoon is a marine nature reserve with a unique ecosystem; over 60 species have been recorded, including the redmouth goby, otherwise only found in Portugal.

8mi/13km SW of Skibbereen on the R 595.

Baltimore★

This picturesque fishing village faces a myriad of islands offshore in sheltered Roaring Water Bay. There is always boat traffic animating the horizon. Overlooking the piers are the ruins of an early-17C fortified house.

Sherkin Island★

Access by ferry (see Addresses).
The island is home to the remains of an O'Driscoll stronghold, a ruined friary, some lovely beaches and a marine research station.

Cape Clear Island★★

Access by ferry (see Addresses).
Great colonies of guillemots, cormorants, shearwaters, petrels and choughs attract ornithologists to this remote rock, Ireland's southernmost inhabited island. Whales, turtles, sharks, seals and dolphins all can be seen in the waters around here.

ADDRESSES

KINSALE

STAY

⊖ **Kilcaw Guesthouse**– *1mi E on the R 600.* ☏*021 477 4155. www.kilcawhouse.com.* *7rm.* A modern guesthouse in seven acres of land. The breakfast room has a farmhouse feel while the sitting room, with its open fireplace, offers a restful sanctuary.

⊖⊖ **Desmond House** – *42 Cork St.* ☏*021 477 3575. www.desmondhousekinsale.com.* *4rm.* This centrally located Georgian town house has huge luxury bedroom suites with super king-sized beds and full-sized bathrooms all with whirlpool bathtub and shower.

EAT

⊖ **Dalton's** – *3 Market St.* ☏*021 477 7597.* The emphasis at this pub is firmly on the food (especially seafood) with a menu that blends international influences garnered from the owner's experiences abroad.

⊖⊖ **Max's Wine Bar/Seafood Restaurant**– *Main St.* ☏*021 477 2443 http://maxs.ie/ Closed mid Dec.* Quaint and intimate, with exposed beams, wood flooring and a small conservatory, the menu is sophisticated French with an Irish accent and features carefully sourced local produce with deft use of herbs.

⊖⊖ **Toddie's** – *Summercove.* ☏*021477 2131; www.thebulman.ie. Closed Mon eve.* Part of the Bulman pub, Toddie's features a delightful terrace. The interior is very attractive with clever artworks. Comprehensive modern menus.

SPORTS AND LEISURE

Good facilities for yachting and deep-sea fishing.

EVENTS AND FESTIVALS

The Kinsale Food Festival (*www.kinsalerestaurants.com*) is held in mid October when visitors sample the delights created by the international chefs of the Kinsale Good Food Circle.

SIGHTSEEING

Historic Kinsale Walking Tours – *Guided tours (1hr) Mar–Oct, daily 11.15am, also May–Sept Mon–Sat 9.15am. €7. Start from outside the Tourist Office.* ☏*021 477 2873. www.historicstrollkinsale.com.* For more tours, visit *www.kinsale.ie/ acwalk.htm.*

Kinsale Harbour Scenic Cruises ☏*086 250 5456; www.kinsaleharbourcruises.com.* *€13. Cruises operate daily Mar–Oct.*

SKIBBEREEN

STAY

⊖⊖ **West Cork Hotel** – *Ilen St.* ☏*028 21277. 34rms. www.westcorkhotel.com.* Most rooms offer river views at this very comfortable and spacious luxury hotel. Friendly, efficient staff and an excellent restaurant (⊖⊖). Superb value.

⊖⊖ **Bridge House** – *Bridge St.* ☏*028 21273. http://bridgehouseskibbereen.com.* *3rms.* You can't miss the beautiful flower-decked façade of this small house. This unusual B&B is bursting with antiques and theatrical touches, which may be a little overwhelming for some, but does have the merit of providing a very personal touch. The owner, Mona, is a fabulous hostess.

ENTERTAINMENT

West Cork Arts Centre (*North St., Mon–Sat 10am–4.45pm.* ☏*028 22090. www.westcorkartscentre.com*) – Regular arts events, films and contemporary art exhibitions.

BALTIMORE

EAT

⊖⊖ **Rolf's** – *Baltimore Hill.* ☏*028 20289, http://rolfscountryhouse.com. Closed Mon and Tue lunch.* Charming restuarant in farmhouse courtyard converted to a hotel and cottages.

SPORTS AND LEISURE

Sailing at Baltimore (temporary marina in summer) and Schull.

SIGHTSEEING

Ten Island Tours– Nature cruise around the Baltimore archipelago. ☏*028 20218/ 087 263 8470. www.tenislandtours.com*

Baltimore–Cape Clear Island Ferry – Operates daily (weather permitting); ☏*028 39159/41923. www.cailinoir.com.* The same boat is used for twilight tours of Fastnet Rock.

Mizen Head and Bantry Bay★★

Leaving the softly rolling hills of the South, you approach harder land, deep bays, moors and rocky outcrops. The two peninsulas, Mizen Head and Sheep's Head, end in high cliffs beaten by the winds, in sharp contrast to the small towns of Bantry and Glengarriff, where the Mediterranean-like vegetation makes the visitor forget the rough seas beyond.

Info: Old Court House, Bantry. ✆027 50229, www.bantry.ie.

▷ **Location:** Bantry lies between Cork and Killarney on the south shore of Bantry Bay between Skibbereen and Glengarriff.

🕐 **Timing:** Allow one day.

🚗 DRIVING TOUR

MIZEN HEAD★★
Tour of 35mi/56km west of Skibbereen. Allow one day.

Punctuated by the villages of Ballydehob, Durrus and Schull, this peninsula is made up of a series of inviting places to visit and is notable as the most southerly point of mainland Ireland, perfect for a one day excursion.

▷ From Skibbereen take the N 71 west. After 10mi/16km turn left.

Ballydehob
The main street, lined with brightly painted houses, slopes steeply down to Roaring Water Bay. The 12-arch railway bridge, part of the Schull and Skibbereen light railway which closed in 1947, has been converted into a **walkway**.

▷ Take the minor road north up to Mount Gabriel and Schull.

Mount Gabriel★
It is a stiff climb to the aircraft tracking station at 1,339ft/408m. During the Bronze Age, copper was mined here in large quantities.

▷ Take the road south to Schull.

Beyond the pass there is a fine view of Roaring Water Bay and Schull.

Schull (Skull)★
The name of this pretty little market town, meaning "school", comes from a monastic centre of learning (10C). Schull is home to the Republic's only **planetarium** (🕐 *star show (45min): Jul–Aug Mon, Wed, Fri & Sat 8pm; ⊛ €6; ✆028 28315; www.schullcommunity college.com*).

The Invasion That Never Was, 1796

An expeditionary force of 15,000 French troops, commanded by General Hoche, accompanied by the Irish rebel Wolfe Tone, set sail from Brest intent on invading Ireland and expelling the British. Fog and adverse winds prevented most of the fleet from entering Bantry Bay. Then a storm blew up, impeding any attempts at landing, so the ships retreated. Had the soldiers managed to come ashore, things might well have been very different, as only a scratch force of militiamen commanded by Richard White, owner of Bantry House, could be mustered.

Ten French warships were lost; the frigate *La Surveillante* was scuttled on January 2, 1797. The 17cwt/863kg French anchor, recovered by a trawler in 1964, sits by the N17 south of Bantry; a captured French longboat is now in Dún Laoghaire.

▶ Continue west; in Toormore turn left onto the R 591 to Goleen and Crookhaven. Turn right (sign) at the entrance to the village of Goleen.

Goleen

The road follows a rocky landscape, across moorland and meandering creeks to Goleen and its tiny port.

▶ From Goleen follow the winding R 591 which in places, clings precariously to the coastline.

Crookhaven

The little resort of Crookhaven was once a busy fishing harbour where mailboats stopped en-route to America and the West Indies, copper was shipped from nearby Brow Head, and Marconi's transatlantic telegraph station was put into operation in 1902.

▶ Take the minor road along the east side of Barley Cove.

Barley Cove

The deep inlet lined with a **sandy beach★** between the cliffs makes this a fine holiday resort, especially popular with surfers.

▶ Cross the causeway at Barley Cove and turn left to Mizen Head.

Mizen Head★★

10min steep descent on foot from car park.
The storm-battered cliffs of Mizen Head mark the southwesternmost tip of Ireland. In 1910 the Irish Lights fog signal station was built here and the **Mizen Head Signal Station Visitor Centre** (*⏰open daily mid-Mar–Oct 10.30am–5pm, Jun–Sept 10am–6pm; Nov–mid-Mar Sat–Sun 11am–4pm, Feb Sat-Sun 11am-4pm; ⊛€7.50; ✕; ✆028 35115/35225; www.mizenhead.ie)* presents the work of the station and of lighthouse keepers, local marine life, wrecks, the famous Fastnet Yacht Race and the building of the Fastnet Rock Lighthouse *(SE – 9mi/14km).*
The most stunning part of the visit, though is the **bridge**, renovated in 2010, across the rocks to the signal station. Surreal rock formations and foaming seas give a lasting impression of just how remote and weather-battered this place is.

SHEEP'S HEAD★★

Approx 30mi/48km.
Smaller than the Mizen Peninsula, but just as beautiful and more remote, this narrow slip of a peninsula, deserted even at the height of the summer season, offers some spectacular seascapes and low purple hills.

Mizen Head

© matthibcn/iStockphoto.com

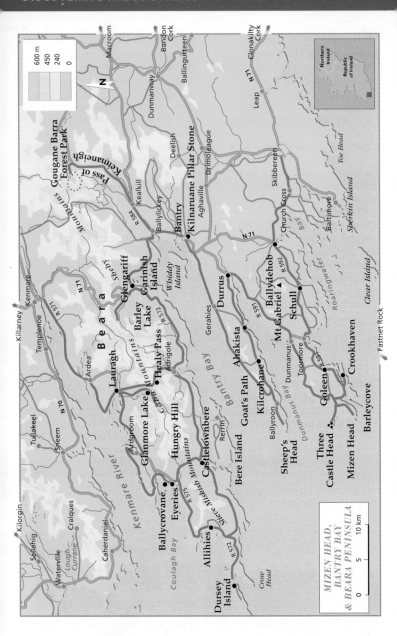

Sheep's Head Way

Sheep's Head Way is a long-distance, waymarked walking route which traces a loop at the beginning of Bantry and traverses the tiny peninsula. Some 55mi/88 km in length, the route has no difficult sections and can be broken into several days' walks, the longest one being 10mi/16km. Maps are available in Bantry and Kilcrohane.

By car, starting from Durrus, the road follows the coastline to the village of

Kilcrohane. At Kilcrohane the road splits. One route takes you on to the head of the peninsula, through increasingly rocky and remote moorland.

At the car park you can carry on to the end of the peninsula on foot (care is needed: the path is rocky and often very windswept) for some breathtaking views. Head back to the village and take the other route northwards by a stunning coastal route back to the N 71 just east of Bantry.

BANTRY BAY AREA★
Approx 40mi/64km

A superb area of coastal roads, forestry, mountains and lakes. After the wild and deserted landscapes of the peninsulas of Mizen Head and Sheep's Head, the Bantry Bay area surprises by its soft climate and its quasi-exotic vegetation, the sweep of its pretty coastline ill preparing the visitor for the Beara Peninsula.

▶ As you approach Bantry from the South, turn right at the Westlodge Hotel (sign).

Kilnaruane Inscribed Stone
On the hilltop stands a 9C stone pillar, possibly the shaft of a high cross. Carved panels depict a boat with four oarsmen, a figure at prayer, St Paul and St Anthony of the Desert.

Bantry★
The market and fishing town of Bantry *(Beanntraí)* was the scene in 1796 of a dramatic episode in British and Irish history, when an attempted French invasion from Bantry Bay was frustrated by foul weather.

Bantry House★ (& ⓘ *open Apr–May, Sep-Oct, Tue-Sun 10am–5pm, Jun-Aug daily 10am-5pm;* ⌂ *house and garden €11; gardens and Armada Centre €5;* ✕; *☎027 50047; www.bantryhouse.com)* is a splendid Georgian mansion of 1740, full of treasures including curiosities from Pompeii. The gardens are superb, comprising sweeping lawns, formal gardens and wonderful views out to sea. The East Stables houses an exhibition on the **Bantry French Armada:** (ⓒ *see "The Invasion That Never Was" box).* It is also possible to stay overnight at the house.

ADDRESSES

⌂ STAY

⌂ **Stanley House** – *Colla Road, Schull. 4 rms. ☎028 28425. www.stanley-house.net.* Modern, but characterful house in an elevated position with excellent bay views.

⌂⌂–⌂⌂⌂ **Sea View House** – *Ballylickey, Bantry. ☎027 50073. www.seaviewhousehotel.com.* Outside town, on the road to Glengarriff, this 4 star 19C country house hotel is set in private and well tended grounds offering large grandly furnished rooms and excellent food in its restaurant.

ⓨ/EAT

⌂ **O'Connors Seafod Restaurant** – *Wolfe Tone Square. ☎027 556 64. www.oconnorseafood.com.* Well-run, harbourside restaurant, with a compact, bistro-style interior featuring model ships in the windows and modern art on the walls.

SPORTS AND LEISURE
Bantry's inner harbour, with two slipways and safe anchorage, is an ideal location for sailing, water-skiing, wind surfing, canoeing, scuba-diving and swimming. An indoor pool, children's and toddlers' pool, and leisure centre facilities at the **Westlodge Hotel** in Bantry are open to the public throughout the year.

EVENTS AND FESTIVALS
The two highlights of the year are: **Bantry Mussel Fair** in May, and **West Cork Chamber Music Week** *(www.westcorkmusic.ie/chambermusicfestival),* in late Jun, early Jul.

Beara Peninsula★★

The Beara Peninsula, projecting some 30mi/48km into the Atlantic, has some wild and beautiful mountain, moorland and coastal scenery. Less affected by tourism than the neighbouring peninsulas of County Kerry, this is the wildest of all the peninsulas of the south-west and offers perhaps the most spectacular views. Its central spine of the Caha and Slieve Miskish Mountains, with Sugarloaf and Hungry Hill as their highlights, forms the backdrop to life on the peninsula. It is a land of tiny farms, perched on pockets of fertility set in sweeping, rock-strewn hillsides. Rarely visited and as wild as Ireland gets, the North Coast makes an interesting driving route with views northwards of the Ivearagh and Dingle Peninsulas.

- **Michelin Map:** p269
- **Info:** www.bearatourism.com
- **Location:** The peninsula between Bantry and Kenmare, see map p270.
- **Don't Miss:** The dramatic route of the Healy Pass.
- **Kids:** The beach at Allihies and the boat ride to Garinish Island
- **Timing:** Two days would allow for a slow tour of the peninsula, with a stop at Allihies.

GLENGARRIFF (AN GLEANN GARBH)

Little more than a high street, Glengarriff has been a resort of international renown since the mid-19C, famed for its mild climate and exotic flora. The **Eccles Hotel**, built in 1833 as a coaching stage, accommodated Queen Victoria on her visit to southwestern Cork and George Bernard Shaw wrote part of *St Joan* here, en route to Garinish Island.

There are pleasant walks along the wooded shore of the Blue Pool in the northwest corner of Glengarriff Harbour. The best view of Glengarriff is from the southwest at **Shrone Hill** (919ft/280m).

AROUND GLENGARRIFF
Glengariff Woods★

Just outside Glengariff village on the N 71. Open daily. www.glengarriff naturereserve.ie.

This is an ancient oak woodland set in 741acres/300ha of parkland, once

Beara Peninsula

© Trish Punch/Getty Images

GETTING AROUND

BY SEA – Garinish Island: Ferries operate from Glengarriff Mar–Oct. Blue Pool Ferry. €10. ℘027 63333. www.bluepoolferry.com.
Harbour Queen Ferry. ℘27 63116. www.harbourqueenferry.com. €12.
Bere Island Ferry – Operates from Castletownbere and Bere Island third week Jun to third week Sept. Call for price and times. ℘27 75009. www.bereislandferries.com.

BY ROAD – Driving tours: Kenmare Coach and Cab Co offer day trips round the Ring of Kerry, Ring of Beara and Garinish/Glangariff. ℘064 41491. www.kenmarecoachandcab.com.
Dursey Island Cable Car – Operates from Ballaghboy year-round, Mon–Sat 9–11am, 2.30pm–5pm, 7pm–8pm; Sun 9–10.30am, 1pm–2.30pm, 4pm–5pm (Jun–Aug only), 7pm–8pm. Arrive 30min before departure.

owned by Lord Bantry, then for a time a forestry plantation, but now a nature reserve. There are pretty, undemanding footpaths through the woods to a waterfall and along the Glengarriff River and a short climb up to Lady Bantry's Lookout with its spectacular views over the Caha Mountains. Fishing permits for trout and salmon can be bought in Glengarriff. Some rare flora and fauna live here and the park is home to some Kerry cattle, a native breed.

Ilnacullin (Garinish Island)★★

Access by Garinish Island Ferry (see Getting Around). (Dúchas). ◐Open Apr–Oct, 10am–5.30pm (Jul–Aug Mon-Fri 9.30am-5.30pm, Sat 9.30am-6pm, Sun 5.30pm, Oct 10am-4.30pm). Hiking trail (1hr 45min). €5 landing fee. ℘027 63040. www.heritageireland.ie.
Ilnacullin (or *Ilaunacullin*), also known as Garinish Island, (or Garnish Island), lies in Glengarriff Harbour. The English landscape designer Harold Peto turned it into a meticulously planned 37 acres/15ha garden for the Belfast-born MP, Annan Bryce. Italianate formality and Classical pavilions contrast well with the austere mountain backdrop and the lush planting of exotic species. A path leads to the **Martello Tower**, which at 135ft/41m above sea-level is the highest point on the island.

Bamboo Garden ★★

Glengarriff. ◐Open daily 9am–7pm. €6. ℘027 63975. www.bamboo-park.com.
The bamboo is ideally suited to the climate, so 30 different species and 12 types of palm thrive here. There are fine views of Glengarriff Harbour and Bantry Bay from the Tower and waterfront.

THE SOUTH COAST OF THE PENINSULA★

Travelling west of Glengarriff this part of the peninsula forms the northern shore of Bantry Bay. The road follows the ragged coastline, with minor roads down to pebble beaches, to Castletownbere.

Bere Island

The coastal road skirts Bere Haven, a sheltered passage between Bere Island and the peninsula, which was used as a harbour by the English Navy until 1938, when Churchill had to return ownership of the harbour to Ireland. Opposite, Bere Island, with its pretty rural landscape and waymarked walking route around the island, is connected to the mainland by ferries, which leave from the quayside in Castletownbere.

Castletownbere

The town prospered in the early-19C when rich copper deposits were discovered at Allihies, but was badly affected by the Potato Famine. By the late 19C, it had become an important fishing port: today fish processing is a substantial industry.

Dursey Island ★

Access by cable-car
(see Getting Around).
The island's isolation was broken when Ireland's only cable railway was strung across the strait in 1970, capable of carrying six passengers, or a cow, or sheep and its minder! Dursey *(4mi/6km long)*, has one village (Kilmichael), one road and large nesting colonies of birds.

THE NORTH COAST OF THE PENINSULA★★

As wild and windswept as Ireland gets, this rarely-visited part of the peninsula, with its tiny colourful villages, makes a pleasant afternoon drive.

Allihies ★

The peninsula became known for its rich **copper mines**, worked by a predominantly Cornish workforce, and bestowing prosperity on 19C-Allihies. Old engine houses and spoil heaps are visible among the many invisible dangerous abandoned mineshafts.
The **Allihies Copper Mine Museum** tells the story (*open Easter–Oct daily 10.30am–5pm, check times/days in winter. €6; 027 73218; www.acmm. ie). **Ballydonegan Strand** (1mi/1.6km south)* is a beautiful golden sand beach made of crushed stone from the mines.

Eyeries

This typical pretty Irish mountain settlement, winner of Ireland's Best Kept Towns award 2012, is renowned for its soft tangy Milleens cheese.

Ballycrovane Ogham Pillar Stone★

Donation to enter the field.
In a field stands the tallest pillar stone in Ireland (15ft/5m high); the Ogham inscription—MAQI-DECCEDDAS AVI TURANIAS—of the son of Deich descendant of Torainn—was probably added later.

Lauragh

In Lauragh, visit **Derreen Gardens★** (*open Apr–Oct, 10am–6pm (Aug Fri–Sun only); €7; 064 83588)*. These lush, mature gardens were planted by the fifth Lord Lansdowne beside Kilmakilloge Harbour, an inlet on the south shore of the Kenmare River. The woodland is richly underplanted with azaleas and rhododendrons, as well as rare New Zealand tree ferns.

Glanmore Lake★

Not far from the gardens a sign indicates the way to Glanmore Lake. There are pleasant strolls around the lake on a good day and some brooding mountain scenery.

Healy Pass★★

The road is particularly steep near Glanmore Lake.
Opened in 1931, the road climbs through a series of tortuous hairpin bends *(7mi/11km)* to the summit; on a clear day there are **views★★** of both shores of the peninsula.

ADDRESSES

STAY

Island View House – *Glengarriff.* *027 63081. www.islandviewhouse.net.* Modern house in a quiet scenic area 150m from the sea front. Self-catering accommodation also available.

Casey's Hotel – *Glengarriff. 027 63010. www.caseyshotelglengarriff.ie.* In the middle of the village, very comfortable rooms and a bar and restaurant.

EAT

Eccles Hotel– *Glengarriff. 027 63003. www.eccleshotel.com.* The bar serves sandwiches, soups and full meals, but for period atmosphere book a table by the window in the restuarant for locally caught seafood and panoramic views of Bantry Bay.

For more options on where to Stay and Eat see p271.

Ring of Kerry★★

The most famous and most-visited of the peninsulas of Southwest Ireland and at the height of summer the road that rings the peninsula can have one too many coachloads for the visitor's comfort. If this occurs, head inland and enjoy the deserted landscape.

KILLARNEY★★

Killarney is an ideal touring centre on the N 22 between Cork and Tralee, not far from Farranfore Airport (north by N 22).

Tourists have been coming to Killarney *(Cill Airne)* for more than 200 years, entranced by its glorious setting of lakes, luxuriant vegetation, romantic ruins and meticulously managed demesnes. All around are rugged mountains, including the **Macgillycuddy's Reeks★★★**, which culminate in the highest peak in Ireland, **Carrauntoohill★★** (3,414ft/1,041m). No visit to the area is complete without making the classic trip into the Gap of Dunloe, a formidable breach rammed by a glacier through the heart of the mountains. The monastery founded on the little island of Innisfallen in the 7C became a centre of learning, where the *Annals of Innisfallen*, one of Ireland's earliest historical chronicles, was composed. The area was subsequently governed by the O'Donoghues, McCarthys and O'Sullivans, who were displaced by Elizabethan settlers like the Brownes and Herberts. It was in the 18C that Thomas Browne, the 4th Viscount Kenmare (1726–95), planned the pre-

sent neat town of slated houses and shops. He also introduced linen and woollen manufacturing and beautified the surroundings by planting trees and providing seats and belvederes. Over time, streams of visitors came, including poets, painters and writers – Shelley found Killarney more impressive even than Switzerland, Macaulay thought Innisfallen "not a reflex of heaven, but a bit of heaven itself"; on the other hand, Charlotte Brontë had the misfortune to be thrown from her horse while exploring the Gap of Dunloe and Thackeray was dismayed by the throngs of touts and guides. Killarney's tourist vocation was confirmed with the visit of Queen Victoria in 1861. In 1932 the Muckross estate was presented by its American owners to the nation as the Bourn Vincent Memorial Park, becoming

---

- **Info:** Beech Rd., **Killarney**, ✆064 663 1633, www. killarney.ie; Fair Green, **Kenmare**, ✆064 664 2615 (seasonal), www. kenmare.com. www.ring ofkerrytourism.com.
- **Location:** The peninsula between Kenmare and Glengarriff.
- **Don't Miss:** The Gap of Dunloe and Killarney National Park, the Ring of Kerry and Skellig Islands.
- **Kids:** Muckross House and Traditional Farm.
- **Timing:** Two days would allow a visit to Killarney and a tour of the peninsula.

GETTING AROUND

BY AIR – Kerry (Farranfore) Airport: Flights to Dublin, Manchester, Stansted, Luton and Frankfurt. ✆066 976 4644. www.kerryairport.ie.
BY SEA – Valentia Island-Renard Point Car Ferry: Operates Apr–Sept, daily 8.30am–10.30pm. ✆066 947 6141.
Skellig Islands Ferry – From Portmagee Pier to the Skellig Islands (45min) daily, weather permitting, at 10am (return departure 2.15pm). €75. ✆066 947 2437/087 23 95470. www.skelligislands.com.

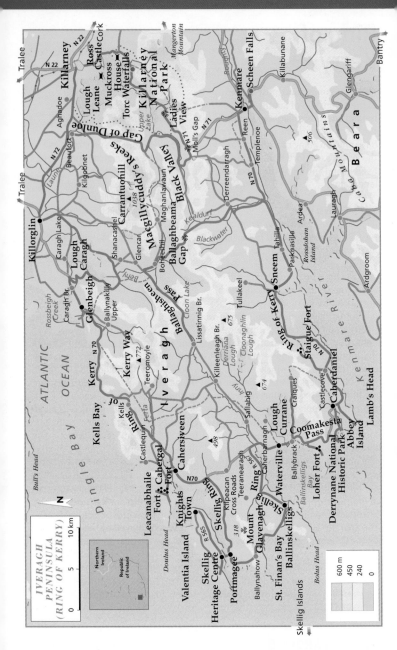

the core of the present National Park, Ireland's first.

Killarney town is thronged with visitors crowding its streets, bars, hotels and shops. Focal points include Market Cross, the intersection of Main Street, High Street and New Street, and Ken-

mare Place, where the jaunting cars wait for passengers.

At the top of New Street, at the junction of High Street on the left, and Main Sreet on the right, is Market Cross, named after the country market that was once held here. Local farming

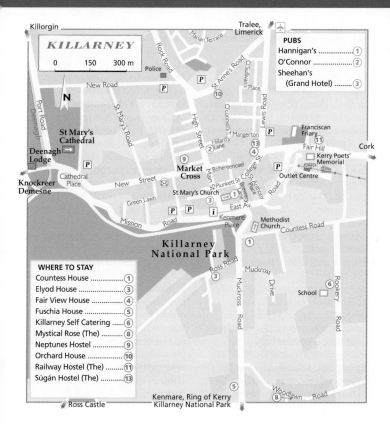

KILLARNEY

0   150   300 m

PUBS
Hannigan's .... (1)
O'Connor .... (2)
Sheehan's
    (Grand Hotel) .... (3)

Killorgin
Tralee, Limerick
Police
New Road
Rock Road
Marian Terrace
St Anne's Road
O'Sullivans Place
O'Connell St
Lewis Road
Port Road
Deenagh
St Mary's Road
High Street
Mangerton
Hilliard's Lane
Franciscan Friary
Fair Hill
Cork
Kerry Poets' Memorial
St Mary's Cathedral
Deenagh Lodge
Knockreer Demesne
Cathedral Place
New Street
Green Lawn
Market Cross
Main St
Bohereencael
Plunkett St
College St
St Anthony's Place
Brewery Lane
Outlet Centre
St Mary's Church
Mission Road
Kenmare Place
East Av.
Methodist Church
Countess Road
Killarney National Park
Ross Road
Muckross
Muckross Road
Muckross Drive
School
Rookery Road
Woodlawn Road
Kenmare, Ring of Kerry
Killarney National Park
Ross Castle

WHERE TO STAY
Countess House .... (1)
Elyod House .... (3)
Fair View House .... (4)
Fuschia House .... (5)
Killarney Self Catering ...... (6)
Mystical Rose (The) .... (8)
Neptunes Hostel .... (9)
Orchard House .... (10)
Railway Hostel (The) .... (11)
Súgán Hostel (The) .... (13)

families brought everything to sell that wasn't essential to their survival to earn a little cash to pay the rent: eggs, milk, butter, peat and cloth woven on home-made looms. Today, Market Cross is the commercial heart of the city, with its shop fronts modernised and its ancient pubs very much alive.

The Early-English **St Mary's Anglican Church**, built in 1870, contains a stained-glass window reproducing Holman Hunt's *Light of the World*. Among its memorials, there is one to the Revd Arthur Hyde, great-grandfather of Douglas Hyde, first president of Ireland. West of Market Cross, a prominent spire (285ft/87m high) marks **St Mary's RC Cathedral★**, designed by Augustus Pugin. Although work began in 1842, it was not consecrated until 1855 as the building was used to provide shelter to famine victims between 1848 and 1853. It was adapted for the new liturgy in 1972–73.

Kerry Poets' Memorial

The personification of Ireland as a beautiful woman *(speir bhean)* was created in 1940 by Seamus Murphy to commemorate Co Kerry's four best-known Gaelic poets – **Pierce Ferriter**, a poet, soldier and musician from the Dingle Peninsula, who refused to submit to the Cromwellians in 1652 and was hanged in 1653, in Killarney; **Geoffrey O'Donoghue of the Glens** (1620–78), who was chieftain of Glenflesk and lived in Killaha Castle, southeast of Killarney; **Egan O'Rahilly** (1670–1728), the greatest of the four poets, who was educated in the bardic tradition and gave his allegiance to the Brownes, as the McCarthys were unable to act as his patrons; **Owen Roe O'Sullivan** (1748–84), who led a roving life as a hedge schoolmaster in winter and an itinerant labourer in summer, as well as serving in the British Army and Navy; to the delight of Admiral Rodney he wrote a poem in English about the

Admiral's victory over the French at Dominica in 1782.

Franciscan Friary

The friary, built in 1860 in a style similar to Muckross Friary (©see Killarney National Park Driving Tour), contains a stained-glass window (entrance hall) by Harry Clarke.

GAP OF DUNLOE★★

There are various ways of exploring the Gap. ⌖Gap of Dunloe Tours operate mid-Mar–Oct. Depart by bus from Killarney at 10.30am to Kate Kearney's Cottage; either travel by jaunting car (€20 extra), pony (€30 extra) or walk (2.5hrs) through the Gap to Lower Brendans' Cottage (lunch extra); boat trip across the three lakes at 2pm; return by bus to Killarney at 4p.m. Tours must be booked in advance; take a rain jacket ⌖Bus and boat €30. ℘064 663 0200. www.gapofdunloetours.com.

By car: from Killarney take N 72 W; after 4mi/6km turn left and continue to Kate Kearney's Cottage, hire a pony and trap or continue on foot before returning to the car park. Boat trips only possible if booked as part of a tour with Dunloe Gap Tours.

By bicycle: make a round trip by hired cycle either via the lakes (cycles are carried aboard a special boat), via the Kerry Way (involving some pushing) or via Moll's Gap.

The jarvies (jaunting car drivers) plying for hire throng the roadsides and the forecourt of **Kate Kearney's Cottage**, (♿🕐open daily 10am until late; ℘064 664 4146; www.katekearneyscottage. com); originally an old coaching inn kept by Kate, who served *poteen* to 19C tourists; the cottage now serves 20C hospitality, including traditional Irish nights.

This excursion, through a deep and narrow rock-strewn gorge, is one of the highlights of a visit to Ireland for many people. The initial crowd of pony traps, riders, cyclists and walkers soon thins out; it is less crowded towards the end of the day and can be entered from the Black Valley to the south. The U-shaped glacial breach (1,500ft/457m deep) is traversed by a narrow track which winds up a series of hairpin bends, past several mountain tarns, to cross a stream before reaching the ruins of a Royal Irish Constabulary strongpoint. Most traffic turns back on reaching the Head of the Gap (794ft/242m). As the track descends into the Gearhameen Valley, where red deer graze, there is a fine view of the Upper Lake, bordered by native oakwoods and backed by Mangerton Mountain (2,756ft/838m).

Upper Lake, Killarney National Park

© Chris Hill/Tourism Ireland

KILLARNEY NATIONAL PARK★★★

3.7mi/6km S of Killarney by N 71.
Killarney National Park *(39sq mi/ 101sq km; Dúchas;* visitor centre open mid-Mar–Sep 9am–5.30pm; last admission 1hr before closing; ✗; ℘064 663 1440; www.heritageireland.ie)* embraces the three lakes – Lower (Lough Leane), Middle (Muckross Lake) and Upper, which are linked by the Long Range River – the foreshore and the mountain slopes south and west.

The original nucleus of the Muckross Estate is now complemented by Knockreer, Ross Island and Innisfallen, formerly part of the Kenmare Estate. Blanket bog on the higher land contrasts with Ireland's largest remaining area of ancient oak woodland and examples of mature yews, alder carrs and arbutus (or strawberry tree), which flourishes in the exceptionally mild climate.

The special character of the park was given international recognition in 1981, when it was designated a UNESCO Biosphere Reserve. An audio-visual show in the visitor centre showcases the Park.

Ross Castle★

1mi/1.6km S by N 71 and a minor road W (sign). Boat trips to Innisfallen Island. (Dúchas) Visit by guided tour only (40min) early Mar–late Oct 9.30am– 5.45pm; Last admission 45min before closing.* Closed 24–26 Dec.* €5. ℘064 663 5851. www.heritageireland.ie.*

The well-restored castle, the last in Munster to hold out against Cromwellian forces (1652) until attacks were mounted from armed boats, was built on the shore of Lough Leane in the 15C by one of the O'Donoghue Ross chieftains. A fortified bawn (a defensive wall surrounding an Irish tower house, whose original purpose was to protect livestock during an attack) reinforced by circular flanking towers surrounded the rectangular keep. The four floors have been restored using medieval techniques and furnished in styles appropriate to the early-15C to late-16C period.

Cycling Killarney

Cycling is an excellent way to see the National Park, particularly around Muckross House. Hire a bike from one of the many outlets in town (the tourist office will give you details).

Within easy pedalling distance of the centre are Ross Castle and Muckross House (though in opposite directions). Cycling lanes go for most of the way to Muckross House (don't forget that you must cycle anti-clockwise around the lake!).

The promontory, known as **Ross Island★**, dotted with copper mines from the early 19C, extends into Lough Leane. Access is along a profusion of tree- and flower-lined avenues. There are fine views of Lough Leane and the islands.

On **Innisfallen★** no trace remains oof the 7C monastery, once so renowned as a centre of learning, but the luxuriantly wooded island still harbours evocative remains of a later abbey with a fine Romanesque doorway.

Knockreer Demesne★

Footpath to Ross Castle.
The grounds of Knockreer House extend westwards from Killarney to the shore of Lough Leane; the entrance from the town is marked by a thatched cottage, **Deenagh Lodge** *(tea room).*

Muckross Friary (Abbey) ★

Open year round until dusk.
Muckross Friary was founded for the Franciscans in 1448 and took 59 years to build. The mid-15C nave and choir, broad central tower and south transept were erected c. 1500.

The 22-arch cloisters and the domestic offices were constructed in four phases. The three-storey building north of the choir probably contained the Sacristy and the Sacristan's lodging.

Muckross Lake with a horse-drawn jaunting car

© Gareth Mccormack/Getty Images

Muckross House, Garden and Traditional Farms★

(Dúchas). ♿☉*House and gardens: open daily, year-round 9am–5.30pm (7pm Jul–Aug).* ☉*Closed Christmas hols.* ☉*Farms: open Jun–Aug daily 10am–6pm. May daily 1pm–6pm. Apr, Sept, Oct Sat–Sun and Bank Hols 1pm–6pm. Last admission 1hr before closing.* ☞*House/farm: €9; house and farm €15.* ✕✆*064 667 0144. www.muckross-house.ie.*

The Elizabethan-style **Muckross House★** in Portland stone was built in 1843 for the Herbert family. Many rooms reflect the taste of the early-20C: the drawing room, library and dining room are all lavishly decorated. The basement is devoted to regional crafts.

The **Traditional Farms★** are a showpiece of early-20C Irish rural life. Animals inhabit the yards and fields and the buildings, from large farmhouse to labourer's cottage, are appropriately furnished with dressers, presses and settle-beds. Indoors, turf fires burn in the hearths and the staff, in period costume, demonstrate the work of a country housewife in the days before electricity and other modern amenities came to the Irish countryside.

The **Muckross Peninsula**, which divides Lough Leane from Muckross (Middle) Lake, contains one of the finest yew woods in Europe and is crossed by nature trails.

Torc Waterfall★

The **cascade** *(60ft/18m)* is one of the highest in Ireland. The viewpoint *(173 steps)* provides a fine view of the lakes.

Ladies View★★

Climbing over the hills to Kenmare, the N 17 enables visitors to enjoy some of the finest panoramas over the Killarney landscape without the need to scale a mountain. Queen Victoria was particularly impressed by the prospect of Macgillycuddy's Reeks and the island-studded Upper Lake. Little has changed since she and her entourage came this way in 1861.

Moll's Gap★

The pass *(863ft/263m)* provides *(north)* a striking view of the Gap of Dunloe in Macgillycuddy's Reeks and *(south)* a glimpse of the Kenmare River.

KENMARE★

Kenmare is located on N 71, a scenic road between Killarney and Glengarriff, and is a good place to stay while exploring Co Kerry.

This small market town, designated a Heritage Town, proclaims itself "The Jewel on the Ring of Kerry". It is charmingly set in a horseshoe of mountains at the point where the Roughty River widens into the long sea-inlet known as the Kenmare River. Kenmare *(Neidín)* is a popular tourist centre, with a wide range of hotels and restaurants and elegant shops (jewellery, linen, delicatessen, books) catering for visitors from many countries, many of whom use it as a starting point for explorations of the Beara and Iveragh Peninsulas.

Kenmare is an 18C planned town shaped like a cross, sponsored by the first Marquess of Lansdowne.

Its two streets, lined with neat stone houses, meet at a triangular space intended to serve as a market-place and now a park. The town's real origin, however, goes back to the energetic Sir William Petty (1623–87), organiser of the Down Survey (&see FINGAL), who encouraged immigration from England and Wales, founded ironworks, and astutely acquired property to the extent that he eventually owned around a quarter of Kerry.

Kenmare Heritage Centre

&⊙Open Easter–Oct, 9.15am–5pm (9am–7pm mid-Jun–Aug). ℘064 664 1233.

Also home to the tourist office, the Heritage Centre traces the history of Kenmare, originally called Nedeen (Neidín in Irish), including the local impact of the Famine and the story of the Nun of Kenmare, a member of the community which established the lace-making industry in the 19C.

On the upper floor, via the door to the left of the Heritage Centre is the **Kenmare Lace and Design Centre** (⊙open Mon–Sat Easter–Oct, 10am–1pm, 2.15pm–5.30pm; winter opening by appointment; ℘064 664 1491. www.kenmarelace.ie) with displays of lace and demonstrations of lace-making.

Stone Circle

The prehistoric circle comprises one central stone and a ring of 15 upright stones.

GLEN INCHAQUIN PARK★★

8mi/14km SW of Kenmare by R 571 and left turn into a single-track lane (5mi/8km). ⊙Open year round dawn–dusk. ⊛€6. ✗ ℘064 668 4235. www.gleninchaquin.com.

Kenmare Lace

Kenmare lace is needlepoint lace introduced from Italy in the 17C. It is particularly difficult because it is worked in needle and thread (linen rather than cotton), according to designs drawn on parchment or glazed calico and outlined with skeleton threads: these are later removed, as is the backing. Raised point is created by using buttonhole stitches over cords or horsehair.

The lane leads into a remote landscape of mountains and lakes, clear streams, glorious sessile oak woodland and wild flowers (laid footpaths). At the head of the glen there is a farmhouse by a spectacular braided waterfall. The views down to the **Kenmare River★** and McGillycuddy Reeks are spectacular.

🚗 DRIVING TOURS

THE SOUTH OF THE PENINSULA★
36km/22mi. Allow half a day.

The first part of the drive, as far as Sneem, follows the **Kenmare River**. The wooded riverbank affords pleasant views of the rugged Beara Peninsular towards the south. The landscape becomes much more spectacular further on, approaching Caherdaniel, where the coastline becomes wild and craggy.

Sneem

Another colourful village, prettily laid out around a square and beside a river, Sneem is a very popular stopover for tourists, with its many crafts and coffee shops. It was also General de Gaulle's last holiday destination before he lost power in 1969. The statue on South Green was erected in memory of Cearbhall Ó Dáiaigh, President of Ireland from 1974 to 1976, who is buried in Sneem.

▷ Follow the N 70 westwards and 17.5 km/ 11mi further on, at Castlecove, turn right in the direction of Staigue Fort (narrow access road).

One of the most famous round forts in Ireland, **Staigue Fort**★ is 2,000 years old (*the Visitor Centre,www.sneem.net/ staiguefort, is expensive and unnecessary*). It was built from undressed stones without the use of mortar on a raised site, which allowed the small community it housed to survey the surrounding area without being seen. The walls, 4m (13ft) thick and 5m (16ft 5in) high, are lined inside with a series of stairways that lead to the parapet.

▷ Rejoin the N 70 as far as Caherdaniel.

Around Caherdaniel★★

Despite its uninspiring appearance, the village of Caherdaniel is worth a stop for the charming sites of the surrounding area.

Begin with an excursion to **Lamb's Head**★★ (*take the road leading off south-west at the bend as you arrive at the village; about 6km/3.7mi round trip by foot or by road*). You will follow a lagoon colonised by birds before reaching a rocky coast. After passing an extraordinary boat-shaped house, which stands above the bay of Derrynane, you will come out at a tiny port.

Return to the village and follow the signs for **Derrynane House**★★ (*Mar–Sep 10.30am–6pm; Oct-Nov: Wed–Sun & bank hols 10.30am–5.15pm, Nov-Dec weekends only 10am-4pm. House ⊕€5; ℘066 947 5113. www.heritageireland.ie.* At the heart of a beautiful park planted with rare species, you can visit the house where Daniel O'Connell – the "Liberator", as he is known – spent his childhood before going to school at Cobh, then to France. This 19C house contains touching mementoes of the famous patriot: personal items, documents, furniture and family portraits, including a bizarre painting in which he is portrayed as Hercules breaking his chains!

After your visit, make for **Derrynane Harbour**★, which is a centre for wind-surfing. Joining the **beach**★★ from the left of the car park, you can walk along as far as **Abbey Island**★, which is accessible at low tide.

In the middle of a marine cemetery invaded by wild grass, the romantic ruins of an ancient abbey, possibly founded by St Finan, look out over a heavenly landscape that includes one of the country's most beautiful beaches.

▷ Rejoin the N 70 and head towards Waterville.

There are lots of parking bays on the road that rises above Derrynane, enabling you to admire the **panorama**★★ laid out below you.

After **Coomakesta Pass**★, the road arrives at Ballinskelligs Bay. On the left, you'll glimpse the outline of a very well-restored round fort dating from around the 9C, **Loher Fort**★ (*drive past it and turn left into the little road after the church*). The exterior fortification (*20m/66ft in diameter with two terraces*), surrounds two buildings, one rectangular, the other circular, where the entrance to a basement would formerly have been. Pleasantly situated facing the sea, the edifice gives you an idea of the restricted life that would have been led by the families who once lived here.

Waterville, despite its superb seaside setting, is disappointing and the long village stretches alongside a road that quickly becomes blocked with touring coaches.

To find a wild and unspoiled landscape, head inland instead, towards **Lough Currane**★ (*1.5km/1mi after Waterville, heading towards Caherdaniel, take the fork in the road that heads inland*). Separated from the sea by an isthmus, this lake, famous for its salmon and sea trout, will appeal to those who love fishing. Its rocky banks and rugged surroundings are worth exploring on a **hike**★ (*16km/10mi round trip; truck road*).

SKELLIG RING★★
40km/25mi, not including Valentia Island. Allow 2hrs.

This, your first escapade off the main roads, is not to be missed. It will take you across harsh, wild landscapes that are bypassed by organised tours because of their narrow roads and sharp bends.

▶ Leave Waterville via the N 70, heading north in the direction of Cahersiveen. After 3km/2mi, turn left and follow the signs for Skellig Ring (R 567).

From Beach to Mountain

The village of **Ballinskelligs** is the beginning of a *gaeltacht* (gaelic speaking) zone.

If you like to go swimming, stop at its sandy **beach★**. Look out for the ruins of **Ballinskelligs Priory** and its little cemetery, daintily posed on the seafront *(free)*. A monastery was established here by the monks of Skellig Michael in the 12C, but the ruins that can be seen today date from the 15C.

Leave the coast temporarily to rejoin **St Finan's Bay★★**, from where, out at sea, you can make out the characteristic profile of the Skellig Islands *(see below)*. The twisting road then climbs the sharp side of Glavenagh Mountain (318m/1,043ft) until you reach a pass

that reveals a marvellous **panorama★★**, before sweeping down towards **Portmagee**, a small, very lively fishing port, whose multicoloured façades look across to Valentia Island.

Skellig Islands cruises★★★

Casey's; ☎066 9472 437, www.skelligislands.com. Sailings only in calm weather. Fares around €75 pers. round trip. Book well in advance to be sure of a place. Take warm waterproof clothing.

Skellig Michael★★★ (or *Great Skellig*), the larger of the two islands, which reaches a peak of 218m/715ft, is home to one of the oldest celtic monasteries. In this spectacular and austerely beautiful setting, the solitude and severity of the monastic life is powerfully tangible. The first monks, who arrived in large rowing boats, were not, however, cut off from the world, as they imported wine from the Middle East and cloth from Europe and North Africa. Although devastated by Viking raids in the early 9C, the community hammered away at its rock and its life continued until the 12C, watching the sea. The monks then abandoned their island and their contemplative life and established themselves at Ballinskelligs.

Founded in the 6C by St Finan, the **monastery** is made up of a group of well-preserved stone buildings that are

Monastery, Skellig Michael

© Caspar Diederik@storytravelers/Tourism Ireland

perched very high on a narrow platform attached to the side of the cliff face. The relics of the church, two oratories and six beehive-shaped cells remain. The exterior walls have salient stones, which no doubt served to hold in place a cladding of insulating earth. The monks gathered rainwater in a cistern and heating was frugally provided with a bit of peat or wood conveyed from the hard earth. In 2015 the island featured prominently in the new *Star Wars* film, prompting a dramatic surge in visitor numbers.

Valentia Island

Allow 2hrs. Access via the bridge at the end of Portmagee quay.

If you want to experience what it's like on the Skelling Islands without actually setting foot on there, visit the **Skellig Experience Centre★★** *(open Jul and Aug, daily 10am–7pm; Mar, Apr, Oct, Nov Mon–Fri 10am–5pm; centre only €5, centre plus non-stopping cruise, daily 2.30pm, around the Skellig Islands €35; www.skelligexperience.com).* This re-creation of a Skellig sea cliff, with life-size models, island sounds, and much more, presents a fascinating history of the islands.

Valentia Island is often overlooked by rushed tourists, but if you have time, walk as far as Bray Head, which faces the cliffs of Skellig Ring *(after the Skellig Centre, turn left and park at the beginning of the footpath leading to the edge of the island and to an observation tower).* At the eastern end of the island, the peaceful port of **Knights Town** *(linked to Cahersiveen by ferry)* is enlivened by an amusing orange clocktower standing on the quayside.

THE NORTH OF THE PENINSULA★

66km/41mi. Allow half a day.

Alternating sandy coves, sheer cliffs and long, pale dunes, the north side offers a view of the neighbouring Dingle Peninsula and the profile of its rugged mountain crests.

Cahersiveen

Neither the town nor the Heritage Centre *(Barracks)* are particularly attention-grabbing, but on the other side of the estuary, at Kiimego West, you should definitely make time to visit two of the most beautiful round forts in Kerry.

▶ Cross the bridge next to Barracks, turn left at the T-junction and look out for the forts on your right. Park, then follow the gravel path.

Near the road, you can make out the huge outline of **Cahergal Fort★**, which, with its two interior stacked terraces, is the largest and better-restored of the two edifices.

Although unobtrusive and invaded by grass, **Leacanabhaile Fort★★** *(follow the road on the right, park and then take the path leading to the fort)* nevertheless possesses lots of charm. The interior of the fortification shows signs of the foundations of six houses and a basement with engraved walls leading to a room.

▶ Return to Cahersiveen and continue eastwards along the Ring of Kerry.

Along the Beaches

After 16km/10mi, a narrow road forks off to the left towards **Kells Bay**, a pretty beach surrounded by trees but unfortunately spoilt by the presence of caravans.

Having rejoined the Ring of Kerry, you follow the coast along a cliff road, which provides views to the North of the Dingle Peninsula. You will drive through **Glenbeigh**, a seaside resort popular with the Irish because of the miles of sandy beaches at **Rossbeigh**, which stretch out 5km/3mi into Dingle Bay.

▶ 4km/2.5mi after Glenbeigh, turn right towards Caragh Lake, then immediately right again towards Glencar.

Lough Caragh★★

The forested landscape around the lake is in total contrast to the coast.

Level with Blackstones Bridge, a beautiful stone bridge spanning the rocky chaos of the Caragh River, is the starting point of a pleasant forest walk. The **Kerry Way★★**, a hiking trail that crosses the county, offers a superb panorama of the portion of Lough Caragh between Glencar and Glenbeigh.

▶ At Glencar, follow the signs to Killorglin.

Killorglin

This lively town is home to **Puck Fair★★** (*www.puckfair.ie*), one of the biggest festivals in Ireland, which takes place every year during the second week of August. Rooted in an old pagan tradition, in honour of the god Lug, the festival (whose name in Irish translates as "billy goat's fair") is celebrated with gusto and coincides with a harvest festival.

ADDRESSES

KILLARNEY

🖾 STAY

Accommodation is best booked in advance during the summer months or expect to queue at the tourist office.

🖙 **Countess House**– *Countess Rd. ℘064 663 4247. www.countesshouse.net.* Pleasant, modern, unfussy rooms. Good value for their central Killarney town location. Internet access for guests.

🖙 **Elyod House**– *Ross Rd. ℘064 663 6544. www.elyodhouse.com. 6 rms.* This centrally located, comfortable modern house is hugely popular thanks in no small part to its charming owners.

🖙 **Neptunes Hostel**– *New St. ℘064 663 5255. www.neptuneshostel.com.* Killarney's largest and best hostel with a good range of room options from dorms to double and single en-suite rooms. Lots of facilities, including free internet access.

🖙 **The Mystical Rose** – *Woodlawn Rd. ℘064 663 1453. www.mysticalrose killarney.com. 6 rms.* It is a 15-minute walk into town from this pleasant house with smartly decorated bedrooms and good friendly service.

🖙 **The SúgánHostel**– *Lewis Rd. ℘064 663 3104. www.suganhostelkillarney.com.* A well-established, compact and well-run hostel with mostly four-bed dorms and popular with backpackers from other parts of Europe.

🖙 **The Railway Hostel**– *Fair Hill. ℘064 663 5299. www.killarneyhostel.com.* Opposite the railway station, this well-equipped hostel has lots of private rooms and a light breakfast for all guests is included. There is a limited amount of free parking.

🖙–🖙🖙 **Orchard House** – *St. Anne's Rd. ℘064 663 1879. www.orchardhouse killarney.com.* Modern but stylish house in a quiet location in the town, with a nice garden.

🖙🖙 **Fair View House**– *College St. ℘064 663 4164. www.killarneyfairview.com.* This 4-star, boutique-style town centre guest house features spacious rooms with free Wi-Fi.

🖙🖙 **Fuchsia House** – *Muckross Rd. ℘064 33743. www.fuchsiahouse.com. Closed Jan–Feb. 9rm.* A small guesthouse with the feel of a country house, from its antique furnished and individually designed bedrooms to the comfortable sitting room and well-tended back garden. Good value.

🖙🖙 **Killarney Self Catering** – *Rookery Rd. ℘064 663 3570. www. killarneyselfcatering.com.* One- and two-bedroom apartments, in two central locations, furnished and equipped to a high standard.

🍽/EAT

🖙 **The Laurels** – *Main St. ℘064 31149. www.thelaurelspub.com.* One of the best of the town's many pubs, little changed in over a century. Live music, a bustling atmosphere and a palpable sense of tradition. The menu offers an extensive selection of the usual pub favourites.

🖙🖙 **Gaby's Seafood Restaurant** – *27 High St. ℘064 663 2519, www.gabys.ie* Gaby's has been in Killarney for a long time and has a reputation for quality underlined by its many excellent reviews.

🖙🖙 **Lord Kenmare's Restaurant** – *College St. ℘064 663 1294.* A cosy place in town and very good value if you opt for the early-bird menu.

🍴🍷 **Treyvaud's Restaurant** – *62 High St.* ☎*064 663 3062. www.treyvauds restaurant.com.* Seafood chowder, beef and Guinness pie, smoked fish, Kerry lamb, ostrich sometimes – plenty to choose from in a restaurant that has gained a very good reputation.

PUBS

There are lots of pubs in Killarney and most of them are unashamedly targetting tourists with traditional music sessions. For a quiet drink you may need to seek out a hotel bar.

O'Connor's – *7 High St.* This family-owned watering hole is the real deal. There's a welcoming atmosphere, home-made soup and sandwiches, and traditional music on Thu–Mon.

Sheehan's – *Main St. www.killarney grand.com.* The bar of the Grand Hotel has regular sessions of traditional music and set dancing, and is popular with visitors.

Hannigan's. *Kenmare Place. www. killarneyinternational.com* The bar of the International Hotel has Irish music nightly during the summer months.

SHOPPING

High Street – The obvious first stop to look for local souvenirs, from jewellery to linen and glassware.

Quills Woollen Market – *Market Cross, High St.* ☎*064 663 2277 www. irishgiftsandsweaters.com.* A family business, established in 1939. Spread over two floors, with a large collection of authentic and typically Irish goods, ranging from Donegal tweeds and Aran handknits to linen and individually designed pieces of jewellery.

Avoca Weavers – *Moll's Gap. 15mi/24km S by N 71, closed mid-Nov–early Mar. www.avoca.ie.* Set in a striking location, this branch of the famous Irish retailer sells their usual stylish and fashionable woollen clothing plus lots of other household items, all made to high-quality traditional standards. Very good café-restaurant here, too.

Kerry Woollen Mills – *Beaufort; 5mi/8km W by N 72; 4mi/6km turn right at sign; after 1mi/1.6km, turn left and then right. www. kerrywoollenmills.ie.* Woollen goods have been produced at the mill here for over 300 years; rugs and blankets for people and horses, tweeds for clothes and furnishings, scarves and shawls, knitwear and knitting yarn, from traditional to cutting- edge designs.

SIGHTSEEING

There are **information centres** at Muckross House and at Torc Waterfall (*summer only*). The **National Park** may be explored on foot, by boat or by bicycle. **Walks** are waymarked at Ross Castle, Muckross House and through the Gap of Dunloe.

There are **boat trips** on Lough Leane, from Ross Castle to Innisfallen Island, or as part of the trip through the Gap of Dunloe.

Jaunts in a horse-drawn **jaunting car** are available from the southern end of the Main Street, or from Kate Kearney's Cottage, or from Muckross House.

KENMARE

🛏STAY

🛏 **The Rosegarden** – *Sneem Rd.* ☎*086 402 3562. www.rosegardenkenmare.com.* The Dutch owners (Jerome is a pastry chef) provide old-school hospitality at their immaculately-kept guesthouse, a 5-min walk from the centre of Kenmare; bedrooms are colourful and cheerful.

🛏🍷 **Sea Shore Farm** – *Tubrid. 1mi. W. Sneem Rd. 6rm.* ☎*064 664 1270. www.seashorekenmare.com. Open Mar–mid-Nov.* This farmhouse B&B is set in grounds of 32 acres/13ha with superb views of the river and mountains. Comfortable bedrooms come in different colour schemes and bathrooms have power-showers.

🛏🍷 **Sallyport House** – *0.25mi S on N 71.* ☎*064 664 2066. www.sallyporthouse.com. Open Apr–Oct. 5rm. No children under 13.* This elegant country house is laid out with lawns and trees, overlooking the harbour and with panoramic views of Kenmare Bay and surrounding mountain; impressive breakfast and very comfortable bedrooms. Antique pieces throughout.

🍴EAT

🍴🍷 **D'Arcy's Oyster Bar and Grill** – *Main St.* ☎*064 664 1589. www.darcys kenmare.com. Closed Mon.* Housed in a former bank, this very stylish town-centre restaurant specialises in seafood on its Modern Irish menu. Striking contemporary bedrooms (😋😋).

😋😋 **The Lime Tree** – *Shelburne St. ℰ064 664 1225. www.limetreerestaurant.com. Open Apr–Oct.* This elegant building has been converted from a 19C schoolhouse with such warm hospitality and outstanding modern Irish cooking that few guests consider truancy. Local artists' work is for sale in the upstairs gallery.

😋😋 **Mulcahys** – *16 Henry St. ℰ064 664 2383. www.mulcahyskenmare.ie. Closed Tue.* The decoration of this modern restaurant features an assortment of Eastern banners and sculptures. The fusion of international cuisine with an oriental touch, particularly Japanese, using fresh Irish produce, makes for an eclectic menu.

😋😋 **Packies** – *Henry Street. ℰ064 41508. www.kenmare.com/packies. Closed Sun and 24 Dec–Feb.* One of the town's established buzzing dinner spots, with its flagstone flooring and exposed stone walls adding to the character. The menu features traditional Irish country cooking, adds a touch of contemporary cuisine and complements it with relaxed and welcoming service.

🎒 STAY AND 🍴EAT

CARAGH LAKE

😋😋😋 **Carrig House** – *left at 2.5mi/ 4km W of Killorglin on N 70, then right at Caragh Lake School. ℰ066 976 9100. www.carrighouse.com.* Close to the lake and well away from the traffic on the N70, this idyllic spot is perfect for anyone wanting a retreat in the countryside and a leisurely stay of two or more nights. The restaurant is delightful and offers good food in a relaxed setting.

PORTMAGEE

😋😋 **The Moorings** – *turn right for Portmagee 3mi/5km E of Caherciveen on the N 70 heading towards Waterville, then onto the R 565 and bear left before the bridge over to Valentia. ℰ066 947 7108. www.moorings.ie.* Overlooking the harbour and Valentia Island, this is a great place to stay, or just to call in for a meal or a drink. The best bedrooms

are those with seaviews and for food, there is a choice between the bar menu or the restaurant; seafood always takes pride of place but local lamb is also a favourite with guests.

WATERVILLE

😋 **The Old Cable House** – *Milestone Heritage Site, Waterville. ℰ066 947 4233. www.oldcablehouse.com.* Polished floors, unpretentious Irish cooking, friendly service and a lot of history distinguish The Old Cable House. Free internet access and terrific sea views.

😋😋 **The Smugglers Inn** – *Cliff Rd., Waterville. ℰ066 947 4330. www.the-smugglers-inn.com.* This guesthouse and bar enjoys a clifftop location next to the Waterville championship golf course and includes golf packages in its tariffs. You can eat in the bar or, weather permitting, in the garden overlooking the sea. The restaurant serves more formal meals and, not surprisingly, the emphasis is on fresh seafood. The bedrooms are decorated in a homely style and there is a large sitting room for guests with magnificent views of the sea and mountains.

SPORTS AND LEISURE

The Beara Way – Rarely rising above 1,115ft/340m, these old roads and tracks form a loop *(122mi/196km)* round the Beara Peninsula that may be walked with moderate ease. The Way begins in Glengarriff and heads west to Allihies, taking in Bere Island and Casteltownbere before heading back along the north coast to Kenmare.

The tourist office in Casteltownbere *(St. Peter's Church by the town square, behind Breens pub; ℰ027 70054)* is a good source of information on the Way, as is the website *www.bearatourism. com/bearaway.html.* It takes over a week to complete the Way, so most walkers choose a section or two.

The Bere Island section is one self-contained section that takes less than a day and does not pose the problem of returning to your transport. A more demanding, but also more rewarding, section of the Way is the route that starts at Allihies and returns to the village, taking in Dursey Island.

Dingle Peninsula★★

The Dingle Peninsula is extreme western Ireland at its most spectacular and atmospheric; a Gaelic-speaking area with sheer cliffs, harsh-looking mountains, an intricate network of tiny stone-walled fields and an extraordinary concentration of ancient stone monuments: ring-forts, beehive huts and inscribed stones. Brandon Mountain (3,121ft/951m) on the north coast, the second-highest in Ireland, is clothed in blanket bog and takes its name from St Brendan of Clonfert, a 6C monk, who is reputed to have set out on a transatlantic voyage from **Brandon Creek**, the narrow sea-inlet at the west foot of the mountain. The north coast has deserted sandy beaches and the ancient town of Dingle.

- **Info:** Strand Street, **Dingle**, ☎066 9151 188. Ashe Hall, Denny Street, **Tralee**, ☎066 712 1288, www.tralee.ie. www.dingle-peninsula.ie.
- **Location:** Dingle is the main town on the Dingle Peninsula, 40mi/65km west of Killarney via the N 70.
- **Don't Miss:** Slea Head, Gallarus Oratory and the view from Connor Pass. A walk along Stradbally Strand.
- **Kids:** Dingle Oceanworld Aquarium. Fungie the dolphin. Stradbally Strand – Ireland's longest beach. Crag Cave.
- **Timing:** Allow at least a day in Dingle and another day of touring.

A BIT OF HISTORY

Extensive Bronze-Age monuments have been recorded on the northern side of the Conor Pass near Cochlane. Later, the possibilities of the great natural harbour of Dingle were quickly realised by the Anglo-Normans; in 1257, Henry III of England imposed customs duties on exports. The peak of its commercial importance was reached in the 16C when Dingle had particularly strong trading links with Spain; in 1583, the town received permission to build a wall of enclosure.

GETTING AROUND

BY SEA – Blasket Islands Ferry: Boats depart for Great Blasket every 30min Apr–Sept from 10am to 17.30pm, with two ferry companies, ☎066 915 1344, www.blasketisland.com, and ☎086 335 3805 or 087 231 6131, www.marinetours.ie; €25 round trip; €35 eco-marine tours spotting birds and marine life.

In the same year a long period of local rule by the house of Desmond came to an end when Gearóid, the rebel Earl, was killed.

Three years earlier, 600 Spanish and Italian troops sent to aid the Desmond Rebellion had been massacred by government forces at Dún an Óir on the West side of Smerwick Harbour. Following the rebellion of 1641 and the Cromwellian wars, Dingle declined significantly as a port for nearly a century, although during the late 18C it had a substantial linen industry.

TRALEE

Tralee is situated at the neck of the Dingle Peninsula, between Dingle, 31mi/52km west, and Limerick, 64mi/106km northeast.

At the head of its bay, the county town of Kerry is a flourishing, workaday place with a range of traditional and modern industries. Not particularly oriented to tourism, it is nevertheless an important gateway to the Dingle Peninsula, treating its visitors to an ambitious and

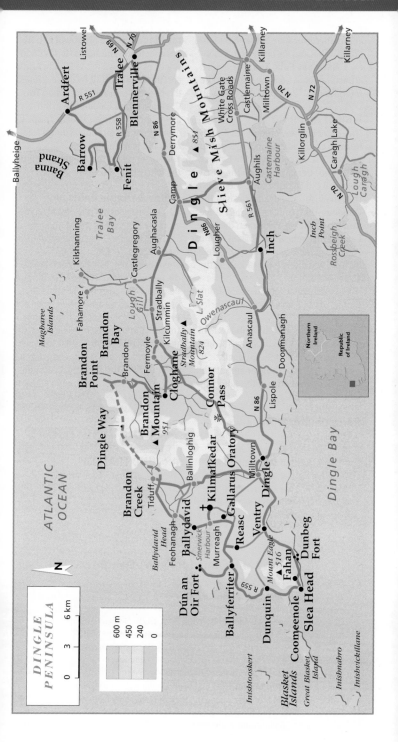

informative evocation to the "Kingdom of Kerry". It is also the home of the country's **National Folk Theatre**, which attracts hopefuls from the Irish diaspora for the annual "Rose of Tralee" festival.

A Bit of History

Tralee *(Trá Lí)* grew around the Anglo-Norman castle built by John Fitzgerald in 1243. His descendants, the Earls of Desmond, became one of the most powerful Old English clans, "more Irish than the Irish", and deadly rivals of the Ormonds. The Geraldine/Fitzgerald line came to an end in 1583 when the 15th Earl, who had rebelled with Spanish and Papal help, was betrayed and executed; his head was displayed on a spike at the Tower of London. Tralee and the Desmond estates were granted to Sir Hugh Denny, whose family held sway here for 300 years.

The town suffered badly in the wars of the 17C and now has a largely 18C and 19C character. Strongly nationalistic in outlook, Tralee became an important centre of opposition to British rule in the late 19C/early 20C.

Kerry County Museum★★

⚐⚑*Open daily Jun–Sept 9.30am–5.30pm, Oct–May Tue–Sat 9.30am–5pm. Bank Hols and Sun 10am–5pm.* ⚐*Closed 24–27 Dec.* ⚑€5. ✕🅿 ☎066 712 7777. www.kerrymuseum.ie. Begin your visit at this excellent museum with the introductory audio-visual **Kerry the Kingdom**. **The Medieval Experience** recreates the sights, sounds and smells of the town in the Middle Ages and the **Knights Hall** further explores this period. Learn about local man **Tom Crean**, and his expeditions and bravery in Antarctica. The main galleries display a wide-ranging array of historical artefacts and scale models.

The surrounding **town park** contains the ruins of the **Geraldine castle**.

Tralee & Dingle Railway

⚐*The service has not operated in recent years but it is hoped it will be working 2015–16. Call the tourist office for the latest.* ☎066 712 1288.

The Tralee & Dingle Railway, serving the disparate communities of the Dingle Peninsula, closed in 1953 but the centenary year of its construction was marked in 1991 by the re-opening to passenger traffic of the first stretch *(1.5mi/2.4km)* of the narrow-gauge *(3ft/1m)* line between Tralee and Blennerville. The train is composed of three original carriages drawn by No. 5, last of the original steam locomotives.

🚗 DRIVING TOURS

AROUND TRALEE★
Allow 3hrs, longer if you want to picnic on one of the beaches.

Failure and Fame for Ryan's Daughter

Despite the fact that it was a critical and box-office failure when released in 1970, for many viewers this is one of the most atmospheric and powerful films ever to have been made in Ireland. *Ryan's Daughter* was directed by David Lean and starred Sarah Miles, Robert Mitchum, Trevor Howard and, most memorably, John Mills in his role as Michael, the mute village idiot. He won an Oscar for Best Supporting Actor and created history at the awards ceremony for the shortest-ever acceptance "speech", merely nodding in the character of Michael and picking up his award without saying a word!

Filming on the **Dingle Peninsula** was very difficult and expensive, and it is said that the local economy gained the then princely sum of around £3 million. Stormy weather is prominent in the film and tragedy nearly struck for real when Robert Mitchum almost drowned.

▶ Leave Tralee and head northwest, in the direction of Ballyheige (R 551). After 9km/5.6mi, stop at the village of Ardfert.

Ardfert★

This peaceful village originally belonged to the bishops of Kerry and eclipsed Tralee with its cathedral, churches and Fransiscan abbey. Lacking a port, it was eventually overtaken in importance by its rival, however.

The ruins of the **cathedral**★ and a couple of **churches**★ *(Easter week, then late Apr–late Sept daily 10am–6pm; €5; ℘066 7134711 www.heritage ireland.ie)* form a touching ensemble, a witness to the intense spiritual life of the Middle Ages. There are also some tombs dating from the period of the first monastery (6C), which was founded by St Brendan "the Navigator". The cathedral itself (13C) is now just a large shell open to the sky; nevertheless, you will be amazed by the elegance of its tall Gothic windows. The statue (13C) positioned in a niche in the northwest corner is believed to represent Brendan. On the west side, the romanesque door (12C) has been restored with rather too much enthusiasm, but unfortunately, the Irish system for conserving its heritage does not have the means to call on specialists. The two other buildings also contain the remains of sculptures, one featuring flowers, the other griffins. On leaving the ruins continue along the same road until you reach the car park, to visit **Ardfert Friary**★ *(200m/220yd from the car park; free)*. Planted in the middle of fields, this Franciscan abbey, founded in the 13C and rebuilt in the 15C, retains a beautiful cloister, full of charm and serenity, whose high windows are reminiscent of those of the neighbouring cathedral.

▶ Leave Ardfert heading SW, in the direction of Fenit, then follow the signs for Barrow.

The Beach Road★

After passing a golf course, continue on as far as the car park for **Barrow** **Beach**★. From the clifftop you can see the Slieve Mish Mountains and Mount Brandon on the Dingle Peninsula facing you; on your right, the huge sandy beach stretches for more than 8km/5mi, as far as **Banna Strand**★, where scenes from the film *Ryan's Daughter* (♿ see p290) were shot in 1968. It was also at Banna that Roger Casement landed with arms destined for the 1916 Easter Rising, before being denounced by a local farmer and captured at Ardfert.

Return to Tralee via **Fenit**, a little fishing port and marina.

You will follow the northern bank of Tralee Quay, with a superb **view**★ of Dingle Peninsula.

▶ Drive through the town and follow the signs for Dingle. 2km/1.2mi from Tralee, you will arrive at the village of Blennerville.

Blennerville

At the end of the bay, this village attracts lots of tourists as a consequence of its little steam train, the marina and above all, its huge **windmill**★, built in 1780. Now superbly restored, you can also climb up inside, admire its workings and enjoy the view over the bay.

From 1830 onwards, Blennerville became a port of embarkation for the Americas and the numbers emigrating grew to such an extent that in 1846 a canal was built to allow ships to sail as far as Tralee.

The **Blennerville Visitor Centre**★ *(🕐Jun–Aug 9am–6pm; Apr–May, Sept–Oct 9.30am–5.30pm; ⚹€5)* retraces this neglected episode in the region's history and gives all sorts of details about the lives of the starving emigrants on board ship, notably from letters and other documents of the period that relate their distress. A local association even decided to reconstruct here the *Jeanie Johnston* (♿ see DUBLIN p130); one of the first ships to undertake the journey, it made the crossing from Tralee to Quebec, carrying passengers on the outbound sailing and Canadian timber on the return. The museum guides relate lots of poignant anecdotes – babies born

Road through Connor Pass, Brandon Mountain in the background

© JoeDunckley/iStockphoto.com

during the crossing, a young widow emigrating with her three children…

FROM TRALEE TO DINGLE VIA CONNOR PASS★★

76km/47mi, including the detour to Brandon Bay. Allow half a day.

Along Tralee Bay

Leaving Tralee on the N 86, the road follows the southern stretch of the bay to the foot of the **Slieve Mish Mountains**, which rise to a height of 800m/2,625ft. At Camp *(15km/9.3mi from Tralee)*, follow the signs for Dingle via Connor Pass. After the turning to Castlegregory, the road climbs little by little, rising above **Stradbally Strand** and **Fermoyle Beach**, a long stretch of sandy beach bordered by pastureland. In the distance, you can see the imposing shape of Mount Bandon (951m/3,120ft), which watches over Brandon Bay.

Look out for the signpost for Cloghane/Brandon and turn right here. You are coming to the most secret part of the peninsula, often ignored by passing tourists.

Brandon Bay★

The first village you come to on the road to Brandon, **Cloghane★** is situated at the end of a sandy bay crossed by a river and its beautiful scenery changes with the tides. About 3km/2mi beyond the village, turn right to get to **Cappagh Beach**, a wild place that is perfect for salmon fishing.

Go past Brandon village and follow signs to **Brandon Point★★** via a coastal road that winds its way to the foot of Mount Brandon, between low stone walls and small fields, where sheep and horses graze. At the end of the road, park your car and take the footpath on the left, which runs beside impressive cliffs. Many walks are possible in the surrounding area: you could climb to the top of **Brandon Mountain★★** *(from Cloghane)*, walk along part of the **Dingle Way★★** westwards *(between Brandon and Brandon Point)* or from **Lough A Dúin★★**, southwards to the heart of stony, desolate mountains *(as the region is a walkers' paradise, locals have gathered all the information necessary, available at Cloghane).*

▶ Retrace your steps and continue as far as the Connor Pass road.

Connor Pass★★

You will gradually climb above a peaty valley, crossed with lakes, rivers and a multitude of steams and waterfalls that make their way between enormous grey rocks. The road clings to the mountainside before arriving at the pass, which, at a height of 456m/1,498ft, is the highest in the country. From the car park, admire the **panorama**★★★ of the peninsula's two coasts, grey and austere to the north, green and gentler to the south. The road then descends to Dingle (8km/5mi).

Dingle★★

The port of Dingle is well sheltered at the end of a natural cove. Its Irish name, *An Daingean*, means fortress, which refers to the role that the town played in the Wars of Rebellion. From the arrival of the Normans onwards, the town centred on fishing and trade, principally with Spain. Many Spaniards also took up residence here, but they were regarded with suspicion and not permitted to live within the town walls.

Walking along Green Street, you will notice plaques above some of the doors, indicating their presence. Little by little, however, it seems the charm of these beautiful foreigners won over the townspeople of Dingle, and the dark hair and eyes of some of the locals are often attributed to the influence of Spanish blood. Although today Dingle is fairly touristy, things quieten down after 6pm when the touring coaches head off elsewhere. The town makes an excellent base, from where you can tour around the peninsula. You can also organise hiking trips, cycling tours or excursions on horseback from here.

There's not a great deal to interest visitors in Dingle itself apart from the rows of colourful façades, the bustle of activity at the quayside when the fishing boats return in the evening, and the national sport of pub crawling. The village has been known to boast that it has as many pubs as inhabitants. If the story doesn't quite hold true, there are at least enough to mean you'll be spoilt for choice (more than 50 for 1,500 inhabitants!). Make time, too, for a stop at **Café Liteartha**, a bookshop and café, where people come to read the paper or meet up over a tea or coffee.

Since 1983, Dingle's most famous attraction, a real tourist trap, has been the presence of **Fungie the dolphin**. The creature has frequented the bay since he was a youngster, but must have got old or tired of clowning around with the tourists, as he's less playful these days. There are several organised boat trips (see "Dingle's Famous Flipper" box).

Near the port, in the direction of Ventry, **Oceanworld** (10am–5pm (7pm Jul-Aug); €14, child €9.50; 0 66 915 2111, www.dingle-oceanworld.ie) continues the theme of marine wildlife with a fine Gentoo Penguins exhibit, Sandtiger Sharks, Amazon displays, a touch tank, and an underwater tunnel where you can watch sharks and tropical fish glide past.

FROM DINGLE TO BRANDON CREEK VIA THE COAST★★

40km/25mi circular tour, leaving from Dingle. Allow one day with stops.

Leave Dingle heading west towards Ventry and Slea Head (R 559).

On the Road to Slea Head

On reaching **Ventry Bay**, you rejoin the seafront. Unfortunately, this superb site is rather spoilt by the caravans parked up behind the beach.

Continuing along the road towards Slea Head, stop on your left at the **Celtic and Prehistoric Museum** (30min guided tour: Mar–Oct 10am–6pm; €4), home to an intact Woolly Mammoth skull, with tusks still attached, the only complete skeleton of a baby dinosaur, a large nest of dinosaur eggs, an interesting collection of fossils, prehistoric and Bronze-Age tools, Celtic jewellery and much more.

After a little detour inland, the road rejoins the coast, on the south side of Mount Eagle (516m/1,693ft), passing Dunbeg Fort and the Fahan site.

Fahan★

The scenery here is exceptionally beautiful: black cliffs, capped by bright green meadows, a patchwork of fields covering the hillside, and one of the most amazing archeaological sites in the country. The Fahan site contains more than 400 dry-stone huts grouped in small clusters,

Coomeenole Beach and Bay, Slea Head

© Chris Hill/Tourism Ireland

some circular forts, including **Dunbeg Fort**, and some underground passages. These huts in the form of beehives are called *clocháns* in Irish. Their origin remains mysterious but it is likely they date from pagan times or from the very beginning of the Christian era.

Further groups of *clocháns* scatter the route as far as the point. Kiosks owned by local landowners are open in summer and charge visitors €3 per site.

The area is interpreted at the **Dún Beag Fort Visitor Centre** (🕐open Mar–Nov daily 10am–6pm, 7pm summer; ☜ €3; ✕; ℘066 915 9070/9755, www.dunbeg-

fort.com) on Slea Head Drive. On a large bend, the road is crossed by a river. Shortly afterwards, you reach Slea Head.

Slea Head★★

The point commands a magnificent view. The precipitous cliffs are impressive; in clear weather the peaks of Valentia Island are clearly visible to the South, while to the West you can see the outline of the Blasket Islands and to the North, the sweep of the enchanting **Coomeenole Beach**, where certain scenes from *Ryan's Daughter* (🕯see p290) were shot.

Dingle's Famous Flipper

Dingle's most unusual resident is a male bottlenose dolphin, named **Fungie** by the locals. He weighs in at around 250lb (114kg) and measures around 13ft/4m long. Fungie was first spotted in 1984, escorting the town's fishing boats to and from the port. Since then he has been studied regularly by many cetacea experts and enthusiasts and has developed into a playful, even mischievous, companion to humans. A small cave under the cliffs at Burnham is thought to be his home.

During the summer months Fungie is often seen taking garfish in the harbour mouth, another oddity as this has never before been recorded as part of a dolphin's diet. During the winter months he has to travel further afield for his food. Dingle Boatmen's Association (👥🚶℘066 915 2626 or 915 1967, www.dingledolphin.com; €16, child €8) organise **boat trips** throughout the day year-round (weather permitting) to see Fungie. These depart from The Pier and last approximately 1hr; there is a "no-show money back guarantee", which rarely has to be paid out.

Blasket Island Authors

The early 20C Blasket islanders were literate in both Irish and English, and were encouraged by their visitors to develop their literary talents and evoke their elemental way of life before it vanished. Among the better-known works are three novels translated from Irish: *Twenty Years A-Growing* by Maurice O'Sullivan, *Peig* by Peig Sayers and *The Islandman* by Tomás Ó'Criomhtain, described by E. M. Forster as "an account of Neolithic life from the inside." Another fine account, albeit from the point of view of an outsider, is *Western Island* by the English author Robin Flower.

After Coomeenole, the cliffs become less high and the landscape greener, as far as Dunquin *(5km/3mi from Slea Head)*. Be careful about approaching the edge: the cliffs are slowly eroding and part of the road collapsed into the sea some 20 years ago.

Dunquin

Perhaps the most memorable aspect of this village is its pier, a narrow stone ramp fixed to the cliff, surrounded by clear, green water, from which boats leave for **Blasket Islands★** *(See Getting Around; Trips only take place when the sea is calm and are very popular during the summer months)*. Uninhabited since 1953, they retain ruins that speak volumes about the harshness of life on the islands. It was, tragically, the death of a young man, due to the inability of rescue services to reach him quickly after he fell ill, that precipitated the exodus of the already declining population to the mainland.

Today, these islands are a paradise for birds and rabbits as well as small numbers of rare sheep and seals. The beach at Great Blasket is one of the most beautiful in the West of Ireland.

Finish your tour of the islands in Dunquin, on the tip of the peninsula, with a visit to the **Blascaod Centre★★** *(open daily early Mar–late Nov: 10am–6pm; €5; ; 066 915 6444/915 6371, blasket.ie/en)*. This museum sensitively presents the daily life of the islanders, their exodus to America and the extraordinary literary wealth of the island that was the birthplace of many writers and poets *(see Box above)*; their works are for sale in the little bookshop).

Follow the road as far as Ballyferriter, admiring en route, on the coastline, the strange profile of the "Three Sisters" (a group of three adjacent cliff peaks).

Ballyferriter

This village is home to some of the most beautiful monuments of the peninsula *(very well signposted)*, which are scattered around the countryside surrounding the village.

The small **Músaem Chorca Dhuibhne★** *(open 7 days from Easter Sat onwards, then early Jun–mid-Sept 10am–5pm; the rest of the year by request; ; €2.50; 066 915 6333)*, meaning Museum of the Dingle Peninsula, explores the flora, geology, heritage and traditions of the area.

About 5.5km/3.5mi to the North of the village *(well signposted)*, the old fortified promontory of **Dún an Oir Fort** could be made the focus of a lovely walk around the Smerwick Bay. It was the theatre of a fierce battle (1580) between the Irish and their allies (the Italians and the Spanish) against the English. The latter prevailed and in the dreadful reprisals that followed, 600 men, women and children were massacred. A memorial to the victims of the massacre stands at Dún an Óir.

Returning to the village, take the R 559 eastwards and, after 2km/1.2mi, follow the signs on your right for **Reasc Monastery★**. This ancient 6C monastery is enclosed by a circular surrounding wall, which also contains relics of a chapel and several huts that would have served as cells for the monks. Particularly noteworthy are the ten or so crosses engraved on the floor of the site,

Gallarus Oratory

© Chris Hill/Tourism Ireland

which display beautiful primitive Celtic motifs of pre-Christian inspiration.

Away from the road between Bally-ferriter and Ballydavid, the **Gallarus Oratory★★** (*open daily mid-Jun–late Aug 10am–6pm; ℘066 915 5333; www. heritageireland.ie*) is a remarkable example of primitive Christian architecture (*see ARCHITECTURE*). Its form is that of the inverted hull of a boat and its clearly designed angles and its impeccable stonemasonry, superbly preserved without the help of mortar for nearly 1,200 years, is something to be admired. An unofficial **visitor centre** screens a film on the construction techniques of this type of oratory and on the different sites of the area.

Following the R 559 in the direction of Ballydavid, look out, on your right, for the signpost to **Kilmalkedar Church★**, a 12C Romanesque church. Notice the door with its sculpted geometric motifs and the heads, in particular that on the archway, which depicts the holy founder of the monastery. Also noteworthy are an ancient sundial, a stone engraved with the Latin alphabet.

After this cultural journey, head for **Ballydavid**, a little village, with a tiny quay, in the back of beyond. A lovely smell of the sea, a soft sandy beach and an unobstructed view of the ocean and of the "Three Sisters", as well as a village shop, two pubs and peace and quiet.

▷ End your tour of the point by following the signposts to Brandon Creek.

Brandon Creek

Brendan the Navigator would have left from here to make the first transatlantic voyage in the 6C. Looking at the high, jagged cliffs and the black, choppy sea, you have to wonder at his incredible courage.

The Brendan Voyage

St Brendan the Navigator was a seafaring monk who, in the 6C, set sail for the New World from Brandon Creek, at the foot of Brandon Mountain on the Dingle Peninsula. His account of the voyage, *Navigatio,* written in medieval Latin, was long thought to be fanciful until, in 1976, Tim Severin built the *Brendan* and proved that the earlier voyagers *could* have reached America several centuries before Christopher Columbus. The 20C adventure, which substantiates the 6C narrative, is retold in *The Brendan Voyage.*

Not far from here, near the hamlet of Ballinlohgig, a footpath leads up to the top of **Mount Brandon**. Pilgrimages are still made to the remains of the chapel, situated at the top of the mountain, where a Mass is read on the closest Sunday to the Feast of St Brendan *(16 May)* and the last Sunday in June.

▶ Follow the signposts to return to Dingle via the main road.

FROM DINGLE TO TRALEE VIA INCH★
56km/35mi. Allow 2hrs, or more if you want to picnic on the beach at Inch.

▶ At Dingle, take the road for Tralee via the south of the peninsula, heading in the direction of Anascaul (N 86). Before Anascaul, turn right on the road heading towards Inch and Castlemaine (R 561).

Inch★
After leaving the N 86, in the direction of Inch, you will cross a narrow gorge before rejoining the coast, with the **Iveragh Peninsula★★** in front of you. You will see **Inch Strand**, a long spit of sand and dunes that seems to cut across the far end of the bay. Here, the huge waves of the Atlantic break on the shore, one after the other, for mile after mile to the great delight of surfers. Cars are allowed access to the beach, so feel free to drive onto the firm sand: it's the only way to avoid the hordes of picnickers at the edge of the beach.

▶ Leaving the beach at Inch, rejoin the R 561 heading east in the direction of Castlemaine. 8km/5mi further on, you will reach the village of Aughils. Watch out for a little road on your left, signposted "Scenic Route to Camp".

The Scenic Route to Camp★★
⚠ *Warning: this 8km/5mi-long road is quite narrow and windy, and therefore drivers with caravans or motor homes are officially advised against using it.* You are now entering the heart of the **Slieve Mish Mountains**, leaving a splendid view behind you; you will cross deep valleys thrust between desolate mountainsides. Eventually, the road ends at the village of **Camp**, on a bend near the bridge, over the Finglass River.

▶ Retrace your steps, returning to Tralee via the N 86.

ADDRESSES

TRALEE

🏨 STAY

🛏 **Denton** – *Oakpark Rd.* ✆*066 712 7637. www.dentontralee.com.* Central modern house with tea-and-coffee-making facilities in each room.

🛏 **Finnegans Hostel** – *17 Denny St.* ✆*066 712 7610. www.finnegans. hostel.com. 40 beds in rooms and dorms.* Built by the Denny family in 1826 from the stones of the old Town Castle, the building was recently converted into a hostel making the most of the original features.

🛏🛏🛏 **Ballyseede Castle Hotel** – *8km from Tralee on the Kilarney Road. 23rm.* ✆*066 712 5799. www.ballyseede castle.com.* This picturesque castle has 16C-origins and bags of character, as well as splendid views of the castle grounds from bedroom windows. The restaurant serves dinner (🍴🍴) every evening (book in advance) and a grand lunch on Sundays. Weddings are regularly held here, so check this when making enquiries or a booking.

PUBS

Kirby's Brogue Inn – *Rock St.* ✆*066 718 1998. www.thrbrogue.ie.* A popular watering hole in the town, with food served in the bar and a separate restaurant area. Lively atmosphere mosts nights with regular live music.

Sean Og's – *Bridge St., www.sean-ogs.com.* A traditional pub well-known for live music and a lively atmosphere. Accommodation is also available here.

SPORTS AND LEISURE

Beaches – Tralee Bay (west and north). The **Aqua Dome** *(open Jul–mid-Aug daily 10am–10pm/9pm Sat & Sun; mid-Aug–Jun*

Mon–Fri 10am–10pm, Sat–Sun 11am–8pm; €15, €12 child; ℘066 712 9150; www. aquadome.ie) is fun for a rainy day visit with the kids. Adults can also relax and chill in the Adult Only Health Suite.

Horse races take place at Tralee and Listowel during the festivals.

Greyhound racing is held every Tuesday and Friday at Tralee.

DINGLE

⌂ STAY

◍◍ **Captains House** – *The Mall, Dingle ℘066 9151 531. www.captainshousedingle. com. 9rm.* A warm welcome is guaranteed at this B&B with a distinctive homely feel and a well-tended garden.

◍◍ **Greenmount House** – *Upper John St., Gortonora. ℘066 915 1414. www.greenmounthouse.ie. 12rm.* Request one of the superior rooms at the top of this B&B overlooking the town. A highlight is the sumptuous breakfast served in the conservatory.

◍◍ **Heatons** – *The Wood. ℘066 915 2288. www.heatonsdingle.com. 16rm.* Excellent position by the water, a five-minute walk from town. Elegant bedrooms decorated to a high standard and an extensive breakfast menu.

◍◍ **Pax House** – *Upper John St. ℘066 915 1518. www.pax-house.com. 12rm.* Fabulous views of Dingle Bay from an elevated position a short walk from the town centre. Clean and roomy accommodation. Very highly rated.

◍◍◍ **Emlagh House** – *Off N 86. ℘066 915 2345. www.emlaghhouse.com. 10rm.* Luxury country house, with very spacious, individually themed bedrooms with antique furniture. Wonderful bay views, some rooms feature a private patio.

⌂ EAT

◍◍– ◍◍◍ **Out of the Blue** – *Waterside. ℘066 915 0811. www. outoftheblue.ie.* Strictly seafood-only but probably the best you will find on the Dingle Peninsula. There is a neat little wine bar at the front, where you can study the menu – it changes daily, according to what comes off the boats.

Be sure to book ahead because space is limited and demand is high. There is a "Special Fish Deal" 5.30–6.45pm Monday–Friday.

PUBS

McCarthy's Bar – *Goat St. www.facebook. com/McCarthysdingle.* The best place in town for live music.

SHOPPING

John Weldon – *Green St. ℘066 915 2522. www.johnweldonjewellers.com.* Gold and silver jewellery featuring the finest Celtic knotwork.

The Weavers Shop/Siopa na bhFíodóirí – *Green St. ℘066 915 1688. www.lisbethmulcahy.com.* Weavings, hangings and tapestries by the Danish-born Lisbeth Mulcahy.

Louis Mulcahy Pottery Workshop – *Clothar, Ballyferriter. ℘066 915 6229. www.louismulcahy.com.* One of the last workshops making every piece by hand at their studio on the Dingle Peninsula. Lovely cafe here too.

SPORTS AND LEISURE

Beaches – At Ventry Harbour, Smerwick Harbour, Stradbally Strand.

Rambling – Make the pilgrimage up the **Saint's Road** *(7mi/12km)* from Kilmalkedar up the southwest face of Mount Brandon to the oratory and shrine dedicated to St Brendon on the summit.

ENTERTAINMENT

National Folk Theatre of Ireland *(Siamsa Tíre)* – *Tralee. ℘066 712 3055. www.siamsatire.com.* This theatre company draws on the rich, local Gaelic tradition to evoke the seasonal festivals and rural way of life in past centuries. The ultra-modern theatre building is shaped like a ringfort.

St John's Theatre and Arts Centre – *Listowel. ℘068 22566. www.stjohns theatrelistowel.com.* Hosts a lively programme of drama, dance, music and art. The centre also holds the Listowel tourist information office.

The long years of economic stagnation that Ireland suffered until the 1990s were at their worst in the West of the country. For decades, population drift was away from this region, where those who had a farm to inherit looked forward to little money and long hours and those without had little option but to leave to find work. The "Celtic Tiger" (Ireland's economic boom between 1995 and 2007) changed all that. In the boom years, a cottage in the West of Ireland was everybody's dream – when the abandoned farm cottages were all bought up, large estates of holiday homes began to appear. Thankfully, planning regulations restricted building, particularly in the Gaeltacht (Irish-speaking) regions. As the "Celtic Tiger" era is now too a matter of the past, today's visitors to the West of Ireland will enjoy unspoilt beaches, a sound tourist infrastructure, well-preserved ancient remains, rare and delicate flora and fauna and empty roads, especially in the relatively unvisited Connemara area of Galway and the counties of Mayo and Limerick.

Co Clare

With the Atlantic Ocean and Galway Bay forming its western border and the Shannon River and Lough Derg at its eastern and northern perimeters, County Clare has a long maritime history and some of the most attractive scenery in Ireland. In the North of the county the stark limestone karst scenery of The Burren dominates the landscape while further south is drumlin-dominated, with the pretty county town of Ennis, surrounded by more productive farming land. The Shannon estuary is both an important shipping port and home to a population of dolphins.

Tourism is an important industry in County Clare and it is an excellent place to stay for a few days, with organised walks in The Burren with its unusual geology and rare flora, beaches with excellent watersports facilities, many ancient archaeological sites to visit and a long musical tradition, which can be encountered in any of the tiny villages along the coast, but especially at Doolin. Lough Derg is a watersports centre and cruising on the Shannon is another important element in the economy of the county. The Aran Islands can be visited from Clare

Co Limerick

On the other side of the Shannon estuary from County Clare, Limerick is a very different place to visit. The estuary is its only coastline. Its predominating industry is agriculture, dairy farming in particular. Limerick city, evolving as a major Irish port and now an important university town and industrial centre, is well worth a visit for the Hunt Museum and for the cathedral, with its beautiful carvings. Many tourists fail to visit the county, lured on by the call of Clare to the North and Cork and Kerry to the South, but the county and city have a lot to offer the discerning visitor: the attractions and culture and history of the city itself and the archaeology and scenery of Lough Gur.

Co Galway

County Galway is the second-largest county in the country and is a small microcosm of all that can be enjoyed in Ireland, from the restaurants and nightlife of Galway city to beaches, offshore islands, quiet rural areas and the bleak moorland landscapes of Connemara.

Highlights

1 The tranquillity of a walk around **Lough Gur** (p310)

2 Cruising on the **River Shannon** (p320)

3 Views from O'Brien's Tower of the stunning **Cliffs of Moher** (p323)

4 Cycling around Inishmore, the smallest of the **Aran Islands** (p331)

5 An evening of traditional Irish entertainment in a **Galway pub** (p343)

Dún Aonghasa, Inishmore, Aran Islands

© marco scataglini/age fotostock

Farming predominates, with dairy farming around Galway city: the average farm size is still about 50 acres/20ha: tiny by European standards. The county is divided in half by the huge Lough Corrib, linked to Galway Bay by the Galway River. West of Lough Corrib is Connemara, one of the least-populated areas of Ireland, dominated by the Twelve Pins and Maumturk Mountains, its hillsides covered in coniferous plantation, its economy dominated by open common land and sheep rearing.

Sitting in the mouth of Galway Bay are the Aran Islands, rather more attuned to the 21C than they ever were to the 20C, but still well worth a visit. The county includes the largest Irish-speaking population in Ireland.

Co Roscommon

Roscommon *(Contae Ros Comáin)* can claim Douglas Hyde, the country's first president, as one of its sons and is the home of Queen Maeve, a figure in Ireland's Ulster Cycle of mythical stories. Alternating bogland and dairy pastureland offer quiet, drumlin-dominated scenes in the South and in the North the Curlew Mountains characterise the skyline.

As a county it has many interesting places to visit, from the grand and well-run Strokestown House, to the elegant ruins of Roscommon Castle and the many lakes and river sites for fishing and boating.

Co Mayo

County Mayo is the third-largest of the Republic's counties and over the course of its history experienced the highest emigration rates, beginning with the Famine and falling to its lowest population figures as recently as 1972.

To the East lie counties Sligo and Roscommon and to the West and North, the complex corrugated coastline of the Atlantic and Clew Bay, Blacksod Bay and Killala Bay. The county has a strong maritime tradition and was home to Ireland's famous pirate queen, Grace O'Malley. Two of Ireland's largest loughs, Corrib and Mask, are within the county's boundaries and linked by underground streams in the limestone bedrock as well as a canal, built in the 19C as a Famine Relief project, which quickly became useless as the canal waters sank into the limestone rock.

Like the surrounding counties, Mayo is a place of small cattle- and sheep-rearing family farms, while fishing is still an important source of income, as is peat production. South of Clew Bay is Croagh Patrick, where an annual pilgrimage is made to honour the saint, and in the East of the county is Knock, where thousands of pilgrims visit the Marian Shrine each year.

Limerick ★★

Astride the River Shannon at its lowest fording point, Limerick *(Luimneach)* is the main administrative and commercial centre of the mid-West region and the third-largest city in Ireland. Its three historic quarters are still quite distinct: medieval Englishtown on King's Island defended by one of the most formidable castles in Ireland; Irishtown, forming the modern city centre, and the Georgian district of Newtown Pery, laid out on a grid pattern during the 18C.
The atmosphere created by a particularly turbulent past, with extremes of wealth and poverty, deeply marked Limerick but today the compact city is a more welcoming place than it has ever been.

LIMERICK TODAY

Limerick really isn't a town dedicated to tourism and this can be a refreshing change after the thatched roofs, Heritage Centres, Irish stew and tour buses. This is a real Irish city, accommodating to visitors, but certainly not fawning over them; a university town with industrial estates, an important harbour and three colleges of further education. The excellent Hunt Museum makes any visit here well worth the trip.

A BIT OF HISTORY

City of Sieges – In 922 Vikings from Denmark sailed up the Shannon, landed at Great Quay (now Long Dock) and established a base on King's Island, from which they plundered the rich agricultural hinterland. For over a century the town was repeatedly attacked by Irish forces until Brian Ború, High King of Ireland, sacked it and banished the settlers. In 1194, the Normans seized control of the region, raising the great fortress of King John's Castle, building city walls and peppering the countryside with hundreds of strongholds.
In 1642 Limerick was besieged by the Cromwellians, followed by a momentous siege after the Battle of the Boyne

- ▶ **Population:** 94,192.
- **Info:** Arthurs Quay. ☎061 317 522. www.limerick.ie.
- ▶ **Location:** Limerick is 62mi/100km south of Galway, on the N 20.
- **Don't Miss:** The Hunt Museum and an excursion to Bunratty Castle.
- **Kids:** King John's Castle and Bunratty.
- **Timing:** Allow a day or two here; Limerick is a good starting point to explore West Ireland.

GETTING THERE

BY AIR – **Shannon International Airport:** ☎*061 712 000.* *www.shannonairport.ie.*

in July 1690, when James II fled to France and the defeated Jacobites withdrew to Limerick. Eventually, under the bold leadership of Patrick Sarsfeld, the Williamites abandoned their siege at the

The First Limerick

The origin of the term limerick in poetry, meaning a five-line poem, usually witty, sometimes rude, and originally popularised by Edward Lear, is obscure.

In the 18C a rustic school of Gaelic poetry flourished along the banks of the River Maigue. **Aindrias Mac Craith**, a local schoolmaster was possibly jointly responsible for the invention of the limerick; in playful poetic conflict with a fellow-poet and tavern-keeper, one Seán Ó Tuama, he wrote:

O'Toomey! You boast yourself handy
At selling good ale and brandy,
But the fact is your liquor
Makes everyone sicker
I tell you that, I, your friend Andy.

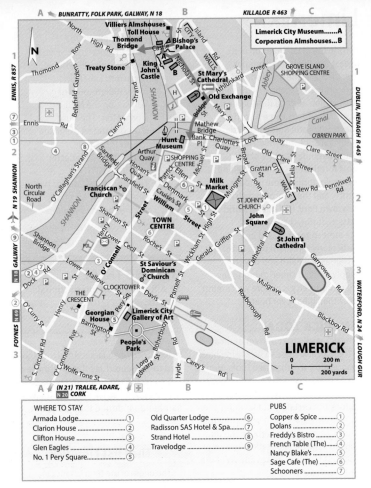

Limerick City Museum.......A
Corporation Almshouses...B

LIMERICK

0   200 m
0   200 yards

WHERE TO STAY		
Armada Lodge	1	
Clarion House	2	
Clifton House	3	
Glen Eagles	4	
No. 1 Pery Square	5	
Old Quarter Lodge	6	
Radisson SAS Hotel & Spa	7	
Strand Hotel	8	
Travelodge	9	

PUBS	
Copper & Spice	1
Dolans	2
Freddy's Bistro	3
French Table (The)	4
Nancy Blake's	5
Sage Cafe (The)	6
Schooners	7

end of August. The following year another Williamite army, led by General Ginkel, returned to the attack while an English fleet blockaded the Shannon. Sarsfield sued for peace, which was granted on surprisingly generous terms by the **Treaty of Limerick**. The Irish were given safe conduct to France and Roman Catholics in general were guaranteed various rights and privileges, including the freedom to practise their religion. Ratification of the Treaty by the Irish Parliament was, however, only partial and the Penal Laws enacted from 1695 were seen by Roman Catholics as a betrayal.

18C to 20C – Despite a considerable agrarian revolt in the region in the 18C, the City Corporation decided that Limerick no longer needed to be fortified, so most of the city walls were demolished in 1760. The 18C also marked the last flowering of the old Irish culture. As the Great Famine and subsequent emigration devastated the local population in the 1840s, Gaelic ceased to be the vernacular language of Limerick.

In the early 20C the city and county became strongholds of nationalism and working-class radicalism. Three of the leaders of the 1916 Easter Rising came from the Limerick district, including **Eamon de Valera** (1882–1975), Prime Minister (*Taoiseach*) and President of the Republic.

In 1919, at the start of the three-year War of Independence, a general strike took place to protest against British military rule.

WALKING TOUR

HISTORIC CIRCUIT★★
Allow 3hrs.
As **King's Island** was almost encircled by the Shannon and the Abbey River, it was an obvious site for the Vikings and Normans to establish their settlements.

St Mary's (Limerick) Cathedral★★
www.cathedral.limerick.anglican.org.
This transitional Romanesque Anglican cathedral, founded in 1168 by Dónall Mór O'Brien, King of Munster, is the oldest surviving building in Limerick. Parts of the King's palace are incorporated in the original cruciform church.
The 15C black oak choir stalls and splendid carved misericords are unique in Ireland; the high altar reredos was carved by the English father of Patrick Pearse (*see DUBLIN*); the North transept contains the fine 15C **Arthur Memorial** *(below the window)* commemorating the cathedral Treasurer Geoffrey Arthur (d. 1519), and a small, rectangular lepers' squint *(right);* the South transept contains the 15C Galway-Bultingfort tomb.

Hunt Museum

© Brian Morrison/Tourism Ireland

Farther along Nicholas Street are seven Tuscan columns, bricked up to form a wall, all that remains of the Old Limerick Exchange, built in 1673.

▶ Turn down Bridge Street and cross Matthew Bridge.

Hunt Museum★★★
♿🕐*Open year-round Mon–Sat 10am–5pm (2pm Sun & bank hols).* 🕐*Closed Good Fri, Easter Sun, 24–26 Dec, 1 Jan.* ⌨€5. ✕ ☎*061 312 833.*
www.huntmuseum.com.
The 18C Custom House designed by Italian architect Davis Duchart provides a fitting home for this outstanding collection of art and antiquities amassed during the lifetimes of John and Gertrude Hunt. The expertly selected items span every age and include works of every scale. Highlights include the wooden carved *Apollo – Genius of the Arts*, a small bronze *Horse*, attributed to Leonardo da Vinci, and a startling self-portrait by Robert Fagan (c. 1745–1816), a painter of the English school and a dealer in antiquities in Rome. The archaeological collection is drawn from ancient civilisations in Egypt, Greece and Rome, as well as Irish treasures such as the Cashel Bell and Antrim Cross.
The Jewellery Gallery displays the Mary, Queen of Scots Cross. Religious Art is dramatically exhibited in the Treasury: among the silver and precious stones is a Greek coin, traditionally thought to be one of the "Thirty Pieces of Silver" given to Judas Iscariot.

▶ Walk over the pedestrian bridge, past the County Court House (1809) and back to Nicholas Street.

Limerick City Museum/ Jim Kemmy Municipal Museum
♿🕐*Open Tue–Sat 10am–1pm, 2.15pm–7pm.* 🕐*Closed Bank Hols.* ☎*061 417 826. www.limerickcity.ie/ CityMuseum. http://museum.limerick.ie.*
The Limerick City Museum gives a comprehensive account of the city and its history. An excellent collection of 18C

King John's Castle

© Brian Morrison/Tourism Ireland

silver, tambour, needlepoint and tape lace recall important Limerick crafts. The brass-topped limestone Nail from the Old Exchange was used to settle commercial transactions – from which may come the expression "paying on the Nail". Finds from excavations in the Abbey River are also displayed.

👥 King John's Castle★★

♿🕐*Open daily 9.30am–5pm (6pm Mar –Apr, 6.30pm Jun-Aug).* ⊛€10.50. ✆*061 360 788. www.heritageisland.com* This was once the most important Norman stronghold in the West and remains a fine example of medieval fortification (1200–16). Instead of a keep, it has massive round towers protecting the gateway; the walls would originally have been taller to withstand siege machines, but in 1611, the towers and the wall-walks were lowered to accommodate

cannons and the diamond-shaped gun bastion was added. Today touch-screen technology will connect you to tales of siege and warfare, CGI animations and ghostly projections bring back past inhabitants, visitors can try on historic costumes and 3-D models, while discovery drawers and audio visuals will all delve into the castle's history. In the courtyard is a medieval campaign tent, a blacksmith's forge and scenes from a 17C siege. Costumed guides reveal the secrets and scandals of castle life. The sentry walk on the battlements provides good views of the Shannon and the city.

Bishop's Palace

🕐*Open by arrangement.* ✆*061 313 399. www.limerickcivictrust.ie.* The oldest-surviving dwelling in the city, the Palace was designed in the Palladian style by Francis Bindon (c. 1690–1765),

---

Eamon de Valera

Eamon de Valera (1882–1975), born in New York to a Spanish father and Irish mother, was largely brought up by his uncle near Kilmallock. One of the leaders of the 1916 Rising, de Valera only escaped execution because of his American birth. He was imprisoned by the British, then later also spared by the Free State authorities after siding with the Republicans during the Civil War. He founded the Fianna Fáil party in 1926, became Prime Minister *(Taoiseach)* in 1932, and kept Ireland neutral in World War II. Between 1959 and 1973 he served as President of the Republic, steadfastly nationalist in his politics, but conservative when deciding how Ireland should develop.

a native of Limerick. It now houses the Limerick Civic Trust.

Limerick is unusual in having two sets of almhouses: the **Villiers Almshouses** (1826), north of the castle, were built in the Bishop's Palace garden by James Pain for 12 poor Protestant widows with an annual income of £24.

The **Corporation Almshouses**, also known as the 40-shilling (equivalent to £2) Almshouses, for 20 widows, were erected by the Limerick Corporation in 1691.

Thomond Bridge

The Gothic-style **Toll House** with castellated parapets dates from 1839 when the bridge was rebuilt.

The **Treaty Stone** (on the west bank of the river), is a block of limestone on which the 1691 Treaty of Limerick is said to have been signed; it was moved here in 1865 from outside Black Bull Pub, where it had been used as a mounting-block.

TOWN CENTRE

The old Irish quarter on the south bank of Abbey River, outside the walls of the English Town, now forms the **town centre** of modern Limerick. The district to the South is a fine example of 18C town planning with broad parallel streets lined with **red-brick terraces** – named **Newtown Pery** after Edmond Sexton Pery (1719–1806), Speaker of the Irish House of Commons.

People's Park

&⊙Open daily 8am–dusk. ⊚€5. ℘061 496 200. www.limerickcivictrust. ie/georgian. http://www.limerick.ie.

This is the focal point of the Newtown Pery district and was built by the Pery Tontine Company in 1838.

The **Georgian House★** at No. 2 Pery Square has been restored as a splendid example of Georgian architecture and décor. It also houses the **Carrol Collection** of family heirlooms and military memorabilia dating between the late-1700s and the 1920s.

The military careers of five generations of this remarkable family start with the

Limerick Lace

Lace making was introduced to Limerick in the 1820s by the English and reached its peak in the 19C when 900 women were employed locally. The elaborate Celtic patterns were outlined on machine-made cotton net in thin or thick thread and infilled with decorative stitches.

legendary exploits of Major-General Sir William Parker Carrol in the Peninsular War and progress through the Boer War and both World Wars.

The **Limerick City Gallery of Art** (&⊙open Mon-Wed, Fri-Sat 10am–5.30pm, Thu 10am–8pm, Sun noon–5.30pm; ✕; ℘061 310 633; www.gallery. limerick.ie) underwent a major redevelopment in 2012. It holds the National Collection of Contemporary Drawings, as well as a growing collection of leading 18C–20C Irish art (Sean Keating, Jack B. Yeats and Evie Hone) and visiting exhibitions.

At **St Saviour's Dominican Church**, stands the 17C statue of Our Lady of Limerick. This was brought from Flanders in 1640 and presented to the Dominicans as a mark of atonement by a Limerick merchant, whose uncle had sentenced the Irish politician and soldier Sir John Burke to death for allowing a priest to say Mass during a time of severe religious persecution.

Milk Market

The open area, on the corner of Ellen Street and Wickham Street, accommodates a bustling Saturday market, where home-grown local produce has been traded since 1830: today it is the gourmet area of Limerick. **William Street** and **O'Connell Street** are prime shopping areas. The **Franciscan Church** (1876–86), with its fine Corinthian portico, was extended in 1930 with a richly decorated apse.

Bunratty Castle

© Fáilte Ireland

John Square★

The square, laid out in 1751, is bordered by terraces of three-storey houses once occupied by wealthy citizens. On the fourth side stands **St John's Church** (1843). The neo-Gothic Roman Catholic **St John's Cathedral★** on the edge of what was the old Irish town dates from 1861. The spire *(280ft/85m)*, completed in 1883, is the tallest in Ireland.

NORTHWEST OF LIMERICK
Bunratty Castle & Folk Park★★

7mi/11km W by N18. ♿ ☛*Castle open by guided tour only, Apr–Oct 9am–5.30pm (6pm Jun–Aug); Dec–Mar 9.30am–5.30pm. Last tour 4pm.* ⊙*Folk park: same hours. Last admission 45min to 1hr 15min before closing. Irish Night: Apr–Oct 7pm; Medieval banquet: year-round nightly 5.30pm, 8.45pm (reservation required for both).* ⊙*Closed Good Fri, 24–26 Dec. Castle and Folk Park* ⊛€15 *(€12 winter) ; medieval banquet €59; Irish Night €49.* ✆*061 360 788. www.shanon heritage.com. www.bunratty.ie*

The most splendid **tower house** in Ireland commands a formidable position on the main road between Limerick and Ennis, at the point where the Bunratty River flows into the Shannon Estuary. It was built in 1460 by the powerful O'Brien family on the site of earlier fortifications. In the 1950s, it was restored to its 16C state to display the superb **Gort Furniture Collection** of furniture and tapestries from the 14C–17C. In the evenings medieval-style banquets are held in the Great Hall, which has a fine **oak roof**.

The **Folk Park** is a very convincing recreation of country life, set at the turn of the century when traditional practices were dying out. There is a blacksmith's forge, flour mill and houses of different regional types – a mountain farmhouse and a more elaborate thatched Golden Vale farmhouse. The **Village Street** contains 19C shops: a pawnbroker, pub, post office, hardware shop, grocery store, draper's and printing workshop, equipped with hand-set type and a hand-operated press. The whole park is staffed by costumed characters.

Bunratty House, built in 1804, is a local adaptation of the Georgian box house so common in Ireland. In its farmyard is displayed the **Talbot Collection of agricultural machinery**.

Craggaunowen Centre★★

Off the R469 near the village of Quin Co. Clare, signposted off the N18 Limerick Galway route. ♿⊙*Open end-Mar–mid- Sept 10am–5pm (4pm last admission).* ⊛€9 *(€8 online).* ✗✆*061 360 788. www.shannonheritage.com.*

Craggaunowen recreates aspects of Ireland's past with the restoration and re-constructions of earlier forms of dwelling houses, farmsteads, hunting sites and other features of everyday life during the Pre-historic and Early Christian eras. As well as a ringfort, a togher (wooden marsh track), the artificial island of a crannóg, there is also a reconstructed 15C castle.

A highlight is **The Brendan**, a replica wood-and-leather *curragh*, sailed across the ocean in 1976 by Tim Sever in order to prove that St Brendan did at least have the means to have made his claimed crossing of the Atlantic (see *DINGLE PENINSULA, box*).

Note the patch where the leather hull was holed by an ice floe. A **tower house** is used to display items from Hunt's extensive antiquarian collection (more can be found in the Hunt Museum in Limerick).

On the estate live Wild Boar (*Porcus sylveticus*) and early breeds of Soay sheep.

Quin Franciscan Friary★

Quin. Open Tue-Fri 10am-5pm, Sat-Sun 9am-4pm. Last admission 30 mins before closing. 065 682 8366.

The extensive ruins of the friary, built c. 1430 by Sioda McNamara, include the **cloisters**, the tower and the south transept. The remains of an earlier ruined

Norman castle (1280–86) include three round towers, erected over of an even earlier monastery.

Ennis★

N 18 from Galway to the North, Limerick to the South. Arthurs Row. 065 682 8366. www.visitennis.ie.

Ennis is proud of its distinguished beginnings. Its origins can be traced back to the 13C, when the O'Brien family, kings of Thomond and descendants of the great Brian Ború, built their royal residence nearby. Because of its central position Ennis became the county town

Quin Franciscan Friary

© Chris Hill Photographic/Tourism Ireland

Thatched roofs in Adare

© M. Siepmann / imagebroker / age fotostock

of Clare during the shiring of Ireland in the reign of Elizabeth I.

In 1610 the town was granted permission to hold fairs and markets; two years later it received a corporation charter from James I.

Known as the "Banner County", Co Clare has a long history of dogged nationalism, the veritable heartland of Irish traditional music. There is evidence of both in the little county town of Ennis, with its narrow, winding streets and colourful shopfronts.

Ennis Friary★

(Dúchas) &Open Easter–Sept 10am–6pm, Oct–Nov 10am–5pm. €5. 065 682 9100.
www.heritageireland.ie.

The Friary was founded by an O'Brien in the 13C, and by the 14C had become one of Ireland's foremost institutions of learning, with over 600 students as well as hundreds of friars. Now a picturesque ruin, it has a superb east window but is most noteworthy for its sculpture. An **Ecce Homo** shows Christ with the Instruments of the Passion; St Francis is depicted with stigmata. The Creagh tomb (1843) in the chancel consists of five carved panels showing the Passion, taken from the MacMahon tomb (1475), and figures of Christ and the Apostles from another tomb.

Clare County Museum

&Open Jun–Sept 9.30am–5.30pm (9.30am–1pm Sun). Oct–May, Tue–Sat 9.30am–1pm, 2pm–5.30pm. Closed Sat on bank hol weekends. 065 682 3382. www.clarelibrary.ie.

Housed in an imaginatively redesigned former convent school, the *Riches of Clare* exhibition traces the history of this particularly distinctive county via four themes – Earth, Power, Faith and Water – using a variety of state-of-the-art techniques to interpret the carefully selected range of items on display. Among them is a *shelagh-na-gig*, a gorgeously carved panel from the wreck of an Armada galleon, and a striking banner of 1917, celebrating the election victory that confirmed Sinn Fein as a force to be reckoned with.

Cathedral

The Roman Catholic Cathedral, dedicated to St Peter and St Paul, was built between 1831 and 1843 in a Tau-cross (letter T) shape; the tower with its spire was added 1871–74.

SOUTHWEST OF LIMERICK
Adare★★

10mi/17km SW of Limerick on the N 21 Tralee road. 🅘 *Adare Heritage Centre.* 061 396 666. www.adareheritage centre.ie.

This tiny town in fertile wooded countryside at the tidal limit of the River

Irish Palatines

In 1709, following two invasions, a bitter winter and religious oppression, many German Protestants left the Rhineland area known as the Palatinate, and travelled to England where the government promised to subsidise their ongoing journey to Carolina, USA. However, funds ran out and many were stranded in London. The Dublin government offered to take the 821 families, and landlords were offered subsidies to accept them. The majority settled on the estate of Lord Southwell in Rathkeale, where their names – Bovenizer, Corneille, Delmege, Miller, Rynard, Piper, Sparling, Stark, Switzer, Teskey – sounded a foreign note. These industrious people introduced new farming practices, and being pious people, mostly **Lutherans** or **Calvinists**, they responded enthusiastically to the preaching of **John Wesley**, who visited them on several occasions from 1756 onwards.

Maigue is often described as the prettiest village in Ireland, with its unusual rows of pretty, colour-washed cottages, with overhanging thatched roofs built in the mid-19C by the local landowner, the Earl of Dunraven, who succeeded in making his corner of West Limerick resemble something from the English shires. Adare (*Átha Dara*) is a designated Heritage Town.

The **Heritage Centre Historical Exhibition** (&⊙*open daily Apr–Oct 10am–5pm; €5; ✕; ℰ061 396 666. www.adare-heritagecentre.ie*) traces the history of Adare from the 13C to the present day with realistic models and audio visuals. The square tower and south wall of the present RC **Church of the Most Holy Trinity** on Main Street were part of a monastery, the only house in Ireland of the **Trinitarian Order**, constructed about 1230 by Maurice Fitzgerald, 2nd Baron of Offaly. The 50 monks were put to death in 1539 at the Dissolution of the Monasteries. The ruins were restored by the 1st Earl of Dunraven and enlarged in 1852. The **dovecot** at the rear (restored) dates from the 14C.

Adare's Anglican **Parish Church★** is fashioned from the nave and part of the choir of a 14C Augustinian priory. The exuberantly neo-Gothic **Adare Manor** (1832) by the River Maigue, now a hotel, was designed in part by James Pain and **Augustus Welby Pugin**.

Adare Manor

© George Munday/Tourism Ireland

Lough Gur

© Shannon Development/Fáilte Ireland

Adare Friary

Access via Adare Golf Course;
ask at the Club House.
The evocative riverside ruins marked by **Kilmallock Gate** are those of the Franciscan friary founded by the Earl of Kildare in 1464 and extended in 15–16C.

Rathkeale

7.5mi/13km W of Adare by N 21.
The Norman tower of **Castle Matrix★** was built in 1440 by the 7th Earl of Desmond. The Great Hall houses a fine **library** and objets d'art. The castle also houses an **international arts centre** and the **Heraldry Society of Ireland**. It was at Castle Matrix that the poet Edmund Spense and Walter Raleigh met in 1580 and began a lifelong friendship. &♿🕐*Open by appointment.* ✆*069 64284.* The **Irish Palatine Museum & Heritage Centre★**(&♿🕐*open Jun, Tue & Thurs 2pm–5pm;* 👝€5; *Genealogy service;* ✕🅿; ✆*069 63511; www.irishpalatines. org)* presents photographs, documents, articles and artefacts relating to the German Palatine Protestant settlers, their innovative farming methods, their impact on Methodism and their dispersion throughout the English-speaking world.

Newcastle West★

16mi/26km W of Adare by N 21.
This thriving market town, known for its spring water, takes its name from the **castle** that belonged to the **Knights Templar** before passing to the **Earls of Desmond**. The strategic importance of **Desmond Castle** *(Halla Mór; Dúchas;* &♿🕐*open Apr–early Oct, 10am–6pm/5.15pm last tour;* 👝€5; ✆*021 477 4855; www.heritageireland. ie.),* also known as Adare Castle, had already dwindled by the time much of it was demolished by Cromwell's forces. A square tower stands in the inner ward of the early 14C stronghold surrounded by a moat. The upper storey of the building in the southwest corner of the outer ward was the **great hall.** The banqueting hall, now known as **Desmond Hall**, with an oak minstrel's gallery (restored) and a hooded fireplace (reconstruction), stands over a 13C vaulted stone chamber, lit by ecclesiastical lancet windows. Nearby are the ruins of **St Nicholas Church** (11C) and **Desmond Chapel** (14C).

SOUTHEAST OF LIMERICK
Lough Gur★

12mi/20km S of Limerick on the R 512.
Set among low hills, horseshoe-shaped Lough Gur is the largest water body in Co Limerick and the area around the lake is one of the longest-inhabited districts in Ireland. It has an exceptional wealth of stone circles, standing stones, burial chambers and cairns. Artefacts, relics and models of stone circles and burial chambers are on display in the

All-Ireland Hurling Championship

An ancient game with modern rules, hurling is said to have been played for the first time in 1272 BC, when 54 players battled it out before the battle of Moytura near Cong, on the border of Galway and Mayo. Legend has it that the native Irish *(Fir Bolg)* won the match, but 27 of the players died during the game and in the following battle, 4,000 men lost their lives. The All-Ireland Hurling Championship, held in Croke Park, Dublin each September, is a little less bloody than the first match, but passionate nonetheless and now considered to be the fastest field sport in the world. Teams compete for the Liam McCarthy Cup, named after a prominent player and organiser and first presented in 1921. The original cup was replaced in 1992 by a sturdier version. It is held for a year by the winning team – Kilkenny have had that honour 35 times. Teams of 15 players take part in a series of county matches over the summer months, playing according to rules first set out in the late-19C by the GAA (Gaelic Athletic Association) during the Gaelic Revival.

The game's dominance has moved from the West to the counties of the South and East in the last 100 years, with Kilkenny, Cork and Tipperary being the dominant counties. Originally the championship was played in a series of knockout games by the winners of each county competition but in order to make the game more popular a more complex system of qualifying matches has been introduced. In 2014, 12 counties and 14 teams competed for the Liam McCarthy Cup throughout the summer, with the final played between Tipperary and Kilkenny in front of 82,000 fans in Croke Park.

© The Irish Image Collection/Design Pics/Photononstop

thatched hut housing the **Lough Gur Heritage Centre** *(&⃝open daily Mar–Oct Mon–Fri 10am–5pm, Sat–Sun noon–6pm, Nov-Feb 10am-4pm, Sat-Sun noon-4pm; ✑€5; ✆061 385 186; www.loughgur.com)*, which also screens a video illustrating the life of Neolithic people in this region.

The best way to get an impression of the ancient ways of life of this area is to take a walk around the lough, stopping at the various sites: Grange Stone Circle, the largest and best preserved stone circle in Ireland, is especially worth seeking out. It consists of 113 orthostats in a perfect circle, the post hole at its centre, used 2,200 years ago to draw out the circumference of the circle, is still visible. The largest stone is thought to have been brought here from 3mi/5km away. The circle is aligned to sunrise at the summer solstice. Rituals involved at this place can only be speculated on, but the discovery of thousands of shards

311

of beaker pottery at the site suggests the pots may have been deliberately smashed in some symbolic ritual.

Kilmallock★

21mi/34km from Limerick on the R 512. Kilmallock developed around its 7C abbey and become a pre-eminent town in the province of Munster, with town walls, a castle and four gates. In 1568, it was burnt down to prevent it being taken by the English; a century later, after Cromwell's departure, its extensive walls had gone and many of its buildings lay in ruins.

By the river stand the ruins of the 13C Dominican **Kilmallock Abbey★**.

At the entrance to the abbey is a small town **museum** (🕐 *open 11am–3pm; 𝄢063 91300).* The walls and arches of the nave and south transept of the 13C Roman Catholic **Collegiate Church★**, dedicated to St Peter and St Paul, are largely intact; the tower is part of an ancient round tower.

A substantial section of the medieval **Town Walls** can be seen between the Collegiate Church and **Blossom's Gate** – the only one of five still standing. The **King's Castle**, a 15C tower house, occupies the site of an earlier fortress.

ADDRESSES

LIMERICK

STAY

🛏 **Clifton House** – *Ennis Rd. 1.25mi NW on R 587. 𝄢061 451 166. Closed 21 Dec–2 Jan. 16rm.* Simple well-priced accommodation, set in an acre of landscape gardens, a 15-min walk from town.

🛏 **Glen Eagles** – *12 Vereker Gardens, Ennis Rd. 𝄢061 455 521.* Basic, but adequate accommodation with a friendly host, only a few minutes walk from the city centre.

🛏 **Old Quarter Lodge** – *Little Ellen St., Ennis Rd. 𝄢061 315 320.* City-centre location for this small, but comfortable guesthouse. There is a pub on one side so try and get a room on the other side for a quieter night.

🛏-🛏 **No. 1 Pery Square** – *Pery Sq. 𝄢061 402 402. 5rm.* Overlooking People's Park and a stone's throw from the Limerick City Gallery of Art, this is the finest boutique hotel in town. Rooms include handcrafted brass beds, free-standing tubs, and rainfall showerheads.

🛏 **Travelodge** – *Coonagh Roundabout, Ennis Rd. 𝄢061 457 000. www.travelodge.ie. 40rm.* Charmless, but functional and good-value, especially for families, when all that is needed is somewhere to sleep for a night. There is car-parking.

🛏 **Armada Lodge** – *Ennis Rd. 𝄢061 326 993. www.armadalodgebandb.com. 5rm. Open Feb–Dec.* Well furnished, clean and comfortable family-run B&B 10-min walk from town.

🛏-🛏 **Clayton Hotel** – *Steamboat Quay. 𝄢061 444 100. www.claytonhotellimerick. com. 158rm.* This landmark hotel by the side of the River Shannon in the centre of the city has style and a contemporary edge to its design. A good range of leisure facilities, a bar and the Sinergie restaurant.

🛏-🛏 **Limerick Strand Hotel** – *Ennis Rd. 𝄢061 421 800. www.strand hotellimerick.ie. 184rm.* Just across the Sarsfield Bridge, with good views from the bedrooms on the higher floors, this modern hotels attracts business travellers but the leisure facilities appeal to a wider audience.

🛏-🛏 **Radisson Blu Hotel & Spa** – *Ennis Rd. 𝄢061 456 200. http://www. radissonblu.ie/hotel-limerick. 154rm.* A smart and modern hotel with a sense of design that distinguishes it from many Limerick hotels. The bedrooms are stylish and comfortable and there is a good restaurant and two bars, as well as a spa, indoor swimming pool and sauna. A 15-minute walk from the city centre.

🍽 EAT

🍽 **The Sage Cafe** – *67 Catherine St. 𝄢061 409 458. www.thesagecafe.com. Closed Sun.* The fact that queues form here over lunchtime gives some idea of The Sage Cafe's popularity, so consider arriving for an early or late meal during the day. Closing time is 5pm. Excellent breakfasts are also served.

🍽 **Copper & Spice** – *2 Cornmarket Row. 𝄢061 313 620. www.copperandspice.com.* Ring the bell to gain admission to this modern restaurant offering Asian (mostly Indian and Thai) and Pacific (Japanese) food, with many vegetarian dishes, though meat-eaters will have no trouble finding something agreeable on the menu. Open from 5pm and a take-away service is also available.

⊜⊜ **The French Table** – *1 Steamboat Quay.* ☎*061 609 274. www.frenchtable.ie. Closed Mon.* There are views of the river from this pleasant restaurant. Expect the likes of chicken cordon bleu, braised rabbit with mustard. Good service and an all-French wine list.

⊜⊜ **Freddy's Bistro** – *Theatre Lane.* ☎*061 418 749. www.freddysbistro.com. Closed Sun-Mon.* Set in a restored 19th-century coach house, this restaurant drips atmosphere through its exposed brick walls and dark wooden beams. Run by three sisters who keep the menu fresh and inventive, it's one of Limerick's finest eateries.

PUBS

Nancy Blake's – *Upper Denmark St.* ☎*061 416 443.* A typical Irish pub with live traditional music most nights of the week.

Dolans – *Dock Rd.* ☎*061 314 483. www. dolans.ie* Probably the best-known pub in the region. It offers a comprehensive menu specialising in seafood, but what really draws the crowds is the live music and or comedian every night. There are several rooms and a variety of traditional and folk, rock and blues, tribute bands and originals; the top acts play in Dolan's Warehouse, which has hosted Mumford & Sons, Christy Moore, Kasabian, Franz Ferdinand and The Saw Doctors.

Schooners – *Steamboat Quay, Dock Rd.* ☎*061 318 147.* Boasts a super location beside the Shannon, with a terrace in summer to watch the boats go by. Live concerts are held at the end of the week.

ENTERTAINMENT

69 O'Connell Street – ☎*061 774 774. www.limetreetheatre.ie.* This multi-functioning arts centre hosts a programme of theatre, dance, visual arts, music, film and comedy.

SHOPPING

Arthur's Quay Shopping Centre – *Arthur's Quay* – ☎*061 412 462. www.arthursquay-shopping.com.*

Housing more than 30 stores, where you will find hand-knit and machine-made sweaters and clothing by Irish designers in linen, tweed and cotton.

Limerick Lace is now rare, though a few people still hand-make the delicate fabric on request. Enquire at the tourist office.

SIGHTSEEING

Walking Tours – *Angela's Ashes tour,* based on the popular novel by Frank McCourt about the wretched life of the poor in Limerick during his childhood. Depart from the tourist office 2.30pm daily during summer, Arthur's Quay. *Call Noel Curtain for times and prices.* ☎*087 2351339. www.visitlimerick.com.*

ADARE

🛏STAY

⊜ **Berkeley Lodge** – *Station Rd. 6rm.* ☎*061 396 857. www.adare.org.* Simple, clean accommodation very competitively priced and centrally located. True "home from home" feeling. Bedrooms at the rear of the house are quieter.

⊜–⊜⊜ **Carrabawn Guesthouse** – *Killarney Rd., 0.5mi SW on N 21. 8rm.* ☎*061 395 947. www.carrabawnadare.com.* A welcoming and immaculately-kept guesthouse, 10 minutes' walk from the town centre.

🍽 EAT

⊜⊜ **White Geese Restaurant** – *Main St.* ☎*061 396 451. www.thewild-geese.com.* The most cottagey of all the places to eat in Adare and with a fine menu of seafood, poultry, meat and game. The early-bird menu is well worth considering, but book ahead. Good vegetarian options.

⊜⊜ **White Sage Restaurant** – *Main St.* ☎*061 396 004. www.whitesage restaurant.com. Dinner only, closed Sun & Mon (open Bank Hol Sun).* The cottage setting and white stone walls makes the White Sage an especially appealing place for a leisurely dinner. The early-bird menu offers the best value for a three-course meal.

TRACING ANCESTORS

The Irish Palatine Heritage Centre at Rathkeale provides a **genealogical service** (www.irishpalatines.org).

Shannon Valley★

Connected to the East Coast by the Grand Canal and the Royal Canal, and to the North by the Shannon Erne waterway, the River Shannon was once a vital transportation route. In modern times it serves as a transport route for motor cruisers carrying holidaymakers, its waters are home to water fowl, the banks smothered in wild flowers. Along its quiet course through the countryside from Limerick to Carrick-on Shannon, the river widens into small lakes. Today's tranquil scene belies the area's turbulent past: Viking raids, the invasion of the Normans, flourishing monasteries and the dominance of the Anglo-Irish. If only rivers could speak, the Shannon might recount much of Irish history!

- 🛈 **Info:** www.discover theshannon.com.
- ◐ **Location:** From Castleconnell, a few miles northeast of Limerick, to Roscommon, 16mi/26km south of Boyle, in County Sligo.
- 👁 **Don't Miss:** Strokestown Park House and Famine Museum or the Heritage Town of Killaloe.
- 👪 **Kids:** Boat trip to Holy Island.
- ♿ **Also See:** Co Offaly for a Driving Tour to Slieve Bloom Mountains.

CASTLECONNELL★

11mi/18km NE of Limerick on the N 7.
This once-small village, only a few miles from Limerick, has succumbed to the need for housing in the city and become a small suburb with estates of modern housing around its borders. This does not however detract much from its sleepy, pretty atmosphere and its main street, filled with elegant 19C-buildings. There are some easy walks in the area, along the river and across the bridge into County Clare to a waterfall. Permits can be bought for salmon fishing, or if it is a really hot day there is **The World's End**, a deep pool in the Shannon where locals go to swim.

🚗 DRIVING TOURS

LOUGH DERG★

A drive around the Shannon Valley visiting some picturesque countryside and the ruins of ancient religious orders.

◐ From Castleconnell drive E on a minor road (crossing N 7); turn left

GETTING AROUND

BY SEA – Holy Island Ferry:
Operates (weather permitting) from Mountshannon pier. *Open May–Oct 9.30am–6pm. €8 (boat and tour).* ☎086 87 49710.
BY SEA – If you would like to explore, the Shannon self-drive cruisers are for hire from Emerald Star ☎07 196 27633. *www.emeraldstar.ie.*

onto R 503; E of Newport turn right (sign); car parks both sides of the river.

Clare Glens★

The Clare River descends in a series of lovely **waterfalls** through wooded glens.

◐ Continue S on minor road to Murroe; turn in through the park gates.

Glenstal Abbey

◐*Grounds open daily* ☎061 621 000; *www.glenstal.org.*
Impressive grounds and lakes surround the castle, now used as a Benedictine monastery and school *(private)*. The modern **church** is known for its surrealistic decor and for the Ikon Chapel in the crypt.

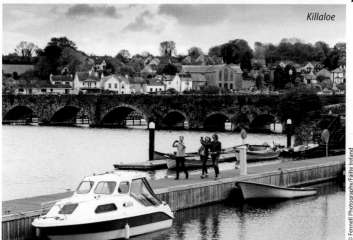

Killaloe

© Fennell Photography/Fáilte Ireland

▶ Return to R 503 and continue E. At the crossroad near Inch turn left onto R 497. Drive N via Dolla to Nenagh.

Nenagh

Little survives of the **Anglo-Norman castle★** built c. 1200, save the colossal circular keep *(100ft/30m high)*, the finest in the country, and the 13C hall (restored).

▶ From Nenagh take R 494 W. Beyond Portroe turn left (sign) into minor road.

Graves of the Leinstermen

The group of prehistoric stones on the west face of Tountinna *(1,512ft/461m)* may be one of the first inhabited places in Ireland. There are commanding **views★** over much of Lough Derg to Slieve Bernagh.

▶ Continue along minor road. Turn left into R 494. In Ballina turn right to Killaloe.

Killaloe★

🛈 *The Bridge.* ℘*061 376866.*
www.discoverkillaloe.ie.
Killaloe *(Cill Dalua)*, delightfully sited on the west bank of the Shannon, is a pretty village and a designated Heritage Town, with steep narrow streets, a cathedral

Shannon Harbour

The junction of the Grand Canal and the Shannon is now a popular mooring for **river cruisers**. The area provides excellent coarse fishing and birdwatching when rare birds, including the corncrake, visit the Shannon Callows' wet grasslands.

and an ancient stone bridge. It is also a watersports centre of international importance.

St Flannan's Cathedral★
The Dónall Mór O'Brien's austere, aisleless **cathedral** of 1185, on the site of a monastery founded in the 6C by St Molua and dedicated to his successor, was rebuilt in 1225 in the Romanesque/ Gothic transitional style that you see today. Its outstanding features include an elaborately carved 12C **Romanesque doorway**, a 12C High Cross from Kilfenora in the Burren, and a cross shaft carved c. 1000 bearing a unique dual inscription in both **Ogham** and **Viking Runic script**.
Beside the cathedral stands the vaulted nave of **St Flannan's Oratory**, a little 12C Romanesque church incorporating a loft beneath its steeply sloping stone roof.

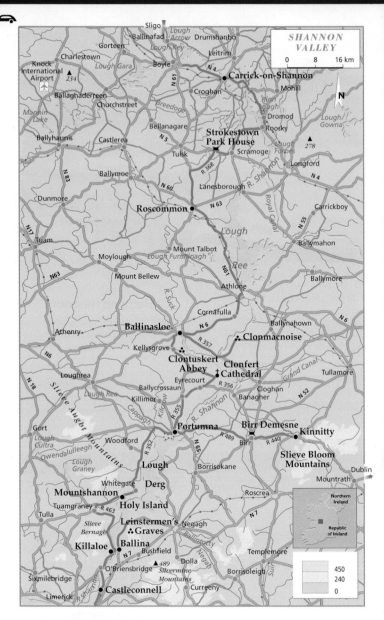

Brian Ború Heritage Centre

The Bridge. ⅃ ⏰ *Open late Apr/early May–mid Sept daily 10am–5pm.* ⌨ *€3.20.* 🅿 ✆ *061 376 866/360 788. www.discoverkillaloe.ie.*

Displays trace the history of Killaloe from the birth of Brian Ború, High King of Ireland (1002–14), through many years of fishing and cruising, to the Civil War and local modern projects such as the building of the Ardnacrusha Dam.

▷ Continue N on R 463.

Tuamgraney

The village is known as the birthplace of the novelist, Edna O'Brien. At the south end of the village stands a 15C tower house and St Cronan's Church (Anglican), which is believed to be the oldest church in continuous use in Ireland or Great Britain.

The West portion, with its lintelled doorway, dates from c. 969; the East end of the building is 12C; note the Romanesque windows.

It now houses the **East Clare Heritage Centre** (&. ○ open May–Oct, see website for times; ✆ 061 921 351; www.discoverireland.ie), which documents local history, including the life and times of Brian Ború.

The **Memorial Park** (330yd/300m West of the village), is planted with indigenous trees and shrubs to commemorate the victims of the Great Famine of 1845–52.

▷ Continue N on the R 463.

Mountshannon

This pretty village, its main street boasting a few quaint multi-purpose shops, a weaver's cottage, an old forge and a Protestant church, has a modern park leading to the little harbour, from where boat trips to Holy Island can be arranged.

Holy Island★

&. See Getting Around for boat travel to Holy Island.

The island, with its extensive and evocative remains of a 7C monastery, is a good excuse for a short trip on Lough Derg. As well as the remains of no fewer than six churches, there is a **round tower** (80ft/24m high) and a curious **bargaining stone** with a hollow channel, through which men would shake hands to seal an agreement.

▷ From Mountshannon take the R 352 to Portumna. (The road bridge over the Shannon is raised at regular intervals to allow the passage of vessels on the river).

Portumna★

The little township of Portumna (Port Omna) is a major crossing point on the River Shannon, where it enters Lough Derg. Occupying part of the shoreline,

Shannon–Erne Waterway

This canal was built (1847–58) as the **Ballinamore–Ballyconnell Navigation** by the engineer John McMahon to join the River Shannon with Lough Erne: the final link in a waterway system devised to enable barges to travel between Dublin, Belfast, Limerick and Waterford. Competition from the railway and a lack of industry meant that the scheme failed and the canal was abandoned in 1869. By 1880, it was derelict. The course (40mi/65km) includes 16 locks and 34 stone bridges as it runs through Lough Scur, St John's Lough, Garadice Lough and along Woodford River. It joins the River Shannon in **Leitrim** (4mi/8km north of Carrick by R 280).

Portumna Forest Park has a deer herd, nature trails, a marina and an observation tower; the bird life, both migratory and resident, is abundant.

Portumna Castle & Gardens★

(Dúchas) &. ○ Ground floor and formal gardens only: open Apr–mid-Oct, 9.30am–6pm; weekends only in late Oct (until 5pm). Last admission 45min before closing. ☞ €5. ✆ 090 974 1658. www.heritageireland.com.

This early-17C castle was for centuries the seat of the Burke family. Long derelict, but now restored to its full splendour, it is a handsome example of the sophisticated, semifortified residence that replaced the tower houses and castles of medieval times. The approach passes through a series of formal gardens. The Gothic Gate houses an exhibition about the story of the castle and its occupants; the 17C walled kitchen garden is planted with fruit trees, flowers, herbs and vegetables.

▷ See p194 for a sidetrip to Slieve Bloom Mountains via Birr and Kinnitty.

▷ Drive 17mi/27km NE of Portumna via the N 65, R 355, R 356 via Eyrecourt and a minor road east.

Clonfert Cathedral★

🔑 *Key available from the house to the right of the cathedral.*

The original 12C church was built on a monastery founded in 563 by St Brendan the Navigator. It is justly famous for its great **west doorway★★**, a masterpiece of Hiberno-Romanesque decoration in red sandstone, aptly described as "the apogee of the Irish Romanesque mason's love of ornamentation" (P. Harbison). The door arch itself is in six orders, while above them a geometric design of triangles, alternating with grotesque human and animal heads and foliage, sits above a colonnade with more human faces. The sixth order, topmost, is 15C as is the tower, south transept and sacristy.

The grounds *(through the rear churchyard gate; turn left)* contain an **ancient yew walk**, probably planted by the monks in the shape of a cross.

▷ Return to Eyrecourt and just beyond it, turn right onto the R 355.

West doorway, Clonfert Cathedral

© Chris Hill Photographic/Tourism Ireland

Clontuskert Augustinian Priory

10mi/16km SE of Aughrim by N 6 to Garbally and S by R 355; 5min on foot from roadside 🅿 *(left).*

The first monastery here was founded by **St Baedán** (d. c. 809). By the end of the 13C, the **Augustinians** had established one of the richest monasteries in the diocese. Most of the present ruins are from the 15C.

▷ To visit Clonmacnoise, follow the R 355 to Ballinasloe, then the R 357 to Shannonbridge before turning north on the R 444.

Clonmacnoise★★★

🕙 *See p194.*

ROSCOMMON AND AROUND

A drive through the countryside of Roscommon, taking in its main attractions.

Roscommon

The history of this county town, the monastery and the district is illustrated in the **Roscommon County Museum** (♿ 🕙 *open Jun–Aug Mon–Sat 10am–5.30pm; Sept–May Mon–Fri 10am–4pm;* ☎*090 662 5613)* housed in a former Presbyterian chapel.

Roscommon Dominican Friary

This ruined friary, established in 1253, still has an effigy of its founder, Felim O'Connor, his feet resting on a dog; below is a panel with vigorous carvings of well-armed mail-clad gallowglasses, the fearsome mercenary warriors imported from the west of Scotland in the 14C.

▷ North of town on the N 61. 2min on foot from the car park across a field.

Roscommon Castle★

The impressive ruin of an enormous Norman castle, built in 1269 by Robert de Ufford and originally protected by a lake or swamp, suggests it had massive walls and round corner bastions.

Strokestown Park House

© Derek Cullen/Fáilte Ireland

▶ Continue on the N 61 and turn right at Four Mile House onto the R368.

Strokestown★

A particularly fine example of an estate village and now a Heritage Town, Strokestown has a broad main street running up to the fanciful Gothic arches of the entrance to Strokestown Park House.

A Bit of History

Confiscated from its original owner, O'Connor Roe, land at Strokestown was granted to Capt. Nicholas Mahon (d. 1680), a Cromwellian officer. In 1845, as the Great Famine began, the property passed to Major Denis Mahon, who acquired an unenviable reputation as a heartless evictor of his destitute tenantry, more than 3,000 in total, many of whom perished aboard the notorious "coffin ships" sailing to America.

On November 2, 1847 he was shot dead by two assassins; that evening, bonfires were lit in celebration on the nearby hills.

Strokestown Park House and The Irish National Famine Museum★

&⚲ Open daily year-round 10.30am–5.30pm (4pm Nov-mid-Mar). ☞House by guided tour only: noon, 2.30pm, 4pm;

John McGahern

The author of *Amongst Women*, which won the Booker Prize in 1991, was brought up in Cootehall, went to school in Carrick-on-Shannon and now lives near Mohill. McGahern is a master at describing provincial life and examining the effect of people's interest in, or indifference to their neighbours' lives.

winter only 2.30pm. House and garden. ☞€13.50; garden only, €9. ✕ ☎071 963 3013. www.strokestownpark.ie.

The house, a fine Palladian mansion designed by Richard Castle in the 1730s, consists of a central three-storey block with a pillared portico, linked by curving corridors to the service wings. The well-preserved interiors give an impression of a comfortable and sociable rather than ostentatious life.

As well as spits and a trio of ovens for baking, roasting and smoking, the great **kitchen** has a dresser filled with Belleek pottery and is overlooked by a gallery from which the housekeeper could supervise her underlings.

The **Famine Museum,** established here on account of Strokestown possessing one of the most complete archives relating to the Great Famine of Ireland (1845–51), presents an excellent account of this grim period.

CRUACHAN DISTRICT

▶ Take the R 368 north to Elphin.

Elphin Windmill
🌀 *guided tour only, year-round Mon–Fri 2pm–6pm, Sat–Sun 10am–6pm. Call to confirm.* ⊛€5. ☎087 216 1559. This early-18C windmill has an unusual conical thatched roof and sails made to face the wind by means of cartwheels running on a circular track.

▶ From Elphin take the R 369 west; turn left onto the N 61; in Tulsk turn right onto the N 5 to Rathcroghan and then first left onto the minor road to Castelplunket and Ballintober.

Ballintober Castle
The ruined castle was inhabited well into the 19C. The high walls, fortified by a polygonal tower at each corner and originally surrounded by a moat, enclose a large, rectangular courtyard. Two projecting turrets guard the entrance gate.

▶ Take the R 367 south; turn right onto the N 60. In Ballymoe turn left and left again onto the minor road to Glinsk.

Glinsk Castle
The four-storey ruins suggest a fine fortified house, built by the Burkes c. 1618–30.

▶ Continue SE through Creggs and on R 362. Before joining N 63, turn left and left again onto a private drive.

Castlestrange Stone★
In a field *(right)* is a rounded granite boulder decorated with a curvilinear Celtic-style La Tène design from 250 BC.

▶ Turn left onto the N 63 towards Roscommon.

ADDRESSES

🛏 STAY
⊜⊜ **Bush Hotel** – *Carrick-on-Shannon. ☎071 967 1000. www.bushhotel.com. 60rm.* Old-fashioned hotel with modern amenities and a lively atmopshere; a good base for exploring the area. A decent restaurant and two bars.

⊜⊜ **Ciuin House** – *Hartley, Carrick-on-Shannon. ☎071 967 1488. www.ciuinhouse.ie. 15rm.* Within walking distance of the town, this luxury modern guesthouse is more like a small hotel. Fully licensed and a good restaurant, with outdoor seating for sunny days.

🍴 EAT
⊜⊜ **The Oarsman Bar & Cafe** – *Bridge St, Carrick-on-Shannon. ☎071 962 1733. www.theoarsman.com. Dinner Thu–Sat, lunch and bar menu Tue–Sat.* In fact it's a restaurant and gastropub, serving high quality Modern Irish cuisine, with a garden area for eating outdoors.

SIGHTSEEING
Moon River, *Main St, Carrick-on-Shannon* – Cruises on the Shannon usually lasting one hour Saturday night party cruises all year, 9.30pm boarding and sailing until midnight. ☎071 962 1777. www.moonriver.ie.

👥 **Cavan and Leitrim Railway** – *Dromond. See website for dates and fares. Trains run Sat–Mon 10am/Sun 1pm–5pm.* ✕☎071 9638599. www.cavanandleitrim. com. Narrow-gauge steam railway.

SPORTS AND LEISURE
Killaloe is a watersports centre of international importance.

TRACING ANCESTORS
Tipperary North Genealogical Service is housed in the Governor's House in Nenagh. *Open Mon–Fri 9.30am–5pm.* ☎067 33850.

The Burren★★★
and West Clare

Covering much of County Clare, the austere limestone plâteau of The Burren *(Boireann – Place of Rock)* is one of Ireland's strangest but most compelling landscapes. Six thousand years of human occupation have largely denuded The Burren of its trees, except for a few stunted hazel and willows, but in spring and early summer, the bleak scenery is coloured by extraordinary carpets of diverse flowers, with Mediterranean and Alpine species flourishing side by side. Standing out on the bare rock, signs of former human habitation are everywhere: dolmens dating back to 3,000 BCE, literally hundreds of Iron-Age ring forts, ancient cooking places, the remains of 15C tower houses and early churches. In summer evenings, as the sun sets over the pale Burren rockscape, an alien-looking glow covers this ancient and very beautiful place, adding to the sense of wonder and mystery that impresses itself on most visitors at some time or other during their visit to the region.

WEST CLARE
Kilrush★
Overlooking the sheltered waters of the Shannon estuary, the second-largest town in County Clare retains something of the character it had when laid out by the Vandeleur family in the 18C.

In the 19C Kilrush *(Cill Rois)* prospered as a port and became the favourite summer resort of wealthy people from Limerick. Today it is a designated Heritage Town and a gateway to the beaches and cliffs of the Loop Head Peninsula. In summer, families of bottle-nosed dolphins can be seen in the Shannon Estuary.

Vandeleur Walled Garden
Ferry Rd. ◑*Open Apr–Aug 10am–7pm. Sep–Mar 9.30am–5pm. Last admission 30min before closing.* ✕*℘065 90 51760. www.vandeleurwalledgarden.ie.*

Info: Cliffs of Moher, Liscannor, Co Clare. ℘065 708 6141. www.discoverireland.ie.

Location: The Burren covers the northern part of Co Clare, extending south from Ballyvaughan to Ennistimon and Corofin.

Don't Miss: The Cliffs of Moher.

Timing: It could take several days to explore The Burren!

Kids: Exploring Aillwee Cave.

GETTING AROUND
BY SEA – Shannon Car Ferry: From Killimer; 5.5mi/8.8km E of Kilrush. *℘065 90 53124. www. shannonferries.com.* Vehicles and passengers to Tarbert (south shore)
Ferry to Scattery Island: From Kilrush Creek Marina. *Apr–Oct. ℘065 905 1327. www.discoverdolphins.ie/ scattery.html.*

The Vandeleurs, a family of Dutch origin, settled in Kilrush in 1688 and were responsible for building the town in the 18C, but in the 19C they acquired an unenviable reputation as harsh landlords. These magnificent woodlands *(420 acres/168ha)* and the old walled garden are all that remain of the Vandeleur family seat.

Scattery Island★
Accessible by boat from Kilrush (☞see Getting Around, opposite). ◑*Visitor Centre open second week June–late Aug daily 10am–6pm. ℘065 682 9100. www.heritageireland.ie.*

In the 6C Scattery island *(some 2mi/3km out in the estuary)* was chosen as the site of a monastery by St Senan. Legend relates that the saint first had to rid it of a terrible monster; more certain historically is the monastery's fate at the hands of the Vikings, who raided it on more than one occasion. There are evoca-

Loop Head Lighthouse

tive ruins of five medieval churches, but the most imposing structure is the tall *(115ft/33m)* **round tower**, with its doorway unusually at ground level.

Kilkee *(Cill Chaoi)*

8.5mi/13.5km NW of Kilrush by N 67.
This seaside resort is set on Moore Bay, with a long promenade embracing a wide horseshoe-shaped sandy beach. Horse races are held on the sands at low tide on the last weekend in August. Duggerna rocks at the entrance to the bay are accessible at low tide.

Loop Head Peninsula

West of Kilrush and Kilkee, the land forms a peninsula, terminating in Loop Head. The treeless landscape is divided into fields by earthbanks rather than the hedges or flagstones found farther inland. The peninsula feels a million miles away from civilisation.

On the South Coast, **Carrigaholt Tower House** was built in the 16C by the McMahon family, who once controlled the peninsula.

The North Coast is much wilder, with spectacular cliffs, stacks and puffing holes. Near Moneen a huge natural arch, the **Bridge of Ross★** *(sign)*, formed by the action of the sea, is visible from the edge of the cliffs.

Loop Head is surmounted by the lighthouse *(277ft/84m above sea-level)* which was built on the headland in 1854. It is the third light on the site; the first, built in about 1670, was one of four stone-vaulted cottage lights which had a coal-burning brazier on a platform on the roof.

Bridge of Ross

🚗 DRIVING TOURS

WEST CLARE COAST
Round trip of 80mi/128km.

Ennistimon *(Inis Díomáin)*
The **waterfalls** on the River Cullenagh are visible from the seven-arch bridge, the river bank *(through arched entry in the Main Street)* and from the grounds of the Falls Hotel. The town itself is noted for its traditional shop fronts with Irish writing.

▷ Head west from Ennistimon on the main road for a couple of miles.

Lahinch
A long beach and some good pubs for live music are two attractions of this little seaside town.

▷ Take the N 67 S and then turn right onto the R 482.

Detour to Spanish Point
Named after the many Spanish sailors wrecked here in 1588, this quiet seaside town is another draw for surfers and golfers.

Cliffs of Moher★★★
&♿🕐*Site: Open daily. Visitor Centre: open daily. 9am-dusk, open later some weekends and bank holidays - see website. ⊚€6 (book online for a discounted rate).✕ 📞065 708 6141. www.cliffsofmoher.ie.*
These great dark sandstone cliffs *(600ft/182m high – nearly 5mi/8km long)* are among the country's most stunning natural sights. Rising sheer from the Atlantic, the Cliffs of Moher are home to one of the major colonies of cliff-nesting seabirds in Ireland. The best view is from **O'Brien's Tower**, built in 1853 by Cornelius O'Brien. The **Atlantic Edge Exhibition** is an exciting new interpretive centre at the centre of the underground building. You will "walk on water" as you enter, then explore Ocean, Rock, Nature and Man-themed areas. The Clare Journey is an aerial tour of the Cliffs; a winding tunnel leads to

The Ledge theatre, housing a virtual reality cliff face adventure, and so on.

▷ NW on the R 478.

Doolin
Famous for traditional Irish music in its pubs and very crowded in summer.

THE BURREN COAST ROAD★★★
38mi/62km from Doolin to Kinvarra (including the detours).

If you do not have much time to spend in The Burren, this route will give you a glimpse of the region's spectacular geography. On the coastal side, the terrain is made up of a series of smooth, flat stone terraces lined with long crevices, with a few pebbly coves dotted along the shore. Inland, fields grazed by donkeys, cows and sheep are few and far between. Above the road, **Slieve Elva** *(345m/1,132ft)* is a mass of bare limestone. In this incredible landscape, the rocks resemble a jumble of stone chimneys, canyons and plâteaus split by valleys, scattered with strange giant stones. As you wander though these stone mazes, it is not unusual to come across some of the most exotic species of Mediterranean or alpine flowers, such as the blue gentian, burnet rose, wild geraniums and orchids.
To travel even a short distance through this tangle of rocks means plenty of detours and scrambling, but you will be rewarded with the feeling of having been transported to another planet, amid the silence of the rocks.

▷ Drive 8.7mi/14km N of Doolin on the R 479.

Fanore
Among all these rocks, visitors will be surprised to discover dunes and a beach of golden sand at Fanore. This is also a good spot for a swim, but unfortunately, the hordes of caravans and holiday bungalows mean the village is noisy and packed in the summer.

Botanising

The best months to view the 1,000 or so species of flowering plants and ferns in The Burren are May or June, but there is something to enjoy in every season. Rarer plants favour the more extreme habitats – the sunniest, shadiest, driest or wettest – look for cracks (grikes) shallow enough to admit light, but deep enough to give shelter. Keep to naked limestone or grassy hill slopes, avoiding the cultivated farmland.

Caher River Valley★★

Just before you cross the river, turn right towards the hills and along the Caher River Valley. Snaking its way between the rocky terraces, the road offers a chance to head out into the landscape of The Burren.

▷ Afterwards, retrace your steps and continue along the coast road to Black Head.

Black Head★

From this large rocky mass jutting out to the sea, with its landscape of bare limestone cliffs, you might be able to spot dolphins or seals. A little lighthouse down on the slope marks the southern entrance to Galway Bay.

The most athletic will want to climb the hillside to **Cathair Dhún Iorais**, an iron-age fort that offers an exceptional **panorama★★**.

Further on, by the water's edge, you will see the tall, square tower of the 16C **Gleninagh Castle** (closed to visitors).

In the hamlet of Cregg, a hiking path heads up into the hills, between Gleninagh and Cappanawalla Mountain, to a **viewpoint★★** looking out over the bay and the rocky scenery, before joining the Burren Way to the South.

Back on the coast road, you will notice a strange little building on your right. This Is the **Pinnacle Well**, a communal well where women used to come to draw water. As a holy well, it is said to bring luck to anyone who walks three times around it and makes three wishes.

As you travel onwards, the scenery becomes greener and before you arrive in Ballyvaughan, you will find trees growing by the roadside.

Ballyvaughan

This little port tucked into a bay has become a magnet for tourists. Some pretty cottages and a series of deep inlets in the coastline mark the transition as you head deeper into Galway Bay, where the coast is bordered by green fields partitioned with low walls.

Coast road through Black Head

© Chris Hill/Tourism Ireland

After 4mi/6.5km on the Galway road, take a right turn for Corcomroe Abbey.

Corcomroe Abbey★

The ruins of this Cistercian abbey, founded around 1180, blend harmoniously with the limestone of the surrounding Burren. The monks dedicated their abbey to St Mary of the Fertile Rock, perhaps in response to the abundance of flowers in the stony countryside. There are carved capitals and fine vaulting in the choir and transept chapels. William Butler Yeats set his verse play *The Dreaming of the Bones* here.

Back on the main road, continue towards Galway for another 9.3mi/15km to Kinvarra.

Kinvarra

This port tucked away at the far end of Galway Bay attracts fans of traditional Irish music *at the* **Cuckoo Fleadh** *(first weekend in May; www.kinvara.com/ cuckoo),* as well as admirers of traditional **Galway Hookers** boats. These heavy

craft, black, pot-bellied and with brown sails navigate this sheltered stretch of water at the **Gathering of the Boats Festival** *(www.kinvara.com/cruinniu)* in mid August.

At low tide, the shoreline reveals seaweed, mud and stones that make it popular with seabirds.

Dunguaire Castle★

Open early Apr–end Sept 10am–4pm. ☞€8.50. ☏061 360 788. *www.shannonheritage.com.*

The muted colours of the landscape are dominated by the austere silhouette of Dunguaire Castle, a tall, four-storey tower built in 1520 by a descendent of the kings of Connaught. After visiting the handful of small rooms with their wickerwork vaulted ceilings, you can enjoy the superb **view★** from the top of the castle, which also holds medieval banquets (*mid-Apr–Oct daily 5.30pm & 8.45pm, Sun 5.15pm & 7.45pm.* ☞€52.50 *online; booking required).*

You will be received by your hosts in period costume, as music plays in the background. Then, after tasting the local brew, a four-course meal (with

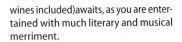

The Burren landscape

The Burren gently inclines south, its outer limits generally marked by steep escarpments. Classic karstic features of limestone pavements and underground drainage systems are accompanied by sink holes, which, when filled by a rise in the water table, become temporary lakes known as *turlach*. Fissures (*grykes*) between the slabs (*clints*) forming the limestone pavements contain enough soil to support a remarkably rich flora. The human impact has been considerable; drystone walls define field patterns and enclosures of immense variety, some dating back to neolithic times, and there is a multitude of tombs, forts and traces of ancient settlements.

The old Celtic practice of booleying – moving cattle and sheep to summer pastures on higher ground or moorland – is practised in reverse: in winter, the cattle are kept on the higher ground, where it remains relatively dry partly due to the Gulf Stream, partly because the limestone absorbs heat and releases it later; then , in summer, when the uplands may suffer from drought, the animals are kept near the homesteads, where they can be tended and watered.

wines included)awaits, as you are entertained with much literary and musical merriment.

▶ To leave the Burren, return to Galway (17.4mi/28km). Those who have fallen for the region's charms can go on to visit another even more remote and fascinating area. From Kinvarra, follow the signs for Gort, which lies in the heart of vast expanses of stone.

THE INTERIOR★
Allow around 2hrs. 23mi/37km route from Kinvarra to Corofin.

Thoor Ballylee★
On the N 66 between Gort (2.4mi/4km) and Loughrea (12mi/20km).
🕐*Call ☎091 537700 for updates.*
Devotees of Irish literature will want to take a detour to Thoor Ballylee, with its poignant reminders of **W.B. Yeats**, whose work was strongly influenced by the surrounding countryside. In 1917, the poet chose this 16C (originally Norman) tower, with small cottage attached, as his summer home, so he could be close to Coole Park, the residence of Lady Gregory, with whom he founded the Abbey Theatre in Dublin. Unfortunately following the flooding of the Cloon River in 2009, the Thoor was extensively dam-

aged and is closed to the public though there are plans to reopen it.

▶ Head 3km norh on the N 18.

Coole Park
🕐*Visitor Centre open Easter to end May & Sept 10am–5pm, then early Jun–Aug 10am–6pm; last entries 1hr before closing.* ✕ 🕐*Grounds open all year round.* ☎*091 631804. www.coolepark.ie.*
The grounds offer pleasant walks and the walled garden contains the **autograph tree**, where some of Ireland's greatest writers carved their initials, including W.B. Yeats, George Bernard Shaw, J.M. Synge and Sean O'Casey.

▶ Return to Gort and take the R 460 towards Corofin. On the right after 3.7mi/6km, you will reach the ruins of Kilmacduagh.

Kilmacduagh Monastery★
🕐*Key from B&B opposite, deposit required, guide leaflet available. www.all-ireland.com/attractions.*
This monastery, founded in the 7C and then ravaged by the Vikings in the 9C and 10C, is totally ruined, apart from its tower. The surprisingly large complex can be spotted from afar, thanks to the silhouette of the **round tower** (11C or 12C), with its conical roof, which leans

slightly to one side. The tower served as a lookout post to watch for attackers and a refuge in case of attack; the doorway is located high up on the wall and was accessed by a ladder that was then pulled up inside the building. The rest of the monastery site comprises a cathedral (13C), several churches (11C and 12C) and Glebe House (15C), a two-storey building that was used as a residence.

Back on the Corofin road (after 10.5mi/17km), you skirt a little lake and cross more expanses of stone forming huge slabs, between which you will find an abundance of wild flowers in May.

THE SECRET BURREN★

Allow at least half a day.
37.2mi/60km route from Corofin
to Cahercommaun Fort.

Corofin

In the countryside around this unpretentious little town, keen anglers will appreciate the **River Fergus** and the numerous lakes.

In Corofin the old village church contains the **Clare Heritage Centre & Museum** (*open Apr–Oct 9.30am–5.30pm, €4; 065 683 7955, www.clareroots.com*). With a collection of tools and household items used for linen working, butter making and farm work, the museum paints a picture of daily life here in the 19C. It also covers the Great Famine, underlining the suffering of the farmers and the mass emigration that resulted. On the other side of the road is the **Genealogical Research Centre** (*same as museum*).

▷ Head 1.2mi/2km south of Corofin on the R 476 towards Ennis, then follow the sign on the right.

Dysert O'Dea★

The battle of Dysert O'Dea was a decisive victory won by the Irish against the Anglo-Norman invaders in 1318, which freed County Clare from English control for almost two centuries.

In the fortified 15C **Dysert O'Dea Castle** tower, the **Clare Archaeological Centre**

(*open May–Sept daily 10am–6pm; €4; 065-6837401, www.dysertcastle. com*) shows a film on local history including the impressive archaeological remains in the surrounding fields. In the middle of the adjacent field is **St Tola's High Cross★**. This superb 12C monumental cross is a perfect example of Celtic art, with its geometric motifs and Scandinavian influence (Viking invaders frequently settled in Ireland). On the lower section, you can see Biblical scenes, such as Adam and Eve and Daniel in the lions' den. Above these is the figure of a bishop and Christ.

At the end of the field, at the foot of a ruined 11C **round tower,** which was demolished by Cromwell's soldiers, the vestiges of an 11C **Romanesque church** have a very peaceful aura about them. The magnificent **sculpted doorway★★** is decorated with a row of strange heads and adorned with columns with complex, interlacing designs.

▷ Return to Corofin and continue on the R 476 towards Kilfenora. After 1.9mi/3km, you will reach the hamlet of Killinaboy.

Killinaboy

Those with a taste for unusual religious art should take a right turn in the village towards **Killinaboy Church** (11C or 12C), which used to be home to a community of nuns. The gable opposite the entrance is decorated with a double-barred cross (often the sign of a relic of the True Cross brought back from the crusades), but the strangest feature is above the South door, where you can see a **sheela na gig**. These images are connected to the Pagan fertility cult and are found on many Celtic buildings.

Some 3mi/5km along the Kilfenora road, you will pass the slightly sinister ruins of **Leamaneh Castle**, the vestiges of a tower belonging to the O'Brien family, which was enlarged in the 17C.

Kilfenora★

The village has its own céilí band and hosts set dancing evenings twice a

Poulnabrone dolmen

© Chris Hill/Tourism Ireland

week. As well as these weekly festivities, the village makes for an interesting visit. At the **Burren Centre**★ (⏰open mid-Mar–Oct 10am–5pm, Jun–Aug, 9.30am–5.30pm; ✕; ⮑€6; ✆065 708 8030, www.theburrencentre.ie), an exhibition and a film help to explain the unique geology, flora and fauna of The Burren, as well as the history of its most important monuments. Guided walks also set out from here.

Close to the centre of the village, the partially-ruined 12C **cathedral**★ retains some fine architectural features, such as the carved bishop's head above the door, a finely-crafted window and some capitals decorated with figures. On either side of the nave are 14C tombstones decorated with effigies of bishops in high relief. The third, which is engraved, also dates from the same period.

Most interesting of all are the three large crosses outside the cathedral, including the famous **Doorty Cross**★★, which unfortunately has been badly eroded. On its east face, which is the best preserved, you can make out a bishop standing above two other figures. The west face has almost been worn smooth, but you can just see a figure of Christ. A second cross, which is very simple and has no ring around it, stands in the North of the enclosure.

To find the third cross, follow the little path running from the cathedral to the field. Its east face is decorated with a figure of Christ, interlacing designs and an animal figure.

▷ From Kilfenora, head NW on the R 476 to Lisdoonvarna (5mi/8km).

Lisdoonvarna

The town is famous for its **sulphur springs** and its Matchmaking Festival (⟡see box above), the first attracting those in search of a health cure, the second, farmers dressed to the nines!

▷ From Lisdoonvarna, head NE on the N 67 towards Ballyvaughan (16km).

After 5mi/8km, the road begins its descent of **Corkscrew Hill**★★, which offers a magnificent panorama over the hills and terraces of The Burren.

▷ Just before you get to Ballyvaughan, take a right-hand fork, almost doubling back on yourself, onto the R 480. Continue for 0.9mi/1.5km, then park.

👫 Aillwee Cave★

&⟡Visit cave by guided tour only (30min), year-round daily 10am–5pm/5.30pm (6.30pm Jul–Aug). ⏰Closed 24–6 Dec, 1 Jan. Cave ⮑€12, child €5. Birds of Prey ⮑€8, child €6. Wolf's Den free 30min crafts demos 11am,

4.30pm; 2hr courses €30. Combo tickets available, see website for prices. ⓔdiscounted prices online. ✕ ☏065 707 7036. www.aillweecave.ie.

This fascinating cavern features weirdly shaped stalactites and stalagmites and a **waterfall★** which is impressively flood-lit from below. At the back of the Highway, the largest chamber, is a vertical drop. The **visitor centre** explains the formation of the cave and its discovery in 1940 by a local herdsman.

Two other popular attractions here are the **Burren Birds Of Prey Centre**, featuring two or three flying displays a day, and the **Wolf's Den**, a living, primitive-crafts village and tool museum where visitors learn from locals skills of wilderness survival and techniques in the art of Woodland Crafts.

▷ The R 480 continues south, flanked on either side by ring forts and tombs. Look out for the sign for Poulnabrone on your left (after 3.7mi/6km).

Poulnabrone★★

In the midst of this rocky landscape, this huge 5,000 year-old dolmen is a wonderful example of a megalithic tomb which held between 16 and 22 adults and 6 children, with their pottery and jewellery. The best time to visit is early morning or dusk, when the low angle of the light accentuates the air of mystery. Around 0.6mi/1km further on, on the right-hand side, behind a house, is **Caherconnel Fort** (ⓞopen Mar–Oct, 10am–5pm (Jul–Aug 6pm); , €7, www.caherconnell.com), a ring fort that would have been inhabited by a farmer and his family (up to 25 people) at the beginning of the Christian era. A **visitor centre** interprets the site as well as that of the nearby ancient megalithic tombs of Poulnabrone and Poulawack Cairn. **Sheepdog demonstration**s are also given (call/see website for times/dates).

▷ Around 1.5 km beyond the dolmen, turn left towards Carran (5.5km).

Brides for Bachelors

Lisdoonvarna is the scene in September of a famous – or notorious – Matchmaking Festival, whose original function was to provide partners for lonely lads living on isolated farms deep in the countryside. For several days the little spa town is filled with revellers, less intent nowadays on the serious business of finding a bride, than on having a raucously good time.

The Match-making Festival takes place from late August to early October with dancing, singsongs, evening pub sessions and walks (www.matchmakerireland.com).

To the east of the village, you can visit the **Burren Perfumery** (ⓞopen May, Jun, Sept, 10am–6pm; Jul–Aug 9am–7pm; Oct–Apr, 10am–5pm; ✕; ☏065 708 9102, www.burrenperfumery.com), a perfume distillery that uses local flowers. An audio-visual explains the production process and, of course, there is a shop.

▷ Head south out of Carran, and at the junction, take the left-hand fork onto the little road that takes you back to Killinaboy. After around 2km, look out for the sign for Cahercommaun.

Cahercommaun Fort★★

ⓞOpen as Caherconnel Fort, above; www.caherconnell.com.

Perched on top of an escarpment, this three-walled fort is one of the finest in the area. It was probably built in the Iron Age and occupied until the 9C.

Finds discovered at the fort include Roman artefacts demonstrating the existence of contacts with people overseas, as well as evidence of its former occupants, who were livestock farmers.

ADDRESSES

🛏 STAY

Fergus View – *Kinaboy, Corofin. 3.25km/ 2mi north of Corofin on Kifenora Rd.* ✆*065 683 7606. www.fergusview.com. 6rm.* Farmhouse accommodation with good breakfasts. Self-catering in an adjacent stone cottage is also available.

Ballyvara House – *Doolin.* ✆*085 888 8581. www.ballyvarahouse.ie. 11rm.* Close to the village and with excellent facilties including games room with pool table, tennis court, and children's playground.

Sheedys Country House Hotel & Restaurant – *Lisdoonvarna.* ✆*065 707 4026. www.sheedys.com. 11rm.* Superb little hotel with large and elegant bedrooms. A lovely garden and a delightful bar add to the attractiveness of Sheedys. The restaurant (🍽🍽) is open to non-residents.

🍴 EAT

Linnane's Lobster Bar – *New Quay, opposite The Burren Centre.* ✆*065 707 8120. www.linnanesbar.com.* Perched on the rocks, above Galway Bay. Pews and pine tables and a menu that makes the most of local seafood; from chowder to mussels, crab cakes to fresh lobster.

Vaughan's – *Kilfenora.* ✆*065 708 8004. www.vaughanspub.ie.* Live music most nights and set dancing in the barn (Sun 9.30pm); hearty Irish pub grub served in the restaurant, or sandwiches at the bar.

ENTERTAINMENT/NIGHTLIFE

Irish Traditional Music – **Doolin** has an international reputation for its music; other places where you'll find sessions in summer are Ballyvaughan, Kilfenora, Lisdoonvarna and Ennistimon.

SHOPPING

The **Burren Smokehouse** in Lisdoonvarna sells fish, cheese and other gourmet items. *Visitor Centre open 9am/10am (Sun 11am)–5pm (6pm May– Sept; 4pm Jan–Feb).* ✆*065 707 4432; mail order service. www.burrensmokehouse.ie.* **Burren Perfumery** (♿*see Driving Tour*).

SPORTS AND LEISURE

Seaside Resorts – To the south at **Liscannor**, **Lahinch** (long, sandy beach with lifeguard) and **Milltown Malbay**; also to the north at **Fanore** *(S of Black Head)* and at **Finavarra** *(NE of Ballyvaughan)*.

Burren Way – Walking trails between Ballyvaughan and Liscannor *(26mi/42km)* in the Caher Valley, mostly on green roads, through Doolin and along the Cliffs of Moher before turning inland to Liscannor. Good walk from Lisdoonvarna south across the bog at Cnoc na Madre. **Beaches** at Cappa and Brew's Bridge.

Marina at Merchant's Quay in Kilrush with 120 berths, a boatyard and yachts for hire.

Fishing in the Shannon Estuary and off the Atlantic Coast.

FESTIVALS

The **Willie Clancy Summer School** *(July)* Milltown Malbay: major festival for all music, song and dance, particularly of the elbow *(uilleann)* pipes. *www.willieclancyfestival.com*

The Cumann Merriman annual summer school is held in **Ennistimon** to celebrate the work of Brian Merriman (b. 1749 in Ennistimon), whose poem *The Midnight Court* is widely regarded as the greatest comic poem in Irish Literature. *www.merriman.ie.*

SIGHTSEEING

Aran Islands – From Doolin there is a ferry to the Aran Islands. ✆*065 707 4455. www.doolinferries.com.*

Dolphin & Whale watching trips – depart from Kilrush Creek Marina. *(€26* ✆*065 90 51327; www.discoverdolphins.ie.)* and from Carrigaholt *(€35;* ✆*065 90 58156; www.dolphinwatch.ie). The latter also do whale-watching trips (€40).*

Both operators: Jun–Aug; also Apr–May and Sept–Oct, subject to demand and weather.

Aran Islands★★

Keeping watch over the mouth of Galway Bay are the islands of Inishmore, Inishmaan and Inisheer, great slabs of limestone linked geologically to the Burren on the mainland. People have inhabited these lonely isles since ancient times, using the limestone to build great prehistoric forts like Dún Aonghasa and Dún Conor, as well as the close-knit network of drystone walls bounding tiny, flower-rich fields. Tellingly evoked in the writings of J. M. Synge and Robert Flaherty's classic semi-documentary film *Man of Aran*, the islanders' traditional, extremely harsh way of life lasted until relatively recently. The islands remain a stronghold of the Gaelic language.

A BIT OF HISTORY

The Aran Islands rise in natural terraces from a flat sandy shore facing Galway Bay to high cliffs *(300ft/91m)* confronting the Atlantic. They get less rainfall than the mainland and are never touched by frost. Despite the lack of soil, wild flowers thrive but trees are rare: the traditional crops of rye and potatoes were grown on artificial soil created laboriously over the years by layering sand and seaweed on the bare rock.

Traditionally, the white-washed cottages were thatched with straw tied down against the wind. Fishing and farming were the main activities; cows would graze the summer pastures in Connemara and winter on Aran, unlike the ponies, which wintered in Connemara and worked on Aran in summer months. Illicit whiskey and peat were imported by boat from Connemara in exchange for potatoes and limestone.

The Aran Islands have been inhabited for centuries: the ruins of great stone forts date from prehistoric times, while in the early and medieval Christian period (5C–16C), the Aran monasteries prospered as centres of culture. Today, tourism is the

▶ **Population:** 2 000.
🛈 **Info:** Kilronan, Inishmore. ℘099 61263. www.aranisland.info.
◐ **Location:** The three Aran Islands are in the mouth of Galway Bay. The smallest, Inisheer is the closest (5mi/8km) to the mainland; the largest, Inishmore, lies about 7mi/11.3km from the coast of Connemara.
◉ **Don't Miss:** An excursion to see the stone cliff-top fort Dún Aonghasa.

dominant industry, ensuring the survival of traditional crafts, notably the distinctive cream-coloured **Aran knitwear**.

INISHMORE★ *(ARAINN)*

The largest island *(9mi/14.5km x 2.5mi/ 4km)* is served by one road running north from the airstrip along the shore of Killeany Bay *(Cuan Chill Éinne)*, to **Kilronan** *(Cill Rónáin)* and then west to the remote hamlet of Bun Gabhla overlooking **Brannock Island** *(Oileán Dá Bhranóg)* and the lighthouse. The old tracks and walls (7,000mi/11,265km) run

Words and Images

The Gaelic-speaking islanders are talented music-makers and storytellers, skills encouraged by the austere life on Aran as portrayed by Liam O'Flaherty (1896–1984) in *Thy Neighbour's Wife* (1924). Local stories feature in JM Synge's play *Riders to the Sea* set on Inishmaan, and in *The Playboy of the Western World*. WB Yeats urged Synge to study the islands and 'express a life that has never found expression;' the result was *The Aran Islands* (1907), made into a film in 1924. *Stones of Aran: Pilgrimage* by Tim Robinson (1935–) is more factual.

GETTING THERE

BY AIR – There are flights to all three islands from Connemara Regional Airport at Inverin (20mi/32km W of Galway by R 336); they can also be reached by ferry from Rossaveal (23mi/37km west of Galway, and from Doolin in The Burren (Inisheer only).

Aran Islands Air Service: Operates regular flights: up to eight per day in summer; three in winter (9min). *091 593 034 (Stobart Air). www.aerarannislands.ie*

BY SEA – Rossaveal: Aran Islands Ferry – Operates two-five sailings per day. €25 Return. Online booking service; bus service from Galway City Centre. *091 568 903. www.aranislandferries.com*

Doolin (Co Clare)–Aran Islands Ferry – Operates (weather permitting) Apr–Oct: to Inishmore (45min), three times daily, Return €20; to Inisheer (20min), up to five times daily, Return €15; to Inishmaan, Return €25. See website for details. *065 707 4455, 707 4189 (Doolin Ferry Co). www.doolinferries.com*

GETTING AROUND

The best way to explore **Inishmore** is on foot or by hired bicycle. A regular, but infrequent bus service operates along the island's main road, and minibus operators meet planes and ferries, offering tours of the principal sights. As well as the Tourist Information Centre by the harbour in Kilronan, the Aran Heritage Centre and the Visitor Centre below Dún Aonghasa are useful sources of information. Buy the meticulously-crafted *Map of the Aran Islands* by Tim Robinson to get to know the landscape in detail.

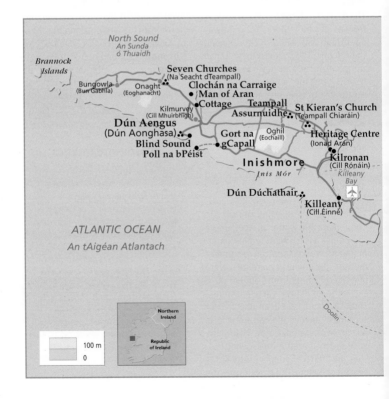

from northeast to southwest following natural rifts and man-made ruts created by the carting of seaweed from shore to field.

At the roadside stand square pillars topped with crosses erected in memory of islanders who died abroad or at sea. The Atlantic waves constantly batter the grim, southwestern cliffs and send spectacular spurts of spray through the "puffing-holes" at the island's eastern extremity. On the northwestern shore, by Port Chorrúch, lives a colony of seals.

Kilronan *(Cill Rónáin)*

The Aran Heritage Centre, **Ionad Arann** (⏱*open Apr, May, Sept, Oct 11am–5pm; Jun–Aug 10am–7pm;* ⊛*€3.50 for film and exhibition;* ℘*099 61355; www.visita-ranislands.com; www.galway.net*) introduces the landscape, monuments, traditions and culture of the islands. Note the currach, the seemingly frail craft made of hide or canvas stretched over a frame of laths and powered by blade-less oars. There is an exhibition and a "Man of Aran" film.

Dún Aonghasa★★★

4.5mi/7.2km W of Kilronan; 10min on foot from Kilmurvy (Cill Mhuirbhigh) Visitor Centre (Dúchas). ⏱*Open daily Jan-Mar, Nov-Dec 9.30am-4pm, Apr-Oct 9.30pm-6pm* ⊛*€5 (no charge after hours).* ✕ ℘*099 61008. www.heritageireland.ie.*

This great drystone fort in a spectacular setting is one of the finest prehistoric monuments in Europe, with three lines of defence. Between the outer and middle wall, stone stakes spike the ground, set at an angle to impede attack.

A square tunnel in the thickness of the wall leads into the inner compound. The inner wall, which has steps up to wall walks, follows a semicircle, beginning and ending on the cliff edge.

Dún Dúchatair★

2mi/3km SW of Kilronan.

The Black Fort is a splendid example of a promontory fort, with a massive curving wall 20ft/6m high and almost as thick, guarding the headland.

South of Kilronan

On the south shore of Killeany Bay stands the ruins of **Arkin's Castle** *(Caisleán Aircín),* a tower house probably built by John Rawson, to whom the islands were granted by Elizabeth I in 1588.

On the coast south of the airstrip, stand the early ruins of **St Eany's Church** *(Teaghlach Éinne).* **St Enda** is said to be buried here on the site of a monastery he founded (c. 490) from which his reputation as a teacher spread far and wide.

A path climbs the hill past St Eany's oratory (6C–7C) with a narrow north door and a slim east window. From **St Benen's Church** *(Teampall Bheanáin),* there is a good **view** of Killeany Bay and of the mainland.

ARAN ISLANDS

0   1   2 km

N

ARAN ISLANDS
Oileáin Árann

Rossaveel

Galway Bay

Gregory's Sound
Sunda Ghríora

Dún Chonchúir
Pier   Rossaveel
Synge's   Dún Fearbhaí
Chair   (Dún Fearbhai)
(Cathaoir Synge)

St Cavan's
Church
(Teampall Chaomháin)
Inishmaan
Inis Meáin   Dún Formna
Foul sound
An Sunda
Salach
Inisheer
Inis Oírr

Doolin

Dún Dúchatair, Inishmore

© Juan Carlos Muñoz/age fotostock

St Kieran's Church (Teampall Chiaráin)

1mi/1.7km NW of Kilronan.

Halfway down the slope to the shore stands a small ruined church dedicated to **St Kieran of Clonmacnoise**, home to four cross-inscribed stones and St Kieran's Well.

Seven Churches

5.5mi/8.8km NW of Kilronan.

Tucked away in a hollow on the north coast overlooking a small bay is an ancient monastic site, also known as *Na Seacht d'Teampall*, the Seven Churches. In fact, only two ruins are churches: the larger, **St Brecan's Church** *(Teampall Bhreacáin)*, marks the grave of St Brecan *(opposite west door)*. The other structures are thought to be outbuildings or pilgrim hostels. In the southeast corner of the graveyard is a stone inscribed to seven Roman saints.

INISHMAAN★★ (INIS MEÁIN)

Inishmaan *(3mi/5km x 1mi/2km)* is the most remote of the three islands.

A bleak and bare rocky plâteau slopes northeast to a sandy shore, providing little shelter to the isolated houses. Inishmaan exercised a particular fascination for J. M. Synge, who is said to have loved one particular spot called **Synge's Chair★** *(Cathaoir Synge)* on the western cliffs overlooking Gregory's Sound *(Sunda Ghrióra)*.

The island's main monument is the huge prehistoric fort **Dún Conor** *(Dún Chonchúir)* perched on high ground, keeping watch over the narrow valley: its main enclosure is contained by a thick wall *(17.5ft/5.65m)*.

A second stone fort, **Dún Moher or Dún Fearbhaigh**, overlooks the landing pier at Cora Point.

INISHEER★ (INIS OÍRR)

The smallest Aran island is mainly populated along its north coast. The ruins by the airstrip are those of **St Cavan's Church** *(Teampall Chaomháin):* its east window dates from the early 10C; the chancel arch and south door are medieval.

The grave of **St Cavan**, brother of St Kevin of Glendalough, lies nearby *(NE)*. Among the central settlements stands **Dún Formna★**, a stone fort containing the ruins of a tower house, probably built by the O'Briens in the 14C and destroyed by the Cromwellians in 1652.

ADDRESSES

🕮 STAY AND ¶/ EAT

🍽 **Fisherman's Cottage** – *Inishere.* 𝒫*099 75073. www.southaran.com.* Stay here for peace and quiet. Restaurant open for lunch, coffees and dinner.

🍽🍽 **Aran Islands Hotel** – *Kilronan, Inishmore.* 𝒫*099 61104. www.aranislands hotel.com. 22rm.* Modern hotel with restaurant and musical entertainment in the summer.

SHOPPING

Aran Sweater Market, *Kilronan* – Wide range of the famous sweaters, with their distinctive family stitches and patterns. 𝒫*064 662 3102. www.clanarans.com.*

Galway★★

The largest town in the West of
Ireland bestrides the Corrib River
as it enters Galway Bay. Galway
(Gaillimh) has grown from a medieval
core of narrow streets into a buzzing
cathedral and university city
sustained by modern industries and
a thriving port. It is also well placed
as a centre for excursions westwards
into the wild, mountainous country
of Connemara, while east and south
lies the fertile Galway plain. This
location, together with the city's
own dynamic character, draws
cosmopolitan crowds of visitors to
its busy streets, which take on an
almost Mediterranean air when the
summer sun contrives to shine.

A BIT OF HISTORY
City of the Tribes – The Anglo-Normans
were attracted by the sheltered anchorage strategically located midway along
Ireland's western coast. The city was
founded on the east bank of the river
in the 12C by the de Burgo (later Burke)
family, who encouraged immigration
from England and Wales. Defensive
walls were built and Galway prospered
on trade with France, Spain and the West
Indies. As an Anglo-Norman enclave in
the midst of an often hostile region,
the city excluded the native Irish, who
had their own settlement outside the
walls. Cromwell called this oligarchy of
Anglo- Norman families who controlled
the city from the 15C onwards "the Tribes
of Galway" and the name lives on. Prosperity did not, however, survive the religious disputes of the Reformation and
their political consequences. After two
lengthy sieges – by the Cromwellians in
1652 and William of Orange's forces in
1691 – Galway went into decline.
The Claddagh – Long before the
arrival of the Normans, an Irish-speaking community with its own traditions
and elected leader, known as the King,
thrived in a fishing village on the west
bank of the Corrib River. Its name – the
Claddagh – derived from the Gaelic *clad-
ach* meaning a rocky or pebbly shore.

▶ **Population:** 79 504
(Galway City).
Info: Forster Street.
☏091 537 700.
www.discoverireland.ie.
▶ **Location:** Roughly halfway
along the West Coast at
the head of Galway Bay
with Connemara north
and The Burren south.
Take the Galway City Bus
Tour's open-top hop-on,
hop-off bus tour to get your
bearings (€10, pay on the
bus or at the tourist office;
www.galwaybustours.ie).
Kids: Atlantaquaria,
Glengowla Mine.
Don't Miss: One of
Galway's major festivals;
Lough Corrib.

GETTING THERE
BY AIR – **Galway Airport** at
Carnmore (3.7mi/6km SE of Galway
via the N 17) – ☏091 755 569.
www.galwayairport.com.

The men fished by night and the women
sold the catch on the Spanish Parade.
Picturesque scattered whitewashed
thatched cottages were replaced in the
1930s by a modern housing scheme. The
Claddagh finger ring, formed by a heart
held by two clasped hands, is popular
throughout Ireland.
Gaelic Galway – The city adjoins the
most extensive Gaelic-speaking region
in Ireland: the Aran Islands, Connemara
and the Joyce Country. The 19C revival
of interest in the language drew many
visitors to the region; two of the oldest
Gaelic summer schools were founded at
the turn of the century at Spiddal *(west)*
and Tormakeady on the west shore of
Lough Mask. Since the establishment
of the Republic, the Gaelic character
of the region has been reinforced:
University College, Galway, founded

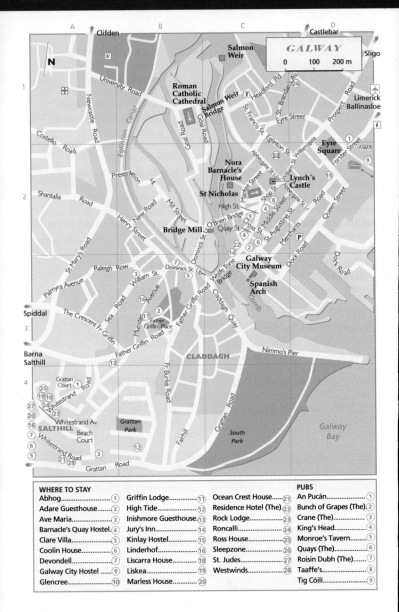

GALWAY

0   100   200 m

WHERE TO STAY

Abhog	1	
Adare Guesthouse	2	
Ave Maria	3	
Barnacle's Quay Hostel	4	
Clare Villa	5	
Coolin House	6	
Devondell	7	
Galway City Hostel	9	
Glencree	10	
Griffin Lodge	11	
High Tide	12	
Inishmore Guesthouse	13	
Jury's Inn	14	
Kinlay Hostel	15	
Linderhof	16	
Liscarra House	18	
Liskea	19	
Marless House	20	
Ocean Crest House	21	
Residence Hotel (The)	22	
Rock Lodge	23	
Roncalli	24	
Ross House	25	
Sleepzone	26	
St. Judes	27	
Westwinds	28	

PUBS

An Pucán	1
Bunch of Grapes (The)	2
Crane (The)	3
King's Head	4
Monroe's Tavern	5
Quays (The)	6
Roisin Dubh (The)	7
Taaffe's	8
Tig Cóilí	9

in 1849 as Queen's College, was made a bilingual institution in 1929. Today it is an important centre for Gaelic culture with a state-sponsored Irish Theatre *(Taibhdhearc na Gaillimhe)* launched by Micheál Mac Liammóir and his partner, Hilton Edwards. In 1969 the offices of the Gaelic Development Authority were moved to Furbogh *(Na Forbacha – 5mi/8km west of Galway by R 336)* and in 1972, Gaelic Radio began operating from Costelloe *(Casla – further west by R 336)*.

Literary Galway – Galway City and its environs have produced or fostered several literary personalities: Patrick O'Connor (1882–1928), who wrote short stories in Gaelic, Nora Barnacle (1884–1951), who lived in Bowling Green and married James Joyce, and Frank Harris (1856–1931) were natives of the city. Violet Martin, the second half of the Somerville and Ross partnership, lived at Ross House on the west shore of Lough Corrib. In 1896, Edward Martyn, who lived at Tullira Castle in south Galway, introduced William Butler Yeats to Lady Gregory; they co-founded the Irish Literary Theatre, which later became the Abbey Theatre in Dublin.

THE OLD TOWN★
Spanish Arch
The arch, recalling the city's links with Spain, may have been part of a bastion, incorporating four blind arches, one of which was opened in the 18C to give access to a new dock beside Eyre's Long Walk. Part of the medieval **town wall** *(20yd/20m long)* is visible on the south side, as are the tidal quays of 1270.

Galway City Museum★
⌖ⓘ*Open Tue–Sat 10am–5pm.* ✕
⌖*091 532 460.*
www.galwaycitymuseum.ie.
This striking modern complex, opened in 2006, is home to imaginative exhibitions relating to the history of Galway City. Suspended in the atrium is the Galway hooker (the local fishing boat), *Máirtín Oliver.*
Other highlights are the city corporation Irish-made sword and mace and the statue by Albert Power, RHA of

Patrick O'Connor (Padraic O' Conaire, 1882–1928) and a rare 17C altar piece.

St Nicholas' Church★
This collegiate church dedicated to St Nicholas of Myra, the patron saint of sailors, is said to be the largest medieval church in Ireland still in use today. Recent research claims that Christopher Columbus visited the church in 1477, during a stay in the area probably prompted by the legendary voyage of St Brendan to the New World (ⓘ*see DINGLE PENINSULA, box).*
The **exterior** has gargoyles and carved mouldings; the **interior** includes a medieval water stoup, a font and numerous tombstones.
Around the corner on Market Street, behind the church, is the city's famous **Lynch Memorial**, on the site of the old jail. It commemorates the drastic action of Judge James Lynch. In the 1490s, in a fit of jealousy, his son Walter murdered a Spaniard who was a guest in their household. This was a heinous crime, given the duty of care, and Walter was sentenced to death. However, the boy was very popular locally and an appeal was made on his behalf by the townsfolk, who refused to execute him. His father consequently took the law into his own hands and hanged Walter himself, from the jail window. A skull and crossbones

Galway International Oyster and Seafood Festival

Galway Bay

The Irish romance of Galway Bay is famously alluded to in The Pogues and Kirsty McColl's evergreen Christmas song *Fairytale of New York*, in the line, *the boys of the NYPD choir were singing Galway Bay*. This is most probably a reference to the traditional song *Galway Bay* by Arthur Colahan:

If you ever go across the sea to Ireland,
Then maybe at the closing of your day,
You will sit and watch the moon rise over Claddagh
And see the sun go down on Galway Bay.

carved into the stone below the window marks the spot. It is claimed this is where the term "lynching" originated.

▶ Walk around to the north side of the Church and into Mary Street.

Nora Barnacle's House

🕐*Closed to the public* ☎*091 564743.* Nora Barnacle, wife of James Joyce, lived in this cottage before she moved to work in Dublin, where she met and married Joyce. It functioned until mid-2012 as a musuem but is presently closed. Call for the latest news.

Lynch's Castle

This splendid 16C mansion belonged to the most powerful of the 14 "tribes". The grey stone façade has some fine carved gargoyles, hood mouldings over the windows and medallions with the family crest (the lynx) and one with the coat of arms of Henry VII.

Lynch's Castle

© Derek Cullen/Failte Ireland

Kirwan's Lane

Just off Quay Street, this is one of Galway's last remaining late-medieval lanes and recently been redeveloped as a residential area. It was here that the Galway MP Richard Martin built a 100-seater theatre for his actress wife in 1783. Among the many famous people who trod the boards was the great republican patriot, Wolfe Tone.

EYRE SQUARE

The focal point of the modern city, Eyre Square was officially renamed the **Kennedy Memorial Park** after the US President visited Galway in 1963, but its original name has always been in common use. The Square underwent a major redevelopment, completed 2006, and incorporates a major shopping and leisure centre.

There are several monuments: the **Browne doorway** removed from a wealthy merchant's 17C town house; cannons from the Crimean War presented to the Connaught Rangers; and a statue of **Liam Mellows**, a Sinn Féin politician, who took part in the 1916 Easter Rising and was executed by the Free State army during the Civil War.

ON THE BANKS OF THE CORRIB
Salmon Weir Bridge

The bridge was built in 1818 to link the old prison (1802–1939), on the cathedral site, with the **County Courthouse** (1812–15), where the Franciscan Abbey stood.

Upstream is the **salmon weir**; beyond are the pontoons of the late-19C viaduct of the old Galway–Clifden railway.

Roman Catholic Cathedral★

The huge neo-Romanesque cathedral, dedicated to Our Lady Assumed into Heaven and St Nicholas, was designed by John J. Robinson in 1957 and defies all the precepts of architectural modernism. It is built of black Galway "marble", the local limestone. Above the altar in St Nicholas' Chapel *(east transept)* are early-17C carved stone plaques, rescued during the Cromwellian troubles from St Nicholas' Church.

Salthill

🛈 *℘091 520 500.*

Once a small seaside resort, Salthill has now been swallowed up by Galway City. Reached by following the shoreline to the west, Salthill offers sandy beaches and a lively nightlife.

EXCURSIONS

Annaghdown Church and Priory

12mi/20km north of Galway via the N 84; in Cloonboo turn left to Annaghdown.

St Brendan of Clonfert founded this convent for his sister: the existing 15C Cathedral incorporates earlier decorated stonework, including a fine doorway and window (c. 1200).

The middle of the church is the oldest part (11C or 12C). The ruined priory *(west of the graveyard)* is a good example of a fortified monastery, built c. 1195.

Tuam

20mi/32km northeast of Galway via the N 17. 🛈 *℘093 25486 or 24463. www.tuam-guide.com.*

The tiny city of Tuam, boasting two cathedrals, is the ecclesiastical capital of Connaught and the market centre for northern Co Galway. In the 12C, when the O'Connor kings of Connaught were High Kings of Ireland, it was virtually the capital of the whole country. Its present layout, with all the streets converging on the central diamond, dates from 1613, when it was given borough status by King James I.

St Mary's Cathedral★ stands in a walled enclosure, on the site of a monastery founded late in the 5C by St Jarlath. The original cathedral dates from 1130, most of the present building, however, including the hexagonal spire *(200ft/61m)*, is the result of a neo-Gothic rebuild by Sir Thomas Deane (1860) around parts of the 12C Irish-Romanesque red sandstone chancel. The shaft of a high cross in the north aisle is inscribed with prayers for an O'Connor king. The 14C building east of the cathedral, badly damaged by the Cromwellians, has been restored to its original castellated style to serve as a Synod Hall. West of the town centre, Irish yews grow among the tombstones of **St Jarlath's Churchyard** and around the ruins of the 13C parish church, dedicated to Tuam's patron saint.

A 17C corn mill on a tributary of the Clare River *(west of North Bridge)* houses the **Mill Museum** *(🕐open May–Oct Mon–Sat 10am–5.30pm; ∞donation requested; ℘093 24141, www.tuam-guide.com)* with three sets of mill-wheels driven by an undershot spur wheel. A video provides an insight into the history of Tuam and its locality.

The cruciform neo-Gothic **Roman Catholic** Cathedral of the Assumption *(℘093 24250; www.tuamparish.com)* was one of the first major Roman-Catholic places of worship to be built in the 19C, initiated in 1827, a year before the Emancipation Act set off a wave of church construction. Funds were subscribed by the local inhabitants, regardless of denomination. Its profusion of spikes and spires prompted one 19C tourist to memorably describe the sight of the cathedral as putting him "in mind of a centipede or a scorpion thrown on its back and clawing at the sky". The Stations of the Cross are 17C, the modern stained glass is from the Harry Clarke Studios.

Knockmoy Abbey★

20mi/32km northeast of Galway via the N 17 and N 63. In Knockmoy village turn left. After crossing the river, turn right and park by the cemetery (15min walk there and back).

Set in fields on the north bank of the River Abbert are the substantial ruins of an abbey founded in 1189 for the Cister-

👥 Atlantaquaria

On the seafront promenade of Salthill, this is Ireland's National Aquarium, home to the country's largest display of indigenous marine and fresh water life. Highlights are the touch pools, and the conger eels that weigh up to 66lb/30kg.

The exhibits have been designed to mimic the various habitats of the area.

The highlight of the centre is the ocean tank, 120 tonnes of seawater and about 200 animals behind thick glass walls. Inside, is a variety of native Irish fish including cod, wrasse and shark. The tank has its own food chain: the fish and sharks are fed with locally caught squid, herring and crab, while other crab live in the tank, picking up the debris from the tank floor.

Another tank mimics the estuary where the River Corrib's fresh water mixes with the salt water of Galway Bay. Plaice, flounder, eels and grey mullet lie camouflaged on the bed of the tank.

At the splash pool, home to sea bass, every 40 seconds a surge of water mimics the ebb and flow of the waves at the beach.

The large, shallow ray pool is home to some five species of ray as well as dogfish, while the three touch pools have to be the highlight for children who can handle starfish, crabs and other denizens of the deep.

Other tanks mimic the environment of a stream bed, where young salmon fry are nurtured, a weir, a millpond and the murky environment of the harbour.

(Open Mon–Fri 10am–5pm, Sat–Sun 10am–6pm. Closed Oct–Feb Mon–Tue, except bank hol Mons and school term hols. €11.50; child €7.50. ✕ *℘091 585 100. www.nationalaquarium.ie).*

---

cians of Boyle by Cathal O'Connor, king of Connaught.

The church, with nave, a transept with two chapels and **chancel**, has some fine stone carving and a 13C tomb niche. A grill protects a rare **fresco** (1400) of the medieval legend of the Three Live Kings (dressed for hawking) and the Three Dead Kings (the inscription reads: "We have been as you are, you shall be as we are").

Athenry

13mi/21km east of Galway via the M 6.

Now a peaceful little market centre and a designated Heritage Town, in 1316 Athenry *(Baile Átha an Rí)* was the scene of one of Ireland's most savage medieval battles, when an Anglo-Norman force massacred a huge army of native Irish. The bloody encounter is commemorated in the town's 14C seal, which features the severed heads of the Irish chieftains displayed on spikes above a gateway. This was probably the North Gate, still the main feature of the defensive walls built in the early 13C by the town's founder,

the Anglo-Norman nobleman, Meiler de Bermingham.

Athenry Heritage Centre

&🕐*Open 10.30am–5pm (Fri 12.30pm-5pm), closed Sat.* ⊜*General admission €5 , Medieval Experience €8. ℘091 844 661. www.athenryheritagecentre.com.*

This lively interpretive centre within a 19C church, traces the history of the town. Its interactive **Medieval Experience** features hands-on exhibits of weaponry, armour, dressing up in medieval costume and Have-A-Go Archery.

Athenry Castle

(Dúchas) &🕐*Open early Apr–early Oct daily 9.30am–6pm, Oct-Nov Mon–Thu 9.30am–6pm.* ⊜*€5. ℘091 844 797. www.heritageireland.ie.*

Built c. 1250, the castle was destroyed in 1597. Among the ruins is a central keep with a vaulted undercroft. The main entrance, at first-floor level, is enclosed within massive walls and towers.

Dominican Friary

Down by the river on the east side of town are the ruins of a 13C-friary. In 1574 it was confiscated and burned by the Burkes; in 1627 it reverted to the friars. After restoration in 1644, the complex became a university, then in 1652, the friars were expelled by Cromwell.

Loughrea

14mi/22km SE of Athenry via the M 6 and N 65.

The town on the north shore of Lough Rea, facing the **Slieve Aughty Mountains**, was built around a Norman stronghold (c.1300) constructed by Richard de Burgo.

The local **Carmelite Priory**, now in ruins, is where General St Ruth, killed at the Battle of Aughrim, is said to be buried.

Part of one of the medieval **town gates** can be seen on the edge of the cathedral precinct.

The neo-Gothic **St Brendan's Cathedral★**, head church of the Roman-Catholic diocese of Clonfert, was designed by William Byrne in 1897. Beyond a rather dull exterior is a richly decorated interior and Celtic Revival arts and crafts furnishings.

The **Clonfert Diocesan Museum** (& ⊙open Mon–Thu 2pm–4pm (call to confirm); ℘091 841 212; if the museum is locked, enquire at the Cathedral Presbytery; P ℘091 841 212) displays vestments, missals and church plate.

ADDRESSES

⌖ STAY

GALWAY, EAST OF THE CORRIB

⊝ **Barnacle's Quay Hostel** – *10 Quay St. ℘091 568 644. www.barnacles.ie. 109 beds and 5rm.* This very friendly, very clean hostel is in the heart of the city's pedestrianised area. Breakfast Included, laundry (8€), Internet and lots of other freebies.

⊝ **Galway City Hostel** – *Frenchville Lane, Eyre Sq. ℘091 535 878. www.galwaycity hostel.com. 77 beds in dorms or private rooms.* Recently renovated hostel opposite the station. Light breakfast included; Internet access (1€/h).

⊝ **Kinlay Hostel** – *Merchants Rd, Eyre Sq. ℘091 565 244. www.kinlaygalway.ie. 150 beds and 12rm.* The best hostel in town, right in the city centre, is housed in a large, spotless building with a reception area that would grace many a hotel. Renovated in 2012 it features spacious, bright rooms and dorms. Friendly welcome. Laundry (charge), lockers, left luggage, Internet (3€/h) and free continental breakfast.

⊝ **Sleepzone** – *St Brendan's Ave. ℘091 566 999. www.sleepzone.ie. 200 beds in dorms and private rooms.* A laid-back hostel in a good location. Large kitchen, free Internet access, money changing, lockers, TV room and laundry (charge).

⊝ **The Residence Hotel** – *Quay St. ℘091 569 600. www.theresidencehotel.ie. 20rm.* Elegant and tastefully decorated hotel right in the heart of Galway's Latin Quarter, with a lively bar downstairs playing live music every weekend. Rooms are intimate and comfortable, but can be on the small side.

⊝⊝ **Jury's Inn** – *Quay St. ℘091 566 444. www.jurysinns.com/hotels/galway. 130rm.* Typical international hotel, but very well equipped. Rooms in the centre of town, overlooking the bay.

GALWAY, WEST OF THE CORRIB

⊝ **Griffin Lodge** – *3 Father Griffin Place. ℘091 589 440. www.griffinlodgegalway. com. 8rm.* A 5-min walk to the city centre, so close enough to enjoy the action and get a good night's sleep. A clean, attractive and comfortable choice.

⊝ **Linderhof** – *25 Munster Ave. ℘091 588 518. 4rm.* The perfect address: spotless, peaceful location 5min walk from the city centre, with Galway's best pubs on your doorstep. Better still, you will be welcomed like an old friend by your charming hostess, who will give you the best tips on what to see and do.

⊝ **Glencree** – *20 Whitestrand Ave. ℘091 581 061. www.glencreebandb.com. 4rm.* B&B close to the bay with pleasant simply furnished rooms.

⊝ **Roncalli** – *24 Whitestrand Ave. ℘091 584 159. www.roncallihouse.com. 6rm.* A comfortable B&B run by a charming couple who are very proud to have accommodated Bill and Hilary Clinton's daughter, Chelsea. Award-winning breakfasts.

⊝ **Abhog** – *28 Grattan Court, Father Griffin Rd. ℘091 589 528. 15min walk* *west of the city centre.* Pretty rooms offer guaranteed peace and quiet.

☐ **Devondell** – *47 Devon Park, Lower Salthill.* ✆*091 528 306. www.devondell.com. 4rm.* Pleasant modern guesthouse with antique-style furnishings including brass beds.

☐ **Liskea** – *16 Whitestrand Ave., Salthill* ✆*091 584 318. 4rm.* Simple but well-kept B&B, home-made bread and scones.

☐ **Ave Maria** – *11 Beach Court, Grattan Rd.* ✆*091 583 319. 5rm.* Set back from Grattan Rd., but still has sea views. Pretty rooms and charming owner.

☐ **Coolin House** – *11 Seamount, Threadneedle Rd.* ✆*091 523 411. www.coolinhousesalthill.com. 4rm.* Modern Georgian style B&B just off Salthill promenade. Pleasant rooms.

☐ **Clare Villa** – *38 Threadneedle Rd, Salthill.* ✆*091 522 520. 6rm. 3km from the centre, served by the bus (stop opposite).* Quiet and bright, large B&B with spacious rooms in pastel colours.

☐ **High Tide** – *9 Grattan Park, Salthill.* ✆*091 584 324. 5rm.* Slightly set back from the front, but facing the bay. A warm welcome and good breakfast choices including fish options. Highly rated.

☐ **Liscarra House** – *6 Seamount, Threadneedle Rd, Salthill.* ✆*091 521 299. 5rm.* Very highly rated, very comfortable B&B, run by a lovely couple who welcome you with tea and scones. Large breakfast.

☐ **Rock Lodge** – *Whitestrand Rd., Salthill. (15min walk from city centre).* ✆*091 583 789. www.rocklodgegalway.com. 6rm.* Nice, bright rooms.

☐ **Ross House** – *14 Whitestrand Ave., Salthill.* ✆*091 587 431. www.galwaybandb.com. 4rm.* A peaceful location, the house and décor are modern. There is a pleasant flower-filled patio at the back.

☐ **Marless House** – *Threadneedle Rd. Salthill.* ✆*091 523 931. www.marless house.com. 6rm.* Warm welcome and pleasant rooms in this large, rather formal neo-Georgian house.

☐ **St Judes** – *110 Lower Salthill Rd.* ✆*091 521 619. www.st-judes.com. 6rm.* Imposing family home a cut above most of the other guesthouses in this area. Rooms are elegant and refined, some with lovely period fireplaces. 15min walk from city centre, bus stop (5 mins to town) very close.

☐ **Inishmore Guesthouse** – *109 Father Griffin Rd, Lower Salthill.* ✆*091 582 639. 8rm.* A pretty little house smothered with flowers. Nice, peaceful rooms in a residential street 15mins from the city centre.

☐☐ **Adare Guesthouse** – *9 Father Griffin Place.* ✆*091 582 638. adare@iol.ie.* A large, very comfortable guesthouse 5min from the city centre and not much further from the sea.

☐☐ **Ocean Crest House** – *6 Ocean Wave (on the sea front).* ✆*091 589 028. www. oceanbb.com. 9rm.* Comfortable rooms (one with a jacuzzi) in a large, smartly furnished house on the seafront.

☐☐ **Westwinds** – *5 Ocean Wave.* ✆*091 520 223. www.travelaccommodation.co.uk/ westwind.htm. 8rm.* Large, comfortable B&B looking out over Galway Bay.

⛐ EAT

☐☐ **Nimmo's/Ard Bia** – *Spanish Arch, Long Walk.* ✆*87 236 8648 or 091 539 897. www.ardbia.com.* Located in the 18th Century Customs House by the banks of the river Corrib. Good value, refreshingly simple, unfussy dishes utilising quality local produce. They have produced their own cook book.

PUBS

GALWAY, EAST OF THE CORRIB

Taaffe's – *Shop St.* This pub is popular during the day for its live music *(daily between 5pm and 9.30pm).* Lively atmosphere with very varied crowd.

The Quays Bar – *11 Quay St.* ✆*091 568 347. www.louisfitzgerald.com/quaysgalway.* Hugely popular multi-room space with all kinds of music and a fascinating ecelectic interior featuring lots of old church artefacts.

The Bunch of Grapes – *Quay St.* The ideal place to begin your evening. The kind of a bar where people come for a chat or just for a pint, and the atmosphere is usually nice and welcoming.

King's Head Pub & Restaurant – *High St.* http://thekingshead.ie. Historical pub with a reputation for live music. Typical pub grub is served in its restaurant.

An Pucán – *Forster St.* www.anpucan.com. Traditional music and set dancing are the staples of this lively historic pub.

Tig Coili – *Main Guard St.* Convivial locals' pub. Excellent traditional music daily at 6pm and 9pm.

GALWAY, WEST OF THE CORRIB

Monroe's Tavern – *Fairhill Rd and Dominick St. www.monroes.ie.* A vast pub that is almost always packed, thanks to its brilliant traditional music. A new venue on the second floor stages live music nearly every night of the week from some of the country's best covers and tribute bands as well as original Irish artists. Friendly atmosphere.

The Roisín Dubh – *Dominick St. www.roisindubh.net.* This is where the big names in comedy and music play, so standards are high. Silent Discos, DJs, open mic nights, rock music, trad music and lots more every single night.

The Crane – *Sea Rd. (southwest of Dominick St). www.thecranebar.com* Some people just come to this typically Irish bar for a pint and a chat, but most come to watch undiscovered musicians playing free acoustic sets (mostly but not exclusively trad Irish) in an atmospheric intimate setting. If you take your music seriously this may be the best spot in town.

ENTERTAINMENT

Druid Theatre – *Flood St. ℘091 568 660. www.druid.ie.* Groundbreaking productions of classic and new dramatic works, drawn extensively from the Irish dramatic repertoire, in an intimate recently refurbished space.

Irish Theatre *(An Taibhdhearc na Gaillimhe)* – *Middle Street. ℘091 563 600/562 024. www.antaibhdhearc.com (in Gaelic only).* Stages Irish productions in Gaelic only, though you don't need the language to enjoy its Irish music and dance shows during August and early September.

SPORTS AND LEISURE

Galway Bay Sailing Club – *℘091 794 527. www.gbsc.ie.* Cruiser sailing, dinghy sailing, windsurfing.

Bow Waves Sailing & Powerboat School – *℘091 560 560. www.bowwaves.com.* Power and sail.

EVENTS AND FESTIVALS

Galway is famous as Ireland's festival town, with more events than any other provincial town and of a quality and size that rival even the largest festivals in Dublin and Belfast. For details of the **Oyster Festival**, the **Hookers Regatta Festival** (a hooker is a type of local boat), the famous **Arts Festival** the **Jazz Festival** and the children's **Baboro Festival** (*see Calendar of Events*).

In addition to these events is **Galway Races** (*seven consecutive days starting from the last Monday in July; www.galwayraces.com*). One of the world's top horse-racing meetings it features Ladies Day, Mad Hatters Day and all sorts of other race-related fun.

Rather more laidback is the **Film Fleadh** (*July, www.galwayfilmfleadh.com*) and the **Galway Early Music Festival** (*May, www.galwayearlymusic.com*).

Athenry Annual Medieval Festival *(weekend nearest 15 August)* – Open-air theatre and concerts, and fireworks.

SIGHTSEEING

Boat trips to Lough Corrib (*see Driving Tour) – Corrib Cruises operates various options between Cong, Inchagoill Island, Oughterard and Ashford Castle. ℘091 557 798. www.corribcruises.com.*

Services to the **Aran Islands** by air (*℘091 593 034, www.aerarannislands.ie*) and by sea (*℘091 568 903. www.aranislandferries.com*).

Galway Races
© Tourism Ireland

Connemara★★★

The largest Gaeltacht (Irish-language area) in Ireland, with many road-signs in Gaelic only, Connemara is a wild and beautiful region of mountains, lakes, tumbling streams, undulating bog, sea-girt promontories, unspoilt beaches and panoramic views. Its beauty and remoteness, together with its traces of a traditional way of life, have attracted a large crafts community who are happy to introduce visitors to their handweaving, knitting, screen printing and carving, marble inlay, jewellery and pottery.

A BIT OF HISTORY

The mountains at the heart of Connemara are the **Twelve Bens** or **Pins**, that culminate with Benbaun (2,388ft/728m). The sharp grey peaks of quartzite rock resistant to weathering rise sharply out of the blanket-bog. The Bens are drained by mountain streams and ringed by a chain of lakes, where trout are plentiful. Between the foot of the Twelve Pins and the southern coastline extends the level **Connemara Bog** dotted with innumerable tiny lakes. On a bright day the stretches of water act like mirrors reflecting the sun; in the rain, it all turns to water.

In this remote region with unyielding soils and harsh climate the people of Connemara lived in settlements dotted along the coast, resisting invaders and colonisation. For centuries the ferocious O'Flaherty clan held sway until dislodged by Cromwell, whose ruthless troop stayed on in their stronghold on Inishbofin. The population was decimated by the Famine but its Irish-speaking, peasant culture survived, exercising great fascination on Gaelic revivalists and on nationalists like Patrick Pearse.

Throughout Connemara's history, enterprising individuals have doggedly tried to implement improvements: **John D'Arcy**, a member of a long-established Galway family which had originally settled in Ireland in the reign of Eliza-

- ☷ **Info:** Galway Road, Clifden; ✆095 21163. www.discoverireland.ie/Places-To-Go/Connemara.
- ◖ **Location:** Connemara comprises all of County Galway, to the west of Galway City and occupies the broad peninsula between Killary Harbour and Kilkieran Bay. The unofficial capital of Connemara is Clifden.
- ⊛ **Don't Miss:** The scenery along the cliffs north of Clifden Bay and around Lough Corrib.
- ◔ **Timing:** Allow at least three days; longer if you wish to explore Connemara's many walking trails.
- ♙♙ **Kids:** The underground chambers of Glengowla Mine.

GETTING AROUND

BY SEA - Ferries and various cruises from Cleggan to Inishbofin. ✆095 45819. http://inishbofin islanddiscovery.com.

beth I, moved to the estate he inherited in 1815 and set about developing the new harbour town of Clifden, constantly importuning the authorities for funds to build roads to link his new settlement to Galway and Westport. The Galway road was completed in the 1820s, running through miles of uninhabited countryside between the Twelve Bens and the Connemara bog, built by labourers who had to be supplied with tents and cooking utensils.

Although a railway line to the area was eventually opened in 1895, it closed in 1935. Another reformer nurtured in this wild land was **Richard Martin**, also known as "Humanity Dick", who founded the Society for the Prevention of Cruelty to Animals; his family home, **Ballynahinch Castle** on the south shore of Ballynahinch Lake, is now a hotel.

🚗 DRIVING TOURS

THE COASTAL ROAD FROM GALWAY TO CLIFDEN
78mi/126km.

From Galway follow the R 336 towards Spiddal *(An Spidéal)* for about 10mi/17.5km. On the other side of the bay you can see the hillsides of The Burren. At 11mi/18.5km further you arrive at a crossroads; to the left the road goes to Rossavel *(Rhos á Mhil)* and to the right it crosses a wild landscape to Oughterard *(Uachter Ard)* and Lough Corrib. Follow the coast to Costello *(Casla)* and take the left fork towards Carramore *(An Cheathrín Rua)*.

Villages along the coast
At Carraroe *(An Cheathrú Rua)*, with its pretty beaches, you will be able to see "Beyond the Pale", an open air exhibition of the metal sculptures of Edward Delaney, a contemporary artist who works locally and whose works decorate many of the county's towns.

▷ From Costello take the R 336 and follow it for 20mi/32km to Screeb

Cross, then turn left on the R 340 to Gortmore (An Gort Mór), located 2mi/4km further. Watch for the signs for Rosmuc and Pearse's Cottage.

Patrick Pearse's Cottage
7mi/11.3km north of Kilkieran. (Dúchas). ⚐🕐*Open Winter 9.30am-4pm, Summer 9.30am-6pm;* ⚒€5. ✆*091 574 292. www.heritageireland.ie.*
On the west shore of Lough Aroolagh is the tiny thatched holiday cottage built by **Patrick Pearse** (1879–1916), one of the leaders of the 1916 Rising (*⚐see DUBLIN*), where he studied the Irish language.

▷ Return to the R 340

Carna Peninsula
Offshore *(south)* lies **St MacDara's Island**, where the 6C saint founded a monastery. The little church (c. 10C, restored) built of huge stone blocks, has distinctive projections on the gable ends known as *antae,* bend inwards that meet at the roof ridge, possibly aping timber cruck construction. The island can be reached by boat from **Carna**, a lobster fishing village, which holds celebrations on the saint's feast day (16 July), sailing over to St MacDara's island for Mass, followed by a series of regattas.

Roundstone harbour

© Chris Hill Photographic/Tourism Ireland

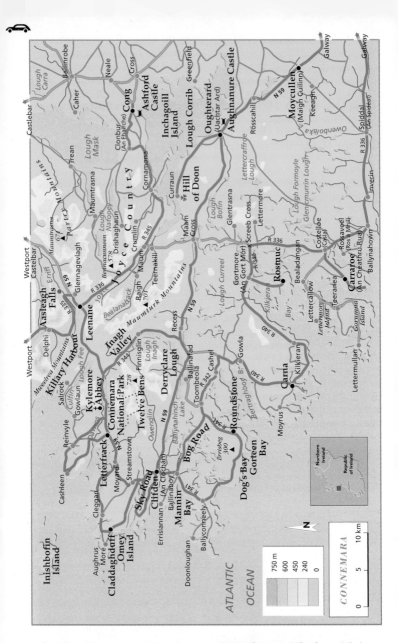

● Follow the R 340 coastal road northwards through Gowla and take the R 341 westwards and then south again, following the coast to Roundstone.

Roundstone (Cloch na Rón)★

The delightful harbour village created by **Alexander Nimmo** (⊙ see "Alexander Nimmo" box) was originally populated with fisherfolk from Scotland.

On the south side of the town is the **IDA Craft Village**, where Malachy Kearns' workshop makes the traditional *bodhrán* (goatskin drum).

Some 2mi/4km from the village in the direction of Ballyconneely the beach, one of the most beautiful of the area, stretches out along Gorteen Bay, followed a little further on by **Dog's Bay★**. It only takes a couple of hours to reach the summit of **Mount Errisbeg** from the village of Roundstone. It is not a demanding climb and the route begins by taking the path that goes along the side of O'Dowd's pub. This path turns into a track and leads you to the top, from where there are magnificent views of the Connemara landscape.

▶ Return to Roundstone and continue towards Galway for 4mi/6km, then take a left turn towards Clifden.

The Bog Road, a minor, very rough road, crosses a magic landscape of brown peat bogs, interlaced with a multitude of black lakes.

▶ This road finishes in Ballinaboy, at the mouth of Mannin Bay with another pretty beach. On the right, the R 341 carries on towards Clifden, the R 340 coastal road.

FROM GALWAY TO CLIFDEN VIA LOUGH CARRIB

49mi/79km (without detours). Allow 2hrs (a day including the boat trip).
If you are in a hurry you should choose this route, shorter but just as beautiful, to get to Clifden via Oughterard. If you have the time to spare, an excursion to the lake would be very rewarding.
Lough Corrib★★, the second-largest lake in Ireland *(36mi/58km long)*, is dotted with islands and **drumlins**, including Inchagoill island, the site of a 5C-monastery.
Beyond Moycullen *(Maigh Cuilinn)* and its Connemara marble factory (*✆091 555 102*), making all kinds of jewellery and other items from the green marble, the NR 59 joins Lough Corrib.

Aughnanure Castle

© Brian Morrison/Tourism Ireland

Aughnanure Castle★

5min walk (there and back) from the car park. (Dúchas) 🐾Tours *(45 min) early Mar–late Oct 9.30am–6pm.* ♿€5. ✆091 552 214. *www.heritageireland.ie/en.*
These formidable ruins of a tower house and bawn, probably built by Walter de Burgo, are defended but also undermined by the Drimneen River.
The circular **watch tower** is all that remains of the original bawn wall.
Most of the **Banqueting Hall** has collapsed into the river, leaving the east wall with its decorated windows. The **keep** rises through six storeys from a

Alexander Nimmo (1783–1832)

Alexander Nimmo was a Scot who came to Ireland in 1809 to assist in surveys into the economic potential of Connemara's bogland. Fortunately for the natural beauty of the area, his scheme for converting the bogs into farmland was never implemented. However his legacy to the area is the village of Roundstone plus Connemara's highway network and a number of piers and harbours.

battered base to Irish-style crenellations with a machicolation on each side. From the roof there is a fine view of Lough Corrib.

▷ Continue northwest on the N 59.

Oughterard (Uachtar Ard)★

This attractive town on the west shore is famed for its excellent fishing.

The road north runs parallel to the shore to **Curraun** (8mi/13km there and back), where the **view** of the lake and its backdrop of mountains is truly spectacular.

Beyond Oughterard (2mi/3km on N 59) you come to Ireland's only show mine, the **Glengowla Mine** 👤👤 (underground tours, 55min, 10am–6pm; tours run every 20min in high season; €10.50; 091 552 021 or 552 360; www.glengowlamines.ie). This silver and lead mine reaches down 70ft/20m, and is complete with its original timbers and many other features. Mining started in 1851 and was suspended in 1865. During that short period, 5,866sq ft/545sq m was "stopped" to produce 390 tonnes of lead containing 61.6lbs/28kg of silver. The underground tour explores large marble chambers and caverns studded with lead and silver pyrite, veins of calcite and quartz, in addition to other precious materials.

On the surface, the powder magazine, blacksmith's workshop and the agent's cottage have been restored and contain items rescued from the mine. A hand windlass and a horse-gin have been reconstructed.

Inchagoill Island★

Boat tours depart from Oughterard. Jun–Sept 11am, 2.45pm and 5pm and returning at the same times, 15€, 30mins crossing. The 11am boat continues to Cong (see p352) on the other side of the lake (€28; 1hr 30mins). For information ask at the tourist office.

In the middle of Lough Corrib, this island preserves the ruins of two churches. St Patrick's Church, reputedly built by the saint in 450 AD, preserves Europe's second-oldest Christian inscription (dating from 470 AD). The more interesting is an ornate Augustinian church built by the monks of Cong in 1178.

▷ Galway–Clifden Road, Maam Cross (An Teach Dóite) and Recess (Sraith Salach).

Galway–Clifden Road

Maam Cross (An Teach Dóite) and **Recess** (Sraith Salach) are two popular angling villages; beyond lie the many islands of **Derryclare Lough**. In the glaciated valley between the Maumturk

Clifden

© Chris Hill Photographic/Tourism Ireland

Sky Road

© Chris Hill Photographic/Tourism Ireland

Mountains *(east)* and two of the Twelve Pins, Bencorr and Derryclare *(west)*, lies **Lough Inagh**. The road curves around the foot of the **Twelve Bens★**, the twelve myth-laden peaks of Connemara, which rise to your right. The very fit can climb Ben Lettery, starting from the youth hostel of the same name *(on the right, 2mi/3km after the crossroads towards Roundstone)*, to enjoy the amazing views from the top.

CLIFDEN AND THE NORTH OF CONNEMARA★★

40mi/65km.

In the small town of Clifden, the capital of Connemara, you rejoin the crowds of tourists alive to the pleasures of a small, but lively and unpretentious destination.

Clifden

Sited at the head of a long sea-inlet and still consisting mainly of John d'Arcy's original triangle of broad streets, Clifden is the heart of Connemara. In August, people flock to the Clifden Connemara Pony Show, a major event in the local calendar. Ireland's native pony breed is celebrated at the **Station House Museum** (&Ⓒ*open May–Oct Mon–Sat 10am–5pm, Sun noon–6pm;* ᴁ*€2;* ℘*095 21494; www.connemara-pony.net/station.htm)*, together with local history

and two events that (briefly) put Connemara "in the forefront of communications technology": the opening of the Marconi radio station in 1905 at nearby Derryginlagh and the first transatlantic flight, which concluded with Alcock and Brown's crash-landing in Derryginlagh bog.

▶ From Clifden take the cliff road west.

Sky Road★★

A steep and narrow road climbs along the cliffs on the north side of Clifden Bay past the site of Clifden Castle, John D'Arcy's house. Looking south across Clifden Bay, you can see the round hump of Errisbeg (987ft/300m). As the road bears northwest over the ridge, a magnificent **view★★** stretches northwest along the coastline and offshore islands. The road descends in a curve to the head of Kingstown Bay and then continues inland along the south shore of Streamstown Bay.

▶ Leave Clifden on the N 59 towards Westport. After 2mi/3.5km, turn left towards Claddaghduff.

Omey Island★

At the village of Claddaghduff you can join, at low tide *(check the times of the*

tides at the pub in Claddaghduff), this small island of beautiful sand beaches and rocks, sheltering some houses. Races of Connermara ponies take place on the beach in summer.

▷ Take the road to Cleggan, a small, lively fishing port, 4mi/6km along the road.

Inishbofin Island★★
Ferry from Cleggan
(⊙see Getting Around).
The Island of the White Cow, where St Colman of Lindisfarne founded a monastery in the 7C, is nowadays inhabited by farmers and fishermen. The fort was used by Grace O'Malley, whose ancestors seized the island from the O'Flahertys in the 14C, then by Cromwell, who expelled the monks and interned Catholic priests there.
A great walk can be enjoyed on Inishboffin by following the road that heads west from the harbour. After about 20 minutes you reach a small beach at the island's westerly end. From here, walk over to the northern shore and join the path near the metal cross that heads back to a lake and then south to rejoin the road you arrived here on.

Connemara National Park
(Páirc Náisiúnta Chonamara)★
(Dúchas). ♿⊙*Visitor Centre open daily: Mar–Oct 9am–5.30pm.* ✕
℘095 41323 or 41054.
www.connemaranationalpark.ie.
The park (4,942 acres/2,000ha) preserves some of the finest scenery in the Twelve Bens range of mountains with areas of heath, blanket bog, grassland and natural oak and birch woodland. The flora includes Mediterranean, alpine and arctic species. The **red deer** and the **Connemara pony,** Ireland's only native pony, roam the park. From Diamond Hill (1,460ft/445m) there is a good view of the Polladirk River.
The visitor centre in **Letterfrack** village offers a good introduction to the park, including a 15min audio-visual presentation and information on walking trails and guided walks.

▷ Continue north on the N 59.
In Letterfrack make a detour left to Renvyle.

Renvyle Peninsula
From **Renvyle (Currath) Castle,** a ruined tower house belonging to the O'Flaherty, clan with a spiral stair and huge fireplace, there is a good view

Connemara National Park

© Tourism Ireland

of the Mweelrea *(Muilrea)* Mountains *(northeast)* and offshore islands – Inish-bofin *(west)*, Inishturk and Clare Island *(north)*. Renvyle House, nearby, was once home to the Dublin wit and socialite, Oliver St John Gogarty, who loved his "long, long house in the ultimate land of the undiscovered West."

▶ Return to the N 59 and continue east.

Kylemore Abbey★

&♿🕐*Visitor Centre, Abbey & Church Apr–Aug open daily 9am–6pm (7pm Jul-Aug); Sep-Oct–Mar 9.30am –5.30.* 🕐*Closed Good Fri and Christmas week.* ✆€13 (10 percent discount online).* ✗ ✆*095 52001. www.kylemoreabbeytourism.ie.*

The Irish name *Coill Mhór* refers to the "big wood" on the north shore of Lough Pollacappul at the foot of Doughrough Mountain. The turreted and crenellated neo-Gothic castle, built (1860–67) of Dalkey granite, now houses a community of Irish Benedictine nuns and a convent school. The lavish mansion was built for the Manchester financier, MP and socialite, Mitchell Henry (1826–1901). The history of the castle and convent is retold with photographs and a 12min film. The **Gothic church★** dating from 1878 (*5min walk*) is a replica of Norwich Cathedral.

The magnificent 6acre/2.5ha **Victorian walled garden★** (*shuttle bus*) is restored to its late-19C state when it was one of the most admired in Ireland. A stream and belt of trees divide the flower garden and geometrical parterres from the vegetable garden and its laid-out lazy-beds.

The buildings comprise a castellated bothy, a head gardener's house and spectacular glasshouses.

The Abbey's extensive **Craft and Design Shop** is famous for its homemade jam and its Pottery Studio.

▶ Turn right, off the N 59, heading south on the R 344.

Kylemore Abbey

© Big Smoke Studio/Tourism Ireland

Inagh Valley★★

This valley is crossed by one of the prettiest roads in Connemara, framed in the North by the tops of the Maumturk Mountains, culminating at 2,296ft/ 700m, and in the South by the Twelve Bens.

▶ After Lough Inagh, the road heads towards Derryclare Lough, through a

Cong's dry canal

Lough Mask and Lough Corrib are linked by the River Cong, which runs mainly through caves and underground channels in the limestone. The idea of creating a navigable waterway between the two great lakes seemed about to come to fruition, when men doing relief work during the Famine laboured for six years to dig a canal (4mi/7km) with three locks. In March 1854, work was suspended; costs had risen, new railways threatened competition and attempts to fill the canal came to nothing when the water drained away into the porous limestone rock. No vessel has ever floated on Cong's dry canal.

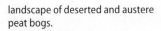

landscape of deserted and austere peat bogs.

CONG AND JOYCE COUNTRY
Allow half a day.

Cong
Access by boat from Oughterard (see "Inchagoill Island", p349) or by road. ⓘ *opposite the Abbey.* ☎ *094 954 6542.* *www.congtourism.com.*

Once the seat of the kings of Connaught, the attractive little settlement of Cong *(Conga)* sits close to the ruins of a famous abbey, on the narrow neck of land separating Lough Corrib and Lough Mask, on the Mayo-Galway border. It is a popular base for exploring the lakes, the mountains of Connemara and Joyce Country to the West. The Wilde family had a holiday house on the shore of Lough Corrib; in 1867 Oscar's father, Sir William Wilde, wrote an antiquarian guidebook, *Lough Corrib, its Shores and Islands*, still in print today.

Cong was put back on the map in 1952 when the *The Quiet Man*, starring John Wayne, was made there. At the time, the film was expected to prove a flop and the finance provided on the understanding that the cast would agree to making a Western afterwards as a way of recovering the costs. Call in at the tourist office for a *Tour Guide to the Quiet Man* that identifies various locations associated with the film, including the shop that was used as a pub, and where in the film, the horse automatically pulls up.

Cong Abbey★
The Augustinian abbey, beautifully set by the river, was founded in the 12C, probably by Turlough O'Conor, King of Connaught and High King of Ireland, on the site of an earlier monastic foundation (6C–7C). It features some very fine examples of stone carving, a lovely Romanesque doorway, **cloisters** (c. 1200), a sculpted **chapter house** and the Guest Refectory with a twisted chimney stack remain.

The **Cross of Cong**, the famous gold cross which is believed to have once contained a relic of the True Cross of Christ, is now in the National Museum in Dublin. West of the abbey grounds on an island in the river is the **monks' fishing house** (12C), with a hole in the floor through which a net could be lowered. When a fish was caught, a bell rang in the kitchen.

Quiet Man Heritage Cottage Museum
🕐 *Open Easter to mid-Oct 10am–5pm.* €5. ☎ *094 954 6089.* *www.museumsofmayo.com.*

The interior, a typical 1920s Irish cottage, is furnished as a replica of the house used in the film. Upstairs is a local collection of historic artefacts dating back to 7000 BC.

Ashford Castle
Pedestrian entrance south of the Abbey; vehicle entrance on R 346 east of Cong. 🕐 *Grounds and gardens open to non-guests daily, 9am–6pm.* €5. ☎ *094 954 6003. www.ashford.com.*

The Guinness family transformed the 13C castle, built by the de Burgos into a huge baronial residence of great sumptuousness in the 19C. It is now a luxury hotel with formal gardens, a golf course, and equestrian, falconry and fishing facilities.

Captain Boycott

From Lough Mask House (on the eastern shore of the lake) **Captain Charles Boycott** administered the estates of Lord Erne with a severity that made him extremely unpopular with his tenants. In 1880, after evicting a number for non-payment of rent, Parnell's Land League made him the first victim of the process that subsequently bore his name. The wretched man and his family were shunned and ostracised, and the land could only be worked by Ulstermen protected by troops. Boycott fled to England, securing lexicographical immortality.

Killary Harbour

© Big Smoke Studio/Tourism Ireland

10mi/16km SE of Cong by R 346 and R 344.

Ross Errilly Abbey★

Although in ruins, Ross Abbey, on the banks of the Black River, is one of the best-preserved Franciscan friaries in Ireland, founded around 1351 and extended in 1496 at a time when the Franciscans felt the need to take control of an idle and corrupt official church. In 1596 the complex was requisitioned by the English for use as barracks. Then, in 1656 it was looted by the Cromwellians, in 1753 the last monks moved away.

Among its fascinating features, note the **cloister buildings**, a second court-yard with a postern gate for entry after dark and the **kitchen**, with its big round **fish tank** and huge fireplace backing onto a large circular oven in the adjoining **bakery**. The **central tower** (70ft/21.5m), probably added in 1498, provides good **views★**.

Joyce Country★

This beautiful area takes its name from a Welsh family which settled in the mountains between Lough Mask and Lough Corrib after the Anglo-Norman invasion in the 12C. **Lough Nafooey★** lies at the foot of Maumtrasna (2,207ft/671m), while **Lough Mask** stretches towards the Parry Mountains (*west*).

The road crosses what is known as Joyce Country – named after the river that skirts the road and not the writer – a very green valley, framed with abrupt hills, often obscured by mist and clouds.

Leenane

The small village of Leenane sits at the head of **Killary Harbour★**, a narrow fjord surrounded by mountains. At The **Sheep and Wool Centre (formerly Leenane Cultural Centre)** (*open Mar–Oct, 9.30am–6pm (5.30pm, Aug-Oct); €5; 095 42323. www.sheepandwoolcentre.com*) you can learn how fleece is transformed into woollen cloth. Leenane was used to film scenes from John B Keane's *The Field* and a short walk leads one to the **Asaleagh Waterfall**, where the church scene was filmed.

East of Leenane flows the River Erriff. At this point the Aasleagh Falls are formed, a waterfall that you can reach at the end of a beautiful walk upstream. The philosopher Ludwig Wittgenstein (1889–1951) discovered this corner of Ireland when he needed to escape academic life at Cambridge University. For six months he lived in a cottage at Rosroe, near the mouth of Killary harbour, working on what would become *Philosophical Investigations*.

ADDRESSES

🛏 STAY

Letterfrack Lodge – *Letterfrack.*
*℘095 41222. www.letterfracklodge.com.
11rm.* Self-catering B&B hostel in dorms or en-suite rooms in a beautiful rural setting. Lively, informative hosts. Excellent value.

Dolphin Beach Country House – *Lower Sky Rd, Clifden. ℘095 21204. www.dolphinbeachhouse.com. 9rm.* Comfortable, modernised farmhouse in a secluded location overlooking the bay and sandy beach. The welcoming hosts produce excellent home-cooked dinners (🍽) and award-winning breakfasts featuring local produce.

The Quay House – *Beach Rd, Clifden. ℘095 21369. www.thequay house.com. 14rm. Open mid-Mar–mid-Nov.* The elegant harbour master's house, the oldest building in Clifden (1820) has been converted into a very stylish town house hotel. Breakfast is served in a lovely conservatory.

Ballynahinch Castle Hotel – *Ballynahinch. ℘095 31006. www.ballynahinch-castle.com. 37rm/ 3 suites.* The castle lies in a vast estate of 450 acres/183ha featuring scenic walks, salmon and trout fishing, sailing, shooting, horse-riding and golf. Log fires, quiet reading rooms and fine dining in the outstanding **Owenmore Restaurant** (🍽) and more casual, but still high quality dining in the **Fisherman's Pub** (🍽).

🍴 EAT

Burke's Bar & Restaurant – *Clonbur. ℘094 954 6175. www.burkes-clonbur.com. Mon–Sat 1pm–5pm; Apr–Sept 6pm–9pm daily.* Superior pub food served in a traditional countrified bar with red gingham tablecloths.

O'Dowds – *Roundstone. ℘095 35809. www.odowdsseafoodbar.com.* This lively pub is famous for its locally-sourced seafood and is especially busy at weekends with family lunches.

Ashford Castle – *℘094 9546003 (see Driving Tour).* Luxurious dining in a sumptuous setting.

SHOPPING

For crafts try the **IDA craft village** at **Roundstone** (see *South Connemara driving tour*), the craft shop at **Kylemore Abbey** (see *North Connemara driving tour*) and, for woollen goods, the **Leenane Cultural Centre** (see *North Connemara driving tour*).

SPORTS AND LEISURE

BEACHES
There is a long, sandy beach on the north shore of Clifden Bay, west of the harbour.

DIVING
Scubadive West – *Renvyle. ℘095 439 22. www.scubadivewest.com.* Ireland's leading PADI dive centre.

SEA ANGLING
In Clifden, at Letterfrack and at the **Roundstone Sea Angling Centre**. *℘095 359 52. www.seaanglingwest.net.*

FRESHWATER FISHING
In Lough Corrib, Lough Mask, Lough Nafooey, in the Joyce River, at Maam Cross and Recess.

RAMBLING
Visitors intending to walk in the hills should be properly equipped (map and compass, stout waterproof footwear, warm clothes and food) and should notify someone, preferably at the **National Park Visitor Centre** of their route and expected time of return. The National Park Visitor Centre offer guided walks during July and August.

EVENTS AND FESTIVALS

Connemara Pony Show – Clifden *(August).* Over 400 ponies from all over Ireland are on show at the Clifden Showground. *www.cpbs.ie.*

Galway International Oyster Festival – *last weekend September. www.galway oysterfest.com.* Four days and nights of music, partying and oysters in Galway City.

SIGHTSEEING

Connemara Sea Leisure: Sightseeing cruises and sea angling cruises depart from Derryinver quay on the Renvyle Peninsula. Cruises throughout the day; fishing trips at 6pm. *℘095 43473. www.crocnaraw.co.uk/Ballinakill.html.*

South Mayo★ and Westport★★

With its desolate mountains and vast beaches, Co Mayo is wilder even than neighbouring Connemara. South Mayo is home to Croagh Patrick, where every year thousands of people come to honour the patron saint of Ireland. Knock is another pilgrimage site and the modern airport of the same name serves pilgrims who come to see the place where, in 1879, people claimed to see a vision of the Virgin Mary.

WESTPORT★★

50mi/81km Northwest of Galway.
Westport *(Cathair Na Mart)*, a designated Heritage Town, occupies an attractive site on the meandering Carrowbeg River and is an excellent centre for touring the west coast of Mayo. The town was planned and built c. 1780, with more than a touch of Georgian elegance and charm, for the local landlord, John Denis Browne, of Westport House, one of Ireland's great country houses. Until the arrival of the railway in the 19C, Westport Quay was a busy port lined with imposing 18C warehouses.

Info: James Street, Westport. ℘098 25711. www.discoverireland.ie/west. www.westport tourism.com.

Location: This part of West Ireland has its own regional airport (close to the Sligo border). The N 5 bisects North and South County Mayo.

Kids: Westport House family attractions.

Don't Miss: Westport House, Ballintubber Abbey, and the scenic drive around the Murrisk Peninsula.

GETTING AROUND

BY AIR – Ireland West Airport Knock
Charlestown, Co Mayo. 9mi/14.5km northeast of Knock by N 17. ℘094 936 8100. www.irelandwestairport.com.

Town Centre★

The focal point of this neat Georgian town is the **Octagon**, where the weekly market is held. From here, James Street descends to the river past the **tourist office and Heritage Centre**, with informative displays and splendid models of the town and the nearby holy mountain of Croagh Patrick.

Westport

© David Lyons/age fotostock

The Brownes of Westport

Twelve generations of Brownes have lived at Westport, all documented in the 400-year family archive. The family is descended from Sir Anthony Browne of Cowdray Castle in Sussex, whose younger son John came to Mayo in the reign of Elizabeth I. The first house was built by Col. John Browne (1638–1711), a Jacobite bankrupted by the Williamite victory, married to the great-great-granddaughter of Grace O'Malley. Their grandson, John Browne (1709–76), was brought up an Anglican to avoid the Penal Law sanctions and ennobled as Earl of Altamont.

John Denis (1756–1809) was made Marquess of Sligo at the time of the Act of Union in 1800. The 2nd Marquess, Howe Peter (1788–1845), a friend of Lord Byron, returned from a tour of Greece in 1812 with the two columns from the doorway of the Treasury of Atreus in Mycenae; in 1906, they were presented to the British Museum.

The leafy North and South Malls follow the river, spanned by three bridges. In South Mall is **St Mary's Church**, rebuilt in the 20C as a spacious, basilica-like structure, with stained glass by Harry Clarke and Patrick Pye.

In contrast, **Holy Trinity Church** is a neo-Gothic building, with a pencil spire and an interior decorated with ornate mosaics illustrating scenes from the Gospels.

🏛 Westport House★★

🕐House & Gardens open daily Jun–Aug 10am–6pm, May & Oct 10am–4pm (extended hours school hols). Mar, Nov, Dec see website for dates and times.
🕐Closed Jan & Feb, and late Jun–early Jul for Westport Festival of Music and Food. House & Gardens: €13. House and Pirate Park: €21, child €16.50 (10 percent discount online). 🍴 📞098 277 66. www.westporthouse.ie.

The house is the work of several architects: Richard Castle designed the east front (1730), Thomas Ivory was responsible for the south elevation (1778), and James Wyatt added the west front c. 1780; the columns on the south date from 1943. The lake was created in the 18C by damming the Carrowbeg River and the garden terraces were built in the early 1900s.

A **tour** of the interior reveals an elegant décor with several distinctive features – the Pompeian frieze and cloud-painted ceiling in the drawing room commissioned by the 2nd Marquess in about 1825; a collection of **family portraits** in the Long Gallery; doors made of mahogany from the family estates in Jamaica; Waterford glass finger bowls; 18C silver dish rings and a unique **centrepiece** of bog oak and beaten silver; the **Mayo Legion Flag** brought to Mayo in 1798 by General Humbert; an **oak staircase** by James Wyatt and **marble staircase** installed by Italians; *The Holy Family* by Rubens and 200-year-old wallpaper in the **Chinese Room**. The basement **dungeons** of the O'Malley Castle, originally on this site, have now been turned into an attraction for children and is part of the **Pirate Adventure Park**, a mini-theme park for younger children. Other attractions include slides, a flume ride, an indoor soft play area, a galleon to clamber aboard, bumper cars, elegant swan pedaloe boats on the lake, and pitch and putt.

The pirate theme comes from the 16C **"Pirate Queen", Grace O'Malley,** (🔖see "Pirate Queen" box, p361) as the house was, and still is, privately owned by the Browne family, who are direct descendants of her. An exhibition inside the house will tell you all you need to know about this extrordinary character. The old **walled garden** contains a mulberry tree planted in 1690.

Clew Bay Heritage Centre

♿🕐Open Mon–Fri 10.30am–2pm, Jun–Sept Mon–Fri 10am–5pm, Sun (Jul–Aug only) 3pm–5pm. €5. 📞098 26852. www.museumsofmayo.com.

This small museum on Westport Quay is endearingly cluttered with items relating to local history and colourful characters associated with the area: the pirate Grace O'Malley (*see "Pirate Queen" box, p361*), John MacBride (1868–1916), executed in Kilmainham Gaol for his part in the Easter Rising, and William Joyce, who broadcast from Germany as Lord Haw-Haw during World War II.

EXCURSIONS
Ballintubber Abbey★★
13mi/20km SE of Westport by R 330; after 11mi/18km turn left. ♿⏱*Open year-round daily 9am–midnight.* ✆*Donation.* ☞*Tours by arrangement* ✆*€10.* ☎*094 903 0934.* *www.ballintubberabbey.ie.*

Mass has been continually celebrated for over 750 years at this wonderful Romanesque abbey. Founded in 1216 by Cathal O'Conor, King of Connaught, for a community of Augustinian canons, the abbey lost most of its conventual buildings when it was sacked in 1653 by the Cromwellians, who destroyed its timber roof. Note, however, the 13C west door and window, and 13C piscina, with a carved head in the Lady Chapel. The de Burgo chapel (now the Sacristy) contains the tomb of Theobald Burke, Viscount Mayo, who was murdered in the locality in 1629.

The **Cloisters** are in ruins but elements have survived of the 13C Treasury and

The Apparition at Knock

One wet August evening in 1879 two village women said they saw Mary, Joseph and St John bathed in light against the south gable of the church. Another 13 people, aged 6 to 75, were called to share the vision. A church commission examined all the witnesses and accepted their account. Pilgrims came in droves, cures of the sick and disabled were reported. In 1957, the church was affiliated to the Basilica of St Mary Major in Rome and special indulgences granted to pilgrims. On the centenary of the apparition, in 1979, Pope John Paul II paid the first papal visit to Ireland.

Chapter House and of the warming room, with under-floor heating ducts and an external fireplace.

The abbey is the rallying point for the revived pilgrimage *(20mi/32km)* to Croagh Patrick.

Knock
31mi/50km East from Westport via the N 5 and N 60.

Until the late 19C Knock *(An Cnoc)* was a quiet little village set on a wind-swept ridge – the Irish word "cnoc" translates

Ballintubber Abbey

© Tourism Ireland

into English as "hill" – in the middle of a vast and inhospitable bog. Today, it has become one of the world's great Marian shrines, attracting 1.5 million pilgrims a year, many of them during Knock Novena week in August, when the Statue of the Virgin is carried in procession in the grounds to celebrate the anniversary of the Apparition.

The striking white modern building on the road in front of the basilica is **Ireland's National Marian Shrine** (*℘094 938 8100. www.knock-shrine.ie*).

Church of the Apparition

The south gable of the church where the Apparition was seen (*see "The Apparition at Knock" box*) is now protected by glass, as early pilgrims used to take away pieces of the wall plaster, believing it to have miraculous powers.

Basilica of Our Lady, Queen of Ireland★

The huge, hexagonal church (over 48,000sq ft/4,500sq m), was designed by Dáithí P Hanly to hold 12,000 people and consecrated in 1976. The external ambulatory has 12 pillars of red Mayo granite and 32 pillars of stone from each of the 32 counties of Ireland. Inside, hangs a large Donegal hand-knotted tapestry of the apparition, designed by Ray Carroll. The central space accommodates the high altar; the rest is divided into five chapels dedicated to the Sacred Heart, St John the Evangelist, Our Lady of Knock, St Joseph and St Columba. The partition walls hold replica church windows from each of the four provinces of Ireland.

Knock Museum

&*Open May–Oct 10am–6pm, Nov–Apr noon–4pm.* *Closed 25–26 Dec.* ∞€5. ✕ 🅿 *℘094 938 8100. www.museumsofmayo.com.*
This folk museum houses a well-presented display illustrating the development of the Knock shrine; life in the West of Ireland in the 19C; the Papal visit in 1979 and the life and achievements of Msgr. James Horan, parish priest from 1963 to 1987.

Castlebar

12mi/19km from Westport via the N 5 and R 311.
This is the county town and commercial centre of Mayo, set on the Castlebar River. It is best known for being the place where the French General Humbert and his Irish peasant allies put a far superior British force to ignominious flight in 1798 in an episode gleefully referred to thereafter as the "Castlebar Races". Another famous local rebel was John Moore, the leader of the short-lived "Republic of Connaught". He was captured at Castlebar, died in prison and is buried by the 1798 memorial in **The Mall**.

Museum of Country Life★★

Open Tue–Sun 10am–5pm (2pm Sun). *Closed Good Fri, 25 Dec.* ✕ 🅿 *℘094 903 1755. www.museum.ie.*
Some 50,000 items from the National Museum's collections are displayed in a Victorian-Gothic mansion and a stunning, purpose-built four-storey curved, stone-clad block, blended (in theory) with the terraced landscape of Turlough Park. The richly-varied collections eschew any hint of sentimentality to present traditional life in the Irish countryside until the late 20C. Displays address the physical realities of the countryside, the unremitting cycle of work, the home, the role of women, the community, folklife and folklore.
The imposing ruin of a medieval Fitzgerald stronghold guards the approach to the park. On the far bank of the Castlebar River, the hilltop is marked by a fine round tower and a roofless church indicating the site of a monastery founded by St Patrick.

🚗 DRIVING TOURS

FROM KILLARY HARBOUR TO WESTPORT

A journey of 47mi/75km, with a detour of 22mi/36km to Silver Strand

Killary Harbour★

In fact, despite its name, this is a magnificent fjord, a narrow arm of the sea

Michael Davitt (1846–1906)

Davitt was born during the Great Famine. When he was four years old, his family was evicted for non-payment of rent and emigrated to Lancashire in England. Five years later, he was working in a woollen mill; a bad accident there meant his right arm had to be amputated. He went to a Wesleyan School; at 16 he was employed in a printing business, following evening classes in Irish history at the Mechanics' Institute. He joined the Fenian movement and rose to become secretary in Northern England and Scotland until he was arrested and imprisoned for seven years for smuggling arms.

He returned to Co Mayo (1878) and helped tenants to get better treatment from the landlords. Then he persuaded Parnell to join the movement, and the Mayo Land League was formed in Daly's Hotel in Castlebar August 16, 1879. The Irish National Land League was formed in October. During the ensuing Land War, Davitt and others were arrested under the Coercion Act (1881). On his release, he abandoned the spotlight to work as a reformer, teacher, writer and social thinker, defending the rights of agricultural labourers and trade unionism. He helped to form the GAA and travelled widely. His books – *Leaves from a Prison Diary* (1885), *The Fall of Feudalism in Ireland* (1904), and other writings – examine working conditions in Australia and South Africa.

(13 fathoms/24m deep) extending inland (8mi/13km) between high rock faces; it broadens out opposite Leenane on the South shore.

Delphi

The 2nd Marquess of Sligo renamed his fisheries, on the Bundorragha River near Fin Lough, after visiting Delphi in Greece.

There is a direct route to Westport. The Scenic Road winds its way for 12mi/20 km through deserted mountain scenery, forested areas and wild moorland to join the N 59 at Liscarney.

Doo Lough Pass★

The road, constructed in 1896, descends from the pass to **Doo Lough** (2mi/3.2km long), which is enclosed by the **Mweelrea (Muilrea) Mountains★★** (2,668ft/817m) *(west)* and the **Sheeffry Hills** (2,504ft/761m) *(east)*; at the southern end of the lake rises Ben Gorm (2,302ft/700m).

Killeen

A cross-inscribed stone stands in the northwest corner of the graveyard.

Turn right at the crossroads; after 0.5mi/0.8km turn right and park.

Bunlahinch Clapper Bridge★

Beside a ford stands an ancient clapper stone footbridge of 37 arches constructed by laying flat slabs on stone piles.

Return to the crossroads. Either go straight across or turn right to make a detour (10mi/16km there and back) to Silver Strand.

Silver Strand★★

The vast sandy beach (2mi/3.2km) is sheltered by dunes.

Take the road towards Roonagh Quay for the ferry to Clare Island.

Clare Island★

Clare Island Ferry (see Addresses). Bicycles for hire at the island harbour. http://ecofarm.ie/island.
Bounded by 300ft/90m cliffs and rising to 1,512ft/461m at the summit of Mount Knockmore, the massive bulk of Clare Island commands the entrance to Clew Bay. Grace O'Malley spent her childhood in the castle by the quay; she may be buried in the Carmelite friary, which was founded on the island by the O'Malleys

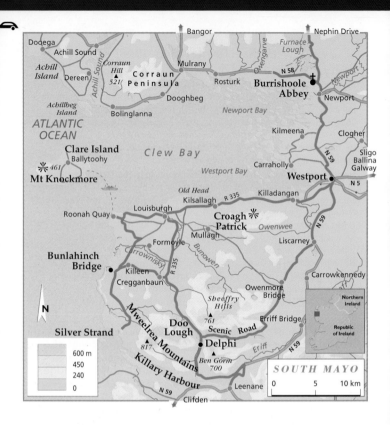

in 1224, although the ruins are of later date. The sandy beach near the harbour is safe for bathing and used for water sports. Traditional Irish music is played in the island pubs.

From Roonagh Quay head southeast through Askillaun to Louisburgh, about 8mi/12km

Louisburgh

The central octagon of this charming little 18C town on the Bunowen River was laid out by the 1st Marquess of Sligo, whose uncle Henry had fought against the French at the Battle of Louisburgh in Canada.

The **Granuaile Heritage Centre** (open Mon–Fri 10am–5pm; €4; 098 66341) traces the family tree of the O'Malleys, the history of the clan and their territory, and the life of Grace O'Malley, "the Pirate Queen" (see "Pirate Queen" box, p361).

From Louisburgh head towards Westport. After 8mi/13 km stop in the car park for Croagh Patrick.

Croagh Patrick★

2hr on foot to the summit.
The distinctive conical mass of Ireland's sacred mountain (2,503ft/763m) dominates Clew Bay and its countless islands. According to legend all the snakes in Ireland plunged to their death when St Patrick rang his bell above the mountain's steep southern face. Up to 100,000 pilgrims, some of them barefoot, climb the stony slopes to the summit on the last Sunday in July ("Reek Sunday") in his honour. Traditionally, the climb was completed by torchlight, possibly an echo of the old Celtic festival of Lughnasa. Recent excavations have shown that the narrow plâteau at the top was occupied by a pre-Christian hillfort, then by a Early Christian oratory; the present one dates from 1905.

Granuaile, the Pirate Queen

Granuaile, also known as **Grace O'Malley** (1530–1603), gained fame for resisting English rule as a female pirate. From her strongholds in Clew Bay, where the many islands made pursuit difficult, she commanded a fleet of privateers who preyed on ships in Galway Bay, imposing pilot charges or confiscating cargoes. She had two sons and a daughter from her first marriage to Donal O'Flaherty, who owned castles at Ballynahinch and Bunowen in Connemara. Her second marriage (1566) to Iron Richard Burke gave her Carrigahowley Castle, where she brought up her youngest son, Theobald Burke. In 1574 she successfully repelled an English attempt to besiege the castle.

In 1593 she sailed to Greenwich to successfully petition Elizabeth I for the release of her brother, Donal-Na-Piopa, and son, Theobald Burke, who had been arrested in order to try to exert control over O'Malley. Burke was later made Viscount Mayo by Charles I in 1627.

The superlative **panorama**★★ of sea and mountains is ample reward for the rigour of the climb, best begun from the **Croagh Patrick Information Centre** (&◔*open 17 Mar–May 10am–6pm, Jun–Aug 10am–7pm, Sept–Oct 11am–5pm, Nov–17 Mar (call for times);* ✕; ✆098 64114; www.croagh-patrick. com), which gives essential information about the mountain as well as useful tips for the ascent.

On the opposite side of the road to the Centre, John Behan's startling modern sculpture of a "coffin ship" constitutes the **National Famine Monument**.

Westport
&*See Westport, p355.*

NORTH OF WESTPORT
25mi/40km. Allow half a day.

▷ From Westport take the N 59 north.

Newport
The charming little angling resort is dominated by its disused railway viaduct (1892), now converted into an unusual walkway across the Newport River. The broad main street climbs the north bank to St Patrick's Church (1914), which contains a particularly spectacular **stained-glass window** by Harry Clarke.

▷ Continue north on the N 59; after 1mi/2.4km turn left.

Burrishoole Abbey★
The ruins of a Dominican Friary, founded in 1486, lie by a narrow inlet where the waters of Lough Furnace drain into the sea. A squat tower marks out the church. The east wall is all that remains of the cloisters. In 1580 the friary was fortified and garrisoned by the English.

▷ Continue north on the N 59; after 2.5mi/4km turn left.

Carrigahowley Castle (Rockfleet)
This 15C/16C four-storey tower house is built on flat rocks beside a sea-inlet commanding Clew Bay. In 1566, the owner, Richard Burke, married Grace O'Malley (&*see box, above*).

▷ Take the N 59 east; after 1mi/1.6km turn left.

Furnace Lough★
A narrow switchback road loops north between Lough Furnace and Lough Feeagh. Where the waters of Lough Feeagh run over the rocks into Furnace Lough, there is a salmon leap where the numbers of fish moving up and downstream are monitored. There is a **view** north to Nephin Beg (2,065ft/628m).

▷ Continue west on N 59 and R 319.

ADDRESSES

🏠 STAY

WESTPORT

🛏 **Ashville House** – *Castlebar Rd. 2mi E on N 5.* ℘*098 27060. http://homepage. eircom.net/~ashville. May–Aug. 9rm.* This guesthouse is a couple of miles outside of town but it may be worth it for the tennis court, large garden and suntrap terrace. A warm welcome is assured.

🛏 **Augusta Lodge** – *Golf Links Rd. 0.5mi N off N 59.* ℘*098 28900. www.augusta lodge.ie. Closed one week at Christmas. 10rm.* There's a clue in the name. Not only is this guesthouse close to the local course but the owner has his golfing memorabilia displayed in the lounge, along with a wall-mounted map highlighting all of Ireland's courses. The Lodge even has its own putting green.

🛏 **The Wyatt Hotel** – *The Octagon.* ℘*098 25027. www.wyatthotel.com. Closed 23–27 Dec. 49rm.* Contemporary lodgings in a traditional building in the heart of the town. Its busy bar is a popular local spot and the restaurant (🍴🍽) menu features assorted influences from around the world. Bedrooms are attractive and comfortable. Excellent value.

CASTLEBAR

🍴– 🍴🍽 **Lynch Breaffy House Hotel & Spa** – *2mi/4km outside Castlebar on the Claremorris Rd.* ℘*094 902 2033. www.breaffyhouseresort.com. 125rm.* This grand 19C manor house has been converted into a very smart hotel complex and spa. Terrific value.

LEENANE

🛏🍴🍽 **Delphi Lodge** – *Leenane. 8.25mi NW by N 59 on Louisburgh Rd.* ℘*095 42222. www.delphilodge.ie. Closed 20 Dec–6 Jan. 12rm. Cottages also available.* Dwarfed by the surrounding mountains and nestling by the lake, this Georgian sporting lodge boasts an unrivalled setting and is much-loved by holidaying fishermen. Communal dinner (🛏🍴🍽) around the large polished table allows guests the chance to discuss the one that got away.

🍴 EAT

WESTPORT

🍴 **Matt Molloy's** – *Bridge St.* ℘*098 26655. www.mattmolloy.com.* The eponymous Matt Molloy is a member of the celebrated Irish folk band, The Chieftains, and nightly live music plays a big part in this town centre pub. It is lively, noisy and atmospheric; the quintessential Irish pub experience.

🍴🍽 **Sage** – *10 High St.* ℘*098 56700 www.sagewestport.ie. Closed Mon, Tue (call ahead).* Simple neighbourhood bistro, with bubbly service and a laid-back feel. The menu focuses on Italy (though not exclusively so), so you'll find homemade pasta, risotto and plenty of seafood. Portions are huge.

🍴🍽 **An Port Mór** – *Brewery Pl, Bridge St.* ℘*098 26730. www.anportmor.com. Closed Monday except Jul-Aug & bank hols.* Compact interior with shabby-chic, Mediterranean-style décor. Classically based menu showcases local produce in elaborate dishes; seafood specials on the blackboard.

CASTLEBAR

🍴 **Cafe Rua** – *New Antrim St.* ℘*094 902 3376. www.caferua.com. Open Mon–Sat 9am–6pm.* Winner of *Good Food Ireland Cafe of the Year* in 2012–13, this splendid cafe/deli uses locally sourced products. Their ready-to-go salads in the summer are great.

SPORTS AND LEISURE

Sailing, fishing, walking and horse riding; sandy beaches to the southwest (Silver Strand).

Castlebar International 4 Days' Walks – *Held late Jun–early July.* ℘*094 902 4102. www.castlebar4dayswalks.com.*

SIGHTSEEING

Clare Island Ferry – *Operates from Roonagh Quay (20min) Jul–Aug, 6 times daily; May, Jun and Sept, 4 times daily. There and back €17.* ℘*098 23737, 086 8515 003, 098 25212 (winter); www.clareislandferry.com.*

North Mayo★

and Achill Island★★

The north of Mayo is not one of the better-known parts of Ireland. Its landscape is characterised by low mountains and turf bogs, an area scantly inhabited, and unspoilt by progress. Achill Island attracts visitors drawn to its scenery and beaches, but for the rest of the area expect wide empty roads through bleak desolate bogland and brooding landscape.

Besides the beautiful Achill Island, the chief draw here are the Céide Fields, a rare prehistoric site.

ACHILL ISLAND★★

Population: 2,701.

Approached by a bridge from the Corraun Peninsula, Achill Island is Ireland's largest (36,223 acres/14,659ha) – a wonderful mixture of sandy bays and spectacular cliffs dominated by two peaks, Slievemore (2,204ft/671m) and **Croaghaun★★★** (2,192ft/667m).

Once poor and remote, its economy dependent on emigrants' remittances, the island's fortunes waxed as it attracted artists and writers such as the painter Paul Henry and German Nobel Prize winner Heinrich Böll.

> **Info:** Cathedral Rd, **Ballina**, ✆096 70848; Achill Sound, **Achill Island**, ✆098 20705. www.achilltourism.com.
>
> **Location:** Ballina is 61mi/98km north of Galway. Achill Island is on the West Coast of Co Mayo and is accessible only by road.

Today, stimulated by the excellent conditions for surfing, boating and sea angling, tourism has brought prosperity.

On the shore of Achill Sound, south of the bridge, stand the restored ruins of **Kildavnet (Kildownet) Church** (c. 1700), which contains Stations of the Cross in Gaelic and is dedicated to Dympna, an Irish saint who sought shelter on Achill in the 7C. **Kildavnet** *(Kildownet)* **Castle**, a square, four-storey 15C **tower house**, commanding the southern entrance to Achill Sound, was one of the strongholds of the redoubtable Grace O'Malley (◐*see box p361*); there are traces of a boat slip.

Trawmore Strand★ has a splendid sandy beach backed by cliffs. **Keel** is the main resort; at the southeastern end of its long beach the cliffs have been sculpted into bizarre forms. **Keem Strand★**, too, has a lovely sandy shore,

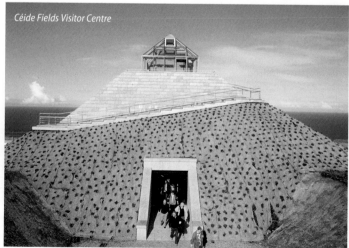

Céide Fields Visitor Centre

© Designpics/Photoshot

The Year of the French, 1798

In August 1798 a force of 1 067 French revolutionaries under General Humbert landed at Kilcummin in Killala Bay and Humbert appointed John Moore as President of the Provisional Government of Connaught in Killala; as the French advanced inland they were joined by enthusiastic, but ill-equipped Irishmen. Their first success was at Ballina; then they met General Lake and his vastly superior force of militia and yeomanry. Although outnumbered, General Humbert routed his opponent and the ignominious retreat of General Lake's cavalry became known as the **Races of Castlebar**. At Carrignagat, they had their third victory. Humbert moved southeast, hoping to avoid the English army and join up with the United Irishmen, but the latter had been defeated; he was defeated at Ballinamuck, near Longford. The French were taken prisoner, while the Irish were hanged as traitors.

The 1798 Rebellion was re-enacted in Killala in 1981 for the film version of Thomas Flanagan's historical novel, *The Year of the French*.

sheltered by the great mass of Croaghaun, whose northwestern face plunges spectacularly seaward forming one of the most awesome sea-cliffs in Europe, best viewed by boat.

Between Keel and the little north coast resort of **Doogort** are the remains of abandoned settlements.

🚗 DRIVING TOURS

NORTH MAYO COASTLINE
Bangor to Killala 93mi/150km

The North Coast of Co Mayo confronts the Atlantic with a line of dramatic sea cliffs, broken only by **Broad Haven**, a wide bay of sandy coves, narrow sea-inlets and tiny habitations, enclosed by **Benwee Head** (829ft/253m – *east*) and **Erris Head** (285ft/87m – *west on the Belmullet Peninsula*). Inland, the country is largely covered in Atlantic blanket bog (400sq mi/1,036sq km): its turf is extensively harvested by machine to fuel the power station at Bellacorick, which is supplemented by wind turbines.

Belmullet

This practical, basic little town *(Béal an Mhuirthead)*, in one of the least populated areas of Europe, was a latecomer to the Irish scene, founded in 1825 by William Carter, a local English landlord. Its market rapidly became an economic

hub for the local area. The town is distinguished by its two bays and by a canal built in the 19C, which runs between them, originally built for small boats to pass through.

The town has everything you might need if you wanted to stay – some decent pubs, accommodation but there is little to keep you here. There is sea and freshwater fishing on nearby Cross Lake and boat hire to be arranged, plus trips to the tiny islands of Inishkea.

Mullet Peninsula

This tiny strip of land projecting into the Atlantic is 19mi/30 km by 8mi/12km at its widest, narrowing to 164ft/50m at Elly Bay. It is home to several villages and encloses Blacksod Bay and Broadhaven Bay. The area is part of the Mayo Gaeltacht and there are several language schools on the peninsula. For the visitor the attractions are the sandy, empty beaches at Elly Bay and Mullaghroe, a growing reputation for watersports and some pleasant walks along the coast. Several promontory forts have survived the lashing Atlantic winds along the western coast.

The waters of Blacksod Bay are the last resting place of *La rata*, a Spanish ship sunk there in 1588.

▷ From Belmullet take the R 313 then turn left and follow the coast along the

R 314 . At Glenamoy turn left towards Portacloy.

Benwee Head★★

This is the northwest extremity of Ireland, populated largely by sheep. The deserted sandy beach here is surrounded by high cliffs. From the little quay at the western end of the beach a path *(take great care on along the cliff edge)* will take you to Benwee Head, overlooking a series of rock stacks known as the Stags of Broadhaven.

▶ Retrace your route to Glenamoy then rejoin the R 314 . Céide Fields is 5mi/8km west of Ballycastle.

Céide Fields★★

(Dúchas) ♿ ⟶ *Visit by guided tour only (1hr), early Apr–early Nov 10am–5pm (6pm Jun–Sept). Last tour 1hr before closing.* ☺*Be sure to dress warmly and wear walking shoes.* ⬤ €5. ✗ ☎096 43325. www.heritageireland.ie. Most of North Mayo is covered by blanket bog, a desolate and seemingly unwelcoming landscape. However, this conceals fascinating evidence of settled and productive prehistoric occupation. Using iron probes and bamboo markers, archeologists have mapped several square miles of fields laid out by the Neolithic people who lived near the Céide Cliffs over 50 centuries ago and who were contemporaries of the tomb builders of the Boyne Valley.

In fact, these are not only the most extensive Stone-Age monuments in the world, but the stone-walled fields, extending over thousands of acres, are almost 6,000 years old and the oldest known in the world.

The centrepiece of the strikingly-modern **visitor centre** is a large, twisted 4,400 year-old Scots pine found in the vicinity; displays explain the geology and evolution of the bog, reaching depths of 13ft/4m. Parts of a primitive plough and postholes suggest how the Stone-Age farmers might have cleared the land of primeval forest and piled stones to create enclosed fields and houses. A bonus is that the centre is located beside **spectacular cliffs** and rock formations and a viewing platform is on the edge of the 110m/361ft high cliff.

▶ Stay on R 314 to Ballycastle and then north on a minor road.

Downpatrick Head★

The projecting headland is undermined by the sea, which comes up through a **blow hole** *(fenced off)*.

Just offshore stands Dunbriste, a rock stack surmounted by a prehistoric earthwork, probably detached from the

Moyne Abbey

© Timothy Kirk/Dreamstime.com

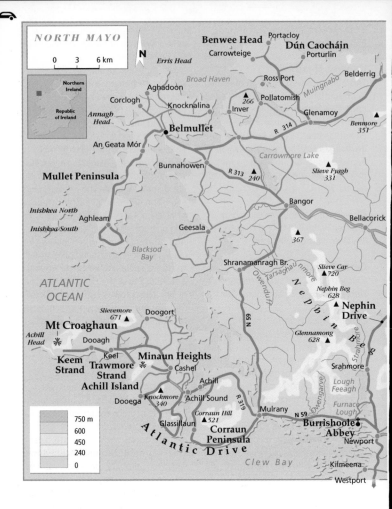

mainland in 1393. The views are superb, taking in *(E)* Benbulben and the Dartry Mountains north of Sligo, *(SE)* the Ox Mountains *(Slieve Gamph)*, *(SW)* the Nephin Beg Mountains, *(W)* the cliffs to Benwee Head and the Stags of Broadhaven offshore.

▶ Retrace your route to Ballycastle and rejoin the R 314.

Killala★

Killala *(Cill Ala)* is a quiet seaside resort overlooking Killala Bay at the mouth of the River Moy, and Bartragh Island, a narrow sandbank. It has a sandy beach and plenty of sports facilities. The harbour warehouses are a reminder of its importance in the past, most notably as it was here that the French first halted when they invaded in 1798. Traces of occupation are still to be seen.

St Patrick's Cathedral – The present Anglican **cathedral** was erected in 1670 by Thomas Ottway, Bishop of Killala, using stone from the ruined medieval cathedral, including the south doorway and Gothic east window. The great 12C **round tower**, built of limestone (84ft/25m high) was recapped in the 19C.

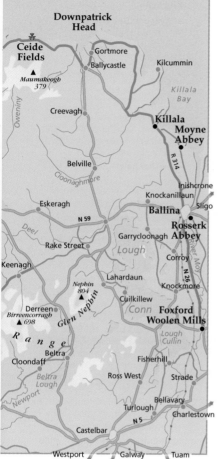

◗ Continue S; on reaching the Rosserk River, turn left.

Rosserk Abbey★

The abbey on the Rosserk River, a tributary of the Moy, was the first Franciscan house to be built in Ireland and its ruins are some of the best preserved in the country.

◗ Return to the T-junction and turn left; continue south.

Ballina

Busy Ballina, the largest town in North Mayo, offers good salmon fishing on the River Moy.

The **Cathedral of St Muredach** on the east bank was built in the 19C, next to the ruins of a late-14C Augustinian **friary**.

Foxford Woollen Mills★

🕐 *May–Oct 10am–6pm (noon Sun), Nov–Apr 10am–6pm (2pm Sun).* ✎Last tour 5.30pm. ✗🅿 ℘094 925 6104. www.foxford-woollenmills.com

The mills were set up by the Irish Sisters of Charity in 1890. The nuns are no more, but the famous Foxford blankets, rugs and tweeds continue to be sold. A presentation about the history of the mill is followed by a self-guided tour of the 1930s' machinery and a view of the many stages of production. The mills also hold two art galleries.

◗ From Ballina drive through Castleconor for 9mi/14km.

Inishcrone *(Enniscrone)*

This is a popular family seaside resort on the east coast of Killala Bay.

The local speciality is a traditional Irish seaweed bath at the elegant Edwardian **Kilcullen Seaweed Baths** (🕐open Jun–Sept 10am–8pm, Oct–May noon/Sat–Sun 10am)–8pm. ☜€25 (€32 per couple); ✗; ℘096 36238; www.seaweed.ie/baths).

MOY ESTUARY
20mi/32km.

The coast road around the estuary of the salmon-rich River Moy passes close to the exceptionally picturesque ruins of two 15C Franciscan establishments, and continues to North Mayo's largest town, Ballina, and Inishcrone beyond.

◗ From Killala take the coast road S.

Moyne Abbey★

The extensive remains of the Franciscan friary at Moy include cloisters, sacristy, chapter-house, kitchen, refectory, church and splendid six-storey tower.

ADDRESSES

🛏 STAY

ACHILL

🛌 **Stella Maris** – *Keel. 8rm.* 📞*098 43297. www.stellamarisachill.com.* A modern house in the village with exuberant, decorative period-style bedrooms (some with four-poster beds).

🛌 **West Coast House** – *School Rd, Dooagh. 4rm.* 📞*098 43317. www.achill westcoasthousebandb.com.* Modern house with pleasant bedrooms and great views. Fine dining (🍴🍴) with fresh local seafood a speciality.

🛌 **Woodview House** – *Springvale, Achill Sound.* 📞*098 45261. 4 rms.* Scenic surroundings, lovely views of the bay, small rooms.

🛌🍴 **The Bervie** – *Keel. 14rm.* 📞*098 43114. www.bervie-guesthouse-achill.com.* This beautifully restored coastguard station sits right in front of the beach. Attractive bedrooms, superb evening meals (🍴🍴).

🛌🍴 **Joyce's Marian Villas** – *Keel. 20rm.* 📞*098 43134. www.joycesachill.com.* An old house, well renovated in the centre of Keel village with breathtaking surroundings overlooking Keel beach and the Minaun Cliffs. Guests are welcomed with tea and scones.

BALLINA

🍴🍴 **Twin Trees Hotel & Leisure Club** – *Downhill Rd.* 📞*096 21033. www. twintreeshotel.ie.* Within walking distance of town, this family-friendly roadside hotel was voted Best Three Star Hotel in Ireland by *Hotel & Catering Review* in 2012. It features an 18m indoor pool, jacuzzi and steam room. Fine dining (🍴🍴) in the restaurant.

BELMULLET

🛌 **Kilcommon Lodge Hostel** – *Pollatimish.* 📞*097 84621. www. kilcommonlodge.ie.* Adorable cottage, nestled at the foot of a hill and ideally located for hikers. Dorm beds, private and family rooms; 4 course evening meals available. A good range of facilities.

KILLALA

🛌 **Avondale B&B** – *Pier Rd. 096 32229.* By the quayside, a small, unpretentious house with a pretty garden. Home baking and friendly owners.

🍴 EAT

ACHILL

🛌 **The Beehive** – *Keel.* 📞*098 43134.* Self-service food throughout the day, with outdoor tables on a patio that has views out to sea.

🍴🍴 **The Chalet** – *Keel.* 📞*098 43157.* Seafood has been the speciality of this split-level dining room, overlooking the Minaun Cliffs, since 1956.

🍴🍴🍴 **Ferndale Restaurant** – *Crumpaun, Keel.* 📞*098 43908. www. ferndale-achill.com.* This luxury fantasy-themed B&B extends its ambitions in the kitchen to probably the most eclectic and global menu you will ever come across! Excellent reviews.

BALLINA

🛌 **Brennan's Lane**– *Garden St.* 📞*096 74044. www.brennanslane.ie.* A new addition to the Ballina pub scene, Brennan's Lane has quickly established itself as something special. Tastefully decorated in tones of dark wood and leather, it serves up some delicious and inventive food. Try the monkfish wrapped in banana leaves with ginger.

🍴🍴 **Crockets on the Quay** – 📞*096 75930. www.crocketsonthequay.ie.* This well-known bar and restaurant serves up a menu of superior pub food dishes.

SPORTS AND LEISURE

All sorts of watersports may be found around Killala Bay. There is salmon fishing in the River Moy and in the Deel River at Crossmolina, as well as canoeing on the Moy River at Foxford.

The **seaweed baths** at Inishcrone (🕐*see Moy Estuary Driving Tour*) are a must.

👫 Children will enjoy the flumes and fun pool at **Waterpoint Leisure Centre** (*www. waterpoint.ie*), which also has a full spa for adults.

Farming dominates the Northwest, with tiny cattle- and sheep-rearing farms run by part-time farmers, doing their day job and then returning home to milk the cows and cut the hay, sustained by EU grants, and feeling the cold winds of agricultural reform. This is also border country and even in Sligo you can hear the Northern Ireland accent beginning to emerge. Donegal, Cavan and Monaghan are part of the traditional province of Ulster, dissected from their natural affinities in 1921 when Northern Ireland was created.

Co Sligo

Bordered by the Atlantic Ocean to the Northwest and by Mayo, Roscommon and Leitrim to the West, South and East, County Sligo (*Contae Shligigh*), at 1,795sq km/695sq mi) is Ireland's fifth smallest county and fourth-least populated with 32 people per square kilometre, compared to Leitrim's 16 or Antrim's 199.

In the West of the county is the Ox Mountain range (*Slieve Gamph*) with Knockalongy (*Cnoc na Loinge*) at its highest point, while in the Northeast is the King's Mountain range with the startling Benbulben (*Binn Ghulbain*) rearing out of the landscape. The county town is Sligo, nestling beside the beautiful Lough Gill, where the Northwest's tourists can all be found, enjoying the Innisfree bus and boat tours. Sligo has Ireland's highest concentration of megalithic monuments, Carrowkeel and Carrowmore being essential parts of a visit to the county.

Co Donegal

Donegal (*Contae Dhún na nGall*) is the most Northwesterly county in Ireland, its second-largest in size at

Highlights

1 Climbing **Benbulben** to enjoy uninterrupted views (p375)

2 Taking the picturesque **Lough Gill** Driving Tour (p378)

3 Exploring the remote and rugged **Donegal Coast** (p383)

4 Getting away from it all in the quiet **Northern Peninsulas** (p389)

5 Viewing 20C artwork at the **Glebe House and Gallery** (p393)

4,830sq km/1,864sq mi), and its third least populated at about 28 people per square kilometre. Its only link to the rest of the Republic is the tiny border with County Leitrim, the rest of the land borders counties in Northern Ireland. For this reason the county has long stood apart from the rest of the 26 counties, being more closely connected with Derry, Tyrone and Fermanagh than those of the Republic. It has the highest population of Gaelic speakers in Ireland and also a strong Gaelic cul-

Carrowmore Megalithic Cemetery, Knocknarea in the background, County Sligo

© Alison Crummy/Fáilte Ireland

Malin Head,
County Dounegal

© Chris Hill/Tourism Ireland

ture. Its outstanding feature is the vast, tessellated coastline but almost all the county is mountainous, with the Blue Stack Mountains in the South, the Glendowan and Deryveagh Mountains in the West and the low mountains of the Inishowen Peninsula in the North. The mountainous nature of the region has been held responsible for the county's poor economic development; farms are tiny and hug the lower-lying coastline while undeveloped infrastructure has hampered industrial growth. The county town is Lifford, although Letterkenny is much larger

Co Leitrim

A county in two halves, dissected by Lough Allen, County Leitrim is Ireland's least populated county. Due to Industrialisation, the Great Famine and emigration, population had been in continuous decline from 1841, however, recent years have seen a marked increase in population.

The northern half of the county is made up of limestone mountain ranges – Selcannasaggart and Tievebaun Mountains in the West and Crocknagrapple and Dough Mountains in the East. The county is graced with about 3mi/5km of coastline. The South section is lower-lying, poorly drained and dominated by drumlin hills, but what is bad news for

the small farmers of Leitrim is good news for the tourist. The county offers lush, green countryside interspersed with the calm waters of its loughs. Lough Melvin is a Special Area of conservation and famous for its salmon fishing, Lough Allen offers beautiful views of the Iron Mountains and Lough Gill is home to Parke's Castle and stunning lakeland views.

Co Cavan

County Cavan (Contae an Chabháin) is border country, planted by English and Scottish settlers in the 17C, divided from its natural home in Ulster by the partition. The tiny county town is Cavan (population about 3,500), on the main route between Dublin and Enniskillen. The county's population was decimated by the Famine and it was in economic decline until the late-20C. Tourism and the "Celtic Tiger" have improved matters, in particular the reopening of the Ballyconnell and Ballinamore Canal, creating the Shannon–Erne waterway in 1994. The chief attractions are the loughs, favourites of coarse fishermen, and the rivers Erne and Shannon, both of which pass through the county. Cavan is home to the comedian Dylan Moran, famous for his surreal narratives and teasing of his home town.

Co Monaghan

Tiny and thinly populated, Monaghan borders Northern Ireland counties Fermanagh, Tyrone and Armagh and is part of the historical province of Ulster. In the years leading up to the Famine it had a strong domestic linen weaving industry and was consequently densely populated. As a result the county experienced one of the highest mortality and emigration rates in the country. The eponymous county town, cathedral town of the catholic diocese of Clogher, prospered in the early 19C as a corn and linen market and its surviving buildings are an indication of former wealth. Co Monoghan is the birthplace of the poet Patrick Kavanagh. It is also home to Castle Leslie, the 1870 baronial-style mansion, now an exclusive hotel.

Co Sligo★★

Sligo Town has a lively cultural scene: theatre, music and high-profile art installations at the Model Arts Centre; festivals stud the calendar; the Yeats Memorial Building hosts a famous summer school devoted to the work of the poet and his family. All this urban bustle contrasts strongly with the unspoilt countryside beyond, its fine sandy beaches at Strandhill and at Rosses Point, where there is also a championship golf course.

SLIGO

Sligo *(Sligeach)* is a busy market town and an important shopping and cultural centre for much of the Northwest of Ireland. It stands on the River Garavogue, which drains Lough Gill into the sea. One of its greatest assets is the beautiful and varied surrounds – green and wooded valleys, lofty mountains, sandy seashores and an exceptional wealth of prehistoric monuments.

Sligo and its surroundings are intimately associated with the Yeats family: the portrait painter John B. Yeats, the artist Jack B. Yeats and the poet William Butler Yeats (1865–1939).

A Bit of History

A Turbulent Past – In 807 Sligo was plundered by the Vikings. Following the Norman invasion in the 13C it was granted to Maurice Fitzgerald. Over the following 200 years, its possession by the O'Conors was disputed by the O'Donnells. A fort was built by the Cromwellians. Patrick Sarsfield reinforced the defences so that Sligo was one of the last places to capitulate after the Battle of the Boyne (1690). The Battle of Carrignagat (1798) was fought south of the town.

A Prosperous Port – In the 18C and 19C Sligo developed into a busy trading port, from which many emigrants set out for the New World. Buildings from that period include the warehouses by the docks, the Courthouse (1878) and the Italianate City Hall (1865).

The stone lookout turret, known as the **Yeats Watch Tower** *(no public access),*

- 🛈 **Info:** Ground Floor, Bank Bldg, O'Connell St. ℘071 916 1201. www.sligotourism.ie.
- ▷ **Location:** Sligo is a hub: N 4 to Dublin, N 15 to County Donegal, N 16 to County Cavan); 40mi/64km southwest of Donegal.
- **Don't Miss:** The Lough Gill Driving Tour.
- 🕐 **Timing:** Allow a couple of days to experience the area.

GETTING THERE

BY AIR – **Sligo Airport:** ℘071 916 8280. www.sligoairport.com.

marks the warehouse owned by W. B. Yeats' mother's family, the Pollexfen dynasty of Sligo merchants and sea traders.

Sligo Abbey★

(Dúchas) 🕐*Open Apr–mid-Oct daily 10am–6pm.* ⊛*€5.* ℘*071 914 6406. www.heritageireland.ie.*

The ruins on the south bank of the Garavogue River occupy the site of a Dominican friary, founded by Maurice Fitzgerald c. 1252, damaged by an accidental fire in 1414; the refurbished buildings (1416), spared by Queen Elizabeth on condition that the friars became secular clergy, were torched in 1641 by the Parliamentary commander Sir Frederick Hamilton.

The nave contains an elaborate altar tomb honouring the O'Creans (1506); a 15C rood screen across the 13C chancel containing the 17C O'Conor monument. North of the church are the 13C sacristy and chapter-house and extant parts of the 15C **cloisters★**.

Model Arts and Niland Gallery★

The Mall. ♿🕐*Open Tue–Sat 10am–5pm, Sun 10.30am–3.30pm.* ℘*071 914 1405. www.themodel.ie*

Built in 1862 as a Model School, this contemporary arts centre of national importance includes the **Niland Collection of**

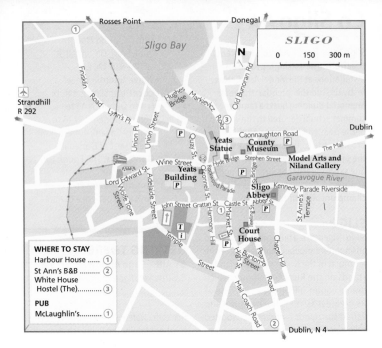

Modern Irish Art, featuring some 200 paintings by such notable artists as Jack B. Yeats, George Russell, Maurice McGonigal, Norah McGuiness, Estella Solomons, Paul Henry, Augustus John and Seán Keating. The Model's contemporary art programme features major exhibitions of national and international artists; see website for details of current exhibitions. Music, both classical and contemporary, and film are also part of the Model's programmes.

Yeats Building

Open: Yeats Photo Exhibition year-round Mon–Fri 10am–5pm. ✗ *071 914 2693. www.yeatssociety.com. Open: Sligo Art Gallery, for exhibitions only, Mon–Sat 10am–5.30pm.* *071 914 5847. http://sligoarts.ie.*

Sligo's most famous family is featured in **The Yeats Photographic Exhibition,** which outlines the Yeats family genealogy, the people and places which were a major influence on the life and career of W. B. Yeats, the man as well as the poet. It includes the film "Yeats Country". Afficionados may also want to request seeing the hour-long film, *Cast a Cold Eye,* which tells the story of Yeats through the eyes of

his son and daughter, Michael and Anne, with comments by Seamus Heaney and other literary figures. In the same building is the Yeats River Café *(open daily until 6pm for coffee, lunch and tea).*

County Museum

Stephen St. *Open May–Sept Tue–Sat 9.30am–12.30pm, 2pm–4.50pm; Oct–Apr Tue–Sat 9.30am–12.30pm.* *071 9111679. http://sligoarts.ie/ VenuesProfile/SligoCountyMuseum.*

The old manse (1851) houses the **Yeats Memorial Collection** of manuscripts, photographs and letters; local antiquities and a large painting "1916", showing Countess Markiewicz and fellow-insurgents surrendering outside Dublin's College of Surgeons (*see box, p375*).

St John's Cathedral

Open Jul–Aug Wed, Sat 2–5pm (see website to confirm). http://sligo cathedral.elphin.anglican.org.

This unusual structure was designed in 1730 by Richard Castle and altered in 1812. A brass tablet *(north transept)* commemorates the mother of W.B. Yeats, Susan, who was married here; the tomb of her father, William Pollexfen, lies near the main gates.

Cathedral of the Immaculate Conception

The highlight of this uninspired neo-Romanesque building (1874) is the 69 stained-glass windows by Loblin of Tours in France, best seen in the early morning or evening light.

WEST OF SLIGO
Strandhill

4mi/6km west of Sligo.

Strandhill marks the end of the peninsula assaulted by Atlantic breakers (☺*good surfing but hazardous bathing*). Here too is Sligo's little airport.

The R 292 skirts the peninsula, offering beautiful views of Ballysadare Bay, and there is a turnoff on the left, signposted **Scenic Drive**, which accesses a **viewpoint**★ car park. From here there is a very pretty walk (*1.2mi/2km, easy enough, muddy in wet weather*).

Knocknarea★

7mi/11km W of Sligo by R 292.
After 6mi/10km bear left; park after 1mi/1.6km; 1hr 30min there and back on foot to the summit.

The approach road climbs up "The Glen", a natural fault in the limestone providing a haven for rare plants. On the summit of **Knocknarea** (1,076ft/328m) is a massive heap of stones (197yd/180m round), visible for miles and providing a fine **view**★★ on a clear day. According to tradition, and W.B. Yeats, this contains the passage grave and tomb of Medb/Maeve, Queen of Connaught in 1C AD; however, it is more likely that she was buried at **Rathcroghan** near Tulsk, Limerick.

Carrowmore Megalithic Cemetery★

3mi/5km SW of Sligo by a minor road.
(Dúchas) ♿ 🕐*Open Apr–Nov 10am–6pm.* ☜€5. ☎071 916 1534.
www.heritageireland.ie.

The area's particular attraction is its outstanding prehistoric monuments and Carrowmore is the largest Stone-Age cemetery in Ireland, having over 60 passage graves, dolmens, stone circles and one cairn marking the largest grave. The most ancient dates from 3200 BC, 700 years earlier than Newgrange. A **visitor centre** contains an exhibition about Stone-Age man and the excavations.

NORTH OF SLIGO
Drumcliff★

Fans of **William Butler Yeats** are regular visitors to the churchyard at Drumcliff, where his great-grandfather had been rector, to pay tributes to the poet. Yeats died in the South of France in 1939 and was buried here in accordance with his wishes. The gravestone carries

Knocknarea

© Alison Crummy/Fáilte Ireland

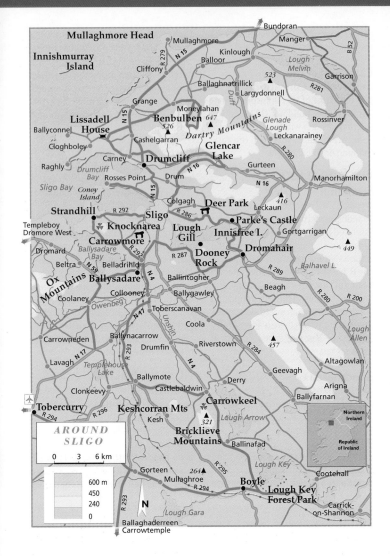

Mullaghmore Head
Innishmurray Island
Mullaghmore
Bundoran
Manger
Kinlough
Balloor
Cliffony
Ballaghnatrillick
Largydonnell
Lough Melvin
523
Garrison
Grange
Moneylahan
Benbulben
647
Lissadell House
526
Dartry Mountains
Glenade Lough
Leckanarainey
Rossinver
Ballyconnel
Cashelgarran
Cloghboley
Carney
Drumcliff
Glencar Lake
Raghly
Drumcliff Bay
Rosses Point
Drum
Gurteen
N 16
Manorhamilton
Sligo Bay
Coney Island
Colgagh
Deer Park
416
Strandhill
R 292
Sligo
R 286
Leckaun
Parke's Castle
Templeboy Dromore West
Knocknarea
Lough Gill
Innisfree I.
Gortgarrigan
Carrowmore
R 293
R 287
Dooney Rock
Dromahair
449
Dromard
Ballysadare Bay
Balhavel L.
Beltra
N 59
Belladrihid
Ballysadare
R 289
Ox Mountains
Ballintogher
Beagh
R 280
R 200
Coolaney
Collooney
Ballygawley
Owenbeg
N 17
Toberscanavan
Carrowneden
Ballynacarrow
Coola
Lough Allen
Lavagh
N 17
Drumfin
Riverstown
R 284
457
Altagowlan
Templehouse Lake
N 4
Geevagh
Arigna
Clonkeevy
Ballymote
Derry
Ballyfarnan
Castlebaldwin
Carrowkeel
Tobercurry
R 294
R 296
Keshcorran Mts
Kesh
321
Lough Arrow
Northern Ireland
AROUND SLIGO
Bricklieve Mountains
Ballinafad
Republic of Ireland
0 3 6 km
Gorteen
264
Lough Key
Cootehall
600 m
450
240
0
Mullaghroe
R 294
Boyle
Lough Key Forest Park
Carrick-on-Shannon
R 293
N
Lough Gara
Ballaghaderreen
Carrowtemple

an enigmatic epitaph he composed himself: *Cast a cold eye On life, on death. Horsman, pass by!*
The site beneath Benbulben (1,730ft/526m) by the Drumcliff River was chosen by St Columba for the foundation of a monastery in c. 575. Its **round tower** was damaged by lightning in 1396; the **high cross** (c. 1000) features biblical carvings.

▶ Just after Drumcliff turn left towards Carney.

Glencar Waterfall

About 8 miles north of Sligo beside Glencar Lake on the Sligo/Leitrim border. Access path right; 5min return by foot.

The waterfall tumbles over the rocks to a sheer drop (50ft/15m). The wind howling in from the Atlantic sometimes blows up the spray (*the cataract smokes upon the mountain side… that cold and vapour-turbaned steep.* W B Yeats "The Stolen Child").

Benbulben

© Chris Hill/Tourism Ireland

Benbulben★★

1730ft/527m.

The dramatic silhouette of Benbulben, a limestone table mountain with a west-facing escarpment like the prow of a dreadnought, dominates the country for miles around. To **climb★** to the summit, follow the trail to the left of Glenvale Farmhouse B&B. On reaching a wall, turn left towards the northwest to the neckline of King's Gully. On reaching the plateau of Benbulben, you can go around the cliffs.

For an approach road, take the N 15 between Sligo and Donegal. After Drumcliff turn right, after a small church with a steeple, to Ballintrillick. Then take the first right and follow the sign to North Sligo and leave the car at the parking area.

Mullaghmore★

N of Cliffony, signposted off the N 15.

The village shelters on the east side of the rocky headland pointing north into Donegal Bay, grouped around the stone-walled harbour and the splendidly picturesque neo-Gothic **Classiebawn Castle** (1856).

Inishmurray Island

11mi/18km offshore; boat from Mullaghmore Pier and from Rosses Point.

St Molaise founded a settlement on this little island in the 6C. The remains of the monastery include the Women's Church *(Teampall na mBan)*; rectangular and "beehive"-style dwellings; the Men's Church; souterrains and stone altars. Elsewhere on the island are pillar stones which may be pre-Christian, 57 inscribed stone slabs and 16 Stations of the Cross, spaced around the rocky perimeter.

Countess Markievicz

Constance Gore-Booth (1868–1927) was the wife of the Polish artist, impresario and boulevardier Casimir Markievicz, who lived in Dublin and Paris.

The couple drifted apart as Constance devoted herself to the Nationalist cause. While Casimir fought on the Allied side in World War I, Constance took part in the Easter Rising. Condemned to death and later reprieved, she was the first woman elected to the House of Commons in Westminster, though she never took her seat.

Lissadell House, Drumcliff Bay

© Derek Cullen/Fáilte Ireland

Yeats' Country

In their youth, the Yeats brothers spent many a summer holiday with their Pollexfen cousins at Elsinore Lodge on Rosses Point, watching their grandfather's ships in the bay from the top of the warehouse now known as the Yeats Watch Tower. Jack Yeats, the only one of the family who spent any part of his life in Sligo – he lived with the Pollexfens from the age of 8 to 16 – once remarked that he never did a painting without putting a thought of Sligo in it. The countryside and its rich legendary associations continued to inspire William throughout his life, recording in verse his visits to Lissadell House on Drumcliff Bay; the calm beauty of the lake isle of Innisfree, the sally gardens he remembers along the Garavogue River. Yeats is buried at Drumcliff, although he chose to live in Galway, Dublin, London and Paris. He died in 1939, in Menton in France and was first of all buried there at his own request and later re-interred at Drumcliff.

The Yeats family also included two daughters, Susan and Elizabeth. Susan was born in County Sligo and both spent parts of their childhood there. The two sisters were artistically talented and were part of the Arts and Crafts Movement of the early 20C, producing embroidered artworks and handprinted books from their studio in Dublin.

The Yeats family connection to Sligo is through their mother Susan Pollexfen, daughter of a wealthy milling and shipping family. John Butler Yeats, a barrister and portrait painter in his own right, spent some summers in Sligo with friends from school, where he met and fell in love with her. The family never settled permanently in Sligo – they had a home in Galway and lived for periods in Dublin and London – but Sligo entered the imaginations of the two brothers and influenced much of their work.

SOUTH OF SLIGO
Carrowkeel Megalithic Cemetery★★

17mi/27km south of Sligo, between Castlebaldwin and Boyle on the N 4.

The bleak hilltop in the **Bricklieve Mountains** (1,057ft/321m) provides a fine **view★★** of the surrounding country. The stone mounds of Carrowkeel Megalithic Cemetery (not to be confused with Carrowmore Megalithic Cemetery, ⚓*see p373*) contain passage graves dating from around 2500 to 2000 BC. On a lower ridge (east) are about 50 round huts, probably dwellings.

As the road south climbs over the Curlew Mountains (867ft/264m), there are splendid **views★** of the lakes *(east)*.

▶ Continue on the N 4, cross the border to Co Roscommon, and turn right on the N 61.

Boyle★

🛈 *King House, Boyle.* ☎*071 966 2145.*

On the River Boyle at the foot of the Curlew Mountains (867ft/264m), this pleasant little town *(Mainistir Na Búille)* has one of the loveliest set of abbey ruins in Ireland and fascinating reminders of one of the most ruthless and ambitious Anglo-Irish landowning dynasties, the King family. The river and the nearby loughs give excellent fishing.

King House★

🕐*Open Apr–Sept, Tue–Sat 11am–last admission 4pm. Also open Easter weekend, bank hol Suns & Mons during season*⊛€5. ✕ 🅿 ☎*071 966 3242. www.kinghouse.ie.*

The Palladian mansion (c. 1730) of the King family was built for Sir John King, a Staffordshire gentleman sent here a century earlier, charged with subjugating the native Irish and rewarded with the lands confiscated from the local ruling clan, the MacDermots.

King House has been carefully restored to accommodate descriptions of the old rulers – O'Connors, Kings of Connaught and MacDermots of Moylurg – and the exploits of the King family who displaced them. The **Boyle Civic Art Collection** is considered to be among the finest collections of contemporary Irish painting and sculpture anywhere.

Boyle Abbey★

(Dúchas) ♿🕐*Open Apr–Sept, daily 10am–6pm (5.15pm last admission).* ⊛€5. ☎*071 966 2604. www.heritageireland.ie.*

A **Cistercian** house was founded here in 1161 by monks from Mellifont. The church, built over several decades, shows the transition from the Romanesque to the Gothic style. Normally frowning on exuberance of any kind, here at Boyle the austere Cistercians gave free rein to their

Boyle Abbey

© Chris Hill/Tourism Ireland

Lough Key Forest Park

© Designpics/Photoshot

masons, who endowed the capitals with carvings of men, beasts and foliage. The abbey buildings were occupied by the Cromwellians, who showed them their usual disrespect; thereafter they served as barracks until the 18C. Information on the monastic life is provided in the **gatehouse**.

▶ 2mi/3.2km E of Boyle by N 4 (still in Co Roscommon).

ᯤᯤ Lough Key Forest Park★

♿⏰*Open Mar–Aug daily (see website for Mar dates) 10am–6pm.Sept–Oct Wed–Sun 10am–6pm Nov–Feb, Fri–Sun noon–4pm. Last admission 1–2hrs before closing. ⊛€7.50, child €5. Lough Key Experience; €18 Boda Borg 2hr pass. €25 adult day pass; €5 child Adventure play area. Combo ticket also available, see website ✕🅿 (€4, free if spend more than €20, inc restaurant). ₰071 967 3122. www.loughkey.ie.*

With its woodlands, bog garden, ornamental trees and estate buildings, this vast forest park (865 acres/350ha) looks out over Lough Key and its islands. Until 1959, it formed part of the Rockingham estate, the demesne of the Earls of Kingston, who built themselves a great house here on the site of a MacDermot castle. In the early 19C, the house was remodelled by John Nash and the estate landscaped by Humphry Repton. In 1959, the house was destroyed by fire.

The **Lough Key Experience** takes visitors on an audio trail through 19C underground tunnels to the top of the five-storey **Moylurg Tower** (132 steps) and along a 300m steel-and-timber **Tree Canopy Walk**, rising 9.8yards/9m above the forest floor, offering panoramic views over the woods, lakes and hills. Younger (and young-at-heart) visitors enjoy the **Adventure Play Kingdom** area, while **Boda Borg** is a cerebral area of finding your way through a maze of rooms solving puzzles and tasks (*min 3, max 5 people per team required to participate; suitable for adults, and children aged 7+*).

New to Lough Key is the **Zipit Forest Adventure** (*www.zipit.ie*) Ireland's first aerial trail activity course, using zip lines, rope bridges, tarzan swings, and climbing walls to manoeuvre through the treetops.

🚗 DRIVING TOUR

LOUGH GILL★

Round tour east from Sligo. 30mi/48km. Allow half a day.

Lough Gill is one of Ireland's loveliest lakes, dotted with islands, fringed by shoreline woodlands, picturesquely set against looming limestone mountains.

Parke's Castle, Lough Gill

© Alison Crummy/Fáilte Ireland

▶ Take the N 4 south; after 0.25mi/ 0.4km bear left to Lough Gill.

Tobernalt
The holy well shaded by trees marks an old Celtic assembly site where a summer festival (Lughnasa) was celebrated.

▶ Continue on the shore road; at the T-junction turn left onto the R 287.

Dooney Rock Forest★
The top of Dooney Rock offers superlative views of the lake and Benbulben.

▶ At the crossroads turn left; after 2mi/3.2km turn left; 2mi/3.2km to car park.

Innisfree Island
W. B. Yeats was especially drawn to this tiny island (*see Addresses*), immortalised in his poem, *Lake Isle of Innisfree*.

▶ Return to the R 287, continue east.

Dromahair
This attractive riverside village sits between the shell of Villiers Castle (17C) and a ruined abbey.

Creevelea Abbey
Park behind the Abbey Hotel; 6min there and back on foot across the bridge.
An avenue of evergreens beside the Bonet River leads to the ruins of a Franciscan friary, which was founded in 1508.

▶ Continue on the R 287.

Parke's Castle★
(Dúchas). ◷*Open early Apr–early Oct 10am–6pm.* ✎€5. ✕ *(summer).* ℘*071 916 4149. www.heritageireland.ie.*
The extensively restored fortified plantation mansion, apparently sitting on the lough waters, was built in 1609 by the Englishman Capt Robert Parke on the site of Sir Brian O'Rourke's former home. In the wall by the shore, a **sweat house** (an early sauna) has been hollowed out. A video presentation provides an overview of the area's history.

▶ Follow the R 286 along the lake to Sligo. At 1.8mi/3km, turn right towards Calry and at the T-junction turn left.

A nice walk through the woods leads to the top of the hill, Deer Park and the neolithic court tomb "Giant's Grave".

▶ Continue west on the R 286 to return to Sligo.

ADDRESSES

SLIGO

🛏 STAY

Harbour House Hostel– Finisklin Rd. *071 917 1547. www. harbourhouse hostel.com.* Just over 10 minutes on foot from the rail and bus station, this hostel has single, double, twin, family and dormitory rooms. Free Wi-Fi in the lobby, free tea and coffee, laundry facilities and a car parking area.

The White House Hostel – Markievicz Rd. *071 914 5160.* Centrally located and with en-suite single rooms in addition to the 31 dorm beds. The reception desk is closed during afternoons.

St Ann's B&B– Pearse Rd (just off the N 4 Sligo–Dublin road). *071 914 3188.* Within walking distance of the town centre and with the benefit of a small outdoor swimming pool.

🍴 EAT

Montmartre – Market Yard. *071 916 9901. www.montmartrerestaurant.ie. Closed Sun, Mon (except bank hols).* It's not 100 per cent French, but the cooking, atmosphere and style of the room have a strong Gallic accent, from the pictures on the walls to the helpful mesdemoiselles providing the service.

PUB

McLaughlin's– 9 Market St. *071 914 4209.* Traditional Irish music and sing-along sessions at night.

SHOPPING

Sligo Crystal – 10mi/16km north at Grange. Open Jun–Sept Mon–Fri 9am–9pm, Sat–Sun 10am–7pm. Oct–May Mon–Sat 9am–6pm. *071 43440.* Factory and showrooms with guided tours; watch craftsmen producing hand-cut crystal.

ENTERTAINMENT

The Hawk's Well Theatre – *071 916 1518. www.hawkswell.com.* A wide range of shows, including drama, children's theatre, contemporary and classical dance, opera, jazz, roots and pop music, comedy and pantomime.

SPORTS AND LEISURE

Strandhill is good for wind-surfing, but bathing can be dangerous. **Rosses Point** (An Ros), a sandy peninsula projecting into Drumcliff Bay, provides a championship golf course and two beautiful sandy beaches for bathing and wind-surfing.

EVENTS AND FESTIVALS

Yeats Annual Winter School – *www.yeatssociety.com.* A weekend, usually late Jan/early Feb, of lectures and the like. For details of other festivals and art events in Sligo see *www.sligoarts.ie/ FestivalsandEvents*.

SIGHTSEEING

Walking Tour – Operates Jun–Aug. from Tourist Office, Temple St. 11am (approx 2hrs) Tue–Fri. *071 9161201.*

Rose of Innisfree Tour Boat – Operates mid-Jun–Sept, from Parke's Castle, to the Isle of Innisfree. Apr, May, Oct, limited sailings. Check website or call for details. *071 9164 266; 087 25988 869 (mobile). www.roseofinnisfree.com.* There are also boat trips offshore to **Inishmurray** from Mullaghmore (north of Sligo). 15 passengers minimum. *071 916 6124 (Lomax Boats).*

BOYLE

🛏 STAY

Abbey House – Abbeytown Rd. *071 966 2385. www.abbeyhouse.net. 5 rms.* This fine Victorian house, set against the lovely backdrop of Boyle's Cistercian Abbey, is located just a five-minute walk from Boyle Town Centre and offers comfortable accommodation in simple rooms.

Rosdarrig House – Dublin Rd. *071 9662 040. www.rosdarrig.com.* A modern house in a rural setting with lovely interiors and stylish bedrooms.

Temple House – Ballymote, 20 min south of Sligo. *071 918 3329. www.templehouse.ie.* This family run luxury Country House B&B, in a classic Georgian mansion, is set in a private estate of over 1,000 acres, overlooking a 13C lakeside castle. Lovely rooms, all with countryside views.

EVENTS AND FESTIVALS

Boyle Arts – King House. www.boylearts.com. Summer festival (late Jul–early Aug) of comedy, storytelling, drama, jazz, classical music and more.

Donegal and the Donegal Coast ★★

Donegal is an attractive town at the mouth of the River Eske, a perfect spot from which to explore the glens and mountains north, the dramatic coastal scenery west and the seaside resorts on Donegal Bay to the south. The town itself is a small place that attracts a large numbers of visitors. It has some lively pubs and there is a pleasant walk along the river.

DONEGAL TOWN
A Bit of History

Dún na nGall (the fort of the foreigners) was established by the Vikings; for 400 years the O'Donnell clan ruled the area until the flight of the Earl of Tyrconnell in 1607. In 1610 it was granted by the English crown to Sir Basil Brooke who rebuilt the castle and laid out the new Plantation town round the triangular Diamond "square". The Irish mounted an unsuccessful attack during the 1641 rebellion; during the Williamite War the town was burned by the Jacobite Duke of Berwick, but the castle held firm. In 1798, two French ships carrying reinforcements for General Humbert's

▶ **Population:** 2 339 (Donegal Town).

▤ **Info:** Quay Street, **Donegal**, ☎972 1148; Main Street, **Bundoran**, ☎072 41350; The Quay, **Dungloe**, ☎074 952 1298. www.donegaldirect.ie

◖ **Location:** Donegal Town is 40mi/60km northwest of Sligo.

☻ **Don't Miss:** A stroll along Rossnowlagh Strand, Cliffs of Bunglass and the views from Glengesh Pass.

♟ **Kids:** A trip to Waterworld, Bundoran.

☻ **Warning:** The coastal roads are narrow and winding, with spectacular views. Only pull over when it is safe to do so.

◷ **Timing:** For a tourist, there is little to see in the town of Donegal itself, but allow at least two days to enjoy the Donegal Coast.

GETTING THERE
BY AIR – Donegal Airport: ☎074 954 8284. www.donegalairport.ie.

Rossnowlagh Strand

© Tourism Ireland

The Irish Navvy

The term navvy is abbreviated slang (often perjorative) for navigator and has been stereotypically applied to Irish labourers for centuries. The term comes from the late 18C when numerous canals ("navigations") were being built in Britain and a navvy came to mean anyone who was manually working on canals, roads and railways. In fact, Irish seasonal and migrant workers were a highly mobile and flexible workforce, vital to Britain's booming 19C economy and economic revival after the Second World War. Many of these men came from Donegal.

army anchored in Donegal Bay, but cut their cables on learning of his defeat. The anchor abandoned by the *Romaine* is now displayed on the quay.

SIGHTS
Donegal Castle

(*Dúchas*) &⃝Open Easter–mid-Sept daily 10am–6pm, mid-Sept–Easter Thu–Mon 9.30am–4.30pm.
Last admission 45 mins before closing.
⃝Closed 25–26 Dec. ⃝€5. 🅿 ☏074 972 2405. www.heritageireland.ie.
Perched on a bluff in the centre of town on the south bank of the River Eske, the original O'Donnell stronghold was largely destroyed by Hugh Roe O'Donnell in 1604 to prevent it falling into English hands. The remains were incorporated into a splendid five-gabled Jacobean mansion with a great hall, furnished in the style of the 1650s.

Donegal Railway
Heritage Centre

⃝Open Mon–Fri 10am–5pm; also Sat–Sun in Summer. ⃝€4. ☏074 972 2655. www.donegalrailway.com.
The old station museum is dedicated to the narrow-gauge County Donegal Railway, run between 1900 and 1959.

Donegal Friary (Abbey)

On the south bank of the estuary overlooking Donegal Bay are the ruins of a **Franciscan house**, once a famous centre for learning founded by Red Hugh O'Donnell and his wife Nuala (1474). Substantial damage was caused by an explosion during the English occupation in 1601.

SOUTH OF DONEGAL
Mullinasole Strand★

This beautiful beach, lined with a forest and facing Donegal Bay, is ideal for swimming, surfing or a picnic.

Rossnowlagh Strand★★

A small village with a large hotel overlook a wonderful beach, some 2.5mi/ 4km long – perfect for swimming, surfing and horse riding. Across Donegal Bay rise the cliffs of the **Slieve League★★★** (⃝see "Climbing Slieve League" p386).

Ballyshannon

Ballyshannon guards an important crossing point on the **River Erne**.
In 1597, the English under Sir Conyers Clifford were defeated here by Red Hugh O'Donnell. Today, it is best known for its popular Folk and Traditional Music Festival (⃝see Addresses).

Four Masters

In the 17C, while taking refuge at a Franciscan house south of Bundoran, **Michael O'Cleary** (b. 1580), a Franciscan from **Donegal Abbey**, and three lay Gaelic scholars compiled the *Annals of the Kingdom of Ireland*, an account of Irish history also known as the *Annals of the Four Masters*. The annals are written in Irish.

The authors are commemorated by the obelisk (1967) in the Diamond, and in the dedication of the Roman-Catholic church built in 1935, of local red granite in the Irish Romanesque style.

Bundoran (Bun Dobhráin)

Bundoran is a major seaside resort with fine views across Donegal Bay to **Slieve League**★★★ and the great square mass of Benbulben rock, north of Sligo.

DONEGAL COAST★★

Facing the full force of Atlantic gales in winter, this remote and rugged coastline of deep sea-inlets, jagged cliffs and sandy beaches is backed by spectacular mountains and blanket bog.

Its pristine landscapes are largely unaffected by modern development; on the north coast the land is divided into fields by walls of huge round stones and dotted with tiny white houses with thatched roofs roped down against the furious winter weather.

🚗 DRIVING TOURS

DONEGAL TO NARAN
70mi/113km. Allow 1 day.

▶ From Donegal take the N 56 west of Dunkineely, turn left to St John's Point.

St John's Point★

The small road that runs along the narrow peninsula offers wonderful **views**★ of McSwyne's Bay, Slieve League on the north coast of Sligo and the silhouette of Benbulben south. Strange rocks, black and flaky, punctuate the route that leads to a lovely cove sheltered from the waves.

▶ Return to the N 56 and continue west. After 3mi/4.8km turn left.

Killybegs

This bustling little town, set on the River Strager, and with a natural deepwater harbour is one of the country's foremost fishing ports and is said to be the most productive port in Ireland. With the decline in fishing stocks the boats are moving further out but at any one time you may still be able to count over 50 boats.

In the mid-19C it became a centre for hand-tufted carpets, celebrated in the local Heritage Centre. Within the gates

of St Catherine's Church, designed by J.B. Papworth c. 1840, *(turn right uphill)* stands the **tomb slab** *(left)* of Niall Mor MacSweeney; allies of the O'Neills, the MacSweeneys originally came to Ireland as gallowglasses (mercenaries) and the slab shows several of these hardy Scottish warriors.

▶ Continue west on the R 263; after 3mi/4.8km turn left onto the Coast Road.

Kilcar Coast Road★

This pretty route introduces you to the most beautiful part of Donegal, with its wild and rugged coastline, dominated by desert hills and streaked with small walls. To the South, on the other side of the bay, you can see the peaks of Sligo on a fine day.

Kilcar *(Cill Cárthaigh)* village is a major centre for tweed (*see Addresses*), set at the confluence of two rivers. Several sandy beaches nearby are ideal for swimming.

▶ Continue west.

At the exit of Kilcar, the **Coast Road** towards Glencolumbkille leads to Carrick, along a deep indentation in the coastline. On the opposite shore, you will see the little village of Teelin at the foot of Slieve League.

The coastal road reaches **Carrick**, where every year in August a notable festival of traditional music takes place.

▶ Leaving Carrick, turn left towards Bunglass and Teelin.

Slieve League★★★

The road leads to one of the most spectacular sights in the whole of Ireland, an awe-inspiring prospect of ocean, mountain and enormous cliffs. After climbing steeply (over 1,000ft/305m) and skirting Lough O'Mulligan, stop at the top to contemplate the view of the **Cliffs of Bunglass**★★★ rising 984ft/300m from the sea, and the sheer south flank of the **Slieve League** sea cliffs (1,972ft/601m). 🚶There are several walking trails of varying difficulty and experienced hik-

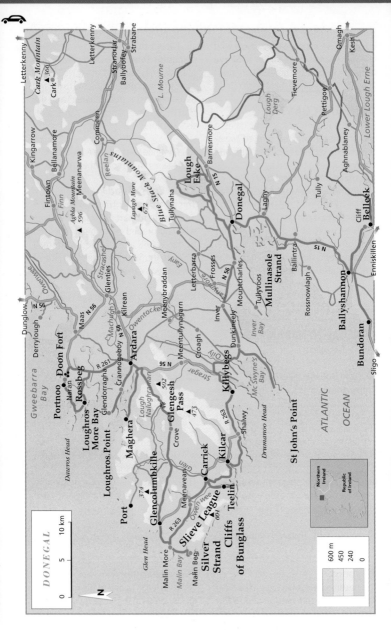

ers can climb to the peak (1,971ft/601m). Whatever the route chosen (&see box, opposite), you will discover unforgettable panoramic views.

◗ Return to Carrick and turn left onto the R 263. After 2mi/3.2km bear left to Malin Beg (Málainn Bhig).

Glenmalin Court Cairn

In marshy ground beside a small stream are the substantial remains of a court tomb, known locally as Cloghanmore, meaning Big Stone.

◗ Continue to the crossroads; turn left along the coast.

Cliffs of Bunglass

© Martin Fleming/Fáilte Ireland

Trabane Strand★

The sheltered sandy bay faces south across Donegal Bay to Benbulben (&see SLIGO).

▶ Return to the crossroads and go straight ahead to Glencolumbkille.

Glencolmcille Folk Village★★

&⊙Open Easter Sat–late Oct daily 10am–6pm (noon Sun). ⊛€5. ✕ ℰ074 974 300 17. www.glenfolkvillage.com.
The folk village was one of the many initiatives undertaken by **Father James McDyer** (1910–87), who resolved to put a stop to the traumatic exodus of emigrants from this poor and remote area. He helped build a community centre, had electricity connected and roads improved. In 1967, he initiated the idea of preserving traditional practises by building a folk village with a cottage for each century, furnished with artefacts donated by his parishioners. The school, craftshop and *shebeen* (illicit bar), which now sells seaweed wine and country wines, were added later.
The actual village of **Glencolumbkille** (*Gleann Cholm Cille*) lies inland from its sandy beaches, guarded by a Martello tower on Glen Head (745ft/227m). In this remote and rugged valley St Columba (*Colmcille*) built himself a house of retreat for quiet prayer. On his feast day (9 June), pilgrims make a penitential tour (3mi/5km) of the glen between midnight and 3am, stopping at Stations of the Cross marked by cairns, boulders, pagan standing stones and early-Christian cross-slabs.
The **Ulster Cultural Institute** (*Foras Cutúir Uladh*), a centre for Gaelic studies, offers a variety of activities and language courses (ℰ074 973 0248; www.oideas-gael.com/en/).

▶ Take the road to Ardara. After 10mi/16km there is a viewing point on the left.

Glencolmcille Folk Village

© Martin Fleming/Fáilte Ireland

© Chris Hill/Tourism Ireland/Fáilte Ireland

Climbing Slieve League★★★

At the tiny, Irish-speaking village of Teelin the road divides and the route to the right is signposted as a walking trail for Slieve League. The route to the left leads to Bunglass and an area for parking cars; from here there are magnificent views of the cliffs and the wild sea below.

The signposted walking trail leads you to **One Man's Pass** and then on to the summit. An alternative route, shorter but more precipitous, begins at the parking area and follows a path to **Scregeighter** (1,010ft/308m) and **Eagle's Nest** (1,060ft/323m), from where a hazardous, narrow path takes you to One Man's Pass.

Whichever route you may decide to take, it is essential that due regard and respect is paid to the weather and on no account should the ascent be undertaken on a windy or misty day – there have been fatal accidents in the past. However, if the weather is fine and you have proper footwear, a head for heights and at least an average fitness, there is no reason not to enjoy one of the best climbs in Ireland.

From the summit of Slieve League there are unsurpassed views that take in Croagh Patrick in County Mayo and Benbulben in County Sligo. Seasoned walkers can continue to Malinbeg (where there is accommodation) along the edge of the cliff from the summit or on a little further to Glencomcille. From Teelin to Mainbeg will take about six hours.

Eagles from Scotland have been recorded on the route from the summit to Malinbeg and you may be lucky enough to see one.

Glengesh Pass★★
Stop at the head of the pass to view the glaciated, green valley, enclosed by steep and rugged mountains. Hairpin bends carry the road down to join the river.

Ardara (Ard an Rátha) ·
Ardara (pronounced with the accent on the last syllable) is an attractive market town on the Owentocker River at the head of a deep sea-inlet, famous for its production of Donegal Tweed.
The **Ardara Heritage Centre** (◐ open Easter–Sept daily 10am (2pm Sun) to 6pm; ✕; ✆074 95 541473, http://new.ardara.ie) celebrates the local tweed industry; weaving demonstrations and Aran knitting tradition.

▷ Take minor road W to Crannogeboy.

Loughros Point★★
The small road that heads west from Ardara takes the visitor through some wild Donegal countryside. There are sublime sea views from Loughros Point across Loughros More Bay.

Maghera★★

Another small road from Ardara opens up views of Loughros Beg Bay and leads to Maghera. Before reaching the parking area on the beach at Maghera you pass **Assarancagh Waterfall★** and the start of a walking trail that leads to Glengesh Pass. The road north from Ardara, the R 261, leads to the twin resorts of **Naran** and **Portnoo**, which face Inishkeel in Gweebarra Bay. They have broad sandy beaches, which are excellent places for cliff walks, surfing, sailing, fishing and golf.

Doon Fort★★

Doon Fort stands in the middle of Lough Doon. It is at least 2,000 years old. During the summer months it is possible to hire a rowing boat to reach the island and explore the ruins.

To reach the fort take the road signposted to Rosbeg on the road for Ardara just outside Narin and then take a right turn a short distance past a school. This accesses a narrow lane, along here look for the sign advertising boat hire to Lough Doon.

▷ Follow the minor road to Rossbeg.

Rossbeg★

Rossbeg is a tiny village close to Tramore Beach and the isolated viewpoint at Dawros Head.

GLENTIES
(NA GLEANNTA)

Glenties is the home town of **Patrick MacGill** (1890–1963), the "Navvy Poet" known for his uncompromising depictions of the hard life led by migrant labourers (*see "The Irish Navvy" box*). At the age of 12 MacGill was sold by his parents to a farmer to be used as a labourer. Two years later he moved to Scotland, where he became a navvy, working on the railway. Despite his lack of formal education he taught himself to read and write and at the age of 19 self-published 8,000 copies of a small book (56pp), printed by *The Derry Journal* which he called *Gleanings from a Navvy's Scrapbook*. By the following year (1911), Patrick was working as a journalist for the *Daily Express* in London. He is honoured in a festival each summer (*July/August*).

St Connall's Church (Roman Catholic), one of Liam McCormick's masterpieces of modern architecture, echoes the landscape between Big Glen and Wee Glen, with marvellous use of natural light and collection of rainwater for the water gardens. St Connell Caol established a monastic settlement on Inishkeel Island in the 6C.

Opposite the church is the excellent **St Connell's Museum & Heritage Centre** (*open year-round Mon–Sat 10am–1pm & 2pm–4.30pm;* €2.50;

Glengesh Pass

© Martin Fleming/Fáilte Ireland

℘074 9551766), which includes the prison cells of the late-19C courthouse and has many artefacts pertaining to the famine in Southwest Donegal and the filming of *Dancing at Lughnasa*.

ADDRESSES

🛏 STAY

🛌 **Abbey Hotel** – *The Diamond, Donegal Town.* ℘074 972 1014. www.abbeyhotel donegal.com. In the very centre of town with a leisure centre (with a pool and gym), nightclub, and popular restaurant and bar. Smart international quality bedrooms. Excellent value.

🛌 **Ardeevin** – *Lough Eske, Barnesmore. 5.5mi/8.8km northeast of Donegal.* ℘074 972 1790. www.ardeevinguesthouse.co.uk. *6 rms.* Peaceful location, with stunning views of Lough Eske. Cosy traditional rooms renovated and updated in 2011.

🛌 **Island View House** – *Ballyshannon Rd, .75mi/1.2km from town.* ℘074 972 2411. dowdsb@indigo.ie. *4rm.* This purpose-built guesthouse enjoys views of the surrounding countryside and lough. Simply decorated with the emphasis on value for money.

🛌🛌 **Ard na Breatha** – *Drumrooska Middle, Donegal Town.* ℘074 972 2288. www.ardnabreatha.com *.6rm.* A delightful guesthouse, part of a working farm, with bedrooms decorated in traditional country-style, an award-winning Modern Irish-cuisine restaurant and cosy bar.

🍴 EAT

🍴 **La Bella Donna** – *Bridge St, Donegal Town.* ℘074 972 5790. *Closed on Mon, reservations advisable at weekends.* www.labelladonnarestaurant.com By the bridge, this is a pleasant Italian-style restaurant serving pizzas and pasta dishes and good Italian coffee.

🍴 **Weaver's Loft** – *The Diamond, Donegal Town (above Magee).* ℘074 972 2660. A long-established central stop for coffee and cakes, lunch or a snack.

🍴🍴🍴 **The Restaurant (Cuisine Art)**– *Harvey's Point Country Hotel, Lough Eske.* ℘074 9722 208. www.harveyspoint.com. The hotel (🍴🍴🍴), voted "Number One Hotel in Ireland 2013" by TripAdvisor is also famous for its food; its Cuisine Art menu offers a gourmet experience.

SHOPPING

The famous woollen **Donegal tweed** is made and sold locally.

Magee of Donegal. *The Diamond.* ℘074 972 2660. www.magee1866.com. Established in 1866 and still going strong as a shop retailing clothes for men and women.

The **Craft Village** on the southern outskirts of the town specialises in contemporary craftsmanship in wood, handweaving, jewellery, glass and stone. *Ballyshannon Rd.* ℘074 972 2225. www.donegalcraftvillage.com.

SPORTS AND LEISURE

Drumcliffe Walk – A pleasant wooded walk from the river bridge in Donegal, downstream along the north bank of the River Eske overlooking the estuary. **Rossnowlagh Strand** is ideal for bathing, surfing and horse riding.

Bundoran town beach can be dangerous but there are sandy beaches for bathing up and down the coast.

👫 **Waterworld** (*Bundoran; open daily Jun–Aug 10am–7pm, Apr–May and Sept, Sat–Sun, also Easter week; €13.50 (inc sauna/steam rooms), €11 for children under 8;* ℘071 984 1172; *www. waterworldbundoran.com*) – Tidal wave, aqua volcano, tornado slide, water rapids, sea-based treatments; seaweed baths and health suite.

Also at Bundoran is **Donegal Adventure Centre** (℘071 98 42418 *www.donegal adventurecentre.net*), one of Ireland's best surf school and outdoor activity centres.

EVENTS AND FESTIVALS

Ballyshannon Folk and Traditional Music Festival – Irish music in marquees, open-air concerts, busking competitions and workshops (*late Jul–early August; www.ballyshannonfolk festival.com*)

SIGHTSEEING

The Waterbus offers 80min tours of Donegal Bay. ℘074 972 3666. www.donegalbaywaterbus.com.

Northern Peninsulas★★

Quiet peninsulas where you can drive, cycle or walk and enjoy spectacular coastal scenery and a sense of being well and truly away from the hustle and bustle of contemporary life. There are few large towns apart from Letterkenny and this is very much part of the appeal for visitors.

 DRIVING TOURS

THE ROSSES★

After the beautiful **Gweebarra Estuary★** comes **Dunglow** (*An Clochán Liath*), an attractive small town regarded as the capital of The Rosses – a bleak, flat rocky Gaelic-speaking region (100sq mi/259sq km) dotted with tiny lakes.

▶ Take the R 259 northwest.

Burtonport *(Ailt an Chorráin)*

The tiny harbour provides regular ferry services *(2mi/3.2km)* to Arranmore Island (*see Getting Around*). Local food specialities are oysters, mussels and lobster.

Arranmore Island★★

Around 800 people live on this unspoilt rock. The scenic attractions are rugged cliffs on the northern and western shores, and several lakes. There are seven pubs, which hold regular traditional music sessions.
Back on the R 259, look on your left for the sign to **Cruit Island**, reached across a small bridge. The island has a succession of sandy beaches and grand views of the bay.

▶ Continue north on the R 259. In Crolly turn left onto the N 56. After 1mi/1.6km turn left onto the R 258; turn left to Bunbeg.

Info: Neil T Blaney Road, Letterkenny, ℘074 912 1160. www.discover ireland.ie.

Location: The N 15 runs between Donegal and Letterkenny, which is linked by N 13 to Londonderry over the border. Letterkenney is the best touring base.

Don't Miss: Glenveagh National Park, Tory Island.

Kids: The Dunlewy Centre.

GETTING AROUND

BY FERRY – **Arranmore Ferry:**
Passenger/car ferry operates from Burtonport to Leadgarrow: 30min crossing, up to eight sailings per day in summer. ℘074 952 0532. *www.arranmoreferry.com.*
Tory Island Ferry: Operates (weather permitting) Bunbeg to Tory Island (1hr 30min). Magheroarty to Tory Island (45min) up to three times per day. ℘074 953 1320. *www.toryislandferry.com.*
Donegal Coastal Cruises: Coastal Cruises from Bunbeg/Magheroarty (Meenlaragh) ℘074 953 1320. *www.toryislandferry.com*

Gweedore

From Gweedore on the N 56, the R 257 heads west and then north to Bloody Foreland.

Bunbeg (An Bun Beag)

Beyond the signal tower on the narrow winding Clady estuary is this lovely little harbour, well protected from the Atlantic storms. Boats sail from here to Tory Island (*see Getting Around*).

▶ Take the R 257 north.

Bloody Foreland Head★★

The headland owes its name to the reddish colour of the rocks, exaggerated in the evening sun. Offshore Inishbofin and its islands point north towards Tory Island.

Tory Island (Toraigh)

Access by boat from Meenlaragh (Magheroarty) and Gortahork (⟲see Getting Around); from Gortahork follow the signs to Bloody Foreshore; right down to the pier.

Although only 7mi/11km from the mainland, bad weather means that Tory Island is frequently cut off; most notably in 1974 when it was inaccessible for eight weeks due to storms and full-scale evacuation plans had been drawn up. This bleak, windswept rock, measuring 2.5mi/4km by around 1mi/1.6km, is largely inhabited by Gaelic-speaking fishermen and ruled since time immemorial by their "king". The population is around 150.

Little is left of the monastery founded in the 6C by St Columba *(Colmcille)* other than a round tower, Tau cross and two ruined churches. At the Tory School of Primitive Art, islanders produce striking paintings in a naive folk style; examples are on show at Glebe House.

▷ Turn left onto the N 56.

Ballyness Bay

The sheltered sea-inlet is overlooked by two Gaelic-speaking villages, **Gortahork** *(Gort an Choirce)* and **Falcarragh** *(An Fál Carrach)*.

▷ At Gortahork, take a right to follow the road south to Donegal. After 5.5mi/9km, turn left towards Dunlewy on the R 251, which runs along the Errigal Mountain.

DERRYVEAGH MOUNTAINS★★

These mountains separate the coastal corners of Donegal from the urban Letterkenny.

Errigal Mountain★★

Errigal, the highest mountain in Donegal, offers extensive views over almost all of Donegal and its neighbouring counties. The tourist route to the summit starts off from the R 251 at the layby before a sign to Altan Farm. There is no regular track in the first section – walkers must climb the lowest part of the southeast ridge and bear left. On reaching the lower screes, follow a faint track winding steeply upwards *(approx 4hr 30min to the summit and back)*.

▲▲ Dunlewy Centre (Ionad Cois Locha)

⏱*Open daily Apr–Oct 10.30am–6pm (Sun 11am).* ☜*€6 (homestead); €6 (boat trip).* ✕ ☎*074 953 1699. www.dunleweycentre.com.*

On the shore of the lake stands an old weaver's homestead which is the focal point of a family-oriented visitor centre, providing tweed weaving dem-

Summit of Errigal Mountain

© Gareth McCormack/Getty Images

onstrations, pony treks, boat trips, an adventure play area, farmyard animals to feed and lakeside walks.

The road from Dunlewy east to Letterkenny (R 251) offers wonderful **views** of the lake and its valley, known as the **Poisoned Glen**. The most likely explanation for the name is that it was once called "Glen of Heaven".

As the Irish for "of heaven" – neimhe – and "of poison" – nimhe – are similar in spelling (if not pronunciation) it is thought an English cartographer confused the two and over the centuries the name has stuck.

Glenveagh National Park★★★

(Dúchas). ◷Open year-round daily 10am–6pm. ⌬Castle open by guided tour only. (5pm last admission) ⌬Castle €7, Minibus between Visitor Centre and Castle €3. ✗ ⌬Cash only accepted. ℘076 100 2537. www.heritageireland.ie. www.glenveaghnationalpark.ie.

The National Park (23,887 acres/9,667ha) consists of Lough Beagh and the surrounding wild landscape of bogs, moorland and rugged mountain, clad in natural woodland of oak and birch. In contrast, the romantic granite castle sits on a promontory beside the lake surrounded by luxuriant gardens.

The estate was created by John George Adair through the amalgamation of several smaller holdings from which he evicted all the tenants in 1861.

The **Visitor Centre** provides information about the park and there is a video about the conservation of the flora and fauna, including the largest herd of **red deer** in Ireland.

The beautiful gardens are designed to provide colour and interest through the seasons. Stone statuary provide a formal note to the **Terrace** (1966) and in the **Italian Garden** (1958). From the long lawn at the centre of the **Pleasure Grounds**, paths lead up to the **Belgian Walk**, which was constructed during World War I by convalescing Belgian soldiers billeted at the house.

Within the **walled garden** is an Orangery (1958), designed by Philippe Jullian.

From the south end of the gardens there is a long **view** up Lough Beagh to the head of the glen below the peak of Slieve Snaght (2,441ft/683m).

The castellated façade of the castle conceals a large Victorian house, designed in 1870 by John Adair's cousin, John Townsend Trench. It was lit by oil lamps until 1957.

◑ Continue south on the R 251.

Churchill and Around

The Regency **Glebe House and Gallery★** houses the **Derek Hill Collection** of some 300 paintings by 20C artists (Braque, Corot, Degas, Picasso, Renoir and Sutherland), notable Irish artists (including J. B. Yeats) and by the inhabitants of Tory Island (⌬see p390), who paint in a primitive style, producing striking "folk" works.

Glebe House (Dúchas; ◷open Easter for 10 days & Jul–Aug daily 11am–6.30pm, Jun–Sept Sat–Thu 11am–6.30pm; ⌬house open by guided tour only, last tour 5.30pm; ⌬gallery free, house €5; ✗ in summer; ℘074 913 7071; www.heritageireland.ie) is richly furnished with Oriental prints, William Morris fabrics, William de Morgan tiles and Wemyss ware pottery; artworks by John Sherlock, Victor Pasmore, Basil Blackshaw, Augustus John, Evie and Nathaniel Hone, Sir William Orpen, Oskar Kokoshka, Cecil Beaton and John Bratby. On the hillside, facing southeast over Lough Akibbon, are the scanty remains of **St Colmcille's Oratory**, a monastery associated with St Colmcille: a holy well, two crosses and the ruins of a church in a graveyard. St Columba, born by Gartan Lough, is commemorated in the **Colmcille Heritage Centre** (℘074 9137306).

Newmills Corn and Flax Mills

(Dúchas). ◷Open late May–late Sept daily 10am–6pm (last admission 5.45pm). ℘074 912 5115. www.heritageireland.ie.

The water-powered corn and flax mill boasts one of the oldest and largest waterwheels in working order in Ireland. A tour explains how the corn was dried and milled, and how the flax was

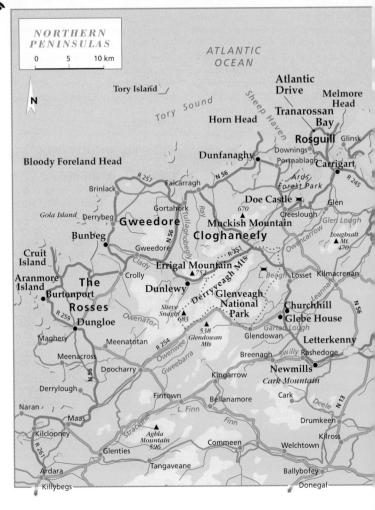

NORTHERN PENINSULAS

0   5   10 km

ATLANTIC OCEAN

Tory Island

Atlantic Drive

Melmore Head

Tranarossan Bay

Horn Head

Tory Sound

Sheep Haven

Rosguill   Glinsk

Bloody Foreland Head

Dunfanaghy

Downings

Portnablagh

Carrigart

Brinlack

R 257

Falcarragh

R 56

Ards Forest Park

R 245

Gola Island Derrybeg

Gortahork

Doe Castle

670

Glen

Creeslough

Glen Lough

Gweedore

Muckish Mountain

Loughsalt ▲ Mt. 470

Bunbeg

Gweedore

N 56

Cloghaneely

Owencarrow

Cruit Island

Clady

Errigal Mountain

R 251

L. Beagh Losset Kilmacrenan

Aranmore Island

Crolly

▲ 752

Derryveagh Mts

Leannan

N 56

Burtonport

The Rosses

Dunlewy

Glenveagh National Park

Churchhill

Glebe House

R 259

Owenator

Slieve Snaght ▲ 683

Letterkenny

Dungloe

Gartan Lough

Maghery

Meenatotan

R 254

538

Glendowan

Owenwee

Glendowan Mts

Breenagh

Swilly Rashedoge

Meenacross

Gweebarra

Newmills

N 56

Doocharry

Kingarrow

Cark Mountain

Derrylough

Fintown

Bellanamore

Cark

Deele N 13

Naran

L. Finn

Drumkeen

Maas

Finn

Kilclooney

Stracashel

Aghla Mountain 596

Commeen

Welchtown

Kilross

R 261

Glenties

Tangaveane

Ballybofey

Ardara

Killybegs

Donegal

---

treated by retting, rolling, scutching and buffering to produce linen thread.

▷ At this point, you can go directly to Letterkenny (3mi/5km from Newmills) or return to Falcarragh (22mi/35km) by turning back on R 251 and returning to the National Park.

Muckish Mountain★★
4hr climb on a steep trail.
Easily identified by its truncated top, this impressive and very rocky mountains is reached by Muckish Gap. Parking spaces are available just after the roadside shrine.

▷ The road then descends to Falcarragh and connects with the N 56 to Dunfanaghy.

NORTHWEST PENINSULAS
106mi/170km from Falcarragh to Letterkenny.

This route connects Falcarragh on the coast with Letterkenny through a succession of jagged peninsulas and some of the most beautiful coastlines in the country.

Horn Head★★

In the lee of Horn Head, the picturesque former fishing port of **Dunfanaghy** was transformed into a resort when the harbour silted up. The **Dunfanaghy Workhouse Heritage Centre** (♿︎○open Jul, Aug & Easter 9.30am–5.30pm, May-Jun, Sept-Oct 9.30am-5pm, rest of year Mon-Wed 9.30am-4.30pm; ∞€5. ✕; ℘074 913 6540; www.dunfanaghyworkhouse. ie) is one of many such built across Ireland in the 1840s, in response to the Great Potato Famine and, at its peak, the Workhouse supported over 600 people. It explains how the Famine devastated the area, highlighting the plight of one Hannah Harraty, who survived hunger, a wicked stepmother, a life of beggary and still reached the age of 90. There is also an art gallery and craft shop here.

Horn Head Scenic Route★★★
30min drive.

This headland, a breeding colony for seabirds, rises to high cliffs (over 600ft/183m) on the north coast; the blow-hole to the southwest is known as "McSwyne's Gun". There are magnificent 360-degree **views**.

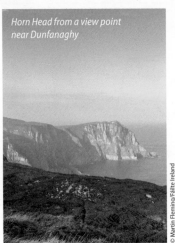

Horn Head from a view point near Dunfanaghy

© Martin Fleming/Fáilte Ireland

Portnablagh

This fishermen's hamlet was transformed by the Portnablagh Hotel (1923).

Ards Forest Park

The park (1,188 acres/481ha), once part of an extensive estate owned by the prominent Stewart family of Scottish descent, includes the north shore of the Ards Peninsula, the Binnagorm headland and Sheep Haven Bay (bathing beaches). It includes a broad variety of woodland, fenland, sand dunes, salt-marsh, a dolmen, ringforts and a lough.

▷ Continue south on the N 56.

Creeslough

Muckish Mountain (2,197ft/670m) stands guard over the village of Creeslough, lending its profile to **St Michael's Church** (Roman Catholic), another of Liam McCormick's outstanding modern churches (1971). Frequent past visitors include artists and writers such as W. B. Yeats, A.E. Russell, Percy French and G.K. Chesterton.

The ruins of **Doe Castle★** stand in a strategic position on a promontory in Sheep Haven Bay, protected by the sea, a rock-cut moat and drawbridge. Built in the 1500s by Scottish mercenaries, the MacSweenys, the stronghold played an important role in local history until after the Battle of the Boyne (1690). A **tomb slab** carved with an elaborate cross may have belonged to one of the Scottish McSweeneys, sometime lords of the castle, moved here from the ruins of the neighbouring Franciscan monastery. A replica of the original is on view.

▷ On leaving the castle turn left over a hump-backed bridge; turn left onto the R 245. At Carrigart (Carraig Airt), follow the R 248 northwest.

Rosguill Peninsula★★

The scenic **Atlantic Drive★★** follows the great curve of sand dunes alongside the Rosapenna golf links before climbing up to **Downies** (*Na Dúnaibh*), renowned for its tweed.

From here it stretches past the deep inlet of Sheep Haven Bay, backed by Horn Head, providing glorious views of the sheltered beach of **Tranarossan Bay★★**, **Melmore Head** and the sandy coves and islands of **Mulroy Bay**.

▷ In Carrigart, take the R 245 east to Mulroy Bay and Millford. Turn left onto the R 246. 2mi/3.2km north of Carrowkeel, fork left onto the coast road.

Fanad Peninsula★

A string of hamlets lines the east shore of Mulroy Bay and Broad Water. North of Kindrum, grass-covered dunes, dotted with white cottages and small lakes, extend to the sandy shore.

The lighthouse on Fanad Head marks the entrance to Lough Swilly. Dunaff Head, the Urris Hills and Dunree Head come into view on the opposite shore. **Portsalon** is a small resort at the north end of Warden Beach.

▷ From Portsalon, take the R 246; after 1mi/1.6km turn left onto the coast road.

Knockalla Viewpoint★

The north end of Knockalla Mountain (1 194ft/364m) provides panoramic **views**.

Lighthouse on Fanad Head

© Chris Hill/Tourism Ireland/Fáilte Ireland

▶ At the junction bear left onto the R 247.

Rathmullan (Ráth Maoláin)

This pretty little place facing Lough Swilly is famous for being the departure point in 1607 of the Irish clan leaders including the earls, Aodh Uî Neill (Hugh O'Neill) and Rudhraighe Ó Domhnaill (Rory O'Donnell), who were leaving Ireland to secure military help from Spain. This episode, which came to be known as "The Flight of the Earls", is cited as the end of the old Gaelic order in Ireland. The story is told in the **Flight of the Earls Heritage Centre** (Ⓞopen Jun–mid-Sept Mon–Sat 10am–5pm, Sun noon–5pm; ⬚€5; ✆074 58229) housed in an old Napoleonic battery beside the pier.

▶ Continue SW on R 247.

Ramelton (Ráth Mealtain)★

This typical plantation settlement, one of Ireland's Heritage Towns, stands on a salmon river flowing into Lough Swilly. Among the 18C warehouses along the quay is the old Steamboat Store.

▶ Take the R 245 south to Letterkenny.

Letterkenny

Large by local standards, and with a good range of facilities, this undistin-guished town on the River Swilly has the longest main street in Ireland and is the seat of the diocese of Raphoe.

The vast Gothic-Revival **Cathedral** has an interior with an uneasy mixture of neo-Celtic carving and Italianate décor.

INISHOWEN PENINSULA★★ (INIS EOGHAIN)

100mi/160km.

This scenic drive follows the coast of the Inishowen Peninsula to Malin Head, the most northerly point in Ireland. The landscape is composed of rugged mountains covered in blanket bog, fringed by steep cliffs or broad sweeps of sand. The peninsula is named after Eoghain, a 5C ruler who was a contemporary of St Patrick. By the 15C the powerful clan of the O'Dochertys held sway, but when their chief was killed in 1608, the land passed into the possession of the Elizabethan adventurer Sir Arthur Chichester, whose family eventually became the largest landowners in Ireland.

▶ From Letterkenny take the N 13.

Grianán of Aileach★★

This pre-Christian circular stone fort crowning the exposed hilltop (ℰsee "The Warrior Coirrgend" box) is among the most spectacular of its kind in the country, though its present form is a late-19C reconstruction. It served as the seat of the O'Neill clan from the

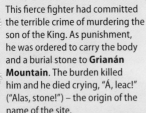

The Warrior Coirrgend

This fierce fighter had committed the terrible crime of murdering the son of the King. As punishment, he was ordered to carry the body and a burial stone to **Grianán Mountain**. The burden killed him and he died crying, "Á, leac!" ("Alas, stone!") – the origin of the name of the site.

5C–11C, but even before then was included in Ptolemy's map of the world as a "royal residence". It was destroyed in 1101 by the King of Munster, Murtogh O'Brien, in retaliation for the destruction of his own royal seat at Kincora. A tunnel pierces the stone wall (13ft/4m thick), which contains small chambers and steps to the ramparts and encloses a circle (77ft/23m in diameter).

From the ramparts is an extensive **view**★★ *(east)* of Derry and the Sperrin Mountains, *(northeast)* of Lough Foyle, *(north)* of the Inishowen Peninsula and *(west)* of Inch Island, Lough Swilly and Knockalla Mountain.

At the foot of the hill is **St Aengus Church**, a magnificent modern building designed by Liam McCormick.

▶ Return downhill to Burnfoot. Take the R 238 north to Fahan.

Fahan Cross-Slab★

On the south side of the village in the old graveyard beside the Anglican church stands a 7C **cross-slab**, decorated with a cross formed of interlaced bands, one flanked by two figures. It marks the site of a monastery founded by St Mura in the 7C and whichsurvived until at least 1098.

▶ Take the R 238 north to Buncrana.

Buncrana

With its long sandy beach facing west across Lough Swilly to the mountains of Donegal, Buncrana *(Bun Cranncha)*

is a busy seaside resort and the largest town on the Inishowen Peninsula. It is crowded in summer with holidaymakers from Londonderry, a mere dozen miles away on the far side of the border.

Approached by a six-arched bridge spanning the Crana River, O'Docherty's Keep is all that remains of the castle built by the Anglo-Normans and later held by the local lords, the "O'Dochertys tall from dark Donegal" (Benedict Kiely).

▶ From Buncranna take the R 238 towards Drumfree and turn left onto the minor road signposted for Fort Dunree.

Fort Dunree Military Museum★

◷*Open Mon–Fri 10.30am–4.30pm, Sat–Sun 1pm–6pm.* ◉€7. ✗ ✆*074 936 1817. www.dunree.pro.ie.*

A drawbridge spans the narrow defile separating this late-18C fort from the desolate headland of **Dunree Head**. The fort itself has been converted into a **military museum** containing the original guns; modern interactive technology and a video explain their role in a coastal defence battery and describe the evolution of the fort from a fortified earthen embankment, built in 1798 under the threat of French invasion, to an important element in a chain of forts on the shores of Lough Swilly defending a Royal Navy base at Buncrana. In 1914 the entire British Grand Fleet sheltered behind a boom in the Lough.

Knockalla Fort is visible across the narrow channel on the opposite shore.

▶ Return to the junction and turn left; at the crossroads, turn left.

Gap of Mamore★★

The road climbs past rocky outcrops to the **viewpoint**★ and sights of Dunaff Head.

▶ Turn left past Lenan Strand to Lenan Head, through Dunaff to Clonmany and continue N on R 238.

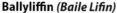

Ballyliffin *(Baile Lifin)*
Beyond Lenon Head, where a gun battery (1895) used to command the entrance to Lough Swilly, lies this attractive holiday village, slightly set back from Pollan Bay and Pollan Strand.

▶ Continue east on the R 238.

Carndonagh High Cross★
At the top of the hill next to the Anglican church stands an 8C **high cross**, decorated with an interlaced cross and a Crucifixion and flanked by two **pillars**: one shows David with his harp. In the graveyard stands a **cross pillar**, known as the Marigold Stone.

▶ Continue north on the R 238 and R 242.

Malin
The 17C Plantation village retains its original layout, including the triangular green.

Lag Sand Dunes★
Massive sand dunes line the north shore of Trawbreaga Bay, the estuary of the Donagh River.

Malin Head★★
The tiny fishing village shelters in the lee of the great headland. On the cliffs stands a tower, originally built in 1805 by the British Admiralty to monitor shipping and later used as a signal tower by Lloyds. North across the sound *(1.5mi/2.4km)* lies Inishtrahull Island, once the site of a hermitage, but now deserted.
The road circles the headland providing dramatic **views★★★** *(southwest)* to Pollan Strand and Dunaff Head.

▶ Take the coast road S via Portaleen to Culdaff and for a detour to Inishowen Head, take the road south from Culdaff to Gleneely and turn left onto the R 238 to Moville, then left onto the R 241 to Inishowen Head.

Inishowen Head★
The headland (295ft/90m) above the tiny harbour next to the lighthouse on **Dunagree Point** commands a fine view east along the Antrim coast to the Giant's Causeway. *(Clifftop footpath to Kinnagoe Bay.)*

▶ Take the coast road south past the golf course.

Greencastle
The beach makes this a popular resort. North of the town, on the cliffs opposite Magilligan Point and commanding the narrow entrance to Lough Foyle, stand the overgrown ruins of a castle. It was built in 1305 by Richard de Burgo, the Red Earl of Ulster, so-called because of his florid complexion. It was captured by Edward Bruce in 1316, fell into the possession of the O'Donnells in the 14C and was granted to Sir Arthur Chichester in 1608; the adjoining fort (1812) was used in the defence of Lough Foyle until the end of the 19C.

▶ From Greencastle take the R 241 south.

Moville *(Bun an Phobail)*
Moville (pronounced with the accent on the second syllable), once a bustling port where emigrant ships set sail for the United States, is now a seaside resort. The granite mass of **St Pius' Roman Catholic Church** (1953) masks its handsome mahogany interior. The cliffs and beaches overlooking Lough Foyle have been incorporated into a landscaped coastal walk, **Moville Green**.

▶ Continue S on R 238, through Quigley's Point and Muff to reach Derry (see p405)

ADDRESSES

THE ROSSES

🛏 STAY

Atlantic House – *Main St, Dunglow.* ☎*074 952 1061. www.atlantichouse dungloe.com. 10rm.* Simple pleasant homely accommodation in central location above the Atlantic Bar pub.

Ostan Gweedore – *Bunbeg.* ☎*074 953 1177. www.ostangweedore.com.* Very well-equipped modern hotel with comprehensive leisure, health and spa facilities; comfortable, luxurious bedrooms and great views over Gweedore. Seafood restaurant and bar menu.

NORTHWEST PENINSULAS

🛏 STAY

Ballyraine Guesthouse – *Ramelton Rd, Letterkenny.* ☎*074 912 4460. 8 rms.* Purpose-built guesthouse, a 15min walk from town, with well-equipped, large bedrooms.

Dergfield House – *Donegal Rd, 0.6mi/ 1km south of Ballybofey.* ☎*074 913 2775. www.dergfieldhouse.com. 5rm.* Very pleasant modern house in own grounds; rooms feature quilts and stripped floorboards, open fire in lounge, all mod cons.

🍴 EAT

The Mill Restaurant – *Dunfanaghy, 0.5mi/0.8km southwest on the N 56.* ☎*074 36985. www.themillrestaurant.com. Dinner only, Tue–Sun.* A converted flax mill in a super location on New Lake, with terrific views of Mount Muckish. A pretty restaurant with Modern Irish cooking. Also has six delightful rooms (🛏) with ensuite facilities.

SHOPPING

The famous **Donegal tweed** is on sale in several centres – Donegal, Kilcar, Ardara and Downies.

Studio Donegal – The Glebe Mill, Kilcar ☎*74 973 8194, www.studiodonegal.ie,* makes and sells hand-woven tweed: throws, clothing, hats.

SPORTS AND LEISURE

Beaches at Naran and Portnoo. Angling in Glenties at the confluence of the Owenea and Stracashel Rivers. Four long-distance, waymarked **coastal paths** – Bealach na Gaeltachta, Dun na nGall – details from North West Tourism Office, Letterkenny (☎*074 9121160*).

EVENTS AND FESTIVALS

International Mary from Dungloe Festival – *Dungloe.* One week late Jul–early Aug (www.maryfromdungloe.com). Music and dancing and outdoor events

TRACING ANCESTORS

Donegal Ancestry Centre – *www.donegalancestry.com.* Online enquiries only.

INISHOWEN PENINSULA

🛏 STAY

Carrickabraghey House – *Shore Road, Ballyliffin.* ☎*074 9376 977. www.dirl.com/ donegal/clonmany.* A simple family-run B&B, with splendid views of Pollan Bay.

Ballyliffin Lodge – *Shore Rd, Ballyliffin.* ☎*074 937 8200. www.ballyliffin lodge.com.* Luxury spa hotel which also features a top class Nick Faldo golf course. Fantastic value.

🍴 EAT

McGrory's of Culdaff – *Inishowen.* ☎*074 937 9104. www.mcgrorys.ie.* Family-run business since 1924, known for locally-sourced seasonal seafood, beef and lamb. Famous for its live gigs in Backroom Bar. Very pleasant well equipped rooms (🛏) too.

MALIN HEAD

🛏 STAY

Malin Head – *Malin.* ☎*074 9370 606. www.malinhotel.ie.* This would be an attractive hotel anywhere, but given the location it is especially appealing and terrific value. Renovation work has transformed it into inviting accommodation and the Jack Yeats Restaurant serves good meals (bar food is also available).

Co Monaghan

Monaghan town *(Muineachán)* **is the commercial centre and the county town of Co Monaghan, once part of the original province of Ulster, projecting into Northern Ireland as far as the Blackwater River. Previously ruled by the McMahon clan, the area was settled by the British in the early 17C and Monaghan town was given its charter in 1613. Its mostly Scottish Presbyterian citizens established a thriving linen industry in the 18C. In the 19C the building of the Ulster Canal and the Ulster Railway brought further benefits, and the town still bears the imprint of these prosperous times, with dignified grey limestone buildings lining its narrow streets.**

- **Info:** The Glen, Monaghan Town. 📞0 47 73718. www.monaghantourism.com.
- **Location:** The county town, Monaghan, is 75mi/120.5km northwest of Dublin; 53mi/80km southwest of Belfast.

MONAGHAN TOWN
St Macartan's (Roman Catholic) Cathedral
This splendid Gothic-Revival landmark was built in 1892, of local limestone, with a soaring spire (250ft/76m) by J.J. McCarthy. The exterior is extravagantly decorated with Carrara marble statues of saints and bishops; the spacious interior contained by a splendid **hammerbeam roof** and ornamented by modern **tapestries** illustrating the Christian life and the life of St Macartan, one of the earliest Irish saints.

Town Centre
The elegant grey limestone **Market House** (1792) was designed by Samuel Hayes, an amateur architect. Church Square *(east)* forms a dignified ensemble, with the **Courthouse** (1830), a handsome Classical building still bearing the scars of the Civil War, and **St Patrick's Anglican Church** (1831), a charming example of Regency-Gothic style. East of Church Square is the **Diamond**, the original marketplace set against the north wall of the 17C castle (long demolished). The **Rossmore Memorial**, an elaborate neo-Gothic drinking fountain (1875), honours the 4th Baron Rossmore.

Museums
Two elegant early-19C terrace houses in Hill Street accommodate the **County Museum** (♿🕐*open Mon–Fri 11am–5pm (noon Sat);* 📞047 82928; www.monaghan.ie). It features exceptional displays on the region and its history, including linen and lace-making, but the museum's greatest treasure is its 12C–14C **Cross of Clogher**.

The **St Louis Heritage Centre** (🕐*open Apr–Oct Thu–Sun 2–4pm;* 📞047 83529) tells the story of the Order of St Louis, founded in France in 1842, and its nuns, who came to Ireland in 1859. There is a **crannóg** *(an ancient partly or completely artificial island, which was once settled)* in Spark's Lake in the convent grounds.

ROSSMORE FOREST PARK
2mi/3.5km S of Monaghan by N 54 and R 189.
Only the foundations of the Rossmore residence remain, though the Earls' **mausoleum** (♿🕐*open 9am–8pm, 6pm in winter;* 📞047 81968) still stands in the grounds of the desmesne, now a Forest Park landscaped with woods and water.

CLONES
12mi/19km SW of Monaghan by N 54.
Right on the border with Northern Ireland, Clones *(pronounced as two syllables)* is a pleasant market town renowned for its angling. It is a typical Ulster plantation settlement, with a long history stretching back to a monastery founded by St Tighernach in the 6C, of which a **round tower**, **monolithic shrine** and a 12C **church** survive.

The **high cross** (c. 10C) standing in the central Diamond, below the Anglican

*Hope Castle,
Lough Muckno Leisure Park*

© Chris Hill/Tourism Ireland

is surrounded by a wooded park (91 acres/37ha) threaded with **nature trails**. The park was originally the desmesne of Sir Edward Blaney, King James I's Governor of Monaghan, whose name lives on in Castleblaney, the little town overlooking the lake's western shore. A later Blaney built the Georgian **Courthouse** and, in 1808, the Anglican church. In the late-19C Blaney Castle was bought by Thomas Hope, a London banker who renamed it "Hope Castle".

ADDRESSES

🛌 STAY

😋😋😋 **Castle Leslie Estate**– *Glaslough.* *℘047 88100. www.castleleslie.com.* Luxury, grandeur and history meet in a fabulous lakeside setting in one of the finest castle-hotels In Ireland; but don't expect TVs, radios, wifi or minibars in the castle's beautiful bedrooms!

🍸 EAT

😋😋😋 **Snaffles Reastaurant**– *Castle Leslie Estate, Glaslough. ℘047 88100. www.castleleslie.com.* Fine dining on the mezzanine floor of one of the top luxury castle hotels in Ireland,this open-plan restaurant is light and spacious with its dramatic hand-carved ceiling and robust oak beams blending effortlessly with a striking wall of contemporary glass.

church (1822), may also be contemporary with the monastery.

The **Ulster Canal Stores** now hosts a display of **Clones lace**, a crochet lace with individual motifs connected by areas of Clones knot.

LOUGH MUCKNO LEISURE PARK

15mi/24km SE of Monaghan on the N 2 to Castleblaney.

Lough Muckno, the largest and loveliest of the lakes in Co Monaghan

Round Tower, Clones

© Monaghan County Council/Fáilte Ireland/Tourism Ireland

Lough Oughter

© IIC / age fotostock

Co Cavan

County Cavan *(An Cabhán)* **is drumlin country – a tranquil, undulating, well-wooded landscape – scattered with countless small lakes. Near to the little county town is Lough Oughter, the largest lake in Co Cavan, fed by the River Erne.**

CAVAN TOWN

There is little to deter visitors in Cavan itself, its places of interest lie outside town. The Roman Catholic **Cathedral** (1942) designed by **Ralph Byrnes** and sculptures by **Albert Power** (1883–1945), is variously described as "sham Renaissance" or "the last flamboyant fling of historicism" and the crenellated **Anglican Church** with west tower

Info: Johnston Central Library, Farnham Street, Cavan. ℰ 049 433 1942. www.thisiscavan.ie.

Location: Cavan town is set at the junction of the N 3 Dublin-Donegal road, 70mi/112km northwest of Dublin.

and steeple by John Bowden, who also designed the Classical **Courthouse**.

BALLYJAMESDUFF

10mi/16km south of Cavan by the N 3, N 55 and a minor road via Cross Keys. This small town, named after Sir James Duff, the commander of British troops

Cavan's Literary Cavalcade

Several famous writers are connected with County Cavan: the playwright **Richard Brinsley Sheridan** was the grandson of Dr Thomas Sheridan, the headmaster of Cavan Royal School and a good friend of Jonathan Swift, who lived at Quilcagh House near Mullagh. An ancestor of **Edgar Allan Poe** (1809–49) emigrated to America from Killeshandra in the mid-18C. William James, a Presbyterian from Baillieborough who settled in America, was the grandfather of **Henry James** (1843–1916). The songwriter and painter **Percy French** (1854–1920), born at Cloonyquin (west of Strokestown), worked in Cavan for seven years as an inspector of loans to tenants. He began penning lyrics while studying at Trinity College, Dublin.

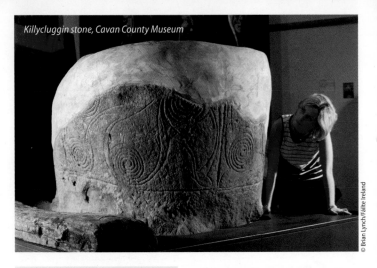

Killycluggin stone, Cavan County Museum

© Brian Lynch/Fáilte Ireland

William Bedell (1571–1642)

William Bedell was born in Sussex, studied at Cambridge and travelled widely in Europe, before being appointed Provost of Trinity College Dublin, in 1627. In 1629 he became Bishop of Kilmore and tried to introduce reforms. During the 1641 Rebellion he was imprisoned by the Confederates for two years in Clogh Oughter Castle.

in the 1798 uprising, clusters around the Market House (1813). It is home to the **Cavan County Museum** (&Open Tue–Sat 10am–5pm; Jul–Aug also Sun 2pm–6pm; ✕; ℰ049 854 4070, www.cavanmuseum.ie). This fine collection includes archaeological artefacts tracing the heritage of County Cavan, including a rare three-faced, pre-Christian Corleck Head and Stone-Age dug-out. Other galleries trace 1950s rural life, art, famine, costume, The Nun's Story, Percy French (&see box, below) and GAA sports.

CARRAIG CRAFT VISITOR CENTRE

Mount Nugent,15mi/24km south of Cavan via the N 3, N 55 and R 154.

Open Apr–Oct, Mon–Fri, 10am–6pm; Sun 2pm–6pm; Nov–Mar by appointment. ⚐€3.50. ✕ ℰ049 8540 179.

The art of basket-making, old and new, is celebrated in this museum shop with donkey creels, pigeon panniers; bee skeps; straw, reed and willow containers for eggs, turf, potatoes, fish, poultry, flowers and more.

KILMORE CATHEDRAL

3mi/5km W of Cavan on the R 198.
By appointment or during services.
The neo-Gothic Anglican cathedral, known as the **Bedell Memorial Church**, is dedicated to **St Felim** (*Fethlimidh*), who brought Christianity to the region in the 6C. The fine 12C Romanesque north doorway may have belonged to an earlier church or to the abbey on Trinity Island in Lough Oughter.

KILLYKEEN FOREST PARK★

5mi/8km west of Cavan on the R 198.
www.cornafean.com/Attractions.htm.
This 600-acre/243-ha Forest Park replicates the patchwork of land and water so characteristic of the River Erne in counties Cavan and Fermanagh.
Marked nature trails thread through the park and there is a wildfowl sanctuary by the Sally Lake. Other facilities include a tennis court, children's play area, bicycle and boat hire.

On Trinity Island, at the southern end of **Lough Oughter**, stands the ruin of a Premonstratensian Priory, established in 1250 by monks from Lough Key.

ADDRESSES

🛏 STAY

🛏 **Rockwood House** – *Cloverhill, Belturbet.* 📞*047 55351. www.rocwood house.com. 4rm.* Lovely stone-built B&B set among woods with a bright conservatory and attractive garden. Bedrooms simply, yet pleasantly furnished. Hospitable owners.

🛏–🛏🛏 **Eonish Lodge Farm Guesthouse** – *Killeshandra, 5mi/8km southwest of Cavan on the N 55 and 2.5mi west of Bellinagh by the N 55, off Arva road.* 📞*049 433 4487. 4 rms. www.eonish lodge.com.* Simple accommodation in a peaceful location, convenient for boating, lake fishing, horse riding and exploring Killykeen Forest Park.

🍴 EAT

🛏🛏🛏 **The Olde Post Inn** – *Cloverhill.* 📞*047 55555. www.theoldepostinn.com.* Fine Dining in the award-winning restaurant of a beautiful turn-of-the-19C guesthouse.

SHOPPING

Cavan Crystal – *Dublin Rd.* 📞*049 433 1800. www.cavancrystalhotel.com.* The second-oldest lead-crystal glass factory in Ireland, is no longer open for tours, but visitors can explore the extensive showroom and extensive contemporary glass gift shop located just inside the door of the Cavan Crystal Hotel on the outskirts of town.

Bear Essentials – *Tiernawannagh, Bawnboy (Marble Arch Caves Global Geo Park).* 📞*049 952 3461. www.bear essentials.ie.* Collectible hand-crafted mohair teddy bears.

SPORTS AND LEISURE

Lough Oughter, a complex of small lakes linked by short rivers, is perfect for **boating** and **canoeing**. **Coarse fishing** takes place on the lake and along stretches of the Annalee, a tributary of the Erne, for roach, bream, hybrids, pike, perch; **trout fishing** on Lough Annagh; **game angling** for salmon and trout. **Watersports** facilities include windsurfing and waterskiing.

EVENTS AND FESTIVALS

Belturbet Festival of the Erne. *www.festivaloftheerne.com.* Live music, a talent competition, marching bands, fireworks, a very popular fancy-dress party and the Lady of The Erne pageant (*late Jul–early Aug*).

TRACING ANCESTORS

Cavan Genealogy Research Centre – *Cana House, Farnham St. Open Mon–Fri 9.30am–4.30pm.* 📞*049 436 1094.*

Angling on Lough Oughter, Clough Oughter Castle in the background

© Tourism Ireland

Carrick-a-Rede Rope Bridge, County Antrim
© G. Gerault/hemis.fr

An area of 14,160 sq km (5,241 sq mi) with a population of over 1.5 million, Northern Ireland has had a tumultuous history. Visitors were once warned about straying into certain areas but today the pretty countryside is no longer marred by road blocks and armoured car patrols and there is a lively, dynamic feeling to the capital city. From the stunning Mountains of Mourne to the iconic Giant's Causeway, and from the ancient city walls of Derry to the high-tech Odyssey Centre in Belfast, there is much to see and celebrate in this reborn part of Ireland.

Highlights

1 A tour of the pubs in the lively city of **Belfast** (p419)

2 Step back in time at **The Ulster Folk and Transport Museum** (p422)

3 The historic City Walls and Tower Museum at **Derry** (p480)

4 The geological wonder of the **Giant's Causeway** (p489)

5 A leisurely Driving Tour of the **Glens of Antrim** (p493)

Co Antrim

Home to the Giant's Causeway and the beautiful Glens of Antrim, this county also claims part of Belfast as its own. The county is one of the most economically developed of Northern Ireland. It has the highest population of any of the counties and its agriculture is far more mechanised than in other parts of the island. Antrim has strong cultural ties with southwest Scotland; many Antrim families originated there; and two ferries still link the areas.

Co Derry (Londonderry)

Sitting on the border with the Republic, the city of Derry experienced some of the worst of the Troubles and much of its architecture suffered bomb damage but the city walls are intact, as is the 1908 Guild Hall, the Catholic Cathedral and the Diamond, the city centre laid out in the early 17C.

The county is landlocked to the Southwest and Northeast but incorporates the long coastline of Lough Foyle to the North and part of Lough Neagh to the South. The River Bann, the long-est and most important river in Ulster, which, in the heyday of linen production powered many linen mills, flows north-wards from the Mourne Mountains, along the eastern border to discharge 80mi/129km later northeast of Cole-raine, a predominantly "planter" town, laid out in 1611. Lough Foyle, a large, shallow sea lough was the determining factor in the development of Derry city, its potential as a seaport making Derry's manufacturing industry and later, its ship building industry, possible. Derry's countryside includes the scenic Sperrin Mountains in the South, Binevagh and Keady Mountains in the North and the Bann, Roe and Foyle Valleys.

Co Down

Traditionally connected more to south-ern Scotland than the rest of Ireland, County Down was settled by lowland Scots before the general plantation of the North. The county town of Downpat-rick is said to be the burial place of St Pat-rick and the town has a strong tradition of celebrating St Patrick's Day. In times past this proved divisive but it is now a genuine cross-cultural experience. The physical landscape of the county includes the Mourne Mountains in the South, from where the River Bann rises, to end its journey in County Antrim. The Mourne Mountains are designated an area of outstanding beauty; they are an important recreational area for the population of Belfast and counties Antrim and Down. Strangford Lough, only 8mi/14km from Belfast, is another important conservation and recreational area in the county. The Lough is home to thousands of birds, seals and some rare sea creatures, as well as a haven for small boats. It is linked to the Irish Sea by only one channel, the Narrows. On the

Lower Lough Erne, County Fermanagh

© Northern Ireland Tourist Board

eastern shore of the Lough is the Ards Peninsula, a pleasant afternoon's drive.

Co Armagh

A small county, landlocked, with Lough Neagh as part of its northern border, and the partly navigable river Blackwater marking the border with County Tyrone, Armagh was once the ancient capital of Ulster. Navan Fort, west of the county town, is an important Iron Age site where the kings of Ulster once lived. Confiscated and settled with English and Scottish settlers in the early 17C, by the 18C Armagh was an important linen-producing area and very densely populated. During the Troubles and with the strongly Republican "bandit country" at the southern end of the county and the headline-hitting Portadown in the North, Armagh's reputation preceded it for many years but in more peaceful times it is a pleasant place to visit, primarily for Armagh city but also for the rolling, drumlin geography, apple orchards and its two forest parks, Slieve Gullion and Gosford Castle.

Co Tyrone

The largest county in Northern Ireland, Tyrone is a very rural county, traditionally poor, with agriculture and linen production being its main industries. At the border with County Derry, the Sperrin Mountains with Mullaglgloghla at their highest point offer stunning scenic tours, hillwalking and quiet country retreats for those who choose to stay a while.

Tyrone's only town of any size is Omagh, the county's main shopping area, its imposing courthouse probably the intended goal for the bomb which wrecked the city centre in 1998, killing 29 people and injuring hundreds more. Other, smaller towns still display their planter origins, with Sion Mills, a designated conservation area, being the most intact.

Co Fermanagh

Known as the "Fermanagh Lakeland", County Fermanagh is renowned for its beautiful Lakeland scenery and activities. The Upper Lough, shallow and calmer than the deeper, Lower Lough, is a maze of islands, many privately owned. In between the two loughs sits Enniskillen. The Lower Lough is a wilder, fiercer place, where high winds can make sailing difficult and whose islands contain some amazing early-Christian remains. The Lower Lough offers watersports such as waterskiing, diving, canoeing and sailing, and several companies offer trips out to the islands. The county's main town is Enniskillen.

Belfast★★

Few cities have such a splendid natural setting; Belfast (Béal Feirste) stands at the mouth of the River Lagan at the point where it discharges into the great sea inlet of Belfast Lough, which is sheltered on both sides by hills. To the West rises the formidable basalt escarpment of Cave Hill and Black Mountain. One of the great industrial and commercial cities of the Victorian era, the capital of Northern Ireland has survived 30 years of Troubles. The fragile peace encouraged a tidal wave of new building and a vibrant cultural life without equal in the rest of the province. Half a million people live within a few miles of the city centre, a third of Northern Ireland's population.

▶ **Population:** 295,000.

▪ **Info:** Belfast Welcome Centre, 47 Donegall Place. ℘028 9024 6609. www.visit-belfast.com. There are information desks at both airports.

◑ **Location:** On the shores of Belfast Lough. For an overview, take the open-top bus tour. www.city sightseeingbelfast.com.

⊛ **Don't Miss:** Titanic Belfast, Ulster Museum, Belfast Zoo, a tour of the Murals.

▲▲ **Kids:** Titanic Belfast W5 (Odyssey Complex), Belfast Zoo.

◷ **Timing:** Allow 3 days.

A BIT OF HISTORY

Norman Castle to Industrial City – Belfast takes its name from a ford by a sandbank *(bealfeirste* in Irish) where the Anglo-Norman John de Courcy built a castle after his invasion of Ulster in 1177. Development only came in the early 17C when a quay was built and trade diverted from Carrickfergus.

The city was settled by hard-working Scottish Presbyterians, followed later by industrious Huguenot refugees, who brought new techniques to the burgeoning linen industry. Cotton spinning was introduced in 1777, shipbuilding in 1791; by the early 19C, industry was booming; and the population multiplied fifteenfold, from under 25,000 to 350,000 over two generations. General engineering flourished, as did distilling, rope-making and tobacco products, but it was the great shipyards that gave the city its distinctive industrial character, with Harland and Wolff – builders of the *Titanic* – becoming the United Kingdom's largest construction and repair yard. In the 20C, Short Brothers produced the Sunderland flying boat and the first VTOL jet; their airstrip in the docks is now used by George Best Belfast City Airport.

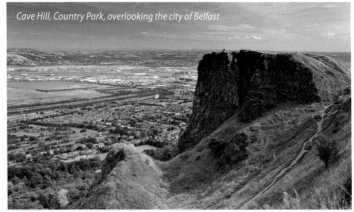
Cave Hill, Country Park, overlooking the city of Belfast

© Northern Ireland Tourist Board

GETTING THERE

BY AIR – Belfast International Airport: Flights to several European and UK destinations. *028 9448 4848. www.belfastairport.com.* 18 mi/29km northwest of Belfast. Airport Express 300 bus shuttles to and from the city centre every 10 mins, journey 30–40min. £7.50 one-way, £10.50 return.

George Best Belfast City Airport – scheduled flights to all over the UK, Jersey, Isle of Man, Malaga, Faro, Palma, Paris. 2mi/3km north east of the city centre. *028 909 3909. www.belfastcityairport.com.* Airport Express 600 to and from the city centre every 20–30min, journey 10–15min. £2.20 one-way, £3.30 return. Buses from both airports terminate at the Europa Bus Centre.

Dissent and Division – The predominance of the Presbyterian Church, its cultural links with Scotland and commercial wealth, underpinned Belfast's early reputation as a centre for intellectual activity and articulated independence. Belfast had the first printing press in Ireland (c. 1690) and published the first Irish newspaper, the *Belfast News Letter*, in 1737 – the oldest morning paper in the British Isles.

It was in Belfast in 1791 that Wolfe Tone helped to found the Society of United Irishmen; in 1792 they published the *Northern Star*, a newspaper which expressed radical opinion and first promoted the idea of the Irish nation, which, in Tone's words, would "substitute the common name of Irishman in place of ... Protestant, Catholic, and Dissenter". To the dismay of the United Irishmen, their ideals, which had sharpened existing divisions, did not survive the failed 1798 Rebellion.

The overwhelmingly Presbyterian city of the late 18C changed as spectacular industrial growth began employing large numbers of Catholics drawn from all over Ireland in the 19C, settling in the **Falls Road** area of the city between the predominantly Protestant working-class districts of Sandy Row and **Shankill Road**. During **The Trouble**s these names became synonymous with extremes of sectarianism and violent conflict. Today they are still divided by sectarian loyalties but now attract visitors by the bus-load, who come to view the murals.

WALKING TOUR

Donegall Square★

The hub of Belfast is Donegall Square: a vast rectangle of grass and gardens peopled with statues, laid out around the City Hall. On sunny summer days every square inch of grass is taken up by picnicking office workers and visitors. Facing onto the Square are a variety of handsome Victorian buildings, notably **Yorkshire House**, with roundels containing low-relief heads of famous men and deities *(south side)*; the elegant block commissioned for **Scottish Provident** (1899–1902), designed by the Belfast architects Young and Mackenzie *(west side)*; an old pink stone linen warehouse (1869) *(north side)*, and the **Linen Hall Library**, (◷open Mon–Sat 9.30am–5.30pm /4pm Sat; ◷closed Bank Hols; ✕; *028 9032 1707; www.linenhall.com),* founded in 1788 as the Belfast Library and Society for Promoting Knowledge. It has a delightfully old-fashioned interior with great views onto the Square, where you can escape the bustle of the city with a newspaper and a cup of coffee. The modern annexe contains various material relating to the Troubles and there is a genealogy section.

City Hall★

◷*Open for free tours Mon–Fri 11am, 2pm, 3pm, Sat 2pm, 3pm. *028 9027 0456. www.belfastcity.gov.uk/cityhall.* The great neo-Renaissance Portland stone building, with its copper-covered dome and corner towers, was designed by Sir Brumwell Thomas and completed

City Hall, Donegall Square

© Northern Ireland Tourist Board

in 1906, at a time when Belfast was at its zenith of industrial and commercial might to mark the city status granted by Queen Victoria in 1888.

Highlights of the **interior** include the grand staircase; a mural of the founding of the city and its principal industries painted by John Luke; a sculpture by Patrick MacDowell (1790–1870), a native of Belfast, of the Marquess of Donegall (1827–53), who devoted the proceeds of his music and poetry to good works; the Council Chamber, panelled in hand-carved Austrian oak; the Reception Hall displaying the original Charter of Belfast granted by James I on April 27, 1613; the Banqueting Hall and the shields of the Provinces of Ireland in the stained glass of the Great Hall.

The grounds of City Hall are notable for their statuary, mostly of famous Belfast men. Sir Edward Harland, who founded Harland and Wolff shipbuilding, is represented here by a statue (1903) by Thomas Brock, while nearby is the **Titanic memorial** (1920), also sculpted by Thomas Brock, which pays tribute to 22 Ulstermen who lost their lives on the ship. Ironically, this included the elite nine-man Harland and Wolff "Guarantee Group", all expert in their fields, who were sent on each maiden voyage in case of problems.

Queen Victoria is represented by a Sicilian marble figure (Thomas Brock, 1903), with figures representing spinning and shipbuilding at her side and education behind her. A cenotaph also stands in the grounds, as does a memorial to the troops of the Royal Ulster Rifles, who were killed during the Korean War.

City Hall gained unwanted publicity in December 2012 when its decision to restrict the number of days the Union flag was flown above the hall became the focus of serious sectarian rioting.

▷ From the northwest corner of Donegall Square, walk west along Wellington Place and cross the road.

Royal Belfast Academical Institute

⌐ *Closed to the public.*

The inter-denominational boys' school on College Square, known as "Inst", was probably designed by Sir John Soane (1814).

▷ Continue left and cross the road.

Church House

& ⊙ *Assembly Hall open for viewing in normal office hours subject to functions; enquire at the reception desk. ✆ 028 9032 2284. www. presbyterianireland.org/about/ churchhouse.html.*

The headquarters of the Presbyterian Church in Ireland was designed by Young and Mackenzie (1905), Belfast architects, in the 15C-Gothic style of a Scottish baronial castle. The massive 131ft/40m-high Clock tower, inspired by St Giles' Cathedral in Edinburgh, contains a peal of 12 bells.

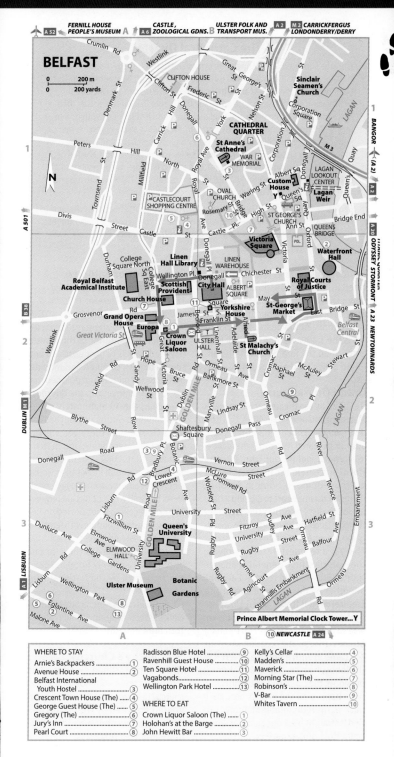

BELFAST

Scale: 200 m / 200 yards

WHERE TO STAY

Arnie's Backpackers	(1)
Avenue House	(2)
Belfast International Youth Hostel	(3)
Crescent Town House (The)	(4)
George Guest House (The)	(5)
Gregory (The)	(6)
Jury's Inn	(7)
Pearl Court	(8)
Radisson Blue Hotel	(9)
Ravenhill Guest House	(10)
Ten Square Hotel	(11)
Vagabonds	(12)
Wellington Park Hotel	(13)

WHERE TO EAT

Crown Liquor Saloon (The)	(1)
Holohan's at the Barge	(2)
John Hewitt Bar	(3)
Kelly's Cellar	(4)
Madden's	(5)
Maverick	(6)
Morning Star (The)	(7)
Robinson's	(8)
V-Bar	(9)
Whites Tavern	(10)

Prince Albert Memorial Clock Tower...Y

The Cathedral Quarter

The area surrounding St Anne's, known as The Cathedral Quarter, is the city's cultural hotspot. Bars, clubs and pubs include the smart Northern Whig, The Mynt, the John Hewitt Bar and The Spaniard, while restaurants include the trail-blazing Nick's Warehouse and Ba Soba Noodle Bar. On the artistic theme there are a host of small commercial galleries and The Black Box with its live music, theatre, literature, comedy and film. The area is also a nightclub mecca, with two of the best places in town; glitzy mainstream Rain, and Kremlin, one of the top gay venues in the UK. The 5-star Merchant Hotel, set in the former Ulster Bank Building in Waring Street, has added its more mainstream seal of approval to the area, adding its Great Room restaurant, Ollie's nightclub and Bert's Jazz Bar to the Cathedral Quarter mix.

Each May the Cathedral Quarter hosts a cutting-edge arts festival (*www.cqaf. com*), with the emphasis on bringing arts to unorthodox places: it also stages the Out to Lunch festival (*same website*) throughout January.

Church House was extensively renovated in 1992 and the ground floor is now a shopping mall while the administrative offices of the Church are on the upper floors. At the heart of the building is the 1,300-seater Assembly Hall, entered on the first floor, with its all-round gallery and pipe organ.

Grand Opera House

Designed by the theatre architect Frank Matcham and opened in 1894, this gorgeous building has a gilt-and-red-plush interior to match its exuberant façade. Its famous neighbour, the **Europa Hotel**, once held the unenviable title of "most-bombed hotel in Europe", thanks in no small part to it being a base for journalists covering the Troubles. Happily, because warnings were always given, no one was killed here.

There is a wonderful story involving the Europa's first general manager, Harper Brown, who received an MBE (Member of the Order of the British Empire) medal from Queen Elizabeth II for keeping the hotel open. Mr Brown was so determined to remain open for business that on one occasion when the IRA came in with a bomb and left it in the lobby, he picked it up and threw it outside in the car park. The bomber saw what happened and in turn, brought it back in. The redoubtable Mr Brown carried it straight back out again, at which point the bomber gave up and left!

Crown Liquor Saloon★

&. ○ *Open year-round Mon–Wed 11.30am–11pm, Thu–Sat 11.30am–midnight, Sun 12.30pm–10pm.* ℘ *028 9024 3187. www.nicholsonspubs.co.uk.*
The Victorian interior of this famous city landmark is richly decorated with coloured glass, coloured and moulded tiles, arcaded mirrors and polished marble. Carved animals top the doorposts of each of the 10 elaborately carved and panelled Snugs or Boothes, lettered from A–J. In these you will find gunmetal plates for striking matches and an antique bell system (this used to be very common in Victorian Houses where servants were employed), which alerts bar staff when drinks are required. The ornate ceiling is supported on hexagonal wooden columns with feathered ornament. Inspired by his travels in Spain and Italy, Patrick Flanagan built the public house as a railway hotel in 1885; it is now owned by the National Trust.

▷ Turn left into Amelia Street and walk eastwards along Franklin Street. Turn right into Alfred Street.

St Malachy's Church★

The austere fortified exterior of this red-brick crenellated Roman Catholic church (1844) gives no hint of the ornate interior enclosed by white stucco fan vaulting inspired by Henry VII's Chapel in Westminster Abbey.

St George's Market

© giulio andreini/age fotostock

▶ Return to the junction; turn right into Sussex Place; walk along Hamilton Street and into East Bridge Street; turn left and walk north along Oxford Street.

St George's Market★

🕓Open Fri 6am–1pm, Sat 9am–3pm
www.belfastcity.gov.uk/markets.
Built between 1890 and 1896, this is the oldest covered market in Ireland and one of the best in the British Isles. It sells a variety of products, including food, clothes, books and antiques, and every Friday morning boasts the largest indoor fish market in Ireland with 23 seafood stalls plus fruit and vegetables, meat antiques, books and clothes.

The Saturday morning Farm & Speciality Food Market is the best day to come, with a huge range of local, continental and specialty foods, while the Sunday market is a mix of the previous two days but with a special emphasis on local arts and crafts.

▶ The front entrance of the market is May Street. This leads west (with your back towards the river) back to Donegall Square.

CITY CENTRE
St Anne's Cathedral★

🕓Open daily 8am–4pm.
No sightseeing Sun 11am–12.30pm during Sung Eucharist service. ℘028 9032 8332. www.belfastcathedral.org.
Belfast's Hiberno-Romanesque Anglican Cathedral (1899–1981), by Sir Thomas Drew, contains a fine Chapel of the Holy Spirit, consecrated in 1932 on the 1500th anniversary of St Patrick's mission to Ireland.

The most remarkable and controversial feature of the church is its **Spire of**

The Seamen's Church

From the Lagan Weir, instead of turning right (towards Waterfront Hall), walk the opposite way along the riverbank, towards the ferries and the **Sinclair Seamen's Church★** *(open Wed 2pm–4pm; ℘028 9080 1240)* dating from 1857. The charming interior of this Venetian-style harbourside church was refurbished on a maritime theme. Early 19C shipyard workers, dockers and sailors would have felt at home in its ship-like interior, with its pulpit shaped as a ship's prow, flanked by navigation lights, ship's binnacle font and the bell of *HMS Hood* calling worshippers to service. The imposing Victorian block next door is the Belfast Harbour Commissioners Office.

Hope, installed April 2007. This relentlessly modern, very slender titanium and stainless-steel clad spike resembles a gigantic knitting needle. The base section of the spire protrudes through a glass platform in the Cathedral's roof directly above the choir stalls, allowing visitors to view it from the nave. In total, it rises 300ft/100m above the ground. To the side of the cathedral three large buoys from Belfast Lough are a reminder of the city's seafaring history.

Victoria Square

Completed in March 2008 at a cost of over £400m, this is the biggest and one of the most expensive property developments ever undertaken in Northern Ireland. The attraction is not the 100-plus shops and restaurants (there is also a multiplex cinema), which are mostly of the chain variety, rather it is the spectacular glass geodesic dome, measuring 115ft/35m in diameter, with its **viewing gallery** (🕘*admission free but ticket required, from the information desk; www.victoriasquare.com*), which not only gives a panorama over the city rooftops, but offers vertiginous views down into the complex itself.

At night the dome glows blue, becoming a landmark. By contrast, just outside the complex on the river side is the relatively tiny but still eye-catching bright yellow ornate Victorian **Jaffe Memorial Fountain**.

THE LAGANSIDE★

The River Lagan heads northsouth through Belfast with the city centre to the East, and across the water the former docklands area – great swathes of deserted and derelict former industrial land. This now hosts one of the biggest urban renewal projects in Europe, most notably the **Titanic Quarter**, which is becoming a new home to shops, offices, housing and leisure facilities, and is now attracting hundreds of thousands of visitors, thanks mainly to Its iconic centrepiece, **Titanic Belfast** (🕘*see below*).

West Bank

The riverside is approached along the High Street – before it was filled in, huge ships once sailed up here, as far as Bridge Street – and ends at the 113-ft/35-m high **Prince Albert Memorial Clock Tower**.

This was built 1867–79 in honour of Queen Victoria's consort (even though he never visited Belfast) and is famous for its lean – 4ft/1.25m off the vertical – due to the fact that it was built on land reclaimed from the river.

To the left, approaching the Lagan is the handsome classical **Custom House** (*closed to the public*) on Donegall Quay. This too is Victorian, built 1854–57 by Charles Lanyon, designer of many of Belfast's finest buildings. In front of the building stands a statue of an orator, a reminder that in the 19C this large square was a "Speaker's Corner", a place of free speech where all sorts of debates were held in the open air.

Across the busy Oxford Street/Donegall Quay road is the riverfront and **Lagan Weir**, marked by **Big Fish**, a 32-ft/10-m long blue ceramic-mosaic salmon by John Kindness, one of Northern Ireland's leading contemporary artists. The fish "scales" are a cladding of ceramic tiles decorated with texts and images relating to the history of Belfast. It was commissioned in 1999 to celebrate the regeneration of the River Lagan and, appropriately, the river is now clean enough for salmon to swim in. A few yards to either side of here, riverboat trips depart, featuring Titanic-related sites (🕾*028 9033 0844; www.laganboatcompany.com*).

Walk along the river bank and on the junction with the bridge is another striking new modern sculpture of a ponytailed woman standing on a sphere. Her title is **The Angel of Thanksgiving and Reconciliation**, though locals refer to her as "the doll on the ball".

Beyond is **Belfast Waterfront Hall** (🕾*028 9033 4400; www.waterfront.co.uk*), a major concert and arts venue, conference centre and city landmark, opened in 1997 as a flagship of redevelopment. It is well worth a visit, even

Politics off the wall? The Murals of Belfast

These mean streets were once feared no-go areas for the police and even the army. Today, however, in a situation that would have been unthinkable a decade ago, the Shanklin and Falls Road are now prime tourist areas. Visitors flock to see their Murals. These giant works of street art/propaganda vary in subject matter from romanticised portrayals of Irish myths and legends (tailored to a political message) to a rather unflattering representation of the late Queen Mother; a heroic representation of IRA hunger-striker and MP Bobby Sands to chilling pictures of hooded gunmen. Perhaps the most memorable is the mural, nicknamed with typical Belfast black humour, *The Mona Lisa*. It depicts a gunman whose rifle is pointing, inescapably, wherever you move, towards the viewer.

The Belfast City Sightseeing bus tour takes in both the Shanklin and Fall Road and gives you a good idea of the murals. If you want to learn more, take a Black Cab Tour (in a London-style taxi cab). The tour, with Billy Scott, a humorous, no-nonsense Belfast Blue badge guide, will tell you all about the city and is particularly good on the areas once dominated by the Troubles (*07798 602401).* A more politically biased option is a tour with **Coiste Political Tours** of Republican West Belfast, with a guide from the ex-prisoner community (*tours Mon–Sat 11am, Sun 2pm from Divis. £10, inc. free glass of Guinness at the end of the Falls Road Walking Tour; 028 9020 0770; www.coiste.ie).*

when there are no performances on, and includes a brasserie overlooking the water.

Opposite the Hall the massive Portland stone **Royal Courts of Justice** (1929–33), scene of many a case in Belfast's recent troubled history, strike a more sombre note.

East Bank (Titanic Quarter)★★★

Towering above the old dockyards the iconic massive yellow **gantry cranes** of the **Harland and Wolff shipyard**, "Samson" and "Goliath", both distinctively marked H and W, are visible from many points in the city (tour guides joke this is for the benefit of visitors and stands for "Hello and Welcome").

Each crane has a span of 460ft/140m and can lift loads of up to 840 tonnes to a height of 230ft/70m, making a combined lifting capacity of over 1,600 tonnes, one of the largest in the world. The dry dock below is the largest in the world, measuring 1,824 ft/556m by 93m/305ft. At its peak Harland & Wolff employed 35,000 men in shipbuilding. Today it employs around 500 people and no longer builds ships. Instead it is involved in overhaul, re-fitting and ship repair, as well as the construction and repair of offshore equipment, such as oil platforms.

Odyssey Complex★

W5 open year-round Mon–Fri 10am–5pm, Mon–Sat 10am–6pm, Sun noon–6pm (Jul–Aug daily till 6pm). £9.80, child £7.50. (charge). 028 9046 7700. www.w5online. co.uk. www.theodyssey.co.uk. www.odysseypavilion.co.uk.

This huge complex is Belfast's landmark Millennium project. For families the main attraction is the hugely entertaining **W5** (Who? What? Where? When? Why?) interactive Discovery Centre. It features over 250 interactive exhibits, experiments and activities, and stages live shows, events and exhibitions daily. The **Odyssey Arena** auditorium can accommodate over 10,000 spectators, who come to see musical superstars and spectacular productions. It is also home to Belfast Giants ice hockey team. The complex also houses The **Odyssey Pavilion**, with an **IMAX cinema,** shops, nightclubs, bars and restaurants.

SS Nomadic

Hamilton Graving Dock. ☏028 9065 9971. www.titanictours-belfast.co.uk. The last surviving White Star vessel afloat, the *SS Nomadic* is a First & Second Class Tender, which carried the wealthiest passengers onto *Titanic*. Launched in 1911, after a long service as a tender, troop carrier and latterly, a floating restaurant in Paris, she fell derelict and was due to be scrapped in 2006. She received a last-minute reprieve, however, and is now undergoing restoration.

♟♟ Titanic Belfast★★

⊙Open Jan-Mar & Oct-Dec 10am-5pm, Apr-May & Sept 9am-6pm, Jun-Aug 9am-7pm. Tickets are based on timed slots available every 20 min. Last admission 1hr 40 min before closing. ☜£18, child £8. ✕ ℗(charge). ☺ Visitors are advised to book tickets online to guarantee entry and also get a 5 per cent discount. ☏028 9076 6399 ticket sales, ☏028 9076 6386 general enquiries. http://titanicbelfast.com. This striking 126-ft (38.5-m) high silver space-age structure houses Ireland's latest major visitor attraction. The design of the building, clad in thousands of 3-D aluminium plates, was influenced by several maritime themes, including ice crystals, ships' hulls and the insignia of the White Star Line. Opened in 2012 to mark the centenary of the world's most famous ship, this is the world's largest Titanic visitor attraction in every sense. Its cavernous interior, marking the site of the slipway where Titanic was built, comprises nine interactive galleries, including a dark ride, underwater exploration theatre and re-creations of the ship's decks and cabins. For many visitors the high point is the **Shipyard Ride** through the Titanic, under construction.

HMS Caroline

Built in Birkenhead in 1914, this light cruiser is the last remaining World War One battleship to have taken part in the epic Jutland Grand Fleet in 1916. It is currently being renovated and is not open to the public.

Titanic's Dock and Pump House

Queen's Rd. ⊙Visitor centre open daily 10am (Fri 9.30am)–4.30pm. ☏Guided tours daily. atnoon, 1pm, 2pm, 3pm. ☜£6 (visitor centre only), £7 to include tour. ✕ ☏028 9073 7813. www.titanicsdock.com. Work began in 1904 on this 880ft/268m long dock, whose walls were 18.5ft thick and which had 332 massive keel-blocks of cast iron to support the weight of the great liners it would hold. At the same time a large outfitting wharf was constructed nearby and the surrounding water dredged to a depth of 32ft/9.7m. Despite its size, the dock still had to be

Titanic Belfast

© Chris Hill/Tourism Ireland

Royal Ulster Academy's annual exhibition, Ulster Museum

© Northern Ireland Tourist Board

extended so its first ship, *Olympic*, could enter in April 1911.

It was here that the engines, boilers and superstructure would be added and work completed on their luxurious cabins and rooms. In October 1911, *Titanic* had to be moved from the dock to the wharf to allow repairs to be completed on *Olympic*, which had been involved in a collision. The delay pushed back the date of *Titanic*'s maiden voyage by nearly three weeks. Had she sailed on time, it is doubtful she would have encountered the fateful iceberg.

Today, guided tours aided by the latest technology and the expertise of experienced guides complete with period sounds and smells and audio-visual presentations, take you back to the glory days of the dock's history.

UNIVERSITY DISTRICT

The area south of the city centre is dominated by Queen's University and the "Golden Mile" lined with busy pubs, bars and all kinds of places to eat, drink and while the night away. In between, clustered around the university are pleasant Georgian and Victorian suburban streets, the Botanic Gardens and the province's most important museum.

Ulster Museum★★

Botanic Gardens. ○*Open year-round Tue–Sun and Bank Holiday Mons 10am–5pm.* ☞*Free highlight tours* 2.30pm (1.30pm Sun). ☎*028 9044 0000. www.nmni.com/um.*

The recently relaunched Ulster Museum is a delight to visit, with a large open, child-friendly, ground floor and a new tower of exhibits called a **Window on Our World** – a series of single objects encased in glass, giving a tantalising glimpse of what else is available and leading the possibly reluctant museum visitor into the galleries themselves. The displays cover world and Irish history and nature, but the real strength of the museum is the **Art Zone**, the museum's art and applied art collections.

Visitors with children may want to visit the museum from the ground floor and travel upwards while those more interested in the art collections should take the lift to the top floor and begin there. The museum's fine art collection includes some major works of international significance, including works by Gainsborough, Reynolds, and Turner. Dutch painting from the 17C is represented with works by Jan Van der Heyden) and Jan Baptist Weenix. However, the bulk of the museum's art holdings is the **Irish collection**, from the 17C to modern times. In the **Applied Art collection**, a history of ceramics includes Ireland's biggest collection of contemporary European pottery, while the museum has a similar collection of contemporary European glassware to complement its historical collections.

In the lower galleries **Nature Zone** has sections on flight, the oceans and marine life, pre-history and fossils; World Cultures has exhibits of African, Asian, the Americas and the ancient world. The **History Zone** covers the history of Ulster set in the wider world, giving an account of The Troubles.

Botanic Gardens

🕐*Open dawn to dusk.* ✕ *(adjacent leisure centre).* ✆ *028 9031 4762. www.belfastcity.gov.uk.*
These lovely gardens *(28 acres/11ha)* slope gently to the River Lagan: they were originally laid out for the study of plants by the Botanic and Horticultural Society, but since 1895 they have been a public park. The beautiful cast-iron and curvilinear glass **Palm House★**was completed in 1840 by Richard Turner, who later collaborated with Decimus Burton on the construction of the Great Palm House at Kew. The **Tropical Ravine House** is also worth a visit.

Queen's University

Queen's College, Belfast was incorporated in 1845 and established as a university in 1908. The red-brick Tudor-style building is reminiscent of Magdalen College, Oxford. If you would like to know more about this handsome erudite establishment, there is a visitor centre at the main entrance (🕐*open Mon-Fri 9.30am-4.30pm, www.queenseventus.com*) and tours can be taken.

ADDRESSES

🏨 STAY

🛏 **Arnie's Backpackers** – *63 Fitzwilliam St.* ✆ *028 9024 2867. www.arniesbackpackers. co.uk. 22 beds.* Small private hostel with four dormitories of four beds and a dormitory of six beds. Kitchen, bike hire, organised tours.

🛏 **Belfast International Youth Hostel** – *22–32 Donegall Rd (at the side of Shaftesbury Sq).* ✆ *028 9031 5435. www.hini.org.uk. 202 beds.* Probably the best address in Belfast for those on a budget, with some double rooms and well-kept dormitories of four to six beds. There is a kitchen and the Causeway Café providing cooked breakfasts. The hostel does not accommodate stag or hen parties, or sports teams, so your chances of a good night's sleep are increased!

🛏 **Vagabonds** – *9 University Rd.* ✆ *028 9023 3017. www.vagabondsbelfast.com. 20 rooms.* Ideally located in The Queens Quarter just minutes from the city centre, this is chic, friendly and cheap. Free breakfast and incredibly friendly staff.

🛏– 🛏🛏 **Pearl Court Guesthouse** – *11 Malone Rd.* ✆ *028 9066 6145. www. pearlcourt.com. 10 rooms.* Beautifully modernised Victorian house with lovely bedrooms in the University part of the city centre. Excellent value.

🛏🛏 **Avenue House** – *23 Eglantine Ave.* ✆ *028 9066 5904. www.avenueguest house.com. 4 rooms.* Very well equipped and smart bedrooms furnished with hand-crafted solid mahogany furniture from the local Eglantine furniture workshop. Free wifi access plus all other mod cons. Good location in a leafy residential avenue yet only minutes from the heart of the vibrant Queen's Quarter.

🛏🛏 **The Crescent Townhouse** – *13 Lower Cres.* ✆ *028 9032 3349. www. crescenttownhouse.com. 11 rooms.* This Regency house in the University Quarter has been converted into a stylish boutique hotel. With oak panelling, the bar has a Gothic feel and the highly-rated brasserie offers imaginative dishes in a lively atmosphere. Excellent value.

🛏🛏 **The George Guest House** – *9 Eglantine Ave.* ✆ *028 9068 3212.* Nice cosy guesthouse housed in a leafy street close to the University Quarter. Warm welcome and good breakfast.

🛏🛏 **The Gregory** – *30 Eglantine Ave.* ✆ *028 9066 3454. www.thegregorybelfast. com. 28 rooms.* Superbly restored large, red-brick, Victorian villa, well maintained, within walking distance of the city centre.

🛏🛏 **Ravenhill Guest House** – *690 Ravenhill Rd.* ✆ *028 9020 7444. www. ravenhillhouse.com. 5 rooms.* Set in a quiet location in the South of the city in the vicinity of the leafy Upper Ormeau and Ravenhill Roads. Individually furnished rooms in lovingly restored Victorian house and an award-winning breakfast.

🛏🛏🛏 **Jury's Inn Belfast** – *Great Victoria St.* ✆ *028 9053 3500. www.jurysinns.com/*

hotels/belfast. Friendly, smart and comfortable medium-sized chain hotel in the heart of the city – ask for one of the side rooms, these overlook the lawns of the Royal Belfast Academical Institution and the hills beyond.

⊖⊜▤ **Radisson Blu Hotel** – *3 Cromac Place, Ormeau Rd.* ✆*028 9043 4065.* *www.radissonblu.co.uk/hotel-belfast.* *89 rooms.* Modern stylish business-oriented high-rise chain hotel with all mod cons, close to the city centre but away from the traffic.

⊖⊜▤ **Ten Square** – *10 Donegall Sq South.* ✆*028 9024 1001. www.tensquare. co.uk.* Small, ultra-chic and very welcoming boutique hotel right in the heart of the city. Attentive staff and all the facilities you need to make your stay a memorable holiday. Lively bar, good restaurant. Some great advance deals online.

⊖⊜▤ **Wellington Park Hotel** – *21 Malone Rd.* ✆*028 9038 1111. www. wellingtonparkhotel.com. 75 rooms.* This smart, modern four-star hotel with all mod cons and excellent restaurant is set in the university district very close to the US Consulate.

⊮/ EAT

⊖⊜ **Coco** – *7–11 Linenhall St.* ✆*028 9031 1150. www.cocobelfast.com. Closed Sat lunch.* Overlooking St George's Market, its glass roof ensures the room is bright and airy. The open-plan kitchen speciality is chargrilled fish and meats.

⊖⊜ **Ginger** – *7 Hope St, Great Victoria St.* ✆*028 9024 4421. www.gingerbistro.com. Closed Sun.* Busy and unpretentious little place, voted Best Restaurant in Northern Ireland 2011 by the *Which? Good Food Guide.* Ample choice from the blackboard menu of daily specials, with influences from around the world.

⊖⊜ **Nick's Warehouse** – *35–39 Hill St.* ✆*028 9043 9690. www.nickswarehouse. co.uk. Closed Sun, Mon.* Set in an old Bushmills warehouse on a cobbled street in the fashionable Cathedral Quarter, downstairs has the buzz, while upstairs is slightly more formal. Nick oversees a busy kitchen, producing carefully prepared modern cooking. Excellent wine list.

⊖⊜▤ **Deanes** – *36–40 Howard St.* ✆*028 9033 1134. www.michaeldeane. co.uk. Closed Sun.* Recently revamped, the

The Crown Liquor Saloon

© Northern Ireland Tourist Board

city's premier restaurant provides original and accomplished fusion cooking, discreet and professional service in elegant, minimalist surroundings.

PUBS

CITY CENTRE

Kelly's Cellars – *30 Bank St* – ✆*028 9024 6058.* This 1720 pub – one of the oldest in the city – tucked away in the financial district, is an atmospheric antidote to the homogeneous modernity of the surrounding development.

Maverick – *1 Union St* – ✆*028 9033 2130. A more radical alternative to the traditional Irish pub* which acts as the flagship establishment for Belfast's Queer Quarter. Formerly 'The Front Page'.

Madden's – *Berry St.* ✆*028 9024 4114.* Low-ceilinged, dark and atmospheric, Madden's is a genuine local's local, known for its live blues and traditional folk music.

Robinson's – *38–40 Great Victoria St.* ✆*028 9024 7447. www.robinsonsbar.co.uk.* Established in 1895 and rebuilt in the 1990s, Robinson's houses six very different venues in one large Victorian building, from traditional boozer to bistro restaurant, hip lounge, gin palace, Titanic-themed bar and nightclub.

The Crown Liquor Saloon – *46 Great Victoria St.* ✆*028 9024 3187.* The city's most famous pub (⌚*see Walking Tour*).

The Morning Star – *17 Pottinger's Entry.* ✆*028 9023 5986. www.themorningstarbar. com.* Classic Victorian gin palace: the downstairs bar has its original mahogany counter, terrazzo floor and snob screens. This pub is famed for its food, great value at lunchtime.

Whites Tavern – *2–4 Winecellar Entry. ℘028 9031 2582.* Dating from 1630, Whites claims to be the oldest tavern in Belfast and it certainly feels that way, with peat-burning fires and historical artefacts liberally dotted around its whitewashed stone walls. Traditional folk music and honest "pub grub" on offer.

John Hewitt Bar – *51 Donegall St. ℘028 9023 3768. www.thejohnhewitt.com.* Located in the Cathedral Quarter, the John Hewitt, although only born in 1999, is a traditional pub in every other sense, with lots of good music, poetry nights, no TV and good pub food each weekday lunchtime.

UNIVERSITY DISTRICT

V Bar – *23–31 Bradbury Place. ℘028 902 33131. www.mclub.co.uk.* Recently revamped and given a smooth, brown décor, the bar beneath the very popular MClub offers bottled beer, wine and some very original cocktails. Very young crowd; students on Tuesdays, DJ in the bar at weekends.

Other historical pubs in the city centre well worth a visit are:
Aether & Echo (*Garfield St*);
The Duke of York (*Commercial Ct*);
The Garrick (*Chichester St*);
Hercules Bar (*Castle St*);
Bittles Bar (*Upper Church Lane*).

ENTERTAINMENT

Belfast Waterfront Hall – *2 Lanyon Place. ℘028 903 334 455. www.waterfront.co.uk.* Excellent venue, attracting top Irish and international acts (⊙*see The Laganside*).

Belfast Empire Music Hall – *40–42 Botanic Ave. ℘028 902 49276. www.thebelfastempire.com.* Contemporary music, jazz, quiz and comedy nights, tribute bands and traditional Irish music and dance. Locals and visitors come to the basement bar for the atmosphere and range of beers.

The Grand Opera House – *Great Victoria St. ℘028 9024 1919. www.goh.co.uk.* Recently given a new extension, Belfast's leading venue for theatre, musicals and opera goes from strength to strength.

The Odyssey – *2 Queen's Quay. ℘028 9045 1055. www.theodyssey.co.uk.* The place for seeing ice hockey and visiting musical superstars (⊙*see The Laganside*), as well as home to a 10-pin bowling alley and two nightclubs.

Ulster Hall – *Bedford St. ℘028 9033 4400. www.ulsterhall.co.uk.* Superb Victorian venue, recently refurbished. Pop concerts, sporting events and a regular venue for the Ulster Orchestra.

SHOPPING

St George's Market – *12–20 East Bridge St. Open Fri–Sat.* Belfast's finest market (⊙*see Walking Tour*).

EVENTS AND FESTIVALS

Titanic Festival –last week Mar. *www.belfastcity.gov.uk.*

Cathedral Quarter Arts Festivals – throughout Jan and early May. *www.cqaf.com.*

Festival of Fools – International Street Theatre and comedy. Early May. *℘028 9023 6007. www.foolsfestival.com.*

Belfast City Carnival – last Sat June. *www.visit-belfast.com.*

Feile an Phobail – Music and dance. Late Jul/early Aug. *www.feilebelfast.com.*

Belfast Festival at Queen's – Three weeks, mid-Oct–early Nov. Claimed to be Britain's second-largest arts festival (after Edinburgh). *℘028 9097 1034. www.belfastfestival.com*

SIGHTSEEING

City Sightseeing Belfast – Open-top hop-on, hop-off bus tours. *Operate year-round Mon–Fri every 30–60min, Sat–Sun every 20–40min, 10am–4.30pm (Nov–Feb 4pm). ℘028 90 321 321. www.belfastcitysightseeing.com.*

Black Taxi Service – Guided personalised tours (⊙*see "The Murals of Belfast" box*).

There are various **themed walking tours** of the city, including:

Belfast iTours – *Mar–Oct Fri–Sun 2pm, Nov & Feb Sat, Sun only; meet Belfast Welcome Centre. ⊙£9. ℘028 9024 6609. www.belfastitours.com.*

Historical Pub Tour of Belfast – *Sat (May–Oct) at 4pm and Thu at 7pm; meet upstairs at Crown Liquor Saloon, Great Victoria St. ℘028 9268 3665 (Judy Crawford). ⊙£6.*

Around Belfast

Belfast city is blessed with an unspoilt hinterland of hills. It sits in a flat-floored glacial trough with the Antrim Plateau and Divis Mountain to the West, and the Castlereagh Hills to the North and the head of Belfast Lough to the Northwest. Since the peace process began, the surrounding towns have been affected by its rapid expansion and the need for out-of-town affordable housing, however Belfast's outer limits are still rural in essence and several sites are well worth a visit.

NORTH OF BELFAST
👥 Belfast Zoo★★

5mi/8km north of Belfast via the A 6. ♿🕐*Open Apr–Sept 10am–7pm. Oct–late Mar 10am–4pm (last admission 2.30pm).* 🎫*£12.50, child £6.25.* ✗ 📞*028 9077 6277.* *www.belfastzoo.co.uk.*

The Zoological Gardens, which opened in 1934, are home to more than 1,200 animals and 140 species, the majority of these critically endangered in the wild. Set in the former Hazlewood Gardens, the zoo eschews cages and enclosures wherever possible and instead surrounds the animals with dry ditches or water-filled moats. There are spacious green areas for the big cats (including Barbary Lions), various types of

ℹ️ Info: Carrickfergus: Carrickfergus Museum & Civic Centre, 11 Antrim Street. 📞028 9335 8049. www.carrickfergus.org. **Lisburn:** 15 Lisburn Square, 📞028 9266 0038. www.visitlisburn.com. **Hillsborough:** The Square, 📞028 9268 9717.
👥 **Kids:** Belfast Zoo, Ulster Folk and Transport Museum

deer, sunbears, apes and kangaroos. An aquatic complex houses penguins, sea-lions and polar bears. Other visitor favourites include elephants, giraffes and gorillas. A large walk-through **aviary** enables visitors to look for free-flying birds in the trees and the latest attraction, **The Rainforest House**, is a walk-through exhibition with tropical landscaping and a constant temperature of 80°F/27°C.

Belfast Castle

4mi/6.4km N of Belfast by the A 6. Turn left into Innisfayle Park to Belfast Castle. 🕐*Open (functions permitting) 9am–10.30pm (6pm Sun).* ✗ 📞*028 9077. 6925. www.belfastcastle.co.uk.*

In a superb location on the lower slopes of Cave Hill, this great mansion in Scottish Baronial style was built by

Belfast Zoo

© Northern Ireland Tourist Board

W. H. Lynn for the Donegall family in 1867–70; the external Baroque staircase was added in 1894.

At an elevation of 122m/400ft, it offers a tremendous panorama of the city.

The **Cave Hill Visitors Centre** tells the story of people on the hill, from Stone Age up to current times and looks at the natural setting, geology and wildlife. An 8-min audiovisual relates the story of Belfast Castle and Cave Hill, while a separate area room has been set up as a 1920s-style bedroom where brides can prepare themselves (the Castle is a favourite place for weddings). A collection of photographs illustrates the changing fashions in weddings at the castle since the 1940s to the present day. The grounds are also home to **Cave Hill Adventurous Playground** (*open year-round Sat–Sun, daily Apr–Sept: see website for times. £2.30. Max age 14*) plus formal gardens and waymarked trails to **Cave Hill Country Park**.

Cave Hill

4mi/6.4km N of Belfast by the A 6. Accessible on foot from Belfast Castle, the Zoological Gardens and various other points across town.

North of Belfast rears the black basalt cliff with a profile likened to Napoleon, known as Cave Hill (1,182ft/360m), which marks the southern end of the Antrim plateau.

The headland, separated by a deep ditch from the rest of Cave Hill, is marked by an ancient earthwork known as **McArts Fort**, which has served as a watchtower, providing refuge for the native Irish hounded by Vikings and Anglo-Normans. In 1795 Wolfe Tone and his fellow United Irishmen spent two days and nights in the fort planning the independence of Ireland.

Fine views extend over Belfast and the lough to County Down and Strangford Lough *(southeast)*, Lough Neagh and the Sperrin Mountains *(west)*.

EAST OF BELFAST
Stormont

4mi/6.4km east of Belfast via the A 20. Grounds (waymarked by nature trails and orienteering walks): Open dawn to dusk. Members of the public can watch Plenary Sittings from the Public Gallery Mon from noon, Tue from 10.30am. Tours (free) Mon–Fri 10am & 3pm (except during summer hols and Christmas recess) 028 9052 1362. www.niassembly.gov.uk.

The Northern Ireland Parliament, a plain white Classical building designed by A. Thornley, stands prominently on a hill surrounded by rolling parkland. Parliament met regularly from 1932 until 1972 when direct rule from Westminster was imposed. In 1999 it became the meeting place of the new Northern Ireland Assembly, which due to constant political wrangling and disagreement has endured several years of suspension and resumption. However, following the historic meeting in 2007 between Dr Ian Paisley (DUP leader) and Gerry Adams (Sinn Fein leader) at Stormont, the Northern Ireland Assembly was restored on May 8, 2007. Powers of policing, a very contentious issue, and justice were handed over to Stormont from Westminster in 2010. **Stormont Castle** *(right)* accommodates other government offices.

Crawfordsburn Country Park

10mi/16km northeast of Belfast on the shores of Belfast Lough via the A 2, then B 20. Park open year-round daily 9am–7pm (Nov–Feb 4.30pm). Visitor centre daily 10am–5pm (Nov–Feb 4pm). Grey Point Fort year-round daily noon–4pm (Dec–Feb Sat Sun). 028 9185 3621. www.doeni.gov.uk

Situated on the southern shores of Belfast Lough, the picturesque village and its coastal country park are named after the Crawford family from Scotland, who bought the estate in 1674.

The Country Park is full of variety, featuring over 2mi/3.5km of coastline, often rugged and rocky, but also including the two best beaches in the Belfast area. There is a deep wooded glen with an impressive waterfall at its head, a pond and wildflower meadows with excellent views over the Lough. The history of the estate and its flora and fauna are comprehensively illustrated in the **Park Centre**, equipped with interactive displays for children.

The **glen walk** (*30min there and back on foot*) passes the old salmon pool before dipping under the handsome railway viaduct of 1865. Upstream is the waterfall, which was used to power corn, flax and saw mills, and from 1850 to generate electricity to light the glen.

Grey Point Fort (*Coastguard Ave, accessible by footpaths within the Country Park – 1hr there and back*) commands the sea approaches to Belfast and was manned by the Royal Artillery during both World Wars. Panels outline its history (1907–63) and a solitary 6in/15cm gun, a gift from the Government of the Republic of Ireland, is mounted in one of the massive reinforced concrete gun emplacements.

∷ Ulster Folk & Transport Museum★★

7mi/11km NE of Belfast in Cultra, Holywood. ⛭🕐*Open Mar–Sept Tue–Sun & bank hol Mons 10am–5pm Oct–Feb Tue Fri 10am–4pm, Sat & Sun 11am–4pm.* ⊚*£9 for each collection, £11 combined ticket (child £5.50/£6).* ✕ ☎*028 9042 8428. www.nmni.com/uftm.* This is one of the most extensive and interesting museums in the whole of Ireland. Bisected by the busy coast road, one section is dedicated to the folk collection, the other to transport.

Folk Museum

A vast, open-air museum is installed in a series of old buildings transferred from the Ulster countryside, where traditional trades, practices and crafts are demonstrated. Costumed staff narrate the story of each structure and explain how the equipment was used for weaving, spinning, agricultural work and cooking. The dwellings, furnished as they would have been at the end of the 19C, range from a one-room farmhouse shared by the family and their cows to a substantial 17C farmhouse with panelled walls. Working premises include a flax-scutching mill, a spade mill, a weaver's

Ulster Folk & Transport Museum
© Northern Ireland Tourist Board

house and more. The village is composed of a school, a market-cum-courthouse, a church and a rectory, together with two terraces of urban cottages, including a shoemaker's workshop and a bicycle repair shop.

In the **Gallery** (*three floors*) the traditional Ulster way of life is illustrated with original domestic, industrial and agricultural implements.

Transport Museum

Examples of virtually every kind of wheeled vehicle used in Ireland in the last two centuries are displayed in their social context.

In the **Irish Railway Collection**, fascinating wall panels evoke the sometimes idiosyncratic history of the railways powered by the beautifully restored engines and carriages; note the wonderful *Maeve (Maebh)*, the most powerful steam locomotive ever to run on Irish rails.

The **Road Transport Galleries**, richly furnished with all types of transport memorabilia, display two-wheelers through the ages. Buses include a lovingly rebuilt 1973 Daimler Fleetline and No. 2 of the Bessbrook and Newry Tramway Co, built in 1885 and still carrying passengers in the 1940s. The final gallery is devoted to *The Car in Society* and ranges from an 1898 Benz Velo Confortable, the oldest petrol vehicle in Ireland, to the legendary **De Lorean motor car** (made famous in the *Back to the Future* movies) produced in Belfast in 1981 by the short-lived De Lorean company. The **Dalchoolin Transport Galleries** present a miscellany of exhibits – shoulder creels and wooden sledges, carts and jaunting cars; horse-drawn vehicles and ships.

The **Flight Experience** is an exciting, interactive exhibition, exploring the history and science of flight, including the important role played by local pioneers. You can "test fly" a range of exhibits, including a full-motion flight simulator ride.

The **Titanica Gallery** honours the great ill-starred liner, built in Belfast.

CARRICKFERGUS

10mi/16km north of Belfast via the A 2. www.carrickfergus.org.

Atop its basalt promontory, the largest and best-preserved Norman castle in Ireland dominates this pleasant seaside town (Carraig Fhearghais) on the north shore of Belfast Lough. A broad promenade runs along the front, between the bathing beach and the Marine Gardens; and a marina packed with yachts and fishing boats now occupies the harbour where, until the development of Belfast, there was once a thriving port.

The district has nurtured three literary figures: Jonathan Swift wrote his first book at nearby Kilroot, while William Congreve and Louis MacNeice lived in Carrickfergus as children.

A Bit of History

The name Carrickfergus (Rock of Fergus) refers to the ruler of the ancient kingdom of Dalriada, Fergus Mór, who was shipwrecked c. 531. The castle was built late in the 12C by the Anglo-Norman, John de Courcy, and completed by Hugh de Lacy c. 1240. Its strength and strategic position conveyed the idea that it was the key to Ulster, indeed to Ireland. In 1315 it was captured after a year-long siege by Lord Edward Bruce from Scotland. The English recaptured and held it for the next 300 years, withstanding many attacks from the local Irish and invading Scots troops.

In 1688 the castle and the town were held for James II by Lord Iveagh but were captured in 1689 by Schomberg. On June 14 the following year, William of Orange landed in Carrickfergus harbour on his way to the Battle of the Boyne.

In February 1760 the town was briefly occupied by a French naval detachment, then in 1778 the American privateer John Paul Jones in his vessel *Ranger* attacked HMS *Drake* in an off-shore engagement. Belfast folk, many of whom sympathised with the American Revolution, gathered in boats to watch the spectacle.

Carrickfergus Castle★★

(HM) ♿ ⏰*Open year-round daily 10am–4pm.* *£5.* ☎*028 933 51273. www.doeni.gov.uk.*

Commanding the seaward approach to Belfast, the great stronghold makes a splendid picture. Initially, it occupied just the tip of the basalt promontory but was extended over the years, protected by the sea on all sides but one.

Carrickfergus Castle

© Northern Ireland Tourist Board

The once-circular **gatehouse towers** built at the same time as the Outer Ward, were cut back some time after the Elizabethan period. The **outer ward** was probably built by Hugh de Lacy between 1228 and 1242 to enclose the whole promontory and to make the castle less vulnerable to attack. Originally it probably contained living quarters but these were replaced in the 19C by ordnance stores supporting gun platforms. The wall enclosing the **middle ward**, now partly reduced to its foundations, was built to improve the castle's defences soon after it had been successfully besieged by King John in 1210. The castle's nucleus was the **inner ward**, enclosed by a high curtain wall, built by de Courcy between 1180 and 1200. The **keep** provided living quarters. Life in the castle is recreated by a large model at the time of Schomberg's siege (1689), a video *Feasts and Fasts* in the Banqueting Hall and with period costume on the top floor.

Standing sentinel over the harbour in front of the castle, the bronze statue of **King William III** was commissioned to mark the Tercentenary of the landing of the King. At barely 5ft/1.5m tall the King strikes a slight figure, though this is believed to be historically accurate.

Carrickfergus Museum
&⏱*Open year-round Mon–Sat 10am–6pm (5pm Oct–Mar).* ✆*028 9335 8049. www.carrickfergus.org/tourism.*
Carrickfergus claims to be the most archaeologically explored town in Northern Ireland and the finds on display here provide a rich glimpse into life in the town from the Medieval period onwards, using a range of media, including audio-visual presentations and hands-on interactives.
The Gallery features special and touring exhibitions.

St Nicholas' Church★
John de Courcy provided Carrickfergus with a church as well as a castle. Centuries of turbulence left the building in a poor state and in 1614 it was heavily restored. The west tower, initiated in

1778, was completed in 1962 as a memorial to both World Wars.
In the north transept is a fine marble and alabaster monument to Sir Arthur Chichester (1563–1625), who as Governor of Carrickfergus played a prominent and particularly ruthless role in the subjugation of Ulster, who fathered the great landowning Donegall dynasty.

Flame! The Gasworks Museum of Ireland
⏱*Call for visiting details.* ✆*028 9336 9575. www.flamegasworks.co.uk.*
Ireland's sole surviving coal gasworks is one of only three left in the British Isles. Opened in 1855, it supplied Carrickfergus with gas until 1965 and was closed in 1987. It is now fully restored. Ascend the working gasholder for panoramic views of the town.

North Gate and Town Walls
Between 1607 and 1610 Carrickfergus was enclosed with defensive walls and ditches by Sir Arthur Chichester, who by this time had been elevated to the rank of Lord Deputy of Ireland. The big arch of the North Gate is still largely 17C despite repairs and alterations; the pedestrian arch and crenellations are 19C. A good stretch of wall survives to the East in Shaftesbury Park.

NEAR CARRICKERGUS
Andrew Jackson Centre
2mi/3.2km N of Carrickfergus via the A 2; turn right onto Donaldsons Ave.
⏱*Open May–Oct Thu, Fri & Sat 11am–3pm, Sun 1pm-4pm, Nov-Apr Fri & Sat 11am-3pm.* ✆*028 933 58049.*
The Jackson family emigrated from Carrickfergus in 1765; their son Andrew, born two years later, went on to become the seventh President of the United States. The Jackson homestead has long since disappeared, but close to where it stood, this restored 17C single-storey cottage, with its earthen floor, preserves the family memory and traces the Ulster-American connection.
The adjoining **US Rangers Centre** presents the story of the elite American force, formed in Northern Ireland in

Hillsborough Castle

© Northern Ireland Tourist Board

June 1942, to spearhead the invasions of World War II.

Dalway's Bawn

6mi/10km north of Carrickfergus.
By the side of the road south of Bally-carry *(left)* stand the remains of a bawn (a fortified wall around an Irish tower house) and three towers, c. 1609.

Whitehead

5.5mi/9km northeast of Carrickfergus.
This little seaside resort, sheltered between the cliffs of White Head and Black Head, has a pebble beach backed by a promenade and two golf courses. The **Railway Preservation Society of Ireland** (*℘028 2826 0803; www.rpsi-online.org)* has a unique collection of steam locomotives and coaches, and operates steam rail tours to all parts of Ireland during the summer season.

Island Magee

6mi/10km north of Carrickfergus via the A 2.
Although not strictly an island, this peninsula (7mi/11km long) feels quite detached from the mainland. The road *(B 90)* provides fine views across Larne Lough. At the northern end of the peninsula, standing incongruously in the front garden of a private house, is the **Ballylumford Dolmen★**, a Neolithic burial monument consisting of four stones supporting a capstone.

From the sandy shores of **Brown's Bay** you can watch the maritime traffic to and from Larne. Farther south are **The Gobbins**, precipitous cliffs (2mi/3.2km) from where local inhabitants were flung into the sea in 1641 by soldiers from the garrison in Carrickfergus.

Glenoe Waterfall

12mi/20km north of Carrickfergus.
The gorge is so deep and well-screened by trees that this well-known waterfall can be heard long before it is seen. The double cascade pours into a deep pool before flowing on under an old stone bridge through the village.

LISBURN

6mi/10km southwest of Belfast.
Lisburn (Lios Na Gcearrbhach) is a size-able industrial and commercial town, now conjoined with Belfast's south-western urban sprawl. It stands on the River Lagan, at the very heart of Ulster's linen-manufacturing district, and in the 19C produced half the linen woven in the province.

The Huguenot Louis Crommelin made Lisburn his headquarters when he was appointed Linen Overseer of Ireland by William III. In 1707 most of the town was destroyed by fire, save for the Assembly Rooms at the top of the market square.

Irish Linen Centre and Lisburn Museum★

&♿○*Open Mon–Sat 9.30am–5pm.*
✕ ⚑ ℘*028 9266 3377.*
www.lisburncity.gov.uk.

Lisburn's Market House now displays exhibitions about the local linen industry, past and present. In the Middle Ages Irish flax was exported to England to be woven; in the 17C English and Scottish weavers helped establish looms in Ireland, largely under the direction of Crommelin, whose portrait hangs in the main hall. There are live demonstrations of spinning and weaving, a recreation of a family at work in a late-18C–early-19C spinner's cottage and a vivid reconstruction of the weavers' toil in "Webster's", a hypothetical 19C mill, where conditions were tough.

Christchurch Cathedral

The cathedral is a fine example of the Gothic style adopted by the Planters (1623, reconstructed in 1708); in the graveyard *(south side)* is the Crommelin tomb.

Lisburn Castle Gardens

○*Open year-round daily 8am–8pm.*
www.castlegardenslisburn.com.

North of the cathedral is the Castle Gardens, recently restored and enclosed within the surviving walls of the 17C castle.

HILLSBOROUGH★

2.5mi/5km S of Lisburn by minor roads.
This charming little town acquired its Georgian aspect under Wills Hill (1718–92), Marquess of Downshire (from 1789). Hillsborough is famous locally for its September Oyster Festival (*http://hillsboroughoysterfestival.com*).

Hillsborough Castle

&♿⚑○*Open by guided tour only, May–Jun, Sat every half-hour 10.30am–4pm.*
⊛£8. ✆*Call to confirm times and prices.*
℘*028 9268 1309. www.visitlisburn.com.*
This neo-Classical red-brick building with a magnificent 18C wrought-iron screen was the former residence of the Governor of Northern Ireland. Since 1972 it has been the official residence of the

---

Secretary of State and is used for state functions, most importantly for discussions on the Anglo-Irish Agreement.

Hillsborough Courthouse

○*Open: Fort Mon–Sat 10am (11am Sun)–4pm. Courthouse, call for times.*
℘*028 9268 9717. www.doeni.gov.uk.*
The 18C Courthouse houses the tourist office and temporary exhibitions. A permanent exhibition shows courtroom proceedings through the ages.

Hillsborough Fort★ was built by Wills Hill, c. 1630, to command the chief roads in Co Down, on instructions from Col. Arthur Hill, who gave his name to the town. The fort is laid out as a square (270ft/82m x 270ft/82m) with a spear-shaped bastion at each corner to provide flanking fire from heavy cannon. Wills Hill later added the delightful gazebo over the northeast entrance and miniature Gothic fort in the northwest rampart.

The central ditch is part of a circular trench revealed by excavations (1966–69) that prove the site was occupied from c. 500–1000.

St Malachy's Anglican Church (1662) was endowed with its towers and spire, Irish oak furnishings and box pews by Wills Hill in 1760–73.

Rowallane Gardens★

10mi/16km east of Hillsborough: B 178 to Carryduff, B 6 to Saintfield, then A 7 S. (NT). &♿○*Open year-round daily 10am–6pm (4pm Nov–Feb; 8pm May–Aug).* ⊛£5.80. ℘*028 975 10131. www.nationaltrust.org.uk/rowallane-garden.* Rowallane Gardens (52 acres/21ha) are renowned for their azaleas and rhododendrons, planted by Hugh Armitage

Rose Week, Dixon Park

© Northern Ireland Tourist Board

Moore, who inherited the estate in 1903. Over the years he turned the drumlins, with their light, acid soil, into a series of natural gardens, seeding wild flowers to attract butterflies. The Rock Garden Wood is worth seeing, as is the Walled Garden for its display of shrubs and bulbs.

🚗 DRIVING TOUR

LAGAN VALLEY
9mi/14.5km. Half a day.

The River Lagan meanders between Lisburn and Belfast before discharging into Belfast Lough. A succession of woods and landscaped estates now form the magnificent **Regional Park**. The **Lagan Canal** was built to bring coal from Coalisland via Lough Neagh to Belfast and under the Lagan Navigation Company, founded in 1843, it became Ulster's most successful waterway. It eventually closed in 1958.

▷ From Lisburn take the A 1 north; in Hilden, turn right (signposted).

Hilden Brewery Visitor Centre
ⓞ*Open Tue–Sat 10am–5pm.*
Guided tours Call for times and prices. £4.50. ✕ ℰ*028 9266 0800. www.hildenbrewery.co.uk.*

Ireland's oldest independent brewery. If you're here in late August don't miss their beer festival also featuring rock, ska, blues, trad and folk music.

▷ Continue N on the A 1; right under the railway bridge onto the B 103 to Lambeg.

Lambeg
This attractive village, with a delightful suspension bridge, has given its name to the huge painted drums introduced into Ireland from the Netherlands by William III's army, which are played on the Orange Day parades.

▷ Continue on the B 103 to Drumbeg.

Drumbeg Church
Picturesque little Drumbeg has a church on a knoll, reached via a magnificent lych gate and path shaded by yews. The present cruciform church (1870), with a shallow apsidal chancel, has an interesting wooden roof.

▷ Continue north on the B 103.

Dixon Park
The famous rose trial grounds (11 acres/4ha) contain some 30,000 roses set in a park with woods, meadows and a tranquil Japanese garden. The final judging

takes place during **Belfast Rose Week** (mid-July).

◐ Continue north on the B 103. At the roundabout turn right onto the dual carriageway, then right again.

Malone House

&.◐Open year-round Mon–Sat 9am–5pm, Sun 11am–5pm. Call to confirm. ℘028 9068 1246. www.belfastcity.gov. uk/malonehouse.

Three houses have occupied the hilltop overlooking the Lagan crossing: the present one was probably designed by William Wallace Legge, who later bought the lease of the whole demesne.

◐ On leaving the park, turn right; after crossing the bridge, turn right. Take the road along the south bank to Edenderry (signposted).

Edenderry

Five terraces of red-brick cottages and a chapel down by the river form part of a fascinating 19C industrial village built for the workers of the local weaving mill.

◐ Return to the last T-junction; turn right onto Ballynahatty Road; after 1mi/1.6km turn right (signposted "Giant's Ring").

Giant's Ring

The Ring is a huge, circular bank of gravel and boulders (600ft/183m in diameter) around a megalithic chambered grave. Its true purpose is unknown, but it was used as a racecourse in the 18C.

ADDRESSES

⌂STAY

⊜ **Dobbins Inn Hotel** – High St, Carrickfergus. ℘028 933 51905. www.dobbinsinnhotel.co.uk. 15 rooms. Situated in the town centre, this is one of Ireland's oldest hostelries. There is popular bar with open fire, a good restaurant (Las Rosas &see opposite) and stylish very well equipped modern bedrooms . Super value.

⊜ **Knockagh Lodge** – 236 Upper Rd, Greenisland. Carrickfergus. ℘028 908 61444. www.knockaghlodge.com. 24 rooms. Close to the village of Greenisland, with grand views over Belfast Lough, Knockagh Lodge has a comfortable lounge and a pleasant restaurant.

⊜⊜ **Loughshore Hotel** – 75 Belfast Rd. Carrickfergus. ℘028 933 64556. www.loughshorehotel.com. 68 rooms. A modern, well equipped hotel, popular with business types, conveniently located for Belfast Airport (10mi/126km away) and as a starting point for exploring the coast of Antrim.

ⵆEAT

⊜ **The Courtyard Coffee House** – 38 Scotch Quarter, Carrickfergus. ℘028 933 51881. www.courtyardcoffeehouse.co.uk. Mon–Sat 9am–4.45pm A minute's walk from the seafront ideal for homemade Irish Stew or a salad, afternoon tea, or just a coffee break.

⊜ **Las Rosas Restaurant** – Dobbins Inn Hotel. High St, Carrickfergus. ℘028 933 51905. www.dobbinsinnhotel.co.uk. A comfortable restaurant serving traditional pub-style food.

⊜⊜ **The Plough Inn** – 3 The Square, Hillsborough. ℘028 9268 2985. This attractive old traditional pub is the most comfortable place in Hillsborough for a relaxing drink. Their Simply Seafood restaurant featuring modern and traditional dishes gets rave reviews.

PUBS

Northgate –59 North St, Carrickfergus. ℘028 933 64136. A pleasant pub serving hearty lunches.

SIGHTSEEING

Fergusons Irish Linen Factory – Banbridge. See Irish linen at its various stages of production including design, weaving, specialist cutting and hemming and ornamenting. There is a shop and interpretive centre (see website for opening hours; factory tours available by appt, no min number of persons required; £3–£6 per person; ℘028 4062 3491; www.fergusonsirishlinen.com).

Walks – Lagan Canal towpath walk from Lisburn to Belfast (9mi/14.5km).

Lough Neagh★

Ten rivers converge on this broad and tranquil lough, which is the largest body of fresh water in the British Isles (153sq mi/400sq km). It is drained by just one of these, the Lower Bann, which flows north to the sea just downstream from Coleraine. Despite its size, the lake is never more than 50ft/12m deep and has little impact on the surrounding flat countryside. Only in Antrim Bay is the shore lined with woodland; elsewhere, it is low and marshy, virtually roadless, and sometimes infested with (non-biting) midges. Together with its tiny northern neighbour, Lough Beg, Lough Neagh is a site of international importance for wintering wildfowl and nature reserves have been established on many of its islands.

Info: Lough Neagh Discovery Centre (*see below*) reception area. www.discoverloughneagh.com.

Location: 15mi/24km W of Belfast. There is no shore road; only a few minor roads reach the water's edge.

Kids: The refurbished Lough Neagh Discovery Centre.

LOUGH NEAGH DISCOVERY CENTRE

South shore; Oxford Island; sign at Junction 10, M 1. &Open Mon–Fri 9am–6pm (5pm Oct–Easter), Sat–Sun 9am–5pm (Sun 6pm Easter–Sept). ✗ 028 3832 2205. www.oxfordisland.com. This modern, child-friendly interactive centre provides information on the wildlife and history of the lake; great views from the mezzanine level of the restaurant.

Five hides and several footpaths provide ample opportunity to watch out for birds along the shores of the lough, in the woodlands and water meadows of the island. Guided walks around the wildlife areas can be booked in advance.

AROUND LOUGH NEAGH

In clockwise order from the southeast:

Peatlands Park

South shore; sign at Junction 13 on the M 1. &Open 9am–9pm (4.30pm Nov–Mar). Info centre and narrow-gauge railway: open Jun–Sept Sat, Sun & Bank Hols 1–5pm. railway £2. 028 3885 1102. www.ehsni.gov.uk. www.discovernorthernireland.com.

Lough Neagh viewed from Oxford Island

© Northern Ireland Tourist Board

This old hunting park is the best place in the North to learn about Ireland's long relationship with peat: the **narrowgauge railway** provides a scenic tour of the site; **turf cutting** by hand and machine is demonstrated at the outdoor turbary station while the **bog garden**, two small lakes, an orchard and woodland provide nature-lovers with a place to enjoy unusual flora and fauna. Each July the Park hosts the **Northern Ireland Bog Snorkelling Championships;** visitors are welcome to come along and try out this unique sport!

Maghery

The village has a lakeside country park from which Coney Island, a densely wooded island, can be visited by boat.

Kinturk Cultural Centre

Open daily 2pm–5pm, 7.30pm–11pm. £1. Boat trips and guided tours. 028 8673 6512. www.ireland.com.
Learn about the long-established local eel industry (*see box, right*).

Ardboe Cross★

East of Cookstown via the B 73.
The finest high cross of its kind in Ulster stands in an evocative spot at the entrance to a graveyard around the ruins of a 17C church. It is decorated with biblical scene, probably carved in the 10C to mark the site of Ardboe Abbey, founded around the 6C. From Ardboe Point is an extensive **view★** of Lough Neagh, Slieve Gallion and the surrounding mountains.

Bellaghy Bawn

North shore; in Bellaghy. (HM).
Open, Sun noon–4pm. Closed Christmas–New Year. 028 7938 6812. www.discovernorthernireland.com.
This 17C fortified house and bawn was built by the Vintners' Company in 1619; exhibitions relates to local history, the Ulster Plantation and the poetry of Seamus Heaney, born nearby in 1939. Much of Heaney's work, notably his *Lough Neagh Cycle*, is marked by the memories of the local people and landscapes.

ANTRIM

Situated on the shore of Lough Neagh, 20mi/32km NW of Belfast. Market Sq. 028 9442 8331.
The former county town of Co Antrim (Aontroim), traditionally known for its linen-spinning, is linked to Belfast by rail and motorway and expanded rapidly in the last decades of the 20C. Located on the Six Mile Water, a fine trout stream, the town's greatest asset is its proximity to the broad waters of Lough Neagh.

Pogue's Entry Historical Cottage

East end of the main street. Call to check opening times 028 9448 1338.
This simple cabin was where Alexander Irvine (1863–1941), spent his childhood. Irvine became a missionary in the Bowery in New York and his book, *My Lady of the Chimney Corner*, is all about his mother's struggle against poverty.

Antrim Castle Gardens

Open year-round Mon–Fri 9.30am–5pm (9.30pm Tue, Thu), Sat–Sun 10am–5pm. 028 9448 1338 www.antrim. gov.uk (click tourism tab).

Slemish Mountain

Beyond the Market Place and the Court House (1726), a magnificent Tudor gate leads to the former demesne of the Clotworthys, ennobled as Lords Massarene in the 17C. The garden is a rare example (unique in Ulster) of a Dutch-style landscape, with ornamental canals, a cascade, geometric parterres and high pleached (formally trained) hedges of lime and hornbeam. Inside Clotworthy House is a Garden Heritage exhibition.

Round Tower★

From the High Street 10min on foot north along Railway Street and Station Road.

Among the trees of Steeple Park stands a fine example of a round tower (90ft/27m), one of the best preserved in Ireland, probably built c. 900 as part of an important 6C monastery that was abandoned in 1147.

AROUND ANTRIM

Patterson's Spade Mill

5mi/8km SE of Antrim by the A 6 via Templepatrick. (NT).   *Open by guided tour only, noon–4pm: St Patrick's Day weekend (Sat–Mon). Easter Week (daily). mid-Apr–late May & Sept Sat–Sun only. Jul–Aug Sat–Wed & bank/public hols.* *£5.50.* *028 9443 3619. www.nationaltrust.org.uk/ pattersons-spade-mill.*

The only surviving water-powered working spade mill in the British Isles was founded in 1919; five generations of Pattersons worked at the mill until 1990. The tour includes all the stages involved in producing spades in the traditional way, as completed by two men.

Ballance House

11mi/17km S of Antrim via the B 101, A 26 and A 30 to Glenavy. *Open Apr–Sept Sun, Wed, Bank Hols, 2pm–5pm.* *Closed 12 Jul.* *£3.* *028 9264 8492. www.visitlisburn.com.*

This is the birthplace of John Ballance (1839–93), who emigrated to Birmingham and then to New Zealand, where he became a journalist and rose to become the first Liberal prime minister. Partly furnished in mid-19C style, the house is a fascinating museum devoted to the Ulster-New Zealand connection.

Templetown Mausoleum

Templepatrick; 5mi/8km E of Antrim on the A 6. Park at the end of the drive. (NT). *Open 11am–6pm.* *028 9064 7787.*

A walled graveyard encloses the mausoleum, a triumphal arch designed by Robert Adam in the Palladian style c. 1770 for Sarah Upton in memory of her husband Arthur. Tablets honour subsequent generations of Uptons entitled Viscount Templetown.

The name Templepatrick derives from an earlier church dedicated to St Patrick, who is supposed to have baptised converts at a nearby Holy Well in about 450.

Slemish Mountain

16mi/26km NE of Antrim on the A 26 to Ballymena, A 42 east and B 94. After 1mi/1.6km turn left; after 3mi/4.8km turn right (Carnstroan Rd); after 0.25mi/0.4km turn right. From the car park 1hr there and back on foot.

The Slemish Mountain (1,437ft/438m) rises abruptly from the flat landscape of the Ballymena plain. On St Patrick's Day (March 17), it is a place of pilgrimage since tradition has it that **St Patrick** spent six years there in captivity herding swine for the local chieftain Miluic. The fine **view** takes in the ruins of Skerry Church *(northwest)*.

Arthur Cottage

17mi/27km NW of Antrim via the A 26 to Ballymena and B 62 to Cullybackey. Cross the river and turn sharp right onto a narrow lane. ○Open Jul-Sep Fri, Sat, 11am-4pm. ℘028 2563 5900. www.ballymena.gov.uk/tourism.

At the end of the lane stands an isolated one-storey cottage; from here the father of Chester Alan Arthur, 21st President of the USA, emigrated in 1816 to Vermont, where he became a Baptist clergyman. Traditional crafts, local agricultural and domestic implements, a display on Chester Alan Arthur's family and 19C emigration from Ireland are all on show during the summer.

Gracehill

11mi/18km northwest via the A 26 to Ballymena and the A 42.

This attractive Georgian village was laid out by a group of Moravian settlers from Bohemia fleeing religious persecution. Begun in 1759, the community built a central square, a church, the minister's house and communal houses for single men and women. Men and women sat on separate sides in church and were buried in separate sections of the graveyard.

ADDRESSES

ANTRIM

STAY

⊜ **Brackenleigh B&B** – *51 Belfast Rd, Antrim. ℘028 9446 6613.* Purpose-built modern establishment, close to Antrim Technology Park and within walking distance of the town. Good facilities in the rooms.

ENTERTAINMENT

Clotworthy Arts Centre – *Antrim Castle Grounds. www.discovernorthernireland.com. ℘028 9448 1338.* Exhibitions of painting, photography and sculpture; talks and lectures; courses and workshops.

SPORTS AND LEISURE

Watersports are available from the marinas at Antrim, Ballyronan and Kinnego and at the Craigavon Watersports Centre (*www.craigavonactivity.org*)

There is an **RSPB reserve** at Portmore Lough (*www.rspb.org.uk*) and **nature reserves** at Reas Wood in Antrim, Oxford Island, Peatlands Park, Washingbay Wetlands near Dungannon, and Randalstown Forest.

Fishing Permits are available from tackle shops.

Permits and **gillie services** for the Lower Bann are available from Bann System Ltd, Coleraine ℘028 7034 4796.

Antrim Forum Leisure Centre – Swimming pool, badminton, bowling, tennis etc. *www.antrim.gov.uk/antrimforum.*

SIGHTSEEING

Lake Cruises are available on Lough Neagh and Lough Foyle aboard The *Maid of Antrim. http://www.loughneaghcruises.co.uk.*

Ards Peninsula and Strangford Lough★★

The inland sea of Stangford Lough, with its 80mi/142km of coastline, has a tranquillity and beauty disturbed only when the tides rip through the narrow channel linking it to the Irish Sea. The Lough was formed when the sea level rose at the end of the Ice Age, drowning the drumlins – the most characteristic features of its landscape – and converting them into countless whale-backed islands. The lough lends itself to sailing and boating, supports an exceptional wealth of bird-life, while its shores and islands are rich in historical remains. Extending south from Bangor to Ballyquintin Point, the Ards peninsula encloses the broad waters of Strangford Lough. This is one of Ireland's best grain-producing regions. The breezy **coast road** follows the bare shoreline past sandy beaches and occasional rocky outcrops. **Portavogie** shelters one of Northern Ireland's three fishing fleets. The southern end of the peninsula presents an austere landscape of marsh and heath.

- **Info:** 31 Regents Street, **Newtownards**; ✆028 9182 6846. The Stables, Catle Street, **Portaferry**; ✆028 4272 9882. Tower House, 34 Quay Street, **Bangor**; ✆028 9127 0069.
- **Location:** Strangford Lough lies 10mi/16km SE of Belfast at its closest point. Bangor, at the top of Ards Peninsula, is situated 15mi/24km E of Belfast via the A 2.
- **Don't Miss:** Mount Stewart Gardens and the view from the hill here.
- **Kids:** Exploris at Portaferry, the beach at Bangor.

MARINE NATURE RESERVE

The whole of the Lough is a **Marine Nature Reserve**, the first in Northern Ireland managed by public bodies including the National Trust and the RSPB. The old Irish name for the lough was *Lough Cuan*, but the Viking name – Strangford means "violent fjord" – prevails, acknowledging the regular spectacle of 350 million tonnes of sea water racing through the strait between

Strangford Lough

© Northern Ireland Tourist Board

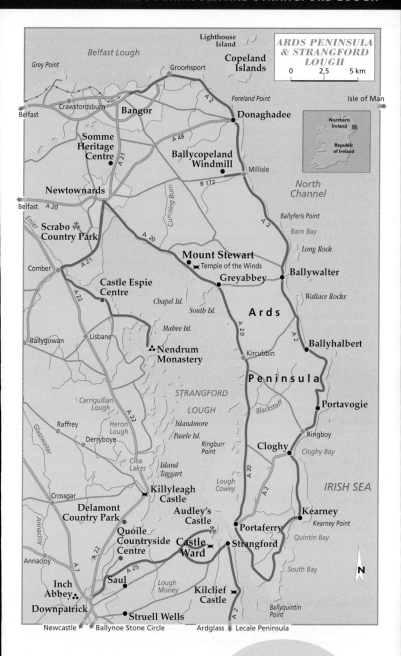

ARDS PENINSULA & STRANGFORD LOUGH

0   2,5   5 km

Portaferry and Strangford village as the tide changes.
Conditions in the lough itself vary between the exposed eastern shore on the Ards Peninsula and the sheltered western shore.

🚗 DRIVING TOUR

ARDS PENINSULA
Approx 56mi/90km. Allow 2hrs for drive (not including visit times).

Bangor

Looking out over Belfast Lough at the northern end of the Ards Peninsula, Bangor (Beannchar) is Northern Ireland's foremost **seaside resort**, well-stocked with Victorian hotels and guest houses. It originally began as one of Ireland's most important monastic settlements, reformed in the 17C as a Plantation town. Today it largely serves as a dormitory town for Belfast commuters.

A Bit of History

Bangor Abbey, founded by St Comgall in 558, became one of the most famous abbeys in western Christendom, sending its missionary monks to found monasteries in Ireland and abroad. In the 9C Comgall's tomb was desecrated in Viking raids; Malachy, appointed abbot in 1124, built a stone church and introduced the Augustinian Order. In 1542 the abbey was dissolved.

On the accession of James I in 1603, Bangor was granted to Sir James Hamilton, later Viscount Clandeboye, who created a town with settlers from his native Ayrshire. In 1620 he was granted a warrant to establish a maritime port, including the nearby creeks. In 1689 the Duke of Schomberg landed at Groomsport, his army of 10,000 men probably coming ashore at Bangor or Ballyholme. The Duke spent a night with the Hamiltons before setting off for the Battle of the Boyne, where he was subsequently killed.

In 1710 Sir James's estates passed by marriage to the Ward family of Castle Ward on Strangford Lough. Two generations later, Col. Robert Ward improved the harbour, promoted the textile industry and founded a boys' school. Bangor's role as a seaside resort, complete with pier, started with the arrival of the railway in 1865.

Old Custom House and Tower

The Tower House (now home to the Tourist Information Centre) was built by Sir James Hamilton in 1637 with financial assistance from the Crown, in the Scottish Baronial style with flanking watchtowers, a crow-stepped gable and a quarter-round corbelled turret.

Bangor Abbey Church

The 14C tower is the only section to survive the dissolution of Bangor Abbey in 1542.

North Down Museum★

Open year-round Tue–Sat, (also Bank Hol Mon and Mon during Jul–Aug) 10am–4.30pm. Sun noon–4.30pm. ✗ ▣ *028 9127 1200. www.northdownmuseum.com.*

The Centre is housed in part of Bangor Castle, a mid-19C Elizabethan-Jacobean revival style mansion. An exhibition of evocative artefacts and models celebrates Bangor's eventful past and development into a popular seaside resort. There is also an informative section promoting the 15mi/26km coastal walk.

Somme Heritage Centre

With the outbreak of the World War I (1914), many Irishmen set aside their political differences and volunteered for service in the British army. Irish units suffered terrible losses in the Somme offensive of 1916: 5,000 men from the Ulster Division were killed in the first two days alone. The Centre commemorates the sacrifices made in battle with a "time tunnel" and an uncanny recreation of the trenches complete with terrible sights and sounds. *(3mi/5km south of Bangor via the A 21. Open Apr–Jun & Sept Mon–Thu 10am–4pm, Sat 11am–4pm; Jul–Aug Mon–Sat 10am–5pm. Oct–Mar Mon–Thu 10am–4pm.* ✗ *Last tour 1hr before closing. Closed Dec 20–mid-Jan. £5.75. 028 9182 3202. www.irishsoldier.org. www.heritageisland.com.*

▷ 4.5mi/7.2km E of Bangor via the A 21, A 2 and B 511.

Groomsport

This is an attractive little seaside resort and fishing village complete with sandy beaches. Two original fishermen's dwellings, **Cockle Row Cottages** (⊙*open daily Jun–Aug 11am–5pm, Apr–May Sat–Sun only;* ℘*028 9127 1200; www. northdowntourism.com*) now illustrate life for a fisherman and his family at the turn of the last century. Entertainment is staged every weekend from 2–4pm.

▷ Rejoin the A 2 and drive for 4.4mi/7.1km along the coast road.

Donaghadee

Picturesque winding streets lead to the **parish church** which dates from 1641. The huge harbour, now full of leisure craft, was built in 1820 to accommodate the mail ships, which were transferred to Larne in 1849. From the 16C to 19C Donaghadee–Portpatrick was the most popular route between Ireland and Scotland as it is the shortest crossing (21mi/34km).

The Norman **motte** near the shore was probably raised by William Copeland, a retainer of John de Courcy; it is crowned by a stone building (1818) providing a fine **view** of the Copeland Islands and the coast of Galloway.

Copeland Islands

Accessible by boat from Groomsport or Donaghadee.

The nearest and largest island was inhabited until the 1940s. A modern lighthouse was built on Mew Island in 1884. **Lighthouse Island** is now a wildlife sanctuary in the care of the National Trust, populated by buzzards, golden eagles, resident seals, dolphins, porpoises, basking sharks, minke whales and killer whales.

▷ Leave Donaghadee on the A 2 in the direction of Portaferry. Turn right at Millisle village, drive onto the B 172 for 1mi/1.6km.

Ballycopeland Windmill

© Northern Ireland Tourist Board

Ballycopeland Windmill★

⊙*Open Jul–Aug daily 10am–5pm.* ℘*028 9181 1491. www.doeni.gov.uk.*

In the late 18C, when grain was grown extensively in the Ards Peninsula, the landscape was thickly dotted with windmills. This rare survivor at Ballycopeland was probably built between 1780–90 and worked until 1915. The complex includes the mill (back in working order), the miller's house with an explanatory display, a dust-house and kiln.

The Coastal Road

This route skirts some sandy beaches before arriving at Ballywalter, a small, quiet fishing port, whose chief focus of interest is **Ballywalter Park**, a currently occupied Stately Home open to the public by appointment, which hosts the annual Irish Game and Country Living Fair in May each year. The gardens include many species of rhododendron. Admission is expensive, considering what is up for viewing, but in summer you can stop to pick your own strawberries from the grounds.

2.5mi/4km further on, while passing the village of **Ballyhalbert**, you can see the ruins of a Norman castle and a church. The next stop on the route is **Portavogie**, whose trawlers specialise in fishing for shrimp and herring, which are often on sale at the quayside when the boats come in.

The route continues past the beautiful sandy beach of **Cloghy**, near which is a renowned golf course, before arriving at the tiny fishing hamlet of **Kearney**, with its lovely restored cottages.

▷ Now cross the southern tip of the peninsua to reach Portaferry.

Portaferry

A busy coastal town until the mid-19C, Portaferry is today a yachting and sea angling centre famed for its sunsets. **Portaferry Castle** (○*open Easter–Aug Mon–Sat 10am–5pm; www.doeni.gov. uk*) was probably built early in the 16C by the Savage family. Its stables house the tourist information centre while the keep is now home to "Art in The Loft", exhibitions by local craftspeople.

Exploris★ (▲▲ ○*Closed for refurbishment util 2016, call or see website for details. ℘028 4272 8062; www.exploris.org.uk*) presents the varied marine life of Strangford Lough and the Irish Sea. It has a touch tank where children enjoy getting "hands-on" with (non-stinging) stingrays and open-sea tanks, which attract passing seals and basking sharks. There is also a seal sanctuary.

▷ Head N on A20.

Grey Abbey★

(HM). ○*Open year-round Tue–Sun noon–4pm (Nov–Feb Sun only). ℘028 9181 1491. www.discovernorthern ireland.com.*

A Cistercian abbey was established in 1193 by Affreca, wife of John de Courcy, for monks from Holm Cultram Abbey in Cumbria. Its church, one of the first in Ireland to exhibit traces of the dawning Gothic style, has a magnificent **west door** (1220–30) with elaborate moulding and dog-tooth decoration. Damaged in the Elizabethan wars, the abbey church was restored and served as the parish church. The small **visitor centre** displays descriptions of monastic life and the abbey; a herb garden stocks medicinal plants typical of a Cistercian garden.

▷ Continue N on the A20.

Mount Stewart★★★

(NT) ♿○*Formal and lakeside gardens: Open year-round daily 10am–4pm (mid-Mar–Oct 6pm). House: ☞open by timed tickets guided tour only, except bank hols when freeflow: mid-Mar–Oct daily noon–5pm. ⊜House tour and gardens £9.50. ○Temple of the Winds: Open mid-Mar–Oct Sun 2–5pm. ✕ ℘028 4278 8387. www.nationaltrust.org.uk.*

A celebrated landscaped park and dramatic views across Strangford Lough help make this palatial mansion one of Ireland's premier visitor attractions.

Gardens

The old demesne acquired by the Stewarts was soon landscaped with fine parkland trees, including a number of exotic species planted by Edith, Lady Londonderry. Having consulted

Soldiers and Statesmen

Mount Stewart owes its name to the Scottish family who settled on the banks of Strangford Lough in 1774. They acquired vast fortunes from substantial property holdings, including their immensely profitable coal mines in northern England. Robert Stewart was made Marquess of Londonderry in 1816, but his elder son, Lord Castlereagh (1769–1822), is better known for having served as leader of the House of Commons and attending the Congress of Vienna in 1815 as foreign secretary. The family's eminence was maintained in part by entertaining the British Establishment in London, across England and at Mount Stewart, rallying support for the Unionist cause.

Mount Stewart

© Northern Ireland Tourist Board

Sir Edwin Lutyens and Gertrude Jekyll, she laid out a series of formal gardens that effectively link the house with its surroundings.

The huge Irish yews by the house overlook the geometrical **Italian Garden**; the **Dodo Terrace** is ornamented with droll stone animals bearing nicknames that allude to Lady Edith's London set. The **Spanish Garden** echoes the ceiling pattern in the **Temple of the Winds**, while the **Sunk Garden** honours Gertrude Jekyll, with its orange, blue and yellow-flowering plants. The **Shamrock Garden** celebrates Ireland with a topiary harp and Red Hand of Ulster bed.

The parkland beyond is planted with exotic trees and shrubs. The hill overlooking the artificial **lake** (1846–48), provides a superb **view** over Strangford Lough. A genuine miniature Japanese pagoda stands beside the **Ladies' Walk**, an old path to the dairy and kitchen gardens.

The Londonderrys' sumptuous **residence** was built in two stages: the west wing in 1805 (George Dance), the main part in 1825–35 (William Vitruvius Morrison). The interior is richly furnished with family portraits, Irish and English furniture, as well as a collection of porcelain and Classical sculpture.

Temple of the Winds

Inspired by the Temple of the Winds in Athens, this pleasure pavilion, designed by James "Athenian" Stuart in 1783, stands on a mound with a fine prospect of Strangford Lough and Scrabo Hill (topped by a tower commemorating the 3rd Marquess of Londonderry). The elegant banqueting room has a superb inlaid floor echoing designs in the ceiling. The servants' quarters, unusually, are underground.

▷ Continue N on the A20.

Newtownards

An ancient priory predates the modern dormitory town (pronounced *newton-ards*) annexed to Belfast, which was refounded in Plantation times.

Today the spacious market square, a handsome Georgian town hall in Scrabo stone and a distinctive market cross (1635) survive from the 17C, as do the unremarkable priory ruins and the burial vault of the Londonderry family. There is a fine collection of of 13C **cross slabs**★ inscribed with foliage crosses. These come from nearby Movilla Abbey, once one of the most important abbeys in Ulster.

▷ From Newtownards take the A 20.

Scrabo Tower

© Northern Ireland Tourist Board

Scrabo Country Park

(HM) ⏱*Tower: open year-round Sat–Sun noon–4pm (Nov–Feb Sun only).* ℘*028 9181 1491.*
www.discovernorthernireland.com.

The upper end of Strangford Lough is dominated by **Scrabo Tower** on Scrabo Hill, the 135-ft/41m-tall centrepiece of this popular country park. Dolerite, a form of volcanic lava extruded at the same time as at the Giant's Causeway, has protected the underlying sandstone from erosion. Both rocks have been quarried in the past: the dark dolerite for Mount Stewart, the light sandstone for many Belfast buildings.

Both were used in Scrabo Tower, which was built in 1857 to commemorate the 3rd Marquess of Londonderry (1778–1854), a compassionate man who showed much concern for his tenants during the Great Famine. There is a video and display about the park in the tower; on a clear day **views**★★ *(122 steps – viewing maps)* extend as far as the Scottish coast and the Isle of Man.

▶ Continue south on the A 22; in Comber take the A 21; turn left up a steep minor road.

Wildfowl and Wetlands Trust (Castle Espie Centre)★

♿⏱*Open Feb–Oct daily 10am–5pm (5.30pm May–Aug Sat–Sun). Nov–Jan daily 10am–4.30pm .* ✕🅿 *£8.* ℘*028 9187 4146. www.wwt.org.uk/visit-us/castle-espie.*

The protected area on the west shore of Strangford Lough includes freshwater lakes, flooded clay and limestone quarries. These are now home to endangered species bred in captivity and a broad range of wild species. In winter, thousands of wildfowl arrive here from the Arctic. A series of walks through the wetlands lead to a sustainable garden, a crannog and several hides from where brent geese can be observed.

A very rare feature of the wetlands is the limekiln lagoon, a shallow coastal lake whose fertile calcareous waters and mudflats support some rare wildlife, including otters, pipistrelle bats and rare wainscot moths.

ADDRESSES

BANGOR

🏨 STAY

😊😊 **Cairn Bay Lodge** – *278 Seacliffe Road. 1.25mi/2km East.* ℘*028 9146 7636. www.cairnbaylodge.com. 5 rooms.*
A detached Edwardian house, sympathetically decorated with feature wood panelling. The sitting room is particularly attractive while the dining room overlooks the beautifully landscaped gardens with panoramic views of Ballyholme Bay. Beauty therapy; gourmet breakfast.

⌒⌒ **Shelleven House** – *59–61 Princetown Rd.* ℰ*028 9127 1777. www. shellevenhouse.com. 11 rooms.* A large Victorian terraced house with many of its neat, traditionally decorated bedrooms enjoying views over the town or sea.

☖/EAT

⌒⌒ **The Jamaica Inn** – *188 Seacliff Road.* ℰ*028 9147 1610. www.jamaicainn. co.uk.* A cosy seaside bar and restaurant with a great outdoor terrace. Friendly and attentive staff serve decent pub-grub fare.

⌒⌒ **Donegans** – *37 High St.* ℰ*028 9146 3928. www.donegansrestaurant.co.uk.* This rural-themed pub, with turf-burning ranges specialises in steaks and chicken, with oriental touches. Regular live music.

⌒⌒ **Grace Neill's** – *33 High St, Donaghadee.* ℰ*028 9188 4595. www. graceneills.com. Restaurant closed Mon.* The oldest pub in Ireland (1611), full of atmosphere; traditional and contemporary cooking.

SPORTS AND LEISURE
Safe, sandy beaches, seawater pool, marina, waterfront fun park, golf.

SIGHTSEEING
Bangor Bay Cruise – *MV Blue Aquarius, Bangor Marina* ℰ*07779 600 607. www. bangorboat.com. Daily in summer 2pm.* ⌒*£6 cruises, £17 fishing trips.*

Belfast Lough Cruise – Daily sea fishing trips, pleasure cruises, day trips to the Copeland Islands (Jun–Sept). ℰ*028 9188 3403. www.nelsonsboats.co.uk.*

Downpatrick★
and around

Historic Downpatrick (Dún Pádraig) owes the first part of its name to a pre-Christian fort (*dún* in Irish), built on the prominent site now occupied by the cathedral, but the town is above all famous for its associations with the patron saint of Ireland. Traditionally held to be St Patrick's burial place, it developed into an ecclesiastical city with many religious foundations. Despite losing its status as a county town in 1973, Downpatrick is still a busy market centre serving the surrounding agricultural area, which to the South is known as the Lecale Peninsula.

A BIT OF HISTORY
As well as the hill now crowned by the cathedral, Downpatrick boasts a second mound, in fact a great Iron Age earthwork, known as the **Mound of Down**, which rises from the marshy levels north of the town. The tree-covered mound sheltered an urban settlement destroyed by the Norman knight, de Courcy, in 1177 as a first step in his conquest of East Ulster. In the 18C,

- **Info:** St Patrick Centre, 53a Market Street, Downpatrick. ℰ028 4461 2233. www.discover northernireland.com.
- **Location:** Between the Mourne Mountains and Strangford Lough, 23mi/37km south of Belfast via the A 7.
- **Don't Miss:** Castle Ward house and grounds.
- **Kids:** Seaforde Gardens and Tropical Butterfly House.

when Downpatrick was the administrative centre for the whole county, great improvements were made to the physical appearance of the town by the Southwell family, who had acquired the demesne of Down through marriage to Lady Betty Cromwell, last of the line to whom the land had been granted by James I in 1617. Until modern times Downpatrick was almost entirely surrounded by water and marshy ground, its narrow medieval thoroughfares – English, Irish and Scotch Streets – converging on the town centre where the market house once stood.

SIGHTS

Saint Patrick Centre

&♿🕐*Open year-round Mon–Sat 9am–5pm, also Sun 9am–5pm Jul–Aug. St Patrick's Day 9am–7pm.* ⌾£5.75. ✕ ℘*028 4461 9000.*
www.saintpatrickcentre.com.
The story of Ireland's patron saint is told by a series of interactive displays which also features the impact of Irish missionaries in Europe.

English Street

The red-brick Venetian-Gothic Assembly Rooms (1882) were designed by William Batt of Belfast. The **Customs House** (no. 26) was built in 1745 by Edward Southwell. The Clergy Widows' Houses (nos 34–40) date from 1730 and 1750, but were altered in the early 19C.
The low, two-storey edifice (right), was originally conceived to hold prisoners; its vaulted cells were converted in 1798 into the **Downe Hunt Rooms**: they house records from 1757. The Courthouse (1834) is the sole section of the new prison complex to survive.

Down County Museum★

♿🕐*Open Mon–Fri 10am–5pm, Sat–Sun noon–5pm.* ℘*028 4461 5218.*
www.downcountymuseum.com.
The old Down County prison, built between 1789–96, was where Thomas Russell was executed for his part in Robert Emmet's 1803 rebellion. When the prison moved, these premises were taken over by the South Down Militia, then by the army until the mid-20C.
The display in the former **Governor's House** in the centre of the courtyard traces the history of Co Down from 7000 BC and describes the local wildlife.
A **Son et Lumière show** (shown at regular intervals throughout the year) dramatises episodes from the history of the gaol and its prisoners. The show is projected onto the wall of the cell block and features the stories of its most famous prisoners, including the United Irishman Thomas Russell, hanged here in 1803.

The Mall

To avoid the deep dip between the Cathedral and English Street, in 1790. the road was raised some 15ft/5m. Well below road level stands the **Southwell Charity**, a school and almshouses founded in 1733 by Edward Southwell, secretary of state for Ireland, who by his marriage in 1703 became Lord of the Manor of Down. Opposite are the **Judges' Lodgings** (nos 25 and 27), two late-Regency houses built soon after 1835.

Down Cathedral★

♿🕐*Open Mon–Sat 9.30am–4pm.* ⌾*Donation requested.* ℘*028 4461 4922. www.downcathedral.org.*
No traces of the monastic complex founded by St Patrick survive, although a round tower stood on the site until 1780. In the 12C, John de Courcy replaced the incumbent Augustinians with a community of Benedictine monks from Chester, rebuilt the abbey church and interred the supposed relics of St Patrick, St Colmcille and St Brigid here, changing the dedication to St Patrick and renaming the town Downpatrick to please the native Irish. This building was destroyed by Edward Bruce in 1316 and its replacement built by the English in 1538. The present building largely dates from the early 19C, built using the stone on site and incorporating the chancel of the abbey church. The original dedication to the Holy and Undivided Trinity was restored in 1609 by James I.
Inside, there are various remarkable features: the granite font was once used as a watering trough, two unusual figures in ecclesiastical robes flank the Chapter Room door, the choir screen is unique in Ireland, the splendid Georgian-Gothic organ given by George III.
Outside in the graveyard, south of the cathedral, stood a stone bearing the names of the three saints said to be buried in the same plot; this was replaced in the early 20C by a great slab of granite, simply inscribed with the name Patrick.

Downpatrick and Country Down Railway

🕐 See website for dates and times of operation. ✕ ☎ 028 4461 2233. www.downrail.co.uk.

Steam locomotives from the 1920s and 30s, or diesels from the 60s carry passengers in 50–100-year-old carriages from Downpatrick to the tranquil ruins of Inch Abbey, approximately 2mi/3km away. There are also guided tours of exhibitions and workshops. Real enthusiasts can book a day's experience on the footplate, driving a diesel train, or firing and driving a steam locomotive.

EAST OF DOWNPATRICK

SAUL

From Downpatrick take the minor road east for 2mi/3.2km to Saul.

St Patrick's Memorial Church

The hilltop site, where St Patrick is said to have made his first Irish convert (👆 see "St Patrick's Saul" box), now accommodates a church, built of Mourne granite in 1932 to commemorate the 1,500th anniversary of St Patrick's landing near Saul, designed in the Celtic-Revival style by Henry Seaver of Belfast, incorporating a characteristic Irish round tower. There are few traces of the original medieval abbey, but its graveyards hold two cross-carved stones and two small **mortuary houses**.

St Tassach's (Raholp) Church

4mi/6.4km east of Downpatrick.
The ruins of this 10C/11C church stand on the spot where Bishop Tassach is said to have administered the last sacrament to St Patrick.

Struell Wells★

2mi/3.2km southeast of Downpatrick.
A popular place of pilgrimage from the 16C until the 1840s, these Wells were once pagan places of worship (streams and springs were important to the Celts) but are now strongly associated with Saint Patrick.

The site, in a secluded rocky hollow by a fast-flowing stream, comprises five

---

St Patrick's Saul

When St Patrick returned to Ireland in 432 to convert the people to Christianity, his ship was carried by the wind and tide into Strangford Lough and up the River Slaney, now a mere stream, to land near Saul. He converted the local chief, Dichu, who gave him a barn (*sabhal* in Irish, pronounced Saul) to use as a church.

St Patrick grew attached to Saul and returned there to die in 461; some records even state he was buried in Saul, rather than in Downpatrick.

---

buildings: an unfinished 18C church; a circular Drinking Well with a domed roof built on a wicker supporting arch; a rectangular Eye Well with a pyramidal corbelled roof; a Men's Bath-house, plus a stone roof and a dressing room with seats next to the bath and a Women's Bath-house without a roof – its dressing room is in the men's bath-house. Although the oldest of these buildings dates only from c. 1600, there is written reference to a chapel on the site in 1306.

Slieve Patrick

3mi/4.8km east of Downpatrick. 15min there and back on foot to the summit.
A statue of St Patrick was erected on the top of the hill in 1932 to commemorate the 1,500th anniversary of his landing near Saul. The path up to an open-air altar is marked by the Stations of the Cross. From the top there is a fine **view** over the surrounding countryside and the drumlin islands of Strangford Lough.

NORTH OF DOWNPATRICK

Inch Abbey★

2mi/3.2km NW of Downpatrick via the A 7, after 1mi/1.6km turn left.
This abbey, built on an island in the marshes, is now accessible by road. The daughter house of the Cistercian abbey at Furness in Lancashire, it was founded c. 1180 by John de Courcy. Among the ruins are the remains of a 13C church

Inch Abbey

© M. Siepmann / imagebroker / age fotostock

and detached buildings presumed to be an infirmary *(southeast)*, a bakehouse and a guesthouse.

Killyleagh

7mi/11km north of Downpatrick on the A 22.

The picturesque turreted **castle**, redesigned in 1850 by Charles Lanyon, has two circular towers (13C and 17C). The original castle, built by de Courcy, was acquired by the O'Neills and destroyed by General Monk in 1648. Killyleagh was the birthplace of **Sir Hans Sloane**, whose collections formed the nucleus of the Natural History and British Museums in London.

♟♟ Delamont Country Park

🕙 *Open: Park 9am–dusk. Railway: Jun–Aug and Bank Hols daily noon–6pm, rest of year Sat–Sun noon–dusk.* ⊜*£2.50, child £1.50.* ✕ 🅿 *(charge).* 🕿 *028 4482 8333. www.delamontcountrypark.com.*

The park contains a walled garden with formal beds and extends to the shore of Strangford Lough. A spacious bird hide is ideal for bird watching; the longest miniature railway in Ireland, boat trips, a blue-flag beach and an adventure playground are more fun for children.

SOUTH OF DOWNPATRICK

Ballynoe Stone Circle

3mi/5km south of Downpatrick. Park opposite the old railway station (east); 6min there and back on foot by the track (west) between the fields.

Low close-set stones encircle an oval mound which contained a stone cist at either end, in which cremated bones were found (1937–38). The Stone Circle was probably built by the late-Neolithic Beaker people, c. 2000 BC.

Killough

7mi/11km S of Downpatrick by B 176.

A broad central avenue runs through this peaceful village on the edge of a deep sea-inlet. In the 17C it was known as Port St Anne after Anne Hamilton, whose husband, Michael Ward of Castle Ward, developed the port to facilitate the export of lead and agricultural products from his estates.

St John's Point

10mi/16km S of Downpatrick via the B 176, A 2 and a minor road.

The ruins of a 10C/11C pre-Romanesque church mark the site of an early monastery. A lighthouse stands on the southernmost point of the Lecale Peninsula.

WEST OF DOWNPATRICK

Clough
6mi/10km southwest of Downpatrick via the A 25.
North of the crossroads stands a stone tower (13C with later additions) surmounting an Anglo-Norman earthwork castle, once enclosed by a wooden palisade.

Loughinisland Churches
5mi/8km west of Downpatrick via the A 2 and a minor road north.
Three ruined churches stand on what was originally an island overlooking the lake. The middle one is the oldest (13C); the largest 15C; the third bears the date 1636 over the door, but may be earlier. The initials PMC stand for Phelim Mac-Cartan, whose family owned property in the area and are probably buried here.

👥 Seaforde Gardens and Tropical Butterfly House★
9mi/14.5km west of Downpatrick via the A 25 and A 2 north. ⏰*Open Easter–Sept Mon–Sat 10am–5pm, Sun 1pm–6pm.* ✆*Garden: £4.95, Butterfly House and garden £8.50, child £4.85.* ✘ ✆*028 4481 1225. www.seafordegardens.com.*
The gardens are situated in the historic demesne of Seaforde, which has been a family home for almost 400 years.
The old walled garden, dating from the 18C or possibly earlier, has been revived with a large hornbeam **maze** and a **tropical butterfly house**. The latter contains hundreds of free-flying exotic butterflies as well as parrots, reptiles and other creatures. The Pheasantry is a deep dell planted with great rhododendrons and exotic trees. Across the lawns and parallel with the maze are two avenues of Eucryphias. The garden also holds the National Collection of Eucryphias, with over 20 varieties grown here. These white or pink Southern hemisphere trees are one of the glories of the garden in late summer and autumn.

🚗 DRIVING TOUR

TOWARDS LECALE PENINSULA
16mi/26km

A splendid region with a number of tourist attractions, the Lecale Peninsula is a spur of land spanning the west coast of Strangford Lough from Strangford to Downpatrick, and inland to Ballynahinch in the North and Dundrum in the West. To the East is the Irish Sea.

▶ From Downpatrick take the A 25 in the direction of Strangford, then follow the route markers to Quoile Countryside Centre.

Quoile Countryside Centre
♿⏰*Open year-round Sat–Sun noon–4pm (Nov–Feb Sun only). Castle island bird hide year-round daily 10am–4pm.* ✆*028 4461 5520. www.doeni.gov.uk.*
In 1957 a barrage was built at Hare Island, excluding the sea from the Quoile estuary, turning the tidal flats into a freshwater lake with sluice gates. The Nature Reserve comprises 494 acres/200ha of woodland, grassland and reedbed habitats enjoyed by birds and otters. From **Quoile Quay**, which was built in 1717 by Edward Southwell and served as a port for Downpatrick until 1940, the road reaches **Quoile Castle**, a late-16C tower house inhabited by the West family until the mid-18C.
The **visitor centre** provides descriptions of the local history, flora and fauna.

▶ Return to the A 25 and continue towards Strangford.

👥 Castle Ward★★★
(HM). ♿⏰*Grounds: Open Apr–Sept 10am–8pm, Oct 10am–5pm, Nov–Mar 10am–4pm). House:* ♿ 🔊*Admission by guided tour only, noon–5pm: daily mid-Mar–early Apr & Jul–Aug; early Apr–Jun Wed–Sun; Sept–Oct Sat–Sun. Also open all bank hols and public hols House, grounds and wildlife centre:* ✆*£8.18, child £4.09.* ✘ ✆*028 4488 1204. www.nationaltrust.org.uk/castle-ward.*

© Northern Ireland Tourist Board

Castle Ward

This 18C house, surrounded by superb parkland, and overlooking Strangford Lough, is an odd but endearing architectural compromise between the conflicting tastes of Bernard Ward, later the first Lord Bangor, and his wife Anne. The main façade is Palladian, the garden front is Gothick; the interiors exhibit a similar dichotomy.

The entrance to the **house** (1760–75) opens into the hall, exuberantly decorated with stuccowork. The rooms on the northeast side reflect the Gothick style favoured by Lady Bangor – the boudoir **fan vaulting** is modelled on Henry VII's Chapel in Westminster Abbey; window panels in the saloon are deemed to be 17C Flemish. In contrast, the **dining room** on the Classical side of the house has 18C panelling and Chippendale chairs (c. 1760).

When the new house was built, the formal gardens were replaced by a naturalistic landscape of grass, trees and deer park around such features as the **Temple Water★**, created in 1724, and the **ice house** on the east bank, close to where the former early-18C house stood. The Walled Garden, which originally provided the house with cut flowers and produce, now contains pens for the **Wildfowl Collection**.

Children can dress up and play with period toys in the Victorian Past Times centre, visit the horses, pigs and hens in the farmyard and let off steam in the adventure playground. The farmyard itself has become a major visitor attraction in recent times, as it featured heavily in HBO's Game of Thrones in the scenes set at Winterfell.

The 17C **tower house**, known as Old Castle Ward on the lake shore, was the first dwelling built on the estate by a Ward; today it is surrounded by farmyard buildings – the original 18C mill, once a tidal mill, was later adapted to be powered by the Temple Water. One building houses the **Strangford Lough Wildlife Centre**.

Ward Family

Late in the 16C Bernard Ward from Capesthorne in Cheshire bought the Castle Ward estate from the Earls of Kildare. In 1610 Nicholas Ward built a tower house, Old Castle Ward, by Strangford Lough. In the 18C the Ward estates extended from Castle Ward to the coast of Dundrum Bay; nothing remains of the 18C house built by Michael Ward, a good landlord who promoted the linen trade, developed the lead mines on his estate, built the new town and harbour of Killough and became a Justice of the Court of the King's Bench in Ireland.

In 1812 the property passed to Robert Ward, who preferred to live at Bangor Castle. Then, in 1827 the 3rd Viscount Bangor (a title bestowed in 1781) started to restore the estate. In 1950 the house was received by the state in lieu of death duties and presented to the National Trust.

The estate's latest venture is **The Clear Sky Adventure Centre** (www.clearsky-adventure.com), including kayaking, canoeing, coasteering, archery, rock-climbing, abseiling, orienteering, mountain biking and clay-pigeon shooting. There is also a heavy Game of Throne influence here - dress up in character costume and practice on the Winterfell replica archery range.

Ardglass Golf Club

© Northern Ireland Tourist Board

▷ Continue towards Strangford and follow signs for Audley's Castle.

Audley's Castle

The ruins of this 15C gatehouse-type **tower house** stand on a spit of land projecting into Strangford Lough. It was built by the Audley family, who sold it in 1646 to the Wards of Castle Ward. The hamlet of Audleystown was demolished in the 1850s and the inhabitants are thought to have emigrated to the US.

Audleystown Cairn
Walk across the fields.
The cairn, which is retained with drystone walling, is a dual court tomb with a forecourt at each end opening into galleries. Excavations in 1952 revealed 34 partly-burned skeletons, Neolithic pottery and flint implements.

▷ Continue on and into Strangford.

Strangford Castle

At the heart of this picturesque harbour town stands a 15–16C **tower house** (HM. ⏰*Key at house opposite*). An internal wooden stair climbs the three storeys to a very narrow roof walk from where there is a fine **view** of the ferry running between the Narrows and Portaferry.

▷ Make a detour (2.5mi/4km) south by the A 2 coast road.

Kilclief Castle

(HM) ♿⏰*Open Jul–Aug, daily 1–5pm.* ☎*028 9023 5000. www.discovernorthernireland.com.*
This 15C gatehouse-style **tower house**, with two defensive projections, was built to guard the entrance to the Narrows.

▷ Continue S on A 2 to Ardglass.

Ardglass

Little Ardglass is attractively located in a natural harbour, home to one of the province's fishing fleets. In the 15C it was an Anglo-Norman enclave, the busiest port in Ulster, protected from the native Irish by numerous fortified buildings. The finest of those standing is **Jordan's Castle**, an early-15C tower house overlooking the harbour, which, in the Elizabethan era, withstood a three-year siege under its owner, Simon Jordan, until relieved by Mountjoy in June 1601. It was restored in 1911 by F. J. Bigger, a solicitor and antiquarian from Belfast, and now houses his collection of antiquities.

King's Castle and Isabella's Tower are predominantly 19C. A row of fortified warehouses along the harbour front is now the clubhouse of the local golf course.

ADDRESSES

🛏 STAY

🍽🍽 **The Mill at Ballydugan** – *Drumcullen Rd, 2.5mi/4km southwest of Downpatrick. ☎028 4461 3654. www.ballyduganmill.com.com. 11 rooms.* Set in a peaceful village, this late-18C flourmill has been sympathetically converted into a very well-equipped B&B with a café and a fine-dining restaurant, all featuring exposed beams and roaring open fires.

Mourne Mountains★

The highest granite peaks in Northern Ireland rise dramatically from the sea and plain of Co Down to Slieve Donard and extend westwards to Carlingford Lough and north into rolling foothills. The Kingdom of Mourne, the strip of land between the mountains and the sea, is a region of small fields divided by drystone walls, where for centuries a life of farming and fishing continued largely undisturbed by external events. Nowadays the mountains and coast are a favourite holiday area, with good beaches and lovely scenery enjoyed by hill walkers and climbers.

Info: 10–14 Central Promenade, **Newcastle**, ✆028 4372 2222. 28 Bridge Street, **Kilkeel**, ✆028 4176 2525.

Location: The Mourne Mountains are bounded by the Newry-Downpatrick road, A 25, and the coast road, A 2.

Don't Miss: Castlewellan Forest Park.

Kids: The Peace Maze at Castlewellan Forest Park.

NEWCASTLE

The town "where the mountains of Mourne sweep down to the sea", as immortalised in verse by Percy French, began to develop in the early 19C when seaside holidays became fashionable. From the tiny harbour a long promenade of hotels, shops and amusement arcades face onto the long, sandy beach of Dundrum Bay.

The town's Roman Catholic church (1967), **Our Lady of the Assumption**, is a modern circular structure with striking stained glass.

Donard Park, on the banks of the Glen River, is a good point from which to start the steep but steady climb to the summit of **Slieve Donard**, named in honour of Donard, a local chieftain supposedly converted to Christianity by St Patrick.

AROUND NEWCASTLE

Tollymore Forest Park★

♿⏱*Open 10am–dusk.* *£4.50 per car. www.nidirect.gov.uk/tollymore-forest-park.*

The main mansion at the heart of this vast landscaped demesne straddling

Mourne Mountains

© Northern Ireland Tourist Board

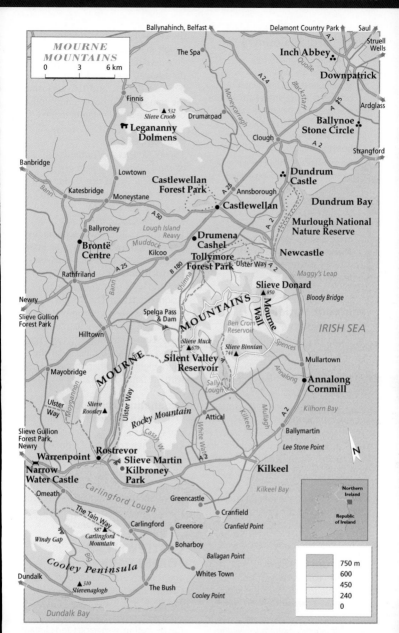

the salmon-rich River Shimna is long gone, but several follies and bridges are preserved in the province's first Forest Park (1955).

There is a hermitage, the extravagantly decorated Gothic and Barbican Gates, and the church-like Clanbrassil Barn (now an **information centre**); trails thread past splendid specimen trees and through an avenue of Himalayan cedars, an azalea walk and conifer plantations. The local fauna includes foxes, otters, badgers, red squirrels, pine martens, moths, butterflies and many birds.

Brontë Country

Among the rolling northern foothills of the Mourne Mountains stands the ruined cottage *(plaque)* where Patrick Brunty (O'Pronitaigh), the father of the famous literary sisters, Charlotte, Emily and Anne, was born in 1777.

He may have changed his name to Brontë before leaving Ireland in 1802 (to study theology at Cambridge), inspired perhaps by Lord Nelson, who was made Duke of Brontë (1799), after a place in Sicily, by Ferdinand, King of Naples, in recognition of his assistance in recapturing Naples from the French.

Murlough National Nature Reserve

2mi/3.2km E of Newcastle by A 2. (NT).
🕐*Park: dawn to dusk. Information Centre mid-Mar–late Oct 10am–6pm; daily Apr–Sept: other times Sat–Sun. Also open Bank Hols.* ⮕*£4 per car.* 📞*028 4375 1467. www.nationaltrust. org.uk/murlough.*

The magnificent sand dunes between the Carrigs River and Dundrum Bay, which reach a height of 100ft/30m, provide sanctuary to migratory birds and a broad range of plants. There are traces of early human habitation, including an ancient tripod **dolmen** (8ft/2.5m high). The reserve also contains an excellent beach.

Dundrum Castle★

4mi/6.4m east of Newcastle on the A 2; in Dundrum turn left uphill to car park. (HM). 🕐*Open Mar–Oct Tue–Sun noon–4pm; Nov–Feb Sun only. Call for possible extended summer opening times.* 📞*028 3885 3955. www.discovernorthernireland.com.*

The ruins north of the town show how the castle's strategic position and natural defences were supplemented by an impressively deep rock-cut ditch. Building was probably initiated by John de Courcy c. 1177 so that the approach to the Lecale Peninsula and Strangford Lough could be defended. There is an unusual circular keep *(fine views from the parapet)* and Lower Ward, added between the 13C and 15C, enclosing the remains of a once-grand house built by the Blundell family in the 17C.

Brontë Centre

1.5mi/2.5km north of Rathfriland, off the B 25 in Drumballyroney (signposted). ♿🕐*Open 17 Mar–Aug Fri–Sun & Bank Hols noon–4.30pm.* ⮕*£3.* 📞*028 4062 3322. www.banbridge.com.*

The hamlet's little white schoolhouse and church now function as an interpretative centre for the life and work of **Patrick Brontë** (*see "Brontë Country" box)* and his three famous daughters. A signposted tour, **The Brontë Homeland Drive** starts at Drumballyroney Church and School near Rathfriland, 10 miles south of Banbridge. It is well signposted along the 10-mile/16-km route, which highlights other sites associated with the family in the area.

Legananny Dolmen

11mi/18km N of Newcastle via the A 50 and side roads from Castlewellan.

The dolmen consists of a huge slanting capstone delicately balanced on three unusually low supporting stones. It is sited in a theatrical setting on the southern slope of Slieve Croob (1,745ft/532m), with a magnificent view of the Mourne Mountains.

CASTLEWELLAN FOREST PARK★★

4mi/6.4km N of Newcastle by the A 50. 🕐*Open 10am–dusk.* ⮕*£2 pedestrian, £4.50 per car. www.nidirect.gov.uk/ castlewellan-forest-park-2.*

Castlewellan, a spacious and elegant little market town, was laid out in 1750 around its two squares by the Earl of Annesley.

The **forest park** is based on the demesne developed by the Annesley family from the mid-18C, its splendid tree collection forming the basis of the national **arboretum**.

Castlewellan Forest Park

© Outdoor Recreation NI/Northern Ireland Tourist Board

The Annesleys, descendants of an Elizabethan army captain, were successors in this part of Ulster to the Magennis clan, who lost their landholdings after the 1641 rising. The core of the estate is not so much the Scottish baronial style castle built in granite and now used as a conference centre, but the superb **Annesley Gardens**, enclosed by a wall and ornamented by two fountains. The mile-long lake provides excellent fishing, while along its shores a 3mi/5km **Sculpture Trail** features pieces created from natural materials.

There is an ice-house on the south shore and a pagan standing stone, now covered with Christian symbols, on the north bank.

From the highest point, Slievenaslat (896ft/273m) provides magnificent views of the Mourne Mountains. The largest and longest permanent hedge maze in the world, the **Peace Maze** 👤👤 was opened in 2001.

Drumena Cashel and Souterrain★

1mi/2km southwest of Castlewellan

A good number of Early-Christian farm enclosures, or cashels, have survived in the Mourne Mountains. This well-preserved example consists an oval space encircled by a drystone wall, containing the foundations of a house and a T-shaped underground tunnel called a souterrain, which can be entered.

SILENT VALLEY RESERVOIR★

♿ 🕐 *Visitor Centre: Open daily May–Sept 10am–6.30pm, Oct–Apr 10am–4pm. 🚗£4.50 car, £1.60 pedestrians. Shuttle to/from Ben Crom £1.20 return. ✖(Apr–Sept weekends & bank hols). www.niwater.com/silent-valley.*

The Mourne Mountains have few natural lakes so the reservoirs supplying Belfast and Co Down since 1933 have altered the landscape, many would say for the better.

The Silent Valley scheme on the Kilkeel River took 10 years to complete and holds 136 million cubic metres of water. The catchment is protected by the extraordinary 22mi/35km linear **Mourne Wall**, beautifully constructed in rough mountain granite between 1910–22, providing seasonal relief work to as many as 2,000 local men.

There is a pleasant walk *(2hrs there and back on foot)* to the dam, which provides a superb **view**★ of the reservoir below Slieve Binnian (2,441ft/744m). From the east end of the dam the path continues north to **Ben Crom Reservoir** (3mi/4.8km), while the path at the opposite end returns down the valley past **Sally Lough**, through a grove of conifers and over a wooden footbridge spanning the Kilkeel River.

Spelga Pass and Dam★

From the dam there is a wonderful **view** north over the foothills of the Mourne Mountains to the rolling hills of Co Down. The reservoir (which provides fine angling for brown trout) flooded the summer pastures, known as Deer's Meadow, in 1959.

🚗 DRIVING TOUR

ALONG THE COAST FROM NEWCASTLE TO NEWRY

▶ From Newcastle take the A 2 south.

Bloody Bridge

It is thought that the name for this scenic bridge comes from an incident at the time of the 1641 uprising when a group of government prisoners, en route to be exchanged for captured rebels, was murdered by a soldier called Russell after he suffered a panic attack.

▶ From the A 2 turn south by the police station towards the shore.

Annalong

Annalong's early-19C restored **corn-mill★** (♿🕐call for times; ∞£2.10; ☎028 4376 8736) is driven by a back-shot breast-shot water-wheel and is the last of some 20 mills in the Kingdom of Mourne, which once milled wheat and oats or scutched flax. The Exhibition Room describes the history of milling.

Kilkeel

The little town is full of interest, with stepped pavements and different levels, but its true colours are really seen when the boats of Northern Ireland's largest fishing fleet land their catch at the quayside.

Green Castle

(HM). 🕐*Open Jul–Sept daily 10am–5pm (Sept Sat–Sun only).* ☎*028 9181 1491. www.doeni.gov.uk.*
The ruins of a mid-13C Anglo-Norman stronghold are set on a low outcrop of rock extending into Carlingford Lough. The **Royal Castle**, consisting of a large rectangular keep within a four-sided walled enclosure with D-shaped corner towers, was surrounded by a moat cut in the rock. It was besieged by Edward Bruce (1316) and used as a garrison in Elizabethan times. From the top of the keep there is a fine view to Cranfield Bay, which has good sandy bathing beach, up Carlingford Lough and the mountains of the Cooley Peninsula in the Republic.

Rostrevor Forest Park

The pine forest covering the south bank of the Kilbroney River and the steep northwest slopes of **Slieve Martin** (597ft/182m), is ideal for walking – to the **Cloghmore**, a great glacial boulder, and to the **viewpoint★** high above Rostrevor Bay.

Rostrevor

This attractive little town on Carlingford Lough enjoys a temperate climate allowing palm trees and mimosa to thrive.

Warrenpoint

The town is both a port equipped to take container traffic and a pleasant resort, with a vast central square, used for markets and festivals, and a promenade facing south down Carlingford Lough between the Mourne Mountains and the Cooley Peninsula.

Narrow Water Castle Keep

2mi/3.2km north of Warrenpoint on the A 2. 🕐*Open Jul–Oct Sun, Mon, Wed, Fri 10am-5pm.*
The castle keep occupies a strategic position on a promontory command-

---

Warrenpoint Massacre

In 1979 Narrow Water was the scene of the largest single loss of life for the British Army since World War II when 18 soldiers were killed by two IRA bombs.

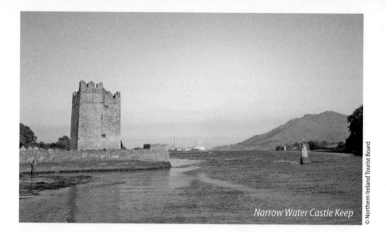

Narrow Water Castle Keep

© Northern Ireland Tourist Board

ing the narrows at the mouth of the Newry River where it enters Carlingford Lough. It was built in the 1650s as an English garrison at the cost of £361 4s 2d. Although restored, it is an excellent example of a **tower house** complete with **bawn**. The Elizabethan Revival castle *(private)* is only open for private receptions.

ADDRESSES

🏠 STAY

🍽️🛏️ **The Cuan** – *Strangford. 9.5mi/ 15km northwest.* 📞*028 4488 1222. www.thecuan.com.* Well-located for Strangford Lough, golfing, sailing and walking, this very comfortable guesthouse with an award-winning restaurant will suit most needs.

🍷/EAT

🍽️🛏️**The Harbour Inn** – *Annalong.* 📞*028 4376 8678. www.harbourinnann along.co.uk.* Located, as its name would suggest in Annalong Harbour this restaurant offers wonderful views of the Irish Sea and dishes to suit all tastes.

SPORTS AND LEISURE

👫 KIDS

Castle and Islands Park, *Newcastle.* – Swings, slides, Slippery Dip, nine-hole pitch and putt course, tennis, boating.

Tropicana – *Newcastle. Open Jul–Aug daily.* Heated outdoor sea-water pools, giant water slide, bouncy castle, etc.

Coco's Indoor Adventure Playground, *Newcastle* – Snake slides, free fall, assault course and soft play activity area 📞*028 4372 6226.*

WALKING

A good base for walking in the Mourne Mountains is the **Mourne Countryside Centre**t *(📞028 4372 4059, www.mournelive.com)* at 10–14 Central Promenade, Newcastle, which is well stocked with walks information and has walking guides for sale (including the essential Ordnance Survey 1:25000 map *The Mournes*). They also organise a programme of hill walks in the summer months, including the **Mourne International Walking Festival** *(last weekend in Jun)*, which starts from Newcastle or Warren Point *(📞028 4372 4059, www.mournewalking.co.uk).*

BEACHES

There are beaches where you can swim at Newcastle and Cranfield.

EVENTS AND FESTIVALS

The **Boley Fair**, traditional sheep fair, in Hilltown *(second week July).* *www.boleyfair.com.*

The **Maiden of Mourne Festival** in Warrenpoint *(early Aug).* *www.maidenofthemournes.com*

Fiddlers' Green Festival – Folk festival at the picturesque town of Rostrevor *(last week in July).* 📞*028 4173 8738. www.fiddlersgreenfestival.com.*

Newry

and Slieve Gullion

Newry (An Tiúr) occupies a commanding position in the "Gap of the North" or Moyry Gap, between the line of hills separating Ulster from the plains of Meath. In the 18C Newry was linked by canals to Lough Neagh and to the sea at Carlingford Lough, becoming for a while the busiest port in the North. Those days are long gone, but its road and railway links to both Belfast and Dublin enable shoppers to come from both sides of the border. Slieve Gullion, together with its attendant circle of lesser heights, known as the Ring of Gullion, dominates the countryside to the West of Newry. It is intimately associated with the legendary Cuchulain, hero of the epic The Cattle Raid of Cooley (Táin bo Cuainlge) and is rich in prehistoric remains.

A BIT OF HISTORY

Turbulent times have erased most of the old town, including the castle built by the Anglo-Norman John de Courcy and all the strongholds that succeeded it. In 1731 work began here on the first inland canal in the British Isles, linking Newry via 14 locks to Lough Neagh. Thirty years later, a ship canal was dug to provide the town with an outlet to Carlingford Lough and the Irish Sea. The town prospered from the trade in linen, coal, building stone and emigrants, as the Georgian town houses and multi-storey quayside mills testify. In 1956, the inland canal was closed and today provides for recreational use.

SIGHTS

Newry Cathedral

Designed by Thomas Duff in 1825 and dedicated to St Patrick and St Colman, Newry Cathedral was the first Roman Catholic cathedral to be built in Ireland following the Act of Emancipation. Inside, it is vivid with stained glass and colourful mosaics.

▶ **Population:** 21,633.

Info: Street, Newry. 028 3031 3i70. www.newry.com.

Location: Newry is 37mi/60km SW of Belfast.

Newry and Mourne Museum

Open year-round Mon–Sat 10am–4.30pm, Sun 1.30–5pm. 028 3031 3182. www.bagenalscastle.com/museum.

Built in the 16C, this is Newry's oldest surviving building and was "discovered" enveloped within the former McCann's Bakery premises. Its museum competently deals with the archeology and history of the area. It has a lovely early 18C panelled room recalling prosperous times and Nelson's cabin table from *HMS Victory*.

🚗 DRIVING TOUR

SLIEVE GULLION★

Round tour of 27mi/43.5km. One day.

▶ From Newry take the A 25 west; after 1.5mi/2.4km turn right onto the B 133 to Bessbrook.

Bessbrook

This early and fascinating example of a planned industrial village has terraces of granite-built, slate-roofed cottages neatly ranged round three sides of two grassy squares. The settlement, complete with churches, schools, shops and a community hall (but significantly, no pub), was built in 1845 by the Quaker linen manufacturer John Grubb Richardson for his flax workers. Bessbrook later inspired the Cadbury family to build the far-larger model settlement of Bournville, near Birmingham.

▶ From Bessbrook take the B 112; turn right onto the A 25. West of Camlough village, turn left onto the B 30.

Cam Lough

From the road there is a fine view of the narrow lake in its deep trough between Camlough Mountain (1,417ft/423m) and Slieve Gullion.

▷ At the crossroads turn left onto a narrow road along the west side of Cam Lough.

Killevy

An ancient graveyard surrounds the ruins of two **churches**, standing end to end. The eastern building is medieval; the western one is earlier (12C), although the west wall, which is pierced by a doorway below a massive lintel, may be 10C or 11C. A granite slab in the northern half of the graveyard is said to mark the grave of St Monenna (also known as Darerca and Bline), who founded an important early nunnery here in the 5C.

▷ Continue south for 1.5mi/2.4km; turn right onto the B 113.

Slieve Gullion Forest Park★★

8mi/13km Scenic Drive. ⊛ *Beware steep gradients and difficult bends.*

The pines, larches and spruce of the Forest Park clad the lower slopes of the southwest face of Slieve Gullion. The visitor centre, housed in old farm buildings, provides information about the park and displays old hand tools. After climbing through the forest, the Scenic Drive emerges on the open slopes of Slieve Gullion; on the left is an extensive view over the treetops; on the right the path, waymarked in white, to the top of the south peak of Slieve Gullion (1,894ft/573m) marked by a cairn; another cairn crowns the lower north peak. The Drive swings left downhill and doubles back along the southwest slope, through the trees and rocks, to a **viewpoint**★★ overlooking a section of the **Ring of Gullion**.

▷ At the exit turn right onto the B 113 and immediately turn left. After 1.5mi/2.4km turn right; after 1mi/1.6km park at the T-junction.

Kilnasaggart Stone

© Northern Ireland Tourist Board

Kilnasaggart Stone

Most of Ireland's cross-decorated pillar-stones are in the West of the country, but this granite example (7ft/2.15m high) in its hedged enclosure *(across two fields)* is the earliest dateable one of its kind, its crosses carved around AD 700. The pillar itself, which marks the site of an Early-Christian cemetery, may in fact be much older, a prehistoric standing stone converted to a new use. It also bears an inscription in Irish stating the site was dedicated under the patronage of Peter the Apostle by the son of Ceran Bic, Ternohc, who died c. 715.

▷ Return to the B 113; turn right towards Newry; after 5mi/8km turn left to Ballymacdermot Cairn (sign).

Ballymacdermot Cairn

Beside the road *(right)* on the south slope of Ballymacdermot Mountain are the remains of a Neolithic court grave: two burial chambers with an antechamber and a circular forecourt enclosed in a trapezoidal cairn. Fine **views** extend southwest across the Meigh Plain to Slieve Gullion and the Ring of Gullion.

▷ Continue for 1mi/1.6km.

Bernish Rock Viewpoint★★

View over Newry to the Mourne Mountains on the eastern horizon.

Armagh and around ★

Ireland's ecclesiastical capital stands on hills surrounded by pleasant countryside and prosperous fruit orchards, planted originally by English settlers who came to populate the early-17C plantation of Ulster. The town, with its many fine Georgian buildings, is dominated by two cathedrals, the seats of Ireland's Anglican and Roman Catholic archbishops.

▶ **Population:** 14,265 (Armagh).

🖩 **Info:** 40 Upper English Street. ✆028 3752 1800. www.visitarmagh.com.

◐ **Location:** Armagh lies between Lough Neagh and the border, 50mi/80km southwest of Belfast via the M 1.

👫 **Kids:** Armagh Planetarium, Navan Centre & Fort (summer), Tayto Potato Crisp Factory.

A BIT OF HISTORY

Armagh, from *Ard Macha* meaning Macha's Height, alludes to the legendary pagan queen who built a fortress on the central hill. Although the major pre-Christian power centre of Ulster was nearby at Navan Fort, Armagh acquired new prominence after Navan's destruction in AD 332. St Patrick arrived in Armagh (c. 445) and made it the centre of the new religion, declaring his new church should take precedence over all other churches in Ireland. In the following centuries Armagh developed into a leading centre of learning: it was here that the famous 9C manuscript, the *Book of Armagh*, now in Trinity College Library, Dublin, was produced; in the 12C, the great Archbishop St Malachy was based here and Armagh's reputation grew such that an ecclesiastical Synod decreed (1162) that only those who had studied at Armagh could teach theology elsewhere in Ireland. The school was dissolved at the Reformation.

👣 WALKING TOUR

The Mall

This distinctive long stretch of grass with a pavilion and cricket pitch bordered by elegant terraces is, to say the least, an unusual Irish urban feature.

Armagh

© H. & D. Zielske/Look/Photononstop

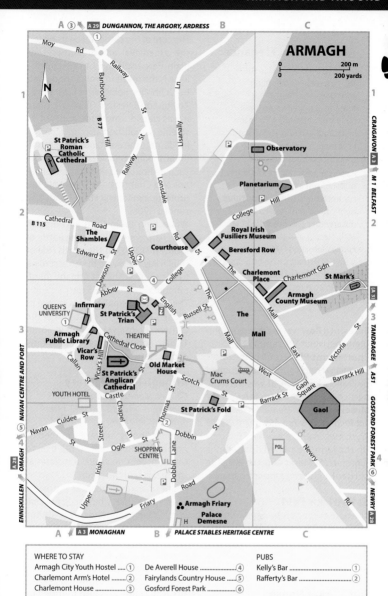

ARMAGH

WHERE TO STAY

		PUBS	
Armagh City Youth Hostel ..... ①	De Averell House .... ④	Kelly's Bar .... ①
Charlemont Arm's Hotel .... ②	Fairylands Country House ..... ⑤	Rafferty's Bar .... ②
Charlemont House .... ③	Gosford Forest Park .... ⑥	

From the 8C it was common grazing land, used for horse racing, bull-baiting and cock-fighting until such activities were stopped by Archbishop Robinson in 1773.

The Classical-style **Courthouse**, at the north end, was designed in 1809 by Francis Johnston. The former **Sovereign's House** now houses the **Royal Irish Fusiliers Museum**, (◐ *open Mon–Fri 10am–12.30pm & 1.30pm–4pm;* ◐ *closed Christmas and New Year;* ℘*028 3752 2911; www.armymuseums.org.uk*) with a splendid collections of flags and standards, uniforms, medals, weapons, silver, portraits and paintings relating to the five units raised in 1793 to fight the French.

Architectural Elegance

During peaceful times in the 18C and early 19C, farming and commerce flourished; Armagh acquired some fine buildings under the patronage of its Anglican Primate: Richard Robinson, later Lord Rokeby, Archbishop from 1765.

Robinson restored the cathedral, built himself a fine palace, commissioned a library and other public buildings, started the observatory and beautified the Mall. He was also the patron of Francis Johnston (1761–1829), a native of Armagh, who he helped to become one of Ireland's leading architects.

Beresford Row was designed by John Quinn between 1810 and 1827. **Charlemont Place**, one of the finest Georgian terraces (1827), was designed by Francis Johnston, as was the Ionic portico gracing the **Armagh County Museum** (◔open Mon–Fri 10am–5pm, Sat 10am–1pm & 2pm–5pm; ℘028 3752 3070; www.nmni.com/acm).
Up the long, tree-lined drive stands Johnston's **St Marks Church** (1811). The old **gaol** at the end replaced barracks.

St Patrick's Fold

The house, which is thought to stand on the site of St Patrick's first church in Armagh, was designed in 1812 for Leonard Dobbin, MP for Armagh (1833–38), by Francis Johnston.

Old Market House

A technical school now occupies the former two-storey Market House, commissioned in 1815 by Archbishop Stuart from Francis Johnston.

St Patrick's Anglican Cathedral★

◔Open year-round daily 9am–5pm (4pm Nov–Mar). £3 donation suggested. ℘028 3752 3142. www.stpatricks-cathedral.org.

The core of the cathedral on its hilltop site is medieval, although its present plain Perpendicular Gothic appearance is the result of works conducted by Archbishop Robinson in 1765, and by Archbishop Beresford (1834–37), when it was clad in sandstone and had its steeple demolished.

Inside, note the outstanding collection of 18C monuments by eminent masters such as Roubiliac, Rysbrack, Nollekens and Chantrey. Outside, note the grotesque medieval stone heads and sundial (1706).

When King Brian Ború and his son Murchard were killed at the Battle of Clontarf (1014), on the north side of Dublin Bay, they were buried according to the King's wishes at Armagh *(north transept)*.

The terrace of small houses known as **Vicar's Row** on the west side of the cathedral close was begun in about 1720 to accommodate female clergy dependants.

Armagh Public Library

◔Open Mon–Fri 10am–1pm and 2pm–4pm. ℘028 375 23142. http://armaghpubliclibrary.arm.ac.uk.
Thomas Cooley's library, founded by Archbishop Robinson (1771), bears a Greek inscription which translates as "the healing of the mind".

Besides many ancient books and manuscripts, the library has a copy of *Gulliver's Travels* annotated by Swift, the Rokeby Collection of 18C engravings and a range of historical maps, including a complete set of 1838 Ordnance Survey Maps of the 32 counties of Ireland. George Ensor's 1774 **infirmary** opposite *(still in use)* was also founded by Archbishop Robinson.

▷ Turn right into Abbey Street.

The Shambles

Archbishop Beresford's meat market (1827) was designed by Francis Johnston.

▷ From Dawson Street, turn left into Cathedral Road.

Armagh Public Library

© Northern Ireland Tourist Board

St Patrick's RC Cathedral★

○Open 10am–5pm (4pm Nov–Mar).
Guided tours, call for times.
℘028 3752 2802.

The twin-spired 19C Roman Catholic
cathedral stands up 44 steps, flanked
by statues of Archbishop Crolly and
Archbishop McGettigan, under whom
it was built. It is a striking Gothic Revival
structure, occupying the most prominent position available, an expression
of growing Catholic confidence built
with the proceeds of countless collections and raffles, and contributions from
royalty and the Pope.

Construction began in 1840, in the Perpendicular style of Thomas J. Duff, but
the Great Famine halted progress until
1854, delaying completion in 1873 but
allowing a change to the Decorated
style favoured by J. J. McCarthy.

The **interior** is lavishly and colourfully
decorated with a painted vaulted roof,
stained-glass windows and wall mosaics;
the spandrels honour Irish saints. The
sanctuary was renovated in 1981–82
by the architect, Liam McCormick.

Palace Demesne and the Garden of the Senses★

*Friary Rd. ○Open Easter Mon & Tue
11am–5pm; Apr–May & Sept Sat 10am
–5pm, Sun noon–5pm (May Bank
Holiday Sat–Sun noon–6pm, Mon
10.30am–5.30pm); Jun–Aug Mon–Sat
10am–5pm, Sun noon–5pm. Last*
*tour 4pm. ○Closed Jul 12. ✗ ℘028
3752 1800. www.visitarmagh.com
(search: The Palace Demesne).*

Between the 17C and the 20C the Palace
Demesne served as the state residence
of the Anglican Archbishop of Armagh.
The **Palace Stables Heritage Centre**
re-enacts life in the palace on July 23,
1786 when Arthur Young, the famous
agricultural improver, and other guests
were entertained by Archbishop Richard Robinson. Costumed interpreters
ensure visitors have a memorable
experience.

The **Primate's Chapel** commissioned
by Richard Robinson is a superb example of Georgian neo-Classical architecture begun by Thomas Cooley (1770)
and completed in 1786 by Francis Johnston. It contains very fine carved oak
panelling and an ornamental plaster
ceiling. The long ruin of the 13C Franciscan **Armagh Friary** is typical.

▲▲ Armagh Planetarium

*College Hill. ♿○Open Mon–Sat
10am–5pm; shows Mon–Fri 2pm, Sat
11am, noon, 1, 2, 3 & 4pm. Last Tue
every month 7–9pm; show 7.30pm.
Check website for programme. Tickets
must be collected from reception at
least 30min before show. ☞£6, child
£5. Booking essential (by phone).
Under-16s must be accompanied by
an adult. ℘028 3752 3689.
www.armaghplanet.com.*

Road Bowls

The ancient Irish sport of road bowling is still played on Sundays in Co Armagh and Co Cork. A heavy iron ball (28oz/794g; 7in/18cm) is hurled along a stretch of quiet winding country road in as few throws as possible; the ball may hurtle through the air at shoulder height. Betting is heavy.

Recently refurbished with the latest digital technology, the Planetarium offers full-colour 3-D 360° star shows projected over its entire huge dome (50ft/15m in diameter).

In the grounds the **Observatory**, founded and endowed in 1789 by Archbishop Robinson is one of the oldest meteorological stations in the British Isles.

EXCURSIONS

⚹⚹ Navan Centre and Fort★

2mi/3.2km west of Armagh on the A 28. ♿⊙*Visitor Centre open 10am–4pm (6.30pm Apr-Sept). Last entry 1hr before close. Fort open year-round freely accessible.* ⊙*Closed Jul 12.* ⊛*£6.60, child £4.40; winter £5.45, £3.30.* ✗ ☎*028 3752 9644. www.armagh.co.uk.*

In the late Bronze Age this impressive earthwork, surrounded by sacred

Navan Fort Centre

© Northern Ireland Tourist Board

places and settlement sites, was the most important place in Ulster, thought to be synonymous with Emain Macha, the capital of legendary Ulster, as mentioned in the **Ulster Cycle** (⊙*see Myths and Lore in Introduction).*

The multi-media displays in the **Visitor Centre★** evoke the world of the Celts and pre-Christian Ireland; archaeological research about the fort and its associated Neolithic sites chart their evolution. The fort itself *(5min on foot from the Visitor Centre)* consists of a massive circular bank and inner ditch around a hill with a high mound on top, flanked by a low circular mound surrounded by an infilled ditch. In summer there are lots of children's activities.

Ardress House★

7mi/11km NE of Armagh on the B 77. (NT) ♿✱*Admission by guided tour only, Jul-Aug Thu-Sun 1–6pm; Easter week daily 1–6pm. Mar-Jun, Sept, all Bank Hol weekends and Mons 1–6pm. St Patrick's Day & weekend noon–5pm.* ⊛*£5.* ☎*028 8778 4753. www.national trust.org.uk/ardress-house.*

Ardress is a simple 17C manor house, enlarged and embellished in the 18C. It was inherited by the architect George Ensor on his marriage in 1760.

The house displays glass from Dublin, Cork and Belfast, and some fine furniture, including Irish Chippendale chairs. The symmetry and proportions of the elegant **drawing room** are enhanced by the delightful stuccowork of Michael Stapleton.

The cobbled **farmyard**, with its central pump, is surrounded by farm buildings equipped with antiquated implements including baskets and bee hives.

The Argory★

(NT) 10mi/16km north of Armagh via the A 29 and a minor road (right). ♿⊙*House open Easter week & Jul–Aug daily noon–5pm; mid-Mar–Jun & Sept Thu–Sun noon–5pm; Oct Sat–Sun noon–4pm.* ⊙*Grounds open year-round daily 10am–5pm.* ⊛*House £5.25, grounds £2.50.* ✗ ☎*028 8778 4753. www.nationaltrust.org.uk.*

The Argory

© The Irish Image Colle / age fotostock

This handsome neo-Classical country house, built around 1824, is little-changed since the early years of the 20C and a tour of the house is a fascinating evocation of an ancient family home. The most extraordinary single object is the cabinet **barrel organ★** of 1820, still in full working order.

The **gardens★**, which extend to the Blackwater River, comprise old roses set in box-lined beds, a sundial dated 1820, yew tree arbours, Pleasure Grounds, a Garden House, a Pump House and a lime tree walk.

Dan Winter's Cottage

6mi/10km NE of Armagh via the A 29 and B 77 to Loughgall. ○*Open year-round daily 10.30am (2pm Sun)– 5.30pm (summer months 8.30pm).* ◎*donation requested.* ℘*028 3885 1344. www.danwinterscottage.com.*

On September 21, 1795, following the affray later called the "Battle of the Diamond" at **Dan Winter's House** *(3mi/5km NE)*, the victorious Protestant Peep O'Day Boys retired to celebrate their triumph at what was Jim Sloane's pub *(halfway up the main street, now part residential, part museum)*.

It was here that the Orange Order was instituted, dedicated to sustaining the "glorious and immortal memory of King William III". The **Sloan House Museum** *(curently under renovation, enquire at*

Dan Winter's Cottage) is overflowing with mementoes of the Order: sashes, caps, waistcoats, banners, guns and pikes used in 1795.

👤👤 Tayto Potato Crisp Factory

11mi/18km east of Armagh via the A 51; factory entrance next to the police station on entering Tandragee. ○*Factory tours, 1hr 30min, must be booked, min. age five years old: Mon– Thu 10.30am & 1.30pm, Fri 10.30am only.* ○*Closed all public holidays.* ◎*£5, child £3, inc 6-pack of crisps.* ℘*028 3884 0249. www.tayto.com.*

The factory is installed in Tandragee Castle, overlooking the town, built in 1837. The factory tour starts in the warehouse and follows the route of the potato on its journey of transformation into neatly-packed wavy golden crisps.

Gosford Forest Park

7mi/11km southeast of Armagh via the A 28 to Markethill. ○*Open 10am–sun-set.* ✕ ℘*028 3755 1277. www.nidirect. gov.uk/gosford-forest-park. www.gosford.co.uk.*

Now in the care of the Forestry Service, the park was formerly the demesne of the Acheson family, the Earls of Gos-ford. The present castle *(private)*, a huge pseudo-Norman pile designed by Thomas Hopper in 1819, was built at the same time as the **arboretum** was

Bloody Battlefields

Two important military engagements involving the O'Neills took place south of Dungannon. At the **Battle of the Yellow Ford** on the River Callan in 1598, Hugh O'Neill defeated the English forces under Sir Henry Bagnall; only about 1,500 Englishmen out of over 4,000 survived.

In 1646 at the **Battle of Benburb** at Derrycreevy, the Scottish army of General Monroe was outmanoeuvred by Owen Roe O'Neill and 3,000 Scots were killed.

planted with exotic trees. The **walled gardens** contain a brick **bee house** with niches to protect the straw hives from damp. The **Gosford Heritage Poultry Collection** aims to preserve rare native poultry breeds once common in the 18C.

Dean Jonathan Swift was a frequent visitor, hence **Swift's Well** and the **Dean Swifts Chair**, an artificial sun trap created by making a semicircular hollow protected by a yew hedge in a south-facing bank.

Dungannon

11mi/18km north of Armagh on the A 29

On its hilltop site, Dungannon (Dún Geanainn) was for centuries a main residence of the O'Neill clan, one of the great families of Gaelic Ulster. Nowadays it is the busy hub of a rich dairying and fruit-growing district, and a manufacturing centre of some importance. One of its oldest industries, textiles, has brought international fame to the Moygashel linen company (founded in 1875).

The Linen Green

🕐*Open year-round Mon–Sat 9.3am–5.30pm.* ✕ 🕾*028 8775 3761. www.thelinengreen.co.uk.*

One of Dungannon's oldest industries is recalled with this designer outlet shopping village built on the site of the former Moygashel linen mill. For non-shoppers the Moygashel Linen Visitors' Centre provides historical interest. Moygashel's history began c. 1795 when Huguenot settlers established the Irish Linen weaving company, weaving some of the finest linens in the world. Their ancestors, the Webb family, came to

own the famous Moygashel Weavers. They were taken over by Ulster Weavers in the late 20C and in 2005, the factory at Moygashel closed.

Parkanaur Forest Park★

4mi/6km west of Dungannon, off A4.

The park's herd of **white fallow deer** are direct descendants of a white hart and doe given by Elizabeth I in 1595 to her goddaughter, Elizabeth Norreys, who married Sir John Jephson of Mallow Castle. The former Burgess family estate boasts several unusual specimen trees, notably two parasol beeches with branches like corkscrews. The woodland is being developed as an oak forest; walks and a nature trail thread through the formal Victorian Garden, by the stone archway and stone bridge on the Torrent River. The farm buildings (1843) contain a display of forestry machinery.

Donaghmore

NW of Dungannon on B 43.

In the centre of this quiet village stands an ancient sandstone cross (AD c. 700–1000), associated with a former abbey, and composed of two different crosses. New and Old Testament scenes ornament the faces.

Castlecaulfield

3mi/5km W of Dungannon, off A 45, follow signs for Auchnacloy.

The stark ruins are those of a Jacobean **mansion** built (1611–19) by an ancestor of the Earls of Charlemont, Sir Toby Caulfield, who commanded Charlemont Fort and whose arms appear over the gatehouse, an earlier structure defended with murder holes above the main door. Although burned by the O'Donnells in 1641, the Caulfields continued in residence until the 1660s.

Moy

S of Dungannon via the A 29.

This attractive Plantation town was laid out in the 1760s by James Caulfield, Earl of Charlemont, modelled on Marengo in Lombardy, which he had visited while on the Grand Tour. The broad central green was once the site of the great monthly horse fairs, which lasted a whole week. From here, the road slopes down to the Blackwater River past the screen and entrance gates to Roxborough Castle (destroyed by fire in 1921), the 19C seat of the Earl of Charlemont. The Blackwater marks the boundary between Armagh and Tyrone, and formed the front line in 1602 between territory held by the rebellious Hugh O'Neill and his English opponents, who fortified it with a great star-shaped stronghold.

Most of the fort was burned down in 1922, though the gatehouse still stands at the end of a short avenue of trees.

ADDRESSES

🛏 STAY

⊖ **Armagh City Youth Hostel** – *39 Abbey St.* ☎ *028 3751 1800. www.hini.org.uk. www.hihostels.com.* A comfortable hostel with good facilities (including free Wi-Fi and a car park) in a modern building, close to the city centre.

⊖ **Fairylands Country House** – *25 Navan Fort Rd.* ☎ *028 3751 0315. www.fairylands.net. 5 rooms.* A smart, if rather uninspiring B&B, with a nice garden and large car parking area, just outside the city on the road to Enniskillen.

⊖⊖ **Charlemont House** – *4 The Square, Moy.* ☎ *07516 093040. www. charlemonthouse.co.uk. 5 rooms.* A grand old house, dating back to the mid-18C, with two double bedrooms and one family room. The decor, with antiques everywhere, has a charm all of its own. Option of room only (⊖).

⊖⊖ **De Averall House** – *47 English St Upper.* ☎ *028 3751 1213. 6 rooms.* Spacious rooms in this Georgian building within walking distance of the city centre. There is a restaurant downstairs, car parking space and a pleasant sitting room. Bedrooms are bright and modern but sympathetic to the period.

CAMPING

Gosford Forest Park – *Markethill (7mi/11km southeast of Armagh via the A 28 to Markethill).* ☎ *028 3755 1277. www.nidirect.gov.uk/gosford-forest-park.* A very pleasant site, with good facilities for tents and caravans.

🍴 EAT

⊖ **Charlemont Arms Restaurant** – *57 English St, Armagh.* ☎ *028 3752 2028. www.charlemontarmshotel.com.* This informal restaurant is part of the Charlemont Arms Hotel and the food is predictably "pub-international" – steak, chicken and some fish – but prices are reasonable and locals like the place.

⊖ **Shambles Bar & Restaurant** – *9 English St Lower. Armagh.* ☎ *028 3752 4107.* A large dining area and a smaller room upstairs in this popular city centre pub.

⊖⊖ **Moody Boar**– *Friary Rd. Armagh.* ☎ *028 3752 9678.* Beautifully designed modern shabby chic restuarant making the most of its lovely setting in the old stables of the Palace Demesne (⚓ *see p458*). Interesting Modern Irish menu.

PUBS

Kelly's Bar – *147 Railway St, Armagh.* ☎ *028 3752 2103.* A congenial pub with live music and DJs.

The Northern Bar – *100 Railway St, Armagh.* ☎ *028 3752 7315.* Food is served from midday to 3pm every day except Sun; musical entertainment at night, from Thursday to Sunday.

TRACING ANCESTORS

Armagh Ancestry – *40 English St.* ☎ *028 3752 1800. www.armagh.rootsireland.ie.* Pre-booking a meeting with a researcher is essential.

Co Fermanagh★★

and Lough Erne★★

Called the Fermanagh Lakeland for a good reason – the county is dominated by two enormous inland bodies of water and their connecting river. Fermanagh is an ever-changing series of vistas; dark brooding waterscapes, wind-tossed trees and marshland one day, followed by brilliant blue skies and multi-coloured flowers reflected in still waters the next. Several of the loughs' tiny islands still bear signs of ancient habitation and religious beliefs. Set between the two loughs and bridging them is Enniskillen, a pretty little town with a sad recent history of the Troubles. It is home to an excellent small theatre, a watersports centre and a castle and museum. Co Fermanagh can also boast two of Ireland's most magnificent country houses, Castle Coole and Florence Court.

ENNISKILLEN★

The principal town of Co Fermanagh (Inis Ceithleann) is a lively commercial and cultural centre, occupying a strategically important island site between Lower and Upper Lough Erne. In the 17C it was one of the main strongholds of the 17C Plantation of Ulster; nowadays it makes an ideal base for exploring Lough Erne, the Shannon-Erne Waterway, the Fermanagh lakes and rivers, and the Sperrin Mountains.

Enniskillen Castle★

&⊙*Open Mon-Fri (and Bank Hols) 9.30am–5pm, Sat 11am-5pm, Sun (Jun-Sept) 11am-5pm. ⊜£5. ℘028 6632 5000. www.enniskillencastle.co.uk.*

🅸 **Info:** Wellington Road, Enniskillen. ℘028 6632 3110. www.fermanagh lakelands.com.

◖ **Location:** Enniskillen, the county town, is situated between Upper and Lower Lough Erne, 50mi/80km west of Dungannon by the A 4 and 12mi/19km from the border.

⊛ **Don't Miss:** Castle Coole, Florence Court, Marble Arch Caves and Lough Erne.

👥 **Kids:** Marble Arch Caves.

GETTING THERE

BY SEA – Devenish Island Ferry: Operates Easter–mid-Sept at 10am, 1pm, 3pm, 5pm from Trory Point, 4mi/6km north of Enniskillen.

Until the 18C Enniskillen Castle was surrounded by water from the Erne. Built in the 15C as a stronghold for the powerful Maguire family (then rulers of Fermanagh), the castle defended the strategic route between Ulster and Connaught across the formidable Erne.

In 1609 it was granted to the English planter Captain William Cole, whose family later moved to nearby Florence Court. Cole laid out the town and made good strategic additions to the castle; Enniskillen held out against the native Irish uprising in 1641 and against Jacobite attacks in 1689.

This historic site houses two museums, **Fermanagh County Museum** and **Regimental Museum of the Royal Inniskilling Fusiliers**. The former has displays on the history, landscapes and

---

The 1987 Enniskillen Bombing

For many outsiders the name Enniskillen still conjures up the dreadful memory of Remembrance Day 1987, when an IRA bomb killed 11 people and injured 61 others as they gathered to commemorate the dead of the two World Wars.

wildlife of the county, while the castle exhibitions unravel the evolution of the castle.

The keep, which incorporates parts of the original 15C fortress, houses the military museum, with displays that trace the history of the prestigious regiment formed in the late-17C.

The **Curved Range** displays information about the ancient monuments and castles of Fermanagh, and the pilgrim's trail to Devenish Island.

Forthill Park

🕐 *Cole's Monument open Apr–Sept 1.30pm–3pm.* 👁 *£1.*

Enniskillen's town park is named after the star-shaped fort built here in 1689 during the Williamite Wars. It has a delightful oriental-looking cast-iron Victorian **bandstand**. The centre of the fort is now occupied by **Cole's Monument**, erected between 1845–57 in memory of General the Hon. Sir Galbraith Lowry Cole (1772–1842), brother of the 2nd Earl of Enniskillen of Florence Court, and a close friend of the Duke of Wellington. Within the fluted Doric column a spiral stair *(180 steps)* climbs to a platform, providing great **views** of the area.

🐾WALKING TOUR

In 1688 the **East Bridge** replaced the drawbridge built by the planters on the site of an old ford in 1614. The **Courthouse** *(left)*, with its Classical portico, was radically remodelled in 1821–22 by William Farrell of Dublin. William Scott's **Town Hall** (1898) and splendid clock overlooks The Diamond.

In the **Buttermarket** *(turn right along Church Street)* the 19C courtyard buildings have been converted into a craft and design centre (👁 *see Addresses*). **St Macartin's Anglican Cathedral** was completed in 1842, although the tower is earlier. The French Gothic Revival **St Michael's Roman Catholic Church** (1875) lacks a spire. Down by the **West Bridge** (completed in 1892) are the Old Militia Barracks (1790) and Enniskillen Castle.

The Cole Family

The Coles came to Ireland from Devonshire in the reign of Elizabeth I. They lived first at Enniskillen Castle and then at Portora Castle.

Sir John Cole (1680–1726) settled at Florence Court, named after his wife, Florence Wrey, a wealthy heiress from Cornwall. Their son, John Cole (1709–67), made Lord Mount Florence in 1760, built the present central block; the wings were added by his son, William Willoughby Cole (1736–1803), later Viscount and Earl of Enniskillen.

CASTLE COOLE★★★

(NT) SE of the town centre by the A 4. ♿🕐*Grounds: Open 10am–7pm (4pm Nov–Feb).* 🐾*House open by guided tour only, Easter week & Jun–Aug daily 11am–5pm; mid-Mar–late May, Sept Sat–Sun 11am–5pm; open all Bank Hol Mons 11am–5pm.* 👁*£5.45 (House tour), £3.50 (Grounds).* ✖ 🅿 *(charge).* ☏*028 6632 2690.* *www.nationaltrust.org.uk.*

Among great oaks and beeches and overlooking its lake, this superb neo-Classical house is perhaps the finest building of its kind in the whole country. It was completed to designs by James Wyatt in 1798 for the **Corry** family, Earls of Belmore, who lived here until the house passed

The Corrys of Coole

John Corry, a Belfast merchant originally from Dumfriesshire, purchased the manor of Coole in 1656, and in 1709 built a new house near the lake incorporating parts of an early-17C castle. In 1741 the estate passed to Armar Lowry-Corry, created 1st Earl of Belmore in 1797, who commissioned Wyatt to design the present house; his son, the 2nd Earl of Belmore, was responsible for the interior decoration and the Regency furnishings.

Castle Coole

© Northern Ireland Tourist Board

into the hands of the National Trust in 1951. Built, decorated and furnished without apparent regard to expense, it has been comprehensively restored to something like its original glory.

The **exterior** consists of a central block containing the formal rooms, flanked by single-storey colonnaded wings with the family accommodation. The pale Portland stone, which lends the façade its particular distinction, was imported from the far-off Dorset quarry via Ballyshannon, where a special quay had to be built. So as not to interfere with the harmony of the composition, the stable yards added in 1817 by Richard Morrison were built out of sight below the level of the house and linked by tunnel.

The spacious feel and sense of proportion in the **entrance hall** are repeated throughout the house. **James Wyatt**'s scheme of decoration and furnishings is best seen in the **library★** and **dining room** where little has changed. The **oval saloon★★**, the most important room in the house, is decorated with elaborate plasterwork; the curved mahogany doors veneered with satinwood are hung on pivots. Wyatt specified the ceramic stoves, which have the same decorative motif as the friezes.

Between 1807 and 1825 some interiors were refurbished by Preston, one of the leading upholsterers of the period; his more flamboyant style is evident in the colours of the hall, staircase and first-floor landing; the hangings and furniture in the drawing room and the saloon and **Bow Room**.

The gold and scarlet decoration and furnishing of the **State Bedroom** were in anticipation of George IV's visit to Ireland in 1821.

FLORENCE COURT★★

8mi/13km S of Enniskillen by the A 4, A 32 and W by a minor road. (NT) ⊙*Grounds: Open 10am–7pm (4pm Nov–Feb).* ☞*House open by guided tour only, 11am–5pm; mid-Mar–Apr & Oct Sat–Sun; May & Sept Sat–Thu; Easter week and Jun–Aug daily.* ☞*Grounds £6, House tour £4.09.* ✗☐ *charge.* ✆*028 6634 8249. www.nationaltrust.org.uk.*

County Fermanagh's second great country house is surrounded by parkland at the foot of Cuilcagh Mountain. Faced in attractive greyish-gold stone, the original three-storey house, probably designed in the 1740s, is flanked by seven-arched colonnades and canted pavilions, which were probably designed in the 1770s by Davis Ducart, a Sardinian, who spent most of his working life in Ireland. The property was transferred, largely unaltered, to the National Trust in 1955.

The interior is charmingly decorated with family portraits, photographs, drawings and other memorabilia, but the glory of Florence Court is the exuberant **Rococo plasterwork★★**, some of it restored after a fire in 1956.

The **Pleasure Grounds** were mostly planted by the 3rd Earl early in the 19C. The walled garden retains some of its original features, although lawn now replaces the vegetable plots.

Since 1975, the estate grounds have been developed as **Florence Court Forest Park**. In the woodlands southeast of the house stands the famous **Florence Court Yew**, also known as the Irish Yew, a columnar-shaped freak, which can be reproduced only by cuttings as seedlings revert to the common type. There are several trails signposted with coloured indicators; the most challenging extends to moorland *(9hrs there and back on foot)* and the top of Cuilcagh Mountain (2,198ft/670m).

♟♟ MARBLE ARCH CAVES EUROPEAN GEOPARK★

11mi/18km south of Enniskillen via the A 4 and A 32, and west by a minor road. ☞☜*Open by guided tour only (75min, comfortable shoes and warm clothes recommended): mid-Mar–Jun & Sept 10am–4.30pm (5pm Jul–Aug), Oct 10.30am–3pm; booking recommended in high season.* ⏱*Closed after heavy rain.* ☜£9.50, child £6.50. ✗ ✆*028 6634 8855.*
www.marblearchcavesgeopark.com.

This spectacular cave system was formed in a bed of Dartry limestone by three streams on the northern slopes of Cuilcagh Mountain, converging underground to form the Cladagh River, which emerges at the Marble Arch and flows into Lough Macnean Lower.

The **reception centre** presents a caving exhibition and a video *(20min)*, covering the same ground as the tour. The **cave tour** includes a short boat trip on an underground lake into a great subterranean decor of stalactites, stalagmites, cascades, draperies and curtains, with picturesque names like Porridge Pot, Streaky Bacon, Cauliflowers, Tusks and Organ Pipes. The longest stalactite (7ft/2m) is named after Edouard Martel, a famous French cave scientist who explored the caves in 1895.

The **nature reserve** consists of the wooded Cladagh gorge created by the collapse of caves eroded by the river. A path *(1hr there and back on foot)* along the east bank links the **Marble Arch** and the **Cascades**, where more water gushes forth.

LOUGH ERNE★★

Wet and wooded, the Fermanagh Lakeland was once the remotest part of a remote province, described by an early-16C traveller as "full of robbers, woods, lakes and marshes" Nowadays it is more accessible, much-frequented by fishermen and increasingly popular for water-based activities, though its vast extent is such that it rarely feels crowded.

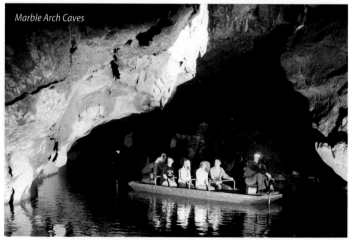

Marble Arch Caves

© Northern Ireland Tourist Board

Fed by the River Erne (50mi/80km long), Lough Erne is divided in two by the narrows around Enniskillen; the Upper Lough is a watery labyrinth of islands and twisting channels, while the glorious expanse of Lower Lough Erne has a more orderly assemblage of islands and a greater share of attractions exploiting its maximum width of 5mi/8km. The Lower Lough also seems to have its own weather and is large enough that in high winds sailing can be as difficult to manage as on the open sea. The Lower Lough is a wildlife reserve and its wooded shores are home to red squirrels, pine martens, otters and badgers.

🚗 DRIVING TOUR

LOWER LOUGH ERNE★★
Round tour of 66mi/106km. One day.

▶ From Enniskillen take the A 32 north; after 3mi/5km turn left to Trory Point.

Devenish Island★
Access by ferry (👜 see Getting Around).
In the 6C Devenish was chosen as the site for a monastery by St Molaise. Devastated by the Vikings, frequently caught up in local feuds and burnt down

in the 12C, it nevertheless survived until early in the 17C.
The picturesque remains enjoy a lovely lakeside setting, while a **visitor centre** (🕐 *open daily Apr–Sept 10am–5pm, see website for rest of year;* 🎫*£2.25 , boat crossing £3;* 📞 *028 6862 1588, www. doeni.gov.uk/niea*) traces the history of the monastery.
Nearest to the jetty are the ruins of the **Lower Church** (Teampull Mór), begun in the early 13C and later extended. The mortuary chapel to the South was built for the Maguire family. The smallest and oldest building, **St Molaise's House**, dates from the 12C, although it is based on an earlier wooden church.
St Mary's Priory dates from the 15C, although the tower is later. An unusual 15C-high cross stands in the graveyard.

▶ Continue north on the B 82, along the east shore of the lake.

Castle Archdale Country Park
🕐*Park: Open year-round daily 8.30am –dusk. Museum and Countryside Centre: Jul–Aug & May Bank Holidays daily 9am–4.30pm; Easter–Jun & Sept Sun only noon–4pm.* 📞*028 6862 1333. www.castlearchdale.com.*

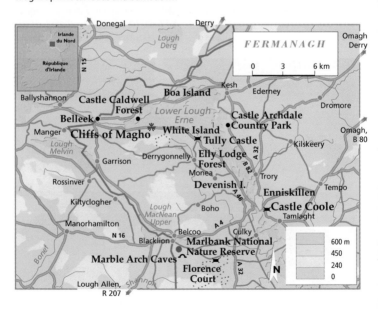

Stone figures, White Island

© Northern Ireland Tourist Board

The fortified residence built in the early-17C by the Archdales, an English planter family from East Anglia, has long since been abandoned but their fine arboretum, 19C pleasure grounds, a cold bath and sweat house, and an old walled garden live on.

The former outbuildings house a Countryside Centre with a display of agricultural implements. A caravan park occupies the site of the World War II base used by the British and Canadian flying boats patrolling the North Atlantic sea lanes, overflying neutral Ireland on the way.

The park has extensive and wonderfully diverse woodlands harbouring a variety of wildlife, while the ruins of **Old Castle Archdale**, near the northeast entrance, include the original gateway of the bawn.

White Island★

⊙*Open Jul–Aug daily 10am–5pm; Jun, Sept, Sat–Sun & Bank Hols only, 10am–5pm.* £3. ℰ*028 6862 1892.*

Within a large, pre-Norman monastic enclosure stand the remains of a 12C church with a handsome Romanesque doorway. Speculation continues to surround the eight 9C/10C **stone figures** set against the north wall: while definitely Christian, they have something of the pagan about them as exemplified by a graphic *sheilagh-na-gig*.

▷ Continue north by the scenic route; north of Kesh bear left onto the A 47. Near the western end of Boa Island park beside the road and follow signs to the cemetery (about 550yd/500m there and back on foot).

Janus Figure★

In an overgrown graveyard sits this squat and ancient stone figure with two faces, staring eyes and crossed arms, possibly from the Iron Age.

▷ Continue west on the A 47.

Castle Caldwell Forest

An important bird sanctuary, the forest covers two long fingers of land at the western end of Lough Erne. The ruined planter's castle (1612) was once owned by the Caldwells. In 1770, family members were entertained aboard a boat by a fiddler whose inebriated state caused him to fall overboard and drown. He is commemorated by the **Fiddler's Stone** at the park entrance.

▷ Continue west on the A 47.

Belleek

⊙*Visitor Centre open year-round Mon–Fri 9am–5.30/6pm; Sat 10am–5.30/6pm (closed Jan–Feb). Sun noon (Mar–June 2pm)–5/5.30pm (closed Jan–Feb).* ⌄*Pottery tours every 30min, Mon–Fri 9.30am–12.15pm, 1.45pm–4pm (last*

Climbing the Cliffs of Magho

© Northern Ireland Tourist Board

*tour Fri 3pm). Sat (Jun–Sept only)
10.30am–12.15pm, 2–4pm. ○Closed
21/22 Dec–4 Jan, 17 Mar. Visitor Centre
open Bank Hols but no tours. ◎£5.
Book online to avoid queues. ✕
℘028 6865 9300. www.belleek.com.*

Belleek Pottery, and its distinctive Parian ware, has an international reputation. The **Guided Pottery Tour** begins where the slip is moulded and trimmed, and continues through the stages to completion and sale in the Visitor Centre.

The Erne Gateway Centre exhibition **ExplorErne** (○*open Mar–Nov daily 10.30am–6pm;* ✕; ℘*028 6865 8866)* introduces visitors to the history, landscapes and ecology of the Lough, from legendary beginnings to the harnessing of its waters to generate hydroelectric power.

▷ Rejoin the A 46 for 10mi/16km towards Enniskillen.

Tully Castle★

(HM) ○Open Easter–Sept daily 10am–6pm. ℘028 6862 1588.

The ruins of a fortified planter's house built in 1613 were left when the castle was captured and abandoned in the rising of 1641. The partially paved bawn is protected by walls and corner towers with musket loops; the rest has been transformed into a 17C-style garden. The three-storey house has a vaulted room on the ground floor containing the kitchen fireplace, an unusually large staircase leading to a reception room on the first floor and a turret stair to the floor above. An abandoned farmhouse, a short stroll from the Castle, has been restored as a Visitor Centre.

▷ Return to the A 46, immediately turn right onto the B 81 towards Derrygonnelly and then follow signs to Lough Navar.

Lough Navar Forest Drive★, in most places a single-track, one-way road, winds through a coniferous forest inhabited by deer, feral goats and squirrels. Numerous picnic areas have been upgraded, and hiking on well-marked paths leads to beautiful viewpoints. Don't miss the **Cliffs of Magho★★★** viewpoint overlooking the North of Lower Lough Erne and Boa Island.

▷ Exit the park and return to the A 46, retracing the route towards Enniskillen.

Ely Lodge Forest offers loughside walks and the beautiful panorama from **Carrickreagh★** viewpoint, reached on foot, 874yd/800m after the car park.

▷ Continue on the A 46 to return to Enniskillen.

Belleek Parian Ware

The pottery was founded in 1857 by John Caldwell Bloomfield, shortly after he inherited Castle Caldwell and felt the need for more income. Being a keen amateur mineralogist, he discovered all the ingredients to make pottery – feldspar, kaolin, flint, clay, shale, peat and water power were available on the estate. At first, only earthenware was produced; Parian ware was refined over 10 years and won a Gold Medal in Dublin in 1865.

ADDRESSES

STAY

⊖⊜⊜⊜ **Lough Erne Resort** –*Belleek Rd – 5mi/8km N of Enniskillen. ☏028 6632 3230. www.lougherneresort.com. 120 rooms.* An award-winning luxury resort situated on a 600 acre peninsula overlooking the Fermanagh Lakelands. Designed as a place of relaxation, the amenities include a world famous golf course (The Faldo Course), an infinity pool, a thermal suite, and a Thai spa.

⊖⊜⊜⊜ **Killyhevlin Hotel** – *Killyhevlin, just S of Enniskillen on the A 4. ☏028 6632 3481. www.killyhevlin.com. 70 rooms.* On the banks of the Erne, this luxury hotel, spa and health club serves both business and leisure travellers. Good views of the mountains and lake from some of the bedrooms. A gym and spa, indoor swimming pool, sauna and steam room. Self-catering lakeside chalets are also available.

EAT

⊖⊜ **Dollakis Restaurant** – *23 Cross St, Enniskillen. ☏028 6634 2616. www. dollakis.co.uk. Closed Sun, Mon.* Small but smart little bistro-style restaurant in the town centre. Dishes from Greece feature on the menu and there is a good range of Cuban cigars.

⊖⊜ **Ferndale Country House Restaurant** – *139 Irvinestown Rd, Cross, Ferndale. 2.5mi/4km N via the A 32. ☏028 6632 8374.* Sophisticated country-house restaurant where the chef owner combines robust Irish cooking with subtle modern influences picked up from his Antipodean travels.

SHOPPING

Buttermarket Craft & Design Courtyard. Made up of 16 art-and-craft units, a coffee shop and a gift shop, housed in a 19C- dairy market.

Belleek Pottery – *See Lower Lough Erne Driving Tour.*

Sheelin Irish Lace Museum & Shop – Bellanaleck. All shop items are hand-made antique lace. *Museum open Apr– Oct 10am–6pm. €£2.50. ☏028 6634 8052. www.sheelinlace.com.*

SPORTS AND LEISURE

The loughs offer a multitude of watersports, from fishing and canoeing to amphibious flying.

Fermanagh Lakeland Tourism – Provides information on all amenities – boat hire, boat charters, fishing facilities and angling licences. *☏028 6632 3110. www.fermanaghlakelands.com*

Melvin Angling Centre – *Garrison on the shores of Lough Melvin. ☏028 686 58194.*

Belleek Angling Centre – *Main Street, Belleek. ☏028 686 58181.*

Lakeland Canoe Centre, Castle Island, Enniskillen – *☏028 6632 4250. www.onegreatadventure.com.*

Lakeland Forum – Sports and leisure centre. *Broadmeadow, Enniskillen. www.lakelandforum.com.*

Share Discovery Village – The largest outdoor activity centre in Ireland, particularly good for disabled visitors: canoeing, yachting, archery, etc. *Lisnaskea. www.sharevillage.org.*

EVENTS AND FESTIVALS

Lady of the Lake – Festival in Irvinestown in mid-July: drama, childrens' entertainment, fishing competition.

SIGHTSEEING

Lough Erne Cruises – There are several operators offering cruises on the Lough and inland waterways: visit *www.fermanaghlakelands.com (click on cruising).*

Upper Lough Erne Cruises *(1hr 30min)* depart from the Share Centre in Lisnakea *(east shore of Upper Lough Erne).*

The principal marinas are on Lower Lough Erne at **Kesh** *(east shore)* and on Upper Lough Erne at **Bellanaleck** *(west shore)* and **Carrybridge** *(east shore).*

Sperrin Mountains★

These lonely, smooth-topped mountains, dividing the Londonderry lowlands from northeastern Ulster, rise to their highest point in Sawel Mountain (2,224ft/678m). Composed of schist and gneiss, they were once covered in magnificent forests, but their upper slopes are now grazed by sheep and clad in blanket bog and purple heather. Woodland is confined to the deep gorges worn by mountain streams. Over the moorland hover birds of prey; the rare hen harrier is sometimes seen and the Sperrins are the only site in Ireland where cloudberry grows. The rocks contain minute deposits of gold, the extraction of which gives rise to periodic controversy about the future of these mountains, which have largely remained outside the mainstream of modern life.

Info: Burn Road, Cookstown, 028 86766 7277. Connell Street, Limavady, 028 7776 0307, www.limavady.gov.uk. Strule Arts Centre, Townhall Square, Omagh, 028 8224 7831. Alley Arts & Conference Centre, 1a Railway Street, Strabane, 028 7138 4444, www.strabanedc.com/leisure-and-tourism. www.sperrinstourism.com.

Location: The Sperrin Mountains are bounded to the West by the A 5 between Londonderry and Omagh, to the East by the A 29 between Cookstown and Coleraine, South by the A 505 between Cookstown and Omagh, and North by the A 2 between Londonderry and Limavady.

Don't Miss: The Ulster American Folk Park.

A BIT OF HISTORY

In the 17C certain areas were granted to four of London's City livery companies – the Drapers, Skinners, Grocers and Fishmongers – who brought in settlers, mainly from Scotland, to inhabit their new towns and villages. In fact, by the early-19C the region was overpopulated, so assisted emigration was introduced and the land re-allocated in holdings of 20–30 acres/8–12ha of neatly-hedged fields. Model farms were established to promote modern methods and roads and bridges, churches, schools and dispensaries built.

COOKSTOWN AND AROUND

Once an important linen centre, Cookstown is now a market centre for the area. Its most notable feature is the extraordinarily long and very broad main street which, under 10 different names, extends north from the River Ballinderry towards the silhouette of Slieve Gallion (1,732ft/528m). This is the result of one of the most ambitious attempts at urban planning ever imposed on the Irish landscape, devised c. 1750 by James and William Stewart, after the original Plantation settlement of Cookstown had been destroyed in the rebellion of 1641. The new street extended south to their own property at Killymoon Castle *(private)*, redesigned by John Nash in 1803; its grounds are now a golf course.

Tullaghoge Fort

From Cookstown take the A 29 south; bear left onto the B 520. Turn left on a blind corner into the car park; it is 10min there and back on foot to the fort.

The tree-crowned earthworks of this hillfort are replete with memories of the ancient rulers of Ulster, having enclosed the residence of the O'Hagans: the chief justices of the old kingdom of Tyrone. It was here that the rulers of Tyrone were inaugurated, the

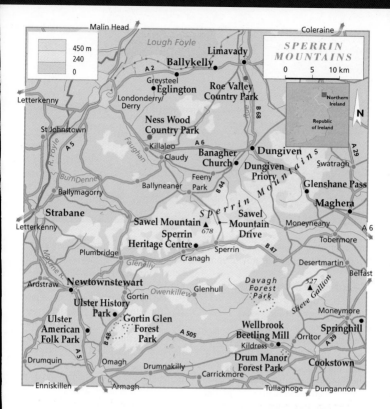

last of them being Hugh O'Neill in 1593. Their stone throne was broken up by Lord Mountjoy in 1602. The **view** from the fort is extensive: southwest to the circular walled graveyard at Donaghrisk where the O'Hagans were buried; east towards Lough Neagh; north to Slieve Gallion, with the River Ballinderry in the foreground and Killymoon Castle in the trees by the river.

Drum Manor Forest Park

West on the A 205 for 2.5mi/4km.
&. &Open 10am–dusk. &£1 pedestrian, £3 per car. ✕ Jul–Aug.
www.nidirect.gov.uk/drum-manor-forest-park.

The old country house of Drum Manor has long been a ruin, but its walled gardens and open parkland now form part of Drum Manor Forest Park. One of the gardens has lent itself perfectly to conversion into a **butterfly garden**, while in the ruins of the manor house an attractive **flower garden** has been created.

Wellbrook Beetling Mill★

4mi/6km west of Cookstown. (NT)
⁜Admission by guided tour only mid-Mar–late Sept 2–5pm Sat–Sun only; open all bank hols and public hols.
&£5. &028 8675 1735.
www.nationaltrust.org.uk/wellbrook-beetling-mill.

The first mill at Wellbrook came into operation in September 1767; the present mill, known as no. 6, dates from about 1830 and worked until 1961.

The drying loft contains an excellent display on the production of linen and the history of the Irish linen industry, while the lower floor houses the seven **beetling machines** turned by an external wooden water-wheel (beetling is the last stage in the production of linen, where the cloth is beaten to close up the weave and give it a smooth sheen). The amount of noise produced by two beetling engines operating for a few minutes explains why deafness was

Beaghmore Stone Circles

© Northern Ireland Tourist Board

common among beetlers, who often-worked early morning to around 9pm.

Beaghmore Stone Circles★

Between Cookstown and Gortin.
10mi/16kms west of Cookstown.
Signposted off the A 505.

Mid-Ulster is particularly rich in pre-historic stone circles. This site, used in Neolithic times, has seven circles from the Bronze Age, comprising quite small stones set on, rather than in, the ground. Six circles are arranged in pairs, with a cairn and a row of stones near the point of intersection. The area enclosed in the seventh circle is studded with close-set stones known as "Dragons' Teeth" – used to calculate the rising and setting of the sun and moon.

Draperstown

13mi/20km north of Cookstown
on the B 162.

This pleasant little town, a classic settlement from the time of the Ulster Plantation in the early-17C, is now a busy market centre in the heart of Sperrin Mountain country.

Springhill★

5mi/8km northeast of Cookstown on the A 29 and B 18. (NT)&🐾🦮 Admission by guided tour only, noon–5pm; Easter week & Jul–Aug daily; Jun Thu–Sat; Mar–May & Sept Sat–Sun only; open all bank hols and public hols; ☜£5.45. ✕🅿 ✆028 8674 8210. www.national-trust.org.uk /springhill.

This attractive country house was the family home of the Conynghams, who came to Ulster from Ayrshire early in the 17C. Built around a deep courtyard flanked by service buildings, it is a rare survivor of the kind of comfortable residence built by Plantation families at this time despite the difficult and sometimes dangerous conditions. The property was altered and enlarged by subsequent generations of Conynghams, who usually followed military careers.

Family portraits hang throughout the house, which is furnished with **fine 18C and 19C furniture**. Note the splendid oak **staircase** with a yew handrail. The older rooms contrast with the more spacious interiors added later, such as the early-19C dining room graced by an Italian marble chimney piece presented by the notorious Earl Bishop of Londonderry. The gun room collection includes flintlocks used during the Siege of Derry and a pair of pikes from the Battle of Vinegar Hill.

The courtyard buildings house an acclaimed **costume collection** of 2,300 articles, from the 18C to the 1930s.

OMAGH AND AROUND

The former county town of Co Tyrone is normally a quiet market town, built on a steep slope overlooking the point where two rivers, the Camowen and the Drumragh, join to form the Strule. Tragically, in 1998, Omagh was the site of the worst single atrocity of Northern Ireland's Troubles when the "Real

IRA", a dissident republican grouping, exploded a bomb in the town centre, killing 29 and injuring over 200 people.

Ulster-American Folk Park★

6mi/8.5km north of Omagh on the B 48.
&♿🕐*Open Mar–Sep Tue-Sun 10am-5pm (Jul-Aug incl Mon), Oct-Feb 10am-4pm (11am Sat-Sun). Open Bank Hols. Last admission 1hr 30 min before closing (all year).* ∞*£9. (£11 on major events days).*
✕ ☏*028 8224 3292.*
www.nmni.com/uafp

Of all the establishments in Ireland celebrating the country's intimate links with America, this extensive open-air museum is perhaps the most evocative. Opened in 1976 as part of the American bicentennial celebrations, it is laid out around the ancestral cottage from which **Thomas Mellon**, of the banking dynasty, emigrated with his family at the age of five in 1818. There is also a Centre for Migration Studies, with a library, extensive database and facilities for research.

The Matthew T. Mellon Information Centre and the **Emigrants' Exhibition** give the historical context for mass emigration, citing life stories of particular individuals who settled in the New World. Various other buildings, some replicas, and others transferred from elsewhere in Ulster or America are laid out in chronological order, starting with the typical 18C and 19C **Ulster buildings**, like a humble cabin from the Sperrins, a complete "Ulster Street" lined with shops, workplaces and Reilly's pub-cum-grocery. The cottage in which Thomas Mellon was born in 1813 was built by his father with his own hands; it was transported here in 1976 to form the nucleus of the park.

The **Ship and Dockside Gallery★** marks the transition to America and features the brig *Union* moored at the Belfast quayside.

The **American Street** with its all-important General Store has a replica of the 1870 First Mellon Bank of Pittsburgh, shielding a series of log cabins and a complete mid-18C stone dwelling, brought from frontier territory in

Ulster-American Folk Park
© Northern Ireland Tourist Board

Pennsylvania, where it was built by an emigrant from Co Donegal.

In the workshops and cottages local people in **period costume** demonstrate the old crafts: cooking, spinning, weaving, the making of baskets, candles and soap; blacksmithing and carpentry. Turf fires burn throughout the year.

Newtonstewart

The village is set near the confluence of the River Mourne and the River Strule. On a nearby hilltop stands **Harry Avery's Castle**, two D-shaped towers from a 14C O'Neill stronghold. There are fine views of the surrounding countryside.

Sion Mills

This model village was established by the three Herdman brothers, who in 1835 started a flax-spinning operation in an old flour mill on the Mourne. The buildings are an appealing mixture of Gothic Revival terraced cottages in polychrome brick and black-and-white half-timbered edifices, of which the most striking are Sion House and the Church of the Good Shepherd, a splendid Italianate Romanesque building (1909).

Strabane

This small town stands at the confluence of the Finn and the Mourne. In the 18C Strabane was famous for printing, celebrated behind the bowed Georgian shopfront at 49 Main Street, where **Gray's Printing Press** (NT. &.⌚admission by guided tour only; six afternoons per year; call for dates; ⌚£2.72; ☏ 028 8674 8210, www.nationaltrust.org.uk/ grays-printing-press) a 19C printing shop has been preserved with its original hand- and foot-operated presses.

The **Wilson Ancestral Home** (⌚admission by guided tour only, Jul–Aug Tue–Sun 2pm–5pm; ☏ 028 7138 4444) is a whitewashed thatched cottage on the South side of town, home to James Wilson, grandfather of **President Woodrow Wilson**. The house contains original furniture, including a cupboard bed by the kitchen fire and curtained beds in the main bedroom. The Wilson family still live in the modern farmhouse behind the cottage.

🚗 DRIVING TOURS

CENTRAL HEIGHTS

A drive from Omagh, taking in Gortin Glen Forest park, the scenic Barnes Gap and then through the heart of the Sperrins on the visually stunning 6mi/10km Sawel Drive.

▷ From Omagh take the B 48 north and follow the signs for Gortin Glen Forest Park from Gortin village.

Gortin Glen Forest Park

🕐Open 10am–dusk. ⌚£1 pedestrian; £3 car. ☏ 028 8167 0666. www.omagh. gov.uk.

This coniferous woodland park is part of the larger Gortin Forest, a commercial plantation. The forest drive (5mi/8km – one way only) offers great vistas over the Sperrin Mountains. Information on trails and where to see Sika deer is supplied in the Nature Centre.

▷ From Gortin go towards Rouskey on the B 46 and travel 2.5mi/4km before turning left into Drumlea Road and following the sign for Barnes Gap.

The **Barnes Gap** carries the road through a narrow cleft in the hills between the valleys of the Owenkillew and Glenelly Rivers.

▷ At the T-junction turn right; at the next T-junction turn left; cross the river at Clogherny Bridge. Turn right and then turn right again onto the B 47.

Sperrin Heritage Centre

🕐Open Apr–Oct 11.30am (2pm Sun) to 5.30pm (6pm Sat–Sun) ⌚£2.70. ☏ 028 8164 8142.

The Centre has been sensitively designed to fit with three adjoining cottages. Videos, computers and exhibitions enable visitors to explore the local flora and fauna, history and culture.

▷ Continue east on the B 47; in Sperrin/ Mount Hamilton turn left.

The **Sawel Mountain Drive★**, a narrow, unfenced road along the east face of Sawel Mountain (2,229ft/678m), the highest peak, passes through the wild and austere beauty of the open moorland; the **views★★** are spectacular.

▷ Continue east on the B 47; in Sperrin/Mount Hamilton turn left. Beyond Dreen turn left onto the B 44 ; turn left onto the B 48 to return to Omagh via Plumbridge.

UPLANDS AND COAST

A drive east and south from Derry, taking in the coast of Lough Foyle, small rural towns, the ruins of some medieval churches and two country parks.

▷ From Londonderry take the A 2 eastwards; turn right.

Eglinton

This elegant little village (1823–25) with its **Courthouse** was developed by the Grocers' Company around a tree-shaded green beside the Muff River, which tumbles down through **Muff Glen**, a narrow tree-lined valley of pleasant walks.

Ballykelly

This community was established early in the 17C by the Fishmongers' Company. The model farm on the North side of the road consists of a two-storey block linked to two one-storey pavilions by curtain walls enclosing a farmyard. Opposite is the Presbyterian Church (1827). The Anglican Church (1795) was built by the Earl Bishop of Derry.

Limavady

The town takes its name from the Irish for "Dogleap", referring to a legend that a dog leaped across the River Roe to warn the local chieftain, O'Cahan, of approaching enemies.

The original settlement was farther upstream (2mi/3.2km) by the 13C O'Cahan castle, in what is now the Roe Valley Country Park. It was re-founded as Newtown-Limavady in the 17C by Sir Thomas Phillips, chief agent of the City of London in Ulster. More recently the famous song, *Danny Boy (The Londonderry Air)*, was noted down by Jane Ross (1810–79), who lived at 51 Main Street. Today, Limavady is a pleasant Georgian market town.

▷ Take the B 68 south.

Roe Valley Country Park★

🕐 *Park: open daily. Visitor Centre: open daily summer 10am–6pm (winter Sun only noon–4pm).* ✕ *℘028 7772 2074. www.discovernorthernireland.com.*

The country park extends along a stretch (3mi/4.8km) of the wild, thickly wooded valley, where the peaty red River Roe runs over rocks and through gorges on its way north to the sea. The **Countryside Centre** at the Dogleap Bridge provides information on the local flora and fauna, old industries and the 17C Plantation. As well as great natural beauty, the park preserves evidence of early industrial activity, particularly related to the linen industry: bleach greens, weirs and mill races, and 18C water-powered mills for sawing wood, scutching flax, weaving and beetling linen. An unusual feature is the stone-built **Power House**

(1896), the site of early success in generating hydroelectric power *(open on request).*

▷ Take the B 192 south to Burnfoot.

Bovevagh Church

In the churchyard of a ruined medieval church stands a **mortuary house** similar to the one at Banagher (🕐 *see below)*; its ruined state reveals the cavity which contained the body and the hand hole in the East end through which the faithful could touch the relics.

▷ Continue south; turn left onto the A 6 and make a detour east.

Glenshane Pass★

The pass between Mullaghmore (1,818ft/555m – south) and Carntogher (1,516ft/462m – north) carries the main Belfast-Londonderry road through the Sperrin Mountains. The northern approach through dramatic mountain scenery overlooks Benady Glen on the River Roe; the southern approach provides a **panoramic view★★** across Lough Neagh in the mid-Ulster plain to Slemish.

▷ Continue east on the A 6. At the north end of the main street turn right into Bank Square.

Maghera

This little town at the foot of the Glenshane Pass has a picturesque ruin, **St Patrick Church** (c. 10C), which boasts an outstanding west door (added c. 12C), with inclined jambs, wonderful floral and animal decoration and a lintel carved with an elaborate Crucifixion scene. In the graveyard stands a rough pillar stone, carved with a ringed cross, which according to tradition is the grave of St Lurach, who founded an important monastery on this site in the 6C *(key from The Bridewell Tourist Information Centre, 6 Church Street; ℘028 79631510; www.magherafelt.gov.uk).*

▷ Return west on the A 6.

Dungiven

Before it was redeveloped by the Skinners' Company, Dungiven was the base of the fierce O'Cahan clan. Just outside the town is an imposing natural strongpoint above the River Roe, the site of a pre-Norman monastery and ruined Augustinian **priory**. The church remains are impressive, but the main attraction is the magnificent **tomb** of the O'Cahan chieftan Cooey-na-Gal, who died in 1385. It consists of an effigy beneath a traceried canopy, protected by heavily armed Scottish mercenaries ("gallowglasses") in kilts. North of the path is a **bullaun**, a hollowed stone originally used for grinding grain – it now collects rainwater, which is deemed to cure warts. The rags tied to the overhanging tree are an ancient tradition, either left as an offering (left when they were full garments, but weathered to rags) or as a good luck symbol.

▶ In Dungiven turn left into a minor road.

Banagher Church

In the graveyard of the ruined church (c. 1100) stands a 12C **mortuary house**, built of dressed stone, probably to house relics disturbed by the addition of a chancel to the church.

▶ Return direct to the A 6, or take the B 74 west through Feeny and Claudy to rejoin the A 6 later.

Ness Wood Country Park★

⏱*Park: open daily. Visitor Centre: open daily summer 9am–4.30pm (winter Sun only noon–4pm).* ✕ ✆*028 7133 8417. www.discovernorthernireland.com.* Here you can walk through 7kms of woodland, parkland and riverside walks connected by bridges and boardwalks. The spectacular 30ft/9m high **waterfall★** was created, together with a series of gorges, potholes and rapids, by the River Burntollet eroding a channel through the metamorphic schist rock since the end of the last Ice Age.

ADDRESSES

STAY

Ballyhenry House – *172 Seacoast Rd, 0.75mi/1.2km north of Limavady. 3rm. ✆028 777 22657. www.ballyhenry.co.uk.* Lovely farmhouse B&B on a working farm estate in Roe Valley with very well appointed characterful trad/modern bedrooms. Ideal base for outdoor activities (fishing, riding, golf, walking) around. Self-catering accommodation is also available.

B&B Tullylagan Country House – *40B Tullylagan Rd, Sandholes, 4mi/6.4km south of Cookstown. 15rm. ✆028 8676 5100. www.tullylagan.com.* Beautiful Georgian-style 19C country house on the Tullylagan River, set in 30 acres of its own private grounds and landscaped gardens. The period-style bedrooms all have an individual personality; popular bar/bistro and award-winning restaurant (😊).

⏧ EAT

Coach Inn – *Railway Terrace, Omagh. ✆028 8224 3330. http://thecoachinnomagh.co.uk.* An easy walk from the town centre, this comfortable place is good for a typical pub meal.

Lime Tree – *60 Catherine St, Limavady. ✆028 7776 4300. www.limetreerest.com. Closed Sun, Mon.* Seasonal produce, modern Irish cuisine; daily fish specials, good wine list. Booking recommended.

SPORTS AND LEISURE

The **Ulster Way** long-distance footpath (*www.walkni.com/ulsterway*) passes through the eastern Sperrins.

The Owenkillew and the Glenelly are both excellent trout streams. Several good angling streams flow north and west down the River Roe and the Foyle tributaries into the Foyle estuary, or southeast into Lough Neagh.

TRACING ANCESTORS

Ulster-American Folk Park★ – *(⏱see Omagh and Around). Centre for Migration Studies: Mon–Fri 10.30am–4.45pm.*

Londonderry/ Derry★

Northern Ireland's second city, close to the border with the Republic, is pleasantly sited on the River Foyle, surrounded by the Sperrin Mountains (southeast) and the wild heights of Donegal (west and north). Almost uniquely in the British Isles, it has kept its defensive walls, erected in the early 17C when the ancient Irish settlement of Derry became a key stronghold in the English Plantation of Ulster and was renamed Londonderry (Doire). A powderkeg during the Troubles, the city has since undergone something of a revival, with renewed economic growth, vibrant commercial activity and an emphasis on tourism, culminating in its selection as UK City of Culture 2013.

A BIT OF HISTORY

Monastic Foundation – According to tradition, the monastery at Derry (from *Doire* meaning "oak grove") was founded in 546 by St Columba. Between 1565–1600, Derry was occupied by the English. During the four-month rebellion of Sir Cahir O'Doherty in 1608, his forces attacked and captured Derry but could not sustain their momentum after his death at Kilmacrenan in Donegal.

▶ **Population:** 105,066.

Info: 44 Foyle Street. ℰ028 7126 7284. www.visitderry.com.

◑ **Location:** Situated on Ireland's northernmost tip, near the border and Co Donegal, and 71mi/115km northwest of Belfast.

☺ **Don't Miss:** A tour of the city walls.

The Irish Society – Under the scheme for the colonisation of Ulster with settlers from Britain, The Honourable The Irish Society was constituted by Royal Charter in 1613 to plant the County of Coleraine, now known as County Londonderry. Most of the land was parcelled out to the 12 main livery companies of London, but the towns of Derry and Coleraine were retained by the Society, which still uses its income from fisheries and property to support projects of general benefit to the community.

Siege of Londonderry – In the uncertainty created by James II's flight to France and William of Orange's landing in Devon, 13 Derry apprentices locked the city gates against the Jacobite regiment led by the Earl of Antrim sent to

City walls

© Northern Ireland Tourist Board

Bloody Sunday

In January 1972, the Northern Ireland Civil Rights Association defied a ban on organised marches to protest against internment without trial. A section of this march was fired on by British paratroopers, killing 13 people, many of them shot through the back, and wounding 13 more, with one person later dying of their wounds. The day became known as "Bloody Sunday".

An inquiry into the deaths in 1972 was a widely regarded as a whitewash and a second inquiry began in 1997. Thirteen years later, on June 15th, 2010 the report summarised that the "immediate responsibility for the deaths and injuries on Bloody Sunday lies with those members of Support Company whose unjustifiable firing was the cause of those deaths and injuries". The British government have acknowledged the soldiers fired without provocation and that the shootings were "unjustified and unjustifiable".

Whether the soldiers involved will face prosecution for their actions is yet to be decided, as is the question of whether others bear responsibility for the tragic events of the day.

garrison the town in December 1688. The citizens declared for William and received an influx of supporters, although food supplies were low. In March, James II landed in Ireland with an army of 20,000 and in April, he besieged the city, erecting a boom across the river which held the relief ships at bay for seven weeks.

The Scottish commander of the city, Robert Lundy, favoured capitulation to what seemed an overwhelming force but advocates of resistance

Lundy

When the Scottish Col. Lundy advised citizens of Londonderry to avoid bloodshed and destruction by surrendering to the superior Jacobite army, he completely underestimated their fighting spirit. In his stead, Major Henry Baker and the Reverend George Walker rallied fellow-Protestants and organised their brave resistance. Ever after, the term "Lundy" has been synonymous with cowardice and treachery, and the wretched colonel's effigy is ceremoniously burned during the Apprentice Boys' annual parade in August.

deposed him and took command. On 10 July a shell bearing terms for surrender was fired into the town by the besiegers; the defenders raised a crimson flag on the Royal Bastion to signify "No surrender", a slogan which continues to resonate with Northern Ireland's Protestant population. The siege lasted 15 weeks, during which the 30,000 people crammed within the walls were reduced to eating cats, dogs, mice, rats and leather; thousands died of starvation. On July 28, 1689 the boom was broken and the relief ships sailed through to the quay. Three days later, the Jacobite army retreated.

Sectors of the City – The character of the Plantation city changed drastically in the 19C. Migrants flocked here from all over Catholic Ireland and by 1900 Protestants were a minority, though careful management of the boundaries of electoral districts and the allocation of public housing continued to deny Catholics control of the city council. While the traditional industry of shirt-making employed many women, male unemployment was rife and housing conditions – notably in the Catholic Bogside district – were among the worst in the United Kingdom.

The city erupted into riot in 1968, the "Battle of the Bogside" ensued in

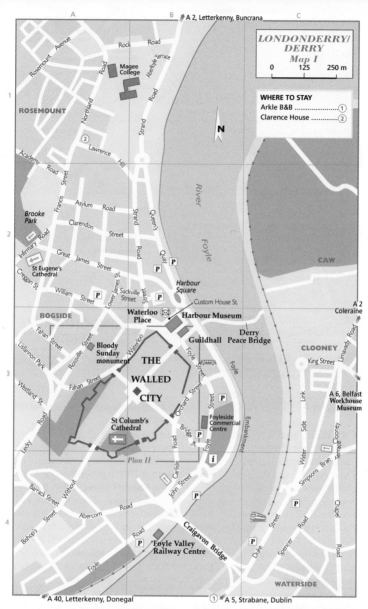

LONDONDERRY/
DERRY
Map I
0   125   250 m

WHERE TO STAY
Arkle B&B .... ①
Clarence House .... ②

1969, and on January 30, 1972 – Bloody Sunday (☞ *see "Bloody Sunday" box*) – paratroopers shot dead unarmed civilians in the violent aftermath of a banned protest march. Ever since, sectarian boundaries have become more pronounced, with Protestants tending to withdraw from the West bank of the Foyle to settle in the Waterside district on the East bank. In 2011 the new **Peace Bridge**, for pedestrians and cyclists, was built across the river, both to improve access for everyone into each half of the city centre, as part of wider regeneration plans, but also to bring the unionist and nationalist communities together.

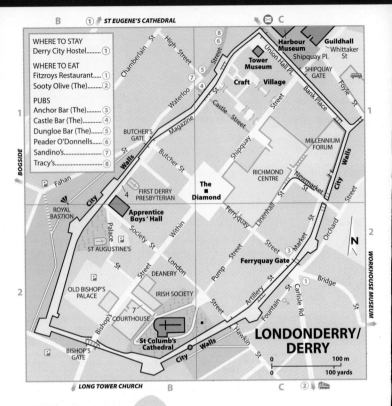

WHERE TO STAY
Derry City Hostel..........①

WHERE TO EAT
Fitzroys Restaurant.....①
Sooty Olive (The)..........②

PUBS
Anchor Bar (The).........③
Castle Bar (The)............④
Dungloe Bar (The).......⑤
Peader O'Donnells......⑥
Sandino's......................⑦
Tracy's..........................⑧

☙ WALKING TOUR

City Walls and Gates★★

ঔ ⏱ *Walls open daily.* ☙ *Various guided walking tours available; enquire at the tourist office and/ or visit www.derrywalls.com, or www.derrybluebadgeguide.com.*

The walls (1mi/1.6km long) enclosing the Plantation town were erected between 1613 and 1618 by the Irish Society. Their near-perfect preservation is remarkable, given they have sustained more than one siege and their vulnerability to gunfire from warships in the Foyle.

A walk around the walls past gateways, bastions, watch-towers and artillery pieces makes for a fine introduction to the city.

▶ Join the wall walk on the East side by Newmarket Street: walk clockwise.

Ferryquay Gate was slammed shut by the 13 Apprentice Boys in the face of the Jacobite troops at the start of the 1688/89 siege.

The present triumphal arch replacing the original **Bishop's Gate** was erected to mark the centenary anniversary of the siege in 1789: it provides a good view down **Bishop's Street Within**, the city's most distinguished thoroughfare, with its cluster of fine late-18C/early-19C buildings, including the red-brick Bishop's Palace (Freemasons' Hall) built by the Earl Bishop, the Greek Revival Courthouse, the Irish Society's headquarters (1764) and elegant Deanery.

The Royal Bastion, overlooking Bogside, is the point where Col. Michelburn hoisted the crimson "No Surrender" flag at the beginning of the great siege. The **Apprentice Boys' Hall** stands on the site of the original Shambles.

From **Butcher's Gate**, Butcher Street leads into **The Diamond**, the characteristic focal point of a Plantation town, where four main thoroughfares meet in front of the Town Hall, in this case

St Columb's Cathedral

© Northern Ireland Tourist Board

replaced by a war memorial. Beyond Butcher's Gate on the right is the **Fifth Province**.

The northernmost corner is marked by the entrance to the **Tower Museum**.

The **Shipquay Gate**, surmounted by five cannon used to defend the city during the siege, straddles another thoroughfare up towards the Diamond.

WITHIN THE WALLS

St Columb's Cathedral★

🕐 *Open Mon–Sat 9am–5pm; Sun for services only.* 👣 *Guided tours £1.50.* ✆ *028 7126 2746.*
www.stcolumbscathedral.org.

The fortified Plantation city was speedily provided with a formidable battlemented late-Perpendicular cathedral, planned in 1613, started in 1628 and completed in 1634. It was the first cathedral to be built in the British Isles since the Reformation. The 191ft/58m spire was added in the early 19C.

Probably its most striking feature is the superb open-timbered **nave roof** supported on corbels carved to represent the Bishops of Derry from 1634 to 1867, and the Revd George Walker, city governor during the Siege. In the porch stands the **mortar shell** containing terms for surrender, which was fired into the city during the Siege; windows in the Choir Vestry *(right)* depict the

Closing of the Gates (1688), the Relief of the City (1689) and the Centenary Celebrations (1789).

The splendid 18C mahogany Chinese Chippendale **bishop's throne** was probably given by the flamboyant Earl Bishop. On the chancel arch above the pulpit is a **Cross of Nails**, a gift from Coventry Cathedral signifying peace and reconciliation. The **chapter house** dates from 1910 and houses a miscellany of historical objects *(for access, ask the Verger).*

Tower Museum

© Northern Ireland Tourist Board

Tower Museum★

🕐*Open daily 10am–5.30pm (Jul–Sept extended hours, call for times). Last admission 4pm.* 👁£4. 📞*028 7137 2411. www.derrycity.gov.uk/museums.*
Excellent displays of artefacts, wall panels and a video explain the story of the Armada shipwreck of *La Trinidad Valencera* in Kinnagoe Bay. Elsewhere, there are comprehensive displays relating to the **Story of Derry**. From the top of the tower there is an extensive view over the inner city and the Foyle.

BEYOND THE WALLS
Long Tower Church★

🕐*Open year-round daily 9am–8.30pm (summer 9pm).* 📞*028 7126 2301.*
The oldest Roman Catholic church in Derry (1784–86) has an lovely Rococo interior with extensive steeply-sloping galleries. It stands on the site of Templemore, a great medieval church built in 1164 alongside the Long Tower (10C) which survived an explosion in 1567. From the churchyard there is a fine view of the Royal Bastion.

Guildhall★

♿🕐*Open daily 10am–5.30pm.*
🕐*Closed Bank Hol Mon.* 📞*028 7137 6510. www.derrystrabane.com.*
The late-Gothic Guildhall with the corner clocktower was erected in 1890 with a loan from the Irish Society. It was severely damaged by fire in 1908 and by bombs in 1972. A reproduction of Follingby's painting of the *Relief of Derry* graces the marble-faced vestibule. Numerous stained-glass windows by Ulster craftsmen make up a visual history of the city, with London scenes on the stairs and early views of Derry in the Great Hall.

Harbour Museum

🕐*Open Mon–Fri 10am-4.30pm (closed for lunch).* 📞*028 7137 7331. www.culturenorthernireland.org.*
The grandiose 19C building, looking finer than ever since its 2011–13 renovation, hosted meetings of the Londonderry Port and Harbour Commissioners. It is now a museum with paintings, models and maritime memorabilia. The dominant exhibit is the largest curragh ever built, constructed in 1963 to re-create the legendary voyage of St Columba to Iona.

St Eugene's Cathedral

🕐*Open year-round daily 9am–8.30pm (summer 9pm).* 📞*028 7126 2894.*
Northwest of the city centre, between a district of elegant Georgian terraces and the green peace of Brooke Park, stands the Roman Catholic Cathedral dedicated to St Eugene in 1873 by Bishop Keely. The building was designed in the Gothic revival style by J.J. McCarthy in 1853 and completed with a cross on the top of the spire in 1903.

Guildhall

© Northern Ireland Tourist Board

Foyle Valley Railway Museum

Open year-round Mon–Fri 10am–4.30pm. www.derrycity.gov.uk/museums.

Londonderry was once the focal point of no fewer than four railway companies, including the Londonderry and Enniskillen, "possibly the least efficient if not the most dangerous railway ever to operate in Ireland", and the County Donegal Railway, the most extensive of all the Irish narrow-gauge systems (125mi/200km). The museum has steam engines, coaches, an old goods wagon, signals, signs and luggage. Excursion trains drawn by diesel car (1934) operate beside the Foyle.

Museum of Free Derry

55–61 Glenfada Park. Open year-round Mon–Fri 9.30am–4.30pm. Apr–Sept also Sat 1pm–4pm; Jul–Sept also Sun 1pm–4pm. £3. 028 71360880. www.museumoffreederry.org.

This intriguing museum is an archive focusing on the civil rights era of the 1960s and the Troubles during the 1970s. Artefacts and documents explain the unrest in the Bogside area, the repercussions of Bloody Sunday and the effects on the local community.

ADDRESSES

 STAY

Derry City Hostel – *Butcher Gate, Magazine St. 028 7128 0542. www.derry-hostel.co.uk.* Centrally-located hostel offering budget accommodation by way of single, double, twin and dorm rooms. Free internet and breakfast included.

Arkle B&B – *2 Coshquin Rd. 028 7127 1156. www.derryhotel.co.uk. 7 rms.* A charming century-old building, 2km north west of the centre. All bedrooms have Wi-Fi and guests also have use of the garden, patio and barbeque facilities. Great value.

Clarence House– *15 Northland Rd. 028 7126 5342. www.clarencehousederry.co.uk.* Built in 1899 and a guesthouse for over 45 years, this is the longest established B&B in Derry.

EAT

Fitzroys Restaurant – *2–4 Bridge St, Carlisle Rd. 028 7126 6211. www.fitzroysrestaurant.com.* Modern restaurant next to the Foyle Shopping Centre; international menu.

The Sooty Olive – *160/64 Spencer Rd. 028 7134 6064. www.thesootyolive.com.* Buzzy new restaurant serving contemporary Irish cuisine.

PUBS

Peadar O'Donnells & Gweedore Bar – *61 Waterloo St. 028 7126 7295. www.peadars.com.* A good pub for trad and contemporary music, very popular with visitors to the city. Upstairs, there is more of a nightclub atmosphere.

The Anchor Bar– *Ferryquay St. 028 7136 8601.* One of the oldest family-run bars in the city. A relaxed place for a drink and musical entertainment at night.

The Dungloe Bar – *41–43 Waterloo St. 028 7126 7716. www.thedungloebar.com.* You can hear local bands and traditional music here; food also served.

The Castle Bar – *26 Waterloo St. 028 7126 6018.* Another pub worth checking out to see what bands are playing during the evenings and weekends.

Tracy's – *1–2 William St. 1 Waterloo St. 028 7126 9700.* One of the older bars in Derry, its thatched roof and interior style does little to hide its proud Irish identity.

Sandino's– *Water St. 028 7130 9297. www.sandinoscafebar.com.* A relaxing modern bar with a varied music programme.

EVENTS AND FESTIVALS

City of Derry Drama Festival (Mar) *www.cityofderrydramafestival.org*

City of Derry Jazz Festival (early May). *www.cityofderryjazzfestival.com*

Banks of the Foyle Hallowe'en Carnival (last week Oct) *http://campaign.derrycity.gov.uk.*

SPORTS AND LEISURE

Cricket, Gaelic football and golf are all popular activities in the area, with cricket clubs in Limavady, Eglinton and Derry City; Celtic Park Gaelic Football Club in Derry; the City of Derry Golf Club (in Prehen), and the Foyle Golf Centre on the outskirts of Derry.

Causeway Coast★

The stunning northern coastline is dominated by the world-famous Giant's Causeway and visitors will be impressed by both the strange and unique rock formations and by the enormous tourist brou ha ha that surrounds them. The Causeway Coast does have other attractions too: Portstewart, Portrush, White Park Bay and Ballycastle are all Victorian seaside towns, some quieter now than others, all with good beaches and much to keep the traveller occupied for a few hours at least. And of course, the much-photographed Carrick-a-Rede Rope Bridge is a highlight in every sense.

Info: Railway Road, **Coleraine**, ℰ028 7034 4723, www.northcoastni. com. Sheskburn House, 7 Mary Street, **Ballycastle,** ℰ028 2076 2024, www. moyle-council.org. http:// causewaycoastalroute.com

Location: The Giant's Causeway is on the coast road, A 2, between Portrush and Ballycastle.

Kids: Dunluce Centre, Leslie Hill Open Farm.

Don't Miss: Giant's Causeway, Dunluce Castle, Carrick-a-rede Rope Bridge, Gortmore Viewpoint and Magilligan Strand.

🚗 DRIVING TOUR

MAGILLIGAN STRAND TO BUSHMILLS

Magilligan Strand

The long stretch of golden sand dunes (6mi/10km) is equipped with sports facilities at Benone. The Point, where a Martello Tower (1812) was built during the Napoleonic Wars to guard the nar-

GETTING AROUND

BY RAIL – Giant's Causeway and Bushmills Railway: Operates a steam locomotive. See website for timetable and prices. ℰ028 20732 844. http:// giantscausewayrailway.webs.com

BY SEA – Rathlin Island Ferry: Summer sailings from 8am–4pm: see website for timetable and prices. ℰ028 20769 299. www.rathlinbally castleferry.com.

Magilligan Strand

© Northern Ireland Tourist Board

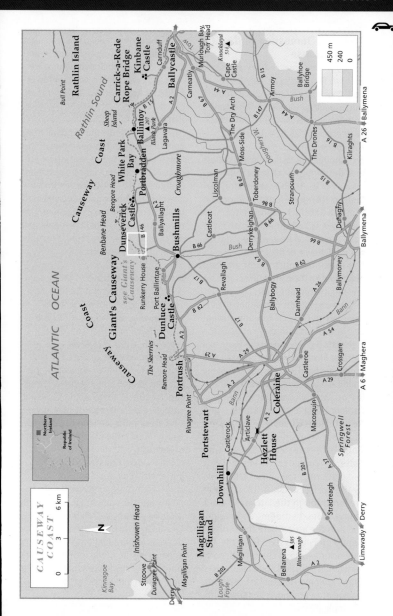

row approach to Lough Foyle, is now a Nature Reserve.

Gortmore Viewpoint★★

High up on the northeast slope of Binenvenagh Mountain, there is a superb **view** of Magilligan Strand across the mouth of Lough Foyle towards the Inishowen Peninsula.

Beyond the Lion Gate, the sea and the strand become visible: where once the Bishop held horse races, the present generation indulges in surfing. The Bishop's Road across the Binevenagh Mountain was built as a shortcut home from Limavady.

Downhill Demesne★ and Hezlett House

(NT) ⏱*Grounds: open all year; House: open late Mar–early Oct daily 10am–5pm.* 🚶*House by guided tour (40min) only: usually Jul–Aug Wed–Sun & Bank Hols, call or see website for details.* ⊛*£5.* 🅿 *(charge).* ✆*028 7084 8728. www.nationaltrust.org.uk.*

Even though the castle is now a roofless shell the demesne still reflects the personality of its flamboyant creator, **Earl Bishop Hervey**. From the imposing **Bishop's Gate**, a charming glen planted with flowers and shrubs, a path leads up to the clifftop from where there is a splendid **view★** of the coast.

The romantic, much-photographed **Mussenden Temple★** erected as a memorial to his cousin, Mrs Mussenden, clearly suggests the Earl Bishop's taste. This elegant Classical rotunda precariously perched on the very edge of the high cliffs is modelled on the Temple of Vesta at Tivoli. Built of local basalt and sandstone from Ballycastle in 1785, the building was used as a library by the Bishop, who allowed the local Roman Catholic priest to say Mass here.

Hezlett House, built in 1691 probably as a clergyman's residence, is a long, single-storey thatched cottage with battered, rough-cast walls, an attic and cruck truss roof. It was taken over by the Hezlett family in 1761. Visitors are led through the kitchen, pantry, dining room, bedrooms and parlour and into the attic where the servants slept. Furnishings date from the 19C and include balloon chairs (with holes for women's bustles) and prayer chairs, allowing women to kneel in hoop skirts. A small museum shows Victorian farming implements.

Portstewart

Portstewart was a fashionable watering place in the 19C and has kept something of its Victorian atmosphere with a picturesque harbour. The landmark O'Hara's Castle, a Gothic-style mansion (1834) was transformed into a Dominican college.

From the promenade, paths lead west along the cliffs to Portstewart Strand (2mi/3.2km). Regular exhibitions, concerts and events are held at the **Flowerfield Arts Centre** (*www.flowerfield.org*).

Portrush

Easily accessible by road and rail from Belfast, Portrush has been one of the North's most popular seaside resorts since early-Victorian times. The natural qualities of its sandy beaches and the nearby coastline are now supplemented by a host of man-made attractions. The town is laid out on a little peninsula which ends in Ramore Head, a notable haunt of bird watchers.

👪 Dunluce Centre

♿⏱*Open Easter week & Jul–Aug daily 11am–5.30pm; Apr–Jun & Sept–Oct Sat–Sun only, noon–5pm.* ⊛*All three main attractions £9 (all ages, min 4 years old).* ✆*028 7082 4444. www.dunlucecentre.co.uk.*

This large family entertainment complex includes Ireland's only "4-dimensional" special effects theatre, the Darklight Laser Drome, a large soft-play adventure area, and a viewing tower (free), which offers a superb panoramic view of Portrush.

Close by, **The Coastal Zone** (⏱*open Easter weekend, Jun Sat–Sun, Jul–Aug daily 10am–5pm, winter weekends only noon–4pm, see website;* 🅿*;* ✆*028 7082 3600; www.discovernorthernireland.com*), located in an old Victorian bath-house, provides an introduction to the ecology and marine life of the locality; visitors can observe the denizens of the seabed from within the "wreck" of the Nautilus.

▶ From Portrush take the A 2 east.

Dunluce Castle★★

⏱*Open year-round daily 10am–5pm (4pm Dec–Jan).* ⊛*£5.* ✆*028 2073 1938. www.discovernorthernireland.com.*

There can be few more romantic sights in Ireland than the jagged outline of ruined Dunluce Castle, perched on its isolated rock stack 100ft/30m above the sea. For years it was the seat of the

Irish branch of the Scottish MacDonnell clan, known as "Lords of the Isles"; the most notable leader was Sorley Boy MacDonnell, a constant irritant to both the native Irish and the English. Despite the use of artillery, the latter failed to expel him permanently from Dunluce, and his descendants were eventually made Earls of Antrim. In the 17C they modernised the castle to provide more comfortable accommodation but when the kitchen collapsed into the sea, they abandoned it.

Beyond the drawbridge and the late-16C gatehouse, with its Scottish-style turrets and crow-step gables, stand the two 14C towers and south wall. The upper yard is dominated by the 17C **great hall**, built in grandiose style with bay windows on the west front. The cobbled **lower yard** is surrounded by service buildings, including the bakery. From here there is a superb **view** of the Causeway Coast.

▷ Continue east on the A 2.

Old Bushmills Distillery★

Factory open by guided tour only, Mar–Oct 9.15am (noon Sun)– 4.45pm (last tour); Nov–Feb 10am (noon Sun)–3.30pm (last tour). For other dates call or see website. Closed Good Fri

Key to the Causeway

West of Portrush the coast is interrupted by the Bann estuary; beyond is a long sand dune extending into Lough Foyle. East of the town more sand dunes give way to strangely weathered and cave-riddled limestone cliffs and the extraordinary volcanic-rock formations of the Giant's Causeway. This geologically important section of the North Antrim Coast has been designated a **National Nature Reserv**e. Detailed analysis of the rocks at Portrush provided the key to the long standing riddle about the origin of such features as the Giant's Causeway.

afternoon, 4 & 12 Jul, Christmas and New Year. No children under eight on the tour. Tour £8, other areas free. During Easter week and some time during early July/Aug no production is in process (call or see website). On Fri afternoon, Sat and Sun there is no bottling process to see. ✕ ☎028 2073 3218. www.bushmills.com.

The original licence to distil was granted to Sir Thomas Phillips in 1608, although

Dunluce Castle

© Alamy/hemis.fr

references to a local distillery date back to 1276. Water drawn from St Columb's Rill, a tributary of the River Bush which rises in peaty ground, is used to produce two blended whiskeys and one malt. The tour includes the main stages in the production of whiskey: mashing, fermentation, distillation, maturing in oak casks, blending and bottling. Tasting takes place in the Potstill Bar; a small museum has been created in the old malt kilns.

GIANT'S CAUSEWAY★★★

(NT) 44 Causeway Rd, Bushmills
Causeway: open daily free. Park & Ride service from Bushmills info centre (£7 to inc Giant's Causeway Visitor Experience) Shuttlebus. £1 each way. Visitor Centre year-round daily from 10am (closing times vary according to season). Open: Giant's Causeway Visitor Experience (book timed ticket online) includes multi-lingual audio guide. £10.50 (£9 online). 028 2073 1855. www.nationaltrust. org.uk/giants-causeway.

Perhaps the strangest and also the most spectacular of Ireland's scenic attractions, the 40,000 basalt columns of the Giant's Causeway have inspired legend, intense scientific debate and endless wonder.

A Bit of History

The Giant's Causeway is the most dramatic geological feature along this coastline. Legends describe it as the work of giants, often in the form of the Ulster warrior Finn McCool. One story tells how he fell in love with a Scottish giantess and constructed a landbridge to reach her. In another tale, he builds the causeway to fight with another giant from over the water, the fierce Benandonner. However, Finn flees when he discovers his rival is bigger than him, dresses as a baby in the cot and waits. When Benandonner arrives to fight, he finds only Finn's wife and "baby". Seeing the size of the "baby", Benandonner panics at how big the adult Finn really must be and races back to Scotland, tearing up the causeway behind him! In fact this geological wonder is the result of a great volcanic eruption some 60 million years ago that impacted on this part of northeast Ireland, western

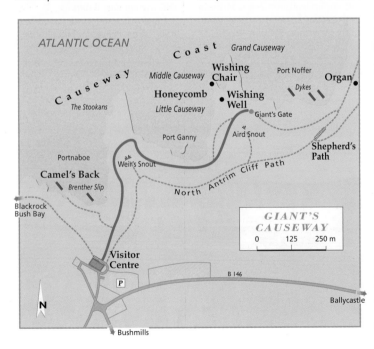

ATLANTIC OCEAN

Causeway Coast

Grand Causeway

Middle Causeway

Wishing Chair

Port Noffer

Organ

Honeycomb

Wishing Well

Dykes

The Stookans

Little Causeway

Giant's Gate

Port Ganny

Aird Snout

Shepherd's Path

Portnaboe

Weir's Snout

North Antrim Cliff Path

Camel's Back

Brenther Slip

Blackrock
Bush Bay

GIANT'S CAUSEWAY

0   125   250 m

Visitor Centre

P

B 146

N

Ballycastle

Bushmills

Giant's Causeway

© L. Decoudin/Michelin

Scotland (producing Fingal's Cave), the Faroe Islands, Iceland and Greenland, when lava exuded through cracks in the chalk mantle, solidifying into layers of hard basalt. The distinctive mass of geometric forms caused during cooling has created a variety of polygonal (four-, five-, six, seven-, eight- and even nine-sided) columns.

The Causeway was first publicised in 1693 by the Royal Society; then, in the mid-18C, the Dublin artist Susanna Drury painted a pair of topographical views (now in the Ulster Museum) provoking great speculation among geologists. Today the Causeway is a World Heritage Site.

🐾 Walking Tour

The Causeway proper extends from the foot of the cliffs into the sea like a sloping pavement, divided into sections by the sea: the Little Causeway, the Middle Causeway and the Grand Causeway.

The columns themselves are split horizontally, forming concave and convex surfaces. Certain features have acquired fanciful references: the **Wishing Well** is a natural freshwater spring in the Little Causeway and the **Giant's Gate** carries the coastal path through the **Tilted Columns**. East across Port Noffer the columns (40ft/12m) of the **Organ★** are visible in the cliff face.

Causeway Coast Way★

The headland known as Aird Snout gives a bird's-eye view of the Causeway, while from Weir's Snout to the West, there is a view across Port Ganny *(east)* to the Causeway and down into Portnaboe *(west),* where a volcanic dyke, known as the Camel's Back, is visible.

It is well worth escaping the crowds by walking to the headland. After Port Noffer comes Port Reostan, where the curved columns of the **Harp** are set in a natural **amphitheatre**.

The next headland has the **Chimney Tops**, three rock stacks formed by the second lava flow. The path enters Port Na Spaniagh where the *Gerona*, part of the Spanish Armada, was wrecked in 1588 with no survivors. Beyond the next headland, the Horse Back, lies Port na Callian; the farther promontory is the **King and his Nobles**, its figures apparently riding in from the sea.

After skirting two bays, the path climbs up past the **Horseshoe** *(left)* to Benbane Head and **Hamilton's Seat**. The spectacular **view★★** extends over the rocks to the mountains of Donegal, Rathlin Island and Mull of Kintyre.

🚗 DRIVING TOUR

GIANT'S CAUSEWAY TO BALLYCASTLE
12.5mi/20km

Dunseverick Castle

Accessible by the B 146 from Bushmills; on foot by narrow clifftop path from the Visitor Centre at Causeway Head (5mi/8km).

On their craggy promontory, separated from the mainland by two defiles, the scanty ruins of Dunseverick recall the ancient kingdom of Dalriada, which included Antrim and Argyll in Scotland. This was a strategic spot on the road from the Hill of Tara to the sea and lands beyond.

White Park Bay★

The small seaside town of Portbradden, once an important salmon fishery, lies at the western end of a 1.8mi/3km sandy white beach backed by towering white cliffs topped by rich green moorlands. The cliffs and surrounding area abound in fossils and archaeological sites. Although tempting, sea bathing is dangerous here because of the strong currents.

The A2 (then the B 15) follows the beach for 1.8mi/3km to the tiny port of **Ballintoy**, nestling at the foot of the cliff and bordered by similar basaltic rocks to those at the Giant's Causeway.

◐ Leave Ballintoy by the B 15 and after 1.2mi/2km look for the car park of the Carrick-a-Rede Rope Bridge, where you continue on foot to the bridge.

👥 Carrick-a-Rede Rope Bridge★★

(NT) From the car park 30min there and back on foot. ◐9.30am-6pm (7pm late Jun-early Sept, 3.30pm Jan-Feb, late Oct-Dec). ⊙£7, child £3.50. ✕ ☎028 2076 9839.
www.nationaltrust.org.uk.
This precarious-looking (yet very safe) bridge was traditionally erected by salmon fishermen every spring to get to their fishery and a fisherman's cottage, recently restored, is open to visitors.

As the migrating salmon head for their spawning grounds in the River Bush or River Bann, they are deflected north by the island (*Carrick-a-rede* means Rock-in-the-Road) straight into the nets.

The bridge (66ft/20m long) sways with each footfall over the spectacular rock-strewn water (80ft/25m below) and a warden ensures that a maximum of eight people only ever cross at one time.

◐ Continue along the B 15.

Kinbane Castle★

Not much remains of the castle built on the long limestone promontory in the 16C. Kinbane, *Ceinn Bán* in Gaelic means "white head", the geology of the headland making the name self-explanatory. Below the castle ruins a hollow is said to be the place where besieging English troops were massacred in the 16C.

From the cliff edge there are spectacular **views★** of Rathlin Island and the Iron Age Dunagregor Fort.

◐ Continue on the B 15 to Ballycastle.

Ballycastle

This attractive little market town, backed by Knocklayd Mountain, has many amenities – a long sandy beach, angling and golf and summer festivities. A stone memorial by the harbour recalls the wireless link between Ballycastle and Rathlin Island set up in 1898 by Marconi and his assistant, George Kemp. The town is best-known for its "Auld Lammas Fair" held over two days in August.

Thought to date back 400 years, it is Ireland's oldest fair. It was once probably a sheep mart but in modern times has expanded to a visiting fairground, with 100 or more market stalls, selling everything from trainers to horses.

From the beach at Ballycastle there are fine views to Rathlin Island and to the Mull of Kintyre in Scotland.

Excursion to Rathlin Island★

Access by boat from Ballycastle (see Getting Around).

The island is separated from Ballycastle by Rathlin Sound (5mi/8km wide). Rathlin is treeless, pitted with shallow lakes and divided into fields by drystone walls. It is surrounded by tall, white cliffs where seabirds breed. From the sheltered harbour, three roads radiate to the outlying homesteads and lighthouses. The traditional occupations are fishing and farming, supplemented in the past by smuggling and now by tourism.

In the 6C St Columba nearly lost his life off Rathlin when his boat was trapped in a whirlpool. In 1306, according to tradition, it was while taking refuge in one of the island's many caves that Robert the Bruce received his famous lesson in perseverance from a spider.

Northern Ireland's only inhabited island has a changing population of around 100. It is only 11mi/17.7km from the Mull of Kintyre in Scotland. Rathlin is a designated Special Area of Conservation and its tall white cliffs are home to breeding colonies of seabirds.

ADDRESSES

🛏 STAY

🍽🍽 **Shola Coach House** – *110A Gateside Rd, Portrush 10rm ☎028 7082 5925.* A boutique bed and breakfast set in a beautifully restored coach house dating back to 1860. Expect plush bedrooms and a warm welcome.

🍽🍽 **Maddybenny Farmhouse** – *Loguestown Rd, Portrush. 3rm ☎028 7082 3394. www. maddybenny.com.* The farmhouse dates back to the middle of the 17C, but is thoroughly modernized. Comfortable rooms are beautifully furnished. Maddybenny also offer s/c cottages and a riding school.

🍴 EAT

🍽 **The Harbour Bistro** – *The Harbour, Portrush. ☎028 7082 2430. www.ramore restaurant.com. Open from 5pm Wed–Sun.* Smart contemporary bar/bistro serving a fairly standard menu of grilled meats, chicken and fish. Its neighbouring sister establishment the **Ramore Wine Bar** (☎028 7082 4313), a relaxed and informal bar with a similar atmosphere and smaller bistro menu.

SPORTS AND LEISURE

Sandy beaches at Portballintrae, Portrush, Portstewart, Castlerock and Magilligan Strand (Benone).

SIGHTSEEING

Portrush Puffer – Road-driven tourist train. *Operates Jul–Aug, Mon–Sat every half-hour 11am–1.30pm, 2pm–7pm, Sun 2pm–7pm – £2.50.*

Open Topper – Open-top bus rides along the Causeway Coast between Coleraine and Giant's Causeway via Portstewart, Portrush, Bushmills and Portballintrae (bus route 177) Jul–Aug. Hopper fare £4.80. Translink: ☎028 703 25400

Excursions by boat – To visit the caves in the limestone cliffs at **White Rock** *(east),* and to **The Skerries**, a chain of offshore islands densely populated by sea birds.

ACCESS AND CLIFF WALKS

From the Visitor Centre to the Causeway takes 10min on foot: in summer there is a shuttle bus service.

Observe the warning signs: freak waves can break over the rocks.

To view the Causeway from above, walk through the Giant's Gate into Port Noffer and climb up the Shepherd's Path *(1hr – 2mi/3km)* and continue along the top to the Visitor Centre. Alternatively, from Port Noffer go up the path (steep steps) to Benbane Head and walk back along the clifftop path *(5mi/8km – 2hr).*

Glens of Antrim★★★

A drive up the Antrim Coast offers a great variety of scenery: seaward are attractive villages, long flat strands, steep basalt or limestone cliffs and a distant prospect of the Mull of Kintyre in Scotland. Inland, are the glens created by the tumbling mountain streams that descend from the uplands of heath and bog, now punctuated by forestry plantations. In the glens, where the underlying sedimentary rocks are exposed, the farms are arranged like ladders climbing the valley sides so that each has a share of the good land near the river and of the poorer, upland pasture.

A BIT OF HISTORY

This once-isolated area, accessed by an old coastal track, was the least anglicised part of the country. The first road dates from 1832, when the Grand Military Road from Carrickfergus to Portrush was built along an ancient raised beach and on a ledge blasted from the basalt and chalk rock.

In the 19C, two narrow-gauge railway lines (3ft/1m) were laid to carry the increasing output of the Glenariff mines in operation from the late-1860s. The Glenariff Iron Ore & Holding Co. line ran from Inverglen down Glenariff to the Southeast end of Red Bay, where the bed of the track is still visible. The other, from Ballymena up the Clogh Valley to Retreat (1876), was never extended farther because of the steep gradient down Glenballyemon to the coast; it closed in 1930.

🚗 DRIVING TOUR

LARNE TO MURLOUGH BAY
70mi/113km. Allow one or two days.

Larne
The southern gateway to the Glens of Antrim, Larne is a busy port with a regu-

---

- 🛈 **Info:** Narrow Gauge Road, Larne, ☎028 2826 0088, www.larne.gov.uk. www.moyle-council.org/tourism. www.causeway coastandglens.com.
- ▷ **Location:** The A 2 runs along the Antrim coast between Ballycastle and Larne at the foot of the nine Glens of Antrim.
- 🚫 **Don't Miss:** Excursions to Glenariff Forest Park and its waterfall, or Murlough National Nature Reserve to admire the view from Benmore.
- 👫 **Kids:** Carfunnock Family Fun Zone.

GETTING AROUND
BY SEA – **Larne Lough Ferry** to Island Magee – *operates (weather permitting) hourly* ☎028 2827 4085.

---

lar ferry service to Cairnryan in Scotland and Island Magee (a peninsula on the east coast of Co Antrim).

Larne has been a regular landing point since the 9C when the Vikings arrived and Edward Bruce sailed here from Scotland to secure an Irish crown in 1315. Twenty-five thousand German rifles and 3 million rounds of ammunition were unloaded in Larne in April 1914 and rapidly distributed to the Ulster Volunteers; clear evidence of the local determination to resist Home Rule by all possible means.

On Curran Point stand the ruins of **Olderfleet Castle**, a square, four-storey tower house, one of three built in the early 17C to protect the entrance to the lough. The **Chaine Memorial Tower** honours James Chaine, a local MP and benefactor.

▷ From Larne take the A 2 north.

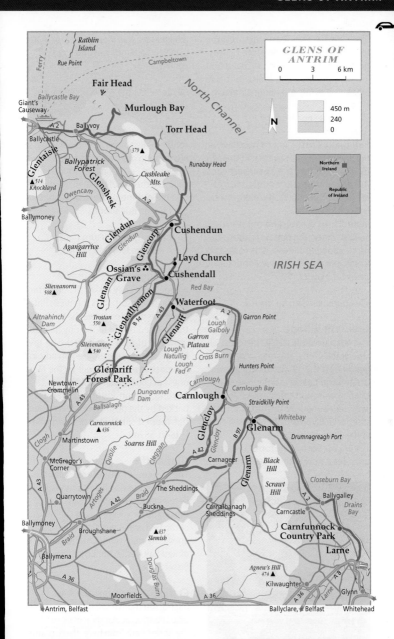

👥 Carnfunnock Country Park (Family Fun Zone)

🕐 *Country Park: open 9am–dusk. See website for attractions opening times.*
🕐 *Fun Zone: open summer daily 11am–5pm Jul–Aug.* 🎟 *Attractions priced individually.* ✕ 🕿 *028 2827 0541. www.carnfunnock.co.uk.*

In a lovely setting of green hills dropping down to the sea north of Drains Bay village, the Park (473 acres/190ha) was once a private demesne. Original features remaining include the walled garden, lime kilns and icehouse. There is a maze and a 9-hole golf course.

The **Family Fun Zone** attractions include mini golf, a miniature railway, bouncy castle, remote control boats and lorries, walk-on-water balls, laser-clay pigeon shooting and bungee running.

▷ Continue north on the A 2.

Ballygally Castle, now a hotel *(www. hastingshotels.com)*, was built in 1625 by James Shaw; the twin bartizans (overhanging, wall-mounted turrets) are original, but the sash windows were later introduced.

Inland rises a natural amphitheatre, Sallagh Braes; the fine walk above the Braes along the plateau edge *(access via Carncastle and Ballycoose Road)* forms part of the Ulster Way.

▷ Continue north on the A 2.

Glenarm Village

This attractive little port is the oldest village in the Glens. The main street runs inland past the 19C barbican gateway of **Glenarm Castle** *(private)*, the seat of the Earl of Antrim, which was begun in 1606 and re-modelled in the Elizabethan style by William Vitruvius Morrison early in the 19C.

The **Forest Park** at the top of the street provides a view of the castle, and there

are pleasant walks by the stream in the upper woodlands beyond the belt of conifers.

▷ Return to the A 2; turn left onto the B 97.

The road runs up **Glenarm**, the southernmost of the Antrim Glens, passing through open farmland, with views of Glenarm Forest on the far side of the valley. At the top of the glen the unmistakable outline of Slemish Mountain can be seen due south.

▷ At the T-junction turn right onto the A 42. Turn left onto the A 2.

Carnlough

A large, sandy bay makes this an attractive seaside resort. Until the 1960s limestone was quarried above the town and transported by rail to the tiny harbour (now full of pleasure boats). The low bridge, former courthouse and adjoining clock tower were built by the Marquess of Londonderry in 1854.

Beyond Garron Point lies **Red Bay**, backed by the distinctive, steep-sided, flat-topped silhouette of Lurigethan (1,154ft/352m).

Glenariff★

The "**Queen of the Glens**", Glenariff comprises broad lush pastures enclosed between steep hanging crags.

Waterfoot★ village lies at the mouth of the Glenariff River. On the headland, above the road tunnel, stand the ruins of Red Bay Castle, built by the Norman Bisset family.

▷ From Glenariff take the A 43 inland. Alternatively, if you want to take the spectacular glen walk to the Forest Park from here, there is an entrance to the Park from Waterfoot on the main Coast Road.

Glenariff Forest Park★

&⚪*Open 10am–dusk.* ⊖*£4.50 per car, £1.50 pedestrians.* ✕ ☏*028 2955 6000. www.nidirect.gov.uk/glenariff-forest-park.*

Glenariff Waterfall

© Northern Ireland Tourist Board

This beautiful forest (2,298 acres/930ha) comprises areas of woodland, peat bog, rocky outcrops, lakes and rivers. The Visitor Centre provides information about the Antrim Glens and has excellent displays on local wildlife, the 19C iron ore and bauxite mines and their railways. The **Ess na Larach waterfall★** *(1hr there and back on foot from the North side of the car park)* tumbles through a wooded gorge created by the Glenariff River.

▶ Continue southwest on the A 43; at the junction turn right onto the B 14.

Cushendall

Cushendall stands at the meeting point of three glens. Its landmark red sandstone Curfew Tower was built as a watchhouse in 1809 by Francis Turnly of the East India Company.

▶ Take Layde Road, the steep coast road going north to Cushendun.

Layd Old Church

The ruins of the church stand in a graveyard romantically sited by a swiftly flowing stream which plunges directly into the sea.
Between 1306–1790 it served as a parish church; note the MacDonnell memorials in the graveyard.

▶ At the T-junction in Knocknacarry turn left onto the B 92 and left onto the A 2.

▶ After 1.5mi/2.4km turn right onto Glenaan Road. Turn left onto a lane; 20min there and back on foot.

Ossian's Grave

The figure of Ossian appears in a number of guises in Irish lore; one of them as an early-Christian warrior-bard, the son of Finn McCool, whose legendary feats are recounted in the Ossianic Cycle.
Revived in the work of the 18C poet James McPherson, Ossian became a hero to the Romantic writers of the late-18C/early-19C, particularly in continental Europe. Whoever he was, it seems unlikely he found his last resting place

here; Ossian's Grave is, in fact, a Neolithic court tomb, enclosed in an oval cairn.

▶ Continue west up the glen.

In **Glenaan**, the Glenaan River flows down from the slopes of Tievebulliagh *(south)*, where Neolithic men once made axe heads from the hard porcellanite rock.

▶ At the crossroads turn right onto Glendun Road to Cushendun.

Glendun★, the Brown Glen, is the wildest of the nine glens; its river noted for sea trout and salmon fishing. The viaduct was designed by Charles Lanyon in 1839.

Cushendun

The houses of this picturesque village (*Cois Abhann Duinne* in Gaelic, meaning "beside the River Dun") cluster at the southern end of a sandy beach flanked by tall cliffs at the mouth of the river Dunn. The village owes its distinctive and rather fey character to Sir Clough Williams-Ellis, the playful architect of Portmeirion in North Wales, who worked here for Ronald McNeill, the first (and only) Lord Cushenden.
The village is intended to look like a Cornish fishing village. There are terraces of small white houses around a square, a number of slate-hung cottages, and a neo-Georgian mansion, Glenmona

Away with the Fairies

Between Knockacarry and Glenaan is **Glencorp**, which translates as "the glen of slaughter/bodies". The derivation of this is uncertain but "The Fairy Hill" on the East slope of Glencorp is called Tieveragh famous locally for being the home of the fairies or "little folk", who are said to emerge in processions on the last day of April (known as May eve). Only believers can see them!

Lodge, which stands in a pine grove facing the sea. The poet John Masefield lived here for a time.

▶ Take the steep and narrow road north. After 5mi/8km, fork right onto Torr Road.

Torr Head is a low promontory, crowned by a look-out post – the nearest point on the Irish mainland to the Scottish coast (12mi/19km), enjoying spectacular views over to the Mull of Kintyre.

▶ Continue northwest along the coast road; after 2.5mi/4km turn right.

Murlough National Nature Reserve

1mi/1.6km to the upper car park; smaller car park lower down the cliff face. ⊙*Information Centre: open Jun–mid-Sept 10am–6pm; mid-Mar–May, Sat–Sun only, 10am–6pm.* ⊚*£4 per car.* ☎*028 4375 1467. www.nationaltrust.org.uk.*

This is the most beautiful bay on the Antrim coast, set in the lee of **Fair Head** *(Benmore)* at the foot of steep and towering cliffs, and overlooked by the rounded peaks of the Mourne Mountains to the South.

It is one of Ireland's most important nature reserves, incorporating 6,000-year-old sand dunes and heath, a habitat for 22 species of butterfly, including the endangered Marsh Fritillary. The area is also an important overwintering site for several species of wading bird and a habitat for seals.

The stone cross is a memorial to Sir Roger Casement.

Waymarked footpaths from the lower car park lead north to some long-abandoned coal mines, before returning along the shore past the remains of the miners' cottages and the ruins of Drumnakill Church; south past an old lime kiln, through a wood to avoid Murlough Cottage *(private)* and ends at Benvan farmhouse.

A second path goes along the clifftop to windblown **Fair Head** *(Benmore)*, from

Beach at Murlough National Nature Reserve

© Bernie Brown/Tourism Ireland

where there are glorious **views★★★** of Rathlin Island *(north)* and the Mull of Kintyre *(northeast)*, before cutting across the rough and often wet ground of the plateau, past a **crannóg** in Lough na Cranagh *(right)*, farm buildings at Coolanlough, to reach Lough Fadden *(left)*. A boardwalk from the car park through the dunes to the **beach**, a long arc of sand, several miles long. An information centre and toilets are located in the car park and are open throughout the summer months.

▶ Return to the coast road, then turn right to Ballycastle.

Bonamargy Friary

The remains of a Franciscan friary (c. 1500, probably in use until the late 17C) sit by a stream, surrounded by Ballycastle golf course. The ruined church was originally thatched and includes the ruins of a chapel, vaults, gatehouse, cloisters and living quarters and graveyard. For a time in the 17C the friary became a refuge for Scots Catholics fleeing the drive to Protestantism in Scotland. It has a vault containing the remains of several MacDonnells, descended from the Scottish MacDonalds, who fought with the McQuillan clan for possession of this part of Ireland. The McQuillans produced a nun, Julia, known for her piety; the round-headed cross in the nave is thought to mark her grave, placed here so that even in death she could practise humility, walked on by the feet of worshippers.

▶ On the edge of Ballycastle turn left onto the B 15; after 0.25mi/0.4km bear right to Dunamallaght Road.

Glenshesk

The road overlooks the Glenshesk River and skirts the southern edge of Ballycastle Forest. From Breen Bridge, at the foot of Knocklayd Mountain, runs waymarked **Moyle Way**, a spur of the Ulster Way long-distance footpath.

▶ Take the B 15 west.

Only the base of the **Armoy Round Tower** (30ft/9m) remains, sited in the graveyard of St Patrick's Church, built in 460 by the monastery founded by Olcan, a disciple of St Patrick.

▶ At the crossroads take the minor road north. Turn right onto the A 44 to Ballycastle.

ADDRESSES

🛏 STAY

⊜– ⊜⊜ **Cullentra House** – *16 Cloughs Rd, Cusendall. ℰ028 2177 1762. www.cullentrahouseireland.com.* A friendly B&B in a modern dwelling with nicely furnished bedrooms and good views from the dining room.

⊜⊜ **The Glens Hotel**– *6 Coast Rd, Cushendall. 20 rm. ℰ028 2177 1223. www.theglenshotel.com.* A small, family-run hotel with good facilities and rooms decorated in fresh light colours.

⊜⊜ **Londonderry Arms Hotel** – *20 Harbour Rd, Carnlough. 35rm. ℰ028 2885 5255. www.glensofantrim.com. 35 rms.* A variety of individually sized and decorated bedrooms (the older-style are preferable), some with sea views, in an old coaching inn, built in 1848. Cosy public areas with open fires for relaxing.

🍴 EAT

⊜⊜ **Harry's Restaurant**– *10 Mill St, Cushendall. ℰ028 2177 2022. http://harryscushendall.com.* Very smart quite formal modern restaurant specialising in the finest sustainable local seafood and Irish beef on an international menu.

⊜⊜ **Frances Anne & Tapestry Restaurant** – *20 Harbour Rd, Carnlough. 35rm. ℰ028 2885 5255. www.glensofantrim.com.* Award-winning restaurant specialising in local Glens of Antrim food: wild salmon, lamb and locally produced vegetables.

INDEX

A

AA (Automobile Association)..........39
Abbeyleix............................ 201
Abbeyleix Heritage House 201
Abbreviations.......................46
Accessibility.........................36
Accommodation 40
Achill Island....................... 363
Activity Holidays 17
Adare.............................. 308
Adare Friary........................ 309
Adventure Sports 21
Ahenny High Crosses 208
Aherlow, Glen of 209
Aillwee Cave 328
Airlines.............................37
Air Travel...........................37
Allihies 274
Altamont Gardens.................. 228
Ancestors (tracing) 55
Andrew Jackson Centre............ 425
Anglo-Irish Ascendancy 64
Anglo-Irish Literature................87
Anglo-Irish Treaty 66
Anglo-Normans......................61
Animals.............................36
Annaghdown Church and Priory 339
Annalong 452
Annes Grove Gardens............... 259
Antrim.............................431
Antrim Castle Gardens.............431
Aran Islands........................331
Aran knitwear......................331
Architecture 67
Ardagh 188
Ardara............................. 387
Ardboe Cross.......................431
Ardee............................. 168
Ardfert............................. 291
Ardgillan Castle 141
Ardglass 447
Ardress House...................... 460
Ards Forest Park.................... 394
Ards Peninsula 434, 435
Argory, The 460
Arklow.............................185
Armagh............................ 456
Arranmore Island.................. 389
Art 83
Arthur Cottage..................... 433
Ashford Castle 352
Athassel Priory 213
Athenry........................... 340
Athy...............................173

B

Ballance House..................... 432
Ballina 367
Ballinskelligs 283
Ballinspittle 264
Ballintober Castle 320
Ballintubber Abbey................. 357
Ballitore 173
Ballycastle 492
Ballycopeland Windmill 437
Ballycrovane Ogham Pillar Stone 274
Ballydavid 296
Ballydehob 268
Ballyferriter 295
Ballygally Castle.................... 496
Ballyjamesduff 401
Ballykelly 477
Ballyliffin 397
Ballylumford Dolmen............... 426
Ballymacdermot Cairn.............. 455
Ballyness Bay...................... 390
Ballynoe Stone Circle 444
Ballyshannon 382
Ballyvaughan 324
Baltimore 266
Baltinglass 174
Banagher 478
Bangor 436
Bangor Trail........................19
Bank of Ireland 113
Banks...............................47
Banshee 99
Bantry 271
Bantry Bay 268
Bantry House 271
Barley Cove 269
Barrow Valley 173
Barryscourt Castle.................. 256
Basic Information 46
Basilica of Our Lady............... 358
Battle of Benburb 462
Battle of the Boyne.................63
Battle of the Yellow Ford........... 462
Battle of Yellow Ford 62
B&Bs...............................41
Beaghmore Stone Circles 474
Beara Peninsula 272

A (right column continued)

Atlantaquaria 340
Audley's Castle.................... 447
Audleystown Cairn 447
Aughnanure Castle................. 347
Automobile Association 39
Avondale 183

Beckett, Samuel........................90
Bective Abbey 160
Bed & Breakfast 40
Bedell, William 403
Behan, Brendan 90
Belfast..................16, 408, 421
    Belfast Castle 421
    Botanic Gardens 418
    Cathedral Quarter..................... 412
    City Hall 409
    Crown Liquor Saloon 412
    Donegall Square 409
    Entertainment 420
    Events and Festivals................... 420
    Grand Opera House 412
    Laganside, The........................ 414
    Murals................................... 415
    Pubs...................................... 419
    Seamen's Church....................... 413
    Sinclair Seamen's Church 413
    St Anne's Cathedral 413
    St George's Market 413
    St Malachy's Church 412
    University District..................... 417
    Zoo....................................... 421
Bellaghy Bawn 431
Belleek 469
Belleek Parian Ware 470
Belleek Pottery.......................470
Belmullet 364
Belvedere House and Gardens 191
Benbulben...........................375
Ben of Howth........................138
Benwee Head 365
Bere Island.......................... 273
Bernish Rock 455
Bessbrook 454
Beverages 60
Bianconi, Charles.................... 207
Binchy, Maeve........................90
Birr 193
Birr Castle........................... 194
Black Abbey, Kilkenny 219
Black Death, The 61
Black Head...........................324
Blarney Castle....................... 252
Blarney Stone 252
Blasket Islands 295
Blennerville.........................292
Bloody Bridge....................... 452
Bloody Foreland Head.............. 389
Bloody Sunday...................... 480
Boating...............................17
Bog of Allen.........................170

Bogs (peat) 102
Bonamargy Friary 499
Book of Durrow 83, 198
Book of Kells 83, 161
Books.................................24
Bovevagh............................ 477
Boycott, Captain Charles............ 352
Boyle 377
Boyle Abbey 377
Boyne, Battle of the 155
Boyne Valley 151
Brandon Bay 292
Brandon Creek 293, 296
Brannock Island 331
Bray 184
Breakfast 60
Bricklieve Mountains 375
Brittas Bay 185
Broad Haven 364
Bród Tullaroan 221
Brontë Centre 450
Brontë Country....................... 450
Bronze Age 67
Browne, Frank....................... 248
Brownes of Westport 356
Brú Ború 211
Brú na Bóinne Visitor Centre 153
Budget Accommodation..............44
Bunbeg............................... 389
Bunclody 228
Buncrana 396
Bundoran 382
Bunlahinch Clapper Bridge 359
Bunratty Castle & Folk Park 306
Burren Coast Road................... 323
Burren, The 321
Burrishoole Abbey 361
Burtonport.......................... 389
Bushmills Distillery 489
Bus Service 37
Buttevant Friary.................... 259

C

Cahercommaun Fort 329
Caherdaniel......................... 282
Caher River Valley 324
Cahersiveen......................... 284
Cahir 213
Cahir Castle..........................213
Cahir House Hotel 214
Calendar of Events 29
Cam Lough 455
Camp Sites...........................41
Canoeing 23

INDEX

Cape Clear Island 266
Car Hire 38
Carlingford 166
Carna Peninsula 345
Carndonagh 397
Carnfunnock 495
Carnlough 496
Car Rental 38
Carrick-a-rede Rope Bridge 492
Carrickfergus 424
Carrickfergus Castle 424
Carrickmacross 167
Carrigahowley (Rockfleet) Castle 361
Carrigglas Manor Hotel 188
Carrowkeel Megalithic Cemetery 375
Carrowmore Megalithic Cemetery . . . 373
Car Travel 37
Casey, Michael 189
Cashel 209
Cashel Heritage Centre 212
Cashel Palace Hotel Gardens 212
Castle Archdale Country Park 468
Castlebar 358
Castle Caldwell Forest Park 469
Castlecaulfield 462
Castlecomer 221
Castleconnell 314
Castle Coole 465
Castledermot 173
Castlekeeran High Crosses 162
Castlestrange Stone 320
Castletown House 172
Castletownshend 265
Castle Ward 445
Castlewellan Forest Park 450
Causeway Coast 486
Cavan 401
Cavan Way 19
Cave Hill 422
Céide Fields 365
Celtic Art 83
Celtic Church 95
Celts 61
Chandler, Raymond 240
Changeling 99
Charles Fort 263
Chieftains 92
Children 28
Churches 48, 68
Churchill 391
Cinema 100
Claddagh, The 335
Clannad 92
Clara Bog 198

Clare County Museum 308
Clare Glens 314
Clare Island 359
Classical Music 21
Clifden 349
Climate 14, 103
Climbing 21
Cloghane 292
Clonakilty 264
Clones 399
Clonfert Cathedral 318
Clonfinlough Stone 198
Clonmacnoise 195
Clonmel 205
Clontuskert 318
Clough 445
Cloyne 256
Coach Services 37
Co Antrim 406
Co Armagh 407
Coastline 104
Cobh 253
Co Cavan 370, 401
Co Clare 299
Co Derry (Londonderry) 406
Co Donegal 369
Co Down 406
Co Fermanagh 407, 464
Co Galway 299
Coirrgend 396
Co Kildare 169
Co Kilkenny 216
Co Laois 201
Co Leitrim 370
Co Limerick 299
Co Longford 188
Co Mayo 300
Communications .46
Co Monaghan 370, 399
Confederation of Kilkenny 63
Cong 352
Cong Abbey 352
Connemara 11, 344
Connemara National Park 350
Connor Pass 292
Conolly, William .172
Consulates 35
Conversion Tables 49
Co Offaly 193
Cooking (classes) .18
Cookstown 472
Coolcarrigan Gardens 173
Coole Park 326
Cooley Peninsula 165, 166

Copeland Islands 437
Copper mines 274
Corcomroe Abbey 325
Cork **11, 15, 244**
   Cork City Gaol 248
   Cork Public Museum 249
   Crawford Art Gallery 247
   English Market 246
   Opera House 247
   Shopping 251
   St Fin Barre's Cathedral 249
   St Mary's Cathedral 248
   St Patrick Street 247
Corlea Trackway 188
Cormac's Chapel 211
Corofin 327
Co Roscommon 300
Cosgrave, William T. 217
Co Sligo 369, 371
Co Tipperaray 205
Co Tyrone 407
Country Houses 74
Country Today, The 52
Courtmacsherry 264
Courtmacsherry Bay 264
Court tombs 67
Co Waterford 235
Co Westmeath 190
Co Wexford 223
Craggaunowen Centre 306
Craith, Aindrias Mac 301
Crawfordsburn Country Park 422
Credit Cards 47
Creeslough 394
Creevelea Abbey 379
Croagh Patrick 360
Cromwellian Settlement 63
Crookhaven 269
Crosshaven 260
Cruachan District 320
Crúibíní 60
Cruising 17, 23
Crutched Friary 160
Cuisine 60
Curracloe 226
Currency 47
Cushendall 497
Cushendun 497
Customs & Excise .35
Cycles (myth/history) 99
Cycling 17, 18, 22

D

Dalkey Village 139
Dalway's Bawn 426
Dance 91
Dan Winter's Cottage 461
Davitt, Michael 359
Delamont Country Park 444
Delphi 359
Demographics 52
Derreen Gardens .274
Derry 479
Derrynane 282
Derryveagh Mountains 390
Desmond Castle 263
Devenish Island 468
Devil's Bit Mountain 209
Devil's Glen 182
Dialling Codes 46
Dingle 293
Dingle Peninsula 288
Dingle Way 19, 292
Discounts 46
Dixon Park 428
Documents 35
Donaghadee 437
Donaghmore 462
Donegal 381
Donegal Castle 382
Donegal Coast 383
Doneraile Wildlife Park 259
Doolin 323
Doo Lough Pass .359
Dooney Rock Forest 379
Down Cathedral, Downpatrick 442
Down County Museum 442
Downpatrick 441
Downpatrick Head 365
Down Survey, The 142
Dowth 155
Draperstown 474
Drisheen 60
Driving 38
Driving Tours 10
Drogheda 151
Drogheda Millmount Museum 153
Dromahair 379
Drombeg Stone Circle 265
Drumbeg 428
Drumcliff 374
Drumena Cashel and Souterrain 451
Drum Manor Forest Park 473
Dublin **6, 10, 14, 16, 110**
   Castle 125
   Chester Beatty Library 126

INDEX

Christ Church Cathedral 126
City Hall 125
College Green. 113
Custom House 129
Drimnagh Castle 137
Dublinia 127
Dublin Writers' Museum. 132
Entertainment 146
Events and Festivals. 148
Excursions 138
GAA Museum 136
Getting There and Getting Around. 112
Glasnevin Cemetery. 135
Government Buildings 120
GPO Building 131
Grafton Street. 123
Guinness Storehouse. 137
Hugh Lane Gallery of Modern Art 132
Irish Jewish Museum 137
Iveagh Gardens 123
James Joyce Centre 134
Kildare Street Club 117
Kilmainham Gaol Museum. 136
Liffey Footbridges. 124
Marino Casino 135
Marsh's Library. 129
Merrion Square 117
National Botanic Gardens. 135
National Library. 121
National Museum (Archaeology). 121
National Museum (Decorative Arts and
    History). 135
Natural History Museum. 120
Newman House 122
Nightlife 147
Northside. 134
Number Twenty-Nine 117
Old Jameson Distillery. 130
Parnell Square 131
Powerscourt Centre 123
Pro-Cathedral. 131
Pubs & Cafes 145
Shelbourne Hotel 120
Shopping. 147
Sightseeing. 148
Southside. 113, 136
Sports and Leisure 148
St Patrick's Cathedral. 128
St Stephen's Green 122
Tailors' Hall. 128
Temple Bar. 124
Tours 148
Trinity College 113
Trinity College Old Library 50, 116

Duiske Abbey 231
Dún Aonghasa 333
Dún A' Rí Forest Park. 167
Dunbrody Abbey. 232
Dunbrody Famine Ship 230
Duncannon Fort. 232
Dundalk 165
Dundrum Castle. 450
Dún Dúchatair 333
Dungannon. 462
Dunganstown. 231
Dungarvan. 239
Dungiven 478
Dunguaire Castle 325
Dún Laoghaire 139
Dunluce Castle 488, 489
Dunmore Cave 221
Dunmore East. 238
Dunquin 295
Dunseverick Castle 492
Durrow, Book of 83
Durrow High Cross 198
Dursey Island 274
Dysert O'Dea. 327

E

Easter Rising 66
East Munster Way 19
Economy. 59
Edenderry 429
Edmund Rice Heritage Centre
    (Kilkenny) 221
Education. 53
Eels. 431
Eglinton 476
EHIC - Health Insurance Card. 36
Éire 66
Electricity. 47
Elphin Windmill 320
Embassies 34
Emergencies 47
Emmet Rebellion. .64
Emo Court 201
Ennis 307
Enniscorthy 226
Enniscorthy Castle. 228
Ennis Friary 308
Enniskillen 15, 464
Enniskillen Castle. 464
Ennistimon 323
Entry Requirements 35
Enya. 92
Errigal Mountain 390
Erris Head. 364

European Health Insurance Card 36
Events 29
ExplorErne 470
Exploris 438

F
Fahan 294, 396
Fáilte 34
Fairylore 98
Famine 64
Fanad 394
Fanore 323
Farm Holidays 41
Farrell, JG 90
Fenit 291
Ferns 228
Ferries 37
Ferriter, Pierce 277
Festivals 21
Fethard 207
Films 25
Fingal 140
Fish 60
Fishing 22
Fleadh Season 31
Flights 37
Florence Court 466
Football 56
Fore Abbey 191
Fort Dunree Military Museum 396
Forthill Park 465
Fota Island 254
Fourknocks 156
Foxford 367
Foyle Valley Railway Centre 484
Free Derry Museum 484
French, Percy 401
Fungie the Dolphin 294
Furnace Lough 361

G
Gaelic 57
Gaelic football 56
Gaelic Revival 58, 88
Gaelige 57
Gallagher, Rory 92
Galway 11, 17, 335
  City Museum 337
  Eyre Square 338
  Lynch's Castle 338
  Nora Barnacle's House 338
  Spanish Arch 337
  St Nicholas' Church 337
Gandon, James 201

Gap of Dunloe 278
Gasoline 39
Geography 101
Getting There and Getting Around 37
Giant's Causeway 490
Giant's Ring 429
Glandore 265
Glass (production) 26
Glebe House and Gallery 391
Glenaan 497
Glenariff 496
Glenariff Forest Park 496
Glenarm Village 496
Glenbeigh 284
Glencar Waterfall 375
Glencolmcille Folk Village 385
Glencorp 497
Glendalough 175
Glengariff Woods 272
Glengarriff 272
Glengesh Pass 387
Glen Inchaquin Park 281
Glenmacnass Waterfall 182
Glenmalin Court Cairn 385
Glenmalur 183
Glenoe Waterfall 426
Glenshane Pass 477
Glenshesk 499
Glens of Antrim 494
Glenstal Abbey .314
Glenties 387
Glenveagh National Park 391
Gliding 21
Glinsk Castle 320
Goldsmith Country 189
Goldsmith, Oliver 189
Golf 22
Gortin Glen Forest Park 476
Gortmore 487
Gosford Forest Park 461
Gothic Churches .70
Gothic Revival 77
Government 58
Gracehill 433
Graiguenamanagh 230, 231
Granuaile 361
Great Famine 64
Greencastle 397
Green Castle 452
Grey Abbey 438
Greyhound Racing 22
Grey Point Fort 423
Greystones 184
Grianán of Aileach 395

INDEX

Groomsport........................437
Guesthouses.................. 40, 41
Gweedore 389

H

Handball............................56
Harry Avery's Castle 475
Hayes, Samuel 184
Health 36
Healy Pass 274
Heaney, Seamus...................90
Heywood Gardens (Ballinakill) 202
High Crosses 86
Highlights 13
Highway Code 38
Hill of Slane 157
Hillsborough 427
Hillsborough Fort 427
Historic Properties 20
History...........................61
Hobson, William................. 240
Hogan, John 248
Holidays (public) 47
Holy Cross Abbey (Cashel) 212
Holy Island........................317
Hook Head Peninsula.............. 232
Hore Abbey 213
Hornhead........................ 393
Horse-Drawn Caravan 17
Horse Racing.................. 22, 57
Horse Riding 17, 22
Hostels 41
Hotels 40, 41
Howth............................138
Hunting..........................22
Hunt Museum.................... 303
Hurling 56
Hurling Championship..............311

I

Illuminated manuscripts..............87
Ilnacullin........................ 273
Inch 297
Inch Abbey 443, 444
Inchagoill Island.................. 348
Inis Eoghain..................... 395
Inishbofin....................... 350
Inishcrone 367
Inisheer......................... 334
Inishmaan 334
Inishmore.........................331
Inishmurray......................375
Inishowen 395
Inistioge 231

Innisfree 379
Inniskeen 167
Inns 40
International Visitors 34
Introduction 51
IRA 65
Irish Agricultural Museum 225
Irish Banquets.....................21
Irish Diaspora 54
Irish Fry.........................60
Irish (language) 17
Irish Linen Centre....................27
Irish National Heritage Park........ 226
Irish National Stud and Japanese
      Gardens.......................170
Irish Palatine Heritage Centre 310
Irish Palatines 309
Irish Potato Famine................65
Irish Republican Army 65
Irish Republican Brotherhood........65
Irish Tourist Board 34
Iron Age 68
Island Magee....................... 426

J

James, Henry...................... 401
James Joyce Museum...............139
Janus Figure 469
Jerpoint Abbey..................... 220
Jim Kemmy Municipal Museum 303
John Square 305
Johnstown Castle 225
Joyce Country..................... 353
Joyce, James 89, 190

K

Kanturk......................... 259
Kate Kearney's Cottage 278
Kavanagh, Patrick 90
Kayaking..........................23
Keane, John B 90
Keane, Molly 90
Kells 161
Kells Priory 221
Kenmare........................ 280
Kenmare Lace 281
Kennedy Arboretum............... 231
Kerry 11
Kerry County Museum.............. 290
Kerry Poets' Memorial 277
Kerry Way........................ 19, 285
Kids 28
Kilbeggan Distillery Experience 192
Kilcar 385

Kilcar Coast Road 383, 385
Kilclief Castle 447
Kilcooly Abbey 221
Kilcullen Seaweed Baths 367
Kildare 169
Kildare (Geraldine) Revolt 62
Kilfane Glen and Waterfall 220
Kilfenora 327
Kilkee 322
Kilkeel 452
Kilkeeran High Crosses 208
Kilkenny 15, 216
Kilkenny Castle and Park 217
Killala 366
Killaloe 315
Killarney 16, 275
Killarney National Park 279
Killary Harbour 358
Killeen 359
Killevy 455
Killinaboy 327
Killorglin 285
Killough 444
Killruddery 180
Killybegs 383
Killykeen Forest Park 403
Killyleagh 444
Kilmacanogue 181
Kilmacduagh Monastery 326
Kilmallock 312
Kilmallock Abbey 312
Kilmokea Gardens 232
Kilmore Cathedral 401
Kilmore Quay 225
Kilnaruane Stone 271
Kilnasaggart Stone 455
Kilrush 321
Kinbane Castle 492
King House 377
King James II 155
King John's Castle 304
Kinnitty 195
Kinsale 261
Kinsale Harbour 263
Kinsale Regional Museum 261
Kinvarra 325
Knitwear 26
Knock 357
Knockalla 394
Knockmoy Abbey 339
Knocknarea 373
Knockreer Demesne 279
Know Before You Go 34
Knowth 155

Kylemore Abbey 351
Kyteler slab 219

L

Lace and Design Centre, Kenmare ... 281
Lace (production) 27
Lady Gregory 89
Lady's Island 225
Lagan Valley 428
Lag Sand Dunes 397
Lahinch 323
Lakes 107
Lambeg 428
Land Acts 65
Lár na Páirce 213
Larne 494
Ledwidge, Francis 159
Leenane 353
Legananny Dolmen 450
Leinstermen, Graves of the 315
Leitrim Way 19
Letterkenny 395
Limavady 477
Limerick 11, 16, 301
Limerick Lace 305
Limerick Museum 303
Linen Board 64
Linen Green, The 462
Linen (production) 27
Lir, Children of 191
Lisburn 426
Lisburn Museum 427
Lisdoonvarna 328, 329
Lismore 239
Lismore Castle Gardens 239
Liss Ard 266
Literary Routes 14
Literature 87
Lodge Park Walled Garden 172
Londonderry 479
Londonderry (Derry) 16
Longford 188
Long house 81
Loop Head Peninsula 322
Lough Caragh 284
Loughcrew Cairns 162
Loughcrew Gardens 162
Lough Dan 182
Lough Derg 314
Lough Erne 464, 467
Lough Gill 378
Lough Gur 310
Lough Hyne Nature Reserve 266
Loughinisland Churches 445

INDEX

Lough Key Forest Park 378
Lough Muckno Leisure Park 400
Lough Neagh 430
Loughrea 341
Loughros Point 387
Lough Tay 182
Louisburgh 360
Lullymore 170
Lundy 480
Lusitania 263
Lusitania Memorial 254

M

MacGahern, John 90
Maghera 387, 477
Maghery 431
Magilligan Strand 486
Mail 47
Malahide Castle 140
Malin 397
Malin Head 397
Mallow 258
Malone House 429
Mamore, Gap of 396
Marble Arch Caves 467
Markievicz, Countess Constance 375
Maynooth 171
McCourt, Frank 91
McGahern, John 319
Meagher, Thomas Francis 240
Meat 60
Media 47, 53
Meeting of the Waters 184
Megalithic Tombs 67
Mellifont Old Abbey 157
Metalwork (production) 27
Michelin Driving Tours 10
Mid-East, The 6, 150
Midlands 12, 187
Midlands, The .6
Midleton 255
Military Road 180
Millmount 152
Minorities 53
Missionaries 95
Mitchelstown Cave 214
Mizen Head 269
Mizen Peninsula 268
Model Arts and the Niland Gallery 371
Moher, Cliffs of 323
Moll's Gap 280
Monaghan 399
Monaincha Abbey 209
Monasterboice 156

Monastic Settlements 68
Money 47
Moone 173
Motte Stone 184
Mountaineering 21
Mount Gabriel 268
Mount Leinster 228
Mountshannon 317
Mount Stewart 438
Mount Usher Gardens 182
Mourne Mountains 448
Movilla Abbey 439
Moville 397
Moy 366
Moy Estuary 366
Moyne Abbey 367
Muckross Friary 279
Muckross House and Farms 280
Mullagh 162
Mullaghmore .375
Mullet Peninsula 364
Mullingar 190
Multyfarnham Franciscan Friary 190
Murlough National Nature
   Reserve .450, 498
Murrough, The 184
Music 20, 91
Myths and Lore 98

N

Naran 383
National 1798 Visitor Centre 227
National Maritime Museum of Ireland 139
National Parks 20
National Parliament 121
Nature 101
Nature Reserves 20
Navan Fort 460
Nenagh 315
Ness Wood Country Park 478
Newbridge House 141
Newcastle 448
Newcastle West 310
Newgrange 153
Newmills 392
Newport 361
New Ross 228
Newry 454
Newspapers 47
Newtonstewart 475
Newtownards 439
Nier Valley 206
Nimmo, Alexander 347
Norman Architecture 70

Norman Castles 72
North Bull Island Interpretive Centre .138
North Down Museum, Bangor 436
Northern Ireland 7
Northern Ireland Tourist Board. 34
North Mayo 363
Northwest, The. 7, 369

O

Oates Conspiracy. 63
O'Brien, Edna 90
O'Carolan, Turlough 91
O'Cleary, Michael. 382
O'Connor, Frank 248
O'Donoghue of the Glens, Geoffrey . 277
Ogham Script 57
Oireachtas, Houses of the 121
Old Midleton Distillery. 255, 256
Omagh 474
O'Malley, Grace. 361
Omeath. 166
Omey Island 349
Opening Hours. 47
O'Rahilly, Egan 277
Orange Order 64
Ossian's Grave. 497
O'Sullivan, Owen Roe. 277
Otherworld 98
Oughterard 348

P

Painting 84
Pakenham 190
Palace Demesne, Armagh. 459
Pale, The. 61, 160
Parachuting. 21
Parkanaur Forest Park 462
Parke's Castle 379
Parking 38
Parnell, Charles Stewart. 183
Parsons, Sir Lawrence. 193
Passage tombs 67
Passports 35
Patterson's Spade Mill 432
Pearse Museum 140
Pearse, Patrick 140, 345
Peat Bogs. 102
Peatlands Park 430
Penal Laws. 96
Penalties (driving) 38
People. 52
Petrol. 39
Petty, Sir William 142
Phoenix Park. 134

Plantation Castles 74
Plantation Period. 74
Planter's Gothic .74
Plunkett, Oliver .163
Poe, Edgar Allan. 401
Pogue's Entry 431
Porcelain (production). 27
Portaferry. 438
Portmagee. 283
Portnablagh 394
Portrush 488
Portstewart 488
Portumna Castle 317
Potato blight. 64
Pottery (production) 27
Poulnabrone 329
Powerscourt 179
Powerscourt Waterfall. 179
Poynings' Law. 62
Prehistory. 67
Proleek Dolmen 166
Pubs. 56
Pubs with Rooms. 40
Punchestown 171

Q

Queen of Ireland 358
Queen's University 418
Quiet Man Cottage Museum 352
Quin Franciscan Friary 307
Quoile 445

R

RAC. 39
Races of Castlebar 364
Rail Service 40
Rakes of Mallow 258
Rambling 22
Rathkeale 310
Rathlin Island 493
Rathmelton 395
Rathmullan 395
Redmond, John .66
Reduced Rates 46
Religion. .53, 94, 98
Renvyle. 350
Restaurants 45
Revolution, The 63
Rice, Edmund Ignatius 221
Rights 53
Ring of Kerry 275
River Liffey. 116
Rivers. 107
Road Bowls 460

INDEX

Road Signs 39
Road tolls 39
Robertstown 171
Rock of Cashel 210
Rock of Dunamase 202
Roe Valley Country Park 477
Roman Catholic Emancipation Act 65
Romanesque Architecture 70
Roscommon 318
Roscommon Castle 318
Roscrea 208
Roscrea Castle 208
Rosguill Peninsula Atlantic Drive 394
Rossbeg 387
Rosscarbery 264
Ross Castle 279
Rosserk Abbey 367
Ross Errilly Abbey 353
Rosses, The 389
Rosslare 225
Ross, Martin 88
Rossmore Forest Park 399
Rossnowlagh Strand 381, 382
Rostrevor 453
Rostrevor Forest Park 452
Rothe House 219
Roundstone .346, 347
Round Tower and High Crosses, Kells .161
Round Towers 68
Rowallane Gardens 427
Royal Automobile Club 39
Ryan's Daughter 290

S

Sailing 23
Saints 94
Sally Gap 182
Saltee Islands 225
Salthill 339
Sarsfield's Ride 14
Saul 443
Sawel Mountain .476
Scattery Island 321
Scenic Routes 14
Schull 268
Scotch-Irish 53
Scrabo Country Park 440
Scuba Diving 23
Sculpture 85
Sea (access via) 37
Seaforde Gardens 445
Season Tickets 46
Seaweed Baths 24
Self Catering 41

Selskar Abbey 224
Set dancing 93
Shannon-Erne Waterway 317
Shannon Harbour 315
Shannon Valley 314
Shaw, George Bernard 88
Sheep's Head 269
Sheridan, Richard Brinsley 401
Sherkin Island 266
Shopping 26
Short Breaks 14
Siege of Kinsale 14
Sightseeing 48
Silent Valley Reservoir 451
Silver Strand 359
Sion Mills 475
Skellig Islands 283
Skellig Ring 283
Skerries Mills 142
Skibbereen 265
Sky Road 349, 350
Slane 158
Slea Head 295
Slemish Mountain 433
Slieve Bloom Mountains 194, 199
Slieve Gullion 454
Slieve Gullion Forest Park 455
Slieve League 385
Slieve Patrick 444
Sligo 11, 15, 371
Sligo Abbey 371
Smoking 48
Sneem 281
Society 53
Somerville and Ross 265
Somerville, Edith .88
Somme Heritage Centre 436
South Coast 261
Southeast, The 6, 203
South Mayo 355
Southwest, The 6, 243
Spanish Armada 62
Spanish Point 323
Spas 24
Speed limit (road) 39
Spelga Pass and Dam 452
Sperrin Mountains 472, 474
Springhill 474
SS Nomadic 415
Stained glass 82
Statutes of Kilkenny 216
St Brendan of Clonfert 296
St Bridget 94
St Canice's Cathedral 219

St Carthage's Cathedral 239
St Colman's Cathedral 253
St Columb's Cathedral 483
St Columcille's House 161
Steeplechase 255
Sterne, Laurence 205
St Fechin 191
St Flannan's Cathedral 315
St John's Point 444
St Kevin 178
St Kieran 197
St Laurence Gate 152
St Mary's Cathedral, Limerick 303
St Mary's Church (Clonmel) 205
St Mel's Cathedral 188
St Mochta's House 167
St Multose Church 261
St Nicholas' Church, Carrickfergus . . . 425
Stoker, Bram 88
Stormont 422
St Patrick's Cathedral, Killala 366
Strabane 475
Stradbally 202
Strandhill 373
Strangford Castle 447
Strangford Lough 434
Strokestown 319
Strokestown Park House and
    Famine Museum 319
Struell Wells 443
Surfing 24
Swift, Jonathan 88, 128
Swiss Cottage 214
Swords (Sord) 142

T

Tacumshane Windmill 225
Taghmon 190
Táin Trail 18
Talbot Botanic Gardens 140
Tara 155
Tayto Potato Crisp Factory 461
Telephone 46
Television 47
Templetown Mausoleum 432
Termonfeckin 158
Thalassotherapy .24
Theatres 21
Themed Tours 14
Tholsel 230
Thomastown 220
Thomond Bridge 305
Thoor Ballylee 326
Timahoe 202

Time 48
Timoleague 264
Timolin 173
Tintern Abbey 232
Tipperary 208
Tipperary County Museum 206
Tipping 45
Tobernalt 379
Tollymore Forest Park 448
Torc Waterfall 280
Tory Island 390
Tourist Offices 34
Tourist Train 18
Tours 10, 14
Tower Houses 72
Town Planning 79
Trabane Strand 385
Traditional Dishes 60
Trains 40
Tralee 288
Tralee & Dingle Railway 290
Tramore 238
Treaty of Limerick 63
Trim 159
Trim Castle 159
Trollope, Anthony 88, 195
Tuam 339
Tuamgraney 316
Tullaghoge Fort 472
Tullamore 198
Tullamore D.E.W. Visitor Centre 198
Tully Castle 470
Tullynally 191
Tweed 27

U

U2 93
Ulster 10, 12
Ulster-American Folk Park 475
Ulster Cycle 460
Ulster Folk and Transport Museum . . 423
Ulster Fry 60
Ulster Museum .417
Ulster-Scots 53
University Residences 41
Useful Words and Phrases 33

V

Valentia Island 284
Vale of Avoca 184
Vale of Clara 183
Valera, Eamon de 304
Vandeleur Walled Garden 321
Van Morrison 92

INDEX

VAT 48
Vegetation 106
Ventry 293
Vernacular Houses. 81
Vinegar Hill 227

W

Wakeboarding .24
Walking. 17, 19
Wallace, Sir Richard. 427
Ward Family. 446
Warrenpoint 452
Waterford. 235
Waterford Coast. 238
Waterford Crystal 26
Waterford Crystal (House of). 237
Waterford Medieval Museum 237
Water Skiing 24
Water Sports. 23
Websites. 34
Wellbrook Beetling Mill. 473
Wesley, John 309
West. 299
West Clare 321
West Clare Coast 323
West Cork Model Railway Village 264
West Cork Regional Museum. 264
Westport 15, 355
Westport House. 356
West, The 7
Wexford 223

Wexford County Museum. 228
Wexford Franciscan Friary 225
Wexford Wildfowl Reserve. 226
What to See and Do 20
When To Go. 14
Where to Eat 44
Where to Go 14
Where to Stay .40
Whiskey 45
Whitehead. 426
White Island 469
Wicklow 184
Wicklow Gap. .182
Wicklow Mountains 175
Wilde, Oscar 88
Wildfowl and Wetlands Trust. 440
William of Orange 155
Willie Clancy Summer School 92
Wilson, President Woodrow. 476
Windsurfing 24
Windy Gap. 166
Woodwork. 27
Words and Phrases 33

Y

Yeats' Country .376
Yeats, William Butler. 89, 374
Yellow Steeple 160
Youghal. 256
Young Ireland Uprising 65

🏨 STAY

Achill 368
Adare. 313
Antrim. 433
Aran Islands. 334
Armagh. 463
Ballina 368
Bangor 440
Beara Peninsula. 274
Belfast. 418, 429
Belmullet 368
Caragh Lake 287
Carlingford 169
Cashel 215
Castlebar 362
Causeway Coast. 493
Clonmel 215

Co Cavan 402
Co Fermanagh 471
Connemara 353
Cork 250
Co Waterford 241
Dingle 297
Donegal 388
Downpatrick. 447
Drogheda. .164, 174
Dublin. 143
Dundalk 168
Galway 341
Glens of Antrim 499
Inniskeen 169
Kells 164
Kenmare. 286

Kildare.................................... 174
Kilkenny 222
Killala..................................... 368
Killarney................................ 285
Kinsale 267
Leenane 362
Limerick 312
Londonderry/Derry 485
Malin Head 398
Mizen Head........................... 271
Mourne Mountains................. 453

Mullingar 192
Shannon Valley 320
Sperrin Mountains 478
The Burren............................. 330
Tralee.................................... 297
Trim 164
Tullamore.............................. 200
Westport 362
Wexford 233
Youghal 260

♀️ EAT

Achill 368
Adare..................................... 313
Aran Islands............................ 334
Ards Peninsula 441
Armagh................................... 463
Ballina................................... 368
Beara Peninsula 274
Belfast.............................419, 429
Caragh Lake 287
Carlingford 169
Cashel.................................... 215
Castlebar 362
Causeway Coast....................... 493
Clonmel 215
Co Cavan 402
Co Fermanagh 471
Co Monaghan.......................... 400
Connemara 354
Cork...................................... 250
Co Waterford 241
Dingle 298
Donegal 388

Dublin.................................... 143
Dundalk 168
Enniscorthy............................. 234
Galway 342
Glens of Antrim 499
Kenmare................................. 286
Kildare.................................... 174
Kilkenny 222
Killarney................................ 285
Kinsale 267
Limerick 312
Londonderry/Derry 485
Mizen Head............................ 271
Mourne Mountains.................... 453
Mullingar 192
Shannon Valley 320
Sperrin Mountains 478
Tullamore.............................. 200
Westport 362
Wexford 233
Wicklow Mountains 186

MAPS AND PLANS

THEMATIC MAPS

Principal Sights . . . . Inside front cover
Driving Tours . . . . Inside back cover
Places to Stay 42–43
Gaelic-speaking Regions 57
Relief map 104–105

MAPS

Dublin

Dublin 114–115, 118–119

The Mid-East

Drogheda 152
Boyne Valley 154
Dundalk 165
Wicklow Mountains 176
Glendalough 177

The Midlands

Clonmacnoise 196

The Southeast

Southeastern Coast 204
Clonmel 206
Rock of Cashel .210
Kilkenny 218
Wexford 224
Waterford .236, 237

The Southwest

Cork 245
Around Cork 253
South Coast 262
Mizen Head, Bantry Bay and
    Beara Peninsula 270
Iveragh Peninsula (Ring Of Kerry) 276
Killarney 277
Dingle Peninsula 289

The West

Limerick 302
Shannon Valley .316
The Burren & West Clare 325
Aran Islands 332–333
Galway 336
Connemara 346
South Mayo 360
North Mayo 366–367

The Northwest

Sligo 372
Around Sligo 374
Donegal 384
Northern Peninsulas 392–393

Northern Ireland

Belfast (Centre) .411
Ards Peninsula and Strangford Lough . . 435
Mourne Mountains 449
Armagh 457
Sperrin Mountains 473
Londonderry/Derry 481, 482
Causeway Coast 487
Giant's Causeway 490
Glens of Antrim 495

Maps: Northern Ireland

Ordnance Survey of Northern Ireland.

The material is Crown Copyright and is reproduced with the
permission of Land and Property Services under delegated
authority from the Controller of Her Majesty's Stationery Office.
© Crown Copyright 2013. Permit number 100507.

Maps: Republic of Ireland

Based upon Ordnance Survey Ireland. Permit number 9015.
© Ordnance Survey Ireland / Government of Ireland

MAP LEGEND

Sight

Highly recommended ★★★
Recommended ★★
Interesting ★

Additional symbols

ⓘ	Tourist information
═══ ═══	Motorway or other primary route
❶ ❶	Junction: complete, limited
▭▭	Pedestrian street
ɪ══ɪ	Unsuitable for traffic, street subject to restrictions
▭▭▭ ----	Steps – Footpath
🚂 🚃	Train station – Auto-train station
🚌 SNCF	Coach (bus) station
━━	Tram
⦿	Metro, underground
ⓅR	Park-and-Ride
♿	Access for the disabled
✉	Post office
☎	Telephone
▭	Covered market
⋅×⋅	Barracks
△	Drawbridge
∪	Quarry
✗	Mine
ⓑ ⓕ	Car ferry (river or lake)
⛴	Ferry service: cars and passengers
⛵	Foot passengers only
③	Access route number common to Michelin maps and town plans
Bert (R.)...	Main shopping street
AZ B	Map co-ordinates

Sports and recreation

🏇	Racecourse
⛸	Skating rink
≋ ≋	Outdoor, indoor swimming pool
🎥	Multiplex Cinema
⚓	Marina, sailing centre
⌂	Trail refuge hut
▭■▭■▭	Cable cars, gondolas
▭+++++▭	Funicular, rack railway
🚂	Tourist train
◆	Recreation area, park
🎢	Theme, amusement park
ⵁ	Wildlife park, zoo
✿	Gardens, park, arboretum
🕊	Bird sanctuary, aviary
🚶	Walking tour, footpath
😊	Of special interest to children

Selected monuments and sights

Symbol	Description
	Tour - Departure point
	Ecclesiastical building
	Synagogue - Mosque
	Building
	Statue, small building
	Calvary, wayside cross
	Fountain
	Rampart - Tower - Gate
	Château, castle, historic house
	Ruins
	Dam
	Factory, power plant
	Fort
	Cave
	Troglodyte dwelling
	Prehistoric site
	Viewing table
	Viewpoint
	Other place of interest

Abbreviations

C	County council offices
H	Town hall
J	Law courts
M	Museum
POL.	Police
T	Theatre
U	University

Special symbols

M3	Motorway
A2	Primary route
	Forest, Country Park, National Park

COMPANION PUBLICATIONS

MAPS

Michelin map 712 –Ireland

Scale 1 : 400 000 - 1cm = 4km -
1in : 6.30 miles, covers the Republic of
Ireland and Northern Ireland, and the
network of motorways and major roads.
This product provides information on
shipping routes, distances in miles and
kilometres, town plans of Dublin and
Belfast, services, sporting and tourist
attractions, and an index of places;
the key and text are printed in four
languages.

Michelin Tourist and Motoring Atlas Great Britain & Ireland

Scale 1 : 300 000 - 1cm = 3km -
1in : 4.75 miles (based on 1 : 400 000),
covers the whole of the United Kingdom
and the Republic of Ireland, the national
networks of motorways and major
roads. This product provides information
on route planning, shipping routes,
distances in miles and kilometres, over
60 town plans, services, sporting and
tourist attractions, and an index of
places; the key and text are printed in
six languages.

Michelin map 713 – Great Britain and Ireland

Scale 1 : 1 000 000 - 1cm = 10km -
1inch : 15.8 miles, covers the whole of
the United Kingdom and the Republic
of Ireland, the national networks of
motorways and major roads. This
product provides information on
shipping routes, distances in miles and
kilometres, a list of Unitary Authorities
for Wales and Scotland; the key and text
are printed in four languages.

INTERNET

Users can access personalised route
plans, Michelin mapping online,
addresses of hotels and restaurants
listed in *The Red Guide* plus practical and
tourist information through the internet:
travelguide.michelin.com
www.viamichelin.com

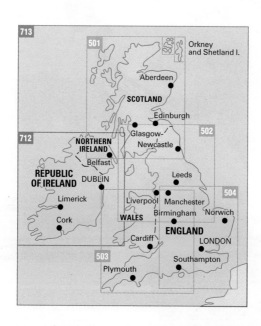

**MICHELIN
IS CONTINUALLY
INNOVATING
FOR SAFER, CLEANER,
MORE ECONOMICAL,
MORE CONNECTED...
BETTER ALL-ROUND
MOBILITY.**

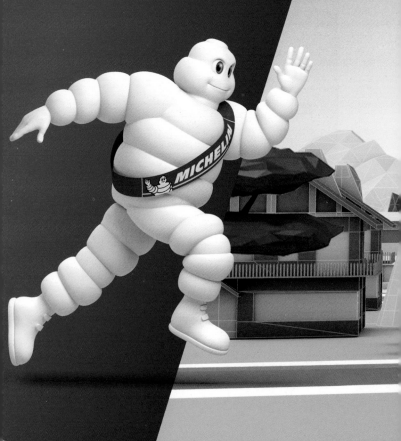

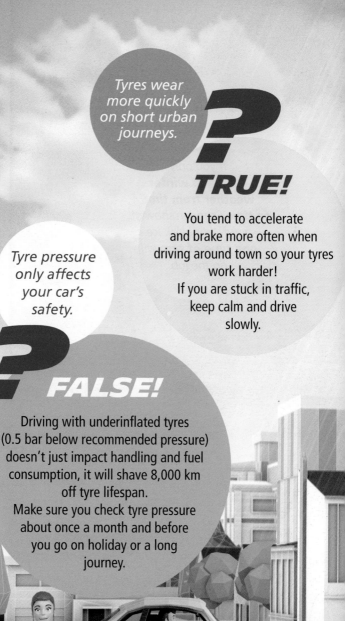

Tyres wear more quickly on short urban journeys.

? TRUE!

You tend to accelerate and brake more often when driving around town so your tyres work harder!
If you are stuck in traffic, keep calm and drive slowly.

Tyre pressure only affects your car's safety.

? FALSE!

Driving with underinflated tyres (0.5 bar below recommended pressure) doesn't just impact handling and fuel consumption, it will shave 8,000 km off tyre lifespan.
Make sure you check tyre pressure about once a month and before you go on holiday or a long journey.

Fitting **2 winter tyres** on my car guarantees maximum safety.

FALSE!

In the winter, especially when temperatures drop below 7°C, to ensure better road holding, all four tyres should be identical and fitted at the same time.

2 WINTER TYRES ONLY =
risk of compromised road holding.

4 WINTER TYRES =
safer handling when cornering, driving downhill and braking.

If you regularly encounter rain, snow or black ice, choose a **MICHELIN Alpin tyre**. This range offers you sharp handling plus a comfortable ride to safely face the challenge of winter driving.

MICHELIN IS COMMITTED

▶ MICHELIN IS **GLOBAL LEADER IN FUEL-EFFICIENT TYRES** FOR LIGHT VEHICLES.

▶ **EDUCATING OF YOUNGSTERS IN ROAD SAFETY,** NOT FORGETTING TWO-WHEELERS. LOCAL ROAD SAFETY CAMPAIGNS WERE RUN IN **16 COUNTRIES** IN 2015.

QUIZ

1 TYRES ARE BLACK SO WHY IS THE MICHELIN MAN WHITE?

Back in 1898 when the Michelin Man was first created from a stack of tyres, they were made of natural rubber, cotton and sulphur and were therefore light-coloured. The composition of tyres did not change until after the First World War when carbon black was introduced. But the Michelin Man kept his colour!

2 FOR HOW LONG HAS MICHELIN BEEN GUIDING TRAVELLERS?

Since 1900. When the MICHELIN guide was published at the turn of the century, it was claimed that it would last for a hundred years. It's still around today and remains a reference with new editions and online restaurant listings in a number of countries.

3 WHEN WAS THE "BIB GOURMAND" INTRODUCED IN THE MICHELIN GUIDE?

The symbol was created in 1997 but as early as 1954 the MICHELIN guide was recommending "exceptional good food at moderate prices". Today, it features on the MICHELIN Restaurants website and app.

If you want to enjoy a fun day out and find out more about Michelin, why not visit the l'Aventure Michelin museum and shop in Clermont-Ferrand, France:

www.laventuremichelin.com